Ignatius of Loyola and Thomas Aquinas

Ignatius of Loyola and Thomas Aquinas:
A Jesuit Ressourcement

Edited by
Justin M. Anderson, Matthew Levering,
and Aaron Pidel, SJ

The Catholic University of America Press
Washington, D.C.

Copyright © 2024
The Catholic University of America Press
All rights reserved
The paper used in this publication meets the minimum requirements of American National Standards for Information Science—Permanence of Paper for Printed Library Materials, ANSI Z39.48-1992.

∞

Cataloging-in-Publication Data is available from the Library of Congress
ISBN: 978-0-8132-3715-2
eISBN: 978-0-8132-3716-9

*Dedicated to the loving memory of our friend, mentor,
spiritual father, and brother
Fr. Joseph W. Koterski, SJ, a true companion of Jesus.*

Contents

Acknowledgements vii

Abbreviations viii

Editors' Preface ix

Chapter 1: The Early Jesuits and Scholastic Theology
Thomas Osborne 1

Chapter 2: Experiencing the Divine according to Thomas and Ignatius
Justin M. Anderson 29

Chapter 3: Ignatius and Thomas on the Ordering of the Passions and the Glory of God
Margaret I. Hughes 59

Chapter 4: The Thomistic Account of Prudence and the Ignatian Account of Discernment of Spirits
Joseph W. Koterski, SJ 79

Chapter 5: Thomas and Ignatius on the Imagination
Nicolas Steeves, SJ 105

Chapter 6: Frequent Communion for the Greater Glory of God: Thomas Aquinas and Ignatius of Loyola
Andrew Hofer, OP 135

Chapter 7: Ignatius and Aquinas on Mary
Theresa Marie Chau Nguyen, OP 167

Chapter 8: Aquinas and Ignatius on the "Hierarchical Church"
Aaron Pidel, SJ 197

Chapter 9: Leading the Blind: Aquinas, Ignatius, and Other Jesuits on Obedience
Sam Zeno Conedera, SJ 217

Chapter 10: "Therefore Israel First": Francisco de Toledo, SJ's
            Thomistic Claims for *Converso* Christians
            Elisabeth Rain Kincaid 247

Chapter 11: Francisco de Toledo on Thomas Aquinas and the
            Possibility of Coerced Faith
            Kevin Flannery, SJ 271

Works Cited 297

Author and Editor Biographies 325

Acknowledgements

This book sprang from a theological conference on "Ignatius, the Thomist" in November 2020, and a debt of gratitude is owed to all those who made that gathering possible, including the benefactors of the Center for Scriptural Exegesis, Philosophy, and Doctrine at Mundelein Seminary. While in the end the gathering had to be on Zoom due to Covid travel restrictions, it still felt like an actual gathering, inasmuch as a real bond sprung up among the participants. The idea of the conference came from conversations between Justin Anderson and Fr. Aaron Pidel, and Matthew Levering eagerly joined in. We also want to acknowledge Hayden Hagerman, a doctoral student in theology at Marquette University, for his work in preparing the draft for publication. John Martino has graciously shepherded the manuscript throughout the process at the Catholic University of America Press. Many thanks to James N. Perry Jr. and Mary D. Perry for supporting the publication of the volume at CUA Press. In the end, we wish to express our deepest gratitude to all of the contributors who have so ably explored the lives and writings of these two saints with the aim of identifying areas of unity and diversity in service to Jesus Christ. We hope that among the beneficiaries will be early Jesuit Studies, Thomistic studies, the broader Church and the ongoing renewal of theology, and the Society of Jesus. Among the contributors, special mention must be made of Fr. Joseph W. Koterski, who was unexpectedly taken to the Lord during the preparation of the volume. Fr. Koterski's contribution fittingly expresses so many elements of his own life and ministry for God's greater glory. All of us have stories of Fr. Koterski's amazing gifts and self-sacrificial labors. May Christ bestow upon our dear friend and esteemed mentor Fr. Koterski the reward for which he yearned—eternal communion with the glorious Trinity.

Abbreviations

Autobiog	The Autobiography of St. Ignatius
CCSL	Corpus Christianorum Series Latina
Cons.	The Constitutions of the Society of Jesus, by St. Ignatius, in any text
CSEL	Corpus Scriptorum Ecclesiasticorum Latinorum
CWE	Collected Works of Erasmus
IHSI	Institutum Historicum Societatis Iesu
MHSI	Monumenta Historica Societatis Iesu. The series of critically edited historical sources of the Jesuits, 124 volumes.
PL	Patrologiae cursus completes, Series Latina
SCG	*Summa contra Gentiles*
SpDiar	The Spiritual Diary of St. Ignatius, 1544–1545
SpEx	The *Spiritual Exercises* of St. Ignatius, in any text
ST/Summa	*Summa Theologiae*
Super Sent.	*Scriptum super Sententiarum*

Editors' Preface

When, shortly after his conversion, John Henry Newman went to Rome in 1846, a Jesuit member of the Curia told him that the thought of Thomas Aquinas was not in favor in Rome. He soon deduced that, in part due to the traditional Dominican opposition to the doctrine of the Immaculate Conception, the reason Aquinas was out of favor was because the Dominicans were out of favor. The leading theologians in Rome were Jesuits—the famous "Roman School." Newman was fine with this situation, since, although in fact (as Owen Chadwick says) "a Thomist might have understood Newman more easily," Newman's "chief friends and advisors in Rome were Jesuits."[1]

This rivalry between Jesuits and Dominicans may seem familiar. Indeed, today's notable theological renewal in Thomistic theology—distinct from the situation in Thomistic philosophy—includes painfully few Jesuit voices. In the domain of moral theology, Nicholas Austin, SJ, has recently made a major contribution with his *Aquinas on Virtue*; and, in historical theology, Gilles Mongeau, SJ, has authored a significant historical study of Aquinas's theological pedagogy. Yet the leading contributors to the retrieval of Aquinas's theology and Thomism these days are Dominicans or laypeople strongly influenced by Dominicans: Jean-Pierre Torrell, Serge-Thomas Bonino, Gilles Emery, Thomas Joseph White, Reinhard Hütter (himself a Third-Order Dominican), and many others. Philosophy is a different situation, since Jesuits have retained a strong voice in Thomistic philosophy, although less so among the younger generation. But the leading lights in Thomistic philosophy continue to include eminent Jesuits, among whom are two collaborators to the current study: Kevin Flannery and Joseph Koterski.

The situation is such today that a young scholar could almost be forgiven for supposing that the history of post-Tridentine theology involves only Dominican theologians having a real interest in Aquinas or Thomism. Ironically, then, it turns out that when Chadwick claimed that Thomists would have understood Newman better, he meant Jesuit Thomists, since Newman ended up finding valuable resources in Francisco Suárez and Francisco de Lugo. We do not mean to downplay the real divisions between Jesuit and Dominican receptions of Aquinas. This would be implausible, given the history from the *De Auxiliis* controversy onward. Discussing one of the leaders of Leonine

---

1. Owen Chadwick, *From Bossuet to Newman*, 2nd ed. (Cambridge: Cambridge University Press, 1987), 168–69.

Thomism (which replaced the "Roman School")—Louis Billot, SJ—Romanus Cessario, OP, has pointed out: "Billot, to be sure, was a Thomist of the Leonine revival, but he was not, I underline, a Thomist of the commentatorial tradition. Those whom he considers authoritative guides for doing theology inhabit mainly the thirteenth century."[2] Billot despised not only classical Dominican Thomists such as Cardinal Cajetan and John of St. Thomas, but also Suárez and other eminent Jesuit representatives. Cessario surveys Billot's views on the political order and on the sacrifice of the Mass and concludes plausibly that had Billot been more open to the Dominican Thomist tradition (Cajetan, Francisco de Vitoria, Domingo Bañez), his viewpoints would have been enriched.

Without downplaying the all-too-frequent polarization between Jesuits and Dominicans, we wish to call attention to the fact that their arguments over the centuries did indeed require both sides to gain knowledge of Aquinas. Aquinas's theology, with its immense richness, cannot be said to have belonged solely to either religious order. It is reasonable to hold that contemporary Jesuit systematics will be impoverished if it stands aside from the ongoing theological retrieval of Aquinas. Aquinas's theology offers an irreplaceable entrance into the Catholic Tradition, as shown most recently by the contributions of forty-four Protestant, Orthodox, and Catholic scholars to *The Oxford Handbook of the Reception of Aquinas*.[3]

Today, Jesuit systematics stands on the shoulders of eminent twentieth-century Jesuit theologians who knew Aquinas's thought profoundly. We think of such figures as Henri de Lubac, SJ, Erich Przywara, SJ, and Bernard Lonergan, SJ, just to name three. The recent publication in English of Lonergan's Latin theology, including his massive and extraordinary treatises on the Trinity and Jesus Christ, has only confirmed the fruitfulness of his Thomism, well known already to readers of his classic work *Grace and Freedom*. Contemporary Lonerganians, led by Jeremy Wilkins, are spearheading the project of learning Lonergan in conjunction with learning Aquinas. For decades, those who studied Lonergan learned almost nothing about Aquinas, resulting in a diminution of his legacy—though Lonergan's own students from the 1960s, such as David Burrell, CSC, and Matthew Lamb, knew Aquinas well.

The retrieval of Przywara's work, led by John Betz and Aaron Pidel, is in its infancy, but its value has already been demonstrated—as has the necessity of knowing Aquinas's philosophy and theology well to be able to apprehend the complexities of Przywara's masterwork, *Analogia Entis: Metaphysics:*

---

2. Romanus Cessario, OP, "Sacrifice, Social and Sacramental: The Witness of Louis Billot, SJ," *Nova et Vetera* 14 (2016): 130–31.

3. See *The Oxford Handbook of the Reception of Aquinas*, ed. Matthew Levering and Marcus Plested (Oxford: Oxford University Press, 2021).

Original Structure and Universal Rhythm. De Lubac's work, similarly, especially with regard to the nature-grace controversy, is suffused with evidence of serious and extensive reading of Aquinas and cannot be well understood by those who lack such background.

Indeed, it is not possible to imagine an accurate telling of the nineteenth century's neo-Thomistic revival that fails to notice that its earliest protagonists were predominately sons of Ignatius. Domenico and Serafino Sordi, Luigi Taparelli, Matteo Liberatore, Josef Kleutgen, and others were tied to both Thomas and Ignatius. The Jesuits continued to contribute prominent Thomists in the twentieth century, including Pierre Rousselot, Frederick Copleston, Joseph de Finance, and Norris Clarke, among many others.

Regarding Ignatius personally, Aquinas's influence seems to have been both direct and difficult to specify. From the earliest days of his conversion, Ignatius was touched by the Dominican community. Ignatius lived and prayed with the Dominicans at their priory for some time while in Manresa, where he received some of his formative experiences. It was to the Dominicans at Salamanca that Ignatius went when he endeavored to study theology and remove himself from the humanistic tendencies overtaking Alcalá. It is unsurprising, then, that, upon arriving in Paris to continue his studies, we discover him studying theology with the Dominicans at their priory on the Rue Saint-Jacques. It is likely here that Ignatius came in direct contact with the works of Aquinas. When it came time to set in order the curriculum of the budding Society of Jesus, Ignatius explicitly stipulated the study of Aquinas's *Summa Theologiae*. Ignatius's directive seems to have been met with acceptance. In March 1549, the Jesuits at the University of Valencia reported studying "almost nothing else except Scripture and Saint Thomas."[4]

Those interested in Aquinas's impact, therefore, will not overlook his influence upon Ignatius himself and through him, the earliest Jesuits. We are not, of course, the first to notice this influence. In his stimulating analysis of Ignatius's spirituality, Hans Urs von Balthasar observes: "Self-abnegation is no less radical in Ignatius than in Francis or Eckhart, but he avails himself of the Thomist metaphysical doctrines of secondary causality and the *analogia entis*, which is now at last taken seriously. By so doing, Ignatius achieves the inner synthesis of the two major parallel currents of the middle ages—scholasticism and mysticism."[5] Balthasar is well aware of other influences on Ignatius—

---

4. ". . . y casi en otra cosa no estudiamos sino es la escriptura y santo Thomás." *Epistolae mixtae ex variis Europae locis ab anno 1537 ad 1556 scriptae*, 5 vols, tom. 2 (1549–1552), MHSI 14 (Madrid: Aügustinus Avrial, 1899), 2:125. John W. O'Malley reports this in his *The First Jesuits*, reissued ed. (Boston: Harvard University Press, 1995), 248.

5. Hans Urs von Balthasar, *The Glory of the Lord: A Theological Aesthetics*, vol. 5, *The Realm of Metaphysics in the Modern Age*, trans. Oliver Davies et al., ed. Brian McNeil, CRV and John Riches (San Francisco, CA: Ignatius Press, 1991), 106.

Dionysius the Areopagite, Augustine, the Rhineland mystics, the *Imitation of Christ*. But he is correct to draw a link to Aquinas, as well. The centrality of the Trinity (three and one), the Incarnate Lord, and the Eucharist in Ignatius's mystical spirituality are what we might expect from a Catholic, and there is no need to insist upon a connection to Aquinas here;[6] yet, we cannot help but note that these mysteries occupy the principal place in Aquinas, as well. Emphasis on the disjunctions between the two saints would miss their deeper unity on so many matters.

In his magisterial introduction to Ignatius's writings, George Ganss, SJ, reflects upon Ignatius's theological formation in Paris, a training that at the very least "was basically Thomistic."[7] It was in Paris that Ignatius "conceived his preferential affection for St. Thomas, which later led him to prescribe 'the scholastic doctrine of St. Thomas' for the scholastics of his Society."[8] Ganss poses the question of what portions of Aquinas's writings were read by Ignatius and upon what texts of Aquinas the teachers of Ignatius lectured. Although we lack documentary evidence to answer this question, Ganss indicates, "it would be natural for Ignatius to seek further light on those ideas of his own which by now had become especially important to him."[9] Indeed, Ganss argues that Ignatius's spirituality bears the imprint of "St. Thomas' comprehensive view of God's plan of creation and redemption," namely, "the procession of creatures from God and their return to him through Christ."[10] Ganss briefly sums up Aquinas's main theological teachings regarding the Triune God who freely created rational creatures so that they might share in his divine beatitude, and who, again out of supreme goodness, healed and elevated human beings to the divine life after the fall, through the Incarnation, redemptive Passion, and Resurrection of Christ. The purpose of the present life is to be configured to Christ's love and thereby to share in his merit and his reward—a reward that consists not in status but in the ability to love God powerfully for eternity. John O'Malley likewise describes the early Jesuits as attracted to Aquinas's views on issues like faith and reason, nature and grace, grace and free will, and the moderation in ascetical practices found in Aquinas's appropriation of the Aristotelian "virtue as a mean" thesis.[11] These theological teachings

---

6. See the chapter on Ignatius—which does not mention Aquinas—in Bernard McGinn, *Mysticism in the Golden Age of Spain (1500–1650)* (New York: Crossroad, 2017).
7. George E. Ganss, SJ, general introduction to *Ignatius of Loyola: Spiritual Exercises and Selected Works*, by Ignatius of Loyola, ed. George E. Ganss, SJ, Classics of Western Spirituality (New York: Paulist Press, 1991), 37.
8. Ganss, general introduction, 37.
9. Ganss, general introduction, 37.
10. Ganss, general introduction, 39.
11. John W. O'Malley, SJ, *The First Jesuits* (Boston: Harvard University Press, 1994), 249.

(admittedly some not solely Thomistic, but certainly themes at the heart of Aquinas's theology) are all present in Ignatius's writings. Ganss concludes that Peter Lombard's *Sentences*, Ludolph's *Life of Jesus Christ*, and Aquinas's *Summa Theologiae* are the "'interpretative sources' which enable us to understand better the theological depth of Ignatius' thought."[12]

John Patrick Donnelly, SJ, has pointed out how impressed Ignatius was by the well-organized curriculum of the University of Paris, in contrast to the looser training he received at Alcalá and Salamanca. He shaped his rules for Jesuit education with this experience in view. Notably, although in the fourteenth and fifteenth centuries the writings of John Duns Scotus and William of Ockham had been dominant, the sixteenth century marked a revival of the thought of Aquinas (Dominicans) and Bonaventure (Franciscans). The path chosen by Ignatius was Thomistic. As Donnelly observes, Ignatius's "choice of Aquinas was critical, given the spread of Jesuit schools. Although only the small advanced classes in those colleges taught philosophy and theology, many leading philosophers and theologians in Catholic Europe came from those schools."[13] By Ignatius's death in 1556, the Jesuits had already founded thirty-three colleges.

In the *De Auxiliis* controversy, Dominican controversialists argued that Ignatius's love for Aquinas had been lost in the Society of Jesus. For instance, Matthew Gaetano has noted the argument made by the early eighteenth-century Dominican theologian Jacques-Hyacinthe Serry that, while Ignatius of Loyola possessed a great zeal for Aquinas's theology, "Ignatius' instruction to follow Aquinas was then weakened under the generalship of Laínez in 1558."[14] Jesuit theologians of the same period, by contrast, insisted either that Aquinas did not resolve the conundrum of predestination or else that the Molinist position ("middle knowledge") was firmly rooted "in the Catholic theological tradition and in Aquinas."[15] Both sides drew important insights from Aquinas, even if the main lines of their considerations of the biblical and patristic testimony to predestination and the goodness of the divine will diverged. Lest such controversies seem otiose—as though today we might be better off without Aquinas—Lonergan's *Grace and Freedom* and numerous other recent studies have shown that reflection on grace necessarily belongs to healthy Christian theology, despite the controversies that inevitably emerge. John Barclay's *Paul*

---

12. O'Malley, *First Jesuits*, 40.
13. John Patrick Donnelly, SJ, "Religious Orders for Men," in *The Cambridge History of Christianity*, vol. 6, *Reform and Expansion 1500–1660*, ed. R. Po-Chia Hsia (Cambridge: Cambridge University Press, 2007), 175.
14. Matthew T. Gaetano, "The Catholic Reception of Aquinas in the *De auxiliis* Controversy," in *Oxford Handbook of the Reception of Aquinas*, 266.
15. Matthew T. Gaetano, "Reception of Aquinas in the *De auxiliis* Controversy," 267.

and the Gift, which investigates grace from the perspective of a Pauline scholar well-versed in later Augustinian controversies (though not the *De Auxiliis* controversy), argues that although "the *priority* of the gift is everywhere presupposed, . . . Paul rarely draws out predestinarian conclusions."[16] This is a highly debatable claim, but it opens up the breadth of Aquinas's vision of the graced life—well beyond the thorny problem of divine priority in moving us to faith and charity—and it similarly opens up the breadth of Ignatius's vision of the graced life.

Aquinas's work can be fruitfully read, in certain of its aspects, by non-Christians, especially Jewish and Muslim thinkers, but also Hindu thinkers and even atheist philosophers who seek to reflect seriously on the most profound metaphysical and anthropological questions. Erin Cline has recently published a book where she proposes that the same point holds for Ignatius's *Spiritual Exercises*, which she deems can be adjusted so as to be of benefit for non-Christians. Whether or not this is true, she has hit upon the core of Ignatius's work—and Aquinas's—when she speaks of the *Spiritual Exercises*' "irreducibly Christocentric content."[17] In his groundbreaking study of Aquinas as a spiritual master, Jean-Pierre Torrell has shown that Aquinas, too, can only be understood as Christocentric, without this in any way undermining his theocentricism: "the whole *Summa* moves toward Christ."[18] Similarly, in a book dedicated to his doctoral director Michel Corbin, SJ, Robert Barron has shown that the "spirituality of Thomas is found, not only in those texts that we tend to recognize as spiritual, but, perhaps most clearly and profoundly, in his doctrine of God, in his Christology, in his understanding of the human person, in his lyrical theology of creation."[19] Barron argues that for Aquinas it is in going out of oneself—*ecstasis*—that human perfection is found, because this is the very pattern of the divine life as exhibited in creation and as revealed powerfully for our salvation in Jesus Christ. Barron's recent introduction to a collection of Jesuit writings finds this same *ecstasis* in Ignatius's spirituality, as Ignatius seeks to detach himself from all worldly things and offer his whole life in service to God.[20]

Of course, not all is commonality here. Ignatius had many sources that influenced him, and so this volume does not aim, as it were, to turn the

---

16. John M. G. Barclay, *Paul and the Gift* (Grand Rapids, MI: Eerdmans, 2015), 569.
17. Erin M. Cline, *A World on Fire: Sharing the Ignatian Spiritual Exercises with Other Religions* (Washington, DC: The Catholic University of America Press, 2018), 268.
18. Jean-Pierre Torrell, OP, *Saint Thomas Aquinas*, vol. 2, *Spiritual Master*, trans. Robert Royal (Washington, DC: The Catholic University of America Press, 2003), 102.
19. Robert Barron, *Thomas Aquinas: Spiritual Master* (New York: Crossroad, 1996), 28.
20. See Robert Barron, introduction to *Ignatian Collection*, by Ignatius of Loyola, Gerard Manley Hopkins, and St. Francis Xavier, ed. Holly Ordway and Daniel Seseske, trans. Louis J. Puhl, SJ (Park Ridge, IL: Word on Fire, 2020), 3–7.

figure of Ignatius of Loyola into a sixteenth-century mystical Thomas Aquinas. The saints' respective historical milieus exclude such an interpretation. Ignatius structured his community at a time when it was necessary to decide how that society would relate to the more modernizing humanist movements swelling in the Church. Perhaps another source of difference is Ignatius's emphasis on mission.

The point of all the above, however, is that there are a number of good reasons to reflect upon "Ignatius the Thomist" and the influence of Aquinas among the early Jesuits. Our task here is something of a thought experiment, carried forward in distinctive but complementary ways by the erudite contributors to this volume. We seek to reflect upon the broad theme of the relation of Ignatius and the early Jesuits to Aquinas, first of all for historical purposes. Given the influence of both Ignatius and Aquinas on the Catholic Church today (and over the centuries since their deaths), it behooves Catholic scholars to reflect upon their points of intersection. Theologically, philosophically, and spiritually, it would be a great impoverishment to neglect the ways in which these two men enrich our understanding of the revelation of the Triune God in Jesus Christ and of the deification in faith, hope, and love that Christ makes possible for us by his Paschal mystery. As Avery Dulles, SJ, observes (in an essay focused on the theology of worship), Aquinas's theology continues to instruct today because he situates his themes "within a theocentric, Christological, and ecclesial framework."[21] The very same can be said of Ignatius.

The structure of the volume imitates in some ways Ignatius's own way of proceeding in his *Spiritual Exercises*. It begins, first, by composing the scene. Thomas Osborne opens with a vista of the historical setting, especially regarding Ignatius and the early Jesuits' position between the debates of humanism and scholastic theology in the sixteenth century. Osborne includes not only Ignatius but also the writings of early Jesuits such as Alfonso Salmerón, Gregory of Valencia, and Gabriel Vázquez—each in relation to Aquinas's scholastic theology.

Ignatius's *Spiritual Exercises* is a time-tested vehicle for God's transformative grace. Several essays treat themes central to, but not exclusively found in, the *Exercises*. At the heart of the *Exercises* is the invitation for the person to attain to the direct experience of God. Justin M. Anderson sets out, therefore, to compare and contrast the ways the experience of the divine can be said to be at the heart of not only Ignatius's *Exercises* but also the Thomistic approach to God. Likewise focusing on religious experience, Margaret Hughes attends to the importance that both Ignatius and Aquinas ascribe to the reordering of

---

21. Avery Dulles, SJ, "The Theology of Worship: Saint Thomas," in *Rediscovering Aquinas and the Sacraments: Studies in Sacramental Theology*, ed. Matthew Levering and Michael Dauphinais (Chicago: Hillenbrand Books, 2009), 13.

passions through prayer. Though Aquinas sketches the metaphysics of affectivity and Ignatius more the experience, they agree that a rhythm of spiritual joy and sorrow characterizes the human pilgrimage toward the beatific vision. Because imagination serves an important function for both Aquinas and Ignatius, Nicolas Steeves, SJ, explores its meaning and role in both saints' writings. While imagination is a topic where commentators have often understood Ignatius's influencers to be predominately Franciscan and/or monastic, Steeves illustrates how Ignatius shares more with Aquinas than is often thought. Equally pivotal to the *Exercises*' popularity throughout the centuries is its method for coming to a discernment, a means of decision-making. Joseph Koterski, SJ, considers the consonance that exists between Ignatius's method of discernment and Thomas's virtue of prudence.

Likewise identifying a theme where Ignatius displays a sensibility more Thomistic than Franciscan, Andrew Hofer, OP, persuasively demonstrates how Ignatius drew, at times even verbatim, from Aquinas's distinctive Eucharistic theology to frame his own position on frequent Communion. Sr. Theresa Marie Nguyen, OP, highlights how both Thomas and Ignatius held the Blessed Virgin Mary in particular esteem. At the base of both Thomistic and Ignatian perspectives, the Mother of God serves a pivotal role both in God's salvific plan and through her mediatory influence.

Several essays investigate Ignatius and Thomas's relationship to the Church. Aaron Pidel, SJ, explores their relation to the "hierarchical Church," a phrase that appears to trace its genesis back to Ignatius's pen. Pidel pushes back against contrasting Aquinas as a Pseudo-Dionysian medieval with Ignatius as a modern apostle of divine immediacy. What is revealed is profound commonality, a certain Thomism in Ignatius. Sam Conedera, SJ, looks deeper into the veracity of claims that Ignatius, and subsequent early Jesuits, held to a "blind obedience" that Thomas would have ardently opposed.

Elizabeth Rain Kincaid and Kevin Flannery, SJ, explore the role faith played in the early Jesuit theologian Francisco de Toledo's thought. Kincaid applies Toledo's Thomistic rationale to support the then-controversial policy of Ignatius to admit *converso* Christians—Iberian converts or their descendants from Judaism—as members of the nascent Society of Jesus. Flannery offers a study of Toledo's complex relationship to Aquinas's reflections on the possibility of coerced faith, especially in light of sixteenth-century condemnations of Erasmus.

While the relationship between Ignatius and Aquinas does not exist without its questions, the effort of discerning consonances, without ignoring contrasts, bears significant fruit. Furthermore, Ignatius's indebtedness to or thematic concurrence with Aquinas is of interest when considering the goals that motivated both men. Discussing the Corinthians' argument about whether they belong to Paul or Apollos, Aquinas writes that there are two differences between Paul and Apollos. The first is found in their respective activities: one plants the words, the other nourishes them and makes them grow. The second difference is that both workers "cooperate outwardly with the work of God who works inwardly."[22] Thus, "he who plants and he who waters are one" (1 Cor 3:8). Aquinas concludes that "since their intention is to be God's ministers, they are one in the harmony of their wills; consequently, it is foolish to have dissensions about persons who are one."[23] If this is a fitting analog for viewing Aquinas and Ignatius themselves, then ascertaining the kind and degree of Ignatius's Thomism becomes an opportunity for dialogue between two figures whose greatest unity comes from worshipping the same Lord and serving this Lord within the same Church.

22. ". . . qui exterius operantur [. . .], ad operationem Dei, qui interius operatur." Thomas Aquinas, *Super Epistolas S. Pauli lectura*, bk. 1, *Super primam Epistolam ad Corinthios lectura*, ed. R. Cai, 8th ed. (Taurini-Romae: Marietti, 1953), c. 3, l.1 (no. 136).

23. Et quia, consequenter, in intentione ministrandi Deo unum sunt per concordiam voluntatis, ideo stultum est de his qui unum sunt, dissentire." Aquinas, *Super primam Epistolam ad Corinthios*, no. 138.

CHAPTER 1

The Early Jesuits and Scholastic Theology

Thomas Osborne

The early Jesuits developed and appropriated the theses and arguments for scholastic theology that were made by scholastic theologians against humanists in the early sixteenth century and were made with particular fervor in the Paris of the 1520s and 1530s. Perhaps Ignatius of Loyola's most famous remark on scholastic theology is in Rule 11 of his "Rules for Thinking, Judging, and Feeling with the Church":

> We ought to praise both positive theology and scholastic theology. For just as it is more characteristic of the positive doctors, such as St. Jerome, St. Augustine, St. Gregory, and the rest to stir up our affections toward loving and serving God our Lord in all things, so it is more characteristic of the scholastic teachers, such as St. Thomas, St. Bonaventure, the Master of the *Sentences*, and so on to define and explain for our times the matters necessary for salvation, and also to refute and explain all the errors and fallacies. For the scholastic teachers, being more modern, can avail themselves of an authentic understanding of Sacred Scripture and the holy positive doctors. Further still they, being enlightened and clarified by divine influence, make profitable use of the councils, canons, and decrees of our Holy Mother Church.[1]

---

1. "Alabar la doctrina positiva y escolástica; porque assí como es más proprio de los doctores positivos, assí como de Sant Hierónimo, Sant Augustín y de Sant Gregario, etc., el mover los afectos para en todo amar y servir a Dios nuestro Señor; assí es más proprio de los escolásticos, assí como de Sancto Thomás, San Bonaventura y del Maestro de las sentencias etc., el diffinir o declarar para nuestros tiempos de las cosas necessarias a la salud eterna, y para más impugnar y declarar todos errores y todas falacias. Porque los doctores escolásticos, como sean más modernos, no solamente se aprovechan de la vera inteligencia de la Sagrada Scriptura y de los positivos y sanctos doctores; mas aun siendo ellos iluminados y esclarecidos de la virtud divina, se ayudan de los concilios, cánones y constituciones de nuestra sancta madre Iglesia." Ignacio de Loyola, *Obras Completas*, 2nd ed., ed. Ignacio Iparraguirre and Candido de Dalmases (Madrid: Biblioteca de Autores Cristianos, 1963), 272; English trans. in *Ignatius of Loyola: The Spiritual Exercises and Selected Works*, ed. George E. Ganss, SJ, Classics of Western Spirituality (New York: Paulist Press, 1991), 212. For the different Latin versions, see Ignatius of Loyola, *Monumenta Ignatiana: Exercitia spiritualia Sancti Ignatii de Loyola et eorum directoria*, MHSI 57 (Madrid: Typis Successorum Rivadeneyrae, 1919),

In the *Constitutions of the Society of Jesus*, he similarly praises both positive and scholastic theology, and he states that Jesuits should especially study the theology of Thomas Aquinas.[2] The language and content of these recommendations reflects Ignatius's experience at the University of Paris, in which scholastic theologians were defending the importance of their discipline against those who wished to reduce theology to the study of biblical languages or the Fathers of the Early Church.

Ignatius's experience at Paris was formative both for his own outlook at that of the Jesuit Order.[3] In his letters in the 1530s, he recommends the University of Paris over other Universities.[4] We will see that this context helps to explain the reason why early Jesuits wholeheartedly adopted Ignatius's defense of scholastic theology, and in particular the theology of Thomas Aquinas. The first, or among the first, of the explicit Jesuit defenses of scholastic theology was written by Alfonso Salmerón (1515–1585), who was one of Ignatius's early companions at Paris. Similar justifications of scholasticism were written by two early Jesuit theologians, namely Gregory of Valentia (ca. 1550–1603) and Gabriel Vázquez (1649–1604). There is a clear line of influence that stems from Ignatius himself.

This historical point is at odds with the claim of some scholars that Ignatius and the early Jesuits were sympathetic towards the rejection of scholastic theology by some humanists. For example, John O'Malley writes, "Although the Jesuits never worked out a theoretical solution to the problem of making scholastic speculation pastorally meaningful, their practical solution was to translate its teachings into a humanistic rhetoric, which meant its transformation."[5] We

---

554–56, 622. For Ignatius's "Rules of Thinking with the Church" in their Parisian theological context, see Philippe Lécrivain, *Paris in the Time of Ignatius of Loyola (1528–1535)*, trans. Ralph C. Renner (St. Louis, MO: Institute of Jesuit Sources, 2011), 85–92; Paul F. Grendler, *The Jesuits and Italian Universities* (Washington, DC: The Catholic University of America Press, 2017), 22–29.

2. Ignatius of Loyola, *Constituciones*, p. 4, cc. 5 and 14, in *Obras Completas*, 492–93, 513. See also c. 6, p. 497.

3. James K. Farge, "The University of Paris in the Time of Ignatius of Loyola," in *Ignacio de Loyola y Su Tiempo: Congreso Internacional de Historia (9–13 Setiembre 1991)*, ed. Juan Plazaola (Bilbao: Universidad de Desuto, 1992), 221–22. Georg Schurhammer gives a detailed account of the early Jesuits at Paris in *Francis Xavier: His Life, His Times*, trans. Joseph Costelloe, 2 vols. (Rome: Jesuit Historical Institute, 1973), 1:108–224. For the Jesuits' adherence to the Parisian model, see especially Lécrivain, *Paris in the Time of Ignatius*, 155–58.

4. Ignatius of Loyola, Epistolae 3 and 20, in *Monumenta Ignatiana ex autographis vel ex antiquioribus exemplis. Series Prima: Sancti Ignatii Epistolae et Instructiones. Tomus primus: 1524–1548*, MHSI 22 (Madrid: Typis Gabrielis Lopez del Horno, 1903), 77–78, 148–49.

5. John W. O'Malley, *The First Jesuits* (Cambridge, MA: Harvard University Press, 1993), 255. For a somewhat similar reading, see Igna Kramp, "Der Jesuit Alfonso Salmerón (1515–1585) als humanistischer Theologe," *Theologie und Philosophie* 90 (2015): 504–27. See also the interpretation of remarks by the early Jesuit Claude Jay in William V. Bangert, SJ, *Claude Jay and Alfonso Salmerón: Two Early Jesuits* (Chicago: Loyola University Press, 1985), 73–75.

will see that Salmerón, Vázquez, and Valentia all recognize the value of humanistic education, but they explicitly resist any attempt to use such education to transform or replace scholastic theology.

The early Jesuits might have had a clearer practical orientation than the members of religious orders to which other theologians belong. These Jesuits may have tended to subordinate education in scholastic theology to preaching and other missionary work. Nevertheless, they held that scholastic theology is needed for their apostolate. Moreover, they did not seem to have unusual views in debates over whether theology is practical or speculative. O'Malley claims that "Jesuits often describe the theology they espoused as 'mystical' and contrasted it with the 'purely speculative' theology of some of their Catholic contemporaries, such as Domingo de Soto."[6] O'Malley refers to Jerome Nadal (1507–1580), a later companion of Ignatius, and Juan Alfonso de Polanco (1517–1576), who was Ignatius's secretary and a historian of the Jesuit Order's early years. Contrary to what O'Malley suggests, neither of them even hints that scholastic theology should be replaced with mystical theology, or that a conflict between the two theologies is possible.

In his writings on contemplation and the cross, Nadal distinguishes between speculative, practical, and mystical theology:

> The study of theology is threefold: one speculative, even in practical things; another practical morally; the third is mystical and spiritual. The zealous in the study of letters, both the good and the bad, both have the first and are accustomed to excel in it, in the way of an innate capacity for the speculative, in this way they are strong for something in this capacity. They have the second who are strong in practical vigor, even if they have not arrived at the spirit and the mystic experience of the spiritual life. Those only have the third who in spirit are prudent in Christ, humble and simple.[7]

There is nothing in this threefold division that would seem surprising or unusual to a scholastic theologian. The distinction between scientific and non-

---

6. O'Malley, *First Jesuits*, 243. See also John W. O'Malley, "Renaissance Humanism and the Religious Culture of the First Jesuits," *Heythrop Journal* 31 (1990): 478; "Renaissance Humanism and the First Jesuits," in *Ignacio de Loyola y su Tiempo*, 391–92.

7. "Studium theologiae est triplex: unum speculativum, etiam in rebus practicis; alterum practicum moraliter; tertium est mysticum et spirituale. Primum et habent et in eo proficere solent literarum studiosi, et boni et mali, modo ingenium sint sortiti speculativum, id est modo aliquid hac facultate valeant. Secundum habent qui practica vi valent, etiamsi spiritum non sint assequuti et vitae spiritualis experientiam mysticam. Tertium soli habent illi qui spiritu sunt prudentes in Christo, humiles et simplices." Jerome Nadal, *Orationis Observationes*, ed. Michael Nicolau, MHSI 90a (Rome: ISHI, 1964), 163. For the work and its context, see especially William V. Bangert, SJ, and Thomas M. McCoog, SJ, *Jerome Nadal, SJ: Tracking the First Generation of Jesuits* (Chicago: Loyola University Press, 1992), 193–206, 216.

scientific practical knowledge is found in Aristotle and most of his scholastic followers.[8] For instance, all virtuous individuals have prudence, whereby they reason correctly about actions. On the other hand, relatively few individuals acquire moral science through study. Similarly, scholastic authors distinguish between the knowledge that is acquired through study and that which is acquired through ordinary and even extraordinary graces. For instance, Thomas thinks that there are several cognitive habits among the gifts of the Holy Spirit, and that these cognitive habits are distinct from the similarly cognitive habits of faith and of theology.[9] Nadal's description of the three kinds of theology reproduces spiritual and theological commonplaces and indicates no new approach in theology. It is unsurprising that not long after the text quoted above, Nadal gives an exhortation to read Thomas Aquinas.[10]

There is similarly no evidence for a special Jesuit mystical theology in the passage that O'Malley finds in Polanco. In his chronicle of the year 1555, Polanco mentions the Dominican Domingo Soto as among those religious who were favorably disposed to the Jesuits.[11] Nevertheless, Polanco mentions later that Soto showed an inability to understand some of the Jesuit teachings and practices on prayer. He writes that this inability makes one "able to discern easily how much a distance there is between speculative and mystical theology; and since in the first the good Father was ably versed and in the posterior little, as it seems, thus he spoke of prayer and contemplation."[12] Polanco is describing how one Dominican, Domingo Soto, failed to understand the Jesuits on prayer because he himself lacked the necessary experience in prayer. Polanco may have thought that the Jesuits in general were more mystical and spiritual than the Dominicans, but he does not, as O'Malley suggests, think that there is a mystical theology that can be substituted for scholastic theology. Both kinds of "theology" are traditionally recognized ways of knowing about God. The first comes from prayer and the second comes from study. The division between knowledge from experience and from study is not new or unique to Jesuits. In 1542, Polanco and

---

8. Thomas Osborne, *Human Action in Thomas Aquinas, John Duns Scotus, and William of Ockham* (Washington, DC: The Catholic University of America Press, 2014), 61–108. For Thomas in particular, see Rafael-Tomas Caldera, *Le jugement par inclination chez Saint Thomas D'Aquin* (Paris: Vrin, 1980), 97–127. For Aristotle, see *Ethica Nicomachea* 6.3–7, 13.

9. See especially Thomas Aquinas, *Summa Theologiae* I–II, q. 68, a. 4, and his partial revision in II–II, q. 8, a. 6.

10. Nadal, *Orationis Observationes*, 165.

11. Juan Alfonso de Polanco, *Vita Ignatii Loiolae et rerum Societatis Jesu historia, auctore Joanne Alphonso de Polanco, ejusdem societatis sacerdote*, 6 vols., MHSI 1 (Madrid: Typographorum Societas, 1894–1898), 5:417.

12. "... ut facile discerni possit quantum intersit inter speculativam et mysticam theologiam; et quia in priori bonus Pater valde versatus fuerat, et, ut videtur, parum in posteriori, sic de oratione et contemplatione loquebatur." Polanco, *Vita Ignatii Loiolae*, 5:419.

another Jesuit were sent to the University of Padua in Italy, in part because it was superior to other Italian universities in Aristotelian and scholastic philosophy.[13] In general, they were dissatisfied with the quality of instruction even in Padua. In theology, a decision was made to focus on Thomas Aquinas's *Summa Theologiae* and Dominican authors such as the commentator Thomas de Vio Cajetan (1469–1534), although the Jesuits also read other scholastic theologians.

Other historians make broader claims that Ignatius and the Jesuits were somehow close to the spirit of Desiderius Erasmus's (1469–1536) program of theological and religious renewal.[14] Historians sympathetic to this view do not usually give very clear indications of what Erasmus's program was. Some connect it to the *devotio moderna* movement that was propagated by the Brethren of the Common Life. But this movement formed the College of Montaigu at Paris, which was the very educational institution against which Erasmus rebelled, and at which Ignatius received his early training.[15] Many scholastic theologians and writers against Erasmus were themselves formed in the *devotio moderna*. Some of these scholars seem to think that similarities to humanist exegesis and the use of humanistic methods is an indication of a new approach to theology that departs from and is a substitute for scholasticism. They appear to accept the extreme humanist view of the debate, namely that it is over whether theology should consist in humanistic biblical and patristic studies or in some scholasticism that is completely separated from them. On this view, scholastic theology is completely separated from humanism. But, scholastic theologians were generally not against the use of humanistic learning. They simply thought that these humanistic methods could not replace scholastic theology.

Historians debate Ignatius's own attitude to Erasmus's version of humanism. Ignatius's companion and first biographer, Pedro de Ribadeneira (1527–

---

13. Grendler, *Jesuits and Italian Universities*, 30–33; Angelo Martini, "Gli studi teologici di Giovanni de Polanco alle origine della legislazione scolastica della Compagnia di Gesù," *Archivum Historicum Societatis Iesu* 21, no. 42 (1952): 225–81. For Thomas Aquinas and Dominican authors, see Martini, "Studi teologici di Giovanni de Polanco," 238–41, 247–50, 273–77.

14. Marcel Bataillon, "D'Érasme a la Compagnie de Jésus," *Archives de sociologie des religions* 24 (1967): 57–81; Terence O'Reilly, "Erasmus, Ignatius Loyola, and Orthodoxy," *The Journal of Theological Studies* 39 (1979): 115–27; John C. Olin, "Erasmus and St. Ignatius of Loyola," in *Six Essays on Erasmus* (New York: Fordham University Press, 1979), 75–92; Jean-Claude Margoin, "Essai de Mise au Point sur l'Érasmisme dans le sillage d'Alcalá et la Lumière de Quelques Travaux Récents," in *Ignacio de Loyola y su Tiempo*, 245–70, at 264–66; Kramp, "Salmerón als humanistischer Theologe," 504–11.

15. I. Rodriguez-Grahit, "Ignace de Loyola et le Collège Montaigu: L'Influence de Standonk sur Ignace," *Bibliothèque d'Humanisme et Renaissance* 20 (1958): 388–401, esp. 399; James K. Farge, "Noël Beda and the Defense of the Tradition," in *Biblical Humanism and Scholasticism in the Age of Erasmus*, ed. Erika Rummel (Leiden: Brill, 2008), 145–46; Lécrivain, *Paris in the Time of Ignatius*, 38–39, 43–44, 56–59.

1611), explicitly states that Ignatius steered his followers away from reading Erasmus.[16] But many historians tend to the view that Ribadeneira and others who wrote later in the sixteenth century read back later Catholic hostility toward Erasmus into Ignatius's earlier remarks.[17] They correctly remark Catholic opinion hardened against Erasmus later, and much of the information about the early Jesuits comes from after this change of opinion. Nevertheless, there is no evidence that Ignatius was friendly to Erasmus's views, and much evidence against it.

Ignatius and the early Jesuits need to be understood in light of the context of the sixteenth-century debates over the nature of theology. Only relatively recently have some historians, such as James Farge and Nelson Minnich, paid adequate attention to the early modern arguments given in support of scholastic theology, and they have not considered in detail the relevant Jesuit writings.[18] Historians who write on Jesuits pass over what the early Jesuits say about scholastic theology or repeat small parts of it out of context. The early Jesuits, like many other scholastic theologians, were not hostile to humanism as such. But they along with other Catholics deliberately rejected and argued against attempts by some humanists to replace scholastic theology with a theology based on philology, patristics, and rhetoric. Before looking at the first explicit Jesuit defenses of scholasticism, it will be helpful to look at the debate at Paris when Ignatius and the early Jesuits were there.

Humanism and Scholastic Theology in the Paris of the Early Jesuits

Although Ignatius and many of his companions had received their earlier intellectual formation in Spain, they came together as a coherent group at Paris, where Ignatius had gone to continue his studies. They were in Paris when the debate over scholastic theology was at its height.[19] Jacques Lefèvre d'Étaples (1450–1536) and Desiderius Erasmus attempted to practice theology by focusing on biblical philology and the writings of early Church Fathers.[20] They

---

16. Pedro de Ribadeneira, *Vita Ignatii Loyolae*, ed. Candidus de Dalmases (Rome, 1965), 172–74, 859–60.

17. Olin, "Erasmus and Ignatius," 77–81; O'Malley, *First Jesuits*, 260–61.

18. Farge, "Nöel Beda"; Nelson Minnich, "Alberto Pio's Defense of Scholastic Theology," in *Biblical Humanism and Scholasticism*, 277–95. Much helpful material can be found in Erika Rummel, *Erasmus and His Catholic Critics*, 2 vols. (Nieuwkoop: De Graaf Publishers, 1989).

19. Farge, "Paris in the Time of Ignatius."

20. Guy Bedouelle, "Attacks on the Biblical Humanism of Jacques Lefèvre d'Étaples," trans. Anna Machado-Matheson, in *Biblical Humanism and Scholasticism*, 117–41; Jan de Boeft, "Erasmus and the Church Fathers," in *The Reception of The Church Fathers in the West: From the Carolingians to the Maurists*, 2 vols., ed. Irena Backus (Leiden: Brill, 1997), 2:542–49; Arnoud Visser,

implicitly and explicitly criticized scholastic theology. Erasmus was the most influential representative of Northern Humanism, and Lefèvre d'Étaples had taught theology at Paris for many years before he left to pursue humanistic studies. By the 1520s this debate over scholastic method became intermingled with issues that arose from disputes with the early Protestants.[21] Francis I, the King of France himself, supported the humanistic side. Traditional Catholic religion and scholastic theology were both under direct attack, but in different ways.

Erasmus and Lefèvre d'Étaples were humanists, but not all humanists were anti-scholastic. "Humanism" is a broad and difficult to define term, and it seems to be applied to the study of classical humanistic disciplines, such as language, poetry, and rhetoric. "Scholasticism" mostly applies to the study of Aristotelian philosophy and theology in the universities and religious houses of studies. How are scholasticism and humanism related? Some humanists, such as Giovanni Pico della Mirandola, were also scholastic thinkers. Paul Oskar Kristeller writes, "In my opinion, it is not so much a question of a group of different philosophical or theological doctrines, as has often been thought, as it is of a group of various studies and preoccupations that touch on philosophical and theological thought in an important but indirect manner and that have other centers of diffusion."[22] The differences between scholastic schools, such as those between Scotism and Thomism, were differences between ways of engaging in the same kind of activity. Erasmus and those trained only in humanistic methods were unable to engage in scholastic theology.

The roots of the controversy in Paris can be seen in an earlier conflict between Erasmus and Maarten van Dorp (1485–1525), who was a Louvain theologian and generally sympathetic to Erasmus. In his *Moriae Encomium* (1511), Erasmus directly attacked those who "only seem to themselves most to be theologians at least, if they speak in a barbarous and low way, and when they stammer so far that they are able to be understood by no one unless he is a

---

"Erasmus, the Church Fathers and the Ideological Implications of Philology," *Erasmus of Rotterdam Society Yearbook* 31 (2011): 7–31. There is a review of the scholarship until 1998 in Charles G. Nauert, "Humanism as Method: Roots of Conflict with the Scholastics," *The Sixteenth Century Journal* 29 (1998): 427–38; Lécrivain, *Paris in the Time of Ignatius*, 45–53.

21. Nauert, "Humanism as Method," 431–37; Erika Rummel, *The Humanist-Scholastic Debate in the Renaissance and Reformation* (Cambridge, MA: Harvard University Press, 1995), 126–52.

22. Paul Oskar Kristeller, "Thomism and the Italian Thought of the Renaissance," in *Medieval Aspects of Renaissance Learning*, rev. ed., ed. and trans. Edward P. Mahoney (New York: Columbia University Press, 1992), 29–91, at 55. One of the best introductions is still Paul Oskar Kristeller, *Renaissance Thought: The Classic, Scholastic, and Humanist Strains* (New York: Harper and Row, 1961), 92–119.

stammerer."²³ In contrast to the works of such scholastic authors, he praised the rhetoric and Latinity of St. Jerome in particular.²⁴ Dorp's subsequent attack on Erasmus is perhaps best known for the response that it provoked from St. Thomas More (1478–1535).

In his Letter to Dorp (1515), More claimed that he and Erasmus were only against scholastic theologians who neglected the Scriptures, and he admitted that many at Louvain did not neglect them.²⁵ Nevertheless, More's overall approach is supportive of those who devote themselves to Scriptures and the Fathers rather than to scholastic disputations.²⁶ In his slightly later Letter to Oxford (1518 or 1519), More defended this patristic approach that he noted was called "positive theology." More's use of the term predates Ignatius's use of it and indicates to some extent what it means. More writes:

> But I certainly deny that theology, that venerable heavenly queen, is so pent up in those narrow limits that she does not also inhabit and dwell in holy scripture as her proper home, from which she makes her pilgrimage through all the cells of the oldest and holiest fathers, Augustine, I mean, Jerome, Ambrose, Cyprian, Chrysostom, Gregory, Basil, and other men like them, whose 'positive' writings, as they are now called with contempt, were the mainstay of theological studies for more than a thousand years after the passion of Christ, before those subtle problems which now command almost exclusive attention were even invented.²⁷

Well before the Protestant Reformation, More defends a theological method that is based on Scripture and the writings of the Fathers. He suggests that such theology was not needed for the first millennium of the Church's history. Moreover, More seems to belittle the "subtle problems" that scholastic theologians

---

23. "... demum maxime sibi videntur theologi, si quammaxime barbare spurceque loquantur, cumque adeo balbutiunt vt a nemine nisi balbo possint intelligi . . ." Desiderius Erasmus, *Moriae Encomium*, in *Opera Omnia*, vol. 4 (Amsterdam: North-Holland, 1969–), bk. 3:158. A looser translation can be found in *The Collected Works of Erasmus* (Toronto: University of Toronto Press, 1974–), 27:130. This translation will be cited as CWE.

24. Den Boeft, "Erasmus and the Church Fathers," 542–47.

25. Thomas More, Letter to Martin Dorp, in *The Complete Works of St. Thomas More*, ed. and trans. Daniel Kinney (New Haven, CT: Yale University Press, 1986), 15:44–49.

26. Daniel Kinney, Introduction to vol. 15 of *Complete Works of Thomas More*, lxxii–xcii.

27. "verum enimuero intra has angustias, augustam illam coeli reginam theologiam, sic coerceri pernego, ut non praeterea sacras incolat atque inhabitet scripturas, indeque per omnes antiquissimorum ac sanctissimorum patrum cellas peregrinetur, Augustini dico, Hieronymi, Ambrosii, Cipriani, Chrysostomi, Gregorii, Basilii, atque id genus aliorum, quibus (ut nunc contemptim vocant) positiua scribentibus, theologiae studium stetit, a Christo passo, plus annis mille, priusquam argutae istae nascerentur, quam iam prope solae uentilantur, quaestiunculae." Thomas More, Letter to Oxford, in *The Complete Works of More*, 130–95, at 140, trans. Kinney at 141.

discuss. From these remarks we can see that criticism of scholasticism predated the Protestant Reformation.

The debate between Erasmus and his critics was originally about the nature of theology. Erasmus thought of himself primarily as a theologian, perhaps because he considered theology to be more of a literary and philological study.[28] Scholastic theologians saw theology as an Aristotelian science that proceeded by examining evidence and opposing arguments.[29] Consequently, scholastics generally thought of Erasmus as a philological expert and not as a theologian. Some or even many were sympathetic to his studies, but they thought them insufficient for theology. On their view, Erasmus, and those like him, lacked the training to understand and provide an opinion on difficult theological issues. On the other hand, Erasmus thought of himself as a theologian. At times, he said that he was criticizing not scholastic theology but rather its abuse, and he even praises some scholastic theologians, such as Thomas Aquinas. Nevertheless, his praise seems insincere in that he never explains why scholastic theology is worthwhile or how scholastic theologians advanced the study of theology as a science.[30]

The University of Paris was traditionally among the more important guardians of Catholic doctrine.[31] In 1521, the theology faculty censured a variety of propositions from Luther's writings.[32] Among these censures were seven statements about scholastic theology. The Parisian theology faculty classified them as being dangerous, false, and in some places near to heresy. In the following years, several humanists criticized both scholastic theology and traditional Catholic practices, such as devotion to the Blessed Virgin Mary, and the payment of stipends for Mass. These humanists had the protection of the French King Francis I through the patronage of his sister Marguerite.

The first controversies were over editions of and commentaries on Scripture.[33] Erasmus had previously published his own Greek version of the New

---

28. C. J. de Vogel, "Erasmus and His Attitude Towards Church Dogma," in *Scrinium Erasmianum*, 2 vols., ed. J. Coppens (Leiden: Brill, 1969), 2:101–32; Kramp, "Salmerón als humanistischer Theologe," 512–17.

29. For the development of this view in early scholasticism, see M-D. Chenu, *La Théologie comme Science au XIIIe Siècle*, 3rd ed. (Paris: Vrin, 1957).

30. Farge, "Noel Beda," 155–56, 156n61.

31. The best accounts of these controversies are in James K. Farge, *Orthodoxy and Reform in Early Reformation France* (Leiden: Brill, 1985), 160–208; James K. Farge, "The University of Paris"; James K. Farge, "Noel Beda"; Bedouelle, "Attacks on Biblical Humanism." But see also Erika Rummel, *The Humanist-Scholastic Debate*, 96–125.

32. César-Égasse Du Boulay, *Historia Universitatis Parisiensis*, 6 vols. (Paris, 1665–1673), 6:126–27; Farge, *Orthodoxy and Reform*, 169.

33. Myron P. Gilmore, "Valla, Érasme et Bédier a propos du Nouveau Testament," in *L'Humanisme Français au début de la Renaisaance*, ed. André Stegmann, Colloque International de Tours (Paris: Vrin, 1973), 175–84.

Testament (1519). Lefèvre d'Étaples published commentaries on and translations of Scripture that seemed to undermine the traditional Latin text and older Catholic commentaries. Although the theologians at Paris were concerned about these and other new translations and commentaries, they did not entirely dismiss biblical philology or positive theology.[34] For example, the syndic of the theology faculty, Noel Beda, recognized the strength of Erasmus's philological work and at first attempted to help him in his enterprise.[35] Similarly, Beda's colleague John Mair thought that the heretics' use of Scripture was an occasion for scholastic theologians to study Scripture more carefully.[36] Nevertheless, the Paris theologians did not think that such studies could replace scholastic theology.

Although Pierre Costurier was among the first Parisian theologians to publish a direct attack on the humanistic biblical studies, Beda expanded the attack and oversaw the theology faculty's overall later censure of Erasmus. Beda had been principal of the College of Montaigu, which was established and influenced heavily by the Brethren of the Common Life. Erasmus had been a student at this college and wrote bitterly against its rigobrs. Beda was no longer principal but remained at the College when Ignatius resided there. Beda and the other allied theologians were concerned not only with Erasmus's biblical studies but also with his editions of the Fathers, as well as with his comments on scholastic theology in his preface to his edition of Hilary of Poitiers's *Opera Omnia*.[37] In this Preface, Erasmus stated "This is indeed the mark of Theological learning: to define nothing beyond what is recorded in Holy Scripture, but to dispense in good faith what is there recorded."[38] He criticized scholastic theology for its complexity, its pointless discussions, and its use of technical languages.

In 1529, Beda published his personal work against the humanists, *Against the Secret Lutherans* (*Adversus clandestinos Lutheranos*). As the title indicates, he thought that the Parisian humanists supported Protestants even though they

---

34. Farge, "Noel Beda," 146. Lécrivain, *Paris in the Time of Ignatius*, 137–46, seems to accept the humanists' caricatures of Beda and other scholastic theologians and does not consider the arguments in favor of scholastic theology.

35. A. Renaudet, *Études Érasmiennes (1521–1529)* (Paris: Droz, 1939), 237–304; Farge, *Orthodoxy and Reform*, 187–96.

36. John Mair, dedicatory preface to *In secundum sententiarum* (Paris: Badius, 1528). The preface has no folio numbers. Farge, *Orthodoxy and Reform*, 179–80.

37. Desiderius Erasmus, preface to Hilary of Poitiers, *Opera Omnia* (Basel: Froben, 1523), trans. John C. Olin and James F. Brady, Jr., in CWE 9:246–74. The original Latin preface does not have folio numbers.

38. "Hoc eruditionis est Theologicae, nihil ultra quam Sacris Litteris proditum est definire, verum id quod proditum est bona fide dispensare." Cited in Desiderius Erasmus, *Ad Censuras Facultatis Theologiae Parisiensis*, in *Desiderii Erasmi Roterodami Opera Omnia*, ed. Jean LeClerc, 10 vols. (Leiden: Peter van der Aa, 1703–1706), vol. 9, col. 927A (CWE 82:255). The Leiden *Opera Omnia* is cited hereafter as LB. See also the text cited in LB, vol. 9, col. 922C (CWE 82:255).

publicly adhered to Catholicism. There were several censures of Erasmus and Lefèvre by the whole faculty in the late 1520s, but they were published and perhaps only made public in 1531. Censure 97 summarizes the central issues:

> It was necessary to assist the weakness of those who think that whatever is set forth in brilliant and splendid language is also true, and that, on the other hand, whatever is written in rude and unpolished language is false, paying no attention to the fact that there is no less difference between one and the other than between jars and what they contain, which is often very great.... It was also necessary to attend to those who think that perfect and peerless theology consists in knowing Greek and Hebrew writings, whereas in fact those who know these languages, if they are not otherwise trained in the discipline of theology, should be considered grammarians, not theologians, just like those who have mastered Latin literature but progressed no further.[39]

The censure directly addresses two of the main humanistic criticisms of scholasticism, namely, that the technical language is barbaric and that philological skill is more important for understanding Scripture than scholastic theology is.

In 1530, Beda reminded the theology faculty that the statutes required students to take some exams in speculative scholastic theology, and not only "positive theology."[40] He did not denigrate positive theology but wished to uphold the place of scholastic theology. In the same year, Francis I appointed royal professors who were unskilled in theology to teach Greek and Hebrew. They were not theology professors, but they seemed to discuss theology. Moreover, Francis I arrested Beda and eventually caused his death under torture. Despite Beda's unhappy end, the theology faculty, as a whole, continued to reject the humanistic approach. By this time, criticisms were levelled against Erasmus in Spain, as well.[41]

---

39. "Huc etiam accedit, quod succurrendum fuit illorum imbecillitati, qui vera esse credunt, qua splendore illustrantur orationis: contra vera falsa, quæ rudi et incompto sermone scribuntur: minime attendentes inter hac et illa non minus esse discrimen, quam inter vasa et ea quæ in illis continentur, quod sæpe maximum est ... Consulendum item fuit iis, qui Græcas nosse et Hebraicas litteras perfectam putant esse et consummatam Theologiam: cum tamen qui eas norunt, si non alioqui in Theologica disciplina fuerint instituti, Grammatici censendi sunt, non Theologi: quemadmodum et qui Latinas profitentur non ulterius progressi." This text from Erasmus's preface is cited in the Parisian censure of Erasmus in LB, vol. 9, col. 922C–E (CWE 82:265). For the original context in the preface, see CWE 9:253.

40. James K. Farge, ed., *Registre des Procès-Verbaux de la Faculté de Théologie de l'Université de Paris de janvier 1524 à novembre 1533* (Paris: Aux Amateurs de Livres, 1990), 235–36. Cf. 235n34.

41. Lu Ann Homza, "Hero or Heretic? Spanish Humanism and the Valladolid Assembly of 1527," *Renaissance Quarterly* 50 (1997): 78–118; Alejando Coroleu, "Anti-Erasmianism in Spain," in *Biblical Humanism and Scholasticism*, 73–92.

At the Valladolid Conference in 1527, Spanish theologians similarly censured Erasmus for his lack of theological knowledge and his writings for their lack of terminological precision.

Ignatius and his companions wholeheartedly adopted this suspicion of humanistic theology. Like other scholastic theologians, they recognized the value of the humanistic studies, but they did not think that these studies on their own were sufficient for theology. Moreover, they saw that the single-minded pursuit of such studies led many at the time away from the Catholic faith. As we have seen, Ignatius worked into his *Spiritual Exercises* the rule in favor of scholastic theology. His *Constitutions* prescribed the study of scholastic theology, and Thomas Aquinas in particular. Moreover, Ignatius used the educational methods of the scholastics at Paris as a model for education within his own order.

In October 1529, Ignatius had left the College of Montaigu for the College of Sainte-Barbe, perhaps because of Juan de Peña, who lectured there on Aristotelian philosophy, or maybe to be closer to Sts. Peter Faber and Francis Xavier, who were students there.[42] He, at first, roomed or in some way lived with all three. Many of those associated with Sainte-Barbe were critical of scholastic theology. Ignatius directed his followers to study with Dominican or Franciscan scholastic theologians. The early Jesuit Nicholas Bobadilla (1511–1590) provides a first-hand account of Ignatius's attitude in his personal memoirs, which were written much later in the third-person:

> The Lutheran heresy began in that time to rage at Paris, and many were burned at the Place Maubert, and those who were studying Greek were becoming Lutheran. Therefore, Master Bobadilla dismissed the goal that he had in Spain, [of studying] the three languages, namely in Greek, Latin, and Hebrew, mostly because he found at Paris a saintly man, Master Ignatius of Loyola, who exhorted him to follow the study of scholastic theology and of the holy positive doctors. He followed his counsel, in hearing theology under Doctor Benedict and Master de Ori, most learned men among the Dominican convent, and among the Franciscans Master de Cornibus, [who is] not praised enough among the theologians.[43]

---

42. Farge, "University of Paris," 231; Schurhammer, *Francis Xavier*, 1:141; Lécrivain, *Paris in the Time of Ignatius*, 60–61, 126.

43. "Eo tempore incipiebat grassari Parisiis hæresis lutherana, et multi comburebantur in platea Mumbert, et qui graecizabant, lutheranizabant; ideo Mag. Bobadilla remisit propositum quod habebat in Hispania, trium linguarum, scilicet græce, latine, et hebraice, maxime quia inuenit Parisiis virum sanctum, Mag. Ignatium de Loyola, qui illum exhortatus ad prosequendum studia theologiae scholasticae et positivae sanctorum doctorum; cujus consilium est sequutus, audiendo theologiam sub doctore Benedicto et Mtro. de Ori, uiris doctissimis apud sanctum Dominicum, et apud franciscanos Mtrum. De Cornibus, non satis laudatum apud omnes

At this time, the term "Lutheran" was a general term for those who eventually came to be known as Protestants. Bobadilla mentions, but does not attribute directly to Ignatius, an apparently common phrase that connected the perhaps exclusive humanistic study of Greek with this heresy: *qui graecizabant, lutheranizabant*. Greek without scholastic theology in that time led to religious error. Most importantly, Bobadilla gives a picture of Ignatius's mind that fits directly with what we know from the *Spiritual Exercises*, which is that Ignatius encouraged both the study of the Fathers (positive theology) and scholasticism. In particular, Ignatius counseled Bobadilla to study with the scholastic theology that was taught by the Dominicans and Franciscans.

Ignatius, and the Order as a whole, always showed a predilection for the theology of St. Thomas Aquinas. However, it is significant that he recommended to his early companions not only Dominican theologians, but also a Franciscan theologian who seems to have been a follower of John Duns Scotus, who was among those authors who were most abused by the humanists. Despite his appreciation of the Franciscan de Cornibus, Ignatius in his writings did not recommend Scotus in the way that he recommended Thomas Aquinas.

We can see from Bobadilla's first-hand account that Ignatius shared the concerns that scholastic theologians had about those who wished to substitute biblical philology for scholastic theology. There is evidence that Ignatius similarly warned St. Francis Xavier away from the same humanist professors.[44] According to Jerome Nadal, Ignatius worked scholastic theology into the *Constitutions* precisely to combat the influence of the more philological and humanistic theology that he saw at Paris. Although Nadal himself had for a time been a student at Paris, he warmed to the Jesuits only much later in his life. Nevertheless, he had first-hand experience of student life in Paris during the 1530s. After his entry into the Order, Nadal was a reliable authority on the *Constitutions*, and he personally knew Ignatius. In his *Scholia* on the *Constitutions*, Nadal writes:

---

theologos." Nicholas Alphonsus Bobadilla, *Bobadillae monumenta: Nicolai Alphonsi de Bobadilla, sacerdotis e Societate Jesu, gesta et scripta ex autographis aut archetypis potissimum deprompta*, MHSI 46 (Madrid: Typis Gabrielis Lopez del Horno 1913), 614–15. Cf. 560–61. For these three theologians, see James K. Farge, *Biographical Register of Paris Doctors of Theology 1500–1536* (Toronto: PIMS, 1980) where they are listed as "Jean (Benedictus) Benoist, OP" (39–40), "Matthieu Ory, OP" (353–356), and "Pierre de Cornibus, OFM" (110–112). For the Dominican and Franciscan Convents, see Lécrivain, *Paris in the Time of Ignatius*, 152–53.

44. For the evidence, see Schurhammer, *Francis Xavier*, 1:168–72. Schurhammer, 171n187, thinks the royal professors are the "*malas compañías*" mentioned in Xavier's *Epistola* 1, in Franciscus Xaverius, *Monumenta Xaveriana, ex autographis vel ex antiquioribus exemplis collecta*, 2 vols., MHSI 16 (Madrid: Typis Augustini Avrial, 1899–1900), 1:204. Lécrivain, *Paris in the Time of Ignatius*, 150, suggests more precisely that it was a group connected with Nicholas Bourbon, who was hostile to Beda and close to the royal professor Pierre Danès.

Father Ignatius saw that many in Paris, and he heard that many in Germany, through the study of Greek literature without theology, were faltering and were carried off to the novelties about the faith. He wished therefore to guard against the danger in us.[45]

Nadal situates Ignatius's own defense of scholasticism within this historical context. He is a first-hand witness to Ignatius's commitment to scholastic theology.

In his *Commentaries* on the *Constitutions*, Nadal explains that the value of studying Greek and Hebrew languages is not for revising the traditional Vulgate version of the Bible, but to better understand and defend it.[46] This study of languages is preparation for or perhaps in addition to the study of philosophy and theology. He notes the importance of Aristotelian philosophy for understanding scholastic theology, and states that, in theology, Thomas Aquinas should be followed unless the common consent might be against him on a point. This study of scholastic theology is the highest part of the Jesuit's education. Even though humanistic learning is a valuable preparation for and even addition to scholastic theology, it is clearly subordinate. In this account, Nadal seems to be describing the early understanding of theology by Ignatius and the early Jesuits, which in turn was the position of the scholastic theologians at Paris in Ignatius's time.

Some of the confusion of contemporary historians exhibit over Jesuits and scholasticism perhaps reflects that the scholars share with the more radical humanists the belief that scholastic theology is meant to be a substitute for devotion and affective preaching. But this belief, that is shared both by some humanists and apparently by later scholars, is one that the defenders of scholastic theology do not share. Some or even many scholastic theologians may have neglected prayer and pastoral work. Many medieval spiritual writers who influenced not only Ignatius but also many of his scholastic contemporaries, such as the author of the *Imitation of Christ* and Ludolph of Saxony (d. 1378), stressed the importance of devotion and pastoral duties over study.[47] Ludolph's *Life of Christ* even contains an account of the damnation of Philip the Chancellor, who was one of the more influential theologians of the early thirteenth

---

45. "Viderat exempla Pr. Ignatius, quod Luteciae plerique, et in Germanía audierat, plures per studia litterarum graecarum absque Theologia evanescebant, et ad novitates fidei abducebantur. Hoc igítur periculum voluit in nostris caveri." Jerome Nadal, *Scholia* pars 4, cap. 6, no. 367, in *Scholia in Constitutiones S.I.*, ed. Manuel Ruiz Jurado (Granada: Facultad de Teologia, 1976), 102. For the context and authority of this work, see Bangert and McCoog, *Nadal*, 207–19.

46. Jerome Nadal, *Commentarii de Instituto Societatis Iesu*, ed. Michael Nicolau, MHSI 90 (Rome: MHSI, 1962), 740–42, 828–29.

47. O'Malley, *First Jesuits*, 264–66; Schurhammer, *Francis Xavier*, 1:175–81.

century.⁴⁸ These medieval criticisms were more about the lives of some scholastic theologians than about scholastic theology. The College of Montaigu, which was criticized so sharply by Erasmus, was a bulwark both of such medieval devotion and of scholastic theology. Both the humanists and contemporary scholars frequently mistake valid criticisms of some scholastic theologians for criticisms of scholastic theology itself.

Like the prominent defenders of scholasticism, Ignatius is not against any using humanist scholarship in theology, but instead against the view such humanistic studies are sufficient for theology. It reflects, or at the very least resembles closely, Beda's criticisms of Erasmus and Lefèvre d'Étaples, and the Parisian theology faculty's censures. Nadal's description of Ignatius fits easily with Bobadilla's account and explains the references to scholastic theology and Thomas Aquinas that can be found in the *Spiritual Exercises* and in the *Constitutions*. The very language of these foundational Jesuit texts reflects Ignatius's experience at Paris and not some later Catholic reaction against Erasmus. As Paul Grendler writes, "The first Jesuits were unanimous in their preference for scholastic theology and distrust and hostility toward biblical theology."⁴⁹ We will see that this same attitude is reflected in some of the earliest Jesuit writings on the nature of theology.

Salmerón's *Commentarii in Evangelicam Historiam, et in Acta Apostolorum*

Alfonso Salmerón was perhaps the most prolific author among Ignatius's early companions at Paris. He completed his master's examination in 1532 in Alcala, and then went with to Paris for further studies along with his friend Diego Lainez, who also joined the Jesuits.⁵⁰ They lived at Sainte-Barbe, where we have seen Bobadilla and Xavier already were. Salmerón formally joined the Jesuits in 1534 and in 1536 received his Master of Arts. Consequently, he is a first-hand witness to the experience of the early Jesuits in Paris during the controversies over humanism. Like most scholastic theologians and the other early Jesuits, Salmerón was sympathetic to humanistic learning but suspicious of or hostile to Erasmus himself.⁵¹ He later played an important role in the devel-

---

48. Ludolph of Saxony, *Vita Christi*, p. 1, cap. 68, in *Vita Jesu Christi*, ed. A.-C. Bolard, L.-M. Rigollot, and J. Carnadet (Paris/Rome: Palmé, 1865), 301. For a translation of this passage, see Schurhammer, *Francis Xavier*, 1:179–80. It is unclear to me whether this particular text was in the version that Ignatius had used.
49. Grendler, *Jesuits and Italian Universities*, 27.
50. Bangert, *Jay and Salmerón*, 155–61.
51. Bangert, *Jay and Salmerón*, 159–62, 342–43. Kramp, "Salmerón als humanistischer Theologe," 517–23, gives examples of Salmerón's commentaries that show a similarity with Erasmus's

opment of the Jesuits and as a theologian at the Council of Trent. It was only when he arrived at Naples in 1565 that he was able to put together his various notes into a publishable form. His *Commentary on the Gospel History and on the Acts of the Apostles* (*Commentarii in evangelicam historiam, et in Acta Apostolorum*) includes a lengthy discussion of how Scripture is best studied.[52] Although Salmerón admits that the study of the original languages and other humanistic tools are helpful, he thinks that scholastic theology is more important for understanding Scripture.

The first volume of Salmerón's *Commentary* contains preparatory material about how to approach the Scriptures. The most relevant sections for our purposes are Prolegomenon XVII, which is on the disciplines of human knowledge generally, and Prolegomenon XVIII, which is on scholastic theology.[53] The human disciplines are not the same as the disciplines that are studied primarily by humanists.[54] They include rhetoric, dialectic, moral and natural philosophy, and metaphysics. In Prolegomenon XVII, he is concerned with defending the uses of these human disciplines in theology in response to those who think that human knowledge is unnecessary for understanding Scripture.

Salmerón first notes that only the teaching of Christ is necessary for the Christian faith and salvation. On the other hand, he notes that "The human disciplines have worth for the more correct understanding of the Sacred Scriptures, and for their fuller understanding, for putting them into the right light and propounding and explaining them fruitfully to others, and fighting against those who speak against them, and they stand out as a great ornament of the Church if, as is right, someone uses them well."[55] He mentions the examples of St. Justin Martyr and Augustine of Hippo, and gives six arguments for this position.[56] His arguments generally note how merely human learning has in the past and now can be used for a higher purpose. The sixth and final argument is against Luther's rejection of dialectics and philosophy as aids to understanding the Scriptures. Salmerón notes that dialectics and philosophy are very well

---

own exegesis. However, she does not address Salmerón's explicit defense of scholastic theology. She does not sharply distinguish between a humanistic theology and the use of humanistic tools by scholastic theology.

52. Bangert, *Jay and Salmerón*, 328–49.

53. Alfonso Salmerón, *Commentarii in Evangelicam Historiam Et in Acta Apostolorum* (Madrid, 1598), 416a–29b. All references are to this edition.

54. Salmerón, *Commentarii*, Prol. XVII:416a–b.

55. "Ad sacram Scripturam rectius, et plenius intelligendam, illustrandamque atque ad aliis eam cum fructu proponendam et explicandam, atque a contradicentibus propugnandam humanæ disciplinæ valent plurimum, ornamentumque maximum Ecclesiæ Dei præstant, si, ut par est, bene quis eis utatur." Salmerón, *Commentarii*, prol. XVII: 418b.

56. Salmerón, *Commentarii*, Prol. XVII:418b–421a.

fitted for being instruments for the arts and sciences, and that they can clearly be used in addition for the study of the Scriptures and Christian Theology.

Salmerón's defense of scholastic theology in Prolegomenon XVIII more or less follows the same lines as his argument in Prolegomenon XVII.[57] He explains in greater detail how scholastic theology uses the human sciences and disputations in order to arrive at a better understanding of Scripture. Salmerón follows the widespread identification of scholastic theology with theology as was practiced by Peter Lombard in the *Sentences*, and then perfected by such theologians as Thomas Aquinas and Bonaventure. In addition to these exemplars, which were mentioned by Ignatius himself, Salmerón lists Albert the Great and Alexander of Hales. Salmerón argues that these scholastic theologians were particularly influenced by two of the more systematic Church Fathers, namely Augustine and St. John Damascene.

In general, Salmerón appeals to New Testament and early Christian practice, and the approval of scholastic theology by Church authorities. William Bangert states, "Focusing on the basically disputatious nature of scholastic theology, 'dialectical theology' (*theologia disputatrix*), Salmerón advanced the unusual viewpoint that it has its origins in Christ."[58] But Salmerón never suggests that the biblical texts feature fully developed scholastic disputations, or that the biblical disputations follow well-developed scholastic dialectic.[59] In response to humanistic critics who held that scholastic theologians erred in holding disputations over religious matters, Salmerón provides historical examples to show that even biblical figures engaged in the disputations that many humanists think are unsuitable for theology. In other words, he wishes to show that theology is not merely about passing on what is revealed without arguments or questions. Among his examples of Christ's disputations and arguments about Scripture, he mentions the early dispute in the Temple. Christ's childhood appearance in the Temple is merely one among many examples of public disputation. Salmerón also refers to the way in which St. Stephen and St. Paul disputed with their adversaries, and more broadly the way in which the Apostles disputed first with the Jews and then with the Gentiles. He merely wishes to show that there are arguments and disputations in the Scriptures themselves, and not that biblical figures learned and taught according to the scholastic method. Salmerón explicitly states that scholastic theology was not perfected until a later period.

Salmerón argues that simply reading what the Fathers wrote will not solve complex theological problems.[60] Scholastic theology orders and condenses

---

57. Salmerón, *Commentarii*, Prol. XVIII:425a–26b.
58. Bangert, *Jay and Salmerón*, 157.
59. Salmerón, *Commentarii*, Prol. XVIII:425a–b.
60. Salmerón, *Commentarii*, Prol. XVIII:425b–26a.

matters that are spread throughout patristic writings. Moreover, scholastic theology gives a way of adjudicating and reconciling disagreements between different Church Fathers. In its ability to take into account such various opinions, it is a good tool for protecting the Catholic faith against heretics. Salmerón seems particularly convinced of its value for easily and accurately refuting heresy. He uses an example taken from classical literature to describe why the early Protestants want Catholics to discard scholastic theology. He recalls how Philip of Macedon, when he was besieging Athens, asked the Athenians to give up Demosthenes and some other prominent citizens in return for peace. Demosthenes told the Athenians the story of the wolf who promised the shepherds that he would not attack the sheep if only the shepherds would remove the sheep dogs. The shepherds gave up their dogs, and the wolf was able to eat the sheep. According to Salmerón, the Protestants similarly argued for peace if Catholics would give up scholastic theology. Their goal was to undermine the Catholic faith more easily.

The use of this classical example perhaps shows a humanistic influence on Salmerón. But he is particularly concerned to address Erasmus's criticisms of scholastic Latin and its use of technical terminology. Like the theologians at Paris, he connects Erasmus's brand of humanism with the early Protestant reformers. Salmerón writes:

> Indeed, this is common to all skills, which concern the body or the soul, that from day to day many new words are collected to impose on things: what is marvelous that this happened in Theology, whose things were unknown at first? And when things and actions are more than words, having grown in their enumeration, it was necessary to devise new names, which in a useful way might represent them to us. No one is ignorant that Cicero, treating physical questions, ventured to do it with praise, as is acknowledge in the book *On Ends*. Now too among the wise it was observed, that they should reach more for things rather than words.[61]

The last quoted sentence reflects a standard criticism of the humanistic theologians which was repeated by the Parisian theologians' censure of Erasmus, which is that they are more concerned with purity of style than with knowledge.

---

61. "Etenim hoc commune est omnibus artibus, quae corpus vel animum concernunt, ut multa indies nova vocabula observatum fuit, rebus imponere cogantur: quid mirum igitur est id fieri in Theologia, cuius res primo erant ignotae? Et cum plures sint actiones, et res quam voces, crescente earum numero, necessarium fuit nova vocabula excogitari, quae eas nobis commode repraesentarent. Nemo ignorat, Ciceronem Physica quaestiones tractantem, id cum laude ausum fuisse facere, ut libro de Finibus confitetur. Id etiam apud sapientes observatum fuit, ut magis rebus quam verbis intenderent." Salmerón, *Commentarii*, Prol. XVIII:426b. Salmerón refers to Erasmus by name in the immediately preceding text.

Salmerón quotes Cicero in order to show that even one of the humanist's preferred stylists was forced to invent new words, on account of the poverty of Latin.

The objection to scholastic terminology is in some way connected with a wish to return to a simpler and supposedly more scriptural Christianity. According to a related line of objection, scholastic theology considers new and useless questions about matters that are too high for human investigation.[62] These matters are more for religious veneration than for study. Scientific investigation into them leads to religious doubt. Although Salmerón does not explicitly mention Erasmus in this context, he may have Erasmus in mind. Erasmus makes this disparagement of scholastic theology in his Preface to Hilary's *Opera*, as well as in his other writings. Salmerón shows how this objection indicates a misunderstanding of theology's nature and role.

Salmerón notes that all sciences proceed from certain principles, and that scholastic theology has as its principles the indubitable articles of faith. Scholastic disputations are not about whether to believe matters of faith, but rather about how best to understand them. Even the Apostles and the Christian Fathers did not use the simplest language but attempted to explain the articles of faith to their hearers. Theology, in the way that other sciences do, moves from the general and confused universal to assertions that are clearer. In response to the objection that scholastic theology is unimportant because it was unknown to the Fathers, Salmerón replies that scholastic clarity and stricter language is necessary to respond to heresies and different difficulties. He writes, "the stupidity of the heretics drives Catholic writers to devise so many distinctions, by which they dissolve their knots, empty out their doubts, and explain their perplexities."[63] Theology, like other sciences, must use precise language as it grows. The use of dialectics and Aristotelian terminology is for the sake of arriving at precise assertions and statements. An attempt to retain merely Scriptural language would hobble theologians in their responses to new problems that arise.

The disagreement among scholastic theologians is not about the principles of faith but about such conclusions. There is disagreement in scholastic theology for many of the same reasons that there are disagreements in human disciplines. Salmerón allows that some scholastic theologians can be excessively disputatious or concerned with matters of lesser importance. Nevertheless, these errors result from the abuse of the method, and not the method itself. He again compares theology with other disciplines, to the extent that the methods

---

62. Salmerón, *Commentarii*, Prol. XVIII:427a–b.
63. "Stultitia Haereticorum Catholicos scriptores ad tot distinctiones excogitandas quibus nodos eorum dissolverent, dubia evacuarent, et perplexa explicarent, compulit." Salmerón, *Commentarii*, Prol. XVIII:427b.

of these other arts and sciences can also be abused. Just as one would not use an abuse of method to condemn all the human arts and sciences, so one should not use a similar abuse to condemn scholastic theology.

Scholastic theology can be compared to the other sciences because of the way in which it is partly human even though it is also partly divine.[64] It is human because it involves human skill in dialectics and draws on philosophical knowledge. Perhaps unlike some of his humanistic Protestants and critics, but like the wider Catholic theological tradition, Salmerón distinguishes sharply between the theological virtue of faith and scholastic theology. Faith is necessary for salvation. Scholastic theology draws clear conclusions from the premises that are articles of faith. By doing so it achieves a greater precision even in its account of the articles. It builds on and does not substitute for faith.

In general, Salmerón develops a defense of scholastic theology that develops according to the general outline that was established by the Parisian theologians. He argues that scholastic theology is a science that is useful for understanding and defending Scripture. It progresses to some extent in the way that other sciences progress. Those who reject scholastic theology would open the Church to the practical danger of being unable to respond to heresy. Moreover, they seem to misunderstand the very nature of theology as a science which proceeds from the indubitable articles of faith to conclusions that clarify and help to defend the faith. Furthermore, the attempts to avoid disputations and use merely Scriptural language contradict the examples of the early Church Fathers and of the Apostles themselves.

Two Early Jesuit Scholastic Theologians: Gregory of Valencia and Gabriel Vázquez

Salmerón's defense of scholastic theology is echoed in the work of two of the Jesuit theologians who worked at the turn of the seventeenth century, namely Gregory of Valencia (d. 1603) and Gabriel Vázquez (d. 1604).[65] The only earlier Jesuit who produced a comparable body of work was Francisco Toletus (1532–1596), who as far as I can determine gave rather unoriginal accounts of the nature of theology. Toletus seems uninfluenced by the controversies over the role of humanistic studies in theology. He simply notes that the common consensus of scholastic theologians is authoritative, and states the Jesuit view that Thomas Aquinas is so authoritative that one should not depart

---

64. Salmerón, *Commentarii*, Prol. XVIII:428a–29b.
65. Franciscus Toletus, Gregory of Valencia, and Gabriel Vázquez are considered together in Bernhard Knorn, "Theological Renewal after the Council of Trent? The Case of Jesuit Commentaries on the *Summa Theologiae*," *Theologial Studies* 79 (2018): 107–22.

from his views unless there is a good reason.⁶⁶ In contrast to Toletus, both Vázquez and Valencia explicitly addressed the humanistic arguments against scholastic theology. They were contemporaries or near contemporaries of Francisco Suárez (1548–1617), whose philosophical and theological work eventually became more or less official among the Jesuits. Although their fame was quickly surpassed by that of Suárez, during their lives they had comparable reputations. Gregory of Valencia received his philosophical and theological formation, which was largely Thomistic, in Spain.⁶⁷ However, he spent most of his early teaching career in Dillingen and Ingolstadt, which were part of the German-speaking territories that the Jesuits were defending against the encroachment of Protestantism. The Jesuit authorities considered him to be one of their leading theologians, which can be seen in their decision to summon him to Rome in order to defend Luis de Molina's account of grace and free will from the charge of heresy in the *De auxiliis* controversy. Gabriel Vázquez's theology was directly in conflict and even in competition with that of Suárez.⁶⁸ He taught originally in Spain and then in Rome, and he returned to Spain in 1592. Among their other writings, Valencia and Vázquez each produced systematic treatments of theology, which were disputations and questions that loosely followed the order of St. Thomas Aquinas's *Summa Theologiae*. Their treatments of scholastic theology occurred in the beginning of these works, since their matter more or less corresponds to what is treated in q. 1 of the *Summa Theologiae*, which is on the nature of theology.

Gregory of Valencia, like Salmerón, is concerned with the distinction between scholastic theology and theology considered in a broader way. Theology in its broader use is "with the application of reasoning, to confirm, persuade, and defend the faith, in the end with whatever way and method he (the theologian) might do this."⁶⁹ More narrowly, theology is the science that is learned and taught by scholastic theologians. Valencia more or less distinguishes between scholastic theology and the theology of the Fathers in the way that Salmerón does:

---

66. Franciscus Toletus, *In I*, q. 1, a. 8, in *Ennaratio in Summa Theologiae S. Thomae Aquinatis*, vol. 1 (Rome/Turin/Paris, 1869), 51b. This particular work of Toletus was not published until the nineteenth century.

67. For his life and works, see Knorn, "Theological Renewal," 113–14, 117–20. There is also a lengthy entry in Carlos Sommervogel, *Bibliothéque de la Compagnie de Jésus*, nouv ed., vol. 8, first part, *Bibliographie* (Bruxelles/Paris: Shepens/Picard, 1898), cols. 388–99.

68. For his life and works, see Knorn, "Theological Renewal," 114–15, 120–22; Sommervogel, *Bibliothéque*, vol. 8, cols. 513–19.

69. Adhibita ratiocinatione, explicat, et confirmat, et persuadet, et defendit fidem, quacunque tandem via et methodo hoc faciat." Gregory of Valencia, *In I*, disp. 2, q. 1, punct. 2, in *Commentariorum Theologicorum Tomi Quatuor*, vol. 1 (Ingolstadt, 1603), col. 8c.

For scholastic theologians do this, with certain questions and arguments in both sides proposed in order, on the basis of the art of examination and the under the guidance of the principles of even natural science, succinctly, briefly, and subtly, speaking without the ornaments of speech. However, the Holy Fathers surpassed the same formerly in effusive and uninterrupted oratory, more nearly in the manner of orators than in that of dialecticians.[70]

This contrast between the rhetorical manner of many Fathers with the scientific approach of the medieval writers is familiar. Valencia recognizes the difference between patristic theology and scholastic theology, but describes it differently from the way that Erasmus would. He thinks that scholastic theology is a development of patristic theology rather than a corruption of it.

Even though Valencia thinks that the writing and use of Lombard's *Sentences* indicated a historical shift in theology, he does not think that its method is unprecedented. Many theologians had similarly attempted to develop and organize theological knowledge. However, Valencia notes that "the method of theology in the time of the Master of the Sentences was reduced to a more perfect form."[71] The New Testament writers and the Fathers sometimes used reason and not merely rhetoric to better understand and explain the articles of faith. Scholastic theology is in continuity with these earlier projects rather than with the more rhetorical or oratorical elements of patristic writing. Neither Valencia nor the other Jesuits are arguing that scholastic theology existed in the early Church as a perfected discipline.

Valencia was particularly concerned with Erasmus's Preface to Hilary's *Opera Omnia*, which, as we have seen, was the object of censure by the Parisian theologians.[72] He considers not so much Erasmus's claim that scholastic Latin is bad, but instead his assertion that the scholastic method leads to curious and empty inquiries. He connects Erasmus's criticisms with those of the Protestants. Valencia states:

> We respond that here we do not wish to defend the vices of certain theologians, but scholastic theology as it is treated by the more serious theologians, such as by D. Thomas and the Master of the *Sentences*, to whom nobody is able to rightly object such vices in disputing. Then we say, even

---

70. "Scholastici enim Theologi id faciunt, propositis ordine certis quæstionibus et argumentis in utramque partem, ex disserendi arte, et ex principiis etiam naturalium scientiarum ductis, succincte et breviter, et subtiliter sine ornamentis dicendi. Sancti autem Patres idem olim præstiterunt fusa et perpetua oratione, et fere magis Oratorum, quam Dialecticorum more." Gregory of Valencia, *In I*, disp. 2, q. 1, punct. 2, col. 8c–d.

71. "Theologiae methodum tempore Magistri Sent. fuisse in formam quandam perfectiorem redactam." Gregory of Valencia, *In I*, disp. 2, q. 1, punct. 2, col. 17b.

72. Gregory of Valencia, *In I*, disp. 2, q. 1, punct. 2, col. 11b, 17c.

among these [other] Theologians, who treat certain questions curiously, even ineptly, there is not one who does not teach many other things seriously and useful, on account of which they should be praised for their intention, rather than blamed on account of some vices. How often is there someone who writes everything correctly?[73]

Salmerón also made this distinction between the correct and incorrect use of the scholastic method. Valencia more precisely notes that some incorrect use of the method can be found even in those writings which are otherwise profitable. He states that we should not condemn all of a scholastic theologian's work on account of some faults, and that we have even less reason to condemn, on such grounds, scholastic theology as a whole.

Valencia defends scholastic theology in general, but he places himself more narrowly in the Thomistic tradition of scholastic theology, especially as it was practiced by Dominicans. He emphasizes the authority of Thomas Aquinas, particularly recommending the work of the great Dominican theologian and commentator on Thomas, Thomas de Vio Cajetan.[74] Furthermore, Valencia took as his theological models the Dominican's Johannes Eck, who was one of the earliest opponents of Protestantism, and the same Dominic Soto whom Polanco mentioned as lacking mystical knowledge. He was against attempts to transform theology.

Against Erasmus and the other critics of scholastic theology, Valencia argues that the scholastic method is better suited for understanding the Catholic faith and persuading others about its truth. Moreover, he stresses that scholastic theology best defends the Catholic faith against attacks. Consequently, although he allows that scholastic theology did not always exist in a perfect form, he holds that it is necessary for the time in which he lives. Presumably, his experience in German-speaking countries exposed him directly to the utility of scholastic theology in arguing against the early Protestant reformers.[75]

---

73. "Respondemus, nos hic non vitia quorundam Theologorum defendere, sed Theologiam Scholasticam, ut tractatur a Theologis grauioribus, ut a D. Thomas et Magistro, quibus ea vitia in disputando nequaquam iure obiici possunt. Deinde dicimus ex his etiam Theologis, qui quasdam quæstiones curiose, aut etiam inepte tractant, neminem esse, qui non alia multa grauiter et utiliter doceat, propter quæ laudari potius illorum institutum debet, quam vituperari propter nonnulla vitia. Quotus enim quisque est, qui omnia recte scribat?" Gregory of Valencia, *In I*, disp. 2, q. 1, punct. 2, col. 17c–d.

74. Gregory of Valencia, "Praefatio Auctoris ad Pium Lectorem," in *Commentarii*, vol. 1. Knorn, "Theological Renewal," 118.

75. The Jesuit St. Peter Canisius, who worked largely in German-speaking areas, similarly suspected a connection between Erasmus and German-speaking Protestantism. See Hilmar M. Pabel, "Praise and Blame: Peter Canisius's Ambivalent Assessment of Erasmus," in *The Reception of Erasmus in the Early Modern Period*, ed. Karl A.E. Enenkel (Leiden/Boston: Brill, 2013), 129–59.

Gabriel Vázquez similarly repeats and develops many of the points that Salmerón made in defense of scholastic theology.[76] Like Valencia, Vázquez in his own theological work follows the doctrine of Thomas Aquinas. He describes Thomas as "the most important and the most acute teacher that God has ever given to us."[77] He makes special use of the Dominican Melchor Cano's (1509–1560) *De Locis Theologicis*, which became the central work on theological sources. Vázquez's use of Cano is significant because Cano was one of the better-known critics of Ignatius and the early Jesuits.[78] Not only Vázquez, but also Toletus and Valencia followed Cano's general account of the number and weight of theological sources.[79] They did not wish to establish an alternative Jesuit theological tradition. Vázquez draws particularly on Book VIII of the *De Locis*, in which Cano considers the authority of the scholastic doctors. He uses Cano to buttress his claim that early Protestants such as Martin Luther and Philip Melanchthon were led into error through their dismissal of scholastic theology.[80] Their contempt of theology led to contempt of many of the Fathers, Councils, and decrees of the Pope.

Vázquez mentions not only John Damascene but also St. Anselm of Canterbury as a forerunner of scholasticism.[81] He attributes the full development of the method not to Lombard, but to Alexander of Hales, Albert the Great, and Thomas Aquinas. He notes that their method was the most useful for bringing together the various theological authorities, and for treating theological matters in an orderly way so that it can be better learned and remembered. More originally, Vázquez notes that the scholastic theologians of Paris were responsible for defending the city's orthodoxy.[82] At least one edition of this text refers to the siege of Paris in 1590 by the then Protestant Henry of Navarre.[83] According to Vázquez, the Parisian theologians strengthened the resolve of Parisians to refuse the acceptance of the heretic Henry as their King.

There is also new material in Vázquez's reply to claims that scholastic theologians are too fond of disputations, and in particular of defending the positions

---

76. Gabriel Vázquez, *In I*, q. 1, a. 1, disp. 3, in *Commentariorum ac disputationionum in Summam S. Thomae tomus primus* (Alcalá, 1598), 13a–18a. All references are to this edition.

77. "Gravissimum, atque acutissimum nobis divinitus datum Doctorum." Vázquez, "Ad Lectorem," in *Commentariorum tomus primus*, trans. Knorn, "Theological Renewal," 120.

78. Terence O'Reilly, "Melchor Cano and the Spirituality of St. Ignatius," in *Ignacio de Loyola y su Tiempo*, 360–80. But the Dominican inquisitors defended Ignatius in Paris. See Lécrivain, *Paris in the Time of Ignatius*, 163–64.

79. Knorn, "Theological Renewal," 124–26.

80. Vázquez, *In I*, q. 1, a. 1, d. 3, cap. 1, nn. 1–2, p. 13a–b. See Melchor Cano, *De Locis Theologicis* (Salamanca: Mathius Gastius, 1563), lib. 8, cap. 1, 265a. Subsequent citations are to this 1563 edition.

81. Vázquez, *In I*, q. 1, a. 1, d. 3, cap. 2, no. 2, pp. 13b–14a.

82. Vázquez, *In I*, q. 1, a. 1, d. 3, cap. 2, no. 3, p. 14a.

83. The reference to the siege is in the 1598 edition, but not in the Lyons edition of 1631.

of their own schools.⁸⁴ Like Valencia, he notes that this error would be due to bad customs rather than to the scholastic method itself. But he appeals to the example of the Dominican Thomists, who were the most ardent in their defense of St. Thomas. Cano had stated that although Thomas's positions should be treated respectfully, they should not be held in the face of better arguments against his positions. Cano refers to Vitoria as an example of this approach. Vázquez, following the directives of his order, agrees that Thomas's positions should be rejected only if there is a good reason. But he emphasizes that scholastic theologians should be concerned more with the truth than with defending the position of any one author, even when that author is Thomas. Perhaps such an approach foreshadows the later eclecticism of Jesuit authors. But it does not open the way to a rejection of scholastic theology.

Vázquez does not mention Erasmus by name, but he seems to have some of Erasmus's censures in mind when he mentions the objections that scholastic theology uses barbarous terms, and that it uses non-Scriptural language in describing mysteries such as the Trinity. Vázquez more than the other scholastics stresses that the humanists themselves fail to follow the examples of their models. For instance, when replying to the claim that scholastic Latin is barbarous, Vázquez writes:

> These (objectors) are devotees of rhetoric and eloquence, who care more for words than things, who, fail to investigate natures and properties of things and lay out their difficulties. To them the very term "scholastic" is something outlandish. In this, clearly, they scarcely follow the teaching of Cicero himself, whom they venerate as an oracle in the art of speaking ... therefore in scholastic writers is sought out not so much the purity of language as the teachings. There are, besides, certain words, which the scholastics frequently use, although they are barbarous, because, for all that, they more easily express what with difficulty is able to be explained in making circumlocutions....⁸⁵

Just as Salmerón did, Vázquez appeals to Cicero's own statement of the problem in the *De Finibus*. Cicero himself recognized that Latin must change when it

---

84. Vázquez, *In I*, q. 1, a. 1, d. 3m, cap. 4, nn. 5–6, pp. 14b–16a. See Cano, *De Locis*, lib. 12, cap. 1, pp. 385a–388a.

85. "Hi sunt Rhetoricae, et eloquentiae addicti, qui magis verbis, quam rebus delectantur, qui rerum naturas et proprietates investigare, difficultates enodare negligunt: quibus ipsum scholasticum nomen invisum est. In quo sane sui Ciceronis, quem ut oraculum in arte dicendi venerantur, doctrinam minime sequuntur.... In Scholasticis ergo scriptoribus, non tam linguae puritas, quam doctrina exquirenda est. Sunt porro vocabula quaedam, quibus Scholastici frequenter utuntur, quae licet barbara sint, quia tamen facilius exprimunt, quod circumloquendo vix posset explicari..." Vázquez, *In I*, q. 1, a. 1, d. 3, cap. 5, no. 8, p. 16a.

incorporates new knowledge. Scholastic theology is an attempt to use a dialectical method and natural knowledge to better understand and explain Scripture. Vázquez, like Salmerón, Valencia, and the Parisian theologians, admits that humanistic studies have value but denies that scholastic theology can be replaced with some more linguistically and scripturally pure theology. Vázquez categorizes the conflict as a disagreement between those who are concerned with merely linguistic matters and those who wish to know what the language is about. As we have seen, this categorization has its roots in the Paris of Ignatius's day and is rooted in earlier debates that preceded the Reformation.

Gregory of Valencia and Gabriel Vázquez both clearly follow the Jesuit tradition of defending scholastic theology and of giving special place to the theology of Thomas Aquinas. They defend scholastic theology in the earlier parts of their systematic works, which is where they discuss the nature of theology. It is not certain how they might be influenced by Salmerón or the Parisian Censures of Erasmus and Lefèvre d'Étaples, but their arguments are similar. Like the first Jesuits, they oppose those who would replace Thomistic theology and scholastic theology in general with biblical philology and patristic learning. They are formed by the foundational documents of the Jesuits, and their arguments follow along the same lines taken by earlier Jesuit participants in the controversy.

Conclusion

This essay shows a consistent Jesuit attitude towards scholastic theology that forms during Ignatius's early years in Paris and is reflected in the writings of Jesuits at least until the end of the sixteenth century. The Jesuit attitude, in particular, reflects the Parisian censures of Desiderius Erasmus and Jacques Lefèvre d'Étaples, and earlier debates between humanism and scholasticism. It might seem to us in hindsight that scholastic theology was never likely to be overthrown in the sixteenth century. But the extreme humanists in Paris had the support of the King, the King's sister, and many members of the academic community. The eventual success of scholasticism would perhaps not have seemed obvious to Ignatius or to his companions.

The critics of scholastic theology saw it as an innovation. They wished to return to an earlier form of theology that supposedly had no need of disputations or specialized vocabulary. Writing against this view, the Jesuits thought that scholastic theology represented a perfection or development of theology that was more or less achieved in the writings of Peter Lombard, although it had precedents in the writings of the Fathers. According to them, disputations have always been a part of Christian theology. Even Christ and the apostles engaged in disputes. Moreover, specialized vocabulary was widely used by the Fathers and even some of the inspired authors. Theology, like any other science or human skill, develops by perfecting techniques and using words more precisely. Even Cicero coined new terms because he recognized the limits of the Latin language as it existed in his time. Scholastic theologians recognized that classical Latin was incapable of easily accommodating developed scholastic thought. It was a language for law and literature rather than for philosophy. Consequently, in order to increase human knowledge, they were forced to expand the vocabulary. Humanists such as Erasmus attempted to return to the inadequate scientific vocabulary of ancient Rome. It is unsurprising that scholastic theologians, not to mention philosophers and scientists, were unwilling to follow him on this point.

The defense of scholastic theology was a characteristic mark of the Jesuits. Ignatius gave scholastic theology a special place both in his "Rules for Thinking with the Church" and in the Jesuit *Constitutions*. Ignatius's first companions give witness to Ignatius's concern to combat attempts to undermine scholastic theology, and in particular the work of Thomas Aquinas. Alfonso Salmerón, one of Ignatius's earliest followers, wrote at length about the value of scholastic theology in combatting error, and he indicated how theology could only fully develop with the use of scholastic dialectics and terminological precision. Three of the greatest Jesuit theologians of the later sixteenth century, namely Franciscus Toletus, Gregory of Valencia, and Gabriel Vázquez, identified themselves as followers of Thomas Aquinas. They even admired Dominicans who were critical of Ignatius, such as Melchor Cano, and those who seemed to lack an appreciation for Jesuit spirituality, such as Dominic Soto. Valencia and Vázquez, in particular, developed arguments about the importance of scholastic theology for refuting heresy, and they showed how scholastic theology was a development of the theological activity of the Fathers and even some New Testament figures.

Ignatius and the early Jesuits lived in a time of theological and religious upheaval. Although they were innovative in their understanding of the religious life, their theological views reflect those of the more traditional scholastic theologians. Ignatius is noteworthy for the way in which he established Thomas Aquinas as a theological authority for the Order. His followers were influenced not only by Thomas Aquinas but also by their Dominican Thomist predecessors and contemporaries. They were not pioneers in Thomistic theology, but they were staunch defenders of it. They struggled against those who would replace scholastic theology with the mere study of biblical languages or a supposed return to the simplicity of the Fathers.[86]

---

86. Special thanks to Fr. James Farge, Nelson Minnich, and Samuel Samson. Michael Boler and an anonymous reader gave helpful remarks on the translations.

CHAPTER 2

Experiencing the Divine according to Thomas and Ignatius

Justin M. Anderson

> . . . for it is not the abundance of knowledge which fills and satisfies the soul, but to feel and taste the matters interiorly.[1]
> —St. Ignatius of Loyola, SJ

> . . . for the one who does not taste, does not know.[2]
> —St. Thomas Aquinas, OP

At the heart of Ignatian spirituality is the understanding that the exercitant will directly experience God. Nowhere is this more evident than in the opening paragraphs of Ignatius's work, the *Spiritual Exercises*. Ignatius opens the *Exercises* with twenty introductory explanations, or "annotations." The second annotation immediately considers the method of prayer and instructs the director to give the exercitant "only a brief or summary explanation" of the points to be contemplated. Ignatius then explains

> For in this way, the person who is contemplating [. . .] by reflecting on it and reasoning about it for oneself, can thus discover something that will bring better understanding or a more personalized concept of the history—either through one's own reasoning or insofar as the understanding is enlightened by God's grace. This brings more spiritual relish [*gusto*] and spiritual fruit than if the one giving the Exercises had lengthily explained and amplified the meaning of the history. For what fills and satisfies the

---

I wish to thank Terence O'Reilly, Bernhard Blankenhorn, OP, Nicolas Steeves, SJ, Thomas Osborne, Aaron Pidel, SJ, and Vivian Boland, OP for their comments that have only bettered this essay.

1. ". . . porque no el mucho saber harta y satisfaze al ánima, mas el sentir y gustar de las cosas internamente." Ignatius of Loyola, *Monumenta Ignatiana*, second series, *Exercitia spiritualia S. Ignatii et eorum Directoria: Nova editio*, bk. 1, *Exercitia Spiritualia*, MHSI 100, ed. Josephus Calveras and Candidus de Dalmases (Rome: IHSI, 1969), 142. English from William F. Longridge, trans., *The Spiritual Exercises of Saint Ignatius of Loyola: Translated from the Spanish with a Commentary and a Translation of the* Directorium in Exercitia (London: Robert Scott, 1919), 7.

2. ". . . quia nullus cognoscit qui non gustat . . ." Sancti Thomae Aquinatis, *Opera omnia*, t. 14: *In psalmos Davidis expositio* (Parmae: Typis Petri Fiaccadori, 1863), no. 9 (p. 266).

soul consists, not in knowing much, but in our understanding the realities profoundly and in savoring them interiorly (SpEx 2).³

Commentator Michael Ivens underscores that "this is a key phrase for understanding the spirituality of the *Exercises*."⁴

Direct, personal experience of the divine is not only at the heart of prayer in the Exercises for Ignatius but also a privileged way for God to communicate to the person His desires and will. This is first evident in the fifteenth annotation, which again urges caution to the director since "it is more appropriate and far better that the Creator and Lord himself should communicate himself to the devout soul" (SpEx 15). This experience is one of the foundational pillars of Ignatian discernment and reveals itself both in the "second time" for making a good discernment (SpEx 176) and in the final contemplation of the thirty-day retreat, the climatic "Contemplation to Attain Divine Love" (SpEx 230–37). Since direct experience of the divine is pivotal both to encounter and to being enlightened regarding choices in one's life, it lies at the root of the enduring draw of the Exercises, and more broadly of Ignatian spirituality. We need not, then, be surprised to read John W. O'Malley comment that "this immediate action of God on the individual is the fundamental premise of the *Exercises*."⁵

---

3. ". . . porque la persona que contempla [. . .] discurriendo y raciocinando por sí mismo, y hallando alguna cosa que haga un poco más declarar o sentir la historia, quier por la raciocinación propria, quier sea en quanto el entendimiento es illucidado por la virtud divina, es de más gusto y fructo spiritual, que si el que da los exercicios hubiese mucho declarado y ampliado el sentido de la historia; porque no el mucho saber harta y satisfaze al ánima, mas el sentir y gustar de las cosas internamente." Ignatius of Loyola, *Monumenta Ignatiana, series secunda: Exercitia spiritualia S. Ignatii et eorum Directoria*, nova editio, tomus I, *Exercitia Spiritualia*, ed. Josephus Calveras et Candidus de Dalmases, MHSI 100 (Rome: IHSI, 1969), 142. Translation from Ignatius of Loyola, *The Spiritual Exercises of Saint Ignatius: A Translation and Commentary by George E. Ganss*, ed. and trans. George E. Ganss (St. Louis, MO: The Institute of Jesuit Sources, 1992), 21–22. All citations of the *Spiritual Exercises* are taken from Ganss's translation unless otherwise indicated. I will follow the standard notation form for the passages in the *Spiritual Exercises* (SpEx) referred to in the text.

4. Michael Ivens, *Understanding the Spiritual Exercises: Text and Commentary, A Handbook for Retreat Directors* (Trowbridge: Cromwell Press, 1998), 3. Nor is Ivens alone in this assessment. Among the instructions to Jesuits on how to give the *Exercises*, the Official Directory of 1599 comments, "Experience shows that in all cases people find more pleasure in, and are more deeply moved by, things they find out for themselves. Hence, it is enough for the director to point out a vein which the exercitant can then mine for himself." Claudio Aquaviva, "The Official Directory of 1599," in *On Giving the Spiritual Exercises: The Early Jesuit Manuscript Directories and the Official Directory of 1599*, ed. and trans. Martin E. Palmer (St. Louis, MO: Institute of Jesuit Sources, 1996), viii.1 (p. 303).

5. Ivens, *Understanding*, 43. Likewise, W. W. Meissner affirms that "the fundamental principle on which the efficacy of the Exercises is based is the direct action of God on the soul." W. W. Meissner, *To the Greater Glory: A Psychological Study of Ignatian Spirituality*, Marquette Studies in Theology (Milwaukee, WI: Marquette University Press, 1999), 130.

While, to denizens of the twenty-first century Christian world, these two points—the exercitant experiencing God and being daily guided by God—may seem exceedingly reasonable, the Ignatian presentation of mystical experience has been put down largely to its Franciscan and Bonaventurean roots.[6] Moreover, these same two elements would come under the heaviest of scrutinies even during Ignatius's life. Those scrutinies hardened into the accusation of heresy and led to multiple ecclesiastical trials of Ignatius, experiences that would ultimately shape the history of Jesuit spirituality and thought for centuries to come. The most vehement of these scrutinies aimed at the *Exercises*, and launched during Ignatius's life, were unleashed by Dominican Thomist's Melchor Cano (d. 1560) and Tomas de Pedroche (d. 1569). Given the common Franciscan attribution and Dominican attacks, we might worthily ask the question: what, if any, relationship might exist between Thomas Aquinas and Ignatius of Loyola on the issues of personal experience of the divine and the influence such experience might have on human action?

Asking the proposed questions means embroiling ourselves in the charges of heresy Ignatius faced from Cano and Pedroche. Because Thomists, like Cano and Pedroche, argued Ignatius's *Exercises* was a work of *alumbradismo*, familiarizing ourselves with some general characteristics of that rather ill-defined coterie as it existed on the Iberian Peninsula between the 1520s and 1530s is necessary. Once the backdrop of *alumbradismo* is stretched out, we will be better positioned to review the particular accusations of heresy themselves. In the second part of the essay, I will turn to examine Thomas Aquinas's own understanding of the experience of the divine and the place, if any, he foresees that experience plays in the process of human action. In closing, we will be able to draw out some points of comparison, looking at the way Ignatius and perhaps the Jesuits, can—and cannot—be called Thomistic.

Ignatius, the Exercises, and the Charges of Heresy

The Alumbrados

The Spanish Inquisition issued its first of many condemnations of the *alumbrados* in 1525.[7] The edict was composed of forty-eight condemned theses

---

6. Hans Urs von Balthasar, *The Glory of the Lord: Theological Aesthetics*, vol. 1, *Seeing the Form* (San Francisco: Ignatius Press, 1983), 373–80. Undeniably, Ignatius was certainly influenced by this Bonaventurian tradition of mysticism likely through Ludolph of Saxony, through his *Vita Christi*, and the medieval tradition of "spiritual senses." Even some of the earliest Jesuits, like Polanco, explicitly defended his "application of senses" with reference to Bonaventure.

7. For a brief but thorough introduction to pre-1525 *alumbradismo* and its link to fears of "Lutheranism" in Spain, see Aaron D. Pidel, SJ, "Jerome Nadal's Apology for the Spiritual Exercises: A Study in Balanced Spirituality," *Studies in the Spirituality of Jesuits* 52, no. 1 (2020): 1–36, esp. 6–9.

attributed to them.⁸ Scholars today agree that *alumbradismo* was a very elastic epithet hardly representing a single, organized group. Though one central group did originate in the Palace of Mendoza in Guadalajara, the *alumbrados* were "a wide, and imprecisely defined category, formulated and theorized by the inquisitors and never admitted to by the accused."⁹

Luis Fernández's 1983 study of the *alumbrados*' relation to Ignatius is still the gold standard among researchers in this area.¹⁰ Fernández discusses five characteristic marks that the *alumbrados* of the 1520s held in common.

First, among *alumbrados*, the doctrine and practice of abandonment prevailed. Adopting a form of quietism, the individual was cautioned to "leave it to God" and to be united to him without doing or thinking anything. It was this immediate and direct contact with God in the soul that would transform the soul. Abandonment then meant a focus on God at work in the soul.¹¹ Here, God is in the soul by his love. This love directs the soul; such that, all done under inner inspiration is infallibly of God regardless of the direction given by the Church, even from one's confessors. This is what it meant, thought the *alumbrados*, to be ruled by the Holy Spirit.¹² With such an emphasis on God's direct influence on the soul, the *alumbrados*, like the Spanish Erasmians around them, focused on discernment of spirits.¹³ Also like the Erasmians, focus on God's

---

8. The condemned propositions resulted from a group of theological consultants called together by King of Spain Charles V and Alonso Manrique, the Inquisitor-General of the Spanish Inquisition. The edict was drawn from the trials of Isabel de la Cruz and Pedro Ruiz de Alcaraz, two principal protagonists of the movement. Among the forty-eight condemned theses there are some that seem particularly close to Ignatius and his experiences. Many of the propositions touch upon the issues of interiority, salvation, and sinning mortally. Of these, Proposition 9—namely, that "the love of God in man is God. And one could abandon oneself to this love of God, which directs people in such a way that they cannot sin mortally or venially"—has long seemed to scholars the crux of *alumbradismo*. The modern Spanish edition of the Edict of 1525 appears in Antonio Márquez, *Los alumbrados: Orígenes y filosofía (1525–1529)* (Madrid: Taurus, 1980), 229–38. The propositions have been translated into English and are taken from Lu Ann Homza, "The Alumbrados in Castile 1525–1532: Document 8, 1525 Inquisition Edict on the *Alumbrados*," in *Spanish Inquisition, 1478–1614: An Anthology of Sources* (Indianapolis: Hackett, 2006), 80–92.

9. Stephanie Pastore, "Jesuits, Conversos, and Alumbrados in the Iberian World," in *The Oxford Handbook of the Jesuits*, ed. Ines G. Županov (Oxford: Oxford University Press, 2019), 269–92, esp. 270. The divergencies were not lost on Melchor Cano. Echoes of them are found in his accusations against Ignatius and the Jesuits.

10. Luis Fernández, "Íñigo de Loyola y Los Alumbrados," *Hispania Sacra* 35 (1983): 585–680.

11. Hence the centrality of condemned Proposition 9. See note 8 above.

12. Scholars here will typically note the difference on this point by two sub-groups of *alumbrados*. The "*Dexados*" are thought to have supported these propositions, though the "Recogidos" did not. Nevertheless, the *Recogidos* did foster openness to the inspiration and operations of God in ways that would have Dominicans looking suspect at Ignatian "indifference" and self-denial.

13. Jean Gerson's work was for this reason of immense interest in Spain during these years. Leading *dexados* translated *De probatione spirituum* into Spanish.

direct influence in the soul led the *alumbrados* to attend to consolation, understood as an effect of this union with God. Consolation in mental prayer was, then, normal and indispensable.

Divine union by abandonment and God's direct, personal, and experiential influence in the person led to nearly all other condemned propositions and characteristics identified by Fernández. Thus, the second alumbradic characteristic was their rejection of all ceremonies, rites, images, and external works. They saw themselves as exempt from fulfilling other laws and were resistant to external and internal works, including liturgical rituals, taking religious vows, and owing obedience to God over obedience to the ecclesial law. These practices, thought the *alumbrados*, pulled one away from God.[14] This turn toward interiority reached even as far as considering the sacraments of the Church superfluous. Of course, this "interior turn" was part of a wider religious shift in the sixteenth century. Melquiades Andrés writes,

> Alumbrados, Erasmians, mystics, and Lutherans insist on the personal relationship between the soul and God, without mediation by persons (priests), institutions (Church), or even the intellect. [. . .] They describe God's directly touching the soul and communicating with it. For them the experience of God is immediate.[15]

This turn, of course, influenced how these groups perceived the hierarchical Church's mission and spiritual authority.[16]

Third, Fernández identifies the *alumbrados* with the idea that their leaders (or *beatos*) were considered both secure in doctrine and impeccable in conduct.

---

14. A point upon which they shared affinity with the Erasmians. In fact, as the persecutions against the *alumbrados* intensified near the end of the 1520s Fernández reports how they got closer to and eventually tried to blend in with the Erasmians who still enjoyed protection due to Erasmus's *Enchiridion militis Christiani*. See Fernández, "Íñigo de Loyola y Los Alumbrados," 586.

15. Melquiades Andrés, "*Alumbrados*, Erasmians, 'Lutherans', and Mystics: The Risks of a More 'Intimate' Spirituality," trans. Esther da Costa-Frankel, in *The Spanish Inquisition and the Inquisitorial Mind*, ed. Ángel Alcalá (Highland Lake, NJ: Atlantic Research and Publications, 1987), 457–94, esp. 459.

16. Consequently, during this time a declaration of fidelity to the hierarchical charism of the Church became for a given mystic or theologian the litmus test of whether they were accounted heretical or not. It is in this context one can view Ignatius's famous "rules for thinking with the Church." O'Malley writes, "Some of the earlier rules in the list clearly take positions contrary to ideas held by the *alumbrados* or attributed to them. With their emphasis on the more institutionalized aspects of religion, the rules can be interpreted as balancing the rest of the text, where these aspects are taken so little into account. They are thus a manifesto of Ignatius's own orthodoxy, frequently impugned precisely on this score. Polanco and others, however, saw them as an 'antidote' to the heretics of the day, and that is what the wording of some of them most obviously suggests." John W. O'Malley, SJ, *The First Jesuits* (Boston: Harvard University Press, 1993), 49. For more on Ignatius's and Thomas's view of the hierarchical Church, see Aaron Pidel's essay in this same volume.

They believed the *beatos* more knowledgeable about Christian teaching than even St. Paul himself. Their purported impeccability issued from the belief that their souls were so united to God that one could not commit a free act to separate oneself from God or that this same union gave him a degree of freedom that the negative precepts of the moral law did not apply.

The fourth and fifth characteristics of the *alumbrados* can be stated simply. They held meetings in private houses instead of churches with both religious and lay participation, both men and women. It was noted that singing was even done by lay women—something that would have been seen as improper. Finally, the group kept secrets among themselves, hiding such things from those otherwise closest to them. They were known, unsurprisingly given the above, to even challenge and defy the advice of their confessors.

Beginning with the Edict of 1525, the *alumbrados* were repeatedly condemned and sought out by the Spanish Inquisition. In the 1520s and 1530s, the investigations and trials moved through two distinct phases.[17] Initially, the Inquisition understood the movement to center on only three people: Isabel de la Cruz, Pedro Ruiz de Alcaraz, and Gaspar de Bedoya. They were condemned and paraded through towns of the Alcarria, the areas surrounding Guadalajara, where they had preached. It would not be long before Ignatius was caught up in the soon-to-be expanding search for *alumbrados*.

Ignatius's Troubles and His Departure from Spain

Many of Ignatius's own experiences of the divine and subsequent activities, as chronicled in his *Autobiography*, can strike an alumbradic note. Of particular importance was his "outstanding illumination" that took place between February 1522 and March 1523 outside Manresa as he gazed at the Cardoner River.[18] There, "the eyes of his understanding began to be opened; not that he saw any vision, but he understood and learnt many things, both spiritual matters and matters of faith and of scholarship."[19] Speaking of this and other mystical experiences, Ignatius later reported that these things strengthened his faith tremendously "so that he thought to himself: if there were no Scriptures to teach us these matters of faith, he would be resolved to die for them, solely because of what he had seen."[20] With these experiences at Manresa, Ignatius's spiritual outlook developed profoundly. He jotted notes in a notebook. At first,

---

17. Pastore, "Jesuits, *Conversos*, and *Alumbrados*," 271.
18. Ignatius of Loyola, "The Autobiography," trans. Parmananda R. Divarkar, in *Ignatius of Loyola: Spiritual Exercises and Selected Works*, ed. George E. Ganss, Classics of Western Spirituality (New York: Paulist Press, 1991), no. 30.
19. Ignatius, "Autobiography," no. 30.
20. Ignatius, "Autobiography," no. 29.

these notes were for himself, but seeing fruit in his spiritual conversation with others, the notes came to constitute the heart of the Spiritual Exercises and even founding features of the Society of Jesus.[21] When Ignatius returned from a pilgrimage to the Holy Land in February 1524, realizing his need for academic training in order to help others, he studied Latin and then entered the University of Alcalá during the summer of 1526 and remained there until leaving for Salamanca in September 1527. Throughout this time, he continued to give "meditations or spiritual exercises, in which he had special ability and efficacy, and the gift of discernment of spirits, and of helping and directing other souls."[22] Such activities would prove dangerous for Ignatius and others, since contemporaneous with these endeavors was the local Church's ongoing struggle with the *alumbrados*.

Ignatius was in fact called before the Spanish Inquisition three times before leaving for the University of Paris in early 1528. Stefanie Pastore indicates that these three trials of Ignatius resulted from the investigations conducted between 1526 and 1527 regarding *alumbradismo*.[23] Probably due to the fact that Ignatius was attracting followers in Alcalá, a good number of them women, and "was engaged in giving spiritual exercises and teaching Christian doctrine," his work attracted the attention of the Inquisition.[24] In 1526, Ignatius was first denounced to the inquisitor at Toledo, Juan Rodríguez de Figueroa (d. 1565), and interviewed.[25] After 17 days in prison, Ignatius was interviewed a second time by Figueroa and released. Several of the questions Ignatius records from that conversation could be traced back to alumbradic tendencies (e.g., whether he enjoined the keeping of the sabbath, regarding his relationship with particular women, especially advice given on God's calling).[26] In total, Ignatius was imprisoned for forty-two days and upon release was told not to speak about the faith until he has studied four more years.

After consultation, Ignatius followed the advice of the Archbishop of Toledo and moved to Salamanca in September 1527 to continue his studies. Within two weeks of arriving in Salamanca, Ignatius found his way into further trouble. The Dominicans in the friary of San Esteban invited him to address them. It is very possible that it was here Melchor Cano first encountered Ignatius. The interviewers were not impressed, and Ignatius and his companion

---

21. George E. Ganss, general introduction, *Spiritual Exercises and Selected Works*, 27.
22. Ignatius, "Autobiography," no. 35.
23. Pastore, "Jesuits, *Conversos*, and *Alumbrados*," 272.
24. Ignatius, "Autobiography," 57.
25. Ignatius, "Autobiography," no. 58. Figueroa questioned Ignatius on two separate occasions. Ignatius himself mentions in his memoirs that he was suspected of being an *alumbrado* when first called before Figueroa.
26. Ignatius, "The Autobiography," no. 61.

went from prison to prison, including three days spent in the Dominican friary itself.[27] From his days spent in San Esteban, Ignatius reports that among the community of Dominicans "there was already some division among them, many showing that they were sympathetic."[28] He reports handing over the *Spiritual Exercises* to the inquisitors, the first time we read of the book as a single work. After being theologically examined, including a query into mortal and venial sin as written in the *Exercises*, and having passed twenty-two days in prison, Ignatius was released. Soon after, he left Spain to pursue studies in Paris, arriving there on February 2, 1528. Following Ignatius's departure from Spain the search, arrests, and flights, surrounding *alumbrados* only intensified.

The Iberian *alumbrado* persecution shifted into another gear when in March 1529 a woman named Francisca Hernández was captured. When Hernández confessed, the inquisitors were alarmed to discover "a complex and fragmented *alumbrado* network, embracing in truth disparate spiritual phenomena."[29] Suddenly, arrests multiplied. What started as a local Guadalajaran inquisition expanded to Toledo, Valladolid, and Alcalá, including apparent *alumbrados* within the university.[30] This in turn triggered multiple notable persons to flee the breaking storm. Mateo Pascual (d. 1562), the rector of the University of Alcalá, and Juan de Valdés (d. 1541) both left for Rome. Meanwhile, Juan de Castillo (d. 1535), Manuel de Miona (d. 1567), and Miguel de Torres (d. 1593), each departed for Paris, where Ignatius himself had already taken up residence since early 1528. Miona had been Ignatius's confessor, and both he and Torres would become Jesuits in the end.[31] Given this historical context, it is easy to see why years later Melchor Cano would regard Ignatius as having fled Spain precisely because he was an *alumbrado*.[32]

---

27. Interestingly, Ignatius reports that the subprior of San Esteban, when learning that Ignatius spoke about virtues and vices without much theological learning, replied that "one cannot speak about these except through learning or through the Holy Spirit. If not through learning, then through the Holy Spirit." Ignatius refused to reply, "because that kind of argument did not seem good to him."

28. Ignatius, "Autobiography," no. 66.

29. Pastore, "Jesuits, *Conversos*, and *Alumbrados*," 271.

30. Of those linked to the University, Pastore names Bernardino de Tovar, Vergara, Juan de Castillo, the Eguía brothers, and Lopez de Celain.

31. On Miona and Torres's connection to *alumbrados* in Spain see Pastore, "Jesuits, *Conversos*, and *Alumbrados*," 273–75.

32. Cano charges Ignatius with just this, writing, "Coming therefore to the founders of this Company who call Jesus, their General is an Inigo, who escaped fleeing from Spain because the Inquisition wanted to catch him, because he was said to be one of the *Alumbrados* or *Dexados* mentioned above. He went to Rome and asked to be judged by the Pope, and there being no one to accuse him, he was released. His companions and Apostles are Torres, Fabro, Salmerón and Laínez." Terence O'Reilly, "Melchor Cano and the Spirituality of St. Ignatius Loyola: The Censura y parecer contra el Insituto de los Padres Jesuitas," *Journal of Jesuit Studies* 4 (2017): 365–94. O'Reilly has

The Dominican Charges

The charges of heresy against Ignatius and the early Jesuits also came in two waves. The first occurred between 1548–1551 with a second, more substantial wave between 1554–1558. Of the first, we have little written record, but it seems to have stemmed from Melchor Cano unleashing an attack in his preaching against Ignatius and the *Exercises*. Simultaneously, the Archbishop of Toledo, Juan Martínez Silíceo (d. 1557), began restricting Jesuits ministering in Toledo, until he eventually forbade their ministry altogether in 1551. While Ignatius could already by July 31, 1548, show papal approval of the *Exercises*, he responded to this first salvo by seeking and obtaining from the Master General of the Dominicans, Romée de Châtillon, a circular letter dated December 10, 1548, to all Dominicans forbidding such attacks on the Jesuits.[33] Eventually, Ignatius would also ask for a letter from Pope Julius III (1550–55) telling Silíceo to desist. The papal intervention was effective, for Silíceo seems to have relented and the first wave subsided.

The second and more significant wave (1554–1558) is traceable to December 1, 1554, the day the Faculty of Theology at the University of Paris condemned the Jesuits. While it did have theological points attached, O'Malley reports that the Paris condemnation was more politically anti-papal than anti-Jesuit.[34] Regardless, its ultimate effect was to embolden others to speak out. Once again, Melchor Cano found his voice. Sometime between 1552–1556, Cano had prepared a treatise—his *Censura y parecer contra el Insituto de los Padres Jesuitas*—and intended to later bring it before Pope Paul IV (1555–59), who shared similar antipathies towards the Jesuits.[35] Therein, Cano charged

---

transcribed Cano's *Censura*, long thought lost, as he found it in a British Museum manuscript in 1992. The *Censura* is composed of fifteen notes, appearing on pp. 385–394. The above citation is from no. 4 (p. 386). Curiously, it was Torres that Ignatius years later would dispatch to meet with Cano and other Spanish persecutors to defuse the accusations of *alumbradismo*.

33. Steward Rose, *Ignatius and the Early Jesuits*, 2nd ed. (London: Longmans-Green, 1871), 326. Not unlike his time with the Dominicans in Salamanca years before, the Spanish Dominicans appeared divided over Ignatius. Dominicans Juan de la Peña (d. 1565), Luis de Granada (d. 1588), and Bartolome de Carranza (d. 1576) each defended Ignatius and the Jesuits in Spain. All three had their own leanings toward a spiritual interiority. On the influence of an "affective spirituality" in the Dominican Order in Spain during these years see: Andrés, "*Alumbrados*, Erasmians, 'Lutherans', and Mystics," 482–86. Andrés also reports de la Peña's words in relation to some of Carranza's propositions. De la Peña wrote: "I have no objection [to this proposition] except that certain very brilliant individuals become dazzled and then take others for Alumbrados with regard to things of the spirit and spiritual freedom." Earlier de la Peña also wrote: "I say this because when we come across some exaggeration by these men, it should not scandalize us or make us suspect that they are not only reckless but heretics as well." Rose, 486.

34. O'Malley, *First Jesuits*, 287–90.
35. O'Reilly, "Melchor Cano 367."

Ignatius with multiple heresies, but especially that of *alumbradismo*. Perhaps having read an early draft of Cano's *Censura*, Silíceo commissioned a review of the *Exercises* in 1553 with Tomas de Pedroche heading the commission. However, when Pedroche returned a verdict against the *Exercises*, Silíceo decided not to press the issue.[36]

What, then, were Cano's and Pedroche's charges against Ignatius and the *Exercises*? We might organize their various accusations into minor and major indictments. Without doubt, even the minor charges—like the fact the Jesuits did not chant the hours in choir, disregarded the tradition of cloister as a community, and neglected bodily penance—would have constituted various telltale signs of deviation from the traditionally accepted path of holiness and of "*alumbradismo*."[37] However, the more substantial, major charges, while having been tallied differently, can be subsumed under two general categories according to our own guiding questions. The first set of charges pivot around a (purported) illicit focus on direct experience of the divine. Originating from this focus, a second set of indictments targets an (supposed) over-reliance on personal internal experiences for decision-making. Cano and Pedroche argue that in both major issues the *Exercises* erroneously instruct others to tempt God.

These Dominicans' first major concern pivots around the promotion of individuals seeking direct experience of the divine. Nowhere is this more obvious, for Pedroche, than in the origin of the *Exercises* themselves. Noting an early Jesuit's words that the *Exercises* came "not so much from books as from the anointing of the Holy Spirit and internal experience," Pedroche writes that Ignatius was a man "of few letters," knowing too little Latin to compose the *Exercises* in that language, having instead to write them in Spanish.[38] Moreover, he points out that Ignatius composed this work "more from the interior experiences of this chest and anointing of the Holy Spirit, than that of books."[39] Emilio Colunga's work introduces us to the backdrop, not only of *alumbradismo*, but

---

36. Pidel notes that the "similarity of Cano's criticism to those of Pedroche suggests Cano's influence on Pedroche." Pidel, "Jerome Nadal's Apology," 12, no. 40. Ignatius had heard of both Cano and Pedroche's report but seemed content to let this second barrage pass by, perhaps as a sign of divine favor to be persecuted. Less content was the early companion Jerome Nadal, who composed a defense of the *Exercises* against Pedroche's report. For Nadal's *Apologia*, see: *Epistolae P. Hieronymi Nadal Societatis Jesu ab anno 1546 ad 1577*, 5 vols. (Madrid, 1898–1905), 4:820–26; Juan Alfonso de Polanco, *Vita Ignatii Loiolae et rerum Societatis Iesu historica*, 6 vols. (Madrid, 1894–1898), 3:501–24 [hereafter abbreviated *Chron.*]; and 4:827–73.

37. Added to these could also be Cano's personal encounters with Ignatius and other early Jesuits.

38. The words come from an unknown source and as an endorsement of the *Exercises* it seems. Tomas de Pedroche's Censura can be found as "Censura Exercitiorum S. Ignatii" in *Chron.*, 3:501–24, this complaint at 504–5.

39. Pedroche, *Chron.*, 3:501–24.

more specifically looks at the suspicion issuing from the Dominican convents on the Iberian Peninsula during the sixteenth century.[40] Colunga points to the tension between intellectualists and mystics. The mystics sought to be renewers, innovators, and popularizers, of spirituality. Counterposed to them were intellectualists who preferred a religiosity taking advantage of the treasures possessed by the Church's age-old wisdom. Intellectualists would have viewed these mystical tendencies, along with the *alumbrados*, as anti-intellectual. It is difficult not to hear behind Pedroche's accusations some overarching suspicion of anti-intellectualism typical among both popularizing mystical renewers, in general, and *alumbrados*, in particular.[41]

While Ignatius' interior life was the origin of the *Exercises*, this Dominican suspicion was further exacerbated by the same work's fostering of a spiritual life built around interior experience. This Ignatian attention to interior motions seemed to its Dominican assailants to risk the exaltation of passive spiritual experience over doctrine and the sacraments. Again, this would have seemed another major similarity between the *Exercises* and the *alumbrados*. Nowhere is this exaltation more palpable than in the expression and thematic centrality of the second annotation. Understood in this context, Ignatius's leitmotif of experience of the divine—"it is not the abundance of knowledge which fills and satisfies the soul, but to feel and taste the matters interiorly"—could not have struck Cano and Pedroche as anything but a typical, anti-intellectual, alumbradic aggrandizement of interior, personal experience over knowledge. Here, they would have discerned a shift in the notion of Christian perfection, a new idea of sanctity.

One further reason Cano took exception to this emphasis on interior experience of the divine was because he saw within it a disregard for the differences among people.[42] He regarded the *Exercises* as urging a spiritual experience not ordinary for most Christians. Terence O'Reilly has pointed out that this was already an over-arching concern for Cano in his longer attack against fellow Dominican Bartolomé de Carranza (d. 1576).[43] Cano

---

40. Emilio Colunga, "Intelectualistas y místicos en la Teología española del siglo XVI," *Ciencia Tomista* 9 (1914): 209–21; 377–94; *Ciencia Tomista* 10 (1915): 223–42. Ignacio Iparraguirre summarizes Colunga's "luminous study" as a further backdrop to the Dominican resistance to Ignatius's *Exercises*. See Ignacio Iparraguirre, *Historia de la Práctica de los Ejercicios de San Ignacio de Loyola en Vida de su Autor (1522–1556)* (Rome: IHSI, 1946): 1:92–94.

41. Pedroche's comment that the *Exercises* were first composed in Spanish is of some note. Colunga points out that intellectualists became concerned that spiritual authors were composing in the common language to popularize their spiritual works. Certainly, the circulation possible from the printing press only exacerbated their concerns.

42. Cano, *Censura y Parecer*, no. 13.

43. O'Reilly writes, "Cano's views on the *alumbrados* may be studied in detail in his lengthy critique of the catechism of Bartolomé de Carranza" O'Reilly, "Melchor Cano," 366. See also

thought it a mistake to encourage all to contemplation first because not all were suitable for it. With different temperaments, come diverse needs. Moreover, contemplation is incompatible with an active life. This, thought Cano, was typical of *alumbrados*: in their chase after interior illumination, they ignored the virtues of the active life. But why would one do such a thing? In another place, Cano argued that the over-emphasis on sanctity identified with mental prayer was insidious and undermined the Christian life. The one who confuses Christian perfection with mental prayer "blasphemes against the wisdom of Christ" who told the rich young man who wished to be perfect, not, "Go and pray mentally," but, "Go, sell your possessions, and give the money to the poor" (Mt 19:21).[44] Placing Christian perfection in mental prayer undermines perfection constituted by the three evangelical counsels. Without respecting the different states of life, the *Exercises* contributed to an equating of the lay state and the "higher states." For these Dominicans, this vocational egalitarianism was again another marker of the *alumbradismo* infesting those who participated in the Exercises. Moreover, for them such suggestions may have reeked of an ill-defined but much feared Iberian "Lutheranism."

No other place in the *Exercises* exhibited such an apparent egalitarianism more than Annotation 15. Therein, Ignatius counsels that "the one giving the Exercises should not urge the one receiving them toward poverty or any other promise more than towards its opposites, or to one state or manner of living more than to another." Again, echoing the leitmotif of personal experience of the divine, he counsels this so as "to allow the Creator to deal immediately with the creature and the creature with its Creator and Lord" (SpEx 15). Pedroche saves some of his strongest condemnatory language of the *Exercises* for this passage. For him, Annotation 15 "clearly contains, affirms, and teaches a reckless, scandalous, and heretical proposition and assertion."[45] However, the Dominicans assailants do not heap scorn on Annotation 15 so much for its (supposed) blatant vocational egalitarianism as for its promotion of "indifference," even before objectively higher states of life. Thus, omission of promoting the higher life was a result of chasing indifference, and this indifference a symptom of the exaltation of personal interior experience. It is this same indifference, urged at critically formative moments in the *Exercises*, including in

---

O'Reilly, "The Spiritual Exercises." The *Qualificación hecha por los Maestros Cano y Cuevas del catechismo [y de otros escritos] 1558–1559* has been published in *Fray Bartolomé de Carranza: Documentos históricos*, ed. J. Ignacio Tellechea Idígoras (Madrid: Real Academia de la Historia, 1981): 6:225–384.

    44. O'Reilly, "The Spiritual Exercises," 384.
    45. Pedroche, "Censura," 509–10.

the "Principle and Foundation," that Pedroche finds especially imbued with *alumbradismo*.[46]

So, for Cano and Pedroche an erroneous emphasis on interior, personal experience of the divine led directly to a misguided doctrine of indifference and consequent anti-clericalism, anti-intellectualism, and shunning of traditional paths of holiness. All these movements, for Cano, constitute the sin of tempting God. As such, those who give the Exercises, thus exalting personal, interior experience of the divine, are guilty of leading souls to tempt God. He writes in his *Censura y Parecer*,

> To this should be added the fact that among the same exercises there are some that are not so wholesome, for at the end of so many weeks are promised grace, and tenderness of heart and spiritual feelings: this seems to place God under an obligation, which is one way of tempting him.[47]

O'Reilly notes that, while arguing against Carranza's catechism, Cano had indicated already the harm in telling lay people that prayer is restful and joyful. Lay people may be tempted to abandon the virtues and charitable acts of their proper state. This, concludes Cano, is a mark of the devil, ever the angel of light.[48]

The question of the temptation of God leads us to the second class of charges flowing from the first. It is the accusation that the *Exercises* encourage an over-reliance on this same personal, interior experience of the divine for making decisions. Ignatius, of course, is known for his method of discernment, very much at the heart of the *Exercises* themselves. This manifests itself, as Pedroche notes, when Ignatius counsels observance of one's history of consolation and desolation as an occasion for making a sound and good election (SpEx 176). Cano's grievance against this sort of counsel can be inferred from his comments about tempting God. If one tempted God in promising interior joy-filled experience, then it was even more so to build an edifice of decision-making on this same foundation. As O'Reilly indicates, Cano's reasoning is more spelled

---

46. In that same place, he writes, "In my view this doctrine is clearly and openly from the dexados and alumbrados. . . . " So certain, he continues by arguing, "if this doctrine is not from the dexados and alumbrados, then I would like to see one that is from them and compare it to this one, and see how far one is from the other." Pedroche, "Censura," 509–10.

47. "Añádese a esto que con los mismos exercicios hay algunos no tan sanos, porque post tot septimanas pollicentur gratiam y ternura de corazón y sentimientos espirituales, que parece obligar a Dios, que es un género de tentarle." Cano, *Censura y Parecer*, no. 13. Translation by O'Reilly, "The Spiritual Exercises," 390.

48. Cano, *Censura y Parecer*, nos. 3, 8. In his *Censura*, Cano typically assigns any good of the Jesuits to a ruse of the devil which had already worked itself out in the *alumbrados*, whom he calls the Jesuits' "first cousins" [*primos hermanos*] (no. 3).

out in his critique of Carranza's catechism on a similar point. He complains that people who make their decisions assuming God's guidance ignore the counsel of learned men. O'Reilly summarizes well,

> To rely, in such a way, on direct divine guidance from God was, in Cano's eyes, to expect an extraordinary grace, and he cited a passage in the New Testament to make his point. St. James, in his epistle, writes: "If any of you lacks wisdom, let him ask God [. . .] and it will be given him" (Jas 1:5). This, observes Cano, is not an invitation to pray for inspiration by the Holy Spirit: that would be to tempt God. Instead it means asking to be led to a teaching representative of the church, in order to receive instruction.[49]

One cannot forget the mark of *alumbrados*, traceable to the tenth proposition of the Edict of 1525, to have rejected the counsel of their confessor.[50] One can easily understand the Dominican concern, especially when among *alumbrados* such "inspirations" even ran contrary to the moral law.

Pedroche also took issue with the Ignatian emphasis of making decisions based upon the experience of consolation for another reason. He queried how, since one does not experience the theological virtue of charity, it makes sense to define consolation as an increase in charity? Yet, this is precisely what Ignatius seems to have done (SpEx 316). Pedroche argues that Ignatius seeks to clarify what is less clear (i.e., the authenticity of consolation) by appealing to something even more opaque (i.e., the experience of charity).

Melchor Cano and Tomas de Pedroche move through several accusations, some deeper and more penetrating than others. Both authors repeatedly drive at what they take to be perceptible associations between the *Exercises* and the Iberian *alumbrados*. I have sought to stylize their heterogeneous charges centered on two deeply Ignatian theses: the importance of a personal, interior experience of the divine and the centrality of that experience in the discernment of God's will. For a more complete understanding, one cannot limit the historical backdrop of their charges to an Iberian *alumbradismo*. Their opposition can further be traced to concerns over a surging emphasis on personal, interior experience in general, of which *alumbradismo* must itself be contextualized. Pastore aptly describes this wider context as a typical sixteenth century Iberian

---

49. O'Reilly, "The Spiritual Exercises," 395. Interestingly, Aquinas employs the same verse from James emphasizing prayer as the means of gaining wisdom. He writes in his *Super Io.*, "hauritorium autem quo aqua sapientiae salutaris hauritur, est oratio; Iac. I, 5: *si quis indiget sapientia, postulet a Deo*." Aquinas, *Super Io. IV*, lect. 2, no. 582. See too similar comments at *Super II Cor. VI*, lect. 1, no. 206; *Summa Theologiae* (ST) II-II, q. 180, a. 3, ad 4.

50. We can discern similar annoyances behind Cano's retelling of the way Pedro Ortiz, when offered the Chair of Sacred Scripture in Alcalá, asked for several days to be guided by the Holy Spirit. Cano, *Censura y parecer*, no. 6.

struggle. At that time, Spain possessed "a religiosity constantly torn between a yearning for orthodox purity and the search for a personal relationship with the divine, independent of imposed rules and rituals."[51] It was a time of shift toward interiority. Sometimes this meant toward a mysticism seen to be at odds with a theology that was especially dogmatic. Nowhere was this dogmatic approach more pronounced than among Cano and the Dominicans in Salamanca. No one was more their intellectual mainstay and master than Thomas Aquinas. It is, then, toward Aquinas's understanding of personal, divine experience that we turn next.

Thomas Aquinas on Experience of the Divine

Among the several discernible ways of speaking about experience of the divine in Thomas Aquinas's writings, we focus on that experience of the divine that might be most akin to Ignatius's own. In short, in what manner, if at all, can Ignatius be called Thomistic when referring to direct experience of the divine? Several recent studies of Aquinas's own "mysticism" or mystical theology will unveil a Thomas speaking ably to our two guiding questions. First, Aquinas does have a way of referring to a direct, personal encounter with the divine. However, his language is certainly not as explicit and frequent as Ignatius's. Thomas more often addresses the cause or related gifts of such an experience, rather than that ineffable experience itself. Second, like Ignatius, Aquinas does address the way experience of the divine can touch and guide one's decisions and acts. While these points can be culled from Aquinas's works, it is not the case that Aquinas left us a straightforward treatment of personal, divine experience. Nevertheless, if we can distill the "solid kernel of what has been handed down to us" by his earliest biographers, we should remind ourselves that Thomas was not someone unfamiliar with such mystical experiences.[52] What Thomas does state regarding experience of the divine might be said to hover around two recurring quotes he repeated on several occasions. The first is from Psalm 34, "Taste and see that the Lord is good . . . ," the other from Pseudo-Dionysius's statement that his teacher, Hierotheos, "learned divine things through experience [*patiens*] of them." We begin by looking at the general structure of this divine experience, then move to its touch upon human decision-making.

---

51. Pastore, " Jesuits, *Conversos*, and *Alumbrados*," 269.
52. Jean-Pierre Torrell, OP, "St. Thomas Aquinas: Theologian and Mystic," in *Christ and Spirituality in St. Thomas Aquinas*, Thomistic Ressourcement (Washington, DC: The Catholic University of America Press, 2011), 18.

A Union Opening to Experience

Before he can speak of experience of the divine, Thomas must speak of union. Nowhere is one's union with God more essentially present in Aquinas's works than in his treatment of the theological virtue of charity.[53] He writes, "Charity, by loving God, unites the soul immediately to him with a bond of spiritual union."[54] Just as it is the definition of love that it unites one to the beloved, so too does charity unite one to God. So interwoven are the notions of unity and love that Aquinas thinks one can discern the proper order of one's loves by comparing the sorts of unions present in one's relationships.[55] Because charity is the supernatural gift "poured out into our hearts by the Holy Spirit, Who is given to us" (Rom. 5:5b), union with God and everything that flows from it will always take place within the context of not only charity, but also sanctifying grace.[56] For Thomas, then, whatever is said about personal experience of the divine must be placed necessarily within the context of this essential right ordering of the person to God by God. Jean-Pierre Torrell states this eloquently. Tying together what Aquinas says on charity, the divine missions, and subsequent experiences with God, he writes, "God does not only come for an encounter with man, He gives Himself also and at the very same moment the possibility of encountering Him."[57]

One of the possibilities available to the person upon having received the theological virtue of charity is an openness to "a certain experiential knowledge" [*quasi experimentalis cognitio*] of divine things.[58] From where does this experiential knowledge come? Here we need to piece together what Aquinas says in disparate parts. For the union is founded in charity and treated there. Thomas treats one of charity's primary effects, the gift of wisdom, in the same place. But here we find a gap. In the *Secunda Secundae*, he moves seamlessly from that union brought about by sanctifying grace and charity to experiential knowledge, which is necessary for

---

53. "Sed caritas importat unionem ad illud bonum." ST II-II, q. 23, a. 6, ad. 3; "Tertium autem studium est ut homo ad hoc principaliter intendat ut Deo inhaereat et eo fruatur. Et hoc pertinet ad perfectos, qui cupiunt dissolvi et esse cum Christo." ST II-II, q. 24, a. 9, c.; "caritas importat unionem quandam ad Deum, non autem fides neque spes." ST II-II, q. 24, a. 12, ad. 5.

54. "Et ideo caritas est quae, diligendo, animam immediate Deo coniungit spiritualis vinculo unionis." ST II-II, q. 27, a. 4, ad. 3.

55. ST II-II, q. 26, a. 8.

56. ST II-II, q. 24, a. 2.

57. Jean-Pierre Torrell, OP, *Saint Thomas Aquinas*, vol. 2, *Spiritual Master*, trans. Robert Royal (Washington, DC: The Catholic University of America Press, 2003), 93.

58. Aquinas writes of this in various forms throughout his writing. Some of the more important passages with reference, not to Christ's or demons' experiential knowledge, see *Super Sent* I d. 14, q. 2, a. 2, ad 3; d. 15, q. 2 a. 1 ad 5; d. 15 q. 5 a. 3 expos.; d. 16, q. 1, a. 2, co.; ST I, q. 38, a. 1; q. 43, a. 2, ad 2; II-II, q. 97, a. 2, ad 2.

wisdom, but he does so without mention of a separate experience. One might conclude that for Thomas there is no experience. Instead, there is only "experiential knowledge" born from charity. If this were the case, then everything he says about experience when treating of the divine missions remains fully removed from the gift of wisdom.[59] However, such a conclusion would not do justice to what he says in other places, especially in his commentaries on Scripture. Thomas devotes a lengthy section in his *Super Iob* to the subject of experience of the divine. Here he speaks of experience, not just experiential knowledge.[60] And again, while commenting on John's Gospel, at Christ's invitation to "come and see" Aquinas explicitly links an experience of God to experiential knowledge of God. Immediately after discussing the experience of God, Thomas indicates four ways such an experiential knowledge of God can be had: by doing good works, by rest and stillness of mind, by tasting the divine sweetness, and by acts of devotion.[61] Certainly, across his works Aquinas gives most attention to the second in his various treatments of the contemplative life. Typically, he links sweetness to experiential knowledge of the divine, however it is attained. Nevertheless, if one takes seriously this Johannine passage, then one should not conclude hastily that the contemplative life, however privileged, is the *sole* way to experience the divine.[62] It seems Aquinas, especially in his Scripture commentaries, does see experiential knowledge having at least one of its sources from an actual experience of the divine. And while it is not mentioned there, this insertion is not disallowed altogether in the *Secunda Secundae* treatment of charity and the gift of wisdom. This leaves us with an open question as to how to understand the role of experiences of the divine after charity's arrival. Regardless of where it is found, for Thomas the most immediate effect of this meeting is this "experiential knowledge," and much depends on how one understands this sort of knowledge.

---

59. Blankenhorn has pointed out the error some, like Garrigou-Lagrange, have made in failing to distinguish between the wisdom of the divine mission of the Son and the wisdom that is a gift of the Spirit. Failing to distinguish these has led these commentators to grant experience of God a more necessary and significant role in Aquinas's theology of the gifts of the Spirit. See Bernhard Blankenhorn, OP, *The Mystery of Union with God: Dionysian Mysticism in Albert the Great and Thomas Aquinas*, Thomistic Ressourcement 4 (Washington, DC: The Catholic University of America Press, 2015), esp. 257, no. 30.
60. Aquinas, *Super Iob XII*, lect. 2 (Leonine 26, p. 81, lines 163–226).
61. Aquinas, *Super Io. I*, 1:15, no. 293. He ties each way to a scriptural reference of encounter. By doing good works to "When shall I come and appear before the face of God?" (Ps. 41:3). By rest and stillness of mind to "Be still and see that I am God." (Ps. 45:10). By tasting the divine sweetness. Here he calls us back to Ps. 33:9. Finally, one encounters God by acts of devotion. "Let us lift up our hearts and hands in prayer" (Lam 3:41). To confirm all of this Thomas cites the Lord's words after His Resurrection: "It is I myself. Feel and see" (Lk 24:39). See also *Super Psalmos*, pr. where Thomas speaks of the fourfold manner by which the soul is elevated to God.
62. ST II-II, q. 180.

Adequate description of this experiential knowledge has been the source of debate among scholars. In the last seventy years, two schools of interpretation have developed. Beginning in the late 1950s, John F. Dedek championed a more affective reading. Under this reading, this experiential knowledge was reduced to "a strongly emotional sense."[63] In this way, experiential knowledge is exalted as something beyond speculative knowledge. For the affective interpretation, experiential knowledge is a knowledge that passes beyond the intellect. The alternative reading leans towards an intellectual interpretation of Aquinas's use of the phrase. This is often attributed to André Combes and Albert Patfoort, though with some differences.[64] Without denying the affective overtones of Aquinas's predecessors and contemporaries, this reading argues that Thomas himself set the phrase within a more intellectual scope.[65]

Thomas's language of experience is drawn from his understanding of the senses.[66] In this way, experience normally means sense experience, which is always about singulars, and consequently, not specifically about knowledge pertaining to universals. The connection to the senses is not unimportant, since Aquinas uses experience in an analogous manner regarding encounter with spiritual, non-sensible realities. Privileged among these senses are Thomas's references to seeing and tasting.[67] What similarity might we discern between Aquinas's use of experi-

---

63. Torrell, *Saint Thomas*, 95. For the affective reading see especially John F. Dedek, *Experimental Knowledge of the Indwelling Trinity: An Historical Study of the Doctrine of St. Thomas* (Mundelein, IL: Saint Mary of the Lake Seminary, 1958); Dedek, "*Quasi Experimentalis Cognitio*: A Historical Approach to the Meaning of St. Thomas," *Theological Studies* 22 (September 1961): 357–90.

64. André Combes, "Le P. John F. Dedek et la connaissance quasi-experimentale des Personnes divines selon Saint Thomas d'Aquin," *Divinitas* 7, no. 1 (1963): 3–83; Albert Patfoort, "Cognitio ista est quasi experimentalis (I Sent, d. 14, q. 2, a. 2, ad 3 m)" *Angelicum* 63 (1986): 3–13; Patfoort, "Missions divines et expérience des personnes divines selon S. Thomas," *Angelicum* 63 (1986): 545–59.

65. One prima facie support for the intellectual reading is Aquinas's inclusion of the word *quasi* in the phrase. Patfoort, however, has shown this not to be Thomas's meaning. Torrell repeats this, commenting: "[I]t seems hard to reduce Thomas's views to either alternative. We certainly cannot eliminate intellectual knowing, properly speaking, from this experience, but it is impossible for the experience not to have simultaneously a no less firm affective dimension. It would be quite strange if, having come to the highest point of its encounter with God on earth, the soul were engaged through only one of its powers." Torrell, *Saint Thomas*, 95.

66. "Experimentum enim est ex collatione plurium singularium in memoria receptorum. Huiusmodi autem collatio est homini propria, et pertinet ad vim cogitativam, quae ratio particularis dicitur: quae est collativa intentionum individualium, sicut ratio universalis intentionum universalium." Commentum in Metaphysicam I, lect. 1, no. 15; see too Ia q. 54, a. 5, co.; see also Super Iob c. 12, lect. 2.

67. As we will explore in greater depth later, Aquinas often refers to Psalm 33's "Taste and see the goodness of the Lord" when speaking of such *quasi experimentalis cognitio*. His extended comments on experience of the divine in *Super Iob* also employs language of sensation. Because of the text of Job, there he employs the senses of hearing and taste. See note 56 above.

ence about sensible objects and spiritual realities? Torrell explains that "Basically, the word experience, borrowing from the vocabulary of the senses, suggests something of direct contact with reality transposed into the realm of divine things."[68] To speak of experience, for Aquinas, is to speak of direct contact.

Thomas is also justified in using experiential language because experience of the divine imparts a knowledge that is something more than mere speculative knowledge. It has an affective dimension.[69] This speaks to not only the kind of knowledge had, but also the nature of the experience: the experience of the divine is anthropologically comprehensive, engaging both intellect and will. Herein, God is grasped as both true and good resulting in a loving knowing. This may even relate to the object of this experiential knowledge. In at least one place, Aquinas refers to "knowledge of the divine goodness or will" as the object of this knowledge.[70]

Such experience of the divine not only engages both intellect and will but exceeds any human ability to rearticulate it fully. Divine experience has a touch of the ineffability of God Himself. Reflecting on the Lord's invitation in the Gospel to "come and see," Aquinas comments that Christ says this "because the dwelling of God, whether of glory or grace, cannot be known except by experience: for it cannot be explained in words. . . . And so he says, 'Come and see.' 'Come' by believing and working; 'and see' by experiencing and understanding."[71] In stressing the connection between love and knowledge, Aquinas never abandons the idea that this knowledge is truly such. He only consistently contradistinguishes it from a merely speculative knowledge. Therefore, one should not injudiciously conclude that the affective reading is correct. Aquinas presents experiential knowledge as more complete knowledge, one that is both cognitive and affective, he does not speak of it as a knowledge altogether beyond reason in a metaconceptual manner. The anthropological root of its ineffability springs rather from the fact that one cannot express it as merely intellectual.

68. Torrell, *Saint Thomas*, 96.
69. ST I, q. 64, a. 5, co.; II-II, q. 97, a. 2, ad. 2.
70. ". . . cognitio divinae bonitatis vel voluntatis . . ," ST II-II, q. 97, a. 2, ad. 2.
71. ". . . quia habitatio Dei, sive gloriae, sive gratiae, agnosci non potest nisi per experientiam: nam verbis explicari non potest; . . . Et ideo dicit *venite, et videte*. *Venite*, credendo et operando, *et videte*, experiendo et intelligendo." *In Ioan. I*, 39, lect. 15, nos. 292–93. Aquinas's commentary on John's Gospel contains other worthwhile references to such affective or experiential knowledge of God. The gist of each of these is experiential knowledge's connection to the will's role, especially through love. See in particular the claim that Christ's knowledge of the Father is said to be affective because of His will's consent [*cognitione affectiva, scilicet per consensum voluntatis ad ipsum*] (I, 39, lect. 15, nos. 292–93). So too the saints know by experience how much God loves us [*sancti cognoscent per experientiam quantum diligat nos*] (XVII, 23, lect. 5, no. 2250), though the world cannot know God by an affective knowledge precisely because it did not love Him [*eum non cognovit cognitione affectiva, quia eum non diligit*] (XVII, 23, lect. 6, no. 2265).

Furthermore, knowledge of the divine is correlated to an enjoyment of the divine realities, even an enjoyment of the divine persons themselves. "By the gift of sanctifying grace the rational creature is perfected so that it can freely use not only the created gift itself, but enjoy also the divine person Himself. . . ."[72] We are reminded that, for Aquinas, experience of the divine is spoken in the context of sanctifying grace. One can experience this only because one has been inducted into the life of the Triune God, and so is given to encounter the One who gives him life. This enjoyment of the divine springs from this new, graced life, and thus the language of taste and sweetness is often called upon. It signals multiple connections, not least of all to contemplation as that by which one tastes and enjoys a delight that "surpasses all human delight."[73] Tasting the sweetness of God is another mark of the experience of the divine and can be said to deepen this experiential knowledge.

Frequently, Aquinas indicates this experiential knowledge using a phrase, slightly modified throughout his corpus, from Pseudo-Dionysius. Thomas uses Pseudo-Dionysius's own example of Hierotheos, allegedly Dionysius's own teacher, who is perfect in divine things for he "not only learns, but also experiences divine things [*non solum discens, sed et patiens divina*]."[74] As we have

---

72. "Ad primum ergo dicendum quod per donum gratiae gratum facientis perficitur creatura rationalis, ad hoc quod libere non solum ipso dono creato utatur, sed ut ipsa divina persona fruatur." ST I, q. 43, a. 3, ad 1.

73. "Delectatio omnem delectationem humanam excedit." ST II-II, q. 180, a. 7, co. Thomas also entertains Augustine's definition of wisdom [*sapientia*] as a "sweet-tasting science" [*sapida scientia*]. ST II-II, q. 145, a. 2, obj. 2 and ad 1 and 2. On the sweetness of this experiential knowledge of God, see also ST II-II, q. 97, a. 2, ad 2 and II-II q. 162, a. 3, ad 1.

74. ST II-II, q. 97, a. 2, ad. 2. Vivian Boland admirably discusses the Thomistic, Dionysian, Neo-Platonic, and even Aristotelian roots of this axiom in his essay "*Non Solum Discens sed et Patiens Divina*: The Wanderings of an Aristotelian Fragment," in *Roma, magistra mundi. Itineraria culturae medievalis: Mélanges offerts au Père L.E. Boyle à l'occasion de son 75e anniversaire*, ed. Jaqueline Hamesse (Turnhout: Brepols, 1998), 55–69. Among other things, Boland indicates the great variety of forms the reference to Hierotheos takes on across Aquinas's corpus. Various forms include "non solum discens sed et patiens divina," "patiens divina didicit divina," "patiendo didicit divina," and "didicit divina ex compassione ad ipsa." Aquinas makes explicit reference to the axiom in various places, including: *Super Sent III*, d. 15, q. 2, a. 1, quaesc. 2; *De ver.* q. 26, a. 3, ob. and ad 18; ST I, q. 1, a. 6, ad. 3; ST I-II, q. 22, a. 3, ob. 1; ST II-II, q. 45, a. 2, co.; q. 97, a. 2, ad. 2.

Bernhard Blankenhorn warns against using the experiential language regarding the missions of the divine persons and the gift of wisdom. Thus, he warns against some interpreters who move too quickly from the "suffering divine things" [*patiens divina*] to "experience divine things." I have used this more modern translation, but without seeking to draw any conclusions for the gift of wisdom itself as Blankenhorn warns. Aquinas's own employment of the same axiom in ST II-II, q. 97, a. 2, ad. 2 within the context of tempting God seems closer to link the axiom with the experience of the divine persons. However, see too Thomas's use of it at ST I-II, q. 22, a. 3, ad 1, where he interprets *passio divinorum* as *affectio ad divina, et coniunctio ad ipsa per amorem*. See Blankenhorn, *The Mystery of Union*, 429.

already seen, this axiom serves to reinforce the idea that there is more than just speculative knowledge of the divine, there is one that is affective, suffered, or experienced.

Moreover, Aquinas typically moves from this suffering of divine things to indicate the subject's connaturality with what is experienced. As Bernhard Blankenhorn indicates, for Aquinas, this means the good experienced imparts an inclination in the appetite of the subject who undergoes this suffering or experience.[75] Aquinas leaves "the good" ill-defined here, because it enables him to pivot. The good that is the end of moral virtue serves to grant a certain connaturality to the virtuous agent. In this way, the chaste or courageous agent becomes a rule unto himself in what it means to act with temperance, courage, etc. However, in an analogous manner, the theological virtue of charity leads to a certain connaturality with the divine. This also leads the agent to judge one's acts according to God's ways. It is from this connaturality, born from the union of charity and an openness to experience with the divine, that one moves to a new manner of navigating one's life.

From Union Arises a New Way to Judge

From the union of charity arises an openness to personal experience of the divine. However, while Aquinas in some places does speak of experiencing the divine, it seems the endowment of experiential knowledge and connaturality with charity is sufficient for Thomas to speak of the gift of wisdom. Thus, from charity Aquinas discerns a connaturality with the divine that enables one to judge the things of God and other things in the light of God. What began by being described as affective or experiential is, as Torrell reminded us, always of the entire creature.[76] For this reason, Aquinas understands the theological virtue of charity as that which perfects and moves the just soul to the intellectual operation of judging rightly according to the gift of wisdom. Whereas the subject of the divine experience was cast in the passive, now that same agent moves towards the active. Like what we saw before regarding merely speculative and experiential knowledge, Thomas again insists that there are two ways of judging rightly. In the first way, one judges rightly through a learned knowledge of morality or theology. Yet, in another way, one judges rightly through an inclination. This inclination is born of love and related to that connaturality with the divine good. Like the chaste or courageous person, this is the one who becomes a rule and measure of right judgment. In this way, Thomas refers to the Spirit teaching Isaac that although Jacob had stolen the blessing of the first born, Isaac

---

75. ST I-II, q. 23, a. 4, co.; Blankenhorn, *The Mystery of Union*, 423.
76. See note 65 above.

was not to take the blessing back.[77] One with the gift of wisdom is capable of receiving an *instinctus* by which the agent judges both divine and creaturely things from the viewpoint of *divina*. "It belongs to wisdom as a gift of the Holy Spirit to judge aright about [divine things] on account of connaturality with them."[78] Aquinas immediately points to the Dionysian axiom.[79] Divine wisdom's capacity to judge, while not identified with experience of the divine, is intimately linked to it. Experience or passive suffering of divine things is the spur towards action. The first task Aquinas points us to is a perfection of the intellect: an ability to rightly judge divine and created realities in light of the *rationes divinas*.

Wisdom in this sense is both speculative and practical, it is both contemplative and in action. Here is one of the differences that arise out of wisdom as a gift of the Spirit rather than an acquired virtue. Endowed with this gift, the recipient "touches God more intimately by a kind of union of the soul with Him" in a way that the virtue does not.[80] Consequently, the gift of wisdom "is able to direct us not only in contemplation but also in action."[81] From judgment of a sapientially moved intellect, one moves towards the ability to order. Here Thomas follows Aristotle in understanding that from right judgment issues the ability to order, and from such a right order comes a tranquility that we call peace. The supernatural character is especially important here, for since the vision of the divine essence is the graced subject's ultimate end, the order proceeding from right judgment according to God's reason is an order capable of ordaining the person towards God, under his inspiration. Acting from such a contemplation, to which wisdom first pertains, one discovers the bitter transformed into something sweet, and toil into rest.[82]

Charity's union, with its concomitant experiential knowledge and connaturality with the divine, first enables the Spirit's gift of wisdom in the *Secunda Secundae*. However, because Thomas speaks of experience's connection to experiential knowledge in other places, one foresees a deepening of what charity

---

77. "... quia in illo stupore quem habuit, factus in extasi, edoctus est a spiritu sancto, quod non retractaret quod fecerat." *Super Heb.* c. 12, lect. 3.

78. "... rectum iudicium habere de eis secundum quandam connaturalitatem ad ipsa pertinet ad sapientiam secundum quod donum est spiritus sancti ..." ST II-II, q. 45, a. 2, co.

79. "Huiusmodi autem compassio sive connaturalitas ad res divinas fit per caritatem, quae quidem unit nos Deo." ST II-II, q. 45, a. 2, co.

80. "... magis de propinquo Deum attingens, per quandam scilicet unionem animae ad ipsum ..." ST II-II, q. 45, a. 3, ad. 1.

81. "... habet quod non solum dirigat in contemplatione, sed etiam in actione." I ST II-II, q. 45, a. 3, ad. 1.

82. "... Nec tamen in actibus humanis ex directione sapientiae provenit amaritudo aut labor, sed potius amaritudo propter sapientiam vertitur in dulcedinem, et labor in requiem." ST II-II, q. 45, a. 3, ad. 3. Thomas speaks of the order of the acts that wisdom moves one to in commenting on James 3:17. See ST II-II, q. 45, a. 6, ad. 3.

grants through subsequent experiences of the divine. These are experiences, in fact, that charity sets in motion.[83] Attention to this facet of Aquinas's understanding makes better sense of his comments that speak specifically of acts of contemplation in his treatment of the gift of wisdom.[84] Moreover, this conclusion would avoid running afoul of what is found in his Scripture commentaries. There we learn that while contemplation is perhaps a privileged place of such encounter it may not be the only means of that encounter.

Some Salient Points regarding Divine Experience in Aquinas

Based on Aquinas's account, and with an eye to Ignatius's Dominican charges, we should point out a few other corollary conclusions in quick succession.

First, Thomas does not foresee a divine experience or wisdom that precludes rational concepts and images. Bernhard Blankenhorn has recently argued that to keep the proper balance between an overly intellectualist and excessively affectionist reading of wisdom means acknowledging that wisdom's judgment is not without the use of images and concepts.[85] This means the Spirit's motion in us has absolute priority, but this motion elicits our active cooperation. To conclude that human nature is only passive under the influence of the Spirit would violate the relationship Aquinas too often underlines elsewhere between nature and grace.

Second, since this divine experience and wisdom do not act outside the employment of concepts and images, neither do they operate independent of faith's articles. The articles of the Creed are not merely a propaedutic for divine encounter that one later leaves behind. As mystical as the experience of God may be, any purportedly infused cognition contradicting or working aside from the articles of faith is not to be trusted. The true gift of wisdom is discerned by its cognitive and affective path of faith, even the articles of faith.[86]

Third, scholars are unanimous: Aquinas foresees direct experience of the divine as possible for ordinary people.[87] Drawn from such an experience's intimate link to the theological virtue of charity, Thomas understands this union

---

83. ST II-II, q. 180, a. 7, co.
84. ST I-II, q. 45, a. 3, co. While this contemplation is graced, it is not necessarily only infused contemplation. Torrell, *Saint Thomas*, 14.
85. Blankenhorn, *The Mystery of Union*, 428–30.
86. Blankenhorn, *The Mystery of Union*, 415.
87. Torrell, *Saint Thomas*, 97–98; Blankenhorn, *The Mystery of Union*, 435 and 465; Heather McAdam Erb, "'*Pati Divina*': Mystical Union in Aquinas," in *Faith, Scholarship, and Culture in the 21st Century*, ed. Alice Ramos and Marie George (Washington, DC: The Catholic University of America Press, 2002), 73–96, esp. 91–95; Patfoort, "Missions Divines," 552; Jacques Maritain, *The Degrees of Knowledge* (London: Centenary Press, 1937), 319; Reginald Garrigou-Lagrange, OP, *Christian Perfection and Contemplation according to St. Thomas Aquinas and St. John of the Cross*, trans. Sr. Timothea Doyle (St. Louis, MO: Herder Books, 1937), 345–72.

with God to be open to all who progress in charity. Blankenhorn points out that this is one feature that separates Aquinas's account from others like Pseudo-Dionysius. Aquinas does not claim that union with God is the result of rarified explicit understanding of all the divine names existing only at a mystical summit. Instead, "the contemplation which refers the soul directly to God increases in proportion with the degrees of charity, and is the natural result of exercising the virtues and gifts in a life of grace."[88] Blankenhorn summarizes,

> ... Aquinas proposes varying degrees of dwelling in the dark cloud and of suffering divine things, degrees determined by growth in grace and charity. [...] Union thus occurs through progressive intensification, not neatly distinct stages. Also, the life of virtue elevated by grace, a grace available to all, replaces a Dionysian monastic theology focused on liturgy and study, although the latter practices are part of the life of virtue. Aquinas quietly takes perfect union beyond the confines of the episcopate, the monastery, and the *studium*.[89]

Consequently, it is part of an authentic Thomistic account that the experience of God is open to the ordinary Christian. "Sanctifying grace is the habitual possibility of living an experiential knowledge of the divine Persons."[90]

Similarly, one need not have a theological education for such an experiential knowledge of God to arise. From the perspective of the gift of wisdom, this is obvious since one's intellect is judging rightly through the connaturality of having experienced divine things. Torrell writes, quoting Aquinas,

> This [knowledge] has nothing to do with intellectual resources, and Thomas sees it to be perfectly realizable for people otherwise deprived of all learned knowledge because "this knowledge from which springs love is found abundantly among those who are fervent in their love of God, because they know the divine goodness as the final end, spreading over them its benefits; and such knowledge cannot be perfect in persons who are not inflamed by this love."[91]

Aquinas, like Aidan Kavanaugh's mythical Mrs. Murphy, expresses his overwhelming partiality for the "little old lady" [*vetula*] who burns with the love of God, over the crustaceous professor of theology who does not.[92]

---

88. Erb, "'*Pati Divina*,'" 91.
89. Blankenhorn, *The Mystery of Union*, 465.
90. Patfoort, "Missions Divines," 552.
91. Torrell, *Saint Thomas*, 98, citing *Super Sent I*, d. 15, a. 4, a. 2, ad. 4. Translation from Torrell's English edition.
92. See Jean-Pierre Torrell, "La pratique pastorale d'un théologien du XIII siècle: Thomas d'Aquin prédicateur," *Revue thomiste* 82, no. 2 (1982): 213–45. Torrell cites *Super Eph.*, cap. 3 l. 5;

Finally, and perhaps most importantly, Thomas encourages us to seek this divine experience. One of the Scriptures that seemed to most evoke this experiential knowledge of God to Aquinas was Psalm 34:9 "O taste and see that the Lord is sweet." Unsurprisingly, then, we find his comments on this Psalm particularly telling. Thomas writes that the Psalmist is "urging an experience" [*hortatur ad experiendum*].[93] In so doing, comments Aquinas, he is exhorting us to experience friendship with God. "Experience comes through the senses, but in different ways," so particularly telling is the Psalmist's highlighting of tasting and seeing.[94] For when something is removed from us and at a distance, we speak of seeing, hearing, or smelling. However, when the object is close to us, we speak of touching and tasting. Aquinas continues,

> For touch senses the outside of the object, whereas taste senses the inside. Now God is not far from us nor outside us, but rather He is in us [. . .]. Thus the experience of divine goodness is called tasting.[95]

From this experience of the divine comes a certitude of understanding [*certitudo intellectus*] and a security of love [*securitas affectus*].

> Now, although in the physical world something is first seen and then tasted, in the spiritual world it is just the opposite, for the one who does not taste does not know. Thus he says first *taste* and then *see*.[96]

Aquinas himself places in the mouth of the divinely inspired Psalmist an urging to experience by tasting how good and sweet the Lord is. Two other places where Thomas invokes Psalm 34 in the *Summa* are in his treatment of the sin of tempting God and on the delight of contemplation. Regarding the first passage, Aquinas replies that tempting God is sinful when doing so issues from ignorance or doubt concerning God's perfection. However, it is another thing altogether when Scripture, namely Psalm 34, tells us "to prove God's will and

---

Symbolum Apostolorum, pr.; Sermon, "Attendite," no. 23. See Aidan Kavanaugh, *On Liturgical Theology: The Hale Memorial Lectures of Seabury-Western Theological Seminary 1981* (Collegeville, MN: Liturgical Press, 1984), 105–6.

93. Aquinas, *In psalmos*, no. 9 (p. 266).
94. Aquinas, *In psalmos*, no. 9 (p. 266).
95. ". . . sed per tactum de extrinseca praesente, per gustum vero de intrinseca. Deus autem non longe est a nobis, nec extra nos, sed in nobis [. . .]. Et ideo experientia divinae bonitatis dicitur gustatio." Aquinas, *In psalmos*, no. 9 (p. 266).
96. "In corporalibus namque prius videtur, et postea gustatur; sed in rebus spiritualibus prius gustatur, postea autem videtur; quia nullus cognoscit qui non gustat; et ideo dicit prius, *gustate*, et postea, *videte*." Aquinas, *In psalmos*, no. 9. In addition to this see Aquinas similar comments at ST II-II, q. 97, a. 2, ad 2.

to taste his sweetness."⁹⁷ This thought brings us back to the purportedly Thomistic-inspired charges against Ignatius.

Is the Heart of Ignatius's Exercises Thomistic?

In what way, then, can we compare and contrast Ignatius's *Exercises* with Thomas Aquinas's theology on divine experience? Since we cannot comment on every similarity and/or difference, mention will only be made of a few.

We began with two questions. They pertained to the *Exercises*' emphasis on direct experience of God's action in the soul and the possibility of directing one's human acts according to this experience. Regarding the first, for both Thomas and Ignatius the person can, and is urged to, directly experience the divine. There is a commonality here, though certainly there are differences. While neither saint gives a theological treatise on the nature of this experience, Aquinas more strongly underscores its link to sanctifying grace and the virtue of charity. While this is certainly not missing from Ignatius's *Exercises*, he, on the other hand, more directly addresses the experience of the divine itself.⁹⁸ Both Thomas and Ignatius look to the experience's effects, one often underlining its subsequent possessions of the agent (e.g., experiential knowledge, charity as root of the experience, gift of wisdom, etc.), the other in action (e.g., acts of service, tears, etc.). This commonality among their difference lays the foundation to find in the two saints common ground in what have been called rival forms of mysticism.⁹⁹

Various facets of this divine experience, facets already presented above, also recommend themselves for our attention. First, both Thomas and Ignatius, like Scripture itself, express this experience in the language of sensation, especially that of tasting and seeing.¹⁰⁰ And while Ignatius may very well be indebted to Franciscan spirituality, especially that of Bonaventure, on this point he is

---

97. ". . . probemus Dei voluntatem et gustemus eius suavitatem." ST II-II, q. 97, a. 2, ad 2.

98. After all, and much to Pedroche's chagrin, Ignatius defines consolation by an increase in charity. See SpEx 316.

99. Erb, "'*Pati Divina*,'" 85.

100. François Marty has recently pointed to irreducible personal dimension that is evoked in this language of sense. He writes, "C'est bien le cœur des Exercices qu'annonce Ignace quand il parle de 'sentir et goûter intérieurement.' Or, l'expérience qui est alors suggérée comme modèle n'est pas celle de l'acquisition d'un savoir, mais celle des sens. Il y a une intériorité dans l'acquisition du savoir, acte de l'intelligence. [. . .] Quand il s'agit de sentir et goûter, nul ne peut le faire à ma place, c'est à chacun de prendre en charge cette expérience. Ainsi en va-t-il du chemin spirituel, car il n'y a pas de modèle standard pour l'écoute du Maître intérieur. C'est alors sur sentir et goûter, avec leur qualification d'intériorité, que le questionnement se déplace." François Marty, *Sentir et goûter, les sens dans les « Exercices spirituels » de saint Ignace*, Cogitatio Fidei (Paris: Cerf, 2005), 11.

closer to Aquinas. For Bonaventure, affective wisdom passes beyond cognition. Blankenhorn summarizes his position reflecting on how Bonaventure understands Moses's encounter before God,

> Moses's mind in darkness becomes utterly passive but not empty, for loving union includes an infused noetic light. The condition for its reception is abandoning all cognition derived from the senses, though newly infused knowledge abides.[101]

Unlike Pseudo-Dionysius and various Franciscan authors, neither Thomas nor Ignatius express this mystical union as something detached from or altogether beyond the concepts and images of human reason. To the contrary, both center their approaches on Scripture and the person of Christ. While commenting on Ignatius's second annotation, Michael Ivens underscores the same un-Bonaventurean point,

> It should be read not as distinguishing between knowledge in an objective sense and the subjective experiences of feeling and relish, but between different levels of knowledge: the knowledge that exists solely or largely on the level of the intellect, and the felt knowledge which involves the affections. The latter is referred to in the Exercises as inner knowledge (see SpEx 63, 104, 333). It can be called inner in two senses: it belongs to the "interior" (or heart) of the person knowing; and it penetrates beyond the immediately obvious to the "inner" mystery of meaning of the person or truth known.[102]

For both Thomas and Ignatius, the one who enters the mystery still retains the active use of his acquired cognition, seen especially in Ignatius' recommendation of the apogeic colloquy.

Second, both Thomas and Ignatius thought such a divine experience could be a common experience. A theological education was not a pre-requisite for that transformative encounter. More can and should be said of the early Jesuit attitude towards the sixteenth century scholasticism they witnessed around them, but both Thomas and Ignatius are similar on the role theological formation would serve.[103] It is not an accident that at the opening of his *Summa*,

---

101. Blankenhorn, *The Mystery of Union*, p. 437. Blankenhorn points us to Bonaventure's *III Sent.*, d. 35, a. 1, q. 3, ad. 5. In a later work Bonaventure writes: "Sed ista excaecatio est summa illuminatio, quia est in sublimitate mentis ultra humani intellectus investigationem. Ibi intellectus *caligat*, quia non potest investigare, quia transcendit omnem potentiain investigativam." Bonaventure, "Collationes in Hexaëmeron" in *Opera Omnia*, vol. 5 (Quaracchi: Collegii S. Bonaventurae, 1891) col. 20, no. 11. See too Bonaventure, col. II, nos. 29, 31.

102. Ivens, *Understanding the Spiritual Exercises*, 4.

103. See Osborne's essay in this same volume.

Thomas calls upon the Pseudo-Dionysian maxim of *patiens divina* when asking whether *sacra doctrina* is a wisdom.[104]

Third, both saints affirm that this personal contact with the divine can and should shape one's subsequent actions. Here again, Aquinas largely references the gift of wisdom that has a practical aspect. But given Thomas's Aristotelian understanding of wisdom's role in order and peace, we find some consonance with the goal, stated in Ignatius's "Principle and Foundation," of ordering all towards the ultimate end of human life. Ignatius is, of course, distinctive in suggesting that one can have recourse to the history of the experience of movements and consolation to discern God's will. Even here though one cannot ignore two unique facets present in Aquinas's own teaching. The first is his innovative way of speaking of grace as moving. The second is his use of the language of *instinctus* for the Spirit's working in us in the gifts. Beginning with his *Summa contra gentiles*, Thomas links this *instinctus* directly to Aristotle's notion of being guided by God as found in the *Liber de bona fortuna*.[105] The subject's consciousness of this movement as divine is not explicitly in Aquinas's *instinctus*, but Robert Augé has recently argued that Thomas can speak about personal experience of movements of God.[106] In both Thomas and Ignatius, there is a recognition of the consonance among God's work in the soul, contemplation, and action.

Regarding our principle two questions, then, we find in Thomas and Ignatius striking similarities, not without their own accents and different emphases. Given our investigation, however, we must avoid two errors. The first posits that Thomas and Ignatius have no authentic and deep-seated harmonies. This error, I think, is justifiably removed by what we have discovered here. The other error lies in too quickly supposing that Thomas's works exercised some direct, historical, and intellectual influence over Ignatius's *Exercises*. Certainly, this last thesis could be held regarding Ignatius's theological education, which in part took place through the Dominicans in Paris, or even of the early defenses and directories regarding the *Exercises*. Moreover, there is evidence that Ignatius did know of Aquinas's teaching on particular topics, and perhaps it would have been natural for him to gravitate to read Aquinas on those topics that most interested him.[107] Consequently, there could be some direct, historical influence

---

104. ST I, q. 1, a. 6, ad 3.
105. Valérie Cordonier, *Aristoteles Latinus, Ethica Eudemica (fragmentum); Liber de bona fortuna, Translatio Moerbekana, Recensio Vulgata, textus praevius praeparatus a Valérie Cordonier*, in "Aristoteles Latinus Database," release 3 (ALD-3), 2016.
106. Robert Augé, *Connaître Dieu par expérience: la connaissance expérimentale de Dieu selon saint Thomas d'Aquin*, coll. Sed Contra (Paris: Artège-Lethielleux, 2016), esp. 97–100.
107. George E. Ganss, general introduction, 37. See Andrew Hofer's essay in this same volume for an example of this on the topic of frequent communion.

in Ignatius's understanding of the experience of God. Nevertheless, such a conclusion would, at this point, still be hasty. What can be said is that the consonance between the two saints is in the very least drawn either from their common intellectual tradition, or their own experiences, but perhaps both.[108]

Though the saints' differences may be more interesting, the point of dialogue is not to discover identical features but to learn and be transformed. There is an evident difference between the objective and subjective balance in mystical experience. If the young Ignatius did lean too far towards the subjective dimension ("if there were no Scriptures to teach us"), then Thomas can function as a corrective, and possibly did in Ignatius's Parisian theological training. Yet, where theology, in particular scholastic-Thomistic theology, becomes too objective, in the sense of being divorced from the subject and experience of the one who practices, then perhaps it is the Ignatian voice we need to hear underscoring the mystical to which theology stands in intimate proximity; "for the one who does not taste, does not know."[109]

---

108. Evidence that, in the least, common tradition can be discovered in Pedro de Ribadeneira's report of Ignatius quoting that Pseudo-Dionysius's axiom of "*patiens divina*" when answering some of Diego Laynez's questions on passivity in contemplative prayer. Pedro de Ribadeneyra, *Monumenta Ignatiana. Series quarta. Scripta de S. Ignatio. Fontes narrativi de Sancto Ignatio de Loyola et de Societatis Iesu initiis*, MHSI 93, ed. Candidus de Dalmases (Rome: MHSI, 1965), 747.

109. "... quia nullus cognoscit qui non gustat." Aquinas, *In psalmos*, no. 9 (p. 266).

CHAPTER 3

Ignatius and Thomas on the Ordering of the Passions and the Glory of God

Margaret I. Hughes

P eter Paul Rubens's well-known painting of Ignatius of Loyola, which depicts him vested for Mass, his face upturned and illuminated, yet with tears flowing from his eyes, seems to embody the beginning of Psalm 42: "As a hart yearns for flowing streams, so my soul longs for you, O God . . . My tears have become my food day and night."[1] This representation of Ignatius's outward appearance echoes what his *Spiritual Diary* reveals about his interior life: Ignatius yearns for God and is consumed by tears. At the end of his *Diary*, he records more than two hundred and forty entries noting only the presence or absence of tears in conjunction with his celebration of Mass.

And yet, in a curious passage, Ignatius writes, "during the greater part of the mass, I experienced much gentle devotion, as I thought that it was more perfect to be without tears, and to find, like the angels, internal devotion and love."[2] Clearly, to judge from the numerous entries in the *Spiritual Diary*, Ignatius understands tears in prayer to be an important indication of the way in which the person in prayer is relating to God. And yet, he also says that it is more perfect to be without tears.[3] One possible explanation of this apparent tension is that the *Spiritual Diary* is simply a record of Ignatius's failures and imperfections. Such an explanation, however, is not consonant with the tone of the record of tears in the *Diary*, which contains no self-recriminations, nor with Ignatius's mention of tears throughout the *Spiritual Exercises*, where he includes tears in the graces for which the penitent should ask, and as indications of the movement of the good spirit.

The ancient Stoics, the modern Jansenists, or the post-modern therapeutic deists would take those tears as a sign of an illness of the soul or of an abnormal psychology. But Thomas Aquinas, some two hundred fifty years before Ignatius,

---

1. Psalm 42:1, 3.
2. Ignatius of Loyola, *Spiritual Diary*, in *Personal Writings: Reminiscences, Spiritual Diary, Select Letters including the Text of the Spiritual Exercises*, trans. Joseph A. Munitiz and Philip Endean (New York: Penguin Books, 2004), March 29 (hereafter, SpDiar).
3. SpDiar, March 29.

provides an account of Psalm 42 that would understand Ignatius's tears as an indication, not of disease, but of spiritual health: tears can be the fruit of devotion, "which is an act of the will whereby a man offers himself for the service of God Who is the last end."[4] When the devout man considers that he has not reached this end, "this consideration causes a certain sorrow in those who do not yet enjoy God fully."[5]

While Western philosophers and theologians have often viewed the passions with suspicion—perhaps with some justification—since the passions can so overwhelm human reason,[6] Thomas Aquinas and Ignatius of Loyola emphasize the importance of the passions, rightly ordered, for a good human life and for human happiness. They have consonant understandings of the passions. These understandings, when taken together, lead to a more robust account of the role of the passions in a good life and to a deeper understanding of the role of the passions in prayer. This essay intends to show that both Thomas and Ignatius hold that the passions play an essential role in prayer, both as part of its perfection and as a means by which man comes to know himself in relation to God so he can participate in shaping himself more fully into an image of God, thereby glorifying Him. When the passions are engaged in prayer, God is glorified.

In order to show that this conclusion is latent in each of Thomas and Ignatius's thought but is illuminated by reading the two together, this essay will first offer a brief summary of Thomas's account of the passions, which considers primarily the causes of the passions, and then suggest that Ignatius supplies a first-hand description of the passions that is not found in, but is consonant with, Thomas's account. Both thinkers understand the passions as involving a bodily movement in response to an object. In human beings, that object can be not only a material, sensed object, but also one that is grasped by the intellect and desired or avoided by the will. Man, therefore, has a unique place in Creation as the only creature that can have a passionate response to God. The next sections of the essay consider the role of the passions in man's life as a whole, which both Thomas and Ignatius conceive of as a pilgrimage on the way to the final end of happiness in the glory of God and which requires a proper ordering of the passions. Finally, the essay concludes with a discussion of the engagement

---

4. *Summa Theologiae* (ST), trans. Fathers of the English Dominican Province (Allen, TX: Christian Classics, 1948), II-II, q. 82, a. 1.

5. ST II-II, q. 82, a. 4.

6. While scholarship on the passions in Western thought is far too extensive to cover here in any depth, Michael Meyer, *Philosophy and the Passions: Toward a History of Human Nature*, trans. Robert F. Barsky (University Park, PA: Pennsylvania State University Press, 2000) and Eva Brann, *Feeling Our Feelings: What Philosophers Think and People Know* (Philadelphia: Paul Dry Books, 2008) offer helpful overviews of the passions in Western philosophy.

of the passions in prayer in both Thomas and Ignatius: specifically, the ways in which they understand the ordering of the passions as necessary for the perfection of prayer and how prayer can help order the passions so that well-ordered passions in prayer contribute to man becoming more fully an image of God and so glorifying Him.

Thomas and Ignatius write in different manners and for different purposes. Thomas writes systematically, attending especially to the order of knowing as he unfurls his investigations of reality so that he may, through his writing, teach others.[7] Ignatius's writings are less systematic. They are shorter, more practical works, and, while certainly engaging the intellect, they are aimed more towards forming the will.[8] This difference in writing style and purpose accounts both for the strengths and deficiencies of their explanations of the passions. While each certainly sees the passions as central to human anthropology and to man's ascent to God, each also offers only a partial account. Reading them together, however, makes clear that, although they emphasize different facets of the passions, they understand the phenomena of the passions in the same way and the importance of the role of the passions in prayer for glorifying God.

Thomas's Account of the Passions

Thomas's explanation of the passions is rooted in his understanding of man as a rational animal. As a living being, man has an animate body that is caused by a soul forming matter, such that he is a living, material, unified whole. As an animal, he has the special capacity of sensation, by which he may be moved interiorly by objects exterior to him. The activity of the senses is passive; the senses are moved by the sensed objects, but do not move them. The motion that the subject undergoes when he senses is entirely in him, not in the sensed object—he changes, but the sensed object does not.

There is, then, in all animals, to greater and lesser degrees, a passive movement of the sensitive appetite that inclines towards the good of sensing and

---

7. Frederick Copleston's "Prefatory Note" to his *Aquinas* (London: Penguin Books, 1955) begins, "Aquinas was a university professor and teacher, and his works bear the impersonal and objective stamp which one naturally associates with writers of his profession." "Impersonal and objective" describes the intellectual nature of Aquinas's writing, with its attention to systematically laying out demonstrations of what is true.

8. As John O'Malley observes about Jesuit preaching in *The First Jesuits* (Cambridge, MA: Harvard University Press, 1993), "When Jesuits preached or delivered 'sacred lectures,' they were not to do so in 'the scholastic manner'" (98). He later adds, "When Nadal commented on the provision of the *Constitutions* about not preaching in the scholastic style, he indicated that the problem with that style was precisely that it was 'speculative' and 'dry'" (100). While, of course, this is not a provision for all Jesuit writing, it does point to an emphasis on the formation of the will, and not simply intellectual instruction.

towards sensible objects that are good for the animal. The passions are movements of the sensitive appetite such that there is a bodily change in response to the sense apprehension of a good or evil. In all other animals but man, however, it is an "appetite arising from an apprehension in the subject of the appetite, but from necessity and not from free-will."[9] Animals undergo passions, but always by necessity and always in response to the material particulars grasped by the sense powers.

Man, however, as not only animal, but also as rational, is moved by more than material particulars. He also is moved by intellectual objects. Just as a sensitive appetite inclines animate bodies towards sensible goods, so an intellectual appetite inclines intellectual beings towards intellectual goods. It does not, however, undergo the sort of material alteration that the movement of the sense appetite entails. It cannot, since it is immaterial.[10]

Among intellectual beings, then, man is unique in his ability to undergo passions. While passions are attributed to both angels and God, these attributions are metaphorical, and not univocal: "When love and joy and the like are ascribed to God or the angels . . . they signify simple acts of the will having like effects, but without passion."[11] Since both angels and God are immaterial, they do not have a sensitive appetite, and so they do not undergo passions. Because God and the angels are intellectual, they have a rational appetite inclined towards the good such that it is possible to attribute to them something like man's passions, but properly speaking, when we use the name of a passion to name the movement of the rational appetite, it is only metaphorical. The movement of the rational appetite on its own is not a passion, since it involves no undergoing, no bodily movement.

Man's passions, then, are a phenomenon unique in all of Creation to him. He can undergo bodily transmutation because he is material; he can be moved by intellectual objects because he is immaterial. Unlike God and the angels, he has sensation, but unlike the other animals, he can understand universals and can direct his sensitive appetite to be in accord with what he understands. Of all beings, only man can respond to God passionately.

Since the passions are movements of the sensitive appetite, which has as its object the pursuit of good and the avoidance of evil, the passions can be distinguished based on their object and the subject's relation to that object: "Passions differ in accordance with their active causes, which, in the case of the passions of the soul, are their objects."[12]

9. ST I-II, q. 26, a. 1.
10. ST I, q. 79, a. 2.
11. ST I-II, q. 22, a. 3, ad 3.
12. ST I-II, q. 23, a. 4.

The appetite inclines towards good and away from evil, and so the most basic distinction between the passions is between love and hate. The object of love is a good; evil is the object of hate. But, in addition to the distinction of objects, there is also a distinction based on the object in relation to the subject. The subject can apprehend those objects simply, or either as present or absent. The absence of the good that is loved causes desire; the presence of the loved good causes joy. The absence of the evil that is hated causes aversion; the presence of the hated evil causes sorrow.

Some goods and evils are particularly difficult to attain. This adds another distinction among passions and another aspect of apprehension that moves the appetite:

> [T]he object of the concupiscible faculty, as stated above, is sensible good or evil considered absolutely. . . . On the other hand, the object of the irascible faculty is sensible good or evil, considered not absolutely, but under the aspect of difficulty or arduousness.[13]

When a good, apprehended but not yet possessed, appears difficult but possible to attain, the response is hope. On the other hand, a good not yet possessed and impossible to attain stirs despair. Likewise, an evil not yet present but difficult and seemingly impossible to avoid evokes fear, while an evil not yet present, difficult but not impossible to avoid, gives rise to daring. And, finally, anger is the response to a perceived injustice.

This is a very brief summary of Thomas's theory of the passions,[14] but at least clear here is that the passions involve a bodily movement that is undergone—it is passive, not active—in response to an apprehended object. The passions may be distinguished by the apprehension of their objects and the way in which that apprehension moves the will such that there is a bodily response. This ability to undergo an interior bodily motion in response to intellectual objects is uniquely human and is an emblem of man's unique place in Creation as the only bodily intellectual beings.

---

13. ST I-II, q. 23, a. 2.
14. There are several book length treatments of Thomas's theory of the passions, including: Diana Fritz Cates, *Aquinas on the Emotions: A Religious-Ethical Inquiry* (Washington, DC: Georgetown University Press, 2009); Paul Gondreau, *The Passions of Christ's Soul in the Theology of St. Thomas Aquinas* (Cluny Media LLC, 2018); Nicholas Lombardo, *The Logic of Desire: Aquinas on Emotion* (Washington, DC: Catholic University Press, 2011); Robert Miner, *Thomas Aquinas on the Passions* (New York: Cambridge University Press, 2009).

Ignatius on the Passions

Thomas defines the passions by their causes. While he also recognizes the physical effects of those causes, he spends little time describing the effects of those causes from a first-person perspective. This omission may seem strange to modern sensibilities, given as we are to understand the passions primarily by how the passions make us feel. As Nicholas Lombardo observes, "The most striking [omission and lacuna of Thomas's account of the passions] is that he does not describe the subjective experience of emotion: his primary interest is the *metaphysics* of affectivity, and not the *experience* of affectivity."[15]

Ignatius, on the other hand, does not explore the metaphysics of affectivity, but does emphasize the experience of affectivity. What he says about the experience of the passions shows a concord with Thomas's causal account while also highlighting the importance of what it is like to undergo the passions.

The passions are first interior movements of man as a composite—matter and form—who can experience a physical feeling, of which Ignatius's *Spiritual Diary* offers several descriptions: "I was at peace and felt such great exultation that there was a pressure in my lungs for the intense love I was experiencing in the Blessed Trinity";[16] "with this movement my hair rose and I felt what seemed a very remarkable burning in every part of my body, followed by tears and the most intense devotion";[17] "I felt considerable relish and warmth";[18] "it seemed moreover as if each vein and part of my body was making itself sensibly felt."[19] Ignatius records his passions with physical, tangible descriptions of bodily sensations.

He also includes in his observations the way in which those interior bodily sensations affect his exterior actions. His *Autobiography* records how as a young man fear came upon him such that "it almost seemed to him he couldn't dress himself." But when that fear gave way to joy, "he began to shout through the fields and to speak with God, etc."[20] Later on, his *Spiritual Diary* shows less impulsive behavior but certainly highlights the way in which Ignatius's passions cause especially the exterior action of crying. For example, "During my first prayer, when I named the Eternal Father etc., there came a feeling of interior sweetness that continued, not without an impulse to weep."[21] And again: "At that point, and later during the Confiteor, I felt new devotion not without the

---

15. Lombardo, *Logic of Desire*, 247.
16. SpDiar, February 19.
17. SpDiar, February 8.
18. SpDiar, February 16.
19. SpDiar, February 18.
20. *Autobiography*, in *Personal Writings*, 79 (hereafter, *Autobiog*). Citations are of paragraph numbers.
21. SpDiar, February 15.

impulse to weep. I began the mass [i.e., the Proper] with great devotion, warmth and tears, at times losing the power of speech."[22]

That the passions should affect external actions—such as not getting dressed, shouting through the fields, or crying—is in keeping with Thomas's location of the passions in the sensitive appetite, which, he says, "is nearer to the outward members than the reason and will," such that the will moves, or at least allows the movement of, the outward members through the sensitive appetite.[23]

Ignatius makes clear, however, that the cause of these bodily sensations is not a particular sense object but rather an object that his intellect presents to his will. As recorded in his *Spiritual Diary*, each passion he describes is a response to his prayer, in which he considers before God the poverty of the Society of Jesus. Like Thomas, Ignatius sees that what elicits the bodily movement—that is, the cause of his passions—is an object understood under the aspect of good or evil.

That he sees that the passions are a response to apprehended objects is clear, too, in the *Spiritual Exercises*. Throughout the Exercises, the retreatant asks for graces that include the undergoing of certain passions. Those passions are always in relation to an appropriate object. For example, in the first week, the retreatant asks for "mounting and intense sorrow and tears for [his] sins,"[24] while in the fourth week he asks "to rejoice in the great joy and gladness of Christ Our Lord."[25] While the retreatant asks for a passion, it is not merely the feeling, or the bodily movement that the retreatant seeks, but rather the bodily movement in response to the object that the retreatant considers with his intellect and responds to appropriately with his will, such that an appropriate movement of the sensitive appetite takes place.

Man, the Pilgrim

While both Thomas and Ignatius clearly embrace the passions as having an essential role in the functioning of the human being—since they both see that the passions are appropriate to what human beings are as material and intellectual creatures—they are not naïve about the dangers that the passions pose to a human being's good. Thomas's objections to the question of "whether every passion of the soul is evil morally," where he acknowledges that the passions are sometimes called "diseases of the soul" and can lead to sin, show that he understands well the reasons for the Stoic rejection of passions.[26] Likewise,

---

22. SpDiar, February 25.
23. ST I-II, q. 24, a. 1.
24. *Spiritual Exercises* (SpEx), in *Personal Writings*, 55. Citations are of paragraph numbers.
25. SpEx, 229.
26. ST I-II, q. 24, a. 2.

Ignatius sees that the passions can stand in the way of man's pursuit of good. For example, in his letter to Teresa Rejadell, offering counsel about growth in prayer, he warns her of "extreme fear of God," which could lead her to separate herself from God, as he knows from his own experience.[27] Part of the phenomena of the passions that Thomas and Ignatius both observe and describe is the need for the passions to be habituated in a manner that is appropriate to reality, to what man is and to his place in Creation.

Thomas's anthropology holds that mature, well-ordered passions are those that are in conformity with reason and, therefore, with reality. Reason is oriented toward the world, such that, through knowing, man takes the world into himself. He knows when he sees reality as it actually is.[28] This includes seeing what is really good as good, and what is really evil as evil. When he knows what is actually good and evil, then he has the capacity to direct his whole self toward what is good and away from what is evil. The passions, being movements of the sensitive appetite toward perceived good and away from perceived evil, are rightly ordered when the perceived good is actually good, and the perceived evil is actually evil, and the strength and motion of the passions are appropriate to the object that moves them. Thus, Thomas writes, "the passions of the soul, insofar as they are contrary to the order of reason, incline us to sin; but insofar as they are controlled by reason, they pertain to virtue."[29]

The passions, located as they are in the sensitive appetite, are not rational. And yet, because "the sensitive powers can be considered in two ways: first, according as they act from natural instinct: secondly, according as they act at the command of reason,"[30] the passions can participate in reason. The passions participate in reason when they are governed by reason. In the well-ordered man, reason rules the passions, and the passions obey what reason dictates.[31]

---

27. "Steps in Discernment" (Letter to Teresa Rejadell, 1536), in *Personal Writings*, 99–107.

28. This position may appear to be at odds with the first of Ignatius's "Rules to follow in view of the true attitude of mind that we ought to maintain [as members] within the Church militant," which states: "Laying aside all our own judgements, we ought to keep our minds open and ready to obey in everything the true bride of Christ Our Lord, our holy mother, the hierarchical Church" (SpEx, 353). But, because Ignatius proposes this rule out of faith in the ability of the Church to always teach what is true, the two positions are not opposed. While our own judgments may be in error, the Church's judgments are not, and so Ignatius's rule has as its aim that each person overcome his own errors by bringing his judgments in line with the Church's so that he may see reality as it is.

29. ST I-II, q. 24, a. 2, ad 3.

30. ST I-II, q. 50, a. 3.

31. See Nicholas Kahn, *Aquinas on Emotion's Participation in Reason* (Washington, DC: The Catholic University of America Press, 2019) for a careful study of what it means for the passions to participate in reason and of the development of Thomas's thought on the matter.

Human beings develop the capacity to reason and the habit of conforming themselves to reason over the span of a lifetime. In this life, man is a "wayfarer," a pilgrim toward his final end. While all things act for an end, man is unique among material things in that his movement toward his final end is self-directed: "Therefore, those things that are possessed of reason move themselves towards to an end; because they have dominion over their actions through their free will, which is the 'faculty of will and reason.'"[32] Part of man's mastery over himself in directing himself toward his final end is to become habituated to mastery over his passions, such that his passions aid him in that motion. In this continued habituation of his whole self—body and soul—toward what is actually good, his whole life is a pilgrimage toward his final end. He is, as Thomas says, quoting Dionysius, a "wayfarer journeying towards happiness."[33]

Ignatius, who frequently refers to himself as a "pilgrim," provides an instance of Thomas's account of man as a wayfarer. Ignatius, in his autobiographical writings, shows that a fundamental part of his pilgrimage is the growing capacity to govern and rule his passions. The very early stages of this pilgrimage brought him—while in his sickbed—to a close examination of his passions, and to the way in which different objects would elicit different passions. He would imagine himself in a variety of circumstances, as a worldly knight or as a humble penitent, and would be moved differently by each:

> One time when his eyes were opened a little, and he began to marvel at this difference in kind and to reflect on it, picking it up from experience that from some thoughts we would be left sad and from others happy, and little by little coming to know the difference in kind of spirits that were stirring: the one from the devil, and the other from God.[34]

This realization leads him to reform his life, and to a deep desire to make a pilgrimage to Jerusalem.[35] From then on, even after his travels to Jerusalem, Ignatius thinks of himself as a pilgrim, as is evidenced by the many times his *Autobiography* refers to him by this title.

The goal of the earthly pilgrimage is the glory of God, as Ignatius lays out in the First Principle and Foundation of his *Spiritual Exercises*: "The human person is created to praise . . . God."[36] We praise God when we recognize God as the supreme good, the source of all other goods, and rejoice in God precisely because of his Goodness. That Ignatius holds that this is man's end is confirmed

---

32. ST I-II, q. 1, a. 2.
33. ST I-II, q. 3, a. 8, ad 1.
34. *Autobiog*, 8.
35. *Autobiog*, 9.
36. SpEx, 23.

at the end of the *Spiritual Exercises*. In the fourth week, the retreatant has become well-ordered enough that he is free to praise, reverence, and serve God. He has done so through the purgation of his sins and making an election in keeping with the service of God, such that he may now "ask for grace to feel gladness and to rejoice intensely over the great glory and joy of Christ Our Lord."[37]

Man glorifies God when he conforms his will to God's will. That this is the ultimate goal of the *Spiritual Exercises*, and all of life, is expressed in Ignatius's "Contemplation for Attaining Love": "Take Lord, and receive all my liberty, my memory, my understanding, and my entire will, all that I have and possess. . . . All is yours, dispose of it entirely according to your will."[38] To glorify God is to participate in making manifest his goodness. Since God wills only what is good, when we conform our wills to God's will, we, too, will only what is good. Furthermore, we become, in a way, like God, since our wills imitate his will. This imitation is a proclamation of the goodness of God. Since we choose only what is apparently good, when we choose to conform ourselves to God's will, we express, through that choice, the goodness of God's will, and so of God Himself.

Thomas concurs with Ignatius that the end of man, and indeed, of all of Creation, is the glory of God: "The entire universe with all its parts, is ordained towards God as its end, inasmuch as it imitates, as it were, and shows forth the Divine goodness, to the glory of God."[39] Human beings, as rational beings, have a special role in the glorification of God, insofar as their imitation of God is not only a likeness, but an image of God.

According to Thomas, man is made "to the image of God." He is an image of God in that he has an intellectual nature, by which he may know and love God. The more his nature is fully actual, the more he knows and loves God, the more fully he is an image of God.[40] Man is "to the image" of God, and not simply the image of God, of course, because he is not a perfect image of God but rather is an imperfect likeness: "Man is said to be both image by reason of the likeness; and to the image by reason of the imperfect likeness."[41] By pursuing his end of becoming more fully an image of God, man glorifies God.

Thomas writes that man's end, the destination of his pilgrimage, is happiness. It may seem, then, that although Thomas and Ignatius both understand man as a pilgrim, they understand two different pilgrimages: one toward happiness, the other toward the glory of God. This is not, however, the case. Ignatius observes that a life lived well, for the service and glory of God, should result

---

37. SpEx, 221.
38. SpEx, 234.
39. ST I, q. 65, a. 2.
40. ST I, q. 93, a. 4.
41. ST I, q. 93, a. 1, ad 2.

in happiness.⁴² An investigation of Thomas's account of happiness indicates that he, too, sees that glorifying God causes happiness.

Happiness, Thomas writes, "can consist in nothing else than the vision of the Divine Essence."⁴³ Man is only completely and fully happy when he possesses his final end, which is the end of his highest powers. Those powers are his rational powers, the intellect and will. The end of the will is the good and of the intellect is the truth. The will is satisfied only by the possession of his complete good, which includes the satisfaction of the intellect. The intellect, aimed as it is at knowing what is true, is satisfied only in knowing all that is true, which requires that he know why all that is is. All that is is because of God. Therefore, man's happiness consists essentially in the vision of God, in which his intellect is completely submersed in the cause of all that is. When man reaches this end and is fully happy, he is more fully an image of God, who is happy in knowing and loving Himself.

Therefore, according to Thomas, man's vision of God, his beholding the essence of God, entails, as well, his praise of God. When he sees God, he necessarily sees the goodness of God, and his will is drawn toward God. That is, the movement of his rational appetite rests in God. In that resting, which is an image of God resting in Himself, he expresses the goodness of God and so glorifies Him.

Thomas and Ignatius again concur in their understanding of the human being. Not only do they agree about what man is, and so what the passions are, but they also both understand man as a pilgrim in this life, on his way to an end. Thomas calls that end "happiness," but his account of human happiness is human activity that gives glory to God. Ignatius calls that end "the glory of God," but recognizes that the glory of God necessarily makes man happy. Both accounts of man's end are in regard to the objective state of man, how man stands in relation to God. But for both thinkers, as the next sections will show, there is an important subjective element of happiness. Happiness necessarily entails joy in response to union with God. Both Thomas and Ignatius hold that the development toward the happiness that glorifies God by becoming more fully an image of God requires a mastery over, and maturation of, the passions, such that man can undergo and express joy in the goodness of God.

The Passions *in Via*

Thomas and Ignatius both understand that, in this life, we do not see God face to face and so cannot be perfectly happy. This life is for the purpose of pre-

---

42. SpEx, 187.
43. ST I-II, q. 3, a. 8.

paring us for that happiness, which comes through anticipating the fulfillment of that happiness as much as possible. Since perfect happiness entails the will directed towards the Good, that is God, man can anticipate perfect happiness through directing his will towards individual goods appropriately, insofar as his choice of those goods ultimately is ordered towards God. Through individual acts that are good, he develops rectitude of will, such that "man obtains [happiness] by many movements of works which are called merits."[44] Doing so leads to what Thomas calls imperfect happiness, which is happiness "on account of the hope of obtaining Happiness in the life to come."[45] The happiness of the wayfarer is a happiness founded in hope for perfect happiness in union with God, which he anticipates by habituating his will towards what is good.

Thomas holds that in order to glorify God—to love him and enjoy him as fully in this life as possible, whereby we praise and glorify him—our passions in regard not only to God but to all other things must be ordered well. It is, he writes, "evident that the first thing to be the object of our desire is the end, and afterwards whatever is directed to the end. Now, our end is God toward whom our affections tend in two ways: first, by our willing the glory of God, second, by willing to enjoy His glory."[46]

This is precisely what Ignatius states in the first principle and foundation. We are created to praise, reverence, and serve God—that is, to love God as the highest good. All other things, that is, all other goods, "are created for human beings in order to help them pursue the end for which they are created. It follows from this that one must use other created things in so far as they help towards one's end, and free oneself from them in so far as they are obstacles to one's end."[47]

Ignatius and Ordering the Passions in Prayer

Ignatius's *Spiritual Exercises* aim at inducing the proper ordering of loves, and passions, in the retreatant. It is divided into four "weeks" of prayer, with each "week" accounting for progression in prayer. An exercitant may accomplish a "week" in but a day or two or may take a month for a single "week." The ultimate goal of the *Spiritual Exercises* is that, as Ignatius writes, "one might seek and find the divine will in regard to the disposition of one's life for the good of the soul."[48] Each week within the *Exercises* advances the exercitant toward a mediate goal that he must accomplish in order to achieve the final

---

44. ST I-II, q. 5, a. 7.
45. ST I-II, q. 5, a. 3, obj. 1.
46. ST II-II, q. 83, a. 9.
47. SpEx, 23.
48. SpEx, 1.

goal of the *Exercises*. It is possible to understand those mediate goals in terms of the passions.

The meditations that Ignatius lays out in the first week all concern sin. The exercitant considers the first sin of the angels, the first sin of man, the sin of men in general, and then his own sin. As in every meditation, Ignatius recommends that the exercitant ask for a particular grace. Throughout the first week, the exercitant petitions for "mounting and intense sorrow and tears for [his] sins"[49] and for "an abhorrence for" his sins.[50] Each of the meditations that Ignatius gives in the first week, and indeed in all of the *Exercises*, begins with a preparatory prayer in which the exercitant asks, "God Our Lord that all my intentions, actions and operations may be directed purely to the service and praise of His Divine Majesty." This prayer is an echo of the first sentence of the First Principle and Foundation: "The human person is created to praise, reverence and serve God Our Lord, and by so doing to save his or her soul."[51] When he asks for the grace of sorrow, abhorrence, and tears towards sin, it is with a view towards conforming his passions, and his whole self, to the reality of being a creation of God ordered toward his praise and service. Sin is the result of disordered affections or attachments,[52] through which one lives and acts in discord with the truth of God as the origin and end of all men. Through developing the disposition of sorrow for sin, the exercitant's passions move him towards God and away from that which holds him back from ever closer union with God.

While the first week forms the passions in accord with the first sentence of the First Principle and Foundation, the second week forms the passions in accord with the second sentence of the First Principle and Foundations: "The other things on the face of the earth are created for human beings in order to help them pursue the end for which they are created."[53] In the second week, the exercitant forms his passions to be rightly ordered toward created goods, by coming to love those goods properly, which he can do now since he has fixed himself so firmly on God as his first beginning and last end. The meditations in the second week center on Christ's earthly life prior to his Passion. The exercitant comes to know Jesus more intimately as he meditates on the way in which God-Made-Man uses, and loves, created goods correctly. Interspersed with these meditations are ones that require the exercitant to examine and to ask for the grace to amend his regard for health, wealth, and status, as well as for fervor in serving Christ. He develops the appropriate loves and hates, desires and aver-

---

49. SpEx, 55.
50. SpEx, 63.
51. SpEx, 46, 23.
52. SpEx, 1.
53. SpEx, 23.

sions, delights and sorrows toward correctly apprehended goods and evils. In this week, the exercitant also examines the goods among which he is choosing and makes an election. Having purified his passions in the first week by attaining a hatred of sin and love for God, he is free, in the second week, to order his passions appropriately toward the goods by which he may praise and serve God.

In the third week, then, he is able to examine his election by joining himself to Christ in his Passion, and by asking for the grace of "grief, deep feeling and confusion because it is for my sins that the Lord is going to the Passion,"[54] and for the grace of "grief with Christ in grief, to be broken with Christ who is broken, and for tears and interior suffering on account of the great suffering that Christ has endured for me."[55] In a way, this is a return to the first week, in which the exercitant also asked for grief for his sins, but now, in the third week, he returns to that petition with his passions having been purified, so that they are now more in conformity with Christ's passions, and the exercitant is free to respond to sin in a way that imitates Christ.

The fourth week continues with asking for the graces to share in and imitate the passions of Christ. Now, however, it is not sorrow, but joy, for which the exercitant prays. In this week he is finally ready, with his passions reordered and purified, to freely rejoice in the Resurrection. He asks for the "grace to feel gladness and to rejoice intensely over the great glory and joy of Christ Our Lord"[56] as he meditates on the mysteries of the Resurrection and Ascension.

This reading of the ordering of passions as a structuring principle of the *Spiritual Exercises* is corroborated by Ignatius's statement at the beginning of the *Exercises*: "In all the spiritual exercises that follow we bring the intellect into action in order to think and the will in order to stir the deeper affections."[57] By Ignatius' own declaration, it is clear that prayer, especially pursued as a spiritual exercise to strengthen the soul in its pursuit of God, necessarily incorporates the passions.

The Ordering of the Passions and the Perfection of Prayer

Thomas, in explaining how the Lord's Prayer is "most perfect," assigns to it an end very similar to that which Ignatius gives to the *Spiritual Exercises*: "Now in the Lord's Prayer, not only do we ask for all that we may rightly desire, but also in the order wherein we ought to desire them, so that this prayer not only teaches us to ask, but also directs all our affections."[58] Like Ignatius,

---

54. SpEx, 193.
55. SpEx, 203.
56. SpEx, 221.
57. SpEx, 3.
58. ST II-II, q. 83 a. 9.

Thomas holds that the prayer of the pilgrim, the wayfarer, should order his loves so that his passions move him first toward God, and then toward other goods for the sake of God. He, too, sees that prayer, while a properly rational activity,[59] involves the passions.

That prayer is a properly rational activity, however, raises Ignatius's conundrum with which this paper began: given that rational activity is the highest activity of man, and that prayer is one of those activities, it seems that prayer would be more perfect without the involvement of the passions. The angels, as Ignatius points out, do not weep, and so, it seems, it would be better if we, too, should "be without tears"[60] when we speak with God. It seems curious that prayer should involve the passive movement of the sensitive appetite, and not simply rational activity.

The beginning of an explanation emerges earlier in this paper: human beings hold a unique place in Creation as the only beings that are both material and spiritual, such that they are the only creatures who can respond to God passionately. Other material beings cannot know God, and other spiritual beings do not undergo passions. Human beings alone are capable of undergoing a bodily response to God.

When a human being's passions are engaged in his prayer, then, he is acting as the kind of thing that he is, as he has been created. His nature, given to him as it is by God, is directed fully toward God, as is appropriate and good. There is more to be investigated here, however: what is the purpose of the passions in prayer? What do they add to prayer that a passionless exercise of the intellect and will lack? Since man has an intrinsic end, his own perfection, and an extrinsic end, the glory of God, there are two considerations here: the role of the passions within the individual who is praying and the role of human prayer and its attendant passions in Creation. Taking up the first will help illuminate the second.

Prayer, the fixing of the heart and mind on God, is a foreshadowing of our final beatitude, in which the heart and mind are fully fixed on and satisfied by the sight of God: "This contemplation will be perfect in the life to come, when we shall see God face to face, wherefore it will make us perfectly happy: whereas now the contemplation of the divine truth is competent to us imperfectly . . . Hence it bestows on us a certain inchoate beatitude."[61] Prayer, then, is essential to a good human life, since it habituates the will toward God as its end and does so through the operation of the intellect coming to understand God, and so growing in a deeper understanding of the goodness of God.

59. ST II-II, q. 83, a. 10.
60. SpDiar, March 29.
61. ST II-II, q. 180, a. 4.

The end and perfection of man, being the contemplation of God, is "the fruition" of God,[62] that is, the enjoyment of God. That enjoyment is first an activity: the operation of the intellect and will resting in the sight of God. But human enjoyment is incomplete without consequent delight in the good being enjoyed. If the passions follow upon the activity of the will, the human being is more completely moved toward what is good: "When the higher part of the soul is intensely moved to anything, the lower part also follows that movement and thus the passion that results in consequence, in the sensitive appetite, is a sign of the intensity of the will, and so indicates greater moral goodness."[63] It is not just the will that should be directed to the good, but the whole human being, as guided by reason. When the appropriate passions follow upon the activity of the intellect and will, then the whole human being is ordered correctly.

Joy in prayer anticipates the beatific vision. The resting of the intellect and will in God necessarily elicits the passion of joy or delight. Delight is, as Thomas puts it, "attendant" on the beatific vision, "For [delight] is caused by the appetite being at rest in the good attained. Wherefore, since happiness is nothing else but the attainment of the Sovereign Good, it cannot be without concomitant delight."[64] The separated soul cannot experience this delight as a passion in the sense of a bodily transmutation. The resurrected body, however, can experience delight, as, Thomas writes, "an overflow into the body,"[65] such that the whole human being is caught up in the sight of God. When there is such an overflow to the body in prayer in this life, man has a glimpse, however shadowy and obscure, of what his final happiness is like.

But, in this life, we are not yet united to God in our final happiness. This is a proper cause of sorrow. Tears, and the sorrow of which they are an effect, are caused by the apprehension of an evil. Since evil is the lack of a good, however, the apprehension of an evil is always in relation to a good. It is possible to sorrow over the lack of a loved good, but it is also possible to sorrow over loving a good that is lacking. The love of conflicting goods can cause sorrow, as, for example, someone who both wants to love and serve God as the supreme good, but who also loves his wealth in such a way that it stands in the way of his loving God. Likewise, the lack of the good of loving what is good, for example, the lack of proper love for God, can also cause sorrow. The cause of sorrow indicates much about what it is the subject understands as good and loves. Sorrow, then, and tears, can be appropriate and perfective of prayer when they are elicited as a consequence of loving God and sorrowing at the lack of complete union with him.

62. ST I, q. 65, a. 2.
63. ST I-II, q. 24, a. 3, ad 1.
64. ST I-II, q. 4, a. 1.
65. ST I-II, q. 4, a. 5, ad 4.

Ignatius is correct, therefore, that it is better to be without tears, insofar as it is better to be in complete union with God. Enjoying final human happiness, the goal of the earthly pilgrimage, is better than being on the way to that goal. Since, in the full and final sight of God, there is no sorrow and so no cause for tears, it is better to be without tears in the beatific vision. But it is also better to be on the way to the final goal than to be stalled or moving away from that goal. Sorrow at the incompleteness of union with God in this life is a sign of love of God. While it is better to be without tears, as it is better to enjoy the beatific vision, in this life, tears can be a sign of devotion because they are an indication of the depth of love of and longing for God.

Prayer, therefore, is perfected when it results—not as an end, but as a consequence—in the undergoing of appropriate passions. The human being is more perfect when he not only recognizes the evil of sin and chooses to avoid it, but also when he undergoes the feelings of sorrow and revulsion toward it. Likewise, the human being is more perfect when he not only recognizes and chooses what is good, but also when he undergoes the feelings of desire and delight in that good. Prayer, while a rational activity, is more complete, more fully human, when the passions result from that activity. The passions, rightly ordered, in prayer, serve to incorporate the whole human being into his praise of God, and so add to the perfection of that activity.

The ordering of the passions in prayer is achieved through the rule of reason over the passions. It is, however, a particular kind of rule: "The intellect or reason is said to rule the irascible and concupiscible by a politic power."[66] Reason is a "royal" or "politic" ruler of the passions.[67] Thomas frequently makes use of the metaphor between a king and his subjects and reason and the passions. He draws a distinction between despotic rule and politic, or royal, rule. The despot rules his subjects as a master does his slaves; his concern is for his own good, and the good of his slaves only insofar as that serves the good of the despot. The slaves cannot rebel and pursue their own good. The royal, or political, ruler, on the other hand, rules subjects who are free to rebel for the sake of pursuing what is good for them: "Now the end which befits a multitude of free men is different from that which befits a multitude of slaves, for the free man is one who exists for his own sake, while the slave, as such, exists for the sake of another. If, therefore, a multitude of free men is ordered by the ruler

---

66. ST I, q. 81, a. 3, ad 2.
67. Discussions of Thomas's analogy between the royal rule and reason's rule over the passions can be found in G. J. McAleer, "The Politics of the Flesh: Rahner and Aquinas on *Concupiscentia*," *Modern Theology* 15, no. 3 (July 1999): 355–65; Tom Ryan, "Aquinas' Integrated View of Emotions, Morality and the Person," *Pacifica* 14 (February 2001): 55–70; Kevin White, "The Passions of the Soul (IaIIae, qq. 22–48)," *The Ethics of Aquinas*, ed. Stephen J. Pope (Washington, DC: Georgetown University Press, 2002), 103–15.

towards the common good of the multitude, that rulership will be right and just, as is suitable to free men."[68]

The royal ruler, he who rules free men well for the sake of the common good, must rule with a view of inclining his subjects toward the good of the polis through reward and punishment: "By his laws and orders, punishments and rewards, he should restrain the men subject to him from wickedness and induce them to virtuous deeds, following the example of God, Who gave His law to man and requites those who observe it with rewards, and those who transgress it with punishments."[69] The good ruler rules the polis by ordering his subjects toward the good. In a healthy city, while the king punishes subjects, it is with the aim of habituating them to the good. He presents the real good to his subjects such that they are inclined to act in accordance with that good, and so respects the freedom of his subjects.

In this metaphor, there is a parallel between free men and the passions. This seems odd, since free men are free because of their will; the sensitive appetite does not have a will. Nonetheless, the sensitive appetite can be "persuaded," not through argument, but through the habituation to real goods. Just as the ruler must habituate his subjects to the pursuit of the good of the polis, through continually placing before them what is actually good, so too does the reason rule the passions through continually placing before them what is actually good, so that they may develop the habit of responding to that good.

And, just as a good ruler must know his subjects so that he knows how to present the good of the polis in such a way that they are moved to pursue it, so too must the human being know the inclinations of his passions so that he knows how to persuade them into a proper ordering toward the good of the whole human being. Although he may, with his rational appetite, incline toward a real good, his passions, if not well ordered, may rebel and pull him toward a good in a disordered way. Simply willing the good is not enough for the good of the human being as a whole; he must, as a whole being, be united in the inclination toward that good. Part of his willing the good, then, is to shape the inclination of his passions toward what is really good. To do that, he must know how his passions are inclined and then continually present to the passions, through his imagination, the evils and goods that will habituate his passions properly, while at the same time restraining disordered actions that may arise from not-yet-ordered passions.

This is the purpose of the *Spiritual Exercises*. In the withdrawal from everyday life, "with one's mind not divided amongst many things but entirely taken

---

68. Thomas Aquinas, *De Regno*, trans. Gerard B. Phelan (Toronto: Pontifical Institute of Medieval Studies, 1949), 10. Citations are of paragraph numbers.

69. *De Regno*, 120.

up with one thing alone, namely, serving one's Creator and doing good to one's soul, one is able to use one's natural powers all the more freely in the diligent search for what one's heart desires."[70] In the intensification of the focusing of the intellect and will on God through the execution of the *Exercises*, the retreatant acts in such a way that he is able to reflect on that activity, so as to see how he relates to God and how he should relate to God.

The passions, especially as they arise in prayer, allow man to know himself better, and so to know where his strengths and deficiencies lie in regard to his ordering toward God. These bodily alterations, because they are material and sensible, are more easily known to the retreatant than the insensible activities of the intellect and will. But these bodily alterations are a result of those activities. Since the passions are a response to the apprehended good, the retreatant's passionate responses in his prayer indicate to him what he understands as good and the strength of his love for that good. Throughout the *Exercises*, as the exercitant prays for graces, he is attentive to the passions that he undergoes and discusses them with his director to track his progress and to make adjustments to his prayer.

The passions in the prayer of the individual help him to order his passions toward what is good and to perfect his prayer, since the perfection of his activity comes from his parts being ordered toward his good as a whole. In engaging in this ordering and perfecting, however, not only does he attain his own, intrinsic good, he also achieves the extrinsic good of the glory of God, which, as Ignatius and Thomas both hold, is the purpose of human life, and, indeed, of all of Creation.

The Ordering of the Passions and the Glory of God

For Thomas and Ignatius, it is especially in prayer that man cultivates his knowledge and love of God and so acts as an image of God. When his reason rules his passions in prayer like a king and not a despot, he is even more fully an image of God, who rules all of Creation like a king and not a tyrant. Just as a king governs his subjects, so reason governs the passions, and God governs Creation: "Therefore let the king recognize that such is the office which he undertakes, namely, that he is to be in the kingdom what the soul is in the body, and what God is in the world."[71] Like Divine Providence ruling the world, "So, too in the individual man, the soul rules the body; and among the parts of the soul, the irascible and the concupiscible parts are ruled by reason."[72] There is a

---

70. SpEx, 20.
71. *De Regno*, 95.
72. *De Regno*, 9.

likeness between the way in which God governs the world and reason governs the passions. Just as God governs the world by ordering all the parts of the world toward the final good which is the glory of God, so too should reason order the passions toward the final good of the human being, which is his happiness and the glory of God. And, just as God governs the world, especially those creatures that are free, not by force and manipulation, but by presenting them with what is good and allowing them to respond to that good, so too the reason rules the passions by presenting to them what is good, so that they may respond appropriately.

When, in the presentation of what is good, an evil also becomes evident, the good ruler of the passions allows for a response of sorrow and tears and recognizes that that response is good because it is appropriate. In doing so, he acts like God governing Creation, who orders all things to what is good, and permits what is evil because that evil is for what is good. Ignatius is correct that it is better, absolutely, not to cry, since the angels do not weep; the angels are higher beings, and, so, how they are and act is better in the order of being in all of Creation. In the order of the human being, however, it is better, and more God-like, to allow tears when there is a genuine evil that should cause sorrow.

When the passions are engaged in prayer, even in sorrow to the point of tears, the human being acts integrally, ordering his whole being toward the glory of God, and becomes more fully an image of God, who orders all things toward his glory. In becoming more fully an image of God, which includes, for man, a well-ordered response of the passions to what is good, man glorifies God.

CHAPTER 4

The Thomistic Account of Prudence and the Ignatian Account of Discernment of Spirits

Joseph W. Koterski, SJ

Does the Ignatian approach to the discernment of spirits rely too much on transient feelings? Is the Thomistic account of the role of prudence in making good decisions too abstract? For those well versed in Thomism, such questions about Ignatian spirituality are not uncommon. Likewise, for proponents of Ignatian spirituality, scholastic distinctions often seem arcane. But as someone deeply appreciative of Thomistic thought and of Ignatian spirituality, I believe that, properly understood, the Thomistic account of prudence and the Ignatian account of the discernment of spirits are not only compatible with one another but mutually beneficial for souls.

The mutual suspicions here remind me of the opening sentence of Tacitus's *Germania*. There he observes that Germany is separated from the Sarmatians and the Dacians by mountains and by mutual dread.[1] Dissipating the caricatures, however, will allow us to see certain real differences while dismissing faulty allegations. To shift from the image provided by the Roman historian to those offered by the American poet Robert Frost, a deeper study of these matters will permit us to say that "good fences make good neighbors."[2]

What is worrisome to some Thomists is that the Ignatian method encourages making important life-decisions on the basis of something as unstable as feelings and desires. Truly, to rest our choices on passing emotions would be risky. But to do that would be to misuse the Ignatian way. If one were to suppose that the *Spiritual Exercises* encourages anyone to make decisions on strong but transient passions, one would misunderstand the program that St. Ignatius devised for differentiating between reliable and unreliable feelings. Properly used, the Rules for the Discernment of Spirits can help us to differentiate

---

1. Tacitus, *Germania* 1: "Germania omnis a Gallis et Raetisque et Pannoniis Rheno et Danuvio fluminibus, a Sarmatis Dacisque mutuo metu aut montibus separatur."
2. Robert Frost, "Mending Wall" (1914), *North of Boston* (Boston, MA: Henry Holt & Co., 1917).

between what comes from God and what comes merely from ourselves—let alone from an infernal source!

The first portion of this essay will offer a review of some important points from the text of the *Spiritual Exercises*. My aim here is to show how the *Spiritual Exercises* and especially the Rules for the Discernment of Spirits can help us to discern the will of God. The exercises of the First Week are intended especially to assist us in becoming *free from* sin and other disordered attachments (including being ruled by unstable feelings), so as to have the *freedom for* making good choices and sound decisions later in the course of the retreat. We will be better followers of St. Ignatius by heeding the worries voiced by the followers of St. Thomas.

Another concern that we need to mention in this section is a worry voiced by some Thomists about the integrity of moral reasoning when Ignatian discernment practices are offered as a justification for moral assessments that amount to ethical consequentialism or situation ethics. Thomists rightly point out that feelings, emotions, and passions do not alter the moral character of an action. The use of Ignatian concepts for this purpose does not show fidelity to the *Spiritual Exercises*.

The second half of the essay will consider certain hesitations that can arise in the followers of St. Ignatius with respect to the Thomistic account of prudence. Can Aquinas's discussions of the workings of prudence and practical reasoning give adequate guidance for decision-making? Is the Thomistic position not overly intellectualist and insufficiently attentive to the affective dimensions of a person's life and to the ways in which God often moves a person to learn about a vocation or to feel God's workings within the soul?

The danger here is for a Thomist to fall into some version of crypto-Stoicism that involves seeing all passions as dangerous. While a Stoic view of Thomism could perhaps be the result of one's philosophical convictions, it seems even more likely to result from some personal discomfort with the emotions. But, whatever the source of one's position, to take such a view of Thomism would neglect Aquinas's careful and repeated distinction between Stoic, Platonic, and Aristotelian stances on the relation between reason and the passions.

This distinction is found in prominent places within the *Summa* as well as in Aquinas's commentaries on Aristotle's *Ethics* and *Politics*. In the Thomistic view, reason can and must make reliable allies out of our appetites and emotions. Cultivating a mindfulness of the distinction between individuals with well-ordered passions and those whose affective and appetitive drives are badly ordered will help the Thomist be a better Thomist. Further, attention to this distinction will also help those trained in the ways of Ignatius dispel the worry that Thomism is not sufficiently sensitive to the stirrings of the spirit for the purposes of spiritual direction. Let us consider each of these points in turn.

The Ignatian Way

It may be helpful to start with an overview of the Ignatian approach to these questions that is provided by the *Spiritual Exercises*.³ This text is a handbook for those giving retreats. In addition to providing topics for mental prayer during a retreat, it contains numerous directives and explanations for how the director of the retreat should proceed. One of its most important features is a series of "rules" for such things as the discernment of spirits (§§313–336), the distribution of alms (§§337–344), dealing with scruples (§§345–351), and thinking with the Church (§§352–370).

After some introductory observations to assist the director and those making a retreat (§§1–22), Ignatius offers an exercise entitled "First Principle and Foundation" (§23). After that we find materials for each of the "four weeks" of the *Exercises* (§§24–229), concluding with an exercise entitled "Contemplation to Attain the Love of God" (§§230–237). There are also supplementary sections on methods of prayer (§§238–260), on the mysteries of the life of our Lord that provide points for use in various prayer periods (§§261–312).

In its full version, this retreat program lasts about a month and is divided into "four weeks." These weeks, however, are not necessarily seven days in length. Rather, a prudent director will urge that the retreatant not move on from one "week" (perhaps better, "stage") to the next until actually receiving the grace that is characteristic of that portion of the retreat. In my experience, it proves far better to go slowly and to wait until God provides the grace that is sought at each stage before going forward. If one needs to break off a retreat at some point, the director can do well to urge the retreatant to take the time necessary for living with the graces received (for instance, to solidify a conversion from a deep habit of sin, or to grow steadily in a new-found freedom from a disordered attachment) before undertaking another retreat some day in which one can resume the search for God's will on a question about a choice of a state of life.

In having diverse "weeks," the *Exercises* resemble the time-honored division of the spiritual journey into the purgative way, the illuminative way, and the unitive way.⁴ Like the purgative way, the first week is focused on becoming free from sin and disordered attachments. In a way that is comparable to the illuminative

---

3. Throughout this paper, I will cite from Louis J. Puhl, SJ, *The Spiritual Exercises of St. Ignatius, Based on Studies in the Language of the Autograph* (Chicago: Loyola University Press, 1951), using the paragraph numbers that are standard for all editions of the Exercises.

4. There are many accounts of these three stages of the spiritual journey, including Jordan Aumann, OP, *Spiritual Theology* (Huntington, IN: Our Sunday Visitor Press, 1980), esp. ch. 3., and Ralph Martin, *The Fulfillment of All Desire: A Guidebook for the Journey to God based on the Wisdom of the Saints* (Steubenville, OH: Emmaus Road, 2006); the three stages constitute the very structure of this book.

way, the second week has us seek the grace of knowing Christ better, loving him more deeply, and following him more closely. In this second week, the *Exercises* focus on the mysteries of Christ from the Incarnation through the public life while offering special exercises that Ignatius devised for finding the will of God in the matters that the retreatant has brought to the retreat for discernment and choice. By seeking to be one with the sufferings of Christ during the Passion and then with the joy of Christ in the glories of the Resurrection, the third and fourth weeks, respectively, correspond to the unitive way.

There are many reasons for using this form of spirituality, whether on a formal retreat or in the course of daily life. The *Exercises* are especially intended to be of help for people trying to become free enough to make important choices, particularly choices about a way of life, about the disposition of their affairs, and about the reform of life. For the present purpose of examining the propriety of understanding our stirrings and feelings, let us concentrate on the "First Principle and Foundation" and on the Rules for the Discernment of Spirits that Ignatius introduces during the First Week and the Second Week.

The First Principle and Foundation

The worry mentioned above about the reliance of the Ignatian approach on something as unstable and fleeting as desires, emotions, and feelings may not show a sufficient understanding of how this method helps differentiate between reliable and unreliable feelings. The first week is designed to prepare an individual for making responsible choices and for discerning the will of God precisely by addressing these questions in a person's life. The First Principle and Foundation (§23) sets the stage for the first week. It provides not merely an opening gambit for this period of the retreat but introduces a sustained quest for the freedom from disordered attachments. The text deserves careful study. It reads:

> Man is created to praise, reverence, and serve God our Lord, and by this means to save his soul.
>
> The other things on the face of the earth are created for man to help him in attaining the end for which he is created. Hence, man is to make use of them in as far as they help him in the attainment of his end, and he must rid himself of them in as far as they prove a hindrance to him. Therefore, we must make ourselves indifferent to all created things, as far as we are allowed free choice and are not under any prohibition. Consequently, as far as we are concerned, we should not prefer health to sickness, riches to poverty, honor to dishonor, a long life to a short life. The same holds for all other things. Our one desire and choice should be what is more conducive to the end for which we are created.

If one were ever to doubt the debt of Ignatius to scholastic thought, the first three paragraphs of this exercise ought to correct that misapprehension. In speaking of "man" in the generic sense of the word, these paragraphs invite those who are praying with them to understand that human beings have a divinely given purpose, such that by praising, reverencing, and serving God they may gain salvation. Further, they direct us to see that we are to use what will be helpful in reaching that end and that we are to rid ourselves of what can only hinder us.

Considered in relation to various other forms of Christian spirituality, the course recommended here is not one of radical renunciation of the goods of this world but one of freedom from disordered attachments. One can see this point in the fourth paragraph, whose key word is "indifferent." In this context the word "indifferent" means neither a state in which we simply do not care nor a state akin to the strategy of classical Stoicism, in which we force ourselves not to care about anything outside of our control. Rather, it means a *freedom from* a disordered attachment to any inclination or any aversion, so that we are *free for* undertaking a permissible course of action or refraining from it, based solely on whether it helps or hinders us in the attainment of the end for which we are created.

It may help to envision this scenario on a spectrum of various inclinations and aversions. The purpose of the following diagram is to help us differentiate individual experiences of an inclination or aversion (the center of the diagram) from more-or-less settled dispositions (habits) of that inclination or aversion, and then (at the far left and far right on the diagram) from disordered attachments to an inclination or an aversion:

Disordered Habits of Inclination	Habits of Inclination	Inclinations	Aversions	Habits of Aversion	Disordered Habits of Aversion

To take some simple examples first, I might be naturally inclined to certain foods (linguini, say, or blueberry pie) and aversion to others (for instance, okra or quinoa). Further, I might have developed habits of following these inclinations and of avoiding the foods to which I feel an aversion. The problem comes not with having inclinations and aversions or with having certain habits and legitimate attachments. Rather, the problem comes with having a disordered attachment to some inclination or aversion, such that I find myself insistent on what I regard as tasty foods even if they become injurious to my health. On the other side of the scale, we could find ourselves in a position in which we refuse to eat something really good for us or if we would be ready to offend a host by refusing some food prepared for us by a family of modest means simply because we have a disordered habit of aversion in regard to certain foods.

Let me propose a different kind of example. I might like research and writing, and I might well have good habits that follow my inclinations in that direction. Further, as a teacher for many years, I have to admit that I have a certain aversion to the ways in which some students carry themselves. We all have certain inclinations and aversions, and certain attachments to our inclinations and aversion. But my habits of inclination and aversion would be disordered if my personal taste for reading and study brought me to the point of taking none of the interest in people that a priest and a teacher needs to take, or if I cannot deal with anyone on account of my dislike for certain types of student conversation (the grade-grinder comes to mind) that I resent for disturbing my office hours.

The specific examples that Ignatius presents in the First Principle and Foundation, it seems to me, can be well understood on this model. I do not think that the fourth paragraph implies that one will not have a natural preference for health over sickness, for a long life to a shorter one (albeit there are some souls who seem to have an inclination to follow St Thérèse of Lisieux in desiring an early death), for riches over poverty, and for honor to dishonor. Nor do I think that there is any problem with cultivating good habits in regard to healthy eating and exercise, to caution about situations that are dangerous to life and limb, to prudent practices in dealing with money and resources, and to the cultivation of a good reputation such that we can be persuasive and influential when we are asked to give our opinions on matters of the day.

Rather, it seems to me that this exercise invites us to seek a poised readiness to risk even our health if that is what is needed to do the will of God. This sort of indifference made countless saints ready to risk their lives by serving the poor during the plagues of their day, much as it has made first-responders, health-care professions, and those in pastoral care today face the dangers of contracting infections when it was their duty to bring medical care or the sacraments to the sick and dying.

Likewise, it is the cultivation of this sort of indifference that often constitutes poverty of spirit, in the sense of treating the resources at our disposal as objects over which we exercise stewardship rather than ownership. And as regards honor, what a pity it would be to have such a disordered attachment to the esteem of, say, *The New York Times* that someone of prominence would not be willing to speak the truth about the faith or its moral doctrine. To make good decisions about any of these cases requires the virtues of veracity and good humor, not to mention real prudence. While one simply cannot fight every fight and while one needs to be careful about offending those with whom we live and work, the reason for not saying the truths that people need to hear should not be a fear that comes from any disordered attachment on our part.

By these examples, I simply mean to indicate the sort of things that might come up in praying on the First Principle and Foundation. The cases that I have mentioned here are relatively simple but quite real. The range of possible topics is considerable. There can be fears and insecurities about one's appearance, about one's natural strengths and weaknesses, about one's education, skills, and qualifications. There can be resentments, angers, and grudges over real and perceived slights. There can be various kinds of wounds, obsessions, and addictions. My point in mentioning such things is not to psychologize what is properly spiritual. It is, rather, a question of working within the Ignatian practice of spiritual discernment (as within the Thomistic tradition of hylomorphic anthropology and moral theory) so as to recognize that each of us is a single, unified person, with various sorts of conditions, corporeal and spiritual, that can make us unfree.

Praying with the First Principle and Foundation during the First Week

If I may here use a term that has a psychological resonance but that is nonetheless entirely appropriate in a sound spirituality, the First Principle and Foundation has a kind of *diagnostic* character. When we meditate and pray during an exercise like this, we are ultimately seeking to be free of disordered attachments. But that liberation does not necessarily come all at once. It might come by the infusion of divine grace instantaneously and in a surprising way. But becoming free to the degree needed for discerning God's will and for making a good choice may well start with seeking the grace of self-knowledge in these matters and the grace to differentiate between the sorts of things that are inclinations or aversions, whether single and transient or habitual, and those that are disordered attachments.

When giving someone the *Exercises*, I find that it is better not to make the First Principle and Foundation a one-time exercise. What can be helpful is to use it recurrently in a variety of ways. One can ask a retreatant to pray it in a simple and straightforward fashion, with an accent on the first three paragraphs, especially in light of the fact that many people in our day do not think that they are the result of divine creation, let alone have a God-given purpose for their lives or that the purpose of their lives are what Ignatius lists here. There is also tremendous value in prayerfully pondering the directives of the second and third paragraphs about our readiness to use whatever helps in the attainment of our end and to be rid of whatever hinders. One needs only to think about the way in which the internet, cellphones, and laptops can be liberating or enslaving.

Often, I suggest that retreatants alternate between periods of prayer of this exercise and on passages from Scripture. My recommendation is that they focus first on the First Principle and Foundation, as explained above. Then, during the next periods of prayer, I propose that they keep the First Principle and Foundation in the background while meditating on an appropriate passage from one of the Gospels. This alternation encourages those praying to let important concerns about unfreedom in themselves surface naturally while pondering stories about how Jesus helped various people face areas of unfreedom they may not have fully understood.

I have, for example, found the Gospel accounts of Peter's replies to the questions of Jesus on the beach after the resurrection (Jn 21:4–19) suitable for this purpose. We might imagine Peter as someone who was expecting to be grilled for having denied that he even knew Jesus after his brash promise that he would never betray him (Mt 26:33–35). To Peter's surprise, Jesus does not even mention the betrayal but instead asks Peter three times whether he loves him. The repetition of the question progressively unnerves Peter, but, somehow, he manages a response. He then hears some unexpected directives from the Lord: Feed my lambs, tend my sheep, feed my sheep.

Given what we know of Peter's life, this conversation seems pivotal. Was he free enough to accept Jesus's forgiveness for his betrayals, or was he still stuck in shame? Was he sufficiently free to leave Galilee behind and become a missionary? Was this fisherman sufficiently detached from his default position of heading out to his fishing boat when the Lord needed him to become a shepherd? Granted that fishermen sometimes die at their task, it is hard to imagine a fisherman dying for the sake of his fish, but not so with shepherds. At various levels, the conversation is striking. It is Jesus's way of freeing Peter from various attachments that he may have had, including the likelihood of a disordered attachment to shame over his failure to live up to his own impetuous assertion of loyalty. For retreatants, there are numerous ways in which unfreedom can lurk in the soul and go unrecognized until the Lord comes to converse with them in prayer.

In my experience with the *Exercises*, the First Principle and Foundation often seems like the tree mentioned in the first of the Psalms. When planted by streams of water, it yields its fruit in its season and its leaves do not wither (Ps 1:3). By this image I mean that we do well to keep the First Principle in mind as a retreat proceeds through the First Week and beyond. While the bracing exercises of the First Week have us imagine the sin of the angels, the sin of our first parents, the case of someone who went to hell because of a single unrepented mortal sin, and the pains of hell, these exercises are not morose.

Like the First Principle and Foundation, the exercises on sin are designed to help us recognize areas of sin and other sorts of unfreedom and to encourage us to respond to divine graces of forgiveness, healing, mercy, and the renewal of our strength. It is in this set of exercises, after all, that we find the directive to place ourselves before Christ on the cross and to speak with him about how he became man for us. We are to reflect on ourselves and to ask: What have I done for Christ? What am I doing for Christ? What ought I to do for Christ? In these questions, and in the conversations with Christ to which we are invited in the First Week, retreatants are given the same sort of opportunity and encouragement that Jesus gave Peter in the conversation on the three questions that we considered above. What Jesus elicited from Peter was not further impetuosity or rash promises, but the growth of humility and truthfulness that makes for greater care in distinguishing which of our emotions and desires are trustworthy and which are not.

The First Week Rules

It is during this portion of the *Exercises* that St Ignatius would have us introduce the retreatant to the Rules of the First Week (§313–§327). Before proposing various rules that offer prudential advice (rules five, six, and eight on how to deal with desolation, rules ten and eleven on how to deal with consolation), Ignatius makes a series of important distinctions, much in the manner of the Angelic Doctor. Some of these distinctions are diagnostic, some definitional, and some designed to help a retreatant think prudently about possible reasons for the onset of desolation.[5]

This set of rules begins with a contrast between the ways that the evil spirit and the good spirit tend to deal with us in the relatively simple cases of those going from one sin to another and of those earnestly striving to cleanse their souls from sin. In the former case, the evil spirit greases the wheels, as it were, by filling the imagination with sensual delights and gratifications while the good spirit rouses the sting of conscience. In the latter case, the reverse is the case. The evil spirit will characteristically afflict us with anxiety, sadness, and fallacious reasoning, while the good spirit gives courage and strength, tears and inspiration (§314–§315).

It is of great significance that right here from the start, Ignatius warns that a feeling of peacefulness or comfort is not by itself a sign of divine approval. There is an objective dimension that needs to be considered in order to give proper guidance. If one subjectively feels peace when objectively going from

---

5. Rules 7 and 9 of the First Week (§§320, 322) take up "the principal reasons" why we suffer from desolation, while Rules 12, 13, and 14 (§§325–27) give prudent advice about certain typical cases of desolation. See also Timothy M. Gallagher, OMV, *Overcoming Spiritual Discouragement: The Spiritual Teachings of Venerable Bruno Lanteri* (Manchester, NH: Sophia Institute Press, 2019).

one mortal sin to another, the first rule identifies the source of that feeling as coming from "the enemy." Only when the subjective experience of peacefulness occurs in a person objectively rising in God's service can the feeling be trusted as coming from God.

The third and fourth rules provide definitions for spiritual consolation and spiritual desolation. As Father Timothy Gallagher explains in his insightful commentary on the Rules for the Discernment of Spirits, we do well here to distinguish between natural consolation and spiritual consolation as well as between natural desolation and spiritual desolation.[6] To wake up feeling chipper or to have the satisfaction of a good meal is admittedly consoling, but this is not necessarily spiritual consolation. Genuine spiritual consolation involves an inner movement of the soul in which there is an increase of faith or hope or charity. Spiritual consolation can include feeling genuine sorrow for our sins as well as interior joy about what is heavenly. Correlatively, to wake up feeling awful or to have a headache is naturally desolating, but spiritual desolation involves some feeling of separation from God, some lack of faith, hope, or love. It might take the form of inclination to what is low or tempting, or a turmoil of spirit, or some form of sadness or sloth.

As will probably be obvious by this point, the resources of the *Exercises* are designed to promote deep and sustained efforts at prayer. The Rules of the First Week, like the First Principle and Foundation, are crafted to assist our prayer and especially our reflection on what happens within us, both during formal periods of prayer and in the intervening times during a retreat (as well as in the normal give-and-take of daily life). In addition to helping us to differentiate between what the good spirit and the evil spirit have aroused in us, they also assist us with realizing when our passions and desires are out of control and when we are operating on the basis of disordered attachments. By bringing together in this first set of rules the need for an objective assessment of our lives along with the need to distinguish between what the good spirit and the evil spirit arouse within us, the *Exercises* give us resources to understand the affective and appetitive moments within us and to become free from being yanked around by wayward feelings and disordered attachments.

Finding Suitable Times for Making Decisions

In the text of the Second Week, Saint Ignatius has provided a series of exercises that follow the life of Christ from the moment of the Incarnation through the public life of Christ. It is for the Second Week that Ignatius devised a

---

6. Timothy M. Gallagher, OMV, *The Discernment of Spirits: An Ignatian Guide for Everyday Living* (New York: Crossroad, 2005), esp. chs. 3 and 4.

number of imaginative exercises for retreatants with important choices to make. In addition to providing these scenarios for prayer about the choices at issue, he also composed a second set of rules for further understanding the movements produced in the soul (§§329–336) and a distinction about the various moments when a sound choice can be made as well as a warning about a time when one should not make a choice (§§175–88).

For Ignatius, one should never make a choice in a time of desolation, for one would be listening to the wrong counsel. The fifth rule of the First Week makes that clear: "In time of desolation we should never make any change, but remain firm and constant in the resolution and decision which guided us the day before the desolation, or in the decision to which we adhered in the preceding consolation. For just as in consolation the good spirit guides and counsels us, so in desolation the evil spirit guides and counsels. Following his counsels, we can never find the way to a right decision" (§318).

The moments at which it is possible to make "a correct and good choice of a way of life" are three: (1) When God so moves and attracts the will that a devout soul without any possibility of hesitation follows what has been shown, as in the case of St. Paul and St. Matthew (§175). (2) When there has been much light and understanding from a steady pattern of consolation, interpreted through the Rules for the Discernment of Spirits (§176). (3) In a time of tranquility, when the soul is not agitated by different spirits and has free and peaceful use of its natural powers (§177).

For this third situation, Ignatius describes in detail a number of ways to proceed. Here it is important to note that even after making use of a series of comparisons about the advantages and disadvantages of taking a particular course and of not taking that course, Ignatius reminds us that "the one who has made [a choice or decision] must turn with great diligence to prayer in the presence of God our Lord and offer Him his choice, that the Divine Majesty may deign to accept and confirm if it is his for His greater service and praise" (§183). From Ignatius's own life we have an explicit example of his own fidelity to this last step. It occurred when Ignatius was working out a portion of the *Constitutions of the Society of Jesus* dealing with poverty. When he did not find the confirmation of God in the way that he was accustomed to experience it when he presented the Lord with a choice made in this third method, he realized the need to re-examine the question and then to present a revised plan to God in prayer.[7]

Among the exercises of the Second Week there are a number that quite clearly echo the theme of the First Principle and Foundation: the Call of the

---

7. For a detailed account of this event and the relevant texts from his *Spiritual Diary*, see *Ignatius of Loyola: Spiritual Exercises and Selected Works*, ed. George Ganss, SJ (New York: Paulist Press, 1991), 217–28 and 240–43 (hereafter, SpDiar).

King (§§91–99) that stands at the entrance to the Second Week, the Meditation on the Two Standards (§§136–148), the Three Classes of Men (§§149–157), the Three Degrees of Humility (§§165–167).

Echoes of the First Principle and Foundation throughout a Retreat

One sees echoes of the First Principle in the Call of the King's portrayal of Christ and particularly the speech by which he invites others to follow him in holding back nothing that is needed for the enterprise (§95). One sees it in the Meditation on the Two Standards when the Standard of Satan envisions a quest for riches, empty honors, and overweening pride while the Standard of Christ calls for a readiness to accept poverty and insults as a route to humility (§146). One sees it in the Three Classes of Men where there is a comparison between those who want to rid themselves of a certain attachment but never get around to doing so, those who want God to come around to their way of thinking so that they do not have to worry about being rid of a certain attachment, and those who want only what God wants and neither wish to retain nor to be rid of what has generated the problem of attachment (§§153–155).

From my experience, the need to return to the themes in the Principle and Foundation does not necessarily come from some failure of the retreatant in dealing adequately with the opening matters at the start of the retreat. Quite the opposite: it is simply that there are some things that are so deep within us that we take them as part of our bedrock, part of the furnishings of our world. It may only come later to light, under the power of grace, that we can come to see these aspects of our reality more clearly. As regards the appearance of these difficulties at some point during a retreat, we may not be able to deal with them adequately until they come into focus for us. Ignatius's approach is not that the First Principle and Foundation is something about which we could ever say, "Been there, done that." It is not something that we do and then leave it behind. Rather, he invites us to keep bringing it back into the picture, so that we can progress to deeper freedom and can assess feelings and emotions for their reliability and trustworthiness.

Distinguishing Reliable and Unreliable Feelings

It may be helpful here to point out something that might help us to avoid a possible misconception about the Ignatian approach. Despite the great amount of instruction Ignatius gives about the method to be used and the order of the exercises, the actual practice of this retreat program is not something that is lockstep or automatic. The text of the *Exercises* is intended as a guide to the one giving the retreat, the better to be able to follow the Lord's stirrings and promptings. One sees the importance of this when one considers the Second Week, especially from the perspective of the problem being addressed in this paper.

For someone to be ready to make a good choice about a way of life or about some amendment of life, one must be adequately free from habits of sin and other disordered attachments. One must come to be in a position where one can reliably use trustworthy feelings, desires, and affections to see what God is intending for us. It will prove highly valuable during this time for such people to focus in on what God has given them to love. The question of making a life decision would be premature for someone still at the stage of the First Week, where the focus has to be on discovering whether there are any such disordered attachments and how one might become free of them.

What often happens is that as the retreat proceeds it becomes clear—sometimes earlier, sometimes later—that the person is not ready to make such an important choice. The better course is to bring the retreat (however long or short) to a halt and to help the person, as well as one can, to identify how to work on whatever issue has been identified. This will be immeasurably better for the person than would be hastening prematurely to a choice that the individual was hoping to make.

When the time comes that the person can consider the matter again and to enter into the stage of the Second Week freely, then there is reason to think that feelings will be trustworthy and that it will be clearer that what God has given them to love—for instance, to go off in the service of the poor, or to receive priestly ordination and to work for the consolation of the faithful through the hearing of confessions, or to seek marriage to a certain person.

In this case, there will be reason to think the feelings are trustworthy and are able to be consulted, much as the Thomist does when considering how to make decisions about prudential matters. For a virtuous person, the feelings and emotions will be mature and faithful allies. In this regard, I do not think that there really is a conflict when the Thomist is being a good Thomist by distinguishing between a virtuous person who has well-integrated desires and passions and a person who has not yet achieved the state of virtue and who must persistently struggle with many wayward passions.

Avoiding a Confusion of the Ignatian Approach with Certain Misuses of Ignatian Concepts

Before we turn to the questions that those trained in Ignatius methods have about Thomism, it may be helpful to note briefly one other worry from the Thomistic side: the suspicion that Ignatian discernment often gets used not only for trying to know the will of God in the ways we discussed above, but for dubious efforts at proportionalist reasoning on questions of moral theology that turn prudential reasoning into utilitarian casuistry.

It is sad, for example, to see some theologians in the Ignatian tradition giving poor arguments on such contemporary questions as whether those who are divorced may remarry without annulment. These efforts should be traced to errors in moral theology or to ignorance of canon law. It would be a caricature to suggest that such fallacious reasoning comes from a proper understanding of Ignatian discernment.[8]

I am quite sympathetic to Thomistic worries here, for real prudence is not a mere calculation of consequences, let alone something that lets strong feelings and emotions distort the scales that we employ on practical moral questions. In my judgment, however, it is a misconception of the Ignatian method of spiritual direction to think that attentiveness to feelings or desires can alter the moral species of an action, or to think that feelings and desires can justify conduct that right reasoning judges morally illicit. It may be that this sort of misuse of the language of Ignatian spirituality in areas where it has no relevance is what makes some individuals allergic to its use within its proper sphere.

The Thomistic Way

Those trained to give spiritual direction by employing Ignatius's teachings on the discernment of spirits sometimes have questions about Thomistic thought. No doubt, some reservations arise in response to Aquinas's way of writing. Becoming comfortable with scholastic modes of expression is admittedly an acquired taste, but the more important questions are not about the style of writing.

I suspect that many of the issues come from the way in which Thomistic ethics and moral theology are typically presented. These texts, after all, cover a massive amount of complex material, including much that is of a highly technical nature. Aquinas's intricate accounts of things like the powers of the soul, the natural and supernatural virtues, and natural law theory manifest the rigorous nature of argumentation that is typical of his reasoning.

Aquinas shows incredible care in making careful distinctions and in setting forth a complex picture of human nature, but the very bulk of his treatment of these matters brings some to see his account as excessively abstract and forbidding. To the extent that retreat masters or spiritual directors are acquainted with Thomism, it may well seem like a trove of reflection across an enormous range of moral questions and problems, but not an especially attractive source

---

8. While it would be a valuable exercise to analyze examples of the misuse of Ignatian concepts within the field of moral theology, I leave that project for a different occasion.

of help for the type of issues and problems they are likely to face.⁹ There seems to be nothing within the Thomistic corpus that is quite like the Ignatian program for the discernment of spirits (a point to be explored below).

Avoiding a Misconception of Thomism as Overly Intellectualist

The size of Thomas's corpus and the detail of his treatment are undeniable. What needs to be corrected, however, is any suggestion that the Thomistic account of the human person and of moral topics is overly intellectualist in character. In fact, the reality is just the reverse. In the area under discussion throughout the first half of this essay, the arena of feelings, emotions, and passions, Aquinas offers many insights that can be of great value for spiritual directors. In both his anthropology and in his moral theory, he invariably exhibits a great balance between the cognitive and the affective dimensions of human nature.

What makes this possible for Aquinas is not only his reverence for what has been divinely revealed about the human condition but also the hylomorphism at the core of his philosophical position. The conviction that God made us to have the passions and that the soul of Christ had the complete range of human passions informs Thomistic theology.[10] Further, the integrative focus of Aristotle's approach[11] enables Aquinas to offer the most sustained treatment of the passions by any medieval author.[12] It is not only large in size but significantly different in character compared to the main alternatives.

Materialists reduce the life of the mind and the life of feelings to biochemical reactions. Substance-dualists tend to regard whatever is bodily as inferior to the mind and have difficulties in explaining how body and mind are connected. By contrast, Aquinas champions a view of the human person as at once spiritual and corporeal and explains it in the terms that he adopted and adapted from Aristotelian hylomorphism.

By his transformation of what he received in light of revelation and ecclesial tradition, he generated a sophisticated vision of the human person as a composite unity. Like other creatures, the human being needs to be explained in terms of a set of paired co-principles that include matter and form, substance

---

9. Valuable as Aumann's *Spiritual Theology* is in many respects, the section on "Discernment of Spirits" (ch. 14) suffers from this problem. It provides a typology of highly technical categories but relatively little by way of how to use them for spiritual guidance.

10. See the magisterial treatment of this theme by Paul Gondreau in *The Passions of Christ's Soul in the Theology of St. Thomas Aquinas*, Beiträge zur Geschichte der Philosophie und Theologie des Mittelalters, neue Folge, vol. 61 (Münster: Aschendorff Verlag Gmbh & Co., 2002).

11. It is only fair to note that Thomas also received inspiration in this area from John Damascene's *De fide orthodoxa* and from Nemesius of Emesa's *De natura hominis* (attributed to Gregory of Nyssa by medieval authors).

12. See the preface to Gondreau's *Passions of Christ's Soul* by Jean-Pierre Torrell, OP, 8–9.

and accidents, essence and existence, and act and potency. The resulting faculty-psychology stresses a rich array of cognitive and appetitive powers ("faculties") and their systemic interconnection in its explanation of human operations and activities.

The Merits of a Hylomorphic Position for Achieving a Balanced Picture

For Thomas, one may still use the traditional terms "body" and "soul" so long as one does not regard them as separate substances. Rather, the rational soul is the substantial form of any human being. Like the substantial form of any organism, its central role is to unify that organism and to animate suitable matter as a living body. While Aquinas regards the rational soul as capable of subsisting after death and thus able to serve as the bearer of our personal identity, he holds that the complete human being will only be reconstituted with the resurrection of the body.[13]

For an organism like the human being, to know anything whatsoever, the cognitive process invariably begins with what our bodily sense organs receive. Our powers of mind can transcend the limits of sense-impressions by their abilities to form universal concepts, to make propositions, and to reason about what we have received, but we always must begin with the sensory data that we received by our powers of sensory perception.

Likewise, the Thomistic account of the will and of the entire realm of human affectivity relies on his core notion of the composite unity of the individual. Our bodily desires and aversions as well as the whole range of feelings and emotions are taken by Thomas as originating in the movements of our sensory appetites. Aquinas subdivides the sensory appetites into concupiscible passions (like or love, hatred or dislike, desire, aversion, joy, and sorrow) and irascible passions (hope, despair, boldness, fear, and anger). The former pertains to the affective inclinations to possess suitable goods that are immediate and easy to attain as well as to avoid apparent evils that can be directly avoided. The latter concern our tendencies toward sensory goods that are difficult to attain and away from sensory evils that are difficult to escape or to counter.[14]

By this hylomorphic approach to human nature, Aquinas envisions a natural relationship between the mental and the corporeal in the appetitive and affective domains as well as in the cognitive. He locates freedom precisely in the power of the will (the rational appetite) to make choices (whether to act or not to act,

---

13. See, for instance, ST I, q. 29, a. 1 ad 5 and q. 89, a.1 c., as well as *In 1 ad Cor. XV* 19, lect. 2, no. 924.

14. A particularly fine account of the Thomistic doctrine of the passions is Kevin White's "The Passions of the Soul (Ia IIae, qq. 22–48)," in *The Ethics of Aquinas*, ed. Stephen J. Pope (Washington, DC: Georgetown University Press, 2002), 103–15.

to act in this way or in that).¹⁵ Unlike approaches that understand human action reductively as the mechanical outcome of pressures and forces, interpreted along the lines of some sort of hydraulic model, the Thomistic account emphasizes the reality of freedom in human choice, not only in the sense of a lack of restraint or coercion but in the positive sense of self-determination.

The Role of the Appetites and Feelings in Thomistic Moral Theory

The general outlines of this Thomistic picture of the human person are well known.¹⁶ For the purpose of this essay, it will be important to focus specifically on the role of desires, feelings, and emotions in Aquinas's account of moral virtue. Thomism understands the passions quite differently than, say, Stoicism and Platonism does.¹⁷ Stoicism shows a thoroughgoing distrust of the affective realm.¹⁸ Platonism tends to relegate affectivity to the body while privileging care for the soul and taking virtue to be knowledge.¹⁹

Interestingly, Aquinas applies the trifold comparison of political and domestic forms of rule according to the relation between the ruler and the ruled that is found in Aristotle's *Politics*²⁰ to the relation between reason and the passions. After likening the Stoic distrust of the passions to the despotic rule of masters over slaves by force and threat of force, and the Platonic insistence that the reason must tutor the passions like parents do children, he compares the Aristotelian approach that is the basis for his own hylomorphic position to the relation between rulers and their free citizens and that between the husband

---

15. See ST I-II, qq. 6–21, esp. a. 13: "On Choice" (*de arbitrio voluntatis*).

16. See, for instance, Steven J. Jensen, *The Human Person: A Beginner's Thomistic Psychology* (Washington, DC: The Catholic University of America Press, 2018). The modest title of this volume belies the masterful sophistication of its treatment of this topic.

17. Aquinas's own comparison between the positions of Aristotle, Plato, and the Stoics is found at ST I-II, q. 24, a. 2 c.

18. For the Stoic distrust of the passions, see Margaret Graver, *Stoicism and Emotions* (Chicago, IL: University of Chicago Press, 2007). One can find this attitude of distrust in many ancient texts, including Cicero's *Tusculan Disputations*, ed. and trans. J. E. King, Loeb Classical Library 141 (Cambridge, MA: Harvard University Press, 1945).

19. On account of the dialogue form that Plato used, it is admittedly more difficult to know his stance on many questions, including his views on feelings, emotions, and passions. For a helpful overview of the topic, see Simo Knuuttila, *Emotions in Ancient and Medieval Philosophy* (Oxford, UK: Clarendon Press, 2004), 7–24.

20. Aristotle, *Politics* I, 12–13 and *Nicomachean Ethics* I, 13. See Aquinas, *Commentary on Aristotle's Politics* bk. 1, lect. 10, trans. Richard J. Regan (Indianapolis, IN: Hackett, 2007), 68–77. See also Aquinas, *Commentary on Aristotle's Nicomachean Ethics* bk. I, lect. 2, trans. C. I. Litzinger, OP (1964; repr., Notre Dame, IN: Dumb Ox Books, 1993), 78–81. Aristotle treats the emotions not systematically in one place but in passing in such works as *Nicomachean Ethics*, *Politics*, and *Rhetoric*. For a systematic overview, see Marlene K. Sokolon, *Political Emotions: Aristotle and the Symphony of Reason and Emotion* (Dekalb, IL: Northern Illinois University Press, 2006).

and wife within a family. In this regard he compares the need for the rational persuasion to the need for the passions to become rational by participation in the direction that right reason sets.[21]

At the core of Thomistic ethics is the Aristotelian theory of the moral virtues as acquired dispositions to choose the mean between the extremes of excess and deficiency as a person of right reason would do. These acquired dispositions can even become "second nature" to us precisely because they are the acquired dispositions of beings that are matter-form composite unities. We are not just minds dwelling in bodies, and not just mindless organisms.

Among the factors that make it possible for Aquinas to hold that these acquired traits make virtuous choices easy, pleasant, and regularly successful is his distinctive understanding of the relation of reason to the passions. It is neither the suppression of all passions nor the instrumentalization of reason in the service of the passions. Rather, he understands the relation of reason and the passions on the political model of the relations between free citizens and the domestic model of the relation of spouses. Following out the suggestion of Aristotle that the sensory appetite "participates in reason to some extent,"[22] Aquinas fills out a sketch of the way in which reason can make reliable allies of the passions.[23]

The analogies here are, of course, not complete identities, for the passions are not persons and Aquinas does not personify them in his accounts. It is not that a desire or a feeling has a mind or a will of its own like a spouse does or like the members of a citizenry do. That is not the point of the comparison. Rather, by using the examples of free and intelligent consent as found in political and domestic relations of love, affection, and providential care, Aquinas holds that the well-ordered passions can participate in the rationality that is typical of human virtue.

The detailed account that Aquinas gives of each of these virtues over the course of the *Secunda secundae* makes it clear that a person with any of these virtues not only chooses the action of excellence but finds it easy and pleasant to do so. A crucial part of the explanation for the regularity of making sound choices is that the person is not fighting wayward emotions or wildly swinging desires but using the energy and strength that the passions provide when they are reason's allies. The suspicion about feelings as unstable discussed earlier

---

21. See ST I-II, q. 24, a. 2; q. 56, a. 4; and q. 59, aa. 1–5, e.g., "Hence, just as the appetite is the principle of human acts, insofar as it partakes of reason, so are moral habits to be considered virtue insofar as they are in conformity with reason," q. 59, a. 2 c. See also Aquinas, *Quaestiones disputate De virtutibus in communi*, a. 4.

22. Aristotle, *Nicomachean Ethics* I, 13, 1102b13–14. See also *Politics* I, 12–13.

23. Aquinas, *Commentary on the Nicomachean Ethics* bk. 1, lect. 13.

would be a legitimate concern in someone who is not virtuous. But we should not conflate the case of those under the sway of unruly passions (e.g., someone who is not temperate) with the case of someone with virtue.

Aquinas finds that the typical movements of our passions show forth the inner connections of the spiritual and the physical (much as our sensory experiences show the same sort of connections in our cognitive operations). In contrast with the theory of moral virtues typical of Stoicism and Platonism, Aquinas explains that the virtues do not come about in spite of the passions or through studied disdain for them. Rather, they come about through the creation of alliance between our reason and our desires, emotions, and feelings.[24]

The Thomistic Account of Prudent Counsel

Understood correctly, Thomas's account of moral virtue invokes a distinction between reliable and unreliable affectivity that is similar to the way in which the passions need to be handled in the Ignatian program for the discernment of spirits.

This is not to say that Aquinas offers what Ignatius does. What attention Aquinas gives to discernment occurs when he considers the charism of *discretio spirituum*. So far as I can detect, Aquinas prefers to handle questions about spiritual direction in terms of the virtue of prudence rather than to formulate anything like the Ignatian "Rules for Discernment of Spirits" when discussing the question of the aid that one person may be able to provide to another in practical matters.[25] In the question devoted to the allies of prudence (literally, "the potential parts of prudence"), there is an intriguing hint in the answer to the first objection of II-II, q. 51, a. 4, where Aquinas says that "sound judgments deals well and truly with all matters covered by the ordinary rules of conduct, but . . . there are other matters to be judged outside this context."[26] Presumably, the reference here points to the account of the charism called *discretio spirituum* that he takes to be a supernatural gift that allows someone blessed with it to know the secrets of hearts or future contingents:

---

24. See Paul Gondreau, "The Passions and the Moral Life: Appreciating the Originality of Aquinas," *The Thomist* 71, no. 3 (2007): 419–50, esp. part 2: "How human emotion becomes rational by participation," 431–42.

25. It seems to me that many Thomists appreciate what Ignatian spirituality provides. There are some disappointing exceptions. A particularly egregious example from an earlier generation is *Religious Vocation: An Unnecessary Mystery* by Richard Butler, OP (1961; repr., Rockford, IL: TAN Books, 2005).

26. ST II-II, q. 51, a. 4, ad 1: "Ad primum ergo dicendum quod synesis est vere judicativa de omnibus quae secundum communes regulae fiunt; sed praeter communes regulas sunt quaedam alia dijudicanda, ut iam dictum est."

> Gratuitous grace is ordained to this, viz., that a man may help another to be led to God. Now no man can help in this by moving interiorly (for this belongs to God alone), but only exteriorly by teaching or persuading. Hence gratuitous grace embraces whatever a man needs in order to instruct another in Divine things that are above reason. Now for this three things are required: First, a man must possess the fullness of knowledge of Divine things, so as to be capable of teaching others. Secondly, he must be able to conform or prove what he says, otherwise his words would have no weight. Thirdly, he must be capable of fittingly presenting to his hearers what he knows. . . . Now, the confirmation of what is above reason rests on what is proper to the Divine power, and this in two ways: first, when the teacher of sacred doctrine does what God alone can do in miraculous deeds. . . . Secondly, when he can manifest what God alone can know, and these are either future contingents—and thus there is prophecy, or also the secrets of hearts, and thus there is the discerning of spirits.[27]

The term *discretio* appears only in the final sentences of this passage. There it designates a divine gift of a knowledge that is beyond the scope of anything we can acquire by our own efforts. As used here, the term does not refer to the kind of guidance that Ignatius gives us for understanding the movements of spirits that we may experience in ourselves or for guiding those under our spiritual care to understand better what they are experiencing. Rather, the context suggests a divine infusion into the soul of a prophet about things that God alone can know, such as the future or the secrets of what is happening in the hearts of other people. While the term used here is *discretio spirituum*, its meaning seems more to be something like the gift of "insight" about the movements of particular "spirits" rather than an acquired skill of "discernment" in the sense that Ignatius speaks about.

To pursue this question a bit further, it is necessary to consider the matter more broadly, for what is at issue is not simply the use of some Latin term that might capture the sense of "discernment," but a consideration of how Aquinas handles the practice of discernment in his own terms, that is, by giving attention to the steps involved in questions of prudence and to the resources provided by its associated gift of counsel.[28] The faculty of practical reason, when made perfect by prudence, has three distinct acts: counsel (by which one considers the possible means to achieve the end), judgment about which is best, and command (when the judgment informs the will's choice, and the person decides to carry out the good action).

---

27. ST I-II, q. 111, a. 4.
28. ST II-II, q. 52.

As in the treatises on faith and hope, the treatise on prudence puts its discussion of the corresponding gift of the Spirit immediately after the main exposition of the virtue. His account of each virtue frequently refers back to the distinctions he made about the various powers of the soul[29] and on the partial acts that together make a complete act.[30]

For Aquinas, *prudentia* is the virtue of practical reasoning, namely, the acquired disposition of practical wisdom by which we can regularly and with ease deliberate well and apply general moral principles to specific situations. It is thus a virtue that is crucial for possessing any other moral virtue. As Josef Pieper explains at length, only someone who is prudent can be just, temperate, or courageous, for one needs to know the truth about human nature in order to know what is good for human beings.[31]

Prudence is not to be confused with cleverness and cunning, or with utilitarian calculations about self-interest, or with fearful tabulation of strengths and weaknesses aiming at self-preservation in the face of danger. Rather, prudence designates a perfected ability (that is, a virtuous character trait) of right reasoning in matters of deliberation and decision. For there to be right reasoning, we need two types of knowledge: (a) knowledge of the universal principles of morality and (b) knowledge of the particulars with which our decisions and the actions that execute those decisions are concerned (that is, the ways and means for achieving the ends of human life, natural and supernatural).

The stages by which we move from knowledge of what is truly good to the achievement of what is good include the process of deliberation, the making of judgments, and decisions. In contrast with the virtue of prudence, there are various forms of imprudence that come from habits of being too swift or too slow as well as from wrongly assessing the truth about things. There are problems, for instance, with being thoughtless (plunging into decision and action without proper deliberation and without attaining well-founded judgments). Likewise, there are problems with being stubborn (not open to the reality of the situation and not docile to what experience can teach) and with being irresolute (inclined to endless and futile deliberation that never reaches a decision, let alone the right one).

Within the *Summa*'s treatise on *prudentia* (ST II-II, qq. 47–56) Thomas devotes q. 49 to giving a list of eight components of prudence (what he considers its "integral parts"): *memoria* (what allows us to profit from past experience),

---

29. With regard to prudence, see especially ST I, q. 79, aa. 11–13.
30. Here see especially ST I-II, qq. 16–17.
31. Josef Pieper, *The Four Cardinal Virtues: Prudence, Justice, Fortitude, Temperance* (Notre Dame, IN: University of Notre Dame Press, 1966). The section of prudence was translated by Richard and Clara Winston.

intelligentia (in practical matters, what grasps the point at issue), *docilitas* (a readiness to learn), *solertia* (the acumen needed to make fair assessments for ourselves), *ratio* (sound reasoning), *providentia* (foresight), *circumspectio* (awareness of relevant circumstances), and *cautio* (the caution needed to avoid hazards).

From the perspective of our question in this essay, none of these discussions provides anything like the program for the discernment of spirits that Ignatius outlines. But each of them individually (and the group as a whole) has great relevance for anyone wanting to do the work of a spiritual director in the Ignatian tradition. Aquinas intends the list broadly as an account of the traits needed for a prudent person, but there is a direct application to our question. Much of the work of discernment and of spiritual direction depends on profiting from past experience. It is for this reason that Ignatius so regularly urges us to review what happened in a period of prayer and to cull the insights of each day and of a whole retreat. The practical work involved in discerning the movements of spirits for ourselves and in helping others requires that we grasp what is at issue and make a fair assessment of what has happened. We are constantly involved in trying to be aware of ambient circumstances and in staying watchful of hazards. Skills like these are needed, for instance, in the proper application of the rules dealing with spiritual desolation.

After treating the various types of prudence in question 50 (e.g., political prudence, the prudence in managing a household, military prudence), Aquinas reviews a number of allied virtues in question 51 (the readiness to be well-informed about practical details and to make sound judgments about them, even on cases outside the normal run of things). In question 52, Aquinas takes up a topic clearly related to the goal of spiritual discernment, namely, the gift of counsel. Drawing on what has been revealed through Scripture,[32] Aquinas sets forth the gifts for which anyone who wishes to undertake spiritual direction must pray. He writes:

> In the search for counsel, one needs to be directed by God, who understands all things. This comes about through the gift of counsel, by which one is guided by advice received from God, just as in human affairs, those who are not sufficient in themselves need the counsel of those who are more wise.[33]

---

32. The whole of question 52 is immersed in references to Scripture, such as Hebrews 4:12, on the need for divine assistance to be able to discern the thoughts and intentions of the heart, or passages like 1 Corinthians 12:10 or Hebrews 5:14, on the need for the grace to God to be able to distinguish between spirits and between what is good and what is evil.

33. ST II-II, q. 52, a. 1 ad 1: "Et ideo indiget homo in inquisitione consilii dirigi a Deo, qui omnia comprehendit; quod fit per donum consilii per quod homo dirigitus quasi consilio a Deo accepto; sicut etiam in rebus humanis, qui sibi ipsis non sufficiunt in iniquisitione consilii a sapientioribus consilium requirunt."

In this way, Thomas sees the possibility for one person to offer sound and helpful advice to another in spiritual matters through the virtue of prudence as well as through the gift of the Holy Spirit called counsel. Aquinas's emphasis is on describing the *habitus* or disposition by which a person will have the resources to provide good advice rather than on outlining practical rules for use in this situation.

It is important to remember that one of the conditions for being able to give or to receive such advice is that our internal affective life be well-ordered. One might call this state "dispassionate" in the sense of being free from disordered outbursts or disorienting coloration of our perception, but it does not imply an internally truncated or desiccated perspective. To be able to give the counsel that others need may well require considerable courage in some situations and to be able to receive and act on that advice may well depend on the moderation associated with temperance.

If this account of the affective and appetitive dimensions were to pass unnoticed, the Thomistic account of the virtues could easily be mistaken for a Stoic or a Platonic position, or for the later Cartesian view. The Stoic position holds choices as judgments and holds all passions suspect. The Platonic position (or at least the position that is taken by Socrates in the dialogues, without the benefit of some interpretive hermeneutic to correct for the common tendency simply to identify Socrates's views with those of Plato) regards virtues as knowledge. Descartes tends to envision the appetites and emotions in mechanical terms as part of the body, with little or no connection to the internal life of the mind.[34]

Avoiding Some Misconceptions

One could easily understand why the proponents of such views would find the Ignatian approach troubling. For the Stoic, all passions are suspect and unreliable. Likewise, for Socrates, there appears to be a thorough-going intellectualism that regards virtues to be a matter of knowledge. If one really knows the right thing to do, one will do it. If one does not do it, one must not have known. This stance is perplexing, for it seems to allow for no way to account for anyone who knowingly goes wrong—that is, for the case of someone who knows the right thing but chooses the worse.

It is precisely for that reason that I would venture that Plato's own position is not identical with views presented dialectically by Socrates. It may be that this is one of the places where Plato deliberately has Socrates take a fallacious position. Presumably, readers are then to see that the Socratic position cannot

---

34. René Descartes, *The Passions of the Soul*, trans. S. H. Voss (Indianapolis, IN: Hackett, 1989).

possibly be correct and that the matter is more complex. In this way it may be like the fallacious proofs for immortality in the *Phaedo* and the curious discussion that learning is recollection in the *Meno*, a dialogue in which the famous geometry episode actually illustrates just the opposite of what Socrates claims that it illustrates.[35] But to argue for this interpretation is a topic for another occasion.

What could rectify the problem we encounter with Socratic intellectualism in matters of virtue (that virtue is knowledge) is understanding the dialogues of Plato as quietly suggesting a view on virtue more like the position that Aristotle explicitly takes. In the final portion of the first book of the *Republic*, for instance, Socrates succeeds in shaming the arrogant Thrasymachus into silence. Before undertaking the elaborate refutation of the position that justice is merely power that constitutes books two through five, Socrates muses on the notion of virtue (*arete*) as consisting in excellence at one's proper function.[36] While he does not formulate the matter in precisely the way that Aristotle does in the second book of the *Nicomachean Ethics*, Plato includes examples in this section that treat the acquisition of virtue to consist of the development of a disposition to choose the mean between extremes.

What is most significant here, as shown above, is that Aquinas takes a hylomorphic rather than a substance-dualist account of metaphysics and philosophy of nature, and more particularly, a hylomorphic anthropology, viz., that the human being is a composite unity. He recasts the terminology of body and soul in the Aristotelian register of matter and form, taken not as separate entities whose connection is difficult, if not impossible, to explain but as paired co-principles.[37] It is this approach that permits him to see human desire and emotion as intrinsic to our matter-form constitution. In every case, the experience of a passion involves some sort of bodily change (what we might note by signs like an increased heart rate, the flush in our face, some hormonal or biochemical change), but for Aquinas the emotions are not reducible to their material component (neurological or biochemical). The proper specification of an emotion needs to include reference to the sensible good to which the person is attracted, or the perceived evil to which the person is averse.

---

35. Plato conveniently gives us some hints in this matter, both in the reservation that Socrates shows about whether the theory that learning is only recollection is right (*Meno* 86b6–c2) and in the passage that compares the winged statues of Daedalus to opinions that are not tied down with right reasoning (*Meno* 97d6–98a7).

36. Plato, *Republic* I, 352d–54a. Note also the mention that virtue might be acquired by practice in the opening lines of the *Meno* at 70a.

37. For a sustained account of the co-principles of Thomistic metaphysics, see *The One and the Many: A Contemporary Thomistic Metaphysics* by W. Norris Clarke, SJ (Notre Dame, IN: University of Notre Dame Press, 2001).

In Summary

This reflection on the Thomistic account of prudence and the Ignatian concept of spiritual discernment has given the occasion for exploring some of the hesitations and the questions that sometimes trouble the proponents of one approach about the other. The main fruit of this examination seems to me that taking seriously the worries that might occupy the mind of someone trained in the Ignatian tradition can help the Thomist to be a better Thomist. And vice versa, the queries about the Ignatian method that trouble a Thomist can help the follower of Ignatius to be truer to Ignatian insights. What we have reviewed here does not show the Ignatian and Thomistic accounts to be the same. But it does make clear how they are deeply compatible.

CHAPTER 5

Thomas and Ignatius on the Imagination

Nicolas Steeves, SJ

Introduction: Apples and Oranges?

Thomists, the cliché runs, don't wield wildly creative imaginations, nor are they often fêted as fanciful folks.[1] Wise, prudent, rational, realistic systematicians: such is their type.[2] Thus, this Roman urban legend, which a Benedictine once gleefully told this Jesuit: a young Dominican friar had asked his famed confrère, Professor Reginald Garrigou-Lagrange, how he handled distractions during mental prayer. "Oh, I never have to deal with any of those," the theologian retorted, "you know full well I have no imagination whatsoever!"

This alleged display of self-deprecating wit, however, is, if anything, strong evidence to the contrary. Garrigou-Lagrange may have built a supposedly unbending neo-scholastic theology of grace,[3] but he clearly knew the metaphysical difference between reality and perception, and the humor he drew therefrom revealed a truly active, realistic imagination. Still more fundamentally,

---

1. On the difficulty of defining "Thomism" and "Scholasticism," see the helpful notes in Thomas Petri, OP, *Aquinas and the Theology of the Body: The Thomistic Foundations of John Paul II's Anthropology* (Washington, DC: The Catholic University of America Press, 2016), 2–3nn2–4. In addition to a definition of Neo-Scholasticism in note 4, he references Gerald A. McCool, *The Neo-Thomists* (Milwaukee, WI: Marquette University Press, 1994), 11, for the Abelardian origin of Scholasticism and James A. Weisheipl, "Thomism," in *The New Catholic Encyclopedia*, ed. Bernard L. Marthaler (New York: McGraw-Hill, 1967), 14:126, for a "good working definition" of Thomism.

2. Much harsher judgements, of course, are passed on what Pope Francis himself decried as the "decadent scholasticism" ("'Avere coraggio e audacia profetica': Dialogo di papa Francesco con i gesuiti riuniti nella 36a Congregazione Generale," *La Civiltà Cattolica* 3995 [2016]: 421) or "manuals of decadent Thomism" (A. Spadaro, SJ, "Intervista a Papa Francesco," *La Civiltà Cattolica* 3918 [2013]: 476) over which he was made to pore. Similar criticism can be found in the writings of Hans Urs von Balthasar, who arguably pays little homage even to Aquinas himself, so unhappy had he felt with the Neo-Thomist *manualistica* forced on him during his studies as a Jesuit scholastic. See Robert Miner, "Thomas Aquinas and Hans Urs Von Balthasar: A Dialogue on Love and Charity," *New Blackfriars*, 95, no. 1059 (2014): 504–24.

3. See Réginald Garrigou-Lagrange, OP, *De gratia: Commentarius in Summam theologicam S. Thomae Iae IIae q. 109–114* (Rome: Marietti, 1946).

Garrigou-Lagrange's theological system itself (however it is viewed today) testifies to a heuristic and hermeneutic imagination[4] that could actively question both observable reality and divine Revelation, so as to come up with plausible, organized answers. No one can be a good architect or a reliable engineer—or a solid, witty systematic theologian—without a high degree of imagination. Such a systematic imagination may seem *prima facie* qualitatively different from the poet's, the painter's, or the mystic's, "lost in wonder, love, and praise,"[5] even on this side of heaven. Nonetheless, it is imagination still, imparted by God to human nature, prone to be perfected and elevated by grace.[6] Even one of Aquinas's driest, most devoted disciples, was highly imaginative.

It would therefore be unfair and simplistic to pit Thomas and Ignatius hastily against each other on the topic of the imagination. To oppose Thomas Aquinas, satirized as an aloof nerd, to Ignatius of Loyola, styled as a starry-eyed, relativistic mystic,[7] is to fall headlong into the trap of a fixed imagin-

---

4. On the multiple functions of the imagination, see Nicolas Steeves, *Grâce à l'imagination: Intégrer l'imagination en théologie fondamentale* (Paris: Éditions du Cerf, 2019), esp. 81–82. Also see Richard Kearney, *The Wake of Imagination: Toward a Postmodern Culture* (London: Routledge 1988), for a philosophical perspective; and Dermot A. Lane, "Imagination and Theology: The *Status Quaestionis*," *Louvain Studies* 34 (2009–2010): 119–45, esp. 135–140, for a theological outlook.

5. Charles Wesley, "Hymn IX," known by its incipit, "Love divine, all loves excelling," in *Hymns for Those That Seek, and Those That Have Redemption in the Blood of Jesus Christ* (London: Strahan, 1747), 11.

6. See Thomas Aquinas, *Summa Theologiae* (ST) I, q. 1, a. 8, ad 2: "cum enim gratia non tollat naturam, sed perficiat"; *Scriptum super Sententiis*, lib. 2, d. 9, q. 1, a. 8, obj. 3: "gratia non tollit naturam sed perficit." All the Latin texts of Aquinas are taken from the website set up thanks to the huge work done by the Pontifical Gregorian University's own Fr. Busa, SJ at www.corpusthomisticum.org. Unless otherwise specified, the English translation from the Latin is my own.

7. How St. Ignatius of Loyola is imaged and portrayed, both in words and in art, has varied immensely over time, and still does. From friend to foe, inside and outside the Catholic Church, the founder of the Society of Jesus is a figure of controversy—as he already was in his lifetime. A cunning, ruthless soldier-*hidalgo* or a meek servant of the papacy? A mystic of the highest kind, repeatedly drawn into God's intimacy by grace, or an ascetical, fully mortified hero? A visionary lawmaker and planner? An emotionally instable man, given to long bouts of tears of grief or mirth? An intellectual or a dunce? An *alumbrado* with covert heretical, Lutheran views or the figurehead of Counter-Reformation Roman Catholicism? For variations in verbal portraits, see Philip Endean, "Who Do You Say Ignatius Is? Jesuit Fundamentalism and Beyond," *Studies in the Spirituality of Jesuits* 19, no. 5 (1987): 1–53; Axelle Guillausseau, "Les récits des miracles d'Ignace de Loyola: Un exemple du renouvellement des pratiques hagiographiques à la fin du XVIe siècle et au début du XVIIe siècle," *Mélanges de la Casa de Velázquez* 36, no. 2 (2006): 233–54. For variations in iconography, see Ursula König-Nordhoff, *Ignatius von Loyola: Studien zur Entwicklung einer neuen Heiligen-Ikonographie im Rahmen einer Kanonisationskampagne um 1600* (Berlin: Gebr. Mann Verlag, 1982). For controversy about the respective roles of asceticism and mysticism in the life of Ignatius and his Jesuit followers, see, e.g., Harvey D. Egan, *The Spiritual Exercises and the Ignatian Mystical Horizon* (St. Louis, MO: Institute of Jesuit Studies, 1976); Egan, *Ignatius*

ary.[8] As this essay will seek to prove, both of them valued the imagination in many positive ways—not least of which, for its aid in knowing and loving God, and thus, being saved. As their biographers evidence, both men led spiritual and intellectual lives that revealed a cogent, conscious use of the imagination.[9]

That is not to say, however, that Aquinas and Loyola used, presented, or accounted for the imagination in identical fashion. An army general victorious in battle uses his imagination as much as (or even more than) the shy, retiring poet, but differently, and with another awareness. Again, an academic trying to grasp, then explain, how the imagination helps acquire knowledge will not speak in the same terms as a spiritual master teaching his disciples how to pray or live their religious life. This applies to St. Thomas and St. Ignatius, and thus raises the question: even if one has already overcome the prejudice that putatively opposes Aquinas and Loyola on their imaginativeness, can one jump over the next hurdle, that it makes no sense to try and match what they wrote on the imagination? Is it just a case of apples and oranges?

The key question here, of course, is: "*What is the imagination?*" Defining the imagination is a formidable task. Any serious academic discussion takes *explicatio terminorum* as a crucial first step, lest it collapse into mere wordplay. As St. John Henry Newman shrewdly commented, speaking from experience, "When men understand each other's meaning, they see, for the most part, that controversy is either superfluous or hopeless."[10] More than controversy, honest

---

Loyola the Mystic (Wilmington, DE: Michael Glazier, 1987). The controversy was whetted by Henri Bremond's seminal work on Ignatian spirituality, which pitted the "mystical school of Lallemant" against the "ascetical school of Alphonsus Rodríguez." See Henri Bremond, *Histoire littéraire du sentiment religieux en France depuis la fin des guerres de religion jusqu'à nos jours*, vol. 3, *La conquête mystique: L'école française*, vol. 5, *L'école du Père Lallemant et la tradition mystique dans la Compagnie de Jésus* (Paris: Bloud et Gay, 1920). A helpful *status quaestionis* is found in Tibor Bartók, SJ, *Un interprète et une interprétation: Le Père Louis Lallemant et sa Doctrine spirituelle au carrefour de l'histoire, de l'analyse institutionnelle et de la pensée d'auteurs jésuites antérieurs et contemporains* (Rome: Gregorian & Biblical Press, 2016), 101–6. Dominican scholars could probably provide a comparably varied depiction and reception of Thomas Aquinas.

    8. On distinguishing a healthy, flowing *imagination* from a sick, fixated *imaginary*, see Steeves, *Grâce à l'imagination*, 22. Also see William F. Lynch, *Images of Hope: Imagination as Healer of the Hopeless* (Notre Dame, IN: University of Notre Dame Press, 1965); Jean-Paul Sartre, *L'imagination* (Paris: Félix Alcan, 1936); Sartre, *L'imaginaire: Psychologie phénoménologique de l'imagination* (Paris: Gallimard, 1940).

    9. For Aquinas, see, e.g., G. K. Chesterton, *St. Thomas Aquinas* (Mineola, NY: Dover Publications, 2009). For Ignatius of Loyola, see *Reminiscences (Autobiography)*, in Saint Ignatius of Loyola, *Personal Writings: Reminiscences, Spiritual Diary, Select Letters including the Text of the Spiritual Exercises*, trans. Joseph A Munitiz, SJ, and Philip Endean, SJ (London: Penguin, 2004), 3–66.

    10. John Henry Newman, "Sermon 10: Faith and Reason, Contrasted as Habits of Mind," in *Fifteen Sermons Preached Before the University of Oxford* (London: Longmans, Green, and Co., 1909), §45.

discussion should be the goal of academic work. The problem with the word "imagination" is that it gets thrown around a lot without ever being clearly delineated. And I would argue that this is truer of the imagination than of many other concepts. Richard Kearney, an Irish-born disciple of Paul Ricœur, dedicated two full books to combing meticulously through the history of the concept of the imagination in Western philosophy: *The Wake of Imagination* and *Poetics of Imagining*.[11] His conclusion? In twenty-five centuries, the West's greatest philosophers have all spoken about the imagination, without ever agreeing on how to define it once and for all.

Caveat lector! My point therefore is not controversy, but a better understanding of what is at stake in my own field of research and teaching—fundamental theology—when studying Thomas's and Ignatius's respective accounts of the imagination. *What do they have to say about the imagination that is relevant to the triple object of fundamental theology—Revelation, faith, and culture(s)?*[12] Philosophers would take a different approach to this issue from a theologian. Thus, while I will not shy away from philosophical analysis, I do not claim to be a specialist, nor do I want to take sides in the internecine wars between Thomist factions in such a way that would preclude my elaborating orthodox theological options.

Granted this caveat, let us now set out to find what Thomas and Ignatius wrote about the imagination. My goal is not to show that Ignatius is a systematic Thomist, but that *the Ignatian and Thomistic approaches to the imagination concur, challenge, and complement each other* in our quest for the One, the True, the Good, and the Beautiful, on our path to knowing and loving God, and thus, being saved.

Therefore, let us be forewarned: our greatest struggle will now be to forsake, as much as we can, what we think we know about the imagination, so as to let Thomas and Ignatius tell us how they see it. If we projected on them our often implicit, romantic view of the imagination as that matchless, spotless creative spark of divine power within our humanity,[13] we would risk totally miscon-

---

11. See note 4 above for the first book. For the second, see Richard Kearney, *Poetics of Imagining: Modern to Post-Modern* (New York: Fordham University Press, 1998).

12. See, e.g., René Latourelle, SJ, "Teologia fondamentale," in *Dizionario di teologia fondamentale*, ed. René Latourelle and Rino Fisichella (Assisi: Citadella editrice, 1990), 1248–58. See also Michael Paul Gallagher, SJ, *Clashing Symbols: An Introduction to Faith and Culture* (London: Darton, Longman and Todd, 1997).

13. In the English-speaking world, an overly enthusiastic, antirationalist, Romantic view of the imagination was ushered in by Samuel Taylor Coleridge, especially in his *Biographia Literaria* (1817), on the wake of Schelling's German romanticism (himself feeding off Kant's account of the transcendental *Einbildungskraft* in the 1781 edition of the *Critique of Pure Reason* and then in the 1790 *Critique of Judgment*): see Steeves, *Grâce à l'imagination*, 56–60. Wordsworth followed suit, celebrating the imagination as "another name for absolute power . . . and Reason in its most exalted

struing them. Let us now therefore take to heart Henri de Lubac's word to the wise, and "check our filter."[14]

This essay has a simple structure. In order to see how much Ignatius agrees with Thomas on the imagination, I will first recount in detail Thomas's account of the imagination within both his philosophy of knowledge and his theology of divine Revelation. I will then examine more briefly how Ignatius's more experiential and mystical account of the imagination, regarding his spiritual life and that of others, concurs with, challenges, and complements Thomas's detailed account. My hypothesis is that *as for the imagination, Thomas ponders and presents a descriptive cognitive system, whereas Ignatius seems to observe and offer a prescriptive spiritual method.*

Thomas and the Imagination: A Descriptive Cognitive System

Simply stated, Aquinas chiefly derives his philosophical view of the imagination from Aristotle, especially the latter's account of knowledge in *De Anima*, Part III. Things get trickier, however, when one realizes that Thomas gives two, slightly diverging accounts of his sense-imagination theory of knowledge. One account is found in *Sententia libri De Anima*, lib. 3, l. 5, and the other in ST I, qq.78 ff.[15] Can those apparently different views be reconciled?

A Preliminary Lexical Detour through Greek and Latin

First, however, we must make a lexical detour. Two distinct Latin words which Aquinas uses in the matter—*phantasia* and *imaginatio*—are often translated as one and the same English word, "imagination." While practical, this single translation for Aquinas's original two terms risks glossing over key hermeneutical disputes. By going further back in time, we'll get a better sense of what lies at stake.

In Latin, *phantasia* is, of course, a Greek loanword, one of two terms which philosophers like Plato and Aristotle had used to describe and critique what modern English, roughly, calls the "imagination." The other term they frequently used was *eikasia*. Now, *eikasia* and *phantasia* express different, com-

---

mood"; while Blake hailed it as the "spiritual fountainhead divine [which] liveth forever." See Kearney, *The Wake of the Imagination*, 177–85.

14. Henri de Lubac, SJ, *Paradoxes of Faith* (San Francisco: Ignatius Press, 1987), 102: "Everybody has his filter, which he takes about with him, through which, from the indefinite mass of facts, he gathers in those suited to confirm his prejudices. And the same fact again, passing through different filters, is revealed in different aspects, so as to confirm the most diverse opinions. It has always been so, it will always be so in this world. Rare, very rare, are those who check their filter."

15. Still other accounts of this matter are to be found in Thomas's *Quaestiones Disputatae de Anima, Quaestiones Disputatae de Veritate*, and *Summa contra Gentiles*. See below.

plementary facets of the imagination. *Phantasia* is a cognate of *phaino* (to shine, to come to light, to appear):[16] it denotes an "objective" view of the imagination, one viewed from the perspective of the imagined object. By contrast, *eikasia* is a cognate of *eoika* (to resemble; in the factitive form: to invent, to create), as well as of the nouns *icon* and *idea*:[17] it thus evokes a "subjective," creative, even artisanal or artistic view of the imagination, one viewed from the perspective of the imagining subject.

In reality, however, this seemingly tidy distinction between an objective imagination and a subjective imagination was never crystal-clear, even for Greek philosophers. This messiness grew when Greek got translated into Latin. *Eikasia* vanished, and *imaginatio* and *phantasia* cohabited in the lexicon of Roman philosophers.[18] Later still, the scholastics, by multiplying the distinctions in the realm of the imagination, caused the confusion to grow. As French *dix-septièmiste* Gérard Ferreyrolles wryly comments: eventually, by early Modernity, "the constant game of reshuffling the functions of the *sensus communis*, the *imaginatio*, the *vis imaginativa*, the *phantasia*, and the *vis cogitativa* now reminded one of a puzzle, a house of cards, and musical chairs, all at once."[19]

Phantasia *and* Imaginatio *in Aquinas's Philosophy of Knowledge*

It is no surprise, therefore, that to this day, Thomist scholars hotly dispute whether *phantasia* and *imaginatio* are one and the same thing for Aquinas. On the one hand, he plainly asserts so in ST I, q. 78, a. 4, co.—"*phantasia sive imaginatio quae sunt idem*"—rebutting Avicenna's prior list of five distinct "interior sensitive powers."[20] On the other hand, the *Sentencia libri De anima* has sometimes been construed as distinguishing between *phantasia* and *imaginatio*.[21]

---

16. See Pierre Chantraine, *Dictionnaire étymologique de la langue grecque* (Paris: Klincksieck, 1968–1980), 1170–71.

17. Chantraine, *Dictionnaire*, 354–55, 455.

18. See Gérard Ferreyrolles, *Les reines du monde: L'imagination et la coutume chez Pascal* (Paris: Honoré Champion, 1995), 124–25: "At least until well into the 17th century, every philosopher elaborated a doctrine about [the imagination] and granted it some, often decisive role in the system he was building. Hence, the extreme complexity of this concept's history, increased by shifts in terminology and inconsistency in [Latin and Greek] translations" (my translation).

19. Ferreyrolles, *Les reines du monde*, 124–25, 139.

20. ST I, q. 78, a. 4, s.c.: "Sed contra est quod Avicenna, in suo libro de anima, ponit quinque potentias sensitivas interiores, scilicet sensum communem, *phantasiam, imaginativam*, aestimativam, et memorativam."

21. See, e.g., the highly technical discussion between Anthony Lisska, Eleonore Stump, and J. R. Weinberg on this issue, with a thorough history of Scholastic subtleties about the imagination, from Aquinas, Scotus, and John of St. Thomas to Ockham, Suárez, and Descartes, in Anthony J. Lisska, *Aquinas's Theory of Perception: An Analytic Reconstruction* (Oxford: Oxford University Press, 2016), esp. ch. 9: "The Imagination and *Phantasia*: A Historical Muddle," 219–36.

Pace other studies of Thomas's cognitive philosophy, I find Robert Pasnau's "Philosophical Study of *Summa Theologiae* Ia 75–89" to be thorough, convincing, and sufficient for my theological needs.[22] I believe that he is right when he asserts that *imaginatio* and *phantasia* are one and the same thing for Aquinas. What does his book's ninth chapter, "Mind and Image," have to say on this issue?[23] Pasnau first reminds us that "Aquinas draws a sharp distinction between the sensory and the rational. The one is material, the other immaterial; the one apprehends particular features of the world, the other the world as universal."[24] For Aquinas, however, it does *not* follow that "the operations of sense and intellect would likewise be segregated."[25] In fact, as Pasnau puts it, "the cognitive processes of a human being are in large part a cooperative venture between sense and intellect."[26] This is where the imagination comes to the fore. Let us now focus specifically on the role of *phantasia* in Thomas's comprehensive philosophy of knowledge.

Thomas asserts that we human beings cannot understand anything without "phantasms" (*phantasmata*), viz. sensory representations provided to the intellect *via* the imagination, on the basis of sensation, with a double purpose: (i) to form concepts and (ii) to "give content to the intellect's actual thoughts even after the relevant concepts have been formed."[27] According to Aquinas himself, phantasms are "the images of bodies"[28] and "the likeness of a particular thing."[29] But one must beware: phantasms are not our ordinary sensory images themselves; rather, they are merely "the leftover impressions from those sensory images."[30]

Where are phantasms found? One would rightly suppose they are found in the *phantasia*, but they are also found in two other internal senses: memory and the cogitative power.[31] Now, phantasms are not identical in these three internal senses. How do they differ in the imagination and in memory? Here, Aquinas draws on Avicenna's notion of intentions as "information not accessible to the external senses": "Phantasia preserves the forms taken in through the senses; it is our storehouse of familiar images, sounds, and so on. Memory, in

---

22. Robert Pasnau, *Thomas Aquinas on Human Nature: A Philosophical Study of* Summa Theologiae *1a 75–89* (Cambridge: Cambridge University Press, 2002).
23. Pasnau, *Aquinas on Human Nature*, 267–95.
24. Pasnau, *Aquinas on Human Nature*, 267.
25. Pasnau, *Aquinas on Human Nature*, 267.
26. Pasnau, *Aquinas on Human Nature*, 267.
27. Pasnau, *Aquinas on Human Nature*, 278.
28. Thomas Aquinas, *Super Sent*, lib. 3, d. 23, q. 1, a. 2, co.: "imagines corporum."
29. ST I, q. 84, a. 7, ad 2: "ipsum phantasma est similitudo rei particularis."
30. ST I, q. 84, a. 7, ad 2.
31. ST I, q. 89, a. 5, co.: "phantasmata, quae sunt in praedictis viribus sensitivis . . . scilicet imaginativa, cogitativa et memorativa." Pasnau quotes other passages in Aquinas to the same effect in *Thomas Aquinas on Human Nature*, 280.

contrast, preserves the *intentions* apprehended through the estimative (or, for humans, cogitative) power."[32] In Pasnau's helpful example, "When you call to mind the generic image (or sound or smell) of an elephant you are using phantasia. When you call to mind an image (sound, smell) of an elephant that you associate with some particular past experience—in the zoo, on safari, and so on—then you are using memory."[33] This theory of phantasms makes plain a first role that the imagination plays in human knowledge: a passive, *"reproductive"* role, in the sense that it reproduces, or represents to the mind an image which was stored on the basis of previous sensation.

According to Thomas, a second role of the imagination is that of "dividing and compounding and forming images of things, even ones that have not been taken in by the senses."[34] This active, *"productive"* role of the imagination builds on the passive, reproductive one. Not only does the imagination take in and store images from the senses, but it also forms new images from those it has in store. Thomas famously exemplifies this with the image of a gold mountain, which we can compound from our separate mental images of gold and of a mountain, although we have never seen one (and likely, never will).[35] Let's quote another example Aquinas makes, for its theological and spiritual implications: "when someone imagines the three divine persons as three human beings,"[36] by analogy from human to divine personhood, the imagination produces a new image, although there is no external sensation of the three divine Persons. In such a case, in Thomas's opinion, the imaginatively pious person could commit a sin if this led to unbelief.

According to Pasnau's convincing argument against Anthony Kenny,[37] one must add that the imagination itself cannot produce sensory experiences based

---

32. Pasnau, *Aquinas on Human Nature*, 280. He is implicitly paraphrasing ST I, q. 84, a. 4, co.: "phantasia sive imaginatio quasi thesaurus quidam formarum per sensum acceptarum ... Ad conservandum autem [intentiones], [ordinatur] vis memorativa, quae est thesaurus quidam huiusmodi intentionum." Italics mine.

33. Pasnau, *Aquinas on Human Nature*, 281. On the subject of memory throughout the Middle Ages, see the two sweeping studies by Mary Carruthers, *The Book of Memory: A Study of Memory in Medieval Culture*, 2nd ed. (Cambridge: Cambridge University Press, 2002); and *The Craft of Thought: Meditation, Rhetoric, and the Making of Images, 400–1200* (Cambridge: Cambridge University Press, 1998).

34. ST I, q. 84, a. 6, ad 2: "phantasia ... est quaedam operatio animae in homine quae dividendo et componendo format diversas rerum imagines, etiam quae non sunt a sensibus acceptae."

35. ST I, q. 78, a. 4, co.: "cum ex forma imaginata auri et forma imaginata montis componimus unam formam montis aurei, quem nunquam vidimus."

36. Thomas Aquinas, *Quaestiones disputatae de malo* q. 7, a. 3, ad 6: "surreptio infidelitatis ... potest esse in imaginatione, puta cum aliquis imaginatur tres personas in divinis sicut tres homines, et movetur subito ad credendum ... talis surreptio est in superiori ratione, et est peccatum veniale." In the absence of rational consent, this is a venial sin.

37. Pasnau, *Aquinas on Human Nature*, 282.

on its images. For Aquinas, the mind simply uses the *sensus communis*, or "*virtus sensitiva*," to do so.[38] In general, he believes that *phantasia* presents or represents images to other faculties, including the intellect.

Pasnau's three short definitions now grant us a clearer view of Aquinas's theory: "*Phantasia*, then, simply is our capacity for storing, rearranging, and presenting generic sensory impressions. *Memory* is our corresponding capacity for handling impressions that have specific associations. *Phantasms* are the impressions contained in each of these so-called treasuries."[39]

The Turn towards Phantasms

Let us now tackle Aquinas's famous "turn towards phantasms" (*conversio ad phantasmata*). This theme, of course, hails back to Aristotle and his celebrated claim in *De anima* III, 7, that "the soul never thinks without a phantasm." Pasnau nonetheless rightfully claims that "Aquinas makes the claim his own to such an extent that it can scarcely be considered Aristotelian."[40] Aquinas discusses the turn towards phantasms at length in ST I, q. 84, a. 7. Here he offers two indications (*indicia*)—neither "decisive proofs," nor true "demonstrations"[41]—of why the turn to phantasms is needed: (i) the fact that our ability to think can be hindered by damage sustained by our bodily organs—especially the brain; and (ii) the common experience that we conjure up internal images of things as *exempla* (viz. pictures or models) when we try to think through a concept.[42] Now, Aquinas makes the very strong claim that "it is *impossible* for our intellect, in this present state of life, . . . actually to understand anything without turning towards phantasms."[43] Pasnau comments that Thomas has previously evidenced that (i) it is useful to do so and (ii) that it often happens, but still has to evidence that it is *impossible to do otherwise*.

38. Thomas Aquinas, *Sententia libri de anima*, lib. 3 passim.
39. Pasnau, *Aquinas on Human Nature*, 283. Italics mine.
40. Pasnau adds, in an endnote, that Aquinas's reinterpretation of this particular claim of Aristotle is "not simply the standard medieval view, either," pointing to Henry of Ghent for a very different hermeneutic and theory of knowledge (*Aquinas on Human Nature*, 447). See also Lisska's discussion of Thomas Hardy Leahey's claim that Aquinas "makes no original contribution to Aristotelian psychology." Lisska, *Aquinas's Theory of Perception*, 225. As a theologian, I must add that the belief that Jesus Christ is the "image of the invisible God" (Col 1:15), joined with bona fide trust in biblical narrative and metaphor, deeply changed how Christian philosophers received and re-elaborated various theories arising from the pagan Greek and Roman philosophy of the imagination. See Steeves, *Grâce à l'imagination*, 45–52.
41. Pasnau, *Aquinas on Human Nature*, 283.
42. See ST I, q. 84, a. 7, co.
43. ST I, q. 84, a. 7, co.: "impossibile est intellectum nostrum, secundum praesentis vitae statum, quo passibili corpori coniungitur, aliquid intelligere in actu, nisi convertendo se ad phantasmata."

How does Aquinas go about proving the necessity of the *conversio ad phantasmata*? For us human beings in this life, he asserts, the intellect must take as its objects *intelligibilia* which are "a quiddity or nature existing in bodily matter."[44] Our intellect does not in fact apprehend particulars, since that is the realm of "sense and imagination."[45] Since we have physical bodies in this life—or rather, as Aquinas asserts, since we are a composite of body and soul—our intellects necessarily abstract universals through the turn to phantasms. Angels, Aquinas adds, do not do so, since they are pure, bodiless spirits.

Of course, we need phantasms because we are not as smart as God and the angels. As Pasnau pithily puts it, "God needs no pictures."[46] Thomas says it more metaphysically: "God, through his single essence, understands all things."[47] Analogically, this applies to angels.[48]

But I agree with Pasnau's contention (vs. Bernard Lonergan and Norman Kretzmann) that, for Thomas, "the need for phantasms only partially arises out of our feeble intellectual state. Phantasms are also particularly well suited for our mode of cognition because of the kind of knowledge we want to have."[49] That is true of three kinds of knowledge: obviously, (i) practical knowledge and the natural sciences, which require an insight into sensible reality; but even (ii) "abstract knowledge in a field such as mathematics, philosophy, or theology, through comparison to natural sensible things"[50]; and more surprisingly still, (iii) theological knowledge that tries to reach "an understanding of God by treating God as the cause of what we can see, more excellent than sensible reality in all positive respects, removed from all negative respects."[51] Simply put, when we think about incorporeal substances such as God and the angels, we do not do so through phantasms of the incorporeal, for they do not exist, but *analogically*, through phantasms of the corporeal objects around us. This, however, must not be taken too far or too

---

44. ST I, q. 84, a. 7, co.: "Intellectus autem humani, qui est coniunctus corpori, proprium obiectum est quidditas sive natura in materia corporali existens."

45. ST I, q. 84, a. 7, co.: "Particulare autem apprehendimus per sensum et imaginationem."

46. Pasnau, *Aquinas on Human Nature*, 283.

47. ST I, q. 89, a. 1, co.: "Deus per unam suam essentiam omnia intelligit."

48. See, e.g., ST I, q. 57, a. 1, co.: "sicut Deus per suam essentiam materialia cognoscit, ita Angeli ea cognoscunt per hoc quod sunt in eis per suas intelligibiles species."

49. Pasnau, *Aquinas on Human Nature*, 290. According to Pasnau, Lonergan and Kretzmann independently suggest that "the turn toward phantasms" is not "an operation of the intellect, but ... merely an intellectual tendency" (289). This theologian confesses this is one of the times where he is bewildered by the sheer technicality and assertiveness of the philosophical claims made by those who wish to interpret Thomas correctly.

50. Pasnau, *Aquinas on Human Nature*, 290.

51. Pasnau, *Aquinas on Human Nature*, 290.

literally, since the imagination might lead us to sin, such as the unbelief that arises "when someone imagines the three divine persons as three human beings."[52]

In a final discussion on the necessity of the turn to phantasms, Pasnau says we sometimes do fleetingly think without phantasms, but never for long. In fact, "the only way to think without phantasms is to receive God's direct assistance, which is precisely what will take place after death."[53] The horizon of Last Things and divine intervention now prods us to move on from Aquinas's *philosophical* account to a more *theological* approach to the imagination in relation to divine Revelation.

Connecting Imagination and Revelation via Aquinas's De Prophetia

In fact, another significant *locus* in Thomas's writings deals both intensely and extensively with the imagination and under a more theological angle: his treatise De Prophetia in ST II-II, qq. 171–174. This study of prophecy forms the last section of ST II-II, "Acts which pertain especially to certain people," a comprehensive study of what we today, favoring the Pauline lexicon, often call "charisms,"[54] while Thomas calls them "*gratiae gratis datae*."[55] While this study is dated 1271–1272, he had also couched an earlier examination of prophecy in more philosophical terms around 1257 in De Veritate q. 12.[56] I will now refer to both studies.

From the perspective of classic fundamental theology, prophecy is viewed not so much as a person's act, but as an occasion to study divine Revelation *ex parte potentiae* (rather than *ex parte objecti*). How does a prophet receive divine revelation? What mode of knowledge is engaged in that process? Surprisingly, most Thomistic philosophers do not scour this part of the *Summa Theologiae* to complete the more philosophical account found in the *Prima Pars*. Thomas's De Prophetia, however, is well worth studying for a better general grasp of how the human imagination operates.[57] French philosopher Serge-Thomas Bonino, in fact, carried out such a study in "Role of the image in prophetic knowledge

---

52. See note 36 above.
53. Pasnau, *Aquinas on Human Nature*, 293.
54. See especially Romans and 1 Corinthians, passim. "In the NT the term charism (*khárisma*) occurs seventeen times, fourteen times in Paul." Enrique Nardoni, "The Concept of Charism in Paul," *The Catholic Biblical Quarterly* 55, no. 1 (1993): 69.
55. ST II-II, q. 171, a. 2, arg. 2.
56. See Serge-Thomas Bonino, OP, "Rôle de l'image dans la connaissance prophétique d'après Saint Thomas d'Aquin," *Revue Thomiste* 89, no. 4 (1989): 533–68, at 540n23.
57. For an in-depth theological synthesis of how, according to Aquinas, the imagination helps receive divine Revelation in the phenomenon of prophecy, see Steeves, *Grâce à l'imagination*, 176–81.

according to Saint Thomas Aquinas,"[58] relying more on the earlier account of prophecy in *De Veritate* q. 12.

Bonino believes that prophecy offers a good example of supernatural knowledge, like faith or the beatific vision. His paper thus returns to the vexed question of how Thomas relates nature and the supernatural based on the principle *gratia non tollit naturam sed perficit*.[59] Does God's revelation to the prophet happen (i) *outside* or *alongside* natural structures of human knowledge; or (ii) *within* them, raising them up to the supernatural end of divine Revelation? We now have to explore the technical details of Thomas's account, insofar as they will help us later to understand how Ignatius concurs with and complements it. The weight and recurrence of the imagination in Ignatius's spiritual life, as told in his autobiography and spiritual diary, as well as his advice in the *Spiritual Exercises*, require that we closely study the Thomistic account of prophecy as a paradigm of how God speaks and reveals himself to human beings.

Thomas articulates two major "acts" of prophecy in *De Veritate* q. 12 as well as in ST II-II, qq. 171–174. The first major act is the vision (*visio* or *revelatio*), while the second, subsequent act is the proclamation (*denuntiatio*) of the message.[60] The *visio* itself has three steps: (i) divine illumination (*lumen propheticum*), followed by (ii) human judgment (*iudicium*—the formal act of prophecy) that the truth revealed in divine light comes from God, and finally, (iii) reception (*acceptio*), the material element of prophetic knowledge.[61]

Now, *De Veritate* q. 18 (on Adam's knowledge *in statu innocentiae*) specifies that divine Revelation does not change natural human knowledge, for, "even in the knowledge of grace through divine revelation, the intellect must always look towards phantasms."[62] Aquinas significantly quotes Pseudo-Dionysius in *Celestial Hierarchies*, Chapter 1: "It is impossible for the divine radiance to shine on us in any other way, than shrouded in a variety of sacred veils."[63] Thus, rightfully concludes Bonino, "supernatural knowledge in this life (of which prophecy is a realization) does not modify the natural mode of

---

58. See note 56 above.
59. See references in note 6 above.
60. Thomas Aquinas, *De Veritate* q. 12, a. 3, co.: "est autem duplex actus prophetiae: sc. visio et denuntiatio." *De Veritate* q.12, a. 13, co. "denuntiatio in prophetia non principaliter, sed consequenter se habet." Full text available at https://www.corpusthomisticum.org/iopera.html.
61. *De Veritate* q.12, a. 9, co.
62. *De Veritate* q.18, a. 5, co.: "etiam in cognitione gratiae, quae est per revelationem divinam, semper intellectus inspiciat ad phantasmata." Translation mine.
63. *De Veritate* q. 18, a. 5, co. "impossibile est nobis aliter lucere divinum radium, nisi varietate sacrorum velaminum circumvelatum." Translation mine.

knowledge; it is supernatural, rather, by reason of its object."[64] To be more precise, this supernatural character of the prophetic object can have two reasons: either (i) the truth that is revealed is rightfully accessible to human reason but was perceived under supernatural light; or (ii) the truth is *per se* unattainable by the natural light of reason alone (say, a mystery like the Trinity or a contingent matter of the future).[65]

Lest we mistake what prophetic, divine Revelation is, however, let us harken to French Thomist Jean-Pierre Torrell, who warns us that it must not be compared to the unveiling of a statue: "To conceive revelation so is to fall into crude anthropomorphism. The human mind is shrouded in ignorance, inattentiveness to spiritual matters, a fundamental inability to grasp the divine on its own; it is this metaphorical veil that the prophetic illumination casts off, by temporarily elevating the prophet to the level of those realities that are usually inaccessible to normal human knowledge."[66]

How, then, can the prophet's reception (*acceptio*) be supernaturally elevated, if, by principle, even divine Revelation does not modify our natural human mode of knowledge? Bonino claims that the imagination's power not only to receive but to create images comes from its proximity to the intellect.[67] Phantasms, to use a helpful Latin distinction, are at once the object "*a quo*" (from which) and "*in quo*" (in which) of the human intellect. This distinction is, I believe, the grounds for Pasnau's earlier claim above that Aquinas intensifies Aristotle's axiom that in this life we cannot think without turning towards mental images. In the realm of natural knowledge, a phantasm is the *a quo* object of the intellect because the intellect receives the phantasm as its intelligible species.[68] As Bonino helpfully rephrases it, "The first role of the phantasm, object *a quo* of natural knowledge, is thus to carry to the intellect the intelligible that is contained virtually in sensible realities."[69] Furthermore, our intellect also needs phantasms "not only when acquiring knowledge, but also when using

---

64. "La connaissance surnaturelle dans l'état de voie (dont la prophétie est une réalisation) ne modifie pas le mode de connaître naturel, mais elle est surnaturelle en raison de son objet." Bonino, "Rôle de l'image," 548.

65. Bonino, "Rôle de l'image," 548.

66. Jean-Pierre Torrell, OP, in Thomas d'Aquin, *Somme théologique*, t. 3 (Paris: éditions du Cerf, 1985), 967n5: "Concevoir ainsi la révélation, c'est verser dans un grossier anthropomorphisme. C'est l'esprit de l'homme qui est enveloppé d'ignorance, d'inattention aux choses spirituelles, d'incapacité foncière à saisir le divin par ses seules forces, et c'est ce voile métaphorique que fait tomber l'illumination prophétique en haussant momentanément le prophète au niveau de réalités habituellement inaccessibles à la connaissance humaine normale."

67. See Bonino, "Rôle de l'image," 550.

68. *De Veritate* q. 10, a. 11, co.: " Mens enim nostra naturali cognitione phantasmata respicit quasi obiecta, a quibus species intelligibiles accipit," quoting *De anima* III.

69. See Bonino, "Rôle de l'image," 553.

the knowledge thus acquired."[70] Images, therefore, play a constant, crucial role in the life of our intellect: "The phantasm is the principle of our knowledge, the place from which the operation of the intellect starts, something not transient, but permanent, a kind of foundation of the operation of the intellect; just like the principles of a demonstration must remain in the entire process of scientific knowledge, for the phantasms, in fact, relate to the intellect as objects in which (*in quibus*) it sees all that it sees."[71] As Bonino shrewdly notes, "Of course, intellectual activity formally transcends the imagination, but it never departs from it in practice, for it is *in* the imagination that the life of the intellect is carried out.... The phantasm is in fact the *in quo* object of the intellect."

How does this impact what roles images play in the act of prophecy? They plainly play a great role as regards the *proclaimed* prophetic message: metaphors, not concepts, are the stuff of prophetic cries. From Isaiah's suffering servant to Jeremiah's almond tree, from Hosea's similes of matrimony and parenthood to Malachi's refiner of silver, Old Testament prophecies brim over with images of ordinary ancient Jewish life that express the paradoxical "simple complexity" of God's extraordinary relation with his people.[72] But how does the prophet know what imagery to use when preaching the divinely revealed message?

Aquinas distinguishes two cases. In the first case, God grants the prophet both divine light and new imagery which the prophet quotes in his subsequent proclamation to the crowds.[73] In the other case, God only sheds new light on the prophet's memory and imagination, and it is up to the prophet to flesh out *ad libitum*[74] the divine message with images that his audience might grasp and cleave to.[75]

Nonetheless, images also play a role *prior* to the public proclamation of the prophecy. As mentioned above, this arises from our composite nature of body and soul: "As long as the soul has its being in union with the body in this life,

---

70. *De veritate* q. 18, a. 8, ad 4: "non solum indiget intellectus noster converti ad phantasmata in acquirendo scientiam, sed etiam in utendo scientia acquisita."

71. Thomas Aquinas, *Super de Trinitate* III, q. 6, a. 2, ad 5: "phantasma est principium nostrae cognitionis, ut ex quo incipit intellectus operatio non sicut transiens, sed sicut permanens ut quoddam fundamentum intellectualis operationis; sicut principia demonstrationis oportet manere in omni processu scientiae, cum phantasmata comparentur ad intellectum ut obiecta, in quibus inspicit omne quod inspicit." Translation mine.

72. See the comprehensive study by Luis Alonso-Schökel, SJ, *The Inspired Word: Scripture in the Light of Language and Literature* (New York: Herder and Herder, 1965). For the biblical imagery mentioned here, see respectively Is 52:13–53:12; Jer 1:13–14; Hos 2; Hos 11; Mal 3:3.

73. See ST II-II, q. 171, a. 2, co.

74. *De veritate* q. 12, a. 12, passim.

75. Though Aquinas slightly hesitates, he decides that the imageless, purely enlightened prophecy is the more excellent of the two cases: see ST II-II, q. 174, a. 2 in its entirety.

the soul does not know even the things whose species are conserved within it without looking at the phantasms. That is also why there are no divine revelations for it except under the species of phantasms."⁷⁶

Of what, therefore, consists the above-mentioned Dionysian "shroud of sacred veils" through which divine radiance shines on us? Of phantasms, the *in quo* objects of prophetic knowledge. Resorting to images is not only a social, didactic necessity required to proclaim the prophecy; it is also a noetic necessity stemming from our natural mode of cognition.

Bonino, however, astutely notes that Aquinas does not apply this necessity at a supernatural level to images as the *a quo* object of the intellect. God may choose to infuse certain concepts directly into the intellect. However, this miraculous mode is not the ordinary mode of prophetic knowledge.⁷⁷ Aquinas noticed that most prophets resorted to imagery in line with their culture and with their personal and social experience. In fact, the supernatural character of the prophet's *acceptio* can arise from a *nova formatio specierum* that is not an (entirely supernatural) *infusio* or *creatio ex nihilo*, but a mere reorganization of previously held mental images. We are able, in fact, to reorganize our mental images on our own, without divine assistance. What makes the new, prophetical order of knowledge supernatural, therefore, is the ordering of these images to represent intelligible truths beyond our intellect, that thus require the gift of *lumen propheticum*. Interestingly for our study of Ignatius, Bonino adds that Thomas, like most scholastics, believed that angels and demons could tamper with our mental images and so redirect our intentions to, or away from, God.⁷⁸ This will come in handy when we consider what Ignatius says about the imagination in his own spiritual experience and as a tool for the prayer of others.

Bonino thus rightfully concludes that, *for Aquinas, the primordial divine gift of prophetic light suffices to make the entire cognitive process supernatural*, although it does not change what is naturally known to man. The divine light strengthens, elevates, and perfects the natural light of the intellectual agent, but does not replace it. Thus, as we fit one piece in the nature and grace puzzle, we also gain a corollary, better understanding of the role of images and the imagination in acquiring knowledge, especially from God.

---

76. *De Veritate*, q. 19, a. 1, co.: "anima . . . quamdiu habet esse coniunctum corpori in statu huius viae, non cognoscit etiam illa quorum species in ipsa reservantur nisi inspiciendo ad phantasmata. Et propter hoc etiam nec revelationes ei aliquae divinitus fiunt nisi sub speciebus phantasmatum."

77. See Bonino, "Rôle de l'image," 558–59.

78. See Bonino, "Rôle de l'image," 561nn116–17. He refers to general Scholastic commentaries on Peter Lombard's second Book of Sentences, distinctions 7–8. Also see *De veritate* q. 12, a. 8, co.: "ipsa formatio specierum in imaginativa virtute proprie Angelis est attribuenda"; *Contra Gentiles* III, cap. 154: "De donis gratiae gratis datae; in quo de divinationibus Daemonum."

Aquinas, More Imaginative than Prejudice Would Have Us Hold

To conclude on Aquinas and the imagination, let's step back for a moment from his account of how the imagination plays in natural and supernatural knowledge. We would be remiss if we didn't realize how much Thomas's theories reveal his own use of the imagination. As Frederick Bauerschmidt puts it, in fact, paradoxically, "Thomas's theological practice is a lot more 'imaginative,' in the modern sense, than his account of *imaginatio* might suggest."[79]

It must first be said that the (post)modern reader scouring Thomas for evidence of a fully "imaginative theology" is in for disappointment.[80] At first glance, indeed, his "*imaginatio*, rather than being the wonderful productive power of the human mind, seems simply a kind of storage facility for sense images; rather than being a factory churning out marvelous (or dangerous) products, it is a humble warehouse of forms."[81] What's more, Aquinas strove to recast theology as an Aristotelian "science (*episteme*), in which ... 'from things already known conclusions about other matters follow of necessity.'"[82] We children of postmodernity do not, however, associate the ensuing syllogistic method with the creative imagination. Many, instead, "value the kind of 'lateral thinking' that we associate today with the religious imagination," as Bauerschmidt deftly suggests, taking his cue from Herbert McCabe, OP.[83]

Nonetheless, *scientia* is not the be-all and end-all of real thought, despite how crucial it is both for Aristotle and Aquinas. "Thomas knows that most human thought is of an intuitive, associative kind," argues Bauerschmidt, aptly noting that, although Aquinas does crown logic as the "*ars artium*,"[84] he also recognizes that poetry and rhetoric, *inter alia*, can help order thought.[85]

As Herbert McCabe points out, the goal of Aristotle's logic is "not to help people to make rational arguments, but to hinder them from making bogus arguments."[86] Likewise, Thomas's *sacra doctrina*—what we call "systematic theology" today—does not purport to help us figure out how we Christians should speak about God, but rather how we should "make sense of the sometimes messy and

---

79. Frederick Christian Bauerschmidt, "Imagination and Theology in Thomas Aquinas," *Louvain Studies* 34 (2009–2010): 169–84, at 169.
80. Bauerschmidt, "Imagination and Theology," 172–73, 180.
81. Bauerschmidt, "Imagination and Theology," 173.
82. Bauerschmidt, "Imagination and Theology," 180, quoting *Super de Trinitate* I, q. 2, a. 2, co. 1: "ratio scientiae consistat in hoc quod ex aliquibus notis alia necessario concludantur."
83. Bauerschmidt, 180n45, quoting Herbert McCabe, *On Aquinas*, ed. Brian Davies, OP (New York: Burns & Oates-Continuum, 2008), 130.
84. Thomas Aquinas, *Expositio Libri Posteriorum Analyticorum*, lib. 1, l. 1, no. 4.
85. See Aquinas, *Expositio*, lib. 1, l. 1, no. 6.
86. McCabe, *On Aquinas*, 130.

misleading ways in which [we] are always already talking."[87] Aquinas also knew that *sacra doctrina* is a science of a very particular, subaltern kind, since it depends on the higher science of God, from which it borrows its first principles.[88] This famously makes faith and theology both more and less certain that other scientific knowledge.[89] Thirdly, Thomas's frequent recourse to *argumenta ex convenientia* shows that his actual practice of theology was often much less rigid than his theory. Thomas was obviously much indebted to his predecessors in philosophy and theology, as well as to the long line of witnesses to the Risen Lord who had handed him down Tradition and Scripture. Nonetheless—or perhaps, more likely, properly *because* he believed in a truly *living* Tradition—he often "ends up with strikingly original positions on any number of theological issues."[90]

In his early 14th century life of Thomas, Bernard Gui writes how the saint often knelt in prayer when a theological question proved especially thorny.[91] Now, surely, such faith and humility testify to a use of divinely illuminated imagination more than any perfectly lined up syllogisms. Could it be that in those moments of supplication and unitive prayer, God granted Thomas a kind of *lumen propheticum* so that he, in turn, could illuminate the minds of so many philosophers and theologians after him, and point them towards God as First Truth?

In terms of what Gabriel Marcel named "creative fidelity"[92] (an often abused or maligned concept), Thomas is a great witness. Bauerschmidt's conclusion is well worth quoting at length for those who struggle to realize how contemporary theology can draw both on *fides ex auditu* and a benevolent but critical *auditus temporis*:

> The sort of originality embodied in Thomas's practice might offer us an alternative to certain modern approaches that seek theological originality in the endless cycle of critique and re-critique of received tradition. While such critique is no doubt necessary at times, it can become as formulaic and stale as the most rigid traditionalism. The true originality of the theological imaginations is found not in novel doctrines, but in the ability, after reflection, to turn back to the tradition of the Church in a new kind of *conversio ad phantasmata*, so as to see it anew and to think it anew.[93]

---

87. Bauerschmidt, "Imagination and Theology," 181.
88. Bauerschmidt, "Imagination and Theology," 182.
89. See, e.g., Avery Dulles, *The Assurance of Things Hoped For: A Theology of Christian Faith* (Oxford: Oxford University Press, 1994), 229–34.
90. Bauerschmidt, "Imagination and Theology in Thomas Aquinas," 183, expanded by explanatory note 57.
91. Bauerschmidt, "Imagination and Theology," 183, expanded by explanatory note 58.
92. Gabriel Marcel, "VIII. Creative Fidelity," in *Creative Fidelity* (New York: Fordham University Press, 2002), 147–74.
93. Bauerschmidt, "Imagination and Theology," 184.

Could our prejudice about Thomas's lack of imagination also have to do with semantic shifts in descriptors of interior senses and faculties since the Middle Ages? In the introduction to her first *magnum opus* on memory in medieval culture, Mary Carruthers masterfully compares how Aquinas's and Einstein's contemporaries painted them as geniuses. As it turns out, while a colleague of Einstein's at Princeton praises above all his imagination, early Dominicans who had known Aquinas first-hand praise his memory.[94] With a warranted sharp jab against the romantic imagination's pretenses, Carruthers reminds us that:

> the nature of creative activity itself—what the brain does, and the social and psychic conditions needed for its nurture—has remained essentially the same between Thomas's time and our own. Human beings did not suddenly acquire imagination and intuition with Coleridge, having previously been poor clods. The difference is that whereas now geniuses are said to have creative imagination which they express in intricate reasoning and original discovery, in earlier times they were said to have richly retentive memories, which they expressed in intricate reasoning and original discovery.[95]

These semantic shifts and "re-labelings," as it were, obviously make our task tougher when it comes to comparing Thomas and Ignatius on the imagination. Ferreyrolles's half-amused, half-desperate sigh at the combination of "a puzzle, a house of cards, and musical chairs, all at once" should not discourage us from turning to Ignatius to study his relation to the imagination. Of course, there is something futile in the very exercise of comparing two great men who lived in very different circumstances and left us an entirely different set of writings. Nonetheless, needs must![96] Let us now try and discover if Ignatius's life and writings warrant the claim that he concurs, challenges, and complements Thomas on the imagination.

---

94. See note 33 above. See Carruthers, *Book of Memory*, esp. 1–8.
95. Carruthers, *Book of Memory*, 4.
96. This echoes with René Lafontaine's preliminary comments as he launched into a comparison of the Christology of the ST's *Tertia Pars* with that of the *Spiritual Exercises*: "As our research is punctuated by the unfolding of the four weeks of the *Exercises*, we will have the opportunity to verify how the Christology of the *Exercises* confirms or contests that of the *Summa*. The extremely opposed literary genre of the two works does not hinder our research, since Jean-Pierre Torrell has demonstrated that Thomas Aquinas proved to be a 'spiritual master,' while Hugo Rahner floated the idea of a Christological understanding of the Ignatian *Exercises* that is more Scotist than Thomist." René Lafontaine, *L'originalité des Exercices d'Ignace de Loyola* (Paris: Éditions Jésuites, 2016), 69. Translation mine. See Jean-Pierre Torrell, OP, *Saint Thomas Aquinas*, vol. 2, *Spiritual Master* (Washington, DC: The Catholic University of America Press, 2003) and note 99 below on Hugo Rahner.

Ignatius and the Imagination: A Prescriptive Spiritual Method?

Three caveats should be granted before we go any further in our examination of Ignatius's relation to the imagination.

Three Caveats

First caveat: do not assume that anything Aristotelian in Ignatius came to him only or chiefly via Thomas.[97] It could have come to him directly from Aristotle, whose texts he surely read;[98] it could also have come via Duns Scotus, whose disciples were rife in Paris when Ignatius was a student.[99] Thomas Osborne's essay in this book, "The Early Jesuits and Scholastic Theology," obviously provides much valuable detailed information on this subject. Nonetheless, Ignatius does explicitly demand in the *Constitutions of the Society of Jesus* that young Jesuits study "the scholastic doctrine of saint Thomas"[100]—the only theologian the *Constitutions* mention by name.

Second caveat: people a tad familiar with Ignatius of Loyola's *Spiritual Exercices* might hastily assume that the Ignatian use of the imagination lies solely in the mind's actively composing "backdrop scenery" and directing "spiritual costume plays," so as to make Gospel scenes more relevant. The truth, of course, is much more nuanced and complex than the caricature I just painted. Ignatius's experience with the imagination was manifold, as his writings attest. That's why this section won't just study his *Spiritual Exercises*, but also his *Autobiography* and *Spiritual Diary*.

Third caveat: in just one or two generations after Ignatius's death in 1556, Jesuits had changed how they used the imagination in prayer. Fancy picture

---

97. See Philippe Lécrivain, "La 'Somme théologique' de Thomas d'Aquin aux XVIe-XVIIIe siècles," *Recherches de Science Religieuse* 91, no. 3 (2003): 397–427.

98. See, e.g., Rogelio García Mateo, SJ, "El pensamiento aristotélico en los *Ejercicios Espirituales* y el influjo de éstos en Descartes," *Gregorianum* 98, no. 4 (2017): 763-83; Ľuboš Rojka, SJ, "Aristotelian Philosophy in the *Spiritual Exercises*," *Gregorianum* 98, no. 4 (2017): 785–94.

99. Hugo Rahner claims that there are "grounds for thinking that when he was at Paris [Ignatius] came very specially under the Scotist influence of the famous Master Petrus de Cornibus. This Franciscan, who wrote a commentary on Scotus, was certainly held in very high esteem among Ignatius's companions at Paris." Hugo Rahner, SJ, *Ignatius the Theologian* (London: Geoffrey Chapman, 1968), 70n31.

100. The Society of Jesus, *The Constitutions of the Society of Jesus and Their Complementary Norms: A Complete English Translation of the Official Latin Texts* (Saint Louis, MO: The Institute of Jesuit sources, 1996), 184. In Rule 11 of the "Rules to follow in view of the true attitude of mind that we ought to maintain [as members] within the Church militant," Ignatius provides a longer list of theologians, "the positive doctors, such as St. Jerome, St. Augustine and St. Gregory . . . scholastics like St. Thomas, St. Bonaventure, the Master of the Sentences," to be praised as a rule. Ignatius, "The Spiritual Exercises," in *Personal Writings*, 357.

albums, like the *Evangelicae Historiae Imagines*[101] by an early Jesuit companion of Ignatius, Fr. Jerome Nadal, were printed and propagated at great cost to help those who made the Spiritual Exercises in their meditations and contemplations. Further, around the same time, although Jesuits continued to refer to Aquinas as an authoritative source,[102] the prolific Spanish Jesuit philosopher and theologian Francisco Suárez changed the metaphysics and theory of knowledge that Jesuits (were) taught by introducing elements drawn directly from Duns Scotus or even Ockham's nominalist theories, sometimes passing them off as faithfully Thomistic.[103] Much later, starting around 1900, prominent Jesuit philosophers and theologians such as Pierre Rousselot, Joseph Maréchal, Karl Rahner, Bernard Lonergan, or François Marty (not to mention Hans Urs von Balthasar), revisited and reshaped the Ignatian understanding of the imagination, including how it is used in prayer.[104] Many scholars of Ignatian spirituality followed suit, once such research lost its stigma.[105] In short, it is nigh impossible for us to read Ignatius with pristine eyes. If I may offer an analogy, to strike our imagination: I once asked my organ teacher what he thought of musical recordings made with baroque instruments. He wryly sighed and added, with a Gallic shrug: "You can play baroque music on period instruments all you want, but once you've heard Wagner, you can't 'unhear' him; you'll never hear Bach the same way."

---

101. See Thomas Buser, "Jerome Nadal and Early Jesuit Art in Rome," *The Art Bulletin* 58, no. 3 (1976): 424–33. Jerome Nadal, *Evangelicae historiae imagines ex ordine euangeliorum, quae toto anno in missae sacrificio recitantur, in ordinem temporis vitae Christi digestae*, ed. IHSI (Sassari: Casa Editrice Scriptorium, 2002). On Jesuit *emblematica*, also see Ralph Dekoninck, "Jesuit Emblematics between Theory and Practice," *Jesuit Historiography Online* (Leiden: Brill, 2017), https://referenceworks.brillonline.com/entries/jesuit-historiography-online/jesuit-emblematics-between-theory-and-practice-COM_192540.

102. See, e.g., Tibor Bártok, SJ, *Un interprète et une interprétation de l'identité jésuite: Le père Louis Lallemant et sa "Doctrine spirituelle" au carrefour de l'histoire, de l'analyse institutionnelle et de la pensée d'auteurs jésuites antérieurs et contemporains* (Rome: Gregorian & Biblical Press, 2016), 256.

103. See Jean-François Courtine, *Suarez et le système de la métaphysique* (Paris: PUF Epiméthée, 1990), 194; 366ff.

104. Of course, this is paralleled by the construction of Ignatian spirituality by Spanish Jesuits as they started the *Monumenta Historica Societatis Jesu* in the late nineteenth century and by French Jesuits such as Alexandre Brou and Joseph de Guibert in the twentieth century. See esp. John W. O'Malley, SJ and Timothy W. O'Brien, SJ, "The Twentieth-Century Construction of Ignatian Spirituality: A Sketch," *Studies in the Spirituality of Jesuits* 52, no. 3 (2020).

105. See Ernest C. Ferlita, "The Road to Bethlehem—Is it Level or Winding? The Use of the Imagination in the *Spiritual Exercises*," *Studies in the Spirituality of Jesuits* 29, no. 5 (1997): 1–23.

Imagination According to the Autobiography

Having written extensively about the Ignatian imagination elsewhere, I shall give a shorter, synthetic account of its chief characteristics here.[106] In order to overcome any "filters" arising from superficial knowledge of the *Spiritual Exercises*, I will preemptively start by looking at how St. Ignatius talks about the imagination in the long story of his life which he dictated to his secretary, the Portuguese Jesuit Luís Gonçalves da Câmara, between 1553 and 1555, having given in to his companions' constant begging to leave them such a narrative, to serve as a testament.[107] Arguably, Ignatius's *Autobiography*[108] is only the third such major work on the timeline of Western literature, more than a thousand years after St. Augustine's *Confessions*, a few centuries after Abelard's *Historia Calamitatum*, soon followed by St. Teresa of Ávila's *Libro de la vida*, completed in 1566 at the behest of her Dominican confessors.

Ignatius's *Autobiography* gives us many instances of times where he used his imagination for spiritual goals. One of its key teachings reminds Ignatius's would-be followers that, despite their genuine, rightful enthusiasm for the *Spiritual Exercises*, the imagination does not just have an active, composing feature: it is also something passive, receptive. Such a claim, of course, is in full agreement with Thomas's account of the imagination as both reproductive and productive. The story of Ignatius's life as told to his disciples thus debunks any suspicion that the Ignatian imagination is such a well-oiled engine that it can almost "force God to appear." Although some self-proclaimed followers of Ignatius may be tempted by such extreme forms of spiritual voluntarism—a Pelagianism of sorts where salvation is wrought without the help of God—the founder made plain that that was not how he met and experienced God.[109] On the contrary, the imagination clearly appears in the *Autobiography* as a meeting

---

106. I hope it is not vulgar of me to suggest that the reader look at chapter 5, "Spiritualité et imagination. 'In obscuro miranda relucent,'" in *Grâce à l'imagination*, 297–334; or "L'immaginazione è preghiera?" *Ignaziana*, 21 (2016): 61–68.

107. See Jean-Claude Dhôtel, SJ, introduction to Ignace de Loyola, *Récit écrit par le Père Louis Gonçalves aussitôt qu'il l'eut recueilli de la bouche même du Père Ignace* (Paris: Desclée de Brouwer-Bellarmin, 1988), 9–41.

108. The English translation which I will use here, by Philip Endean, SJ, is entitled *Reminiscences (Autobiography)*. Francophone Ignatians often call it "*Récit du pèlerin*," based on a 1925 edition by Eugène Thibaut, SJ. Simplicity in the present context suggests using the self-explanatory (albeit imprecise) title *Autobiography* (hereafter, *Autobiog*).

109. See Frederick G. McLeod, "The Use of the Imagination in the Ignatian Exercises," in Centrum Ignatianum Spiritualitatis, *Images and the Imagination in the Ignatian Exercises* (Rome: CIS, 1987), 33–92. Although this paper is remarkable, it does not entirely avert the risk that Ignatius's use of the imagination could be construed as so powerful that, in the wrong hands, it might become manipulative.

point where divine and human liberty play together:[110] God is free to reveal himself; we are free to believe in him.

Ignatius describes vivid visions he had as he convalesced at the family castle in Loyola after a cannonball shattered his leg at the battle of Pamplona.[111] Based on what he was reading at any given time, his imagination becomes a battlefield of its own—entertaining, on the one hand, pleasant but worldly ideas (such as writing love poems and performing great knightly deeds for a lady he would woo) that leave him deeply unsatisfied, and on the other hand, more rigorous but spiritual inspirations that deeply gratify him (imitating, nay, surpassing St. Francis of Assisi and St. Dominic in their penances).[112] Just like Thomas, and any good Christian spiritual master, Ignatius thus realizes that our imagination is a battleground for "angels" and "spirits," "good" and "bad." Ignatius makes no naïve assumptions about the imagination: like Thomas, from his first-hand experience of spiritual warfare, he knows our imaginings can lead us to sin. This spiritual realism is far indeed from the later unqualified enthusiasm that the Romantics showed towards the imagination. The latter can convey a spark of the divine, of course, but it can also light the fires of hell—for instance, when Ignatius is later brought to the verge of suicide, as his conscience is haunted by scruples about his past sins.[113]

The *Autobiography* also shows us that Ignatius, on his sickbed in Loyola, uses his intellect and his will to think about and ponder the mental images he has previously received in prayer or while reading or daydreaming.[114] Memory and the imagination, as described by Aquinas, are thus to provide the phantasms *a quo* and *in quo* the intellect can operate. And so, one night, as he lies awake, a "likeness of Our Lady with the Holy Child Jesus"[115] heals him forever of any carnal thoughts; his inner conversion is now apparent to others, such as his brother.[116]

Ignatius's experience of alternating "good" and "bad" images, leading either to, or away from God, teaches him that *our mind is never imageless*, and that this fact should not sadden us.[117] In order to become better disciples of Jesus, therefore, the issue is not to empty our imagination, as in some strains of ascetical Buddhism, but to chase away bad imagery with good imagery.[118] Now, Igna-

---

110. See Steeves, *Grâce à l'imagination*, 302.
111. See Ignatius of Loyola, *Autobiog*, 13–17.
112. Ignatius, *Autobiog*, 14–15.
113. Ignatius, *Autobiog*, 22–24.
114. Ignatius, *Autobiog*, 14–15.
115. Ignatius, *Autobiog*, 16.
116. Ignatius, *Autobiog*, 17.
117. See Steeves, *Grâce à l'imagination*, 304.
118. Steeves, *Grâce à l'imagination*, 304.

tius gives no details in the *Autobiography* about the likeness of the Virgin and Child: he just notes its effects on his sexual ethics. As the popular saying goes, the devil is in the details.

"Discernment" is a key word in Ignatian spirituality, rooted in Ignatius's reflectiveness and secondary thoughts about his imaginings, starting in Loyola, when he realizes that he must discern, i.e., judge and distinguish, the spirits that are pushing him towards God or away. Ignatian discernment is analogous, I believe, to the Thomist *iudicium* on the gift of prophecy we met above. It is in fact, a common human experience which Scripture itself beholds time and again: within the mystery that we human beings are unto ourselves, other mysterious "voices" speak up within us or among the "prophets"—broadly speaking, God's mouthpieces around us—forcing us to discern, to judge: what spiritual entity is speaking to me?[119] What should I do? In Ignatius's later words, once he realizes it is not God's will that he stay on in his fantasy city, Jerusalem, he ponders, "*Quid agendum?*"[120] At this stage, the power of the mental images and the struggle which Ignatius undergoes in Loyola eventually pushes him to become a pilgrim, headed for the Holy Land.

Another key time of Ignatius's life as regards the imagination is his lengthy stay in Manresa, an otherwise rather unremarkable river valley in Spanish Catalonia, a few months after he has left Loyola.[121] What are the highlights of Manresa for the study of the Ignatian imagination? First, in that lowly place, the spiritual warfare going on in and through Ignatius's imagination waxes. He is tempted by a vain, shimmering image: "something in the air alongside him, which would give him much consolation, because it was very beautiful, enormously so. He couldn't properly make out what it was an image of, but somehow it seemed to him that it had the shape of a serpent, and it had many things which shone like eyes, though they weren't eyes."[122] The image tries to distract him enough that he will quit the path of humble self-denial he has undertaken. He loses courage, becomes scrupulous, and, as mentioned above, is tempted to suicide through imaginary thoughts.

Looking back on his life, some thirty years later, as he dictates his narrative to his secretary, after a wealth of experience and a scholastic education in Alcalá and Paris, he can use his hermeneutic and heuristic imagination to understand how God was acting in his life at Manresa: "At this time, God was

---

119. See Jacques Guillet's first-rate exegetical contribution to *Discernment of Spirits*, ed. Jacques Guillet et al. (Collegeville, MN: The Liturgical Press, 1970), 17–54.

120. Ignatius, *Autobiog*, 36. Differing from their Anglophone *confrères*, the Latin phrase has stuck with Francophone Jesuits to the point that it is left thus in the midst of the French translation (see *Récit*, 104).

121. Ignatius, *Autobiog*, 20–28.

122. Ignatius, *Autobiog*, 21.

dealing with him in the same way as a schoolteacher deals with a child, teaching him."[123] At this point in the *Autobiography*, Ignatius sets aside his habitual narrative style and takes up a systematic exposition worthy of his best Parisian professors—no less imaginative than his storytelling, just differently so. In five consecutive, highly organized theological points, Ignatius explains how God saved him through his imagination. First, by a vision of the Most Holy Trinity as three keys on a keyboard, through an elevation of his understanding, with much sobbing.[124] Second, a joyful understanding of divine Creation through the vision of a white thing, from which some rays were coming out, although Ignatius claims later that he cannot explain it or remember it in detail.[125] Third, the real presence of Christ in the Blessed Sacrament; a vision of the Body of Christ while Ignatius is in a process of converting how he relates to his own body.[126] Fourth, the humanity of Christ as a kind of limbless white body, and likewise for Our Lady. This particular vision gives him a great "confirmation regarding the faith, that . . . if there weren't Scripture to teach us these matters of the faith, he would be resolved to die for them solely on the basis of what he has seen."[127] Fifth and finally, the famed "vision at the Cardoner," by a river, a turning point in Ignatius's life and ministry. "And as he was seated there, the eyes of his understanding began to be opened; not that he saw some vision, but understanding and knowing many things, spiritual things just as much as matters of faith and learning, and this with an enlightenment so strong that all things seemed new to him. . . . And this left him with the understanding enlightened in so great a way that it seemed to him as if he were a different person, and he had another in mind, different from that which he had before."[128] After that, as he kneels in thanksgiving in front of a nearby cross, Ignatius is finally able to chase away for good the vision in the air which had

---

123. Ignatius, *Autobiog*, 25.
124. Ignatius, *Autobiog*, 25.
125. Ignatius, *Autobiog*, 25.
126. Ignatius, *Autobiog*, 25.
127. Ignatius, *Autobiog*, 25. This declaration, which might seem *prima facie* to skate on the brink of heresy, brings to mind the famous assertion by John Henry Newman: "The heart is commonly reached, not through the reason, but through the imagination, by means of direct impressions, by the testimony of facts and events, by history, by description. Persons influence us, voices melt us, looks subdue us, deeds inflame us. Many a man will live and die upon a dogma: no man will be a martyr for a conclusion." Newman, "The Tamworth Reading Room," in *Discussions and Arguments on Various Subjects* (London: Longmans, Green, and Co., 1907), 293; see also Newman, *An Essay in Aid of a Grammar of Assent* (London: Longmans, Green, and Co., 1903), 93. Like Ignatius, Newman connects the reality of the imagination, which touches the heart and can lead a man to accept martyrdom, to the reality of faith. "Dogma" in this case refers *lato sensu* to a firmly held belief, such as in the case of Ignatius's divine revelations.
128. Ignatius, *Autobiog*, 27.

initially tempted him so sorely, by shaking a stick at it, now clearly recognizing it as the devil.[129]

Images, therefore, according to the *Autobiography*, clearly play a great role in Ignatius's knowledge of natural and supernatural things. Of course, the text should not be taken as a naïve, merely factual account of Ignatius's words and deeds. The time in his life when he dictated the narrative, over two long years, in two different languages, to a secretary who presumably had a hand in redacting the text: all these details should make us wary of a fundamentalist reading of the *Autobiography*. The story has a clear scope: to serve as a testimonial and testament to his Jesuit confreres,[130] alongside the booklet of the *Spiritual Exercises* which received papal approval in 1547–1548, and the *Constitutions of the Society of Jesus* that are then slowly taking form. Among many different topics, a particular piece of spiritual and practical wisdom which Ignatius wishes to impart to the members of the Society is his meticulously organized narrative of how he, God, and the devil had met and grown to know one another *via* his imagination.

It is more than likely that, during his studies in Paris (the story of which takes up an entire chapter of the *Autobiography*), Ignatius studied Aristotle and Thomas, who had been restated in the syllabus at the University of Paris after a spell of *post mortem* condemnation, as well as Church Fathers and scholastic authors, not to mention Scripture.[131] Nonetheless, the *Autobiography* gives no detail as to the actual content of Ignatius's studies in philosophy or theology.

The *Autobiography*'s literary genre, and its scope, lend themselves much less still, then, to the sort of theoretical discussion Thomas carries out of how the imagination helps us acquire natural and supernatural knowledge. It is safe to say, however, that the treatment of the imagination in Ignatius's life story *concurs* with Thomas's theoretical discussions. The *Autobiography* also enhances the ethical component of the imagination which Aquinas, to my knowledge, does not expand on, although he does not exclude it. Ignatius's discernment of spirits always leads him to make a decision and act on it: his imagination, swayed by grace, has an eminently practical tone. More generally, Aquinas, following the general Dominican preference for the intellect over the will, does not spend much time analyzing how the imagination connects to human emotions and affectivity. By contrast, Ignatius's feelings and will are well connected

---

129. Ignatius, *Autobiog*, 28.
130. Ironically, though, in view of Ignatius's canonization, Jesuit authorities quickly decided that the text of the *Autobiography* should no longer be circulated and read. Instead, the third General of the Society of Jesus, St. Francis Borgia, asked Pedro Ribadeneira to write an official biography. The original Spanish-Italian text, incredibly, was not published until 1904 in the *Monumenta Historica Societatis Iesu*. The original testament had been set aside for three centuries. See Dhôtel, introduction, 26.
131. Ignatius, *Autiobiog*, 49–55.

to the imagination in the *Autobiography*. Both for ethics and affectivity, therefore, Ignatius's narrative *complements* Thomas's theories and can be further taken to *challenge* contemporary Thomistic ethics to consider giving greater space to the imagination and its relation to emotions.[132]

Imagination According to the Spiritual Diary

The rather short, enigmatic document known as the *Spiritual Diary* gives us other insights into Ignatius's imagination. Even among Jesuits, rare are those who have actually read the diary, which runs some forty pages in Munitiz's and Endean's edition of Ignatius's *Personal Writings*.[133] In his 1987 edition, Munitiz had entitled the book "Inigo: Discernment Log-Book."[134] It is, in fact, a rather dry compilation of diary entries from February 2, 1544, to February 7, 1545, most of which are just mentions of tears (or the absence thereof) at Ignatius's daily Mass. At first glance, therefore, there is not much in that book that could strike the reader's fancy as imaginative. The text we know as the *Spiritual Diary* is all that is left from a bundle of pages[135] that was burned, then was enshrined in a silver reliquary where it stayed, unread, until the early 20th century; it was first published in 1934.

The first half of the *Spiritual Diary*, however, from February 2 to April 4, 1544, offers more substantial entries than "tears" or "no tears." During those two months, Ignatius tried to discern God's will about rules on poverty in the nascent Society of Jesus. He wanted to make a decision, and that desire informed his daily meditation and Mass. The entries for those two months show how comfortable Ignatius felt in the world of visions, in compliance with what Gonçalves da Câmara says in the Epilogue to the *Autobiography*.[136] Nonetheless, an attentive study by Pierre-Antoine Fabre[137] reveals that things were not so simple for Ignatius and his spiritual imaginings during those two months. The title for the entries as of February 12 is "About the Persons Who Hid Themselves," viz. the three Persons of the Trinity, whom Ignatius was desperately seeking to see, in order, allegedly, to make a final decision about Jesuit poverty. He was in fact greatly used to seeing those three Persons, but for nine weeks, God withdrew his favor from Ignatius's imagination—or so it seems.

---

132. See Pamela M. Hall, "Towards a Narrative Understanding of Thomistic Natural Law," in *Medieval Philosophy and Theology* 2 (1992), 56n8, on how Martha Nussbaum has repeatedly criticized Aquinas for disregarding Aristotle's account of the imagination in the field of ethics.
133. See *Personal Writings*, 67–109.
134. Joseph A. Munitiz, *Inigo: Discernment Log-Book* (London: Inigo Enterprises, 1987).
135. Ignatius, *Autobiog*, 63–64.
136. Ignatius, *Autobiog*, 63–64.
137. Pierre-Antoine Fabre, introduction to "Journal des motions intérieures," in Ignace de Loyola, *Écrits*, ed. Maurice Giuliani, SJ (Paris: Desclée de Brouwer-Bellarmin, 1991), 313–18.

Fabre notes that Ignatius had already made up his mind about poverty on February 8, after using his reason (in conformity with *Spiritual Exercises*, [178] ff.) to draw up a chart of pros and cons "in having a fixed income for the churches of the Society of Jesus."[138] Fabre's bold but credible claim is that Ignatius's seeking out the image of the three Divine Persons was really more for his own spiritual enjoyment than for decision-making. Nonetheless, Fabre adds, the very absence of Ignatius's preferred spiritual image, far from quashing his earlier decision, actually confirmed his election of poverty by means of a *poverty of images*. Rather than a "confirmation" of his decision, Ignatius thus obtained a "conformation" to the essential poverty of the Trinity itself.[139]

In fact, however, during those "Trinity-poor" months, Ignatius was not totally deprived of spiritual visions through his imagination. Our Lady, Jesus, and even an unfocused image of the three Divine Persons did take form in his *phantasia*. But the lack of detail and richness in this impoverished imagination led Ignatius to grow in one of the virtues he extols in the *Spiritual Exercises*, respect or reverence,[140] both towards God the Creator and towards his creatures, through spiritual and actual poverty.[141] Ignatius was thus led, by an impoverished imagination of God, to see poverty and the poor with respectful eyes. Actual poverty is baseless if not chosen on the base of the grace of the spiritual poverty which Jesus extols in the Beatitudes.[142]

In short, the *Spiritual Diary* teaches us how *even the absence of images in the imagination can increase the theological virtues* of faith, hope, and charity. Ignatius's desperate attempts at grasping a mental image of the Trinity as he discerned rules of poverty for the Society illustrate how free God is to intervene in the human imagination and correct false imaginings that an evil spirit or human sin have brought about. Even the absence of a particular image, under divine light, can lead to making the right decision according to the Gospel.

In this, Ignatius's *Spiritual Diary confirms* and slightly *completes* Thomas's account of the imagination. In his *De Prophetia*, Aquinas considers how God may reveal a supernatural reality to a person without adding any new images, but simply by giving the *lumen propheticum* that elevates pre-existing images in the prophet's imagination to a supernatural level. Aquinas also mentions how angels and demons can work on a person's imagination to lead her closer to God or farther away. Ignatius confirms this by his diary's details (though he likely would never have dreamed of labelling himself a prophet, even in Aquinas's wide under-

---

138. See SpDiar, 70–72.
139. Fabre, introduction, 315.
140. Ignatius, SpEx, 289.
141. SpEx, 312.
142. Mt 5:3.

standing of the term!). Through his extreme experience and its dry narration, he also completes Aquinas's account by considering how even the absence of an image can move the imagination. It is, of course, noteworthy that Ignatius, by the grace of God, steered clear of the very example of sinful imagining which Aquinas made, viz. self-imagining the three Divine Persons as three human persons. However deprived of God's imaginative revelation of that mystery, Ignatius did not make up for that lack by successfully falling into the sin of irreverent imaginings.

Imagination According to the Spiritual Exercises

Finally, Ignatius's *Spiritual Exercises* provides us with many valuable insights about how the imagination can serve in the spiritual life, so that (i) God reveals himself to us and so that (ii) our faith may grow in response to this intimately revealed new knowledge. In many key meditations and contemplations of the *Exercises*, Ignatius inspires or instructs the "exercitant"[143] to use her imagination. Let us give a synthetic view of his instructions.[144]

The first instance where Ignatius instructs the exercitant to use the imagination actively is the "Meditation on Hell" in the First Week of the Exercises.[145] Many other instances happen in the other Weeks during Gospel-based contemplations, such as the "Call of the Earthly King,"[146] the "Contemplation on the Nativity,"[147] or the nightly "Application of Senses" on the Gospel story contemplated during the day.[148]

What are the qualities of the imagination in the *Exercises*? First of all, Ignatius's imagination is realistic and Christocentric. Ignatius lived in a time where imagery was rife; the late Middle Ages was highly imaginative and visual, sometimes shockingly so.[149] In this context, Ignatius avoids both traps of iconolatry and iconoclasm. He taps into the imagination of those whose spiritual life he would improve, but never imposes on them any particular detailed vision of his. This respect for the exercitant mirrors, one could say, Aquinas's understanding of prophecy, where the prophetic light is more crucial than any novel

---

143. In Ignatian lingo, the person who does or, better, "receives" the *Spiritual Exercises*.

144. For greater detail, see McLeod, "Use of the Imagination," n109; Peter-Hans Kolvenbach, SJ, "Images and the Imagination in the Spiritual Exercises: A Talk Given by Father General on June 30, 1986 to the Members of the IX Course on Ignatian Spirituality Organized in Rome by the Center for Ignatian Spirituality," 11–32.

145. See Ignatius, SpEx, 298–99.

146. SpEx, 303–4.

147. SpEx, 303–4.

148. SpEx, 307–8.

149. See, e.g., chapter 12 of Johan Huizinga, *Autumntide of the Middle Ages: A Study of Forms of Life and Thought of the Fourteenth and Fifteenth Centuries in France and the Low Countries* (Leiden: Leiden University Press, 2020).

mental images. Ignatius's instructions for spiritual directors in the *Exercises* are sober, based on Scripture, but not in a slavish, fundamentalist way. One of the Exercises' key principles is found at the end of Annotation 2: "it is not so much knowledge that fills and satisfies the soul, but rather the intimate feeling and relishing of things."[150] Combined with the "Principle and Foundation" that we must cleave to created things only insofar as they help us towards the end for which we have been created—"to praise, reverence, and serve God our Lord, and by so doing, to save [our] soul"—it is clear that Ignatius calls our imagination to be free in God, through God, and for God.[151] Although Thomas would certainly not contradict Ignatius on the desirability of divine and human freedom, it is not a point that he makes explicitly in his account of the imagination, whether natural or supernatural. Here, Ignatius *completes* Thomas.

Ignatius's goal, in short, is to make divine Revelation more real for the exercitant, so that his faith can also be more real. *Ignatius's focus is not on particular images; it is on setting the imagination on fire for God and for the real.* This is evidenced particularly by the three Meditations on Sin[152] where the subject matter is invisible, incorporeal.[153] Again, here, Ignatius *concurs* with Thomas's philosophical and theological accounts of the imagination, especially the analogical use of phantasms of corporeal objects to ponder the incorporeal.

Let us make a final comment on the text of the *Spiritual Exercises*. It is as dry as a syllogism, albeit in a different way: but it is made to strike the imagination. On a first level, this is because the booklet is to be read by the director, not by the exercitant. On a second level, this apparent paradox should lead us to be wary of our preconceptions about the imagination. We would gladly hold that our imagination is best fired by wild, exuberant descriptions of all sorts in sagas and novels. The biblical text, and more so still, the text of the *Spiritual Exercises*, beg to differ. At times, the less is said, the freer the imagination is, both for God and for us. Poetry, in its interplay of word and silence, of metaphors and allusions, is another great example of this reality.

Conclusion

In his Preface to René Lafontaine's theological *magnum opus* on the *Spiritual Exercises*, Mark Rotsaert comments that this work's goal is not

---

150. See Ignatius, SpEx, 283. On the philosophical and theological implications of this principle, see François Marty, SJ, *Sentir et goûter: Les sens dans les "Exercices spirituels" de saint Ignace* (Paris: Cerf, 2005).
151. SpEx, 289.
152. See SpEx, 294–99.
153. See SpEx, 294, and the detailed research work in Étienne Lepers, SJ, "Rendre visible ce qui est invisible: La comparaison dans les deux premiers Exercices," *Christus* 133 (1987): 100–110.

to know if Ignatius is to be located more in the line of Saint Thomas than in the line of authors from the Franciscan family.... One of the achievements—and not the least—of this thorough theological research is to highlight how much Ignatius's *Exercises* are a text of the Church. During the entire work, the text of the *Exercises* is illuminated by the Church's theological treasure through the ages.[154]

Ignatian scholars today often highlight how much Ignatius was indebted to monastic and Franciscan sources, especially in the *Spiritual Exercises*. The Basque founder nonetheless also implicitly concurs with Aquinas's views on the imagination.[155] He further adds thoughts drawn from experience on how the imagination relates to emotions and ethics, which can complement and challenge the theories of Thomas himself or of those who fill the varied schools of Thomist thought.[156] As for the imagination, then, in conclusion, Thomas does ponder and present a descriptive cognitive system. What Ignatius observes and offers, though, is not so much a prescriptive spiritual method (as I suggested initially), as a realistic experience, whose spiritual, intellectual, and emotional notes connect to an imagination that finds its freedom in Christ.

Carruthers's and Bauerschmidt's sharp comments on imagination, memory, and tradition should spur us on as we try to be faithful but creative theologians with our hearts, eyes, and imagination set on Jesus Christ, "the image of the invisible God." I have argued elsewhere that Christianity is a religion of the imagination because it is centered on Christ, whom Balthasar called the "image of Images."[157] The imagination helps us best when it finds its place as a humble servant, a truly free mediator in the image and likeness of Jesus Christ, the "one Mediator between God and humanity."[158] Despite their differences, Thomas and Ignatius would probably agree with that thesis on the grounds of their common love for Christ—at least, one can realistically imagine them doing so!

---

154. Mark Rotsaert, SJ, preface to Lafontaine, *L'originalité des Exercices*, 1.

155. A recent book agrees and expands on this point: Ludovico Nisi, *Fuori dell'anima: Ignazio di Loyola e l'immaginazione* (Milano: Mimesis, 2020). So ends the section on how the Thomist account of the imagination influenced Ignatius: he "operates an original synthesis between both the Dionysian-Thomistic background and late Medieval imaginative practices, drawn especially from the Cistercian school and the hallmark proponents of the *devotio moderna*" (179).

156. For an introduction to the many schools and "flavors" of Thomism, see the helpful contribution by Tracey Rowland, "Hallmarks and Species of Thomism," chapter 2 of *Catholic Theology* (London: Bloomsbury T&T Clark, 2017), 43–90.

157. See Steeves, *Grâce à l'imagination*, 425–43.

158. 1 Tm 2:5.

CHAPTER 6

Frequent Communion for the Greater Glory of God:
Thomas Aquinas and Ignatius of Loyola

Andrew Hofer, OP

Did Thomas Aquinas influence Ignatius of Loyola in the matter of frequent Communion?[1] This essay reconsiders Ignatius of Loyola's teaching on frequent Communion, a topic of much interest in Ignatian studies, by focusing on Thomas Aquinas and his influence—both explicit and implicit—on Ignatius's Eucharistic life and doctrine. It answers the question affirmatively. Most significantly, it argues that Ignatius continues Aquinas's distinctive teaching that frequent Communion, if practiced rightly, is more praiseworthy and gives God more glory than to abstain from Communion. We proceed in four steps.

First, we consider accounts of Ignatius on frequent Communion to show its significance for his thought and contribution to the Church. In doing this work, we will be attentive to how Thomas Aquinas appears (and does not appear) in the secondary literature on Ignatius and frequent Communion. Second, we recover what Thomas himself taught. This recovery of Thomas's doctrine is important in itself, as it corrects imprecise positions that have arisen in the academy. Edmond Dublanchy, for example, writes in his *Dictionnaire de Théologie Catholique* entry on frequent Communion, "The teaching of Saint Thomas was nearly unanimous among the contemporary and subsequent theologians."[2] Yet if we compare Thomas with other scholastic theologians such as

---

1. I dedicate this essay to the nineteenth-century Jesuits of Osage Mission, now Saint Paul, Kansas, who founded and staffed Saint Francis de Hieronymo Parish, established in 1847, the first Catholic church in what is now the Diocese of Wichita. I thank especially Frs. John Schoenmakers, John Bax, and Paul Mary Ponziglione of the Society for their ministry in my hometown. I thank the volume's editors and anonymous reviewers for their support and suggestions. I am also grateful to Fr. Jonah Teller, OP, for reviewing this essay and providing many helpful corrections, and to Fr. Reginald M. Lynch, OP, for his consulted expertise on the theology of the Eucharist in Aquinas and the sixteenth century. I am responsible for any remaining errors and infelicities.

2. E. Dublanchy, "Communion Fréquente," in *Dictionnaire de Théologie Catholique*, vol. 3, *Clarke–Czepanski* (Paris, 1908), 515–51, at 529 (my translation).

Peter Lombard and Bonaventure, we find Thomas's position to be more distinctive than Dublanchy leads us to believe. After reviewing what both Lombard and Bonaventure teach about frequent Communion, we study what Thomas says in his *Scriptum on the Sentences* and *Summa Theologiae*. Third, we examine select writings from and about Ignatius to show the Thomistic character of his Eucharistic practice, reasoning, use of patristic sources, and desire to help souls. Fourth, we sketch how the magisterium teaches about frequent Communion at the Council of Trent and the landmark document from Pius X's pontificate on the topic, *Sacra Tridentina Synodus* (1905). A brief conclusion summarizes the essay's findings.

With a renewed sense of what Aquinas thought about frequent Communion, when we consider Ignatius on the same topic we see better how he adapts scholastic (and particularly Thomistic) devotion and argumentation for the needs of his own day. In fact, we find that Thomas Aquinas's position on frequent Communion, as it was believed to be the practice of the primitive Church, finds a prominent *ressourcement* ally in Ignatius of Loyola for giving God greater glory.

Accounts of Ignatius of Loyola on Frequent Communion in Historical Context

The second rule in Ignatius of Loyola's *Rules for Thinking, Judging, and Feeling with the Church* stipulates, "We should praise confession to a priest, reception of the most blessed Sacrament once a year, and much more once a month, and still more every week, always with the required and proper conditions."[3] The support of Ignatius for frequent reception of Communion, typically stated in connection with prior confession, distinctively marks his spirituality and pastoral zeal, a charism leaving an imprint on the Society of Jesus. Through the Society's members who have implemented this vision in various ways, Ignatius's thinking has profoundly influenced the practice of the Catholic Church. Arguably, this Jesuit advocacy prepares for Pope Pius X's teaching on frequent Com-

---

3. Autographum: "La segunda. Alabar el confessar con saçerdote, y el resçibir del sanctíssimo sacramento vna vez en el año, y mucho más en cada mes, y mucho mejor de ocho en ocho días, con las condiçiones requisitas y deuidas." See the parallel columns of the Spanish and Latin texts of the *Spiritual Exercises* in *Monumenta Ignatiana*, vol. 1, second series, new edition, of MHSI 100, *Exercitia Spiritualia* (Rome: IHSI, 1969), no. 354; pp. 404, 406. The autograph text of the *Spiritual Exercises* in Spanish was left by Ignatius at his death in 1556, with some thirty-two minor corrections. For a review of the early textual witnesses, see the introduction to the *Spiritual Exercises* in *Ignatius of Loyola: Spiritual Exercises and Selected Works*, ed. George G. Ganss, SJ, Classics of Western Spirituality (New York: Paulist Press, 1991), 117–20. For the translation of the "Rules for Thinking, Feeling, and Judging with the Church," see pp. 211–14.

munion as well as the much further increase in frequent Communion among the faithful present at Mass after the Second Vatican Council.[4]

Jesuit historian John W. O'Malley states in a 1990 essay: "Probably at Montserrat, surely from the *Imitation* at Manresa, Ignatius learned the benefits of frequent Communion. Frequent Communion had been proposed by leading theologians like Jean Gerson in the early fifteenth century. To say the least, it had not caught on even in most convents and monasteries, where generally five or six times a year was considered a safe norm."[5] O'Malley recognizes that the Jesuits "for the most part had nothing new to say about the benefits to be derived from receiving the Eucharist."[6] He continues, "If you want to know what they thought, read the pertinent chapters from the fourth book of the *Imitation [of Christ]*."[7] O'Malley then notes two points of emphasis of the early Jesuits: the Eucharist as nourishment for one's ongoing spiritual pilgrimage and overcoming worthiness-unworthiness arguments from medieval spirituality and theology concerning the Eucharist's reception.[8]

O'Malley's work can be seen within the context of twentieth-century Ignatian scholarship on the history of frequent Communion. After the Decree on Frequent and Daily Reception of Holy Communion on December 20, 1905, during the

---

4. John Hardon writes, "In view of the subsequent major role which his followers were to play in promoting the cultus of the Eucharist, St. Ignatius of Loyola should be regarded as the pioneer apostle of frequent Communion in modern times." See John A. Hardon, SJ, "Historical Antecedents of St. Pius X's Decree on Frequent Communion," *Theological Studies* 16, no. 4 (1955): 493–522, at 498. Hardon notes that before the nineteenth century 220 Jesuits were known to have written one or more ascetical works on the Eucharist, including some exclusively on the subject of frequent communion (500n32). Liturgical scholar Robert Taft writes, "The greatest and most successful liturgical movement in Catholic history is surely the movement for the restoration of frequent communion, sanctioned by Pius X." See Robert F. Taft, SJ, *Beyond East and West: Problems in Liturgical Understanding*, 2nd rev. ed. (Rome: Pontifical Oriental Institute, 1997), 105. For a comparison with other Churches on frequency of communion, see pp. 104–8. Taft calls the Orthodox practice on frequency of communion "less than ideal" (105).

5. John W. O'Malley, SJ, "Some Distinctive Characteristics of Jesuit Spirituality in the Sixteenth Century," chapter 10 of *Saints or Devils Incarnate? Studies in Jesuit History*, Jesuit Studies: Modernity through the Prism of Jesuit History, vol. 1 (Leiden: Brill, 2013), 165–80, at 168–69. This essay was originally published in *Jesuit Spirituality: A Now and Future Resource*, ed. John W. O'Malley, John W. Padberg, and Vincent T. O'Keefe (Chicago: Loyola Press, 1990), 1–20.

6. O'Malley, *Saints or Devils Incarnate?* 169.

7. O'Malley, *Saints or Devils Incarnate?* 169.

8. O'Malley, *Saints or Devils Incarnate?* 169. Lest one think wrongly about what is meant by the second, O'Malley's illustration from Nicolás Bobadilla in 1551 concerns a sinner's repentance from sin, going to confession, and then receiving the Eucharist. To miss the pairing of frequent communion with frequent confession would introduce something foreign to this Ignatian thinking. Frequent confession and communion is the second rule in the "Rules for Thinking, Feeling, and Judging with the Church"; frequent attendance at Mass, chants, prayers, and the Divine Office is the third. Communion was commonly given at times other than during Mass.

pontificate of Pope Pius X, Jesuits offered studies on Ignatius's teaching on Eucharistic reception. Justo Beguiriztáin contributed a little book on Ignatius as apostle of frequent Communion, and never mentions an influence of Aquinas.[9] L. Joseph-Marie Cros, in introducing a translation of the famous text on frequent Communion from the sixteenth-century Jesuit Christopher de Madrid, wrote "Saint Ignace de Loyola et la communion quotidienne" (1522–1557).[10] Cros mentions Aquinas only in reference to the Dominican teachers at the University of Ávila. When the Jesuits arrived in Ávila in 1551, Cros narrates, the practice of frequent Communion was not known. The people communicated once a year, and religious communicated six times a year, or at most, once a month.[11] In his 1955 *Theological Studies* article, John Hardon pairs Thomas and Bonaventure as typifying the medieval attitude toward Eucharistic reception before the Council of Trent: "In order to understand this anomaly [of having the faithful receive Communion at least at Christmas, Easter, and Pentecost] it is necessary to examine the ascetical principles that were currently in vogue, from the early thirteenth century to the Council of Trent." Hardon continues, "It is easy to trace these principles because they were substantially those of St. Thomas Aquinas and St. Bonaventure, who dominated theological thought in the Middle Ages."[12] From these perspectives, one might not suspect that Thomas Aquinas may have motivated Ignatius's fervor for promoting frequent Communion.

---

9. Justo Beguiriztáin, SJ, *The Eucharistic Apostolate of St. Ignatius Loyola*, trans. John H. Collins, SJ (Cambridge, MA: B. Herder, 1955). Cf. his *Ignacio de Loyola: apóstol de la comunión frecuente* (Barcelona: E. Subirana, 1909).

10. L. Joseph-Marie Cros, "Saint Ignace de Loyola et la Communion Quotidienne," *Études* 115 (April, May, June, 1908): 752–65. On p. 752, the first footnote explains, "The pages that follow form the preface of a translation, soon to appear, of a little work directed under the inspiration of Saint Ignatius, by Father Christopher de Madrid, SJ, *De frequenti usu sacramenti Eucharistiae sacramenti libellus*" (my translation from the French). For overviews of Madrid's 1556 work, itself influenced by Ignatius and his trusted Tridentine theologian and papal advisor Alphonsus Samerón, see Hardon, "Historical Antecedents," 500–501 and John W. O'Malley, *The First Jesuits* (Cambridge, MA: Harvard University Press, 1993), 154–55. Madrid's work has been reprinted multiple times. For this research, I consulted this edition: R. P. Christophori Madridii Doctoris Theologi Societatis Iesu, *De Frequenti Usu Sanctissimi Eucharistiae Sacramenti Libellus* (Cologne: Apud Balthasarum Clypeum, 1604).

11. Cros, "Communion Quotidienne," 760. A more recent researcher observes, "There is no doubt that the Society of Jesus played a major role in spreading the practice of frequent communion throughout Europe and beyond. However, that role can be exaggerated and the complexity of the historical record distorted. For instance, Joseph-Marie Cros asserted in 1907 that the reception of the sacrament in Spain was rare and that it was basically introduced there by the Society. . . . Yet the fact is that frequent communion, although not common, was debated with intensity by Spanish theologians." See Rady Roldán-Figueroa, *The Ascetic Spirituality of Juan de Ávila (1499–1569)*, Studies in the History of Christian Traditions (Leiden: Brill, 2010), 146. We will return to Roldán-Figueroa's scholarship later in this essay.

12. Hardon, "Historical Antecedents," 496.

In his 1993 *The First Jesuits*, O'Malley repeats his emphasis of the Jesuit practice of promoting frequent Communion as continuing the teaching of *The Imitation of Christ* and Jean Gerson, believed by early Jesuits and others to be its author. O'Malley writes, "The idea of frequent Communion, therefore, was not new. An effective advocacy originated in the Low Countries in the late fourteenth century, as the *Imitation* suggests."[13] Yet, O'Malley provides here another perspective:

> Despite much opposition, the Jesuits persisted. Why? Ignatius was early convinced that he and his companions were reinstituting in somewhat modified fashion a practice of the 'primitive church,' when the faithful communicated every day. One of his immediate sources for this idea was the *Summa theologiae* of Aquinas.[14]

To support this statement, O'Malley notes the letter of November 15, 1543, to Theresia Rejadella.[15] Neither the letter nor the edition's critical apparatus mentions Aquinas, although the practice of the primitive Church that Ignatius notes is indeed found in ST III, q. 80, a. 10. Referring to early ecclesial custom was common among scholastic theologians in different ways as we will see. *The Imitation of Christ*, however, avoids appeal to patristic authorities. O'Malley's reference leads us to look beyond that fifteenth-century work to the teaching of Thomas Aquinas, whom Ignatius chose for his Society's scholastic formation.

Thomas Aquinas on Frequent Communion for the Greater Glory of God

Any study of frequency of Communion in the thirteenth century must take into account the Fourth Lateran Council's canon *Omnis utriusque sexus*:

> All the faithful of either sex, after they have reached the age of discernment, should individually confess all their sins in a faithful manner to their own priest at least once a year, and let them take care to do what they can to perform the penance imposed on them. Let them reverently receive the sacrament of the Eucharist at least at Easter unless they think, for a good reason and on the advice of their own priest, that they should abstain from receiving it for a time.[16]

---

13. O'Malley, *First Jesuits*, 152.
14. O'Malley, *First Jesuits*, 153.
15. Ignatius of Loyola, Ep. 73, in *Monumenta Ignatiana ex autographis vel ex antiquioribus exemplis, Series Prima: Epistolae et Instructiones*, vol. 1 (Matriti: Typis Gabrielis Lopez del Horno, 1906), 274–76.
16. Fourth Lateran Council, can. 21; text and translation in *Decrees of the Ecumenical Councils*, ed. Norman P. Tanner, SJ, 2 vols. (Washington, DC: Georgetown University Press, 1990),

A modified form of this minimal Easter duty is still in effect for the Latin Church, as seen in the *Catechism of the Catholic Church* and *Code of Canon Law*.[17] A narrow focus on this canon, however, might obscure the debate that occurred among medieval canonists and scholastics regarding frequency of Communion. The canon determines the framework of subsequent pastoral thinking and practice, and it comes from Pope Innocent III, himself influenced by preceding theological and canonical debates.[18]

One way to trace scholastic arguments is to study the twelfth-century *Sentences* of Peter Lombard and subsequent commentaries.[19] In Book IV of the *Sentences*, Lombard addresses the cause of the Eucharist's institution as twofold: for the increase of virtue, namely of charity, and as medicine for our daily infirmity.[20] He provides a fuller array of authorities than anyone else in his time.[21] Almost all quotations are misattributed. Some of his authorities also appear in the *Decretum* and other canonical collections.[22] Lombard first quotes four authorities:

> Ambrose: If as often as Christ's blood is shed, it is shed in remission of sins, then I must always receive it; I, who always sin, must always have medicine.[23]
>
> Augustine: This oblation is repeated every day, although Christ suffered once, because every day we commit those sins without which mortal

---

1:245. For an overview of medieval canon law on communion, see Thomas M. Izbicki, *The Eucharist in Medieval Canon Law* (New York: Cambridge University Press, 2015), especially chapter 3, "Communion: Union with Christ and Unity in the Sacrament," 137–77.

17. *Catechism of the Catholic Church*, 1389 and 2042; *Code of Canon Law*, can. 920.

18. For analysis of Lothar of Segni/Innocent III on matters of communion, see Izbicki, *Eucharist in Medieval Canon Law*, 149–50.

19. I am using Peter Lombard, *Sententiae in IV libris distinctae*, 3rd rev. ed., ed. Ignatius C. Brady, 2 vols. (Grottaferrata: Collegii S. Bonaventurae ad Claras Aquas, 1971–1981). For the translation of Book IV used, see Peter Lombard, *The Sentences, Book 4: On the Doctrine of Signs*, trans. Giulio Silano, Mediaeval Sources in Translation, vol. 48 (Toronto: Pontifical Institute of Mediaeval Studies, 2010). I do not mean to suggest by this focus on Lombard that scholastic theologies of the Eucharist can be reduced to him and his commentators. For a look at the diversity, see Gary Macy, *The Theologies of the Eucharist in the Early Scholastic Period: A Study of the Salvific Function of the Sacrament according to the Theologians c. 1080–c. 1220* (Oxford: Clarendon Press, 1984). Macy dedicates only pp. 122–24 to "Peter Lombard and His School."

20. Lombard, *IV Sent.* Dist. 12, c. 6 (71).

21. Marcia L. Colish, *Peter Lombard*, 2 vols., Brill Studies in Intellectual History, vol. 41 (Leiden: Brill, 1994), 2:580.

22. For Gratian's *Decretum* I am using *Decretum Magistri Gratiani*, 2nd ed., vol. 1 of *Corpus Iuris Canonici*, 2 vols., ed. Aemilius Ludovicus Richter and Aemilius Friedberg (Leipzig: Tauchnitz, 1879).

23. Lombard, *IV Sent.* Dist. 12, c. 6 (71) (Silano, 65; translation altered). Ambrose, *On the Sacraments* IV, c. 6, no. 28. Also in *Decreti Tertia Pars de Consecratione* dist. II, c. 14.

infirmity is unable to live. And because we daily fall, Christ is daily immolated for us mystically.[24]

Gregory: For he gave to us this sacrament of salvation so that we may receive remission through this sacrament because we sin daily and he can no longer die. Daily, he is drunk and eaten in truth, but he remains whole and alive.[25]

Also, Gregory: It is called the mystery of faith, because you must believe that our salvation is to be found in it.[26]

Following this, a question is raised about receiving Communion daily. Here Lombard invokes the authority of Augustine's correspondence with Januarius, but the words are from the *Book of Ecclesiastical Teachings* now known to be by the fifth-century Gennadius of Marseilles. This quotation has great importance for disputes on frequent Communion:

> I neither praise (*nec laudo*) nor blame (*nec vitupero*) daily reception of the Eucharist; but I encourage all to receive Communion every Sunday. But if the mind remains in the thrall of sin, I say that the reception of the Eucharist burdens rather than purifies. And although one is vexed by sin, yet if he does not intend to sin again and makes satisfaction with tears and prayers, let him approach securely; but I say this of one whom mortal sins do not burden.[27]

Lombard immediately follows this with quotations attributed to Pope Fabian (d. 250) and Pope Anacletus (d. ca. 92), both found in Gratian's *Decretum* and not known to be authentic.[28] The first regards reception of Communion at least three times a year, Easter, Pentecost, and Christmas, unless one is impeded by crimes, and the second concerns how all should receive Communion who do not wish to be cut off from the Church.[29] Marcia Colish observes

---

24. Lombard, *IV Sent.* Dist. 12, c. 6 (71) (Silano, 65). Not Augustine, but Paschasius Radbertus (d. 865), *De corpore et sanguine Domini*, c. 9.

25. Lombard, *IV Sent.* Dist. 12, c. 6 (71) (Silano, 65). Not Gregory the Great, but Remigius of Auxerre (d. 908), *De everential missae*.

26. Lombard, *IV Sent.* Dist. 12, c. 6 (71) (Silano, 65). Not Gregory the Great, but Remigius of Auxerre, *De everential missae*.

27. Lombard, *IV Sent.* Dist. 12, c. 6 (71) (Silano, 65–66; translation altered). Not Augustine, but Gennadius of Marseilles, *Book of Ecclesiastical Teachings*, c. 53. Also in Gratian, *Decreti Tertia Pars de Consecratione* dist. II, c. 13.

28. Lombard, *IV Sent.* Dist. 12, c. 6 (71) (Silano, 66). Also in Gratian, *Decreti Tertia Pars de Consecratione* dist. II, c. 16 and c. 10. Notice that Lombard reverses the proper historical order, given in the *Decretum*.

29. Gratian gives a fuller quotation from Anacletus by adding: "For thus even the apostles mandated, and the holy Roman church holds" (my translation). See *Decreti Tertia Pars de Consecratione* dist. II, c. 10.

that, like his English contemporary Robert Pullen, Lombard does not take a stand on the frequency of Communion.[30]

Like so many other theological topics, it is fruitful in this matter of frequent Communion to compare Thomas Aquinas with his older contemporary Bonaventure, especially in their commentaries on the *Sentences*. Such has special warrant in this present research. Ignatius himself, in his *Rules for Thinking, Judging, and Feeling with the Church* favorably names three scholastics: "St. Thomas, St. Bonaventure, [and] the Master of the Sentences."[31] Bonaventure's *In IV Sent.* d. 12, p. 2, a. 2 has three questions.[32] In the first, Bonaventure asks whether we are bound to approach the sacrament of the Eucharist. In his reply, he quotes at length the pertinent canon of Lateran IV. The second asks, "Whether is it better for one who is free to approach frequently or infrequently," and the third pertains to abstaining from reception on account of bodily filth. For our present focus, we consider an argument from glory that Bonaventure gives in the second question.

The second question begins with several arguments in favor of frequent Communion, and then arguments against frequent Communion. One of these latter arguments pertains to the glory of God:

> Again, the glory of God is to be preferred to our convenience. The one who puts aside reception on account of the dignity of the sacramental reception, chiefly gives glory to God. The one who receives on account of the effects of the sacrament, serves his own convenience. Therefore, the one who delays does better than the one who receives.[33]

Bonaventure returns in response to this argument of God's glory by alluding to Augustine's ep. 54, where Augustine writes to the layman Januarius that both Zaccheus, who received the Lord into his house, and the centurion, who

---

30. Colish, *Peter Lombard*, 2:581.

31. In this eleventh rule, Ignatius instructs that we ought to praise both positive and scholastic theology. About the two, he says that it is more characteristic of Thomas, Bonaventure, Peter Lombard, and other scholastic teachers "to define and explain for our times the matters necessary for salvation, and also to refute and explain all the errors and fallacies. For the scholastic teachers, being more modern, can avail themselves of an authentic understanding of Sacred Scripture and the holy positive doctors. Further still they, being enlightened and clarified by divine influence, make profitable use of the councils, canons, and decrees of our Holy Mother Church." Ignatius, "Rules for Thinking, Feeling, and Judging with the Church," *Spiritual Exercises*, 212.

32. For the three questions of article 2, I am using the text of *S. Bonaventurae Opera Omnia*, vol. 4 (Quaracchi: Collegium S. Bonaventurae, 1889), 294–98. Translation taken from Bonaventure, *Commentary on the Sentences: Sacraments*, Works of Bonaventure, vol. 17, trans. J. A. Wayne Hellman, OFM Conv., Timothy R. LeCroy, and Luke Davis Townsend (St. Bonaventure, NY: Franciscan Institute Publications, 2016), 305–15.

33. Bonaventure, *In IV Sent.*, dist. 12, p. 2, a. 2, q. 2, s.c. 4 (Hellman, 309).

did not, honored the Savior and received mercy (Lk 19:6 and Mt 8:8).[34] Bonaventure writes:

> To the last, it must be said that they both render glory to God, both the one who eats with reverence and the one who abstains out of reverence. For just as Augustine says, both the centurion who did not want him to enter his home honored the Lord, and so does Zacchaeus who welcomed him into his home.[35]

Here Bonaventure faithfully reproduces Augustine's teaching to Januarius, without showing any preference for one action over the other. It would be good for us to see that teaching in its original context. In the letter, Augustine gives arguments from imagined opponents, one opposing and the other supporting daily Communion. He writes, "One perhaps settles the dispute between them more correctly who warns them above all to remain in the peace of Christ, but let each do what he piously believes according to his faith should be done."[36] Later in the letter Augustine adds, "This food only refuses to tolerate contempt, just as the manna refused to tolerate boredom. The apostle, after all, says that it is received unworthily by those who do not distinguish this food from other foods by the veneration due to it alone" (cf. 1 Cor 11:29).[37] In the corpus of this question, Bonaventure would prefer people to be warm in their Eucharistic devotion. He says that it is praiseworthy (*laudandum est*) to receive Communion daily if people judge themselves to have the devotion of the primitive Church. He does not stop there but goes on to say that it is also praiseworthy (*laudandum est*) to receive Communion rarely if people judge themselves to be among the frigid in the Church of the final state (*in statu Ecclesiae finali*).[38] If people find themselves somewhere in between, then their practice should be between those two extremes.

Besides commenting more about frequency of Eucharistic reception on the *Sentences* than this brief excerpt, Bonaventure writes elsewhere on the topic, including in his *Instruction for Novices* (ca. 1260).[39] Bonaventure recommends

---

34. See Augustine of Hippo, Ep. 54.4, in *Sancti Aureli Augustini Epistulae I-LV*, ed. K. D. Daur, CCSL 31 (Turnhout: Brepols, 2004), 228–29. I am also using the translation of Ep. 54.3.4 in *Letters 1–99*, trans. Roland Teske, SJ, ed. Boniface Ramsey, Works of Saint Augustine II, vol. 1 (Hyde Park, NY: New City Press, 2001), 211–12. Augustine considered his two epistles to Januarius (*epp.* 54–55) to be so important that he reviewed them as two little books in his *Retractationes* II, 20.

35. Bonaventure, *In IV Sent.*, dist. 12, p. 2, a. 2, q. 2, ad 4 (Hellman, 311).

36. Augustine, Ep. 54.4 (Teske, 211–12).

37. Augustine, Ep. 54.4 (Teske, 212).

38. Bonaventure, *In IV Sent.*, dist. 12, p. 2, a. 2, q. 2, ad 4.

39. I am using the text of Opusculum 20, *Regula Novitiorum*, in *S. Bonaventurae Opera Omnia*, vol. 8 (Quaracchi: Collegium S. Bonaventurae, 1898), 475–90. Translation from *Writings Concerning the Franciscan Order*, trans. Dominic Monti, OFM, Works of St. Bonaventure, vol. 5 (St. Bonaventure, NY: The Franciscan Institute, 1994), 145–75.

daily confession for them, and requires them to confess every third day and make a general confession yearly.[40] As for frequent Communion, he takes a very different approach. Bonaventure says to them: "I will not be so bold as to counsel you on the frequency of receiving Communion, except to counsel Augustine's advice." Bonaventure then quotes from what we now know is Gennadius found in the *Sentences*, "I neither praise nor blame daily reception of the Eucharist...."[41] Gennadius, thought to be Augustine, neither praises nor blames daily Communion, a position we saw in Augustine's *ep*. 54, and Bonaventure continues to follow suit. While we will see certain similarities with Aquinas's approach, Bonaventure was cited by those who opposed frequent Communion in the sixteenth century, according to Christopher de Madrid.[42] We can underscore that Bonaventure is, in a sense, perfectly Augustinian in a position of neutrality.

When Thomas writes his *Scriptum on the Sentences*, he devotes two articles to *In IV Sent*. d. 12, q. 3, one on frequency of Communion and the other on abstention from Communion.[43] The first article has four *quaestiunculae*: the first begins with objections against frequent Communion; the second begins with objections in favor of daily Communion; the third begins with objections in favor of receiving only once a year; the fourth begins with objections in favor of the possibility of communicating more than once daily. Notice the movement of the first through third little question, and especially how the second begins with the opponents who *favor* daily Communion.

In response to the first *quaestiuncula*, Aquinas gives an argument for spiritual nourishment as akin to physical nourishment. It is necessary to take physical food frequently to restore the physical loss due to the body's heat and labor. In the same way, Aquinas reasons, "from innate concupiscence and by the occupation with externals there arises a loss of the devotion and fervor according to which man is recollected unto God; and so it is necessary that these losses be restored many times, lest a man become completely alienated from God."[44]

---

40. Bonaventure, *Instructions for Novices*, c. 3.2 (Monti, 158).

41. Bonaventure, *Instructions for Novices*, c. 4.4 (Monti, 160).

42. Madrid, *De Frequenti Usu*, 25. For analysis, see Roldán-Figueroa, *Ascetic Spirituality of Juan de Ávila*, 127. Comparing Thomas and Bonaventure, Joseph Stadler writes, "St. Bonaventure (1221–1274) had been even more exacting than St. Thomas, and in conclusion had admitted that the condition of proper dispositions for the daily reception of Holy Communion was fulfilled in very few (*paucissimus*) cases." See Joseph Nicholas Stadler, *Frequent Holy Communion: A Historical Synopsis and a Commentary*, The Catholic University of America Canon Law Series 263 (Washington, DC: The Catholic University of America Press, 1947), 14–15. Stadler cites Bonaventure, *In IV Sent.*, dist. 12, a. 2, q. 2.

43. Text and translation of the *Scriptum* taken from Thomas Aquinas, *Commentary on the Sentences Book IV, 1–13*, trans. Beth Mortensen (Green Bay, WI: Aquinas Institute, Inc., 2017) with translation altered at times.

44. Aquinas, *In IV Sent*. D. 12, q. 3, a. 1, qc. 1 (Mortensen, 561).

Here Aquinas strikingly describes devotion as an effect of Eucharistic reception, rather than a cause whose absence would signal that one should not receive.

In response to the second *quaestiuncula*, Aquinas says that two things are required on the part of the recipient: desire for union with Christ, which love causes, and reverence for the sacrament, which pertains to the gift of fear. "Now the first incites one to frequent this sacrament daily, but the second restrains one from it."[45] Aquinas then focuses on the communicant's experience. If one notices an increase of love and no diminishment of reverence, then that one should communicate daily. But if someone notices that reverence is diminished and fervor not much increased, that one should sometimes abstain in order to approach later "with greater reverence and devotion" (*cum majori reverentia et devotione*). Aquinas quotes Augustine's *ep.* 54 regarding Zacchaeus and the centurion, a passage not found in Lombard's *Sentences*, but in Bonaventure's commentary on it as we have seen: "One says that the Eucharist should not be received every day, someone else may approve its daily reception; let each one do what he conscientiously believes should be done according to his own faith."[46] Aquinas's conclusion, like Augustine's, is that mercy follows both Zacchaeus's welcoming Christ and the centurion's protestation of unworthiness to receive the Lord. In this, we find Aquinas similar to Bonaventure in following Augustine's neutrality.

In response to the third *quaestiuncula*, Aquinas reviews the different customs of the Church in light of what he sees as a historical decline of fervor: daily communion at the beginning of the Church, then at least three times a year because of the solemnity of those days, then at least once, at Easter. During Aquinas's time, he complains, many are not found fit even for that. But then he states, "And although one is not permitted to ignore the statutes of the Church, nevertheless it is permitted to communicate many times. Hence Augustine praises receiving Communion every Sunday, and so someone may communicate many times a year."[47] Notice now that Aquinas emphasizes frequent, even weekly reception on Sundays, a practice that the Church permits.

As for the fourth *quaestiuncula*, Aquinas makes an exception for a priest who may need to celebrate Mass more than once a day, but he discourages others from receiving Communion more than once a day. For the concern about the removal of venial sin that may occur many times in a day, he comments that we have other remedies besides receiving Communion.

---

45. Aquinas, *In IV Sent.* D. 12, q. 3, a. 1, qc. 2 (Mortensen, 561).
46. Aquinas, *In IV Sent.* D. 12, q. 3, a. 1, qc. 2 (Mortensen, 561). Cf. Augustine's Ep. 54.3.4.
47. Aquinas, *In IV Sent.* D. 12, q. 3, a. 1, qc. 3 (Mortensen, 562). Mortensen's note identifies this authority of Augustine as his Ep. 54, but it is Gennadius of Marseilles, *Book of Ecclesiastical Teachings*, c. 53.

In the second article, we find also three *quaestiunculae*, each beginning with objections that argue for abstaining from Communion. Aquinas, not surprisingly, is against abstinence from Communion. The most significant arguments occur in the third *quaestiuncula*, which completes his discussion of distinction 12. This response concerns the good. Aquinas affirms that receiving the Eucharist is good by its genus, to take it is good *per se*, and to abstain from it is good *per accidens*, in that it is feared to be consumed inordinately. Since *per se* is better than *per accidens*, he observes that "simply speaking it is better (*melius*) to consume the Eucharist than to abstain from it."[48] Reception of the Eucharist should prevail over abstention, both because of the sacrament's effect and by reason of preparation, however little it may be, and also based on the comparison of the two virtues involved: charity for receiving, and fear for abstaining. Aquinas closes the response with: "But love prevails over fear."[49] Here he goes beyond the neutrality seen in Augustine's *ep.* 54 and some of Bonaventure's teaching, as well as certain of his own earlier formulations in the *Scriptum*.

The final argument of the article appears in the reply to the second objection regarding God's glory. Aquinas entertains an objection that it belongs to true charity to seek God's glory more than one's own benefit. It seems that if one abstains, one does that for God's glory. This is similar to what Bonaventure had considered. But Aquinas replies: "The glory and goodness of God is most in this, that he communicates himself to creatures according to their capacity. And so it seems to belong more to the glory of God (*magis videtur ad Dei gloriam*) that someone should come to Communion than that one should abstain."[50] The reasoning here recalls one tradition and prepares for another. Implicit is the Neoplatonic principle that the good is self-diffusive, an idea loved by Aquinas.[51] As Aquinas affirms elsewhere, "It pertains to the meaning of the *Summum Bonum* that in the highest way he should communicate him-

---

48. Aquinas, *In IV Sent.* D. 12, q. 3, a. 2, qc. 3 (Mortensen, 566).
49. Aquinas, *In IV Sent.* D. 12, q. 3, a. 2, qc. 3 (Mortensen, 566).
50. Aquinas, *In IV Sent.* D. 12, q. 3, a. 2, qc. 3, ad 2 (Mortensen, 566). Similarly, in ad 1, Aquinas emphasizes that although humility may make one abstain, charity is greater than humility.
51. For a study in comparison to the analyses of W. Norris Clarke, SJ, and Norman Kretzmann on *bonum diffusivum sui*, see Bernhard-Thomas Blankenhorn, OP, "The good as self-diffusive in Thomas Aquinas," *Angelicum* 79 (2002): 800–837. Blankenhorn writes, "Thomas Aquinas's teaching on the good as diffusive of itself is a rich and almost ignored aspect of his metaphysics and philosophical theology. It is key to his understanding of the act of creation, the interrelated nature of the universe, and theory of operation" (836). In Aquinas's writing, we see a too-little appreciated application to the communication of God's goodness in the Eucharist. For Aquinas on communication as applied to Christology, see John Emery, OP, "Aquinas's Christology of Communication," in *Thomas Aquinas and the Crisis of Christology*, ed. Michael A. Dauphinais, Andrew Hofer, OP, and Roger W. Nutt (Ave Maria, FL: Sapientia Press, 2021), 171–94.

self to the creature."⁵² By receiving God in Communion, rather than abstaining, we give him greater glory since we are open to God sharing his goodness in the highest way. Also, Aquinas's reasoning foreshadows what would become something of Ignatius's own counsel about deciding what should be done *ad majorem Dei gloriam*. That phrase became emblematic in the Jesuit tradition; its original meaning appears in various forms in Ignatius's writings for choosing to do what is more for God's glory.⁵³ Because God gives us his immense goodness, we can discern what renders greater glory to his majesty than what another action may render.

While Aquinas treats frequent Communion in other places, we focus now on his *Summa*'s treatment.⁵⁴ Even in ST III, q. 79, regarding the effects of this sacrament, Thomas offers an implicit argument for daily Communion in a. 4, on whether venial sins are forgiven in this sacrament. He relates Communion to daily physical food, which we saw in *In IV Sent*. d. 12, q. 3, a. 1, qca 1. He also quotes Ambrose's *On the Sacraments*: "Hence, Ambrose says that this daily bread is taken 'as a remedy against daily infirmity.'" ⁵⁵

In ST III, q. 80, on receiving the sacrament of the Eucharist, Aquinas begins with articles that pertain to the distinction between eating this sacrament sacramentally and spiritually.⁵⁶ He takes for his authority in the *sed contra* Peter Lombard's gloss on 1 Corinthians 11:29 regarding the two types of Eucharistic consumption.⁵⁷ Maintaining the importance of this distinction, Aquinas should

---

52. This pertains to the Incarnation in ST III, q. 1, a. 1, corp.

53. Walter Ong, SJ "A.M.D.G.: Dedication or Directive?" *Review for Religious* (September 1952), reprinted in *Review for Religious* 50, no. 1 (January–February 1991): 35–42. Ong writes, "'Greater,' it will be seen here, enters into the scheme precisely because there is question of comparing alternatives. The famous expression is thus as central as it is to the tradition that comes to us through St. Ignatius because it is inseparably engaged with the Ignatian activity of making a choice" (39–40). The idea appears over a hundred times in the Society's early *Constitutions*. See O'Malley, *First Jesuits*, 18.

54. For other treatments, see Aquinas's collection of authorities in his *Catena on Luke* 11, lect. 1 and his own comments on 1 Cor 11:27–34, where he emphasizes that love is preferred to fear. He recommends that "each one should consider in himself which effect the frequent reception of this sacrament would have in him" (*Commentary on 1 Corinthians* 11, lect. 7, no. 699). If he finds that frequent reception would help him make progress to the fervor of loving Christ and resisting sin, he should receive frequently. But if someone feels less reverence for this sacrament by receiving frequently, he should receive rarely. In other words, it is up to each one's personal experience regarding perceived growth in the spiritual life regarding frequent communion.

55. ST III, q. 79, a. 4, corp.

56. For a Thomistic review of spiritual communion with applications for recent events, see Paul Jerome Keller, OP, "Is Spiritual Communion for Everyone?" *Nova et Vetera* (English) 12, no. 3 (2014): 631–55.

57. Peter Lombard, Gloss on 1 Cor 11:29: "We say that there are two ways for this to be eaten, one sacramental by which both the evil and the good eat, the other spiritual by which only the good eat" (my translation). Aquinas has abbreviated the quotation in the *sed contra*. When

not be understood to mean that a non-sacramental only spiritual eating is the same as a sacramental and spiritual eating. He says that the very receiving of the sacrament brings more fully (*plenius*) the effect of the sacrament than only the desire for the sacrament. Abstaining from Communion, while making a spiritual Communion in mere desire, is not as efficacious as receiving sacramental Communion from desire.

In ST III, q. 80, a. 10, Aquinas asks whether Communion may be received daily. Interestingly, while the objections in his *Scriptum* on Book IV of the *Sentences* were posed as arguments in support of daily reception, these *Summa* objections are posed to be against daily reception. Has Aquinas shifted his own position to be more in favor of daily Communion when he writes the *Summa*? Let us see.

Aquinas's cites what he says is from Augustine, but it is really Ambrose's *On the Sacraments*, in the *sed contra*: "This is our daily bread; take it daily, that it may profit you daily."[58] For the article's corpus, Aquinas distinguishes between the part of the sacrament itself and the part of the recipient. As for the sacrament itself, it is profitable to receive it daily in order to receive its fruits daily. He then identifies Ambrose's *On the Sacraments*, the first of Lombard's authorities, in his treatment of the question: "If as often as Christ's blood is

---

Aquinas cites the Gloss on the Pauline epistles, we should typically think of Lombard's Gloss rather than what became known later as the *Glossa Ordinaria*. Aquinas regularly cites Lombard's Gloss on the Psalms and the Pauline epistles when he names the Gloss on those biblical books.

58. Aquinas here credits Augustine, and Gilby notes, "Sermo suppos. LXXXIV. PL 39, 1908." See *Summa Theologiae*, vol. 59, *Holy Communion (3a.79–83)*, trans. Thomas Gilby, OP (New York: McGraw Hill, 1975), 75n7. The text is by Ambrose, *On the Sacraments* V, c. 4, no. 25. For a summary of the arguments of Otto Faller, SJ, for Ambrosian authenticity that accompany his edited text in CSEL 73, see Saint Ambrose, *Theological and Dogmatic Works*, trans. Roy J. Deferrari, Fathers of the Church, vol. 44 (Washington, DC: The Catholic University of America Press, 1963), 265–67. Also see Deferrari's translation in pp. 269–328. Ambrose probably wrote *On the Sacraments* before 392. Early manuscripts agree that the work is by Ambrose, but the work became identified as by Augustine in the Middle Ages. Cf. Thomas's crediting of Ambrose *In IV Sent.* IV, dist. 12, q. 2, a. 2; q. 3, a. 1, qc. 2, arg. 1. I am assisted by Mortensen, 559n81. For a study of Augustine in comparison to Ambrose in the *Summa*'s questions on the Eucharist, see Thomas Humphries, "'These Words are Spirit and Life': Thomas's Use of Augustine in *Summa Theologiae*, III, 73–83," *Recherches de Théologie et Philosophie médiévales* 78, no. 1 (2011): 59–96. Humphries provides a helpful argument about Aquinas treating Augustine and Ambrose as dueling authorities in terms not of dueling swordsmen but rather of dueling banjos. Unfortunately, the beginning of his first note does not convey how rare frequent communion was in Thomas's day: "At *Summa theologiae* (ST) 3.80.10 Thomas endorses daily reception of the Eucharist on the authority of Ambrose and Augustine, as well as the canonical tradition of the Church, but recognizes the contemporary practice of reception at least on Sundays" (59n1). It seems that Thomas not only tries to return the Church to the early practice of daily communion, he goes beyond Augustine's Ep. 54 and the *Book of Ecclesiastical Teaching* to emphasize that daily communion is objectively more praiseworthy than abstaining.

shed, it is shed in remission of sins, then I must always receive it; I, who always sin, must always have medicine."[59] As for the recipient, Aquinas teaches, "If anyone finds himself prepared daily for this, it is praiseworthy (*laudabile*) that he should receive daily." Aquinas then continues to quote from his patristic source cited in the *sed contra*: "Hence, Augustine after saying, 'Receive daily, that it may profit you daily,' adds: 'So live, as to deserve to receive it daily.'"[60] Aquinas continues that many suffer from impediments to this devotion, from an indisposition of either body or soul, and so he gives a counsel about how it is unrealistic for all the faithful to receive daily. He does not say, however, that abstaining from Communion is also "praiseworthy."[61] Instead, he stresses the possibility and benefit of the practice of daily Communion: "It is not useful (*utile*) for all people to receive this sacrament daily, but whenever (*quotiescumque*) someone should find himself prepared for it."

After concluding the corpus with the familiar patristic passage, "I neither praise nor blame daily reception of the Eucharist," Aquinas himself goes on to praise daily Eucharistic reception in the replies to the objections. Contrasting baptism, received only once, with Communion, Aquinas writes in reply to the first objection, "Since one has daily need of Christ's salvific virtue, one may praiseworthily (*laudabiliter*) receive this sacrament daily." Also, he says that this sacrament is food. We need bodily food every day, so too "it is praiseworthy (*laudabile*) to receive this sacrament daily."[62] That is why Jesus teaches us to pray, "Give us this day our daily bread." Aquinas cites what he believes to be Augustine's exposition on those words in support of daily Communion, but which actually come from Ambrose's *On the Sacraments*: "If you receive daily," namely this sacrament, "daily is it 'today' for you, because Christ rises daily, for it is today when Christ rises."[63] The reply to the second objection emphasizes how Christ's Passion is given daily through the memorial by way of food. This daily food was signified by how God fed the people daily in the Exodus through manna. The reply to the third objection concerns the desire of love for receiving and the filial fear and humility of reverence for abstaining. Aquinas quotes Augustine's *ep.* 54, which we have seen in his and Bonaventure's commentaries on the *Sentences*. Zacchaeus, who received, and the centurion, who did not

---

59. Ambrose, *On the Sacraments* IV, c. 6, no. 28 (Deferrari, 306). Cf. Gratian, *Decreti Tertia Pars de Consecratione* dist. II, c. 14 (Richter and Friedberg, *Corpus Iuris Canonici* 1:1319).

60. Ambrose, *On the Sacraments* V, c. 4, no. 25 (Deferrari, 317).

61. In ST III, q. 80, a. 11, after he mentions in the first objection that the centurion is praised for professing his humility not to receive the Lord, Aquinas replies that the purported humility of altogether refraining from receiving, which in fact would be to disobey the command of Christ and the Church, is not praiseworthy (*laudabilis*).

62. Cf. ST III, q. 79, a. 4.

63. Ambrose, *On the Sacraments* V, c. 4, no. 26 (Deferrari, 317).

receive, both acted rightly and are both models for people determining for themselves about daily Communion. Aquinas adds: "Nevertheless, love (*amor*) and hope, to which Scripture always calls us, are preferred to fear. Thus, when Peter said, 'Depart from me, Lord, for I am a sinful man,' Jesus replied, 'Do not fear'" (Lk 5:8, 10). In other words, Aquinas does not follow Augustine's neutrality in *ep.* 54, as did Bonaventure, but shows how love and hope are greater than fear, which the Lord wants banished.

The fourth and fifth objections concern time: not receiving Communion more than once a day and the ecclesial practices of receiving less frequently through the centuries. The fourth objection observes that the custom of the Church is not to receive multiple times each day, and so it seems that receiving more frequently is not more praiseworthy (*laudalius*). Aquinas replies that although it is true the custom of the Church is not to receive more than once a day, on account of the Lord's Prayer reference to "daily bread," when one who receives once a day, the unity of Christ's Passion is set forth. In reply to the fifth objection, Aquinas emphasizes how in the early Church the faithful would communicate daily. He then gives the canonical review of the decline. Aquinas cites the authorities of Pope Anacletus, Pope Fabian, and Pope Soter before quoting Pope Innocent's decree at the Fourth Lateran Council for reception "at least once a year," that is at Easter. He sees this time in terms of the Gospel passage: "after the increase of wickedness and the cooling of love in many" (Mt 24:12). Aquinas does not stop there at deploring the historical record of the cooling of Eucharistic devotion. He continues, "Nevertheless, it is counseled in the *Book of Ecclesiastical Teachings* to communicate on all Sundays."[64] By adding this, he shows that the Fourth Lateran Council should not be read as discouraging reception every Sunday, a practice advocated in the *Book of Ecclesiastical Teachings*, a work—as we have seen—that neither praises nor blames daily Communion. One can easily see why Aquinas would determine that one may not wholly abstain from Communion, as is asked in the following article.

In concluding this section, we find that, while retaining his pastoral concern for people's individual readiness and the need of each person to consider what would be personally best, Aquinas did shift his emphasis from the *Scriptum* to the *Summa* to be more explicitly in support of frequent, even in daily Communion.[65] Contrasted with what we see in sixteenth-century discussions, the *Summa* does not explicitly tie frequent Communion with preceding confession. Yet it should be noted that Aquinas prepared for his article on daily Communion in

---

64. Gennadius of Marseilles, *Book of Ecclesiastical Teachings*, c. 53.

65. Against the view of knowing precisely one's own state of soul, Aquinas recognizes that we cannot know from our own powers, and with certainty, that we are in a state of grace. See ST I-II, q. 112, a. 5.

part by considering matters of sin in earlier articles of the same question. Following upon the condemnation on one who eats and drinks unworthily (1 Cor 11:29), Aquinas teaches that one in mortal sin who receives Communion commits the mortal sin of sacrilege.[66] He does not explicitly give in the *Summa* the *Scriptum*'s argument that it is more for God's glory to communicate rather than to abstain, which differed from Bonaventure's account that both abstaining and receiving may give glory to God. In the *Summa*, Aquinas does say that daily Communion is praiseworthy, and does not say that rarely receiving Communion is praiseworthy. Giving glory to God is precisely done through actions that are themselves praiseworthy. Some actions give glory to God more than other actions and are thus more praiseworthy.[67] The virtue of religion gives shape to how we receive from God, give to him, and receive again from him.

Moreover, in ST III, q. 80, a. 10, Aquinas retained his respect for caution given in some authorities, but he added comments and scriptural quotations after patristic and magisterial texts in order to support frequent and even daily Communion. He both recovers a sense of promoting daily Communion from the early Church and moves beyond an Augustinian neutrality on whether one should receive daily or not. Seen within the context of the *Tertia Pars*, the *Summa*'s teaching on the Eucharist, which is Christ himself, in some way follows the first article of the *Tertia Pars* on the incarnation through a Dionysian adaptation of *bonum diffusivum sui*.[68] Thus, in his developed teaching Aquinas increases, rather than decreases, his sense of advocating frequent Communion for God's greater glory.

Ignatius of Loyola on Frequent Communion for the Greater Glory of God

Before tracing a Thomistic influence in Ignatius's Eucharistic thinking and practice, we begin with two cautionary notes understood in Rady Roldán-

---

66. ST III, q. 80, a. 4.
67. In fact, only insofar as we give God glory is our action in itself praiseworthy. Put otherwise, those who most give God glory are the most deified. This is why Aquinas concludes his question on religion with an article on whether religion is the same as sanctity. See ST II-II, q. 81, a. 8. For an example of seeing what is more praiseworthy in action, consider the treatment of obedience in ST II-II, q. 104, a. 3, corp. Cf. Jared Staudt, "Religion as a Virtue: Thomas Aquinas on Worship through Justice, Law, and Charity" (PhD diss., Ave Maria University, 2008), 185.
68. For a study, see Andrew Hofer, OP, "Dionysian Elements in the Christology of Thomas Aquinas: A Case of the Authority and Ambiguity of Pseudo–Dionysius," *The Thomist* 72, no. 3 (2008): 409–42, at 422–24. For Pseudo-Dionysius's presence in the *Summa*'s teaching on the Eucharist, see Joseph Wawrykow, "The Greek Fathers in the Eucharistic Theology of Thomas Aquinas," in *Thomas Aquinas and the Greek Fathers*, ed. Michael Dauphinais, Andrew Hofer, OP, and Roger Nutt (Ave Maria, FL: Sapientia Press, 2019), 274–302, at 295–98.

Figueroa's scholarship. As we saw in this essay's introduction, Ignatius of Loyola has been lauded as a pioneer of frequent Communion for modern times. That should be understood within a broader context of Ignatius's time. In addition, those influenced by Thomas Aquinas developed his teaching on this matter in divergent ways in the sixteenth century.

Rady Roldán-Figueroa observes that Ignatius's promotion of frequent Communion must be considered within his time and greater attention should be given to what "frequent" means. He maintains, "In his 1540 letter to the inhabitants of Azpeitia, Loyola recommends monthly reception of the sacrament, and in his other letters to lay people he does not mention daily Communion. Only in his 1543 letter to Sister Teresa Rejadell does he mention daily communion."[69] Comparing Ignatius to Christopher de Madrid, Roldán-Figueroa notes, "Madrid was more assertive about daily communion than Loyola ever was in his own writings."[70] In his advocacy for frequent Communion, Ignatius wrote the Jesuit Juan Nuñes, Patriarch of Ethiopia, that Communion was to be received after one went to confession and "not every day by whomsoever comes to the church."[71] Ignatius's second rule of *Rules for Thinking, Judging, and Feeling with the Church*, which began this essay, can be read precisely against not only a rigorism that discourages sacramental reception but also laxism. Ignatius, after all, advocated weekly Communion in the context of confession and "always with the required and proper conditions." In discussing "frequent communion," we must not impose today's Communion practices on Ignatius himself or on his Society before the changes that Pope Pius X made to the Catholic Church—not to mention what has occurred since the Second Vatican Council.[72]

In addition, Roldán-Figueroa exposes how Spanish Dominican friars in the time of Ignatius, who themselves were within the broad Thomistic tradition, covered the gamut of opinions on frequent Communion.[73] Roldán-Figueroa chooses the Dominican Juan de la Cruz, who authored his *Diálogo sobre la necesidad de la oración vocal* in 1555, as an example of opposition to frequent Communion.[74] Archbishop Bartolomé Carranza represents the moderate position,

---

69. Roldán-Figueroa, *Ascetic Spirituality of Juan de Ávila*, 166.

70. Roldán-Figueroa, *Ascetic Spirituality of Juan de Ávila*, 145.

71. Quoted in Roldán-Figueroa, *Ascetic Spirituality of Juan de Ávila*, 144. We will return to this letter, citing an edition different from the one that author used.

72. A Master of Ignatian spirituality, José García de Castro Valdés, SJ, writes, "Still in 1883, Jesuit Scholastics were not allowed to receive communion more than once a week." See his "Companionship in the Spirit: A History of the Spirituality of the Society of Jesus," *Estudios Eclesiásticos* 91, no. 356 (2016): 87–141, at 126.

73. For an overview of the history of Thomism, see Romanus Cessario, OP, and Cajetan Cuddy, OP, *Thomas and the Thomists: The Achievement of Thomas Aquinas and His Interpreters* (Minneapolis, MN: Fortress Press, 2017).

74. For analysis, see Roldán-Figueroa, *Ascetic Spirituality of Juan de Ávila*, 147–48.

and Domingo de Valtanás propounds the most enthusiastic defense of daily Communion.⁷⁵ Both of these latter men fell afoul with the Inquisition.⁷⁶ In other words, Thomas Aquinas' own Order shows a spectrum on this vital spiritual topic of debate during Ignatius's lifetime.⁷⁷ Some friars were held in suspicion for their writings that, *inter alia*, promoted frequent Communion. Given this caution, we now turn to how Thomas Aquinas influenced Ignatius's life and teaching for our study of frequent Communion for the greater glory of God.

As is well known, Ignatius's conversion of life followed his reading of Ludolph of Saxony's *Life of Christ* and a form of the Dominican James of Voragine's *Golden Legend* during convalescence from injury in 1521–1522.⁷⁸ Ignatius's autobiography relates his inspiration to imitate certain saints, "What if I should do what St. Francis did, and what St. Dominic did? . . . St. Dominic did this, therefore I have to do it; St. Francis did this, therefore I have to do it."⁷⁹ After his healing and stay of about a month in Montserrat in February–March 1522, he came to Manresa, a place of great interior struggle and mystical insight for him. From this time, Ignatius developed a profound Eucharistic life and teaching.⁸⁰

---

75. Archbishop Bartolomé Carranza wrote his *Comentarios sobre el everenti christiano* in 1558, and his confrere Melchor Cano took a lead in opposing him. Dominigo de Valtanás wrote his *Apologia de la frecuentación de la sacrosanta Eucaristía comunión* in 1558. For analysis, see Roldán-Figueroa, *Ascetic Spirituality of Juan de Ávila*, 148–51.

76. For a Thomistic account of Carranza's complex situation, with mention of the accusation against Ignatius, who was brought to the attention of the Inquisition, see Cessario and Cuddy, *Thomas and the Thomists*, 88–89. More recently, Cessario writes of Carranza: "This Spanish Thomist of sorts endured a long ecclesiastical trial and years of house arrest both in Spain and in Rome, where he died in 1576 shortly after having been acquitted of heresy charges." See Romanus Cessario, OP, "Sixteenth-Century Reception of Aquinas by the Council of Trent and its Main Authors," in *The Oxford Handbook of the Reception of Aquinas*, ed. Matthew Levering and Marcus Plested (Oxford: Oxford University Press, 2021), 159–72, at 168.

77. For Cajetan's position, see his comments on ST III, q. 80, a. 10. He introduces that article by describing it as pertaining to "daily celebration" (*In articulo decimo, circa quotidianam celebrationem* . . .). As Father Reginald M. Lynch, OP, has confirmed to me, Cajetan seems to discuss the priestly daily celebration of Mass, whereas Aquinas has in mind the faithful's Eucharistic reception in a. 10. Cajetan expounds on the quotation by Ambrose, thought to be by Augustine—"So live so that you may deserve to receive daily"—quoted in the article's corpus. He writes, "For the one who deserves to receive daily ought daily to be so disposed as to perceive the fruit of the Eucharist. Moreover, the fruit of this spiritual food is not only the actual refreshment of the spirit, but also the increase of grace (*augmentum gratiae*), since we are in a state of increase (*in statu augmenti*) through the entire time of this present life." See *Sancti Thomae Aquinatis Opera Omnia, Tertia Pars a quaestione LX ad quaestionem XC, cum commentariis Thomae de Vio Caietani*, vol. 11 (Rome: Ex Typographia Polyglotta, 1906), 242.

78. *Autobiography*, no. 5 (hereafter, *Autobiog*).

79. *Autobiog*, no. 7 (Ganss, 70).

80. For a fascinating comparison of Ignatius and Michelangelo on Eucharistic beauty, see Ann W. Astell, *Eating Beauty: The Eucharist and the Spiritual Arts in the Middle Ages* (Ithaca, NY: Cornell University Press, 2006), 190–226.

Was Ignatius influenced by Aquinas and the Dominicans at Manresa, where he first began to write the *Spiritual Exercises*? Yes. When Ignatius lived in Manresa for eleven months from March 1522 to February 1523, the Dominican priory of St. Peter Martyr was one of his places where he stayed.[81] The Dominican friars hosted him for perhaps twelve or thirteen days there in a ground-floor cell in April. Ignatius returned in August, and stayed in a different cell, when he was struggling with scruples. He usually attended Mass either at the cathedral or at the Dominican priory during his time in Manresa. His mystical experience of the Trinity on the priory's steps left an indelible impression on his piety, as he himself reports. In his *Autobiography*, Ignatius writes of mystical experiences he had at the priory in connection to the sacrifice of the Mass: "at the elevation of the Body of the Lord, he saw with interior eyes something like white rays coming from above. Although he cannot explain this very well after so long a time, nevertheless, what he saw clearly with his understanding was how Jesus Christ our Lord was there in that Most Holy Sacrament."[82] Among testimonies of Ignatius's mystical experiences reported in Manresa, Antoni Joan Cabrera, doctor and nephew of Gràcia Bechs, who was helping Ignatius, specified that Ignatius experienced a vision of the Body of Christ during Mass when the priest was celebrating at St. Thomas's altar at the priory.[83]

Ignatius came to have great respect for St. Thomas Aquinas's teaching, though it must be said that his interactions with Thomas's Order were rather mixed. After rudimentary studies in Barcelona, Ignatius studied at Alcalá almost a year and a half and then moved to Barcelona where Dominicans suspected him of heresy. He was imprisoned and later released without any condemnation of error. This was by no means the end of conflict with the Dominicans; he was questioned, imprisoned, and released soon after he moved to Salamanca. His experience, it seems, motivated Ignatius to study at length in Paris. Paris was his base from February 1528 to April 1535, during which his studies would have included Aquinas's teaching at the renowned Dominican school of Saint Jacques.[84] O'Malley writes about Ignatius and his first companions there: "At least some of them heard lectures by Matthieu Ory, Thomas

---

81. *Autobiog*, no. 23. Cf. Joan Segarra Pijuan, SJ, *Manresa and Saint Ignatius of Loyola*, trans. Patricia Mathews (Manresa, Spain: Ajunament de Manresa, 1992 [original Catalon edition in 1990, Spanish in 1991]). See especially Chapter 8, "The Dominican Priory," 65–68.

82. *Autobiog*, no. 29.

83. Pijuan, *Manresa and Ignatius*, 66–67, citing J. Calveras, *San Ignacio en Montserrat y Manresa, a través de los procesos de canozación* (Barcelona: Editorial Libreria religiosa, 1956), 194.

84. Ignatius's brief account of his Parisian years in his *Autobiography* belies their importance for the future Society. The *Autobiography* does not tell us "that while in Paris he attended lectures on Aquinas by the Dominicans at the convent of Saint-Jacques" (O'Malley, *First Jesuits*, 28).

Laurent, and Jean Benoist, and Ignatius seems to have been particularly favorable toward the Dominicans."[85] Speculating what from Peter Lombard and Thomas Aquinas most influenced Ignatius during his studies in Paris, George Ganss writes that "it would be natural for Ignatius to seek further light on those ideas of his own which by now had become especially important to him."[86] Surely, frequent Communion was one idea important to him, and we can easily imagine Ignatius reading Aquinas on this subject.

Ignatius's study assisted him in mandating the studies of his Society, as he wanted his men to have a more Thomistic education than he had during his eclectic studies in his Parisian years.[87] The original constitutions of the Society named "the scholastic doctrine of the divine Thomas" (*doctrina scholastica divi Thomae*) after the Old and New Testaments for theology and before mention of positive theology.[88] John O'Malley observes, "the Jesuits would never have selected Thomas unless they found in him elements compatible with their reli-

---

85. O'Malley, *First Jesuits*, 248.
86. George E. Ganss, SJ, general introduction to *Ignatius of Loyola: Spiritual Exercises and Selected Works*, 9–63, at 37.
87. O'Malley writes, "The Jesuits and Ignatius himself . . . rejected the eclectic program the companions followed at Paris and settled on Aquinas." See O'Malley, *First Jesuits*, 249. The Society explicitly came to propose a flexibility to depart from Thomas Aquinas when deemed opportune, and Alphonsus Salmerón claimed that the Society always had that leeway to favor the truth over Aquinas. See O'Malley, *First Jesuits*, 247–48, citing *Epistolae P. Alphonsi Salmeronis*, 2 vols. (Madrid, 1906–7), 2:709–15; cf. Aristotle's preference for truth over friends (and Plato) in *Nicomachean Ethics* I, c. 6 (1096a), and Aquinas's *Commentary on the Nicomachean Ethics*, I, lect. 6, no. 76. Also, see the pertinent analysis of Molina's formation and teaching in Romanus Cessario, OP, "Molina and Aquinas," in *A Companion to Luis de Molina*, ed. Matthias Kaufmann and Alexander Aichele (Leiden: Brill, 2014), 291–323.
88. I am using Sancti Ignatii de Loyola, *Constitutiones Societatis Iesu*, in *Constitutiones Societatis Iesu a Congregatione Generali XXXIV annotatae et Normae Complementariae ab eadem Congregatione approbratae* (Rome: Apud Curiam Praepositi Generalis Societatis Iesu, 1995), part 4, c. 14, no. 464 (pp. 170–71). O'Malley says it is not clear why Thomas was chosen, but suggests as reasons his unquestioned orthodoxy, the organization and comprehensiveness of the *Summa Theologiae*, special favor in Rome, and the Thomistic emphasis on the compatibility between nature and grace. He emphasizes that the first Jesuits would have surely differed from Thomas on account that Thomistic teaching is addressed "to the head, not the heart." See O'Malley, *Saints or Devils Incarnate?*, 188–89. For a prominent distinction by Ignatius himself between positive and scholastic theology, see the eleventh rule in the "Rules for Thinking, Judging, and Feeling with the Church." Given how Aquinas writes about the Eucharist, including in the Office of Corpus Christi and the *Adoro Te*, I wonder if Aquinas's Eucharistic writing would have been considered exceptional to the stereotypical description of Aquinas not addressing the heart. The division between scholastic and positive theology, present very much in sixteenth-century intra-Catholic debates (as well as in intra-Catholic debates of the twentieth century in the form of Neo-Scholastic and *Ressourcement* arguments), would be a poor framework to distinguish the practices of theology in Aquinas's thirteenth century, although some identify a similar rift between monastic and scholastic theology.

gious vision."[89] Here we can consider especially elements of Thomas in their Eucharistic vision.[90]

In Rome, Ignatius became a fervent promoter and member of Santa Maria sopra Minerva's Confraternity of the Most Blessed Sacrament founded by the Venetian Dominican Tommaso Stella, the Minerva's prior, in 1538.[91] After the Minerva gave a petition to Pope Paul III, the Pope issued the bull *Dominus Noster Jesus Christus* on November 30, 1539. In its beginning, the bull recognizes the Confraternity of the Most Sacred Body of Christ at the Minerva instituted by the Order of Friars Preachers, and lists in detail the indulgences and privileges given to the Minerva confraternity.[92] This should be seen against the broader movement of confraternities, including those dedicated to the Eucharist, at the time. A scholar of confraternities in sixteenth-century Italy, Christopher Black, describes the work of "the Corpus Christi or Sacrament confraternity, whose purpose was to encourage frequent Communion and

---

89. O'Malley, *First Jesuits*, 249.

90. In his arguments on the Eucharist and his Corpus Christi office, Aquinas strongly influenced the Latin Rite's Eucharistic doctrine and piety by the early sixteenth century, one of several significant features of his theological preeminence that Ignatius would have recognized. O'Malley writes that Bonaventure "never enjoyed an annual celebration in his honor like the one for Aquinas at the Minerva. For that matter, neither did any other medieval figure, including Francis of Assisi, enjoy such recognition.... However we explain the liturgical preeminence Thomas enjoyed in [Renaissance] Rome, it seems to correspond with the esteem in which his theology was held." See John W. O'Malley, SJ, *Praise and Blame in Renaissance Rome: Rhetoric, Doctrine, and Reform in the Sacred Orators of the Papal Court, c. 1450–1521* (Durham, NC: Duke University Press, 1979), 148. Thomas's mystical conversation with Christ on the Cross—"You have written well of me..."—came to be understood by some as pertaining to Aquinas's writing on the Eucharist. See John W. O'Malley, SJ, "Some Renaissance Panegyrics of Aquinas," *Renaissance Quarterly* 27, no. 2 (1974): 174–92, at 184–85 concerning Albertus Hunacius's praise of Aquinas.

91. I am grateful to Father Cassian Derbes, OP, of Santa Maria sopra Minerva, and its archivist Dott.ssa Fabiana Spinelli, who gave me electronic access to the Minerva archive. To underscore the significance of the Minerva for Thomistic study of the early sixteenth century, it can be noted that Cardinal Cajetan, who died in 1534, chose for his body's resting place "an unadorned grave in the vestibule of Santa Maria sopra Minerva, the church in Rome where Dominicans still guard the body of Catherine of Siena." See Cessario and Cuddy, *Thomas and the Thomists*, 80. For an account of the Most Blessed Sacrament Confraternity movement until 1539, see Giuseppe Barbiero, *Le confraternite del Santissimo Sacramento prima del 1539: saggio storico* (Vedelago: Aer, 1944). Although with Dominican and Thomistic influence and oversight, the Confraternity of the Most Blessed Sacrament was never considered, strictly speaking (*stricte loquendo*), one of the official confraternities of the Order of Preachers. After 1539, other Eucharistic confraternities looked to the Dominican friars at Santa Maria sopra Minerva for the rights and privileges granted to that confraternity by Pope Paul III on November 30, 1539. See Ludovicus I. Fanfani, OP, *De Confraternitaibus Aliisque Associationibus Ordini Fr. Praedicatorum Propriis: In Appendice de Confraternite SS. Sacramentum* (Rome: Apud Domum Generalitiam, 1934), 321–49, especially the Monitum on p. 321.

92. Barbiero, *Le confraternite del Santissimo Sacramento*, 263–68.

devotion to the sacraments by the laity."[93] The Roman Sacrament confraternity promoted Eucharistic piety from the late fifteenth century, and, after its founding in 1501, the Sacrament confraternity at S. Lorenzo in Damasco alla Cancelleria heavily influenced the papal curia.[94] "Further official encouragement came," Black writes, "with the 1539 Bull *Dominus Noster Jesus Christus* issued to the Sacrament confraternity in S. Maria sopra Minerva, which made available numerous indulgences and privileges for the laity of both sexes who venerated the sacrament and took communion frequently."[95] Stella's Minerva confraternity became the most influential Blessed Sacrament confraternity, and Ignatius took an active part to promote it.

In fact, in 1541, Ignatius and five other Jesuits joined that Minerva confraternity at the Church of Santa Maria della Strada, the church in Rome given by Pope Paul III that would be less than thirty years later the site of the Church of the Gesù.[96] About Ignatius entering the Minerva Confraternity and the Confraternity of the Holy Spirit in Rome, O'Malley writes, "He probably joined these institutions because of spiritual benefits like the special indulgences to which members had access, for he does not seem to have played an active part in either of them."[97] Early Jesuits became extremely active in promotion of many confraternities, continuing and transforming what the Dominicans and others had started before them. Peter Faber, for instance, founded a confraternity in Parma in 1539–40, which became known by the Society's own name, Compagnia di Gesù, and included the practice of weekly confession and Communion.[98] It is through this appreciation of the confraternities that we should read the first of the most famous letters of Ignatius on frequent Communion.[99]

---

93. Christopher F. Black, *Italian Confraternities in the Sixteenth Century* (1989; repr., Cambridge: Cambridge University Press, 2003), 29. For Black's description of how "frequent communion" was variably interpreted by confraternities, see p. 97. He also writes, "The Jesuits during their 1617 mission to Genoa introduced monthly general communions in the societies they sponsored" (67).

94. Black, *Italian Confraternities in the Sixteenth Century*, 96.

95. Black, *Italian Confraternities in the Sixteenth Century*, 96.

96. O'Malley, *First Jesuits*, 193. For Ignatius and some companions entering the Minerva's Confraternity of the Most Blessed Sacrament within a study of Jesuits and Italian confraternities, see Lance Gabriel Lazar, *Working in the Vineyard of the Lord: Jesuit Confraternities in Early Modern Italy* (Toronto: University of Toronto Press, 2005), 57–58.

97. O'Malley, *First Jesuits*, 193.

98. O'Malley, *First Jesuits*, 194–195.

99. Ignatius's letters fill twelve volumes of the *Monumenta Ignatiana* and are the largest extant correspondence of any sixteenth-century figure (O'Malley, *First Jesuits*, 2–3). For numerical comparisons of his letters numbered from 1 to 6,742, plus seventy-four additional letters discovered later in the twelfth volume, with other prominent writers of his age, see Ganss, *Ignatius of Loyola: Spiritual Exercises and Selected Works*, 325. We do not have any sermon by Ignatius on frequent communion, as we do not have a single sermon by him (O'Malley, *First Jesuits*, 95).

In August or September 1540, close to the time the Society of Jesus received its first papal approbation in the bull *Regimini militantis ecclesiae* (September 27, 1540), Ignatius wrote the people of Azpeitia, his hometown, and sent them the bull *Dominus Noster Jesus Christus* issued less than a year earlier.[100] Ignatius begins by recognizing his debt for his own beginning of life to Azpeitia, and recalls that he had visited his hometown about five years earlier. The letter shows Ignatius to be animated by the same desires as he had when he visited. He wants the people to experience the peace of the Lord. To have that peace it is necessary to love God and our neighbors for his sake. Indeed, the Apostle Paul says, "The one who has loved his neighbor has fulfilled the law" (Rom 13:8). Ignatius was wondering how he could fulfill these desires, and at this point, he introduces his focus:

> And as a great work presents itself, which God our Lord has wrought through a Dominican friar, a very great friend and acquaintance of ours of many years' standing (*nuestro muy grande amigo y concido de muçhos años*), to the honor and glory of the Most Blessed Sacrament, I determined to console and visit your souls in *Spiritu Sancto*, with the bull which the Señor Bachelor is taking with him, with the other indulgences which the bull contains; and these are so many and of such great value that I could not compute or overrate them.[101]

After that mention of Tommaso Stella and the papal bull the Minerva received, Ignatius urges his fellow townspeople to greater progress:

> I do pray, beseech and implore you for the love and reverence of God our Lord, that with great strength and great affection you should endeavor exceedingly to honor, favor and serve his only begotten Son Christ our Lord in this great work of the Most Holy Sacrament, in which his Divine Majesty is present, in his divinity and his humanity, as great, as entire, as mighty, and as infinite, as he is in heaven.[102]

---

100. Ignatius, Ep. 26, to the Citizens of Azpeitia, in *Monumenta Ignatiana, Epistolae et Instructiones*, 1:161–65. For translation, see that letter, numbered Ep. 10, in *Letters and Instructions of St. Ignatius of Loyola*, vol. 1, *1524–1547*, ed. A. Goodier, trans. D. F. O'Leary (1914; repr., New York: Cosimo, 2007), 43–47, which I am using, but at times altering. Also, I have consulted the partial translation of this letter, and the one to Theresia Rejadella, in "Two Letters of St. Ignatius on Frequent Communion," *The Woodstock Letters* 37, no. 3 (1908): 348–50, which identifies these letters as Ep. 21 and Ep. 48 in Carlos Ramón Fort, *Cartas de San Ignacio de Loyola*, vol 1. See also the partial translations in Beguiriztáin, *Eucharistic Apostolate*, 14–18. For the importance of these two letters, consider the Thomistic scholar Lawrence Feingold's extensive quotations that take up one page in a nine-page review of the entire Catholic history of frequent communion. See Lawrence Feingold, *The Eucharist: Mystery of Presence, Sacrifice, and Communion* (Steubenville, OH: Emmaus Academic, 2018), 561–69, at 565.
101. *Monumenta Ignatiana, Epistolae et Instructionae*, 1:162–63.
102. *Monumenta Ignatiana, Epistolae et Instructionae*, 1:164.

Ignatius wants the people to make some rules in the confraternity so that members confess and receive Communion once a month, voluntarily and without penalty of sin. He urges them to do this because the spiritual profit would be incalculable.

Ignatius then reviews the history of the practice of receiving Communion, which reveals a gradual cooling of devotion. At the beginning of the Church, people received daily. Then the practice became weekly. Much later, when true charity was decreasing even more, all communicated on three principal feasts of the year, leaving people free to do so more frequently. Ignatius then says how so many now receive Communion only once a year, "so great is our coldness and weakness" *(por la nuestra tanta frialdad y enfermedad)*.[103] Such a review echoes Aquinas's in ST III, q. 80, a. 10, ad 5, including the language of coldness, a common image deployed by writers. Ignatius urges, "Let it then be our business, for the love and spirit of such a Lord as ours, and to the great benefit of our souls, to revive and refresh in some measure the saintly customs of our fathers; and if we cannot do all, at least let us do something, confessing and communicating, as I said, once a month."[104] Those who want to do so more frequently are supported by St. Augustine and all the holy doctors, Ignatius continues, giving what were believed to be Augustine's words, which we know come from Gennadius: "I neither praise nor blame daily communion." He emphasizes that the passage goes on to say, "I recommend receiving communion every Sunday." The first part is how Aquinas concluded the corpus of ST III, q. 80, 10, and the second part is what Aquinas added to the end of ST III, q. 80, ad 5. Thus, Ignatius's letter, which promotes the Minerva's confraternity, resembles St. Thomas's teaching in emphasizing the same aspects of a patristic source.[105]

On November 15, 1543, Ignatius wrote from Rome to Sister Theresia Rejadella, a nun with whom he had known since his studies in Barcelona (1523–25).[106] One of the matters Sister Theresia had asked him was about daily Communion. Jesuit Father Justo Beguiriztáin praises Ignatius's reply as containing "a eucharistic doctrine so conformable to the decree of Pius X on

---

103. *Monumenta Ignatiana, Epistolae et Instructionae*, 1:164.

104. *Monumenta Ignatiana, Epistolae et Instructionae*, 1:164.

105. On May 24, 1541, Ignatius writes to his sister a brief letter mentioning frequent confession and communion as well as her spiritual progress in grace "to the greater glory of his Divine Majesty" (*á mayor gloria de su diuina magestad*). Ignatius also gives her sets of blessed beads (*quentas*), which William Young has identified as having been rosaries. For the text, see Ep. 29 in *Monumenta Ignatiana*, 1:170–71, and translated as Ep. 11 in *Letters and Instructions*, 1:48–49, and as Ep. 29 in *Letters of St. Ignatius of Loyola*, trans. William J. Young, SJ (Chicago: Loyola University Press, 1959), 50.

106. Ep. 73, *Monumenta Ignatiana, Epistolae et Instructionae*, 1:274–76. I am using the translation of Ganss, *Ignatius of Loyola: Spiritual Exercises and Selected Works*, 340–41, with my alteration.

frequent and daily Communion that of itself it suffices to place the holy founder of the Society of Jesus in the first rank of the saints and doctors who have written in behalf of frequent communion."[107] It is more strikingly Thomistic than the letter to Azpeitia. The following gives Ignatius's response and adds citations to Aquinas, inserting Ignatius's Spanish with comparisons to Aquinas's Latin at times.

> Regarding daily Communion, we should recall that in the primitive Church everybody received daily (*en la primitiua yglesia todos se comulgauan cada día*),[108] and that since that time there has been no ordinance or document of our Holy Mother the Church or of the holy doctors, either positive or scholastic, against a person's being able to receive Communion daily if so moved by devotion.[109]

Ignatius then continues with three patristic points, all of which he claims are from Augustine. The first is from Gennadius's *Book of Ecclesiastical Teachings*, and the second, mentioned parenthetically, is from that same work. The third is from Ambrose's *On the Sacraments*. All three references are also found in ST III, q. 80, a. 10.

> And while St. Augustine did say that he neither praised nor blamed the daily reception of communion[110] (although elsewhere he exhorted all to receive every Sunday),[111] he states later on, speaking of Christ our Lord's most sacred body, "This is our daily bread; therefore live in such a way that you can receive it every day" (*más adelante dize, hablando del cuerpo sacratíssimo de Christo N. S.: este pan es cotidiano; luego así viuid, como cada día podáis recibir*).[112]

Ignatius next applies these principles to Sister Theresia's case, taking into consideration her conscience, her love, and her experience of spiritual growth:

> This being the case, even in the absence of so many good indications or salutary motions we can rely upon the good and solid witness of your own

---

107. Beguiriztáin, *Eucharistic Apostolate*, 17.
108. Cf. ST III, q. 80, a. 10, ad 5: "in everenti Ecclesia, quando magis vigebat everent fidei Christianae, statutum fuit ut quotidie fideles communicarent."
109. *Monumenta Ignatiana, Epistolae et Instructionae*, 1:275 (Ganss, 340–41). Cf. Aquinas's review of the Church's teachings in ST III, q. 80, a. 10, esp. ad 5.
110. Cf. ST III, q. 80, a. 10, corp.
111. Cf. ST III, q. 80, a. 10, ad 5.
112. *Monumenta Ignatiana, Epistolae et Instructionae*, 1:275–76 (Ganss, 341). Cf. ST III, q. 80, a. 10, sed contra and corpus: "Unde Augustinus, cum dixisset, accipe quod quotidie tibi prosit, subiungit, sic vive ut quotidie merearis accipere."

conscience. That is, given all things are lawful for you in our Lord, if—barring obvious mortal sin or anything you can deem to be such—you judge that your soul derives more help and is more inflamed with love for your Creator and Lord (*que vuestra ánima más se ayuda y más se inflama en el amor de vuestro criador y señor*),[113] and if you receive communion with this intention, having found by experience that this most holy spiritual delicacy offers you sustenance, peace, and tranquility (*hallando por esperiencia que este santissimo manjar espiritual os sustenta, quieta y reposa*),[114] preserving and advancing you in his greater service, praise, and glory, so that you have no doubt about this, then it is licit, and indeed would be better, for you to receive communion every day (*en su mayor seruicio, alabanza y gloria, no dubitando, os es lícito, y os será mejor comulgaros cada día*).[115]

Ignatius closes his letter by recalling God's infinite goodness and his own poverty in goodness. Perhaps in Ignatius's invocation of the *Summum Bonum*, we see something akin to Aquinas's interest in the experience of the divine goodness in the Eucharist:

> On this point and on some others I have spoken at length with Araoz, who will deliver this letter. Referring you to him in our Lord regarding all matters, I close, praying God our Lord by his infinite clemency to guide and govern you in all things through his infinite and supreme goodness (*por la s[u in]finita y suma bondad*).[116]
> Poor in Goodness (*De bondad pobre*), Iñigo[117]

The *Summum Bonum* appears again in a later letter on frequent Communion. In 1545, when writing to Francis Borgia, before Francis became a Jesuit, Ignatius notes that Francis receives frequently. He writes:

> In addition to the great increase of grace the soul obtains in receiving its Creator and Lord, this frequent reception is a very principal and special reason why he does not allow the soul to remain obstinate in sin. As soon

---

113. Cf. Aquinas, *In IV Sent.* D. 12, q. 3, a. 1, qc. 2: "Unde si aliquis experimentaliter cognosceret ex quotidiana sumptione fervorem amoris augeri, et reverentiam non minui."
114. Cf. ST III, q. 79, a. 1: "Et ideo omnem effectum quem cibus et potus materialis facit quantum ad vitam corporalem, quod scilicet sustentat, auget, reparat et delectat, hoc totum faciet hoc sacramentum quantum ad vitam spiritualem."
115. *Monumenta Ignatiana, Epistolae et Instructionae*, 1:276 (Ganss, 341). Cf. Aquinas, *In IV Sent.* D. 12, q. 3, a. 2, qc. 3, sed contra: "multo melius est homini parato accipere quam ex reverentia desistere"; and *In IV Sent.* D. 12, q. 3, a. 2, qc. 3, ad 2: "unde magis videtur ad Dei gloriam pertinere quod aliquis ad communionem accedat quam quod abstineat."
116. Cf. ST III, q. 79, a. 1: "Et inde est quod ex virtute huius sacramenti anima spiritualiter reficitur, per hoc quod anima delectatur, et quodammodo inebriatur dulcedine bonitatis divinae."
117. *Monumenta Ignatiana, Epistolae et Instructionae*, 1:276 (Ganss, 341).

as it falls into sin, even in things which are quite small—granted anything can be called small, when the object is infinite—and, more, the *Summum Bonum* (*summo bien*) straightaway lifts it up, with greater powers, and with greater intention and firmness to serve more its Creator and Lord (*la leuanta presto con majores fuerças, y con major proposito y firmeza de más seruir á su criador y señor*).[118]

This letter can be compared to ST III, q. 79, a. 6. Aquinas says there that Communion's help to the soul can be likened to the two ways that one avoids bodily death. Just as food and medicine preserve the inner strength of a body, so Communion does that for the inner strength of a soul. Also, just as military arms protect a body from an exterior attack, so too Communion equips a soul against attack by the devils. In the reply to the third and last objection of that article, Aquinas says that not only does Communion give a soul an increase in charity and a decrease in cupidity, "it directly confirms the human heart in the good (*in bono*)."[119] While certainly Aquinas is not the only scholastic source available to Ignatius for his teaching (let alone other kinds of sources), Ignatius's counsel to Francis compares favorably to Thomas's teaching.[120]

We close our review of Ignatius's letters with two more. In early 1546, Ignatius gave an exhortation to the Jesuit priests selected to attend the Council of Trent. The Council had opened in December 1545, and Pope Paul III asked Ignatius for three theologians to advise papal legates. Ignatius wrote to his chosen priests an Instruction for the Sojourn at Trent.[121] Its eighth point for helping souls relates: "Exhort those with whom you come into contact to frequent confession, communion, and the celebration of Mass (*á confessar, comulgar y celebrar á menudo*). Have them make the Exercises and perform other works of piety; also encourage them to pray for the council."[122] While

---

118. Ep. 101, to Francis Borgia, in *Monumenta Ignatiana, Epistolae et Instructiones*, 1:339–42, at 341. For a partial translation, see Beguiriztáin, *Eucharistic Apostolate*, 18–19.

119. ST III, q. 79, a. 6, ad 3; cf. ST III, q. 79, a. 1: "Et inde est quod ex virtute huius sacramenti anima spiritualiter reficitur, per hoc quod anima delectatur, et quodammodo inebriatur dulcedine bonitatis divinae."

120. Besides this consideration of goodness, we could also think about how Aquinas considers creation to be very small compared to the Creator. One favorite patristic source for Aquinas on this is Gregory the Great's treatment of Benedict's mystical vision of creation being "*angusta*" (small or insignificant) when seeing the Creator in *Dial.* II.35.6. See ST II-II, q. 180, a. 5, arg. 3; ST II-II, q. 180, a. 5, ad 3; *Quodl.* I, q. 1, arg. 1; *In IV Sent.*, d. 45, q. 3, a. 1, s.c. 2.; *In IV Sent.*, d. 49, q. 2, a. 5, arg. 4; and *De Veritate* q. 8, a. 4, arg. 9. For analysis, see Andrew Hofer, OP, "St. Thomas Aquinas on St. Benedict," *American Benedictine Review* 71 (2020): 410–34.

121. Ep. 123, *Monumenta Ignatiana, Epistolae et Instructiones*, 1:386–89.

122. Translation altered from *Ignatius Writes to His Brethren: Fifty Selected Letters and Instructions of St. Ignatius of Loyola*, with commentary by Joseph N. Tylenda, SJ, https://www.library.georgetown.edu/woodstock/ignatius-letters/letter8#letter, accessed March 1, 2021.

such counsel is not distinctly Thomistic, it should be seen within the context of his previous letters that do convey striking resonances with Thomas Aquinas's thought. Our last letter, one we already saw in passing in Roldán-Figueroa's scholarship, can be a salutary reminder of putting Ignatius's teaching on frequent Communion in perspective. In his instructions in 1555 for ministering to the Ethiopians, he says to the Jesuit who was named Patriarch of Ethiopia about his people, "In bringing them to communion let them know that confession should precede, and that communion is not distributed any day to anyone who comes to the church."[123] Again, while not distinctly Thomistic, it too bears resemblances to Aquinas's pastoral concern of people's readiness. Both Aquinas and Ignatius express due caution regarding frequent Communion. Through these two letters, we see Ignatius's concern for frequent Communion during the Council of Trent. Ignatius died on July 31, 1556, almost eleven years after the opening of the Council of Trent's first session and over seven before the closing of its last session.

Frequent Communion at the Council of Trent and in *Sacra Tridentina Synodus*

Some authors describe the Council of Trent's teaching on Eucharistic reception as Thomistic, while others describe it as Ignatian.[124] Setting up the two as opposed schools of thought on this matter would be a false dichotomy. Reflecting on Trent, John O'Malley bemoans the scholastic influence on the Council's teaching on the sacraments, specifying the *Summa*'s teaching on the Eucharist:

> The theologians and bishops at Trent recognized and tried to observe the difference between dogma (or doctrine) and theology. The former con-

---

123. "y en el comunicarles enderezen que sea después de la confessión, y no cada día quienquiera que uiene á la yglesia." *Instructio P. Ioanni Nunnio et Sociis Data, Pro Aethiopiae ad Ecclesiam Catholicam Reductione*, dated 1555, in *Monumenta Ignatiania, Epistolae et Instructiones*, 8:680–90, at 684–85 (Young, *Letters of St. Ignatius of Loyola*, 385).

124. For a Thomistic connection, without mention of Ignatius, see Joseph Dougherty, *From Altar-Throne to Table: The Campaign for Frequent Holy Communion in the Catholic Church*, ATLA Monograph Series, no. 50 (Lanham, MD: Scarecrow Press, 2010), 6: "Trent could support more frequent Holy Communion because the ideal of it had been echoed for over a thousand years. Trent decreed that all those assisting at the Mass should receive Communion, and in this the council seems to have relied upon Aquinas." For an Ignatian connection, without mention of Thomas, see Beguiriztáin, *Eucharistic Apostolate*, 19: "We should bear in mind that in the publication of these eucharistic chapters of the Council of Trent Fathers Laynez and Salmerón of the Society of Jesus, first companions of St. Ignatius, had a great part. It should in no way surprise us, then, if these chapters are a faithful expression of St. Ignatius's enlightened and benevolent eucharistic teaching."

sisted in the fundamental teachings of the church, the latter in reflection on them, in explanations of them, and in systems to show their coherence with one another. The council was in principle concerned only with dogma, not with theology. Clear though this distinction was in theory, it was difficult to observe in practice. In the decree on justification, however, the council did so relatively successfully. It was less successful in the decrees on the sacraments. Scholasticism was the prevailing theological system at the council simply because the theologians had been trained in it. It left its mark on the sacramental decrees. This outcome is not surprising, of course, because during the Middle Ages the scholastics developed such a thorough theology of the sacraments. That development was nowhere more elaborate than on the Eucharist. Eleven "questions," divided into eighty-four "articles," are devoted to it, for instance, in Aquinas's *Summa Theologiae*.[125]

Regarding frequent Communion, in October 1551, during its thirteenth session, the Council of Trent exhorted all the faithful "to receive frequently that super-substantial bread and that it may truly be for them truly the life of the soul and the unending health of the mind; thus, strengthened by its force, may they be able after the journey of this wretched pilgrimage to reach the heavenly fatherland, there to eat without veil the same bread of angels which they now eat beneath the sacred veils."[126] In September 1562, during its twenty-second session, the Council taught, "The holy council would certainly like the faithful present at each Mass to communicate in it not only by spiritual affection but also by sacramental reception, so that the fruits of this sacrifice could be theirs more fully (*uberior*)."[127]

---

125. John W. O'Malley, *Trent: What Happened at the Council* (Cambridge, MA: Harvard University Press, 2013), 255. For study on Eucharistic sacrifice, see Reginald M. Lynch, OP, "The Reception of the *Summa Theologiae* on the Question of Eucharistic Sacrifice in the Early Modern Period" (Ph.D. diss., University of Notre Dame, 2020). Lynch identifies Cajetan's influence on Trent's teaching on the Eucharistic sacrifice in pp. 292–301.

126. Council of Trent, Session 13, October 11, 1551, Decree on the most holy Sacrament of the Eucharist, c. 8; text and translation in *Decrees of the Ecumenical Councils*, 2:697 (translation altered); cf. that decree's can. 9, on receiving communion at least once a year, at least at Easter. This decree could be used both in support of and in opposition to frequent communion. See Stadler, *Frequent Holy Communion*, 15–16.

127. Council of Trent, Session 22, September 17, 1562, Teaching and canons on the most holy sacrifice of the Mass, c. 6; text and translation in *Decrees of the Ecumenical Councils*, 2:734 (translation altered).

128. It stops before "so that the fruits of this sacrifice could be theirs more fully." For the translation I am using of the Sacred Congregation of the Council, *Sacra Tridentina Synodus*, December 22, 1905, see *The New Liturgy: A Documentation, 1903–1965*, ed. R. Kevin Seasoltz (New York: Herder and Herder, 1966), 11–15; text in *Acta Sanctae Sedis* 38 (1905): 400–406.

The Sacred Congregation of the Council's decree *Sacra Tridentina Synodus* in 1905 begins with that second quotation.[128] This action of Pius X's pontificate gives a landmark in the Church's history of teaching on Eucharistic reception. Interestingly, the decree narrates the historical shift differently from the medieval scholastics and writers of Ignatius's time regarding when frequent Communion became rare. It maintains that the first Christians daily hastened to this table of life and strength for the communion of the breaking of the bread. It continues, "The holy Fathers and writers of the Church testify that this practice was continued into later ages and not without great increase of holiness and perfection." Then the Congregation gives a vague expression for a shift before identifying the particular problem: "Piety, however, grew cold, and especially afterward because of the widespread plague of Jansenism, disputes began to arise concerning the dispositions with which one ought to receive frequent and daily communion." As Cornelius Jansen died in 1638, he cannot be blamed for the scarcity of the faithful receiving Communion frequently in earlier centuries, which Thomas Aquinas, Ignatius, and many others lamented. The Decree's numbered statements conclude, "Finally, after the publication of this decree, all ecclesiastical writers are to cease from contentious controversy concerning the dispositions requisite for frequent and daily communion" (no. 9). Some wonder if after the Second Vatican Council we have lost sight of certain basics that Pius X's pontificate presupposed when it authorized a cessation of controversy concerning dispositions requisite for frequent Communion, matters on which Aquinas, Ignatius, and Pius X would readily agree upon, but this query cannot be adequately considered here.

Conclusion

The exploration above asked if Thomas Aquinas's teaching on frequency of Communion influenced Ignatius of Loyola, lauded as a pioneer for the Church's modern practice. What has been discovered? Was Ignatius a Thomist in this respect? To summarize this study's findings, I offer four theses:

(1) Aquinas argues for not simply frequent but even daily Communion in his *Summa Theologiae*. This continues his teaching, which is different from Bonaventure's, about how receiving Communion gives more glory to God and is more praiseworthy than abstaining from Communion. Choosing actions that would give God greater glory was at the heart of Ignatius's discernment, and we have seen that his counsel for frequent Communion is expressive of that basic concern.
(2) Ignatius benefitted from Thomas and the Dominicans in both his intellectual formation and his devotional practice, and he wanted this to be the case for others. Having been himself educated in Thomistic

theology, Ignatius named Thomas Aquinas as the scholastic master of his Society in its early *Constitutions* (a choice eventually embraced by the Fathers of the Second Vatican Council in *Optatam Totius* 16). Ignatius also promoted membership in the Confraternity of the Most Blessed Sacrament, founded by his friend, the Dominican Tommaso Stella, and run out of the Dominican community of Santa Maria sopra Minerva.

(3) Ignatius's letters on frequent Communion, especially his letter to the nun Theresia Rejadella, in which he advocates for daily Communion, repeats and applies teaching found in Aquinas's own writings.

(4) Some scholars see the movement for frequent Communion as having its roots in Jean Gerson and the *Imitation of Christ*, but we have seen that Thomas Aquinas's teaching, which predates Gerson and the *Imitation*, offers ample resources for the approach Ignatius took in promoting frequent reception of the sacraments. For example, both Aquinas and Ignatius favor a return to the sources of the early Church against the chilled devotion that they notice in their own times.

It would be wrong to claim that Thomas Aquinas was the *only* influence on Ignatius of Loyola regarding the frequent reception of Communion. But we have good reason to conclude that Ignatius and his Society of Jesus were influenced by Aquinas in their Eucharistic teaching, including frequent Communion. The Jesuit Eucharistic zeal is a teaching stitched through with elements already taught centuries before by Thomas Aquinas, especially with his scholastic concern for the practice of the early Church. When we attend closely to the reasoning of Thomas Aquinas, such as his argument in the *Scriptum* that it is more for the glory of God to receive Communion than to abstain, and his greater advocacy in the *Summa* for even daily Communion, with the proper conditions met, we find that Thomas Aquinas's teaching would indeed benefit Ignatius's desire to shape his Society of Jesus in this central concern to help souls in the sacramental life. Choosing to adopt and adapt Aquinas's teaching on frequent Communion seems to be for Ignatius of Loyola *ad majorem Dei gloriam*.

CHAPTER 7

Ignatius and Aquinas on Mary

Sr. Theresa Marie Chau Nguyen, OP

For nearly five hundred years, the prominent sons of Saint Ignatius of Loyola (1491–1556)—from Jérôme Nadal (1507–1580), Ignatius's personal secretary, to the influential Jesuit patrologist Hugo Rahner (1900–1968)—have referred to St. Ignatius as "our Father, the theologian."[1] Avery Cardinal Dulles (1918–2008) examined the question "Is there an Ignatian Theology?" in a lecture series at Boston College on 18 November 1981. The lecture, which was revised and published in *Studies in the Spirituality of Jesuits*,[2] provides a valuable perspective for this volume of essays on the resonance of Thomistic principles in Ignatius's own thought. This essay focuses on the concurrences in Ignatius and Aquinas's Marian thought, and it will proceed in two main sections. The first will examine the prominence of Mary in Ignatius's devotional life, highlighting her part in his conversion and in the founding of the Society of Jesus. This will lead to an exploration of the *Spiritual Exercises*, which, as a seventeenth-century pious hyperbole held, was "dictated" to Ignatius by Mary herself.[3] The second section will elucidate the points of convergence between Ignatius's implicit Mariology and the salient points of Aquinas's own writings on the Blessed Virgin. Engaging Ignatius and Aquinas in dialogue on the Blessed Virgin Mary will reveal both the extent and limits of their concurrence. Herein, one can begin to unearth the points of contact between Ignatius and Mary (which are delightfully plentiful) and between Ignatius and Aquinas, which though less obvious, are also significant.

---

1. Hugo Rahner, *Ignatius the Theologian* (London: Geoffrey Chapman, 1968) 1; Rahner quotes Nadal's instruction concerning the plan of theological studies proposed by St. Ignatius: "He aqui a nuestro Padre téologo."

2. Avery Dulles, "Saint Ignatius and the Jesuit Theological Tradition," *Studies in the Spirituality of Jesuits* 14, no. 2 (March 1982): 1–21.

3. Various works examining this legend include A. Maas, SJ, "Did the Blessed Virgin Help St. Ignatius in the Composition of the *Spiritual Exercises*?" *Woodstock Letters* 24 (February 1895): 52–70; Francis J. Marien, SJ, "Our Lady and the Exercises," *Woodstock Letters* 82 (1953): 224–37; and Maurice Giuliani, SJ, "Le mystère de Notre Dame dans les Exercices," *Christus* 1 (July 1, 1954): 32–49.

The Virgin Mary as "Very Propitious before the Father"
The Lineaments of Mary's Significance for Ignatius's Pilgrim Journey

In the summer of 2006, two professors from Xavier University (Cincinnati, OH) made a ten-day pilgrimage between Spain and Rome, retracing Ignatius's steps and story. With their visit to all of the important Ignatian sites from the Loyola family castle to Ignatius's simple apartment next to the Gesù, Drs. Margo Heydt and Sara Melcher report their great surprise at encountering—in myriad dioramas, statues, and paintings—Ignatius's deep devotional relationship to Mary, which stood in stark contrast to "the minimal emphasis given in most Jesuit history accounts to this secret in the life of Ignatius."[4] They describe their discovery of "the secret agency of Mary as a hidden catalyst in the formation of the Society of Jesus through her influence on Ignatius."[5] Although an appropriate recognition of Mary's role in Ignatius's life is to be found in the standard texts on Jesuit history and its spirituality (such as the works of George E. Ganss and Joseph de Guibert[6]), the surprise of Drs. Heydt and Melcher is not uncommon, especially in the post-conciliar milieu which has not fully received the Second Vatican Council's teaching on Mary and the Church.[7] Similarly, attention to Mary in more recent Ignatian literature is also lacking. Despite this lacuna, a return to the sources on the life and writings of Ignatius robustly show that the Founder of the Society of Jesus had frequent recourse to Mary's intercession and maternal care, especially at crucial moments in his life. In this first section, I provide a sketch of that journey, highlighting details associated with Mary, so as to lay the groundwork for a theological analysis to come.[8]

---

4. Margo Heydt and Sarah Melcher, "Mary, the Hidden Catalyst: Reflections from an Ignatian Pilgrimage to Spain and Rome," in *Jesuit and Feminist Education: Intersections in Teaching and Learning from the Twenty-First Century*, ed. Joceyln Boryczka and Elizabeth Petrino (New York: Fordham University Press, 2012), 37–55, https://doi.org/10.5422/fordham/9780823233311.003.0003.

5. Heydt and Melcher, "Mary, the Hidden Catalyst," 37.

6. Ignatius of Loyola, *Ignatius of Loyola: Spiritual Exercises and Selected Works*, ed. George E. Ganss, SJ, Classics of Western Spirituality (New York: Paulist Press, 1991); Joseph de Guibert, SJ, *The Jesuits: Their Spiritual Doctrine and Practice*, trans. William J. Young, SJ (Chicago: Institute of Jesuit Sources and Loyola Press, 1964).

7. For more on the incomplete reception of Vatican II's Mariology, see Denis Farkasfalvy's discussion in *The Marian Mystery: The Outline of a Mariology* (New York: St. Pauls, 2014).

8. These abounding references to Mary have been documented in Simon Decloux, SJ, "Our Lady in Ignatian Spirituality: Mary in the Spiritual Diary of St. Ignatius," *Centrum Ignatianum Spiritualitatis* 19 (1988): 1–144; see also Louis Bonacci, SJ, *The Marian Presence in the Life and Works of Saint Ignatius Loyola: From Private Revelation to Spiritual Exercises—The Cloth of Loyola's Allegiance* (doctoral diss., University of Dayton, 2002).

Born into a noble Basque family, Ignatius was raised in strong Catholic piety and practice.[9] The Loyolas had a chapel in the family castle and Ignatius would often pray there before the image of the Annunciation.[10] Ignatius's mother died soon after his birth, and his sister-in-law Doña Magdalena filled that maternal role. It was also Magdalena who was Ignatius's primary caretaker during his convalescence following his injury in a battle at Pamplona in 1521. W. W. Meissner's psychological study of Ignatius and Ignatian spirituality posits that the young Iñigo's early trauma at the loss of his mother and the deep attachments he developed for his substitute mother provided "the psychic substratum that fed into Iñigo's conversion experience."[11] Ignatius's transference of the maternal ideal to Doña Magdalena and ultimately to the Virgin Mary would fuel his piety toward Mary as the paragon of virtue and feminine beauty, establishing her place in his spiritual journey.[12] Mary was the noble Lady to whom Ignatius offered himself throughout his life, first as a knight, then as a pilgrim and mystic.

The story of Ignatius's conversion is well known. Oft-recounted are the books providentially given to him to fill his days while bedridden: translations of the *Vita Christi* by Ludolph of Saxony and the *Flos sanctorum* by Jacopo of Voragine. Both works are, in a sense, of Dominican provenance. Jacopo was the Dominican Archbishop of Genoa, and although Ludolph of Saxony was a Carthusian when he wrote his "Life of Christ," he had spent the first half of his life as a Dominican friar, whence he likely received a Thomistic formation.[13] Less commonly known, however, are Ignatius's mystical experiences involving the Virgin Mary during this period of his convalescence. Ignatius reports in his *Autobiography* that he had been granted a vision of "the Mother and Child" as he lay awake one night, and this sight produced in him abounding consolation for a considerable time. Accompanying the experience was Ignatius's newfound disgust with his past life, especially with his offenses of the flesh. With that, as

---

9. For a standard biographical introduction, see Ganss's introduction to *Spiritual Exercises and Selected Works*.

*10. Hugo Rahner, *The Spirituality of St. Ignatius of Loyola*, 18; as cited in Robin Koning, "Revisiting the Marian Dimension of Ignatian Spirituality," in *Mariology at the Beginning of the Third Millennium*, ed. Kevin Wagner et al. (Eugene, OR: Wipf and Stock, 2017), 141.

11. W. W. Meissner, *To the Greater Glory: A Psychological Study of Ignatian Spirituality* (Milwaukee, WI: Marquette University Press, 1999), 22–23. Meissner's analysis is insightful but still in need of further evidence and explanation of how this "psychic substratum" contributed to his cooperation with the grace of his conversion.

12. Meissner interprets the vision of Our Lady and the Child Jesus that Ignatius received during his convalescence to be "the embodiment . . . [and] reflection of his idolized image of his own mother who had died so early, as well as the reflection of the lovely Magdalena toward whom unconscious libidinal impulses had been stirred." *To the Greater Glory*, 30–31.

13. Paul Shore, "The *Vita Christi* of Ludolph of Saxony and Its Influence on the *Spiritual Exercises* of Ignatius of Loyola," *Studies in the Spirituality of Jesuits* 30, no. 1 (1998): 1–32, at 2.

if by the hand of God, Ignatius was released from the hold of carnal desires. He states that "from that hour . . . he never again consented to the least suggestion of the flesh."[14] Beyond the images of Francis and Dominic which he encountered in the *Golden Legend* and which so inspired him toward holy things, it was the Madonna who was the pivotal catalyst for his conversion.

As these graces flowed through the hands of the Blessed Virgin and took hold of Ignatius, he assumed new ideals. His former worldly ambitions were replaced by a firm resolve to serve the Lord, and he explored the spiritual life with great tenacity. He recounts how his conversations with other members of the household thenceforth revolved around Godly topics and how he delighted to record his thoughts in a three-hundred-page manuscript, using red ink for the words of Christ, our Lord, and blue ink for those of "Our Lady."[15] As evidenced here and in Ignatius's later writings, he favored the proper noun "Our Lady" for the Blessed Virgin both for its noble, courtly connotations and its semantic association with Jesus Christ, "Our Lord."[16]

In late February 1522, Ignatius mounted a mule and left Loyola with an image of Our Lady of Sorrows in his prayer book, which he kept with him throughout his journey.[17] Ignatius traveled first to the shrine of Our Lady of Aránzazu in the village of Oñati where he made a vigil, committing himself to living a life like Jesus and vowing perpetual chastity to Our Lady. From there, he set out for Navarrete and Montserrat where he collected a debt from the duke's household. With this money, he gave to the poor and to the restoration of an image of Our Lady at Navarette which had fallen into disrepair.[18]

From Our Lady of Aránzazu to Our Lady of Montserrat and Manresa

In his *Autobiography*, Ignatius recounts an intriguing story about his journey toward Montserrat, where he found himself traveling alongside a Moor and a theological conversation unfolded between them. On the topic of the Blessed Virgin, the man confessed his faith in the virginal conception but refused to concede the idea that Mary remained a virgin in and after giving birth to Jesus.

---

14. Ignatius, *Vita*, 10; cf. Koning, "Revisiting the Marian Dimension of Ignatian Spirituality," 143. All references to Ignatius's autobiography (*Vita*) are from *Spiritual Exercises and Selected Works*, ed. George Ganss.

15. *Vita*, 11.

16. Faithful to Ignatius's own personal preference, this chapter will also employ the title "Our Lady" to refer to Mary.

17. Paul Dudon, *St. Ignatius Loyola*, trans. William V. Young (Milwaukee, WI: Bruce, 1949) 49, 70 as quoted (incorrectly) by Meissner, *Ignatius of Loyola: The Psychology of a Saint* (New Haven, CT: Yale University Press, 1992), 308.

18. *Vita*, 13.

Ignatius argued with his interlocutor to no avail and, after the man rode on ahead of him, indignation took hold of the fiery Spaniard. He felt it was his duty to defend Our Lady and considered riding ahead to stab the Moor and avenge her honor. Yet, as he remained conflicted about whether this was the right course of action, Ignatius gave the decision over to the donkey he was riding. If the donkey chose the path following after the Moor, Ignatius would indeed proceed with his violent machinations. Fortunately, at a fork in the road, the donkey chose a different route and Ignatius continued his pilgrimage.[19]

At the Chapel of Our Lady of Montserrat, Ignatius made a general confession of his entire life and concluded with an all-night vigil before the Black Madonna. It was the eve of the Annunciation, and Ignatius spent the entire night either on his feet or his knees—a great feat since his legs had not yet fully recovered from the battle wounds. After surrendering his sword and dagger to Our Lady, he donned a peasant's garb and left at the break of dawn.

Ignatius arrived at Manresa on March 25, 1522—another Marian feast day. He resided with the poor in the Hospital of Santa Lucía, caring for their bodily and spiritual needs, while often attending Mass at the Dominican priory. Manresa had many shrines dedicated to Mary, and one of Ignatius's favorite places to pray was the chapel of Our Lady of Viladordis.[20] But it was especially in a little cave near the Capuchin priory and on the banks of the Cardoner that Ignatius's spiritual doctrine came to maturity. There, he exercised extreme asceticism, immersing himself in prayer, fasting, and penances.[21] His penitential regimen brought him to deep psychological and spiritual crises, filling him with desolation and suicidal impulses. In the midst of all this, Ignatius likely had a Dominican spiritual director.[22] W. W. Meissner speculates on how this anonymous confessor must have been particularly instrumental in alleviating Ignatius's torment and leading him closer to God.[23]

---

19. *Vita*, 15–16.
20. Meissner, *Ignatius of Loyola*, 308.
21. Cf. SpEx 317. All references to Ignatius's *Spiritual Exercises* (SpEx) are from *Spiritual Exercises and Selected Works*, ed. George Ganss. Cf. Meissner, *To the Greater Glory*, 93. From July to October of 1522, Ignatius suffered a darkness of soul; he was plagued by "turmoil of spirit, inclination to what is low and earthly, restlessness rising from many disturbances and temptations which led to want of faith, want of hope, want of love."
22. Meissner, *To the Greater Glory*, 91–93.
23. Meissner states: "This Dominican priest . . . remains nameless and faceless to the eyes of history, but he undoubtedly served his function well in his efforts to aid the tormented pilgrim. . . . He offered advice and direction to his troubled penitent, probably serving in many ways as an auxiliary ego, assisting the pilgrim to discern more carefully, to integrate and master his overwhelming anxiety. In the midst of the pilgrim's scrupulous torment and depression, the confessor served as a wise teacher who helped the pilgrim to discern what was real from what was fantastic, helped him understand that there was a difference between impulses and graces from God and

These profound experiences contributed no little to Ignatius's spiritual doctrine. He asserts that the Lord graciously dealt with him "in the same way a schoolmaster deals with a child."[24]

Ignatius was formed through great suffering and mystical experiences, including visions of Our Lady. It was specifically while praying the Office of Our Lady at the steps to the door of the Dominican priory one day that Ignatius received a vision of the Trinity. On another occasion, he saw the humanity of Christ, and yet another time, he had a vision of Our Lady.[25] The postulator for the cause of his canonization reports that Mary appeared to Ignatius more than thirty times during his eight-month stay at Manresa.[26]

The Society: From La Storta to Our Lady of the Way

Ignatius began his studies in Paris in 1528, and by the time he received his Bachelor of Arts in 1532, he had an ardent group of companions around him. On the feast of the Assumption in 1532, Ignatius and six confreres pronounced their vows of poverty and chastity in the Chapel of St. Denis of Montmartre. They also vowed to make a pilgrimage to Jerusalem before heading to Rome to offer themselves in service of the Holy Father. All of this took place under the auspices of Our Lady, "helper and protector and special intercessor before her Son Jesus Christ our Lord."[27]

After his ordination to the priesthood on June 24, 1537, Ignatius prepared himself to receive a mission in Rome by forgoing the celebration of Mass for a year. He spent this time praying to Mary, that she might "be pleased to place him with her Son."[28] Near the end of 1538, about ten miles outside of the Eternal City, Ignatius received a profound mystical experience in the Chapel of La Storta.[29] His persistent prayers beseeching the intercession of Our Lady were answered when, in a vision, he saw God the Father and Jesus carrying the Cross.

---

temptations and delusions arising from the influence of the devil. By his advice, and even use of his confessional authority, he also served the important function of softening the severity of the pilgrim's superego." *To the Greater Glory*, 99.

24. *Vita*, 27.
25. *Vita*, 28–29.
26. John A. Hardon, *All My Liberty: Theology of the Spiritual Exercises* (Bardstown, KY: Eternal Life, 1998), 113–14.
27. Simão Rodrigues, *A Brief and Exact Account: The Recollections of Simão on the Origin and Progress of the Society of Jesus* (St. Louis, MO: The Institute of Jesuit Sources, 2004), 13–15, quoted in Koning, "Revisiting the Marian Dimension of Ignatian Spirituality,"145.
28. *Vita*, 96. This prayer already manifests the spiritual hierarchy Ignatius would employ and routinely prescribe: approach the Father through the Son, and the Son through his Mother.
29. Cf. Hugo Rahner, *The Vision of St. Ignatius in the Chapel of La Storta* (Rome: Centrum Ignatianum, 1975).

The Father spoke first to the Son, saying: "I wish that Thou take him for thy servant," and Jesus in turn spoke to Ignatius, saying: "I wish that you be my servant." Then, the Father spoke to Ignatius directly: "And I will be propitious to you at Rome." This vision filled Ignatius with light and consolation, perceiving that it was specifically through the intercession of Our Lady that the vision had been granted. Ignatius subsequently celebrated his first Mass at the Basilica of St. Mary Major on December 25, 1538.

After Pope Paul III's approval of the Society on September 27, 1540, Ignatius continued refining the *Constitutions*. Everyday, he would pray over some particular point and then offer Mass, asking for grace and clarity. This was another period of many mystical visions, "sometimes [of] God the Father, at other times all the three Persons of the Trinity, at other times Our Lady interceding, at other times her confirming [his decisions]."[30] One notes how the *Constitutions of the Society of Jesus* bear the traces of Ignatius's devotion to Mary. It prescribes that the brothers who cannot read should pray the rosary, and all vows were made before "the Virgin Mother and the whole heavenly court."[31]

Ignatius's diary entries between February 1544 and February 1545 regularly call upon the intercession of Jesus and his Mother, often invoked as "the two mediators" who are earnest and "willing to intercede with the Father."[32] The entry on 8 February 1544, for example, expresses Ignatius's desire "to make this offering to the Father through the mediation and prayers of the Mother and the Son." Ignatius often experienced the efficacious intercession of his "two mediators" so palpably that he would sob, being overwhelmed by "a complete security" that the Eternal Father would grant his request because of them.[33] Ignatius was confident in Our Lady's propitious pleading before the Father: "I seemed to feel the Heavenly Father showed himself propitious and kind—to the point of making it clear to me that He would be pleased if Our Lady . . . would intercede."[34] The founding of the Society finds a symbolic culmination in Rome, at the Church of Sancta Maria della Strada (Our Lady of the Way), the name of the first Jesuit parish and the site of the future Gesù Church.[35] "Our

---

30. *Vita*, 100.
31. Ignatius of Loyola, *Constitutiones Societatis Iesu*, in *Constitutiones Societatis Iesu a Congregatione Generali XXXIV annotatae et Normae Complementariae ab eadem Congregatione approbratae* (Rome: Apud Curiam Praepositi Generalis Societatis Iesu, 1995), IV.2.B, 343; V.4.2, 535.
32. Ignatius of Loyola, *Spiritual Diary*, in *Personal Writings*, 73–109; entry 5 February 1544.
33. SpDiar, 13 February 1544.
34. SpDiar, 15 February 1544.
35. There is surprisingly very little scholarship on this Marian icon which was adopted by the Society. The painting, of the Cavallini school, dates c. 1280–1330 and belonged in the mortuary chapel of the Astalli family in Rome. The painting was the only item that was preserved when the mortuary chapel was demolished to make room for the construction of the Chiesa del Gesù. Thereafter, the fresco was enshrined as the main altarpiece of the Madonna chapel, where it

Lady of the Way" thus symbolizes the special dedication Ignatius held toward the Blessed Virgin Mary and her special love for him. She is *the way* for his being pleasingly placed with her Son in service of the Father.

Ignatius's story culminates in Rome where he died on July 31, 1556. His earthly sojourn in the footsteps of our Lord was aided by the constant presence of Mary. Like the essential "rest areas" on the way toward a final destination, Aránzazu, Montserrat, Manresa, and La Storta were special meeting points with Our Lady who confirmed and strengthened the Pilgrim throughout his journey.

The Spiritual Exercises

Peter-Hans Kolvenbach, the 29th Superior General of the Society (1983–2008), states that "not seldom does one come across excellent commentaries on the *Exercises* today with no reference whatever to Our Lady, or at best a quick mention in passing."[36] The comment, made in a paper presented in 1988, remains true over thirty years later. The current state of affairs stands in stark contrast to that popular legend dating to the early seventeenth century which held that Mary had personally dictated the *Spiritual Exercises* to Ignatius. A more moderate version asserted that, just as Mary had played a part in the composition of the *Constitutions*, so too "the Exercises would have been composed in a prayerful consideration by Ignatius, involving regular recourse to Mary's intercession and experience of her presence."[37] Whether dictated verbatim or via prayerful inspiration, the point is, as Kolvenbach himself argues, that Mary is "at the very heart of the *Spiritual Exercises*."[38] This section examines Mary's presence in the *Spiritual Exercises*, following the twofold division of "narrative" and "functional" aspects proffered by the former Jesuit Superior.[39] The narrative element looks at Mary in the scenes of Scripture as the object of contemplation. The functional element looks at her as an agent working within the dynamic of the Exercises. Both elements reveal Mary's inconspicuous but profound role in Ignatius's *Spiritual Exercises*.

---

remains today. See Louis Bonacci, "Santa Maria della Strada," *Marian Library*, https://udayton.edu/imri/mary/s/santa-maria-della-strada.php.

36. Peter-Hans Kolvenbach, *Road from La Storta: Peter-Hans Kolvenbach, SJ, on Ignatian Spirituality* (St. Louis, MO: The Institute of Jesuit Sources, 2000), 33.

37. Koning, "Revisiting the Marian Dimension of Ignatian Spirituality," 148. Theories of authorship have proliferated in different directions. One particularly amusing argument was proffered by a certain Benedictine, Constatino Cajetan, who asserted that the *Spiritual Exercises* was but an adaptation of Garcia de Cisnernos, OSB's own *Exercitatoria*, and thus had nothing to do with any special dictation from Mary.

38. Kolvenbach, *Road from La Storta*, 33.

39. Kolvenbach, *Road from La Storta*, 35.

Mary's Narrative Presence in the Spiritual Exercises

Mary appears throughout the *Spiritual Exercises,* and Ignatius always contemplated Mary in connection with Jesus, her Son. In his meditation on the circumcision of Jesus, Ignatius says: "They gave back the Child *to His Mother,* who had compassion for the Blood which came from her Son."[40] In contemplating Jesus's baptism, Ignatius imagines Jesus taking leave of his Blessed Mother.[41] Ignatius also moves beyond the basic text of Scripture in contemplating the pietà and burial of Jesus, inviting the retreatant to consider "the loneliness of Our Lady, whose grief and fatigue were so great."[42]

The most striking of the narratives, however, is Ignatius's contemplation of Jesus's appearance to his mother after the Resurrection. From the tomb, Ignatius ushers the retreatant "to the house where Our Lady was, after her Son was buried."[43] There, the Risen Christ would make his first post-resurrection appearance to his mother.[44] This extra-biblical scene is key, and its setting in "the house where Our Lady was" inevitably links the post-resurrection scene to Gabriel's Annunciation to Mary: "It is unimaginable that Our Lord should not make his Risen presence known to the one who said 'Yes' to his Incarnation, who had borne him in her womb. . . ."[45] In this way, the retreatant is invited to contemplate how Mary's *fiat* is brought to consummation in the resurrection.

That Ignatius considered the appearance of the Risen Christ to Mary to be *a fact* of salvation history is evinced by his reference to it as "historia" in the 1548 Vulgate text of the *Exercises*.[46] Records from Ignatius's fellow pilgrims on the way to Jerusalem also show that they had visited the site believed to be the place where the Risen Christ appeared to Mary.[47] The tradition of such an apparition was deep-rooted. References to it can be found as far back as Tatian's commentary on the *Diatessaron* (c. 150 AD) as well as the works of John

---

40. SpEx, 266, emphasis added.
41. SpEx, 273.
42. SpEx, 208.
43. SpEx, 208.
44. SpEx, 218–25, 299.
45. Koning, "Revisiting the Marian Dimension of Ignatian Spirituality," 150. The significance of this domestic setting is expounded in Thomas Lucas, SJ's insightful discussion of the shrine and image of Our Lady of Loreto in "Virtual Vessels, Mystical Signs: Contemplating Mary's Images in the Jesuit Tradition," *Studies in the Spirituality of Jesuits* 35, no. 5 (2003): 1–46; see, in particular, 17–21.
46. Philip Endean, "Our Lady and the Graces of the Fourth Week," *The Way Supplement* 99 (2000): 44–60.
47. Cf. Endean, "Our Lady and the Graces," 44nn1–2, with reference to Jean-Claude Guy, "L'apparition à Notre Dame," *Christus* 95 (1977): 356–62 and Peter Füesslis and Leza Uffer, *Peter Füesslis Jerusalemfahrt 1523 und Brief über den Fall von Rohodos 1522* (Zurich: Schulthess, 1981).

Chrysostom (347–407 AD) and Ephrem the Syrian (306–373 AD).[48] Early on, the Pontifical Mass for Easter in Rome was celebrated at the Basilica of St. Mary Major to explicitly honor this appearance of the Resurrected Lord to his mother, and the tradition perdured in medieval Christendom.[49] Ludolph of Saxony includes a discussion of its fittingness in his *Vita Christi*, alongside common theories to explain why Scripture does not report on it. Ludolph suggests that the omission was necessary to avoid dishonoring Mary, whose witness might not have been believed because she was a woman; and that Jesus appeared to those whose faith needed confirmation, but Mary's did not.

Ignatius, however, does not enter into these discussions. He merely states: "This, although it is not said in scripture, is included in saying that he appeared to so many others, because scripture supposes that we have understanding, as it is written: 'Are you also without understanding?'"[50] Ignatius is clearly aware of the potential problems of his use of this non-biblical tradition, and yet he proceeds to incorporate it as a key meditation in the fourth week of the *Exercises*. Ignatius's persistence on the matter seemingly indicates how essential the Blessed Mother is to the dynamic of the *Exercises*, especially for the grace sought in the fourth week, namely, "That we might participate in the immense joy of Christ and his Mother." Whereas at the Annunciation (week one), the Lord dwelt *in* Mary's womb, now in week four, He comes to dwell in an "altogether new form of presence. . . . He lives again and she experiences it as 'Easter,' for thanks to him, she lives again and already rises to a new life."[51] Mary is the prototype of a new creation. The immense joy she experiences in her Son's apparition is the same joy which the retreatant seeks to partake in by the end of the *Exercises*. The retreatant's journey through the *Exercises* engages his/her imagination in an ever-deepening experience of the mystery of the Incarnation, and this experience culminates in the concrete and tangible joy of the Resurrection, embodied in Mary.[52]

Mary's Functional Presence in the Spiritual Exercises

In addition to the narrative elements, Mary is also functionally present in the *Exercises*. Throughout the four weeks, the retreatant is invited to engage Mary in his/her prayer. For example, annotation 98 asks the retreatant to make

---

48. Kolvenbach, *Road from La Storta*, 50.
49. Kolvenbach, *Road from La Storta*, 49.
50. SpEx, 299.2.
51. Jean Laplace, *An Experience of Life in the Spirit: Ten Days in the Tradition of the Spiritual Exercises* (Chicago, 1977), 172; cited in Kolvenbach, *Road from La Storta*, 56.
52. Laplace, *An Experience of Life in the Spirit*, 172; cited in Kolvenbach, *Road from La Storta*, 56.

his/her oblation to Christ specifically "in the presence of Christ's mother and all the heavenly court." Annotation 248 further invites the retreatant to reflect on and to use his/her bodily senses in imitation of Christ and Mary. Later, the retreatant is to meditate on the words of the Hail Mary and the Hail, Holy Queen.[53] The most significant Marian function, though, is Mary's place in the three colloquies which are prescribed at key moments in the *Exercises*.

The Triple Colloquy refers to the spontaneous heart-to-heart conversation with which the advancing retreatant completes particular meditations. The colloquies bear a threefold structure: the first is a prayer to Our Lady requesting that she might obtain for oneself some specific grace from her Son and Lord. This request is followed by a Hail Mary. The second colloquy—addressed to the Son in petition of the same grace—is followed by the *Anima Christi* prayer. The last colloquy is addressed to the Father directly, "that the Eternal Lord Himself may grant it to me," followed by an Our Father. The colloquy's threefold structure is reminiscent of Ignatius's prayer in his *Spiritual Diary*, whereby he consistently offered his petition to "the two Mediators," Jesus and Mary. It is also evidenced in his personal correspondences. In a letter written to Inés Pascual, he states: "May it please our Lady to mediate between us and her Son and Lord," for she "stands between us, poor sinners, and her Son and Lord," that through her intercession "our weak and wretched spirit may be transformed within us into a spirit which is strong and which sings his praises with joy."[54]

The intended movement of the Triple Colloquy is *from Mary to Jesus* to the Father,[55] and it embodies a distinct mediatory structure in which Our Lady is a propitious mediator between human beings and her Son. Robin Koning, SJ, makes a compelling argument against a contemporary adaptation of the Triple Colloquy which replaces the colloquy to Mary with a prayer to the Holy Spirit, fashioning a Trinitarian formulation instead.[56] This contemporary practice has emerged principally as an accommodation for Protestant Christians making the retreat but are uncomfortable with the idea of conversing with Mary. While such an adaptation may seem harmless, it is clearly contrary to Ignatius's explicit prescription.

To suggest replacing Mary with the Holy Spirit in the mediatory structure of the Triple Colloquy is to deviate from the specific structure Ignatius intends, whereby the retreatant first beseeches the Blessed Mother to intercede before her

---

53. Cf. J. Thomas Hamel, "Our Lady's Presence in the Spiritual Exercises," *Review for Religious* 63, no. 2 (2004): 182–91.

54. *Monumenta Ignatiana* I, *Epistolae I*, Letter to Inés Pascual (Madrid, 1903), 72; as quoted in Rahner, *Ignatius the Theologian*, 127.

55. SpDiar, 8 February 1544; 11 February 1544.

56. Koning, "Revisiting the Marian Dimension of Ignatian Spirituality," 154–60.

Son, then that the Son might intercede before the Father, before the retreatant approaches the Father directly. This threefold invocation for one particular grace intends to instruct the retreatant on perseverance in prayer. It is for *one* particular grace that the retreatant seeks *persistently* in the Triple Colloquy, and this persistence both purifies and conforms the retreatant's will to the divine will.

Moreover, the three colloquies are not independent of each other but rather interrelated. The blessed Mother is truly a "propitious intercessor" because she is a unique being: she is human like us, but *perfectly human* like her Son, who, as God-man, is the sole mediator between heaven and earth (1 Tm 2:5). He alone intercedes for humankind before the throne of God specifically in the human nature he received from Mary (Heb 7:25). The blessed Mother thus participates in Christ's mediation in a unique way, a participation which cannot be attributed to the Holy Spirit who is both the very Gift besought and the one who animates every prayer.[57] Any adaptation which replaces Mary with the Holy Spirit in the first colloquy—asking the Holy Spirit to intercede with the Son—would amount to subordinating the Spirit to the Son, a grave theological error![58]

A mystical vision recorded in the *Diary* reveals how Ignatius once thought "that the Blessed Virgin felt ashamed at asking for me so often." Ignatius had falsely perceived that his failings and frequent petitions made the Virgin Mary withdraw from him, and this caused him to weep in great sorrow. However, the heavenly Father appeared and reassured Ignatius, "showing Himself favorable and kindly" and confirming that "it would be pleasing to Him [the Father] *to be asked through our Lady*."[59] Ignatius's vision confirms what the Second Vatican Council centuries later would teach on the fact of Mary's subordinate mediation: "All the salvific influence of the Blessed Virgin originates, not from some inner necessity, but from the divine pleasure" (*Lumen Gentium*, no. 60). Mary's intercession pleases God; it participates in and is subordinate to the unique mediation of Jesus Christ.

Ignatius is adamant that "Mary is very propitious before the Father."[60] Recourse to Mary leads directly to her Son, and in Mary, the retreatant encounters a perfect model of receptivity, a receptivity which relies on the grace of Christ. The Triple Colloquy and Ignatius's devotion to Mary bespeak her essential functional role in both Ignatius's spiritual masterpiece and his own

---

57. St. Paul speaks of the Holy Spirit as a true *intercessor* for us according to the will of God (Rm 8:26–27). R. Koning posits that Ignatius's evident restraint in speaking of the Holy Spirit stems, at least in part, from the Inquisition's censure of the *Alumbrados*, the Illuminated ones, who claimed direct illumination from the Holy Spirit.

58. A similar subordination of the Spirit to the Son emerged in the fourth century in the Pneumatomachian heresy, which was condemned at the First Council of Constantinople in 381.

59. SpDiar, 15 February 1544, emphasis added.

60. SpDiar, 15 February 1544.

spiritual journey. The narrative and functional dimensions complement one another in Ignatius's presentation of Mary as truly "Our Lady," closely associated with "Our Lord" and wholly "propitious before the Father."

Ignatius never wrote a Marian treatise, but her place in his spiritual journey and within the *Exercises* are indisputably important. A distinctive Mariology can be inferred from his life and writing and was indeed witnessed and shared by all the early Jesuits. In testifying to this indispensable role of Mary, Peter Faber (1506–1546) describes how he, like Ignatius, often prayed to Mary that he might become a servant to her Son.[61] Francis Borja (1510–1572), the third Superior General of the Society, also had great devotion to Mary; he entrusted all of his works and decisions to the Mother of God, frequently prayed the rosary, and constantly entreated Mary to be his intercessor.[62] Jerónimo Nadal (1507–1580) argued in his work, *Orationis observationes*, that Mary was an effective intercessor to whom Jesus constantly "refers you back" because she exemplifies the perfect unity of contemplation and action, a Jesuit ideal.[63] Moreover, it was before the icon of Our Lady of the Way that Ignatius and all the early Jesuits prayed before departing for mission. The Marian theme is not a superfluous addendum to Ignatius's legacy but an essential element in his spirituality. Before comparing this implied Mariology to what one finds in the writings of Saint Thomas Aquinas, we briefly consider their medieval context.

Historical Context

Ignatius's devotion to Mary is neither unique nor innovative, but rather, reflective of his historical context. Surveying sixteenth century Europe, one enters a complex historical era of discovery and developments. Christopher Columbus embarked on the voyage to the West Indies in 1492, just one year after Ignatius's birth. A few decades earlier, Johann Guttenberg had invented the printing press, revolutionizing the dissemination of ideas; religious writings thus proliferated and popular devotions grew. Marian piety, in particular, developed with great popular force. The great medieval cathedrals bore the mark of the splendors of Mary, and the many Marian feasts added to the liturgical calendar at this time also reveal a heightened Marian piety. As evidenced in Ignatius's day, pilgrim routes to shrines and chapels built in Mary's honor were

---

61. Pierre Favre, *Memoriale*, in *The Spiritual Writings of Pierre Favre: The Memoriale and Selected Letters and Instructions*, trans. Edmond C. Murphy and Martin E. Palmer (St. Louis, MO: Institute of Jesuit Sources, 1996) no. 96; quoted in Fredrik Heiding, "Our Lady, Lead us to Christ! Early Jesuit Devotion to Mary," *The Way* 50, no. 2 (April 2011): 25–35, at 26.

62. Heiding, "Our Lady, Lead us to Christ!," 27.

63. Jerome Nadal, *Orationis observationes*, ed. M. Nicolau (Rome: IHSI, 1964), nn. 301, 120; 581 and 184.

charted all across Europe. Popular Marian prayers and hymns such as the *Memorare, Salve Regina,* and *Regina Caeli* were all products of the Middle Ages, bearing the imprint of monastic devotion to Mary.

The major religious orders of the Middle Ages, such as the Premonstratensian Canons, Carmelites, and Dominicans, all sought Mary's patronage and exhibited strong Marian devotions associated with their distinct charisms. For example, the Carmelites, also known as the Order of the Brothers of the Blessed Virgin Mary of Mount Carmel, promoted devotion to Mary by way of the brown scapular, and the Dominicans were known for the rosary. However, it could be said that the predominant Marian theology of that era (as distinct from Marian piety) came largely from Cistercian and Franciscan schools of thought.[64] Early Marian treatises came from the pen of Cistercian abbots like St. Isaac of Stella (d. 1169) and, most famously, St. Bernard of Clairvaux (d. 1153). The practice of the Triple Colloquy can be traced back to Bernard himself recommending this manner of prayer.[65] Also very influential was Bernard's "Sermon on the Aqueduct," in which Mary is described as the channel of all God's grace and mercy and the most powerful mediator between Christ and man: "So great a Mediator is Christ that we have need of another to mediate between him and us, and for this we can find none so qualified as Mary."[66] For Bernard, Mary was Queen and Lady above all else. When plague and death ravaged Europe, prayers and supplication were directed to the tender Madonna and mother who had suffered her own Son's death and understood the vicissitudes of life.

Marian devotion in the Middle Ages sometimes tended toward pious exaggeration, however. *A Life of the Blessed Virgin* written in Latin and a separate German work by Wernher the Swiss, both which appeared in the twelfth century, introduced romantic conceptions of Mary which led to further accretions. In the thirteenth century, St. Bonaventure's (d. 1274) *Speculum Beatae Mariae Virginis* continued in the same vein, redirecting the praises of God to Mary. For instance, Psalm 96 is recited thus: "Sing to Our Lady a new song: for she hath done wonderful things. In the sight of the nations she hath revealed her mercy; her name is heard even to the ends of the earth."[67] Another work on

---

64. For an excellent discussion of the development of Mariology in the Scholastic era, see Edward O'Connor, "The Fundamental Principle of Mariology in Scholastic Theology," *Marian Studies Journal* 10, no. 1 (1959), 60–103.

65. Kolvenbach, *Road from La Storta,* 42; with reference to Bernard's *Oeuvres IX,* 346.

66. Bernard of Clairvaux, *Sermons on the Blessed Virgin Mary* (Chulmleigh, UK: Augustine, 1984), 207–8; quoted in Brian Daley, "Sign and Source of the Church," in *Mary on the Eve of the Second Vatican Council* (Notre Dame, IN: Notre Dame University Press, 2017), 34.

67. Bonaventure, *The Mirror of the Blessed Virgin Mary and the Psalter of Our Lady,* trans. Sr. Mary Emmanuel (St. Louis, MO: Herder, 1932), 254.

Mariology, popular because of its attribution to St. Albert the Great (d. 1280), was *Mariale supra Missus est Angelus*.[68] The work extols Mary's preeminence and plenitude of grace to the point of conferring on her a kind of "omnicompetence" over angels, demons, and souls: she was said to possess angelic properties and the universality of all human knowledge, exceeding all the apostles and theologians in the knowledge of the faith.[69] Yet another work falsely attributed to Albert, *De laudibus sancta Mariae*, applied the *Pater Noster* to Our Lady and stated that Mary so loved the world she gave her only begotten Son for the life of the world.[70] These and other such works express a maximalist devotion which—while justifiable to a certain degree[71]—could also lead in the direction of excess. Furthermore, the Protestant Controversy in the sixteenth century exacerbated the maximalizing tendency, as Catholics capitalized Mary's divine privileges as a counterpoint to Protestantism. Ignatius's spiritual doctrine is generally free of these pious extravagances, and the same can be said of St. Thomas Aquinas's Christocentric Marian doctrine, to which we now turn.

Aquinas's Mariology[72]

St. Thomas, no doubt, had great devotion to Mary, and he taught that Mary surpasses even the angels in grace and dignity. The story is told of how, when he was a child, his nurse—wanting to bathe him—had to wrestle from his tiny hands a piece of parchment on which she found the words *Ave Maria*. That precious babe became one of the most prolific theologians of the West, and his Marian thought can be traced in seven key texts. In each of these, we encounter a Christocentric focus which constitutes the fundamental concurrence between Ignatius and Aquinas.

---

68. Cf. Albertus Magnus, *Alberti Magni Opera omnia*, ed. Auguste Borgnet and Émile Borgnet (Paris: Vivès, 1898), 37:1–362; as quoted in René Laurentin, *A Short Treatise on the Virgin Mary* (Washington: Ami Press, 1991), 117. The attribution to Albert was proven false in 1952; cf. B. Korosac, *Mariologia sancti Alberti Magni eiusque coaequalium* (Rome: Academnia Mariana Internationalis, 1954), 14.

69. This last assertion was made by Francisco Suarez (d. 1617) in *Misterios de la Vida de Cristo*, I, disp. 19, 1, 4; quoted in Thomas Thompson, "Recovering Mary's Faith and Her Role in the Church," in *Mary on the Eve of the Second Vatican Council*, 55–78, at 62.

70. The author is known to be Richard of St. Laurent; see *Opera Alberti Magni*, 36.

71. For example, on the idea that Mary's knowledge of faith exceeded the knowledge of all the apostles and theologians, one might consider the theologian's exercise of the Spirit's gift of knowledge, by which he produces more exacting and precise theological formulations. On the other hand, Mary, possessing the greatest intensity of faith and the infused virtues and gifts, would have penetrated the divine mysteries in an even more profound way through the Spirit's gift of wisdom. I am indebted to Fr. John Sica, OP for this insight.

72. For a bibliography of literature on Aquinas's writings on Mary, see G. Roschini, *La mariolgia di San Tommaso* (Rome: Belardetti, 1950), 24–33.

1. *Scriptum super Libros Sententiarum* (1254–1256)
2. *Summa contra Gentiles* (1261–1264)
3. *Expositio in Evangelium S. Matthaei* (1269–1272)
4. *Expositio in Evangelium Joannis* (1269–1272)
5. *Summa Theologiae, tertia pars* (1272–1273)
6. *Compendium Theologiae* (1272–1273)
7. *Devotissima Expositio super Salutatione Angelica* (1273)

A prime example of Aquinas's careful balance deriving his Marian thought from his Christology is ST III. Q. 27, a. 5 in which he addresses the question: *whether Mary's sanctification in the womb resulted in a fullness of grace.*[73] Aquinas answers in the affirmative, that indeed Mary had received the most perfect intensity of grace possible. Then, with his characteristic Christocentrism, he immediately counterbalances, distinguishing her fullness of grace from that of Christ by contrasting it with Christ's superior fullness as the Author of grace. In what follows, I explore the convergence of Aquinas's and Ignatius's Marian thought in three aspects: Mary's maternal mediation; her closeness to God; and the original justice that characterizes her freedom from all sin.

Maternal Mediation

We have seen how, for Ignatius, Mary was an essential and propitious intercessory figure. Aquinas also considers the nature of Mary's intercession and deduces her mediatory efficacy as fundamentally derived from her relationship to her Son. Mary's divine motherhood is the foundation for the fullness of every grace she received. In Aquinas's theology, Mary was "nearest to Christ in His humanity because He received His human nature from her. Therefore, it was due to her to receive a greater fullness of grace than others."[74] It is from this unparalleled fullness that Mary effectively mediates grace to the human race: "She received within her Him Who is full of all grace; and by bringing Him forth, she, in a certain way, brought grace to all."[75] Aquinas comes very close to proffering a theology of Mary as *Mediatrix* here, and what he means by "in a certain way, brought grace to all" is further illumined by his *Commentary on the Gospel of John* (1269–1272).

Aquinas interprets John 1:16, "Of his fullness we have all received, grace upon grace," as applicable to Mary.

---

73. By "fullness of grace" (*plenitudo gratiae*), Aquinas does not mean that there is a measurable, maximum degree of created grace, but that the superabundance of God's favor upon Mary is one which is complete and perfectly increasing to infinity.
74. ST III, q. 27, a. 5, co.
75. ST III, q. 27, a. 5, ad 1.

There is a fullness of superabundance, by which the Blessed Virgin excels all the saints because of the eminence and abundance of her merits. Further, there is a fullness of efficiency and overflow, which belongs only to the man Christ as the author of grace. For although the Blessed Virgin super-abounds her grace into us, it is never as authoress of grace. But grace flowed over from her soul into her body: for through the grace of the Holy Spirit, not only was the mind of the Virgin perfectly united to God by love, but her womb was supernaturally impregnated by the Holy Spirit. And so after Gabriel said, *hail, full of grace*, he refers at once to the fullness of her womb, adding, *the Lord is with you* (Lk 1:28).[76]

There is a clear ordering in the divine dispensation in which Mary's active mediation is derived from her divine maternity. She is not the author of grace, but she is so full of grace that it overflows to the rest of the human race in the fruit of her womb, Jesus Christ.[77] She mediates effectively because she is the Mother of the Author of grace, and from this foundational relationship, God's love and mercy in her life and in the fruit of her womb flow out to all.

Furthermore, in his commentary on the wedding at Cana (Jn 2:1–11), Aquinas explicitly states that "Christ's mother assumed the role of a mediatrix."[78] He explains that Mary is a true mediator on account of two works: (a) she intercedes with her Son, and (b) she instructs the servants to do whatever Jesus says. These are functional works, and we witness in them how Mary mediates between Christ and the peoples. The fine wine is miraculously procured through her intercession and compassionate concern for the newlyweds. Moreover, Mary's role in the miracle is grounded in her relation to Jesus, for she intercedes with *her Son*. In other words, Aquinas's argument reveals a painstaking theological precision. Mary's role as Mediatrix follows upon her divine Maternity. It is through her that God's superabundant love and mercy are bestowed upon the human race in the person of Jesus Christ, the fruit of her womb.

Interestingly, Aquinas does not expound Mary's *spiritual* maternity in relationship to Christ's mystical body in either the *Summa Theologiae* or the *Compendium theologiae*. He principally treats of Mary's personal, maternal relationship to Christ and only elucidates Mary's spiritual mediation of grace in the aforementioned biblical commentaries and in his Lenten sermon on the Angelic salutation. The latter, *Expositio salutationis angelicae*, was preached in Naples in 1273, about a year before his death. Transcribed by Reginald of Piperno, Aquinas's secretary and close associate, the sermon

---

76. Thomas Aquinas, *Expositio in Evangelium Joannis*, c. 1, l. 10, 201.
77. *Expositio in Evangelium Joannis*, c. 2, l. 1, 344.
78. *Expositio in Evangelium Joannis*, c. 2, l. 1, 344.

reveals Aquinas's robust devotion to Mary. He provides an earnest exposition of the "*plenitudo gratiae* / fullness of grace" by which she surpasses even the angels. Aquinas argues that grace filled Mary's sinless soul (such that she possessed every virtue), overflowed to her body (such that she conceived the Son of God), and further overflowed from her soul and body onto all humankind (in spiritual mediation).[79]

This precise theological ordering in Aquinas's understanding of Mary's mediatory influence as subordinate to and derived from her unique maternal relationship to Christ underscores the significance of the ordering of Ignatius's (and Bernard's) Triple Colloquy. As seen in his treatment in the *Summa*, Aquinas assigns precedence to Mary's maternal relationship to Jesus as the foundation for her *spiritual* maternity by which she continues to mediate for all from heaven. The latter is derived from the former; the function is derived from the relation: Mary's historical participation in the mystery of Redemption as Mother to the Son of God becomes the unique source of her "propitiatory intercession."

Although Ignatius does not make this distinction, his own practice and recommendations are in accord with Aquinas's understanding. Applying that understanding to the Ignatian colloquies, the Christian prays to Mary principally because of her unique maternal relationship to Christ, more than because she is the Queen of Heaven and the heavenly treasures. While this may seem to be a pedantic distinction, it is a necessary one because without it, a mere expounding of Marian privileges risks veering off into ahistorical speculation. Contrarily, the essence of Christianity is incarnational. Aquinas models for us the necessity of grounding our contemplation of the Blessed Virgin Mary in the historical realism of the Incarnation.

Ignatius and Aquinas on Mary's Intimacy with Christ

A second point of discernable consonance between Ignatius and Aquinas on Mary is their mutual emphasis on her closeness to Christ. In the corpus of ST III, q. 27, a. 4, Aquinas speaks of the "*singularem affinitatem*" (singular intimacy) shared between Jesus and his Mother, and in ST III, q. 27, a. 5, co., he establishes Mary's fullness of grace on the principle of proximity: "In every genus, the nearer a thing comes to its principle the more it shares its effects.... The Blessed Virgin Mary was nearest to Christ in His humanity: because He received His human nature from her." The fullness of this unique nearness to Christ is the source of Mary's efficacious mediation.

---

79. Thomas Aquinas, *Expositio salutationis angelicae*, *Opuscula theologica*, vol. 2 (Rome: Marietti, 1954), 1114–18.

A similar emphasis on the intimacy of Mary and Jesus is intimated in Ignatius's favorite title for Mary. In the *Spiritual Exercises,* he refers to her as "Our Lady" twenty-seven times, far surpassing thirteen invocations to her as "Mother"; five to the name "Mary," and once each as "Virgin" and "Handmaid."[80] As previously noted, Ignatius's predominant use of "Our Lady" is derived from the title's semantic closeness to "Our Lord," which evokes the close association of Christ and Mary in the work of salvation.[81] The content of this association plays out in Ignatius's consistent coupling of Mary and Jesus as his personal "two Mediators" before God the Father. One can envision how Ignatius might have studied and imbibed the theological principles of Aquinas's Marian thought, and in them, found confirmation of his own spiritual instincts: Mary is an unfailing intercessor because she is perfectly united to Christ, her Son, "Our Lord."

Ignatius records a special mystical experience in his *Spiritual Diary* entry of 15 February 1544, which, without employing precise theological terms, reveals his experience of Mary's role in the mystery of grace. Ignatius says that during the celebration of the Mass, he "was not able to feel her or to see her," but he experienced Our Lady "as being part or portal of such a great grace that I felt in spirit." Ignatius's words are carefully chosen: without seeing her, he experiences Our Lady as *"parte o puerta"* of the graces he received. Mary provides access to the great favors of God and is both the threshold and a "part" of the mystery itself. Ignatius adds: "At the consecration, she showed me that *her flesh is in that of her Son,* with so great an understanding that one is unable to articulate it." While this latter mystical insight cannot be sustained as a literal thesis (i.e., that Mary and Jesus share the same flesh), it nonetheless resonates with Aquinas's emphasis on the priority of Mary's maternal mediation and what he says in ST III q. 31, a. 5, ad 3 on the body of Christ being "formed out of the most chaste and purest blood of the Virgin." Aquinas's discussion in question 31, "On the Matter from which the Savior's Body Was Conceived," draws explicitly from Aristotle's *de Generatione Animalium.* Ignatius would have been well-acquainted with this text from his studies in Paris.[82] However, it appears that there is more than an Aristotelian biological perspective at work in Ignatius's mystical experience. The reality of Mary's flesh as being "in that of her Son," revealed by Mary at the moment

---

80. Kolvenbach, *Road from La Storta,* 34.

81. The use of this semantic significance in the *Exercises* was lost in the Vulgate, which replaced "nuestra Señora" with "the Blessed Virgin Mary"; see Philip Endean's discussion in "Our Lady and the Graces," 54.

82. It should be noted that Aquinas is precise in his application of Aristotelian thought, asserting that it is *from Mary's purest blood* that the Word fashions for himself a human body: "[Christ] is said to have taken flesh from the Virgin, not that the matter from which His body was formed was actual flesh, but blood, which is flesh potentially." ST III, q. 31, a. 5, ad 1.

of the Eucharistic consecration, underscores Mary's unique intimacy with Christ in the sacramental economy. In the Incarnation, the Word took on the flesh taken from the Virgin Mary; in the sacramental order, the Virgin Mary's own flesh is now taken up into her Son.[83]

Moreover, Ignatius's reference to Mary as *"puerta"* echoes the prophecy of Ezekiel, chapter 44, which the tradition has applied to Mary as the Gate of Heaven (*Janua Caeli*). She is *"la puerta"* through which the Incarnate Word passed from heaven to earth, taking his flesh from her purest blood. Furthermore, the Church Fathers of both the East and the West interpreted Ezekiel's oracle of the Temple's closed gate as a prophecy of the virgin birth of Christ: "The Lord said to me: This gate must remain closed; it must not be opened, and no one should come through it. Because the Lord, the God of Israel, came through it, it must remain closed" (Ez 44:2).

Not only is the Virgin an essential *"parte"* of the mystery in which the Son of God takes on human flesh, she is also the closed *"puerta,"* a symbol of her perpetual virginity which becomes the mysterious portal through which God showers his grace upon the world. Mary's virgin motherhood is the guarantor of both Jesus's divinity and his humanity. For Aquinas, "In order that Christ's body might be shown to be a real body, he was born of a woman. In order that his godhead might be made clear, he was born of a woman."[84] Mary is truly both *"parte"* and *"puerta"* of the *admirabile commercium* with which Ignatius came into mystical contact during his celebration of the Mass on 15 February 1544.

The third and final aspect of Aquinas's Marian thought which beckons our attention is the topic of the Immaculate Conception, a topic on which Aquinas and Ignatius diverge. We begin with a survey of the historical context.

Original Justice and the Immaculate Conception

Historical Context

Belief in Mary's perfect holiness originated in the East, and it was disseminated primarily through a liturgical feast honoring Mary's conception. How the feast penetrated into the West is uncertain, though it is clear that the devotion took root in some English monasteries and cathedrals shortly before the Norman Conquest of 1066. After the Normans suppressed the feast in their attempt to reform the English Church, devotion to Mary's conception was

---

83. For the entry in the *Spiritual Diary*, see *Monumenta Ignatiana Series Tertia: Sancti Ignatii de Loyola Constitutiones Societatis Jesu*, vol. 1, *Monumenta Constitutionum Praevia*, MHSI 63 (Romae: Typis Pontificiae Universitatis Gregorianae, 1934), 94.

84. ST III, q. 28, a. 2, ad 2.

revived not only as filial piety but as a proper theological question.[85] Ironically, as history would have it, one of the greatest devotees of Mary, St. Bernard of Clairvaux, could not admit the idea that Mary was conceived without sin. Known as the "greatest lover of the Virgin and champion of her honor," Bernard argued that Mary "received sanctification after the *conceptus,* when already existing in the womb; this sanctification made her nativity holy and free from sin, but not at her *conceptio.*"[86] Scholastic theologians such as Peter Lombard, Albert the Great, and Bonaventure[87] all seriously entertained positive arguments *for* Mary's sinless conception, but at the end of the day, they unanimously conformed to Bernard of Clairvaux's argument that Mary incurred Original Sin at her conception and was later sanctified while still in the womb. Bernard's opinion was held as authoritative and the normative tradition until the arrival of John Duns Scotus (1266–1308). Aquinas also upheld Bernard's position, as evidenced in the *Summa* and the *Compendium Theologiae,* c244. In the latter, he writes:

> If she had not been conceived with original sin, she would not have needed to be redeemed by Christ; then Christ would not be the universal redeemer of man—which would take away from his dignity.

Aquinas on the Immaculate Conception

Aquinas's ill-famed error in teaching that Mary was conceived in sin predates the formal promulgation of the dogma of the Immaculate Conception by six centuries and is posited on the premise of the primacy of Christ. Question 27 of the *Tertia pars* of the *Summa Theologiae* is devoted to Mary's sanctification, discussed in six articles. In article one, Aquinas argues that Mary was cleansed of Original Sin *before birth,* but not of the guilt of that sin befalling humankind precisely because "she could not enter Paradise except through the sacrifice of Christ."[88] In article two, he argues that the Blessed Virgin was not sanctified before animation because such a grace belongs only to a rational creature, and therefore, Our Lady's sanctification simply could not happen before the infusion of the rational soul. Furthermore, if Mary never "incurred the blemish of original sin, she would not have needed redemption and salva-

---

85. Early proponents of belief in the Immaculate Conception were principally from England: St. Anselm (1109), Eadmer (1137), Nicholas of St. Albans (1175), Osbert of Clare (1170), Robert Grosseteste (1253), William of Ware (1300), and John Duns Scotus (1308).

86. Bernard, *Epistola 174* (PL 182, 333); as quoted in Edward O'Connor, ed., *The Dogma of the Immaculate Conception* (1958; repr., Notre Dame, IN: University of Notre Dame Press, 2017).

87. Cf. Albert the Great, III *Sent.* 3.6; Bonaventure, III *Sent.* 3.1.2.2.

88. ST III, q. 27 a. 1, ad 3.

tion which is through Christ."[89] The position put forward in these two articles is that Mary seemingly must have incurred Original Sin at conception if she is to be sanctified by Christ; this sanctification initially took place in her mother's womb before Mary's birth and then was perfected in her miraculous and direct contact with Christ in the moment of his conception in her womb.

One must also take notice of how Aquinas repeatedly couches his argument in tentative terms. In ST III, q. 27, a. 3, he says that the grace of Original Justice (which characterized Adam and Eve's prelapsarian state) *"does indeed* pertain to the dignity of the Virgin Mother." However, the dilemma is that "it also derogates from the dignity of Christ." Moreover, "it *seems unfitting* to say that before Christ appeared in sinless flesh, His Virgin Mother's or anyone else's flesh should be without the fomes."[90] Consequently, Aquinas concludes, "It *would seem better* to say that in the sanctification in the womb the inflammation of sin was not removed in essence from the Virgin but that it was rendered harmless." Aquinas ends his *respondeo* quoting Ezekiel 43:2 to describe this second instance of purification by the Holy Spirit in beautiful, almost lyrical, terms, saying: "Ezekiel suggests this: 'I saw the glory of the God of Israel approaching from the East (that is, from the blessed Virgin) . . . and the earth (that is, her flesh) shone with his glory (that is, of Christ).'"[91] The beautiful splendor of the Virgin's immunity to sin and its effects are likened to the grandeur of the earth illumined by the radiance of the sun. Over and over again, Aquinas maintains a deference to Christ; Mary could not have been entirely immune from Original Sin if that immunity detracted from the dogma of Redemption by Christ.

After Aquinas: Varying Interpretations

Many disciples of Aquinas have proffered various interpretations of Aquinas's position on the Immaculate Conception. The ambiguity stems from his diverse writings over the course of a lifetime in which different positions are expressed. Some scholars concede a straight-forward reading of ST III, q. 27 as Aquinas's position distinguishing between conception in Original Sin (q. 27, a. 2) and later sanctification in her mother's womb (q. 27, a. 1) with a third point of perfection in final glory (q. 27, a. 5). Others argue that Aquinas wavered, explicitly holding the doctrine of the Immaculate Conception early on, later coming to deny it, only to return to affirm it near the end of his life. Yet still others argue that Aquinas explicitly held that Mary *was* immaculately con-

---

89. ST III, q. 27, a. 2, co.
90. "Fomes" or "fomes peccati" refers to the inflammation (literally, "tinder") of sin which characterizes the state of original sin.
91. ST III, q. 27, a. 3, co.

ceived. These latter positions are based on certain statements. Aquinas makes in his *Commentary on the Sentences* and his sermon on the "Angelic Salutation" referring to Mary's absolute freedom from Original Sin, which contrasts with his position in the *Summa* (discussed above). One might, therefore, discern a development in Aquinas's Marian thought.[92]

An early phase is manifested in his composition of the *Commentary on the Sentences* (1254–1256). In the first book, Aquinas affirms that the Blessed Virgin was indeed exempt from both original and actual sin: "*talis fuit puritas B. Virginis, quae peccato originali et actuali immunis fuit*" (such was the purity of the Blessed Virgin who was free of original and actual sin).[93] However, in book three of the *Commentary*, Aquinas locates the time of her sanctification *after* the infusion of her soul and before her birth, whence she was cleansed from original sin and made immune to actual sin.[94]

In the *Summa*, written at the maturity of his career, Aquinas expounded this last perspective, affirming the universality of Redemption wrought by Christ alone, as we have already seen from ST III, q. 27, a. 3, ad. 3:

> *Spiritus sanctus in beata Virgine duplicem purgationem fecit; unam quidem quasi praeparatoriam ad Christi conceptionem, quae non fuit ab aliqua impuritate culpae vel fomitis sed mentem eius magis in unum colligens et a multitudine sustollens.* (The Holy Spirit effected a twofold purification in the Blessed Virgin. The first was, as it were, preparatory to Christ's conception: which did not cleanse her from the stain of sin or fomes, but rather gave her mind a unity of purpose and disengaged it from a multiplicity of things.)

This position is bolstered in the *Compendium Theologiae* (previously quoted) where Aquinas reasserts the necessity of Mary's conception in original sin, saying, "If she had not been conceived with original sin, she would not have needed to be redeemed by Christ; then Christ would not be the universal redeemer of man—which would take from His dignity."[95]

Last, Aquinas's maximal devotion to Mary is conspicuously expressed in his Lenten sermon on the "Angelic Salutation." Critical editions of *Expositio*

---

92. That Aquinas changed his position over the course of his life is the basic position of Reginald Garrigou-Lagrange; see *The Mother of the Savior*, trans. B. Kelly (Dublin: n.p., 1948), 66–71.
93. Aquinas, *Sent.* I, d. 44, q. 1, a. 3, ad. 3.
94. Aquinas, *Sent.* III, d. 3, q. 1, a. 2, 1 ad. 1.
95. Aquinas, *Compendium theologiae*, c. 244. See also: *Parmae*, XVI, 65 and *De malo*, q. 4, a. 6 in *Parmae*, VIII, 292–93; as quoted in O'Connor, *Dogma of the Immaculate Conception*, 193. See also *Quodlibet* VI, a. 7 in *Parmae*, IX, 545–46: "We must not attribute so much to the Mother as to detract from the honor due to her Son, who is 'the Savior of all men,' as the Apostle says."

Salutationis Angelicae have shown that 16 out of 19 codices report Aquinas's assertion that Mary was exempt from all sin, original sin included.[96] The sentence under scrutiny is: *"nec originale nec mortale, nec veniale peccatum incurrit."* Aquinas argues that Mary exceeds the angels with respect to purity, since her purity had been procured for the sake of others, "for she incurred neither Original, nor mortal nor venial sin."[97]

Dominican Father Louis Every (1927–2000) seeks to resolve the conundrum by explaining that these statements are not as inherently contradictory as they may first appear to be. According to Every, Aquinas writes within the framework of an Aristotelian biological perspective in which the conception of the body preceded the infusion of a rational soul by at least a month. Thus, Aquinas's statements attributing original sin to Mary could be read to be referring to the debt of original sin as incurred "antecedently in the body, before perfect animation."[98] Throughout the various interpretations, at least one point is clear: Aquinas firmly believed that Mary was sinless. The principal reason he gives for asserting Mary's conception as tainted with original sin is to preserve the necessity and universality of salvation in Jesus Christ alone.

Ignatius

By the time Ignatius enters the scene over two centuries later, John Duns Scotus's doctrine of Mary's Immaculate Conception, ingeniously developing a notion of preservative redemption, had already taken hold in both popular piety and ecclesiastical circles, even as the theological debates between the Franciscans and the Dominicans continued. At the time of the Council of Basel-Ferrara-Florence (1431–1449)—so called because it had commenced in Basel but subsequently transferred to Ferrara and then again to Florence to improve ecumenical prospects—a group of conciliar fathers in favor of the "immaculist thesis" remained at Basel, and on September 17, 1439, they declared: "We define ... that the doctrine that maintains that the glorious Virgin and Mother of God, Mary, by the power of a singular prevenient grace and the working of the divine will, was *never subject to original sin but was always in a state immune from actual and original fault, holy and immaculate.*"[99] Although this definition did

---

96. Reginald Garrigou-Lagrange, *De Christo Salvtore* (Turin, 1945), 506–8; see O'Connor, *Dogma of the Immaculate Conception*, 45.

97. Aquinas, *Opera Omnia*, Vives Edition (Paris, 1875), vol. 27, Opusculum VI, *Expositio de Ave Maria*, 198–202; repr. in "St. Thomas's Explanation of the Hail Mary," trans. Louis Every, OP, in *Dominicana* 39, no. 1 (1954): 31–38.

98. Every, St. Thomas's Explanation of the Hail Mary," 33n5, 35n9.

99. Heinrich Denzinger-Peter Hunermann, introductory note to *Enchiridion Symbolorum* (DH 1400).

not have the backing of conciliar authority, the consensus that lay behind its promulgation is telling. In 1477, Pope Sixtus IV of the Order of Friars Minor, issued the constitution *Cum praeexcelsa*, inviting all the faithful to "render thanks and praise for the wonderful conception of this immaculate Virgin . . . so that they might become more worthy of divine grace."[100] However, because Pope Sixtus never ruled out the "maculist thesis" as a legitimate theological position, both positions enjoyed the same juridical status, and this enabled the controversy to continue until the official definition of 1854.

There is little evidence indicating whether Ignatius ever encountered or took part in the theological debates between the Franciscans and Dominicans of his time. What is evident is the substantial distance between Ignatius's Spanish surroundings, which took the Immaculate Conception as a matter of belief, and the reigning Thomistic doctrine on the matter. Moreover, the next generation of Jesuits became the ardent leaders of a Marian revival in Italy and Spain in the last years of the sixteenth century. Francisco Suarez (1548–1617) wrote the first systematic mariology, and Hernando Chirino de Salazar (1576–1646) wrote the first great work on the Immaculate Conception in 1618.[101] The spiritual sons of Ignatius intuited their father's Marian spirit. They formed groups with Marian designations, referred to as Congregations or Sodalities, and became the zealous proponents of Mary's Immaculate Conception.

The Council of Trent (1545–1564) did not treat the Marian question but only made one mention of the Blessed Virgin Mary in its decree on original sin, establishing continuity with Pope Sixtus's promotion of the doctrine of the Immaculate Conception:

> This same holy Synod doth nevertheless declare, that it is not its intention to include in this decree, where original sin is treated of, the blessed and immaculate Virgin Mary, the Mother of God; but that the constitutions of Pope Sixtus IV, of happy memory, are to be observed, under the pains contained in the said constitutions, which it renews.[102]

This is a significant indicator of the prevailing ecclesiastical milieu to which Ignatius would have given his assent in the spirit of *sentire cum ecclesia,* and it explains the Society's subsequent advocacy of the Immaculate Conception in adherence to Trent's teaching. Moreover, the Tridentine decree provides a theological focus which draws out the proper meaning of original sin as a depriva-

---

100. DH 1400, *Cum praeexcelsa* (1477). Over two centuries later, Pope Clement XI would issue the constitution *Commissi nobis divinitus* (1708), which prescribed a universal celebration of the feast of the Immaculate Conception.
101. Laurentin, *Short Treatise*, 126.
102. DH 1516, *Decree on Original Sin* (1546).

tion of original justice.[103] Here one comes to an essential common point for both Aquinas and Ignatius.

Original Justice

As previously noted, Aquinas states explicitly: "the grace of sanctification in the Virgin had *the force of original justice* . . . [and] this appears to be part of the dignity of the Virgin Mother."[104] He only refrained from attributing this original justice to Mary because it seemed unfitting to do so as such a state would "derogate from the dignity of Christ" (*derogat tamen in aliquo dignitati Christi*). Other than this, there is no theological reason *intrinsic* to Mary's being by which he would deny her the grace of original justice.[105]

In ST I-II, q. 82, a. 3, Aquinas explains that "the whole order of original justice consists in man's will being subject to God." This "subjection" is found chiefly in the will, "whose function it is to move all the other parts to the end." In contrast to the state of original justice (wherein the will is subject to God), in original sin, the human intellect and will suffer discord, and once the will is turned away from God, "all the other powers of the soul become inordinate." This disorder is the formal element in original sin.[106]

Insofar as Ignatius's *Spiritual Exercises* aims to re-establish the subjective ordering of the soul in accordance with the objective order of Redemption—in essence, re-establishing the proper ordering of the retreatant's will and his or her attachments—it can be found consistent with Aquinas's teaching on original sin as the privation of original justice. For instance, the second week of the *Exercises* begins with a contemplation of the Annunciation scene, titled the "Incarnation." The first point of meditation invites the retreatant to see the condition of humankind in original sin, with the three Divine Persons looking down on earth to see "all nations in great blindness, going down to death and descending to hell."[107] All of this stands in contrast to the serene scene of the humble maiden in a house

---

103. ST I-II, q. 82, a. 1, ad 1.
104. ST III, q. 27, a. 3, co.
105. Had Aquinas been presented with Scotus's idea of preservative redemption as the grounds for the Immaculate Conception, I surmise that he would have embraced it. What was of utmost importance to Aquinas was that Mary be understood in relationship to Christ; rendering Mary as *most perfectly redeemed* by Christ, rather than an *exception* to his work of redemption, would have greatly satisfied Aquinas. Moreover, the idea of "preservation from sin" already imbued his understanding of Mary's being kept from all actual sin by being sanctified in the womb (ST III, q. 27, a. 4), even if he had failed to locate this preservation at the moment of conception.
106. For Aquinas, original sin is concupiscence, materially, but privation of original justice, formally.
107. Annotation 106; taken from *The Spiritual Exercises of St. Ignatius*, trans. Louis Puhl (Chicago: Loyola University Press, 1961), 59.

and room in the city of Nazareth whose simple existence embodies and emboldens the harmony of grace and complete submission to God.

As the retreatant journeys through the *Exercises,* the narrative and functional presence of Mary evokes an awareness and orientation to this harmony. The retreatant's work of freeing himself from his disordered attachments can be anchored in the graciousness of the "Immaculate Virgin who sums up all the perfection of the universe redeemed and restored to its original beauty."[108] As R. Koning states: "It is not simply a matter of having Mary as our intercessor, but also as someone who has received the graces we seek and lived according to them so that we can converse with her about them and be inspired to imitate her. Hence the Triple Colloquy is a carefully structured prayer involving both intercession and imitation."[109] Our Lady's intercession is propitious because she has already received from God the reality of that grace for which we strive. As Aquinas argues in ST III, q. 30, a. 1, Mary offered her consent to the Incarnation on behalf of the world; consequently, all other "*fiats*" to God's will essentially trace the lines of her love and participate in that state of justice, of which she is a living embodiment.

Moreover, even as Aquinas held to the position of Mary's sanctification as taking place only at a point in time following the infusion of her soul, he nonetheless expounded how that sanctification involved an efficacious ordering in original justice. An example of the effect of original justice restored in Mary is found in Aquinas's assertion in his *Commentary on the Sentences* that Mary was so beautiful (i.e., so perfectly sinless and manifesting the order of original justice) that no man could ever look upon her with disordered desire.[110] The unspoiled order of grace within her soul overflowed to her body and further instilled order in the concrete universe she inhabited.

Additionally, a prayer Aquinas writes to Our Lady stands as a spiritual testimony of his own Marian theology and his personal expression of dependence upon her aid, specifically in restoring God's just order to the world.

> Dearest and most blessed Virgin Mary, Mother of God,
> Overflowing with affection,
> Daughter of the Sovereign King, and Queen of the Angels:
> Mother of Him who created all things,
> This day and all days of my life
> I commend to the bosom of thy regard
> My soul and body,
> All my actions, thoughts, wishes, desires, words, and deeds,

---

108. Kolvenbach, *Road from La Storta,* 43.
109. Koning, "Revisiting the Marian Dimension of Ignatian Spirituality," 154.
110. *Sent.* III d. 3, q. 1, a. 2, I ad 1.

My whole life, and my end: *so that through thy prayers*
They may be all ordered according to the will of thy beloved Son. Amen.[111]

Aquinas's prayer to Mary is that she might aid in the re-ordering of every aspect of his being according to the will of Jesus Christ; it is a prayer for the original justice which Mary herself embodies. The same dynamic is implied in the movement of Ignatius's *Spiritual Exercises*.

Conclusion

Returning then to the question of the extent of the concurrences between Aquinas and Ignatius in Mariology, the Blessed Virgin Mother's mediatory influence, her intimacy with Christ, and the original justice that characterizes her sinlessness constitute three essential points of contact. Aquinas's and Ignatius's decisive placement of Marian considerations squarely within Christology underscores their mutual view on Mary's indispensable place in the mystery of her Son's work of Redemption.

In the broader context of Christological thought, however, clear differences between Aquinas and Ignatius are discernible. For example, on the discussion of the necessity of the Incarnation, Jesuits have tended to side with Franciscan theologians who hold that the Incarnation would have happened even if our first parents had not sinned.[112] In this vein of theological development, Mary's role in the mystery of the Incarnation would look very different, and to speculate upon such matters here would take us far afield. My point, though, is that Ignatius does not entertain this avenue of speculation at all. Instead, like Aquinas, he takes his point of departure from the concrete factual state described in Scripture and Tradition: Adam's sin has ruptured man's communion with God, and God has willed for his Son to become incarnate in the Virgin Mary for the salvation of all humankind. Aquinas will expound the intrinsic intelligibility of this revelation, and Ignatius will engage that same reality in such a way as to bring its truth to bear in the transformation of human hearts.

That Jesuit engagement with Thomism over the course of the centuries has waxed and waned, even sparring over specific theological points, is no surprise.

---

111. Thomas Aquinas, *Devoutly I Adore Thee*, trans. and ed. Robert Anderson and Johann Moser (Manchester, NH: Sophia Institute Press, 1933), 21–31; emphasis added.

112. Cf. Rahner's discussion in *Ignatius the Theologian*, 78. For Aquinas's discussion of the necessity of the Incarnation and of faith for salvation, see ST III, q. 1, a. 3 and ST II-II, q. 2, a. 7. Amongst other differences between Thomism and Ignatian thought, A. Dulles also discusses a difference of theological orientation: "Whereas the Thomists commonly define theology in terms of God himself as its formal object, many Jesuits, with Emile Mersch, prefer to define theology in terms of its integral object as the discipline that deals with the 'total Christ'" (Dulles, "Ignatius and the Jesuit Theological Tradition," 5).

Avery Dulles makes a lucid assessment of a key difference between Ignatius's and Thomas's theology when he says:

> Perhaps the most serious accusation that can be leveled against Ignatius' theology is that it tends to instrumentalize the intelligence. The Ignatian devotion to the service of God alone could perhaps lead to a certain supernatural pragmatism. Unlike classical Thomism, which exalts the speculative for its own sake, the Jesuit tradition looks on speculation itself as a form of praxis to be pursued to the extent that it may advance the glory of God and the salvation of humankind.[113]

Ignatius's implicit Mariology is ordered to the practical ends in spiritual growth and conformity to Christ. Its tendency toward a "certain supernatural pragmatism" can be contrasted with Aquinas's Mariology, which is explicitly theological. However, the distinct features of Aquinas's and Ignatius's Marian thought do not present any inherent dichotomy. Ignatius's sublime mystical experiences of the Blessed Virgin are not diametrically opposed to the painstaking theological precision Aquinas seeks in his reflections on the Blessed Mother. Rather, the shared horizons of both thinkers bring to a point the harmony of spirituality and theology which finds a unique embodiment in Mary. Even in Aquinas's theologizing on her, one senses that, for him as for Ignatius, Our Lady was less the object of academic study and more the object of his loving contemplation. What both Aquinas and Ignatius write on the Blessed Virgin Mary evince a powerful love and deep devotion which informed and inspired their respective work. Their mutual focus on Jesus Christ bespeaks a mystical horizon within which Mary was always present. Alongside Ignatius and Aquinas, then, we as contemporary thinkers can contemplate and appreciate the convergence of theology and spirituality in the figure of Mary, and thereby seek to share in the splendor of sanctity and sagacity rooted in Jesus Christ.

---

113. Dulles, "Ignatius and the Jesuit Theological Tradition," 17. Dulles concludes: "In the nineteenth century the Jesuits were among the foremost promoters of the Thomistic revival, but their espousal of Thomism was dictated more by practical considerations than by serious conviction. Thomism was held to be orthodox and serviceable to the universal Church. At a later time, under changed circumstances, Jesuits could abandon Thomism as casually as they had previously embraced it." Dulles' thesis has been further substantiated by the extensive research of Rivka Feldhay; see Feldhay, *From Knowledge and Faith to Science and Religion: The Jesuit Way to Modernity (2003–2005)* (Max Planck Institute for the History of Science, 2003–2005); *Galileo and the Church: Political Inquisition or Critical Dialogue?* (Cambridge: Cambridge University Press, 2008); "The Use and Abuse of Mathematical Entities: Galileo and the Jesuits Revisited," in *A Companion to Galileo*, ed. P. Machamer (Cambridge University Press, 1998), 80–146; and "On Wonderful Machines: The Transmission of Mechanical Knowledge by Jesuits," *Science and Education* 15 (2006): 151–72.

CHAPTER 8

Aquinas and Ignatius on the "Hierarchical Church"

Aaron Pidel, SJ

At first glance, the prospects might seem bleak for discovering deep affinities between St. Thomas Aquinas and St. Ignatius of Loyola on matters of ecclesial hierarchy. In nearly everyone's estimation, Aquinas stands as a parade example of the medieval hierarchical worldview, whereby divine power descends along an all-embracing chain of being, favoring certain privileged channels. Ignatius, by contrast, typically comes off as a patron saint of divine ubiquity and holy immediacy. His contemporary interpreters emphasize not so much his search for God in privileged times, places, and persons (Mass, Jerusalem, relics, etc.) as his exhortation to seek God "in all things."[1] They likewise underscore Ignatius's advice to givers of the Spiritual Exercises to "permit the Creator to deal directly [Spanish: *inmediate*] with the creature, and the creature directly with his Creator and Lord."[2] From such passages it is inferred that Ignatius teaches the "priority of experience over doctrine,"[3] and, presumably, over other mediating structures as well.

But there are good reasons for thinking that Ignatius's worldview is no less "hierarchical" than Aquinas's. A reader as knowledgeable as the great Dominican ecclesiologist Yves-Marie Congar suggests that it was Ignatius who first popularized the phrase "hierarchical Church."[4] Indeed, the neologism appears

---

1. English translation with paragraph numbers: *The Constitutions of the Society of Jesus and Their Complementary Norms* (hereafter: Const), trans. George Ganss, SJ, et al. (St. Louis, MO: Institute of Jesuit Sources, 1996), 288; citations by paragraph number.

2. Ignatius of Loyola, *The Spiritual Exercises of Saint Ignatius: A New Translation, Based on Studies in the Language of the Autograph*, trans. Louis J. Puhl, SJ (Westminster, MD: The Newman Press, 1951), 15; citations by paragraph number. References to the Latin *Versio vulgata* and Spanish autograph version will be taken from: *Monumenta Ignatiana: Exercitia Spiritualia Sancti Ignatii de Loyola et eorum directoria*, vol. 1, *Exercitia Spiritualia*, nova editio, MHSI 100 (Rome: IHSI, 1969).

3. William Reiser, SJ, "The *Spiritual Exercises* in a Religiously Pluralistic World," *Spiritus* 10 (Fall 2010): 135–57, at 150.

4. See Yves-Marie Congar, *L'Église de saint Augustin à l'époque moderne*, Histoire des dogmes, vol. 3, part 3 (Paris: Éditions du Cerf, 1970), 36; *Tradition and the Traditions: An Historical and Theological Essay*, 2 vols., trans. Michael Naseby and Thomas Rainborough (London: Burns and Oates, 1966), 1:176n3.

no fewer than three times in the *Spiritual Exercises*. A representative instance can be found in the first of Ignatius's Rules for Thinking with the Church: "We must put aside all judgment of our own and keep the mind ever ready and prompt to obey in all things the true Spouse of Christ our Lord, our holy Mother, the hierarchical church."[5] Because Ignatius here and elsewhere presents the hierarchical Church as a rule for private judgment, one might be tempted to think that Ignatius meant by "hierarchical" no more than we mean by "magisterial" today. But the remaining Rules for Thinking with the Church turn out to be much more comprehensive. They aim to help the exercitant find the right measure of "praise" due to a variety of religious practices, ranging from frequent reception of the sacraments to making vows of religion to venerating the saints in glory.[6] This suggests that the phrase "hierarchical Church" reflects not only Ignatius's emphasis on doctrinal conformity but his broader conviction that God ordinarily exercises providence through privileged intermediaries—a conviction more typically associated with medieval scholasticism.

This contribution to *Ignatius of Loyola and Thomas Aquinas* will argue, more specifically, that Ignatius understands the "hierarchical Church" much as Thomas Aquinas does. This should hardly be a surprise. For in Ignatius's day no less than in Aquinas's, the word "hierarchy" evoked the legacy of Dionysius the Areopagite, pseudonymous author of the *Celestial Hierarchy* and *Ecclesiastical Hierarchy*.[7] The adjective "hierarchical" no less than the noun "hierarchy" would, therefore, have evoked an image of the Church as a cascade of divinizing energy, emanating from the divine source and perfecting the farthest creatures through a graded sequence of intermediaries. Aquinas, as we will see, stands by a modified version of the Dionysian economy. And Ignatius's way of proceeding in devotion and governance, as we shall also see, proves eminently compatible with Thomas's reception of Dionysius.

To demonstrate these deep "hierarchical" resonances between Thomas and Ignatius, this essay will proceed as follows. It will begin by examining how Aquinas retains Dionysian angelology and ecclesiology in their main outlines while modifying them in particulars. It will then turn to Ignatius, showing the how the Thomistic version of the celestial and ecclesiastical hierarchies finds practical application in the Spanish mystic's rules for discernment of spirits, his

---

5. SpEx, 353. See also SpEx, 170, 365.
6. SpEx, 352–69.
7. Santiago Madrigal Terrazas has convincingly argued in a chapter entitled "La estructura 'jerárqica' de la realidad, el influjo de Pseudo-Dionisio en la teología medieval," that "hierarchy" would have been understood by Ignatius's contemporaries as an allusion to Dionysian ideas. See Santiago Madrigal Terrazas, *Estudios de eclesiología ignaciana* (Madrid: Universidad de Comillas and Desclée de Brouwer, 2002), 253–99.

mediated approach to God in prayer, and his stated rationale for placing Jesuits at the service of the papacy by means of a special vow.

Aquinas's Appropriation of Dionysian Hierarchy

What notion of hierarchy did Dionysius bequeath to Aquinas? Broadly speaking, Aquinas inherited a vision of the saving economy in which God sustains and perfects the cosmos through a ranked series of intermediary agents. According to Dionysius, divine light and energy proceed successively from Jesus, the "Light of the Father,"[8] to each of the nine angelic orders, beginning with the seraphim and ending with the angels.[9] From this celestial hierarchy, the divinizing current then descends to the ecclesial hierarchy, where it passes first through the clerical triad of bishops, priests and deacons, and then through a lay triad of monks, contemplatives, and penitents.[10] Because each hierarchical rank receives illumination according to its own capacity and then transmits this light to the next rank, divine grace and revelation gradually particularize and accommodate themselves to each level, excluding no one. "[The blessed Deity] has bestowed hierarchy as a gift," writes Dionysius, "to ensure the salvation and divinization of every being endowed with reason and intelligence."[11] For Dionysius and the greater part of the Christian tradition, then, the concept of hierarchy stands not for a machinery of oppression but for an economy of what René Rocques calls "uplifting condescension" (*condescendence anagogique*).[12]

Dionysius further analyzes hierarchy's elevating activity into three sub-operations: purifying, illuminating, and perfecting.[13] Every triadic angelic hierarchy exercises this threefold influence over the triad below it, but without any apparent one-to-one correspondence between angelic order and operation.[14] In the ecclesiastical hierarchy, however, Dionysius comes closer to teaching such a one-to-one correlation, assigning each of these three functions predominantly to one or another sacramental action or social order. This is especially true of the clerical

---

8. Pseudo-Dionysius, *Celestial Hierarchy* (hereafter: CH) I, 2; cf. Pseudo-Dionysius, *Ecclesiastical Hierarchy* (hereafter: EH) I, 1; IV, 5. For the Greek text and English translation I have used, respectively, *Corpus Dionysiacum*, vol. 2, *De coelesti hierarchia. De ecclesiastica hierarchia. De mystica theologia. Epistulae*, ed. Günter Heil and Adolf Martin Ritter, Patristische Texte und Studien 36 (Berlin: De Gruyter, 1991); *Pseudo-Dionysius: The Complete Works*, trans. Colm Luibheid, Classics of Western Spirituality (New York: Paulist, 1987).
9. CH, passim.
10. EH V, 6; VI, 1–3.
11. EH I, 4.
12. René Rocques, "Denys l'Aréopagite," in *Dictionnaire de spiritualité*, vol. 3 (Paris: Beauchesne, 1957), 244–86, at 280.
13. CH III, 2–3
14. CH VII, 2.

ranks of deacon, priest, and "hierarch" (or bishop), who represent, respectively, the "one which purifies, the one which illuminates, and the one which brings about perfection."[15] The division of labor is not complete, however, since the perfective power of the bishop virtually includes the illuminating power of priests and the purifying power of deacons.[16] It is a feature of Dionysian hierarchy that a higher order can do whatever a lower order can do, though not vice-versa.

Points of General Agreement

Aquinas's respect for Dionysius as a theological authority soon becomes apparent to even a casual reader. Dionysius, as the author of *On the Divine Names*, is the only extra-biblical author besides Aristotle to whose work Aquinas dedicates a commentary. Aquinas cites him nearly 1,700 times, always with deference.[17] Even the particulars of his worldview find a place in Aquinas's arguments. For instance, when the *Sentence Commentary* replies negatively to the question, "Whether all angels are sent in ministry?," it offers the following reasoning:

> According to Dionysius, this is the inviolably established law of divinity [*lex divinitatis inviolabiliter stabilita*]: that the last things be perfected by the first things through intermediaries. But between us and the first angels there are lower intermediaries. Hence, the action of the first does not reach us immediately but exists through secondary intermediaries. Besides, a proportion is said to exist between agent and recipient. But it is fitting for the lower angels to receive divine illuminations proportioned to us, and through fittingness to our hierarchy. Therefore, it seems that only they are immediately sent to us.[18]

Aquinas thus accepts the general Dionysian picture of the cosmos, according to which divinizing energy reaches us through a non-arbitrary sequence of intermediaries. Only the lower angels are sent to "our hierarchy" because the illuminations of higher angels would be disproportionate to human minds, like ultraviolet light to human eyes, or a dog whistle to human ears.

15. EH V, 4.
16. EH V, 7.
17. On Aquinas's greater deference to Dionysius than to even Aristotle or the "Platonists," see Wayne Hankey, "Dionysian Hierarchy in Thomas Aquinas: Tradition and Transformation," in *Denys l'Aréopagite et sa postérité en Orient et en Occident*, ed. Y. de Andia (Paris: Études Augustiniennes, 1996), 405–38, at 243n41.
18. Thomas Aquinas, *Super Sent* lib. 2, d. 10, q. 1, a. 2, s.c. Latin text of this and other Thomistic works, unless otherwise noted, are taken from *Corpus Thomisticum*, https://www.corpusthomisticum.org/iopera.html. The English translations of Aquinas are also mine, unless otherwise noted. The "law of divinity" translates what Dionysius calls the "all-holy ordinance of divinity" (θεμισμὸς . . . τῆς θεαρχίας ὁ πανίερος). EH V, 4.

Aquinas perhaps accepts so readily the idea that the ministrations of the lower angels are more proportionate to the human intellect because it harmonizes so well with the Aristotelian principle that that the human intellect is sense-bound. The *Summa Theologiae* invokes both Aristotelian and Dionysian principles when responding affirmatively to the question, "Whether an angel can enlighten man?"

> The human intellect . . . cannot grasp the universal truth itself unveiled; because its nature requires it to understand by turning to the phantasms . . . So the angels propose the intelligible truth to men under the similitudes of sensible things, according to what Dionysius says (*Coel. Hier.* i), that, "It is impossible for the divine ray to shine on us, otherwise than shrouded by the variety of the sacred veils."[19]

In concluding that angelic natures can enlighten human persons only through phantasms proportionate to their intellects, Aquinas supplies, as we will see, one of the unstated assumptions behind Ignatius's Rules for the Discernment of Spirits.

Aquinas invokes the *lex divinitatis* to explain the relationship not only between angels and men but between one Christian and another. The *Sentence Commentary* presents the differentiation of the Church into orders as the reflection of a kind of aesthetic "natural law" (*legem naturalem*): "In order that this beauty [*pulchritudo*] not be lacking to the Church, God put order in her, that certain men would give the sacraments to others—assimilated to God by this in their own way, as if cooperating with God—just as also in a natural body certain members influence others"[20] In the *Summa Theologiae*, Aquinas even deploys Dionysius's tripartite division of labor among the ordained. When replying negatively to the question, "Whether all ecclesiastical prelates are in a state of perfection?," he invokes Dionysius's teaching that the role of perfecting—and thus the state of perfection—belongs to bishops alone.[21] Aquinas appears, in short, to take over much of Dionysius's hierarchical framework without demur.

Extending and Nuancing Dionysius

Aquinas's palpable reverence for Dionysius, however, does not prevent him from nuancing and extending his thought in ways that Dionysius himself might not have recognized. Though one could adduce many instances of Aquinas's

---

19. ST I, q. 111, a. 1, co. Latin text and English translation of the Summa Theologiae from Logic Museum, http://www.logicmuseum.com/wiki/Authors/Thomas_Aquinas/Summa_Theologiae.
20. *Super Sent* lib. 4, d. 24, q. 1, a. 1, qc. 1, co.
21. ST II-II q. 184, a. 6, s.c.

creative fidelity to Dionysius, the ultimate goal of establishing points of contact between Aquinas and Ignatius obliges us to focus on three areas: the relationship between angels and Christians *in patria*, the relationship between angels and Christians *in via*, and the role of the bishop within the Church militant. In all cases, Aquinas treats the order of mediation more flexibly than his forebear.

To understand how Aquinas nuances Dionysius on the relationship between angels and Christians in glory, one does well to recall that for Dionysius the order of proximity to God follows the order of natural dignity. Not a few medieval authors influenced by Dionysius, therefore, conclude that even in the state of glory the lowest angelic natures will outrank the most supernaturally exalted humans. To Aquinas, however, this interpretation "seems to savor of heresy, since the blessed Virgin Mary is exalted over all the choirs of angels."[22] Seeking to preserve both Mary's celestial queenship and Dionysius's authority, the *Sentence Commentary* quotes Dionysius against himself, observing how the *Ecclesiastical Hierarchy* teaches a kind of analogy of salvation-historical periods. Just as the legal hierarchy of the Jews adumbrates the ecclesiastical hierarchy, so also the ecclesiastical hierarchy adumbrates the celestial hierarchy.[23] The saints will consequently inherit, according to their merits, places among the nine choirs of angels, with the "Blessed Virgin Mary [being] over all."[24] Dante would give this eschatological arrangement poetic expression in his *Paradiso*.

Having placed Mary above the nine angelic choirs and ranged the saints among them, Aquinas explains the propriety of approaching God through heavenly patrons. Since all of these angels and saints enjoy a proximity to God greater than that of us wayfarers, he observes, "it is fitting for us so to be led back [*reduci*] to God that we might receive his benefits again through the mediation of the saints; that is why we make them intercessors for ourselves before God, and something like mediators [*quasi mediatores*]."[25] Ignatius too, as we shall see, also warmly recommends approaching God through such "mediators."

Turning from the relationship between the angels and Christians *in patria* to their relationship *in via*, we once again find Aquinas carefully nuancing Dionysius. Both the *Celestial Hierarchy* and *Ecclesiastical Hierarchy* strongly imply that we wayfarers, owing to the natural disproportion between divine and human intelligence, would be incapable of receiving any divine influx that had not been "pre-digested" by the lower angels. Thomas, however, expressly anticipates exceptions. When the *Summa* revisits the question earlier mooted in the *Sentence Commentary*, "Whether all the angels are sent in ministry?," it qualifies

---

22. *Super Sent* lib. 2, d. 9, q. 1, a. 8, co.
23. *Super Sent* lib. 2, d. 9, q. 1, a. 8, ad 4. See EH V, 2.
24. *Super Sent* lib. 2 d., 9 q., 1, a. 8, co.
25. *Super Sent* lib. 4, d. 45, q. 3, a. 2, co.

Dionysius's principle that God always communicates himself to inferior creatures via superior creatures: "By divine dispensation, however, this order is sometimes departed from as regards corporeal things, for the sake of a higher order, that is, according as it is suitable for the manifestation of grace."[26] For Thomas, no one can doubt that God bypasses the secondary causality of the heavenly bodies to work miracles. "Nor can anyone doubt that God can immediately reveal things to men without the help of the angels."[27] Though God ordinarily works through mediators and secondary causes, in other words, he sometimes acts immediately to make his existence more manifest.

All of this leads Aquinas to speak of divine providence as embracing a twofold causal order. When treating the question, "Whether the Son of God assumed flesh through the medium of the soul," Aquinas answers by way of a distinction. There is an order of efficient causality by which God is in all creatures "by essence, presence, and power;" and there is an order of final causality by which "lower creatures are directed to God by higher, as Dionysius says."[28] It is according to this latter ordering that God can be said to have assumed flesh through the human soul. A similar distinction between God's immediate and angelically mediated communications, as we shall soon see, informs Ignatius's Rules for Discernment of Spirits.

Aquinas's attitude of creative fidelity to Dionysius surfaces again in his treatment of the bishop as ecclesiastical "hierarch." Here the Angelic Doctor develops Dionysian thought in two ways that foreshadow Ignatius's own sensibility. First, Aquinas, despite generally concurring with the Dionysian teaching that it belongs to the bishop to "perfect" his subjects,[29] complicates the arrow of grace's transmission.[30] For example, when the *Summa* moots the question, "Whether an inferior angel can enlighten a superior angel?," it entertains as grounds for an affirmative answer Paul's words, "You may all prophesy one by

---

26. ST I, q. 112, a. 2.
27. ST I, q. 112, a. 2.
28. ST III, q. 6, a. 1, ad 1. For other references to this distinction between an immediate and hierarchical ordering, see David E. Luscombe, "Thomas Aquinas and Conceptions of Hierarchy in the Thirteenth Century," in *Thomas Aquin: Werk und Wirkung im Licht neuerer Forschung* (Berlin: Walter de Gruyter, 1988), 261–77, esp. 272.
29. For Aquinas's emphasis on the bishop as perfecting through teaching, see Noel Molloy, "Hierarchy and Holiness: Aquinas on the Holiness of the Episcopal State," *Thomist* 39, no. 2 (1975): 198–252, esp. 236–47. For the role of local bishop as perfecter even of friars, see Ulrich Horst, *Bischöfe und Ordensleute: Cura principalis animarum und via perfectionis in der Ekklesiologie des hl. Thomas von Aquin* (Berlin: Akademie Verlag, 1999), 113–38.
30. Dionysius elsewhere reproves the monk Demophilus for chastising a priest, reasoning that Demophilus ought not enforce justice "beyond his worth and order." Letter 8, 3, *Pseudo-Dionysius*, 275. See also Adam G. Cooper, "Hierarchy, Humility, and Holiness: The Meaning of Ecclesial Ranks according to Dionysius the Areopagite," *Nova et Vetera* 11, no. 3 (2013): 649–61.

one, that all may learn and be exhorted" (1 Cor 14:31). If Paul allows even the lowest to prophesy in the presence of the highest, the objection runs, then a lower angel can also enlighten a higher angel.[31] Aquinas handles the objection by explaining the irrelevance of the Pauline passage to angelic mediation:

> The ecclesiastical hierarchy imitates the heavenly in some degree, but by an imperfect likeness. For in the heavenly hierarchy the perfection of the order is in proportion to its nearness to God; so that those who are the nearer to God are the more sublime in grade, and clearer in knowledge; and on that account the superiors are never enlightened by the inferiors, whereas in the ecclesiastical hierarchy sometimes those who are the nearer to God in sanctity are in the lowest grade, and are not conspicuous for science; and some also are eminent in one kind of science, and fail in another; and on that account superiors may be taught by inferiors.[32]

Because the angelic hierarchy follows a difference of nature, whereas the ecclesiastical hierarchy follows only a difference of public charism, one can expect more "contraflow" in the ecclesiastical hierarchy than in the celestial. Here Aquinas gives a theological rationale for the services that Catherine of Siena would later render as unofficial papal admonitor.

The second way Aquinas develops the role of the "hierarch" beyond the warrants Dionysius provides is to create a special rank for the Pope within the episcopal college. For Dionysius, it will be remembered, each diocesan hierarchy terminates in a bishop, but each bishop has no other human superior save Christ.[33] Aquinas, not sharing Dionysius's polycephalous ecclesiology, argues in the *Summa contra gentiles* that is fitting for episcopal *potestas* to culminate in a single highest individual, a Pope. He appeals to Aristotle's judgment that monarchy is the best rule for the multitude,[34] as well as to the fittingness of representing Christ's unique headship through a single hierarch.[35] But he also offers a third, more Dionysian, line of reasoning based on an analogy of heavenly and ecclesiastical hierarchies:

> The militant Church, moreover, derives from the triumphant Church by exemplarity. But in the triumphant Church one presides, the one who pre-

---

31. ST I q. 106, a. 3, arg. 1.
32. ST I, q. 106, q. 3, ad 1. Translation modified.
33. EH V, 4. Dionysius does speak of Peter as vertex and chief of all who speak in God's name (*Divine Names* III, 2), but little indicates that Dionysius ascribes such a preeminence to Peter's successors.
34. Thomas Aquinas, *Summa contra gentiles* (hereafter: SCG) IV, 76.4. English translation: *Summa Contra Gentiles Book Four: Salvation*, trans. Charles J. O'Neil (Notre Dame, IN: University of Notre Dame Press, 1975).
35. SCG IV, 76.7.

sides over the entire universe—namely, God—for we read in the Apocalypse (21:3): "They shall be His people and God himself with them shall be their God." Therefore, in the militant Church, also, there is one who presides over things universally [*praesidet universis*].³⁶

The premise that the Church militant imitates the Church triumphant betrays Aquinas's Dionysian sensibility.

At the same time, Aquinas's failure to cite Dionysius expressly perhaps indicates his reluctance to accept all the implications of the Dionysian hierarchical schema for his characterization of the Pope as "president" of the church militant. After all, if the pope acted in every respect as vertex of a Dionysian hierarchy, he would precontain all divine energies destined for the lower tiers of the ecclesial pyramid. He would thus encroach upon the prerogatives of Christ and Mary. Perhaps for this reason, Aquinas limits the comparison between divine and papal monarchy to the act of "presiding," presenting the pope as a font of jurisdiction rather than of all graces and charisms.³⁷

A motivation for emphasizing the Pope as summit of jurisdictional authority emerges in Aquinas's defense of the Dominican order during the mendicant controversy. The secular clergy felt that roaming friars destroyed the Dionysian sense of order. By appealing to papal commission rather than local episcopal delegation for their itinerant preaching and teaching, they violated the principle that each ecclesiastical station depends on the rank immediately above it.³⁸ Defending his fellow friars in *Contra impugnantes* (1256), Aquinas recalls that Scripture describes the angels who purify Isaiah's lips as "seraphim" (Is 6:6), one of the higher orders not sent out in ministry. The *Celestial Hierarchy* accounts for this *façon de parler* by noting that an angel of lower rank, while remaining in its station, may be said to represent an angelic order many grades superior.³⁹ Aquinas then reasons analogically to ecclesial order: "Therefore, it is not unfitting if in the ecclesiastical hierarchy someone of an inferior order exercise the office of a superior order by his commission [*eius commissione*]."⁴⁰ In case the relevance for the mendicant controversy were not sufficiently clear, Aquinas parallels the seraphim commissioning the lower

---

36. SCG IV, 76.5.
37. Hankey notes how Aquinas "identifies the principal ecclesiastical hierarch with the Roman Pontiff," but gives this power a political cast, making him "head of the Christian republic." "Dionysian Hierarchy in Thomas Aquinas," 437.
38. For background to this debate, see Ulrich Horst, *The Dominicans and the Pope: Papal Teaching Authority in the Medieval and Early Modern Thomist Tradition*, trans. James D. Mixson (Notre Dame, IN: University of Notre Dame Press, 2006), 7–14.
39. CH XIII, 1.
40. Thomas Aquinas, *Contra impugnantes*, pars 2, cap. 3, ad 8.

angels on the one hand to Innocent III commissioning Cistercians to preach in Toulouse on the other.[41] It was an encounter with these same Cistercian papal legates that moved Dominic to make the itinerant "apostolic form" his own life's ideal.[42] The upshot: the Pope, as lone apex of the Church's jurisdictional and doctrinal hierarchy, may legitimately commission friars to preach and occupy university chairs without the prior approval of local bishops.

Painting in broad strokes, then, one might say that Aquinas treats Dionysius's *lex divinitatis* as the default setting for God's dealings with humanity while allowing for exceptions. This is true of the slope of influence between the celestial and ecclesiastical hierarchies, as well as between grades within the ecclesiastical hierarchy. Aquinas innovates on the Dionysian schema most overtly by assigning the Pope a hierarchical grade superior to that of other bishops. At the same time, he interprets this *plenitudo potestatis* not as a claim to mediate all graces destined for the Church, but as an immediate and universal jurisdiction, along with its concomitant teaching authority.[43]

Ignatian Resonances with the Thomistic Reception of Dionysian Hierarchy

When profiled against this Thomist background, Ignatius of Loyola's way of proceeding, as we will see, begins to appear very Thomistic. Prior to a detailed exposition of the parallels, however, it will perhaps be useful to explain why this essay speaks not of Ignatius's reception of Aquinas but of his resonances with Aquinas. Any talk of Ignatius's literary dependence on Aquinas must remain conjectural for two reasons: our inability to determine the contribution of infused knowledge, and our inability to reconstruct Ignatius's exact course of studies.

On the first point, there is always the possibility that Ignatius first received his hierarchical worldview not through formal education but through a mixture of ambient culture and infused knowledge. Ignatius's *Autobiography*, for instance, describes many of Ignatius's early illuminations as a kind of divine initiation into the *lex divinitatis*. Relating how Ignatius found devotion while

---

41. *Contra impugnantes, pars 2, cap. 3, ad 28*. Aquinas elsewhere draws the parallel between Seraphim acting through lower angels and the Pope hearing confessions through priests. See ST I, q. 112, a. 2, ad 2.

42. Humbert Vicaire, *L'imitation des Apôtres* (Paris: Éditions du Cerf, 1963), 72.

43. On the chiefly jurisdictional implications that Aquinas draws from his analysis of the pope as Dionysian hierarch, see the seminal article of Yves Congar, OP, "Aspects ecclésiologiques de la querelle entre mendiants et séculiers dans la seconde moitié du XIIIe siècle et le début du XIVe," *Archives d'histoire doctrinale et littéraire du Moyen Age* 28 (1961): 35–151, 95. On the close relationship between jurisdiction and teaching authority for Thomas, see Horst, *The Dominicans and the Pope*, 9–11.

still convalescing from battle injuries at Loyola (1521), the *Autobiography* recalls, "And the greatest consolation he used to receive was to look at the sky and the stars, which he did often and for a long time, because with this he used to feel in himself a great impetus towards serving God Our Lord."[44] Here it is important to remember that Ignatius would have contemplated the heavens according to the Ptolemaic model, much as Dante had done two centuries earlier.[45] He saw the night sky, therefore, not as a trackless void with occasional clouds of combustible gas, but as concentric spherical intelligences, each moved by the intellectual love of God, each composed of elements ineffably nobler than anything earthly. It was this image of the heavens as a nested hierarchy of intelligent operations that made Ignatius burn to serve God.[46]

When Ignatius takes up residence in Manresa (1522–23), allowing God to treat him "just as a schoolmaster treats a child,"[47] his education in the *lex divinitatis* only intensifies. Indeed, the principal effect of several of Ignatius's mystical experiences seems to have been to render hierarchical processions momentarily visible under the Dionysian figure of descending luminosity. When receiving insight into how God had created the world, for instance, Ignatius "seemed to see something white, from which some rays were coming, and God made light from this." On another occasion, during the elevation of the host at Mass, "he saw with interior eyes something like white rays coming from above."[48] Such experiences left Ignatius feeling like "another man with another mind,"[49] that is, alive to the reality of hierarchical emanation in the orders of both creation and redemption.

Tellingly, the same Dionysian imagery appears in the *Spiritual Exercises*, the retreat manual that Ignatius began to compose during his time at Manresa. The Contemplation to Attain the Love of God, the retreat's summative meditation, invites exercitants to imagine themselves bathed in currents of hierarchical energy: "I will consider how all good things and gifts descend from above; for example, my proportionate power [*medida potencia*] from the Supreme and Infinite Power above . . . just as the rays come down from the sun, or waters from the font [*de la fuente las aguas*]."[50] The whole ensemble of motifs—self-diffusive

---

44. Ignatius of Loyola, *The Autobiography*, in *Ignatius of Loyola: Spiritual Exercises and Selected Works*, ed. George E. Ganss, SJ, Classics of Western Spirituality (New York: Paulist, 1991), 11; cited by paragraph number.

45. Copernicus's *De revolutionibus orbium coelestium* was not published until 1543 and, even then, gained acceptance only slowly.

46. For the effect of the Ptolemaic cosmos on premodern feeling and imagination, see especially C. S. Lewis, *The Discarded Image: An Introduction to Medieval and Renaissance Literature* (Cambridge: Cambridge University Press, 1964), 92–121.

47. Autobiog, 27.
48. Autobiog, 29.
49. Autobiog, 30.
50. SpEx, 237.

goodness, rays and font, proportionate participation—all unmistakably evoke the Western reception of the Dionysian tradition.[51] Some evidence, therefore, points to the idea that God initiated Ignatius into the *lex divinitatis* long before any professors did, giving him a deep feeling for things hierarchical.

At the same time, since Ignatius dictated his *Autobiography* late in life and kept touching up his *Spiritual Exercises* long after Manresa, one cannot exclude the possibility that Ignatius's subsequent education influenced his way of interpreting and recounting these early experiences. Indeed, there are good but not conclusive reasons for thinking that Ignatius encountered scholastic receptions of Dionysius while studying in Paris, the putative city of Dionysius's martyrdom. Historical records show, for instance, that the University of Paris's Theological Faculty stoutly resisted innovation on the Dionysian corpus, whether by addition or subtraction. From 1512 to 1515 its members met intermittently to draft a condemnation of *De auctoritate papae et concilii sive ecclesiae comparata* by the Dominican Thomas de Vío (or Cajetan), whose insistence on the pope's superiority to councils ran counter not only to the faculty's Gallican sympathies but to Dionysian polycephaly. Only the King's fear of straining diplomatic relations with Rome prevented the faculty from issuing a formal censure.[52] Just a few years later in 1521, however, the Parisian faculty did succeed in formally condemning Martin Luther. As grounds for censure, their *Determinatio* pointed *inter alia* to the incompatibility between the German Reformer's priesthood of all believers and Dionysius's hierarchical ecclesiology.[53] It is safe to assume that, when Ignatius arrived just a few years later in 1529, Dionysian ecclesiology was still very much "in the air."

The distinctively Thomist reception of Dionysius would naturally have contributed to this atmosphere. The Basilian historian James Farge notes that the University of Paris in the first half of the sixteenth century was witnessing a kind of "Thomist revival."[54] The Dominican Pieter Crockaert had already replaced Lombard's *Sentences* with Aquinas's *Summa Theologiae* at the Dominican Studium in Paris, whence the innovative pedagogy spread to Spain.[55] And though we cannot be certain how much Ignatius read Aquinas directly,

---

51. Besides relying heavily on light imagery, Dionysius writes that the "source of this hierarchy is the font of life . . . the Trinity which bestows being and well-being on everything" (EH I, 3).
52. James K. Farge, *Orthodoxy and Reform in Early Reformation France: The Faculty of Theology of Paris (1500–1543)*, Studies in Medieval and Reformation Thought 32 (Leiden: Brill, 1985), 117, 223–25.
53. Farge, *Orthodoxy and Reform*, 167.
54. Farge, *Orthodoxy and Reform*, 233n71, 246.
55. Georg Schurhammer, SJ, *Francis Xavier: His Life, His Times*, vol. 1, *Europe (1506–1541)*, trans. M. Joseph Costelloe, SJ (Rome: Jesuit Historical Institute, 1973), 247–49. Ricardo García Villoslada, SJ, finds evidence of the Dominican Studium using the *Summa* from 1509. See *La*

we know that the Jesuit founder aligned his fledgling order with certain aspects of the Parisian Thomist revival. The Jesuit *Constitutions* likewise prescribe the *Summa* as the basic theology textbook for Jesuit colleges.[56] And as we will see below, these same *Constitutions* commit the Society of Jesus to a papalism savoring more of the Thomist school than of Parisian Gallicanism.

In sum, it remains probable but not demonstrable that Ignatius read Aquinas directly. To avoid building castles on sand, therefore, I will describe the parallels between Aquinas's hierarchical theory and Ignatius's religious praxis merely as striking "affinities," bracketing the question of direct historical influence. These affinities include Ignatius's preference for approaching God through his "mediators," his teaching on angelic consolation, and his grounds for devoting the Society of Jesus to the service of the Church under the Roman Pontiff.

Ignatius and his "Mediadores"

Numbering among the many points of agreement between Aquinas and Ignatius on hierarchical order is the latter's habit of approaching God the Father through a sequence of *"mediadores,"* first Mary and then Jesus. This pattern of prayer corresponds closely to the upper reaches of Aquinas's eschatologically adjusted picture of the celestial hierarchy, which, as we saw, assigns Mary a dignity and mediatorial scope falling just below that of Christ and the Father but exceeding that of all other angels and saints. Ignatius both follows this anagogical itinerary— from Mary to Christ to the Father—and teaches others to pray the same way.

Though the *Autobiography* suggests that Ignatius experienced God approaching him through Jesus and Mary very early,[57] it describes his habit of retracing this itinerary back to God only later. This kind of mediated ascent becomes evident, for instance, in the *Autobiography*'s version of the Vision of La Storta (1537), often considered the mystical charter of the Society of Jesus:[58]

> Ignatius had decided to spend a year without saying Mass after he became a priest, preparing himself and praying Our Lady to deign to place him with her Son. One day, a few miles before reaching Rome, he was at prayer

---

universidad de Paris durante los estudios de Victoria, OP (1507–1522) (Rome: Gregorian University Press, 1938), 279.

56. Cons., 464; cited by paragraph number.

57. While receiving his other illuminations at Manresa, Ignatius also sees with "interior eyes the humanity of Christ" in the form of an indistinct "white body, neither very large nor very small," and "Our Lady in a similar form." Autobiog, 29.

58. There are several versions of the Vision of La Storta. For a classic comparative analysis, see Hugo Rahner, SJ, *The Vision of St Ignatius in the Chapel of La Storta*, 2nd ed. (Rome: Centrum Ignatianum Spiritualitatis, 1979), 43–68.

in a Church and experienced such a change in his soul and saw so clearly that God the Father placed him with Christ his Son that he would not dare doubt it—that God the Father had placed him with his Son.[59]

Here we find Ignatius's prayer beginning with Mary, moving to Christ her Son, and culminating in the Father, who places Ignatius with Christ. The Father thus mystically confirms this graduated approach to himself.

Much evidence suggests that Ignatius kept approaching the Father through Mary and Christ. In the *Spiritual Diary* entry for February 8, 1544, for instance, Ignatius recalls presenting God his election for stricter poverty as follows: "praying to her to help me in approaching her Son and the Father, and then praying to the Son to help me in approaching the Father in the company of the Mother, I felt in myself a motion towards the Father or that I was being lifted up before him."[60] At several other places in the *Spiritual Diary*, Ignatius refers to Mary and Jesus simply as the "mediators" (*mediadores*), a designation Aquinas himself applies to the saints.[61]

In complete harmony with the Thomistic ethos of "handing on the fruits of contemplation,"[62] Ignatius's *Spiritual Exercises* invite others to follow Ignatius's ascending itinerary. This is most notable in The Meditation on Two Standards, which invites the retreatant to pray in the form of a "Triple Colloquy." This involves imploring the grace to be received under the standard of the poor Christ, first from Mary, then from Christ, and then from the Father.[63] The fact that Ignatius prescribes this ladderlike ascent for all who make the Exercises suggests that he ascribed a certain universality to the mediation of Mary and Jesus. This comports well with the Aquinas's depiction of Mary and Jesus as penultimate and ultimate "hierarchs" in the celestial hierarchy.

Ignatius's Hierarchy of Consolation

Though Ignatius shows a special sensitivity to Mary and Jesus as mediators, he by no means neglects the hierarchical activity of the angels so prominent in Dionysius and Aquinas. In fact, his Rules for the Discernment of Spirits, a set of criteria for recognizing the origin of affective movements in the soul, presuppose a great deal of medieval angelology.[64] They show little interest in the

---

59. Autobiog, 96.
60. SpDiar, 8; cited by paragraph number. English translation: *Ignatius of Loyola: Spiritual Exercises and Selected Works*, 235–270.
61. SpDiar, 6, 12.
62. ST III, q. 40, a. 1, ad 2.
63. SpEx, 147.
64. SpEx, 313–36.

number and classification of angelic hierarchies, most of which, according to Aquinas's theory, would have exercised no direct influence in human affairs. But they do use, as a diagnostic criterion, one of Aquinas's speculative departures from Dionysius, namely, his position that God may bypass angelic intermediaries for the sake of confirming faith.

Ignatius's acceptance of the fact that God may exercise providence either with or without angelic mediation appears most clearly in the so-called "second-week rules" for discernment of spirits.[65] There Ignatius identifies the origin and indications of what he calls a consolation without previous cause:

> God alone can give consolation to the soul without any previous cause. It belongs solely to the Creator to come into a soul, to leave it, to act upon it, to draw it wholly to the love of His Divine Majesty. I said without previous cause, that is, without any preceding perception or knowledge of any subject by which a soul might be led to such a consolation through its own acts of intellect and will.[66]

In the opening sentence of the next rule, Ignatius then turns to consolation *with* previous cause, identifying its possible instigators:

> If a cause precedes, both the good angel and the evil spirit can give consolation to a soul, but for a quite different purpose.[67]

The resonances with Aquinas's more flexible version of Dionysian hierarchy are plain. In consolation *with* previous cause, the Creator permits his creatures to be moved through the secondary agency of good or bad angels. In consolation *without* previous cause, the Creator bypasses the ordinary hierarchical sequence to move his creature immediately.

It is little noticed that Ignatius, despite associating "previous cause" with an intramental order of causality—the "perception or knowledge of any subject by which a soul might be led to such a consolation through its own acts of intellect and will"—actually has an extramental order of causality in view. Ignatius reasons that spiritual consolation, if it perdures only so long as it is sustained by the soul's "acts of intellect and will," has a proximate angelic origin. Here Ignatius takes for granted the principle of Dionysian and Thomistic angelology mentioned above, namely, that angels give enlightenments proportionate to the human mind, proposing "intelligible truth to men under the similitudes of sensible things."[68] But if angels possess this power by nature, it follows that fallen

---

65. SpEx, 328–36.
66. SpEx 330.
67. SpEx 331.
68. ST I, q. 111, a. 1, co.

angels too can touch the membrane between sense and spirit. Aquinas draws this conclusion explicitly, stating, "Both a good and a bad angel by their own natural power can move the human imagination."[69] This ambiguity obviously suggests that even a generous impulse sustained by recourse to phantasms requires further testing, since demons may disguise themselves as an "angel of light" (2 Cor 11:14).

Though it is sometimes proposed that one can reasonably accept the validity of Ignatius's rules for discernment of spirits without accepting the existence of angels and demons,[70] the opinion remains hard to reconcile with the second-week rules. For unless there exist malign intelligences capable of influencing us through phantasms, it makes little sense to put more trust in consolations without previous cause than in consolations with previous cause. Apart from the possibility of demons masquerading as "angels of light," in fact, it makes far more sense to trust impulses continuous with our psychological operations than bolts from the blue. The "wisdom" of at least some of Ignatius's rules, therefore, hangs together with key premises of Thomistic angelology: that angels, whether good or bad, can influence us only through phantasms; that God exercises providence ordinarily through angelic hierarchies; and that God occasionally bypasses angelic hierarchies for the confirmation of faith.

Special Vow of Obedience to a Thomistic Hierarch

Ignatius's papalism resembles his angelology inasmuch as it too represents a practical orientation consonant with Aquinas's innovative reception of Dionysius. Aquinas, as we saw, crowned Dionysius's ecclesiastical hierarchy with a lone papal vertex, the plenary source of all juridical *potestas* but not of all divine light destined for the Church. Ignatius's twin policies of vowing special obedience to the pope and making "representation" to him suggest a special affinity for the Thomistic theology of the papal monarchy.

An understanding of the papacy quite harmonious with Aquinas's informs Ignatius's so-called "Letter on Obedience." Laying out the metaphysical grounds for religious obedience, the letter observes:

---

69. ST I, q. 111, a. 3, co.
70. John English, SJ, asserts, "In these rules it is possible and necessary to prescind from whether good or evil spirits exist." *Spiritual Freedom: From an Experience of the Ignatian Exercises to the Art of Spiritual Guidance*, 2nd ed. (Chicago, Loyola University Press, 1995), 112. Jules Toner, SJ, thinks one can prescind at least from demons: "The reader who finds Ignatius's treatment of Satan and demons uncongenial can, without painful complexity, readily understand them as personifications of the force of evil in self and in the world; and with this interpretation too Ignatius's Rules will remain wise, valid, and useful." *A Commentary on St. Ignatius' Rules for Discernment of Spirits* (St. Louis, MO: Institute of Jesuit Sources, 1982), 36–37.

It is by this means that Divine Providence gently disposes all things, bringing to their appointed ends [*reduciendo*] the lowest by the middlemost, and the middlemost by the highest. Even in the angels there is subordination of one hierarchy to another, and in the heavens and all the bodies that are moved . . . We see the same on earth in well-governed states, and in the hierarchy of the Church, the members of which render their obedience to [*que se reduce a*] the one universal vicar of Christ our Lord.[71]

Here one finds a statement, emanating from Ignatius's own authority, that appeals to the *lex divinitatis* in all its manifestations. These range from the music of the heavenly spheres, which Ignatius contemplated with such delight at Loyola, to political and ecclesiastical hierarchies. Ignatius reasons that the ecclesiastical hierarchy, being subject to the *lex divinitatis*, must also "reduce to" (*reducirse a*) a single hierarch, "the one universal vicar of Christ our Lord."[72] This language of "universal vicar" evokes not only the medieval Latin idea of ecclesial monocephaly but the specifically Thomist accent on the Pope as origin of universal jurisdiction.[73]

---

71. Ignatius of Loyola, Letter to the Members of the Society in Portugal, March 26, 1553. English translation: *Letters of St. Ignatius of Loyola*, trans. William J. Young, SJ (Chicago: Loyola University Press, 1959), 287–95, at 295. Spanish original: *Obras Completas de San Ignacio*, 806–16, at 815. Ignatius explains nearby that, because of this hierarchical arrangement, even the Superior General must render obedience "to the one whom God our Lord has given as superior, his vicar on earth" (*Letters*, 295).

72. Though Ignatius often worked through amanuenses, the description of the Pope as "[Christ's] universal vicar" (*su universal vicario*) seems to reflect his own devotion, inasmuch as the phrase appears also in his rough-draft treatment of papal missions, or the "Constitutiones circa Missiones." See *Monumenta Ignatiana Series Tertia: Sancti Ignatii de Loyola Constitutiones Societatis Jesu*, vol. 1, *Monumenta Constitutionum Praevia*, MHSI 63 (Romae: Typis Pontificiae Universitatis Gregorianae, 1934), 160. Commenting on the "Letter on Obedience," Michel Olphe-Galliard, SJ, refers the reader to ST II-II q. 104, a.1, where Aquinas compares subordination within the human order to subordination within the natural order of secondary causes. Olphe-Galliard, "La letter de Saint Ignace de Loyola sur la vertu d'obéissance," *Revue d'Ascétique et de Mystique* 30 (1954): 7–28, at 25.

73. Though the Letter on Obedience's emphasis on the pope as "universal vicar of Christ" betrays a certain Thomist accent, it must be admitted that other presentations of the papacy may indicate a Bonaventurian influence. Joseph Ratzinger points out that the language of hierarchical *reductio*, even if not unknown in Aquinas, is more prominent in Bonaventure. Joseph Ratzinger, "Der Einfluss des Bettelordenstreites auf die Entwicklung der Lehre vom päpstlichen Universalprimat, unter besonderer Berücksichtigung des heiligen Bonaventura," in *Theologie in Geschichte und Gegenwart: Michael Schmaus zum sechzigsten Geburtstag*, ed. J. Auer and H. Volk (Munich: K. Zink, 1957), 697–724, at 714–16. Other writings, moreover, suggest what Ratzinger considers a typically Bonaventurian paradigm, according to which Christ and Pope constitute invisible and visible hierarchs of the Church, respectively, with invisible grace following the channels of visible authority (Ratzinger, *Theologie in Geschichte und Gegenwart*, 718–19). In his letter of Feb. 23, 1555 to Emperor Claude of Abyssinia, Ignatius writes: "A member that has been torn from the body

It is the papacy's universal jurisdiction, at any rate, to which the Jesuit *Constitutions* appeal when justifying the special Jesuit vow of obedience to the Pope. Aquinas, it will be remembered, had invoked papal commission to justify Dominican preachers' exemption from local episcopal control. The *Constitutions* intensify this option for mobility by strengthening, via a fourth vow, the bond between the Jesuits and Church's universal hierarch:

> The intention of the fourth vow pertaining to the pope was not for a particular place but for having the members dispersed throughout various parts of the world. For those who first united to form the Society were from different provinces and realms and did not know into which regions they were to go, whether among faithful or the unbelievers; and therefore, to avoid erring in the path of the Lord, they made the promise or vow in order that His Holiness might distribute them for the greater glory of God, in conformity with their intention to travel throughout the world.[74]

The fourth vow thus concerns most directly the pope's plenitude of administrative power, his authority to "distribute them for the greater glory of God, in conformity with their intention to travel throughout the world." And it was this structural feature of the Jesuit order that led the Gallican theology faculty at the University of Paris to oppose the Jesuits in the sixteenth century, just as they had opposed the Dominicans in the thirteenth.[75] In solemnizing this readiness for papal mission with a special vow, Ignatius hoped simply to give the Jesuits a special incentive to use this mobility "for the greater glory of God."

---

does not receive life from the body or movement or feeling [*sentido*] from its head. Thus the patriarch in Alexandria or Cairo, being schismatic and separated from this Apostolic See and its supreme pontiff who is the head of the body of the Church, received for himself neither the life of grace nor authority." Here it seems that the "life of grace" derives from the body, and "movement or feeling" from the Pope as head. But the only head that Ignatius expressly identifies as a font of grace is Christ himself: "For whoever is not united with the body of the Church will not receive from Christ our Lord its head that influx of grace [*influjo de gracia*] which gives life to the soul and prepares it for beatitude." See *Letters*, 367–72, at 369–70; *Obras Completas*, 902–8, at 904–5.

74. Cons., 605.

75. The University of Paris censured the Jesuits in 1554, *inter alia*, for preaching, lecturing, and teaching "in praeiudicium Ordinariorum & Hierarchici ordinis." C. E. Boulay, *Historia Universitatis Parsisiensis*, vol. 6, *Ab Anno 1500. ad an. 1600* (Paris, 1673), 573. At the closing session of Trent, delegates from the Faculty of Paris resisted the motion of the Jesuit General Diego Laínez to define that Peter's successor alone had "full power of ruling, pastoring and governing the universal Church." Farge, *Orthodoxy and Reform*, 235. For the Jesuits' concerted resistance at Trent to any mechanisms of reform that would infringe upon papal *plenitudo potestatis*, see Hermann Josef Sieben, "Option für den Papst: Die Jesuiten auf dem Konzil von Trient, Dritte Sitzungsperiode 1562/1563," in *Ignatianisch: Eigenart und Methode der Gesellschaft Jesu*, ed. Michael Sievernich, SJ, and Günter Switek, SJ (Freiburg: Herder, 1990), 235–53, esp. 242–50.

Though the *Constitutions* might seem to present the special vow of obedience to the Pope as no more than a practical expedient for resolving uncertainty, broader familiarity with Ignatius's spiritual profile suggests that a deep feeling for the *lex divinitatis* guides his preference for this papal solution. Evidence of this sensitivity appears from time to time in his correspondence, as when he explains to the Bishop of Calahorra why he cannot send more Jesuits: "Since we are not, and do not want to be, our own masters, we are content to travel wherever the vicar of Christ our Lord is pleased to send us. Since the heavens echo in his voice, not the earth, I sense in us no laziness, nor even any movement thereof."[76] Ignatius's habitual perception that the "heavens" echo in papal commands informs even the little details of his administration. When certain Spanish theologians accused Ignatius of heterodoxy, for instance, appealing to an error in the Latin translation of the *Spiritual Exercises*, Ignatius resisted amending the text. He could not bring himself to use the Spanish text to correct the Latin, he explained, "because the Latin text had been approved by the Pope."[77] Ignatius never doubts that the Society of Jesus will promote the more universal good by placing themselves at the service of Christ's "universal vicar," regardless of his personal qualities.[78]

Ignatius's palpable reverence for the Apostolic See does not prevent him, however, from giving at least one Jesuit the responsibility of enlightening the Pope when he seems to lack information relevant to governance. "When one of the subjects has been designated for some place or undertaking, and it is judged that the supreme vicar of Christ, if well informed, would not send him to it, the superior general may give him better information, while finally leaving the entire matter to the decision of his Holiness."[79] Ignatius calls this practice of informing superiors "representation," and makes allowance for it at every level of governance.[80] The practice agrees well with Aquinas's more flexible reception of Dionysian hierarchy, according to which ecclesiastical inferiors, being lower in office rather than nature, often find themselves in a position to enlighten their superiors.

76. Letter of Ignatius to Bernal Díaz de Luco, 11 January 1543. See *Monumenta Ignatiana Series Prima: Sancti Ignatii de Loyola Societatis Jesu fundatoris epistolae et instructiones*, vol. 1, *1524–1548*, MHSI 22 (Madrid, 1903), 241.
77. See the entry for April 4, 1555 of the Memoriale of Luís Gonçalves da Câmara, in *Remembering Iñigo: Glimpses of the Life of Saint Ignatius Loyola*, trans. Alexander Eaglestone and Joseph A. Munitiz, SJ (St. Louis, MO: Gracewing, 2004), 185.
78. For more early Jesuit testimonies justifying the vow of obedience to the Pope by reference to the universality of papal office, see Antonio M. Aldama, SJ, *The Constitutions of the Society of Jesus: Missioning*, trans. Ignacio Echániz, SJ (St. Louis, MO: Institute of Jesuit Sources, 1996), 23–27.
79. Cons., 607.
80. For "representation" as the practice of giving information to a superior, whether a Jesuit superior or Pope, see *Letters*, 294–95; Cons., 610.

There is much evidence, in short, to suggest that Ignatius's papal policy tracks Aquinas's papal theology. The special vow of obedience binds Jesuits to the papal office under the aspect that Aquinas accentuates—that is, the pope as font of jurisdiction and unrestricted missioning authority. But despite his reverence for Christ's "universal vicar," Ignatius does not forget that popes, having an intellectual nature no higher than their subjects', often profit even from unsolicited "representations." In both these respects, Ignatius shows strong affinities for Aquinas's adaptation of the *lex divinitatis*.

Conclusion

It is sometimes debated whether Ignatius was the last of the medievals or the first of the early moderns. This study suggests that the transition between the two periods and sensibilities was a gradual one. Ignatius leaves behind some of the florid speculations about the hierarchical structure of reality more typical of high Latin scholasticism, showing little concern either for the number and nomenclature of the angelic choirs or for the exact division of labor into purification, illumination, and perfection. At the same time, Ignatius shows striking affinities for certain aspects of the Thomistic hierarchical worldview, especially those aspects where Aquinas complicates Dionysius's fixed order of mediation. Like Aquinas but unlike Dionysius, Ignatius holds that God may illuminate either immediately or through angelic intermediaries, that Mary outranks the angels, that jurisdictional authority radiates from the Pope as from a principal hierarch, and that ecclesiastical inferiors may nonetheless enlighten their superiors.

It is often assumed that mystical experience tends to explode all religious frameworks, submerging them in the universal solvent of divine immediacy. Ignatius's illuminations, however, do not seem to have had this effect. While it is true that they led Ignatius to seek God "in all things," they nevertheless left him expecting to find God more reliably in some things rather than others. After being transformed by grace into "another man with another mind," Ignatius grows only firmer in his conviction that God wishes to perfect the lower things through a meaningful order of "*mediadores*." In his respect for the *lex divinitatis*, Ignatius was a faithful Thomist.

CHAPTER 9

Leading the Blind:
Aquinas, Ignatius, and other Jesuits on Obedience

Sam Zeno Conedera, SJ

Introduction

"I would like all of you to practice recognizing Christ our Lord in any superior, reverencing and obeying his Divine Majesty in him with all devotion."[1] Such lines from Ignatius's 1553 letter to the Jesuits in Portugal helped make the order he founded famous for obedience, which admirers and critics alike cite as a key feature of the Jesuits's service to the Church across the centuries.

Several contemporary scholars, Geoffrey Hull, John Lamont, and Louis-Marie de Blignières, have blamed Ignatius and the Society for fostering a tyrannical understanding of obedience that has led, among other things, to the abandonment of Church tradition and to the sexual abuse scandals. They allege that a distorted understanding of the obedience subjects owe to their superiors has allowed some churchmen to undermine faith and worship or cover up immoral behavior with impunity. Lamont locates the problem in Ignatius's insistence upon conformity of a subject's will and judgment to the superior's, a position he contrasts with the teaching of Thomas Aquinas. De Blignières regards this conformity of will and judgment as both morally wrong and psychologically impossible.[2] The provenance of these criticisms from the margins of theological discourse is not sufficient cause to dismiss them, for they raise a number of important questions. Are the views of Aquinas and Ignatius on obedience truly alternative, or even contradictory, positions? Is

---

1. Ignatius of Loyola, *Letters and Instructions*, ed. John W. Padberg, SJ, and John L. McCarthy, SJ, trans. Martin E. Palmer (St. Louis, MO: Institute of Jesuit Sources, 2006) (hereafter *Letters*), no. 3304, 413.

2. Geoffrey Hull, *The Banished Heart: Origins of Heteropraxis in the Catholic Church* (New York: T&T Clark, 2010), 134–55; John Lamont, "Tyranny and sexual abuse in the Catholic Church: A Jesuit tragedy," (2018), https://catholicfamilynews.com/blog/2018/10/27/2018-10-27-tyranny-and-sexual-abuse-in-the-catholic-church-a-jesuit-tragedy/; Louis-Marie de Blignières, "L'obéissance du jugement," *Sedes Sapientiae* 126 (2013): 43–69, at 61–62.

there something inherently tyrannical in the Jesuit approach?[3] Here the historical question of the Society's impact on the Church will be set aside in favor of an exploration of the theological issues as well as an examination of the Society's internal debates up to the early decades of the seventeenth century. This task involves not only comparing and contrasting the writings of Thomas and Ignatius, but also examining how several important Jesuit commentators, including Jerome Nadal, Robert Bellarmine, and Francisco Suárez, explained and justified their founder's teaching, sometimes in response to objections from their fellow Jesuits. Although important differences remain between the Angelic Doctor and Ignatius on obedience, Bellarmine and Suárez can provide a partial reconciliation of their teaching, as well as a plausible defense against present-day criticisms.

Ignatius of Loyola

The best exposition of Ignatius's view of obedience is his 1553 letter to the Jesuits in Portugal, the teaching of which appears elsewhere in his correspondence and the order's *Constitutions*.

The first observation that Ignatius makes in the letter is that Jesuits should excel in obedience above all else, for, in the words of Gregory the Great, "it alone implants all the other virtues in the mind and preserves them once implanted." The Jesuit founder does not say explicitly if he means the virtue or the vow of obedience, but his emphasis seems to be on the latter, since he adds that Jesuits should distinguish themselves among other religious orders "in the purity and perfection of obedience."[4]

This purity and perfection has several characteristics. It entails, first, "recognizing Christ the Lord in any superior, reverencing and obeying his

---

3. The charge of tyranny was leveled at Ignatius by one of the order's founders, Nicholas Bobadilla. John O'Malley, *The First Jesuits* (Cambridge, MA: Harvard University Press, 1993), 273, 334. It is worth noting that there has been a reassessment of obedience within the Society of Jesus itself, although according to a different set of priorities than those articulated by Hull, Lamont, and de Blignières. Even before Vatican II, one Jesuit wrote that the conformity of judgment did not necessarily mean agreeing with the superior but only believing that the divine wisdom will realize its designs by means even of human imprudence. Karl Rahner was pushing toward "demythologizing" obedience during these same years, a line that others pursued after the council as well. See Roger Tandonnet, "L'obeissance religieuse, obeisance parfait," *Christus* 7 (1955): 332–49, at 337; Karl Rahner, "Eine ignatianische Grundhaltung: Marginialen über den Gehorsam," *Stimmen der Zeit* 158 (1955–56): 253–67; David Knight, "Joy and Judgment in Religious Obedience," *Studies in the Spirituality of Jesuits* 6 (1974): 131–67. Summarizing the relevant history and studies of the last sixty years, one scholar claims that the Jesuits have reconceived religious obedience in terms of social justice. Antje Schnoor, "Transformational Ethics: The Concept of Obedience in Post-Conciliar Jesuit Thinking," *Religions* 10, no. 5 (2019): 1–16.

4. *Letters*, no. 3304, 413.

Divine Majesty in him with all devotion." That means looking to him not on account of his personal qualities, but because he holds the place and authority of God.[5] Ignatius appeals to Scripture in support of this teaching, beginning with Luke 10:16, "He who hears you, hears me." The activity and contemplation of Martha and Mary Magdalene were holy, but they had to take place in Bethany, which means "house of obedience."[6] Ignatius expresses the same idea in a 1547 letter to the Jesuit College of Gandia as well as Part VI of the *Constitutions*.[7]

The second feature of pure and perfect obedience, and the one central to the present essay, is that it entails the conformity of will and judgment. Mere execution of what is commanded does not really deserve the name of obedience unless it rises to the second degree, which consists of making the superior's will one's own. Ignatius cites Scripture as well as several Fathers, including Gregory, Cassian, and Bernard, in support of this conformity of the will, and says that when a subject tries to draw the superior to his own will it is a dangerous sign of self-love. Such an action entails subverting the order of God's wisdom by making one's own will the rule of his.[8]

The highest degree of a subject's obedience involves "submitting his own judgment to the superior's to the extent that a devoted will is able to influence the understanding."[9] This is what makes it a complete and perfect oblation, a holocaust of the entire person in the fire of charity. Ignatius explains:

> For while the understanding does not enjoy the same freedom as the will and by nature gives its assent to whatever is presented to it as true, nevertheless, in many matters where the evidence of the known truth is not compelling, it can, by the will's intervention, incline to one side rather than the other; and in such matters every truly obedient person should incline himself to think the same as his superior.[10]

Ignatius observes that obedience of judgment is necessary to make obedience of execution and will function properly, since one cannot obey long or enthusiastically without all three.[11] While acknowledging that the will and the understanding function differently, Ignatius nevertheless asserts the power of the

---

5. *Letters*, no. 3304, 413.
6. *Letters*, no 3304, 414.
7. *Letters*, no. 182, 199; *The Constitutions of the Society of Jesus*, trans. George Ganss (St. Louis, MO: Institute of Jesuit Sources, 1970) (hereafter Cons.), 547, 551; cited by paragraph number.
8. *Letters*, no. 3304, 414–15.
9. *Letters*, no. 3304, 415.
10. *Letters*, no. 3304, 415.
11. *Letters*, no. 3304, 417.

former to influence the latter. Conformity of will and judgment is enjoined in letters from 1548 and 1551, as well as in Part VI of the *Constitutions*.[12] A corollary of the conformity of judgment is Ignatius's instruction that subjects should mistrust their own prudence, submitting instead to the judgment of the superior.[13] This idea is echoed in a letter to the scholastics of Coimbra in 1547, where Ignatius says that if they lack discretion, they should make up for it with obedience, whose counsel is sure.[14]

When the Jesuit founder provides practical tips on how to attain the higher degrees of obedience, he uses a term that will become associated with his view in general and which makes for a third feature: blindness. His third way of reaching perfect obedience is as follows:

> taking for granted and believing—very much as we do in matters of faith—that whatever the superior enjoins is the command of God our Lord and his holy will, one proceeds blindly to the execution of the command, without any inquiry and with the force and promptitude of a will eager to obey.[15]

This statement is followed by the image, taken from Cassian, of a man watering a dry stick for a year without asking why. Although Ignatius uses "blindly" only once in the letter of 1553, the term and its variants appear in other letters too: from 1542, 1548, and 1550.[16] Part VI of the *Constitutions* substitutes the images of the obedient man as a lifeless body and a staff in the hand of an old man for the image of watering a dry stick.[17]

Ignatius's views on obedience would not be complete, however, without reference to a fourth feature: limiting conditions. The first of these is that obedience is required so long as nothing is commanded contrary to God.[18] The second is that a subject may, after taking the matter to prayer, represent to a superior when something occurs to him that differs from the superior's view or instruction. Ignatius counsels an attitude of indifference about the outcome, or even a preference for what the superior wills.[19] The limiting condition of sin

---

12. *Letters*, no. 252, 234; *Letters*, no. 295, 241–43; *Letters*, no. 1848, 337; Cons., 550.
13. *Letters*, no. 3304, 416.
14. *Letters*, no. 169, 172. He cites 1 Sam 15:23: "it is the crime of idolatry not to submit, the sin of witchcraft not to obey."
15. *Letters*, no. 3304, 419.
16. *Letters*, no. 52, 87; no. 295, 243; *Monumenta Historica Societatis Jesu: Monumenta Ignatiana: Sancti Ignatii de Loyola epistolae et instructiones* (Madrid, 1903–1911) (hereafter *EI*), vol. 3, no. 1326, 156.
17. Cons., 547.
18. *Letters*, no. 3304, 418.
19. *Letters*, no. 3304, 419–20.

appears in Part VI of the *Constitutions*.[20] The legitimacy of representing is not mentioned in Part VI, where obedience is treated, but Part V does say, "To represent his thoughts and what occurs to him is permissible."[21] Representing also appears elsewhere in Ignatius's correspondence, often in letters focused on the theme of obedience.[22] Thomas O'Gorman is correct to say that while it may not be immediately apparent how representing coheres with what else Ignatius says on obedience, it is an indispensable feature of his teaching.[23]

Although the Society in Portugal was in a serious state of disorder when Ignatius wrote his 1553 letter, other sources show the ideas expressed therein were by no means exceptional, but part of his ordinary teaching. As he says in two letters of 1551, Jesuits should excel above all in obedience.[24] When denying a request for release from vows in 1548, Ignatius refers to the grain of wheat that dies in obedience. Writing to the superior is a matter of obedience, and one should not go to bed before accomplishing this task; if one is summoned by a superior, one should leave off writing a letter or meeting with another person to comply.[25] On top of this, Ignatius was known to back up his understanding of obedience with harsh penances for those who violated it in the least way, especially those in whom he placed the greatest trust.[26]

A final feature of Ignatius's writings on obedience is that he does not appeal to the teaching of any scholastic doctors, but only to Fathers of the Church, especially the Desert Fathers.[27] One possible explanation is that the style and content of the scholastics, including Thomas, does not harmonize as well with his thought.

---

20. Cons., 547, 549.

21. Cons., 543. There are additional references to representing in Parts III and VII. Noting the persistence of this theme in the *Constitutions* and correspondence of Ignatius, Pierre-Antoine Fabre claims that representing plays an indispensable role in "negotiating obedience" in the Society of Jesus. See Fabre, "L'obéissance comme 'représentation' dans la Compagnie de Jésus," in *Negociar la obediencia: autoridad y consentimiento en el mundo ibérico en la Edad Moderna*, ed. Jean-Paul Zúñiga (Granada: Comares, 2013), 189–95.

22. Letters, no. 52, 86–87; no. 295, 239; *EI*, no. 849, 2:528; *EI*, no. 1248, 3:93.

23. Thomas O'Gorman, *Jesuit Obedience from Life to Law: The Development of the Ignatian Idea of Obedience in the Jesuit Constitutions, 1539–1556* (Manila: Ateneo University, 1971), 34.

24. Letters, no. 1848, 337; Letters, no. 1854, 341.

25. *EI*, no. 380, 2:147; *EI*, no. 727, 2:437; *EI*, no. 1326, 3:156.

26. Joseph de Guibert, *The Jesuits, their Spiritual Doctrine and Practice: A Historical Study*, trans. William Young (Chicago: Institute of Jesuit Sources, 1964), 91. Laínez in particular was the recipient of harsh reproval from Ignatius on matters of obedience. Antonio Alburquerque, *Diego Lainez, SJ: First Biographer of Saint Ignatius of Loyola*, trans. John Montag (St. Louis, MO: Institute of Jesuit Sources, 2010), 41–42.

27. Antonio M. de Aldama suggests, however, that a text from Aquinas (ST II-II, q. 104, a. 2, rep. obj. 2) may have inspired some of Ignatius's letters and text P of the *Constitutions*, which speak of obedience to a mere hint of the superior's will, rather than to an order: "Obedience is not a

Thomas Aquinas

When we turn to the teaching of Thomas Aquinas on obedience, we find differences of methodology and content. Aquinas explains the natural virtue of obedience as a foundation for the religious vow, and he is more restrained about the scope of the latter. Although there are references to the topic scattered throughout his writings, the main locus is *Summa Theologiae*, II-II, q. 104. The Angelic Doctor establishes some key points: the legitimacy of obedience of one man to another, in general, and the status of obedience as a special virtue annexed to justice. Like other moral virtues, obedience is a matter of observing the mean between extremes.[28] In the case of obedience, excess is found in the one who insists on fulfilling his own will, thereby not rendering to the superior due obedience, whereas deficiency is on the part of the superior who does not receive obedience.[29]

The proper object of obedience is a precept, which proceeds from another's will. Citing Gregory the Great, Aquinas observes that obedience increases in matters repugnant to one's own will, since in such cases it inclines toward nothing but the precept. In the *Summa Theologiae*, Thomas is careful to place obedience beneath the theological virtues, and praises it because it proceeds from charity and involves contemning one's own will for the sake of God.[30] In the *Commentary on the Sentences*, however, Thomas is more effusive about obedience, calling it the greatest of all virtues and the mother of all virtues, borrowing these expressions from Gregory the Great.[31] *Summa Theologiae*, II-II, q. 186 also identifies the vow (as opposed to the virtue) of obedience as preeminent among the three religious vows, since it entails offering to God one's own will, which is greater than the offering of the body or external goods.[32] Throughout this *quaestio*, Thomas speaks of the vows as the *holocausta* of religious self-offering.[33] Summing up the importance of obedience in Aquinas's thought, Benjamin Brown says that for him it "ingrafts, informs, perfects, and preserves the other virtues," and that the Christian life is more perfect when obligation is involved.[34]

---

theological virtue, for its direct object is not God, but the precept of any superior, whether expressed or inferred, namely, a simple word of the superior, indicating his will, and which the obedient subject obeys promptly." Antonio M. de Aldama, *The Constitutions of the Society of Jesus: Jesuit Religious Life*, trans. Ignacio Echániz (St. Louis, MO: Institute of Jesuit Sources, 1995), 11–12.

28. ST II-II, q. 104, aa. 1–2.
29. ST II-II, q. 104, a. 2, rep. obj. 2.
30. ST II-II, q. 104, a. 3, resp.
31. *II Sent.*, d. 44, q. 2, a. 1.
32. ST II-II, q. 186, a. 8, s.c.
33. ST II-II, q. 186, a. 5, rep. obj. 1.
34. Benjamin Brown, "The Integration of Law and Virtue: Obedience in Aquinas's Moral Theology," *Irish Theological Quarterly* 67 (2002): 333–51, at 346.

Like Ignatius, Thomas distinguishes between degrees of obedience in religious life, although his taxonomy is different. He says that religious are bound to obey in matters pertaining to the regular mode of life, and that this suffices for salvation. If they are willing to obey even in other matters, this belongs to the superabundance of perfection, provided the things commanded are not contrary to God or the rule they profess. Thus, Aquinas distinguishes between an obedience that is sufficient for salvation, and perfect obedience, which obeys in all things lawful.[35] His comments in *Summa Theologiae*, II-II, q. 186 about supererogatory works, however, show that he does not think that religious, as such, are bound to the perfect observance of all the counsels.[36] This suggests that he would not have agreed with the idea of making perfect obedience the baseline expectation of all members of an order, as Ignatius does.

Thomas identifies several cases in which subjects are not bound to obey their superiors. First, when they command something that is against God, then subjects must do as it is written in Acts 5:29: "We ought to obey God rather than men." Thomas does not seem to think that such a case is so difficult to imagine, for he says explicitly that sometimes (*quandoque*) what superiors command is against God.[37] "Indiscreet obedience" is the name Thomas gives to obeying even in matters unlawful.[38] Second, if a lower power commands something contrary to a higher power, the former is not to be obeyed. Third, a subject is not bound to obey when commanded to do something wherein he is not subject to that superior: "His body is subjected and assigned to his master but his soul is his own. Consequently in matters touching the internal movement of the will man is not bound to obey his fellow-man, but God alone."[39] Thomas repeats this idea that obedience only extends as far as the superior's jurisdiction or authority, which is limited by the rule, in *Summa Theologiae*, II–II, q. 186, a. 5 and *Quodlibet* X, q. 5, a. 2, which say that the vow subordinates the subject to his superior in the general ordering of his life, but not in every one of his particular actions.[40] Thomas offers examples of acts

---

35. ST II-II, q. 104, a. 5, rep. obj. 3.
36. ST II-II, q. 186, a. 2, s.c.
37. ST II-II, q. 104, a. 5, s.c. An interesting complication is found in Thomas's statement that men are always bound to obey God, even when he commands something against the customary course of nature, as in the case of Abraham and Isaac. "God can command nothing contrary to virtue since virtue and rectitude of human will consist chiefly in conformity with God's will and obedience to his command." ST II-II, q. 104, a. 4, rep. obj. 2.
38. ST II-II, q. 104, a. 5, rep. obj. 3.
39. ST II-II, q. 104, a. 5, resp.
40. Thomas Aquinas, *Thomas Aquinas's Quodlibetal Questions*, trans. Turner Nevitt and Brian Davies (Oxford: Oxford University Press, 2020), 147.

that do not belong to religion, that is, matters concerning love of God and neighbor, one of which is lifting a stick from the ground.[41] Although he does not cite a source for this example, it is at least curious that it makes for a direct contrast with Ignatius's image of the obedient man watering a dry stick without asking why. Thomas also says that subjects are not bound to obey when they are commanded something impossible, but offers the qualification that the determination of what is impossible should not be left to the subject, but to the superior.[42]

Although the evidence is not very robust, Thomas's treatment of the limiting conditions of obedience indicates that the obedient person need not conform either his will or his judgment to the superior's, since he upholds the interior freedom of the will, and says nothing at all about the conformity of judgment to what is commanded.[43] As one recent commentator observes, "only exterior acts of the will fall under the authority of the superior, those that arise from the end of the community for which he is responsible."[44]

Is it possible to speak of "Ignatius the Thomist" where obedience is concerned? Surely there are significant differences of method, content, and emphasis, and one could make the case, as our contemporary critics of the Society have done, that the idea of conformity of will and judgment is not Thomas's teaching or compatible with it. The Jesuit commentators on Ignatius's concept of obedience, however, may be able to shed more light on this question.

Jesuit Commentators

The principal Jesuit theologians of the sixteenth and early seventeenth centuries range widely in their treatment of obedience. Some, like Gabriel Vázquez, Francisco de Toledo, and Gregory of Valencia, do not treat Thomas's crucial q. 104, or undertake any systematic study of obedience elsewhere in their scholastic commentaries. Other authors, like Peter Canisius and Antonio Possevino, push a strong notion of obedience for the lay faithful and religious in their catechisms and devotional works, but without discussing any special conditions of obe-

---

41. ST II-II, q. 186, a. 5, rep. obj. 4. The other example is rubbing one's beard.
42. ST I-II, q. 13, a. 5.
43. This would also be in keeping with the characteristic tendency of the Order of Preachers to place limits on the superior's will. Basil Cole, "Consecrated Obedience and Spirituality," *Angelicum* 73 (1996): 569–87, at 574–75. Although he acknowledges that an obedient subject has to make the superior's idea the principle of his own action, Labourdette insists that obedience concerns practical rather than speculative judgments and credits Thomas with protecting obedience against the abuse of power. Michel-Marie Labourdette, "La vertu d'obeissance selon S. Thomas," *Revue thomiste* 57 (1957): 626–56.
44. Hughes Bohineust, *Obéissance du Christ, obéissance du chrétien: Christologie et morale chez saint Thomas d'Aquin* (Paris: Éditions Parole et Silence, 2017), 101. My translation.

dience in the Society.⁴⁵ This evidence indicates that at least some learned members of the order did not view the theory of obedience, or its relation to the teaching of Thomas, as a pressing matter. The impression is confirmed by even a cursory examination of the Dominicans of the period, who neither dealt with these specific questions in their commentaries on Thomas, nor accused the Jesuits of having compromised his teaching.⁴⁶ Melchor Cano, Thomas Pedroche, and Alonso de la Fuente launched exceedingly trenchant attacks on the order and its members, but they were mainly concerned about the *Spiritual Exercises* and its alleged connections to *alumbrado* spirituality.⁴⁷ Domingo Bañez famously clashed with Jesuits over predestination, grace, and free will, and Juan de Orellana wrote against Jesuit superiors's alleged abuse of the sacrament of Penance as a method of governance, but neither wrote about obedience per se.⁴⁸

An example of relative indifference to the question may be found in the work of Alfonso Salmerón, who, after Diego Laínez, was the best theological mind among the founding members of the order. His massive commentaries on the New Testament, which have mostly been ignored by historians and theologians alike, have little to say about Jesuit obedience, or indeed about the Society at all.⁴⁹ Although he has plenty of words praising the obedience of Christ and

---

45. Silvia Mostaccio, *Early Modern Jesuits between Obedience and Conscience during the Generalate of Claudio Acquaviva (1581–1615)* (Burlington, VT: Ashgate, 2014), 39, 51–52.

46. One possible explanation for this is the general emphasis on obedience in religious life during the period, not just among the Jesuits, and in the Church more generally. Paolo Prodi, *Il paradigma tridentino: Un'epoca della storia della Chiesa* (Brescia, Italy: Morcelliana, 2010), 169–86; Brad Gregory, *The Unintended Reformation: How a Religious Revolution Secularized Society* (Cambridge, MA: Belknap Press, 2012), 210.

47. See Terence O'Reilly, "The Spiritual Exercises and Illuminism in Spain: Dominican Critics of the Early Society of Jesus," in *Ite Inflammate Omnia: Selected Historical Papers from Conferences Held at Loyola and Rome in 2006*, ed. Thomas McCoog (Rome: IHSI, 2006), 199–228; Terence O'Reilly, "Melchor Cano and the Spirituality of St. Ignatius Loyola: The *Censura y parecer contra el Instituto de los Padres Jesuitas*," *Journal of Jesuit Studies* 4 (2017): 365–94; A. D. Wright, "The Jesuits and the Older Religious Orders in Spain," in *The Mercurian Project: Forming Jesuit Culture, 1573–1580*, ed. Thomas McCoog (St. Louis, MO: Institute of Jesuit Sources, 2004), 913–44, at 924–25. In his summary of the earliest Dominican attacks on the Society, Iparraguire makes no mention of Jesuit understanding of obedience, which in any case may not yet have been well known outside the order. Ignacio Iparraguirre, *Práctica de los ejercicios de san Ignacio de Loyola en vida de su autor (1522–1556)* (Rome: IHSI, 1946), 91–115.

48. Some Jesuits also made this complaint about the use of confession. Michela Catto, *La Compagnia divisa: Il dissenso nell'ordine gesuitico tra '500 e '600* (Brescia, Italy: Editrice Morcelliana, 2009), 130–31. There was also the infamous case of the use of confession by Hernando de Mendoza, whose alleged disobedience may have pushed forward Acquaviva's treatise on Jesuit confessors of princes. Nicole Reinhardt, "Hernando de Mendoça (1562–1617), General Acquaviva, and the Controversy over Confession, Counsel, and Obedience," *Journal of Jesuit Studies* 4 (2017): 209–29.

49. See Sam Zeno Conedera, "Forgotten Saint: The Life and Writings of Alfonso Salmerón, SJ," *Studies in the Spirituality of Jesuits* 52, no. 4 (2020): 1–34.

the Blessed Virgin, or the need for obedience to the Church and to civil authorities, there are only three passages in his sixteen volumes that touch upon, even obliquely, Ignatius's understanding of obedience. First, Salmerón says in his general prologue that he wrote his *Commentaries* submitting his intellect, like a neck, to obedience.[50] Second, he praises St. Joseph for practicing blind obedience toward God.[51] Third, in a commentary on the vestiges of the Trinity found in the virtues, he says, "Obedience is not to be given in deeds only, but also in will and in judgment."[52] The final reference especially suggests that Salmerón agreed with Ignatius's teaching, but the evidence is thin. This is despite the fact that Salmerón was a significant participant in the Society's internal disputes and conflicts well into the 1570s. He briefly served as vicar general of the order in 1561–1562, and was the envoy to the pope during the tumultuous Third General Congregation that elected the Society's first non-Spanish general, Everard Mercurian.[53] Salmerón's eighteen years as provincial in Naples were brought to an end with the appointment of Claudio Acquaviva, under whose direct authority he lived out his final years.[54] In his magnum opus, however, Salmerón remains silent about these events and Jesuit obedience in general.

Jerome Nadal

Very different is the case of Jerome Nadal, who was not an original companion, but nevertheless a close collaborator of Ignatius, and after him arguably the most important expositor of Jesuit life.[55] For years, this man from Mallorca traversed Europe explaining the order's *Constitutions* to its members. He left to posterity a treatise entitled *De Virtute Obedientiae* that pushes Ignatius's teaching in the direction of absolute obedience.[56]

---

50. Alfonso Salmerón, *Commentarii in Evangelicam Historiam et in Acta Apostolorum*, 12 vols. (Cologne: Antonius Hierat and Johannes Gynmnicus, 1612–1614) (hereafter *CEH*), 1:††4r.

51. *CEH*, 3:235.

52. "Obedientia non tantum opera praestanda, sed et voluntate, et iudicio." *CEH*, 9:508.

53. William Bangert, *Claude Jay and Alfonso Salmerón: Two Early Jesuits* (Chicago: Loyola University Press, 1985), 259–62, 330–31.

54. For more on Salmerón's governance of Naples, see Mark Lewis and Jennifer Selwyn, "Jesuit Activity in Southern Italy during the Generalate of Everard Mercurian," in *The Mercurian Project: Forming Jesuit Culture, 1573–1580*, ed. Thomas McCoog (St. Louis, MO: Institute of Jesuit Sources, 2004), 532–57; Esther Jiménez Pablo, "El P. Alfonso Salmerón y el gobierno de los colegios de Nápoles," *Magallánica* 2, no. 4 (2016): 57–79.

55. For a chronological account of Nadal's life and influence, see Juan Nadal Cañellas, *Jerónimo Nadal: Vida e influjo* (Bilbao: Mensajero, 2007).

56. He completed this work sometime in autumn 1562, during a visit to Central Europe. Manuel Ruiz Jurado, *Jerónimo Nadal: El teólogo de la gracia de la vocación* (Madrid: Biblioteca de Autores Cristianos, 2011), 187. The editor of Nadal's treatise notes that some manuscripts attribute the canons on obedience to Ignatius himself. Nicolau believes that the work is entirely Nadal's

Nadal's first point is that obedience in religious orders is greatly different from obedience in any other circumstances, since the former is concerned with striving after perfection.[57] Although his treatise is ostensibly about the virtue of obedience, he begins with a rather sharp delineation of the vow from the virtue and gives most of his attention to the former.

Following Ignatius, Nadal says that obedience should be offered in the external action, in the will, and in the intellect. He adds that this obedience should not only be blind, but also that, once blindness has been attained, the one offering obedience should examine the matter in the fullness of the Spirit and seek to obey not only what has been commanded, but also what has been merely hinted at.[58] Nadal speaks of this virtue in the highest terms, and identifies the superior with God even more closely than does Ignatius, saying that obedience is like the state of original justice, in which all the soul's powers are subordinated to God, and that one should practice obedience as if responding to public revelation. "For whenever I hear a superior speaking, I should feel that it is exactly what it would be were I to hear God himself present to me."[59]

The Mallorcan Jesuit enlists biblical figures to illustrate blind obedience. Lucifer considered his own perfection without the eyes of self-denial and became disobedient, and Eve resisted under Satan's influence the sacred blindness of the command she had been given. By contrast, Christ, though not properly blind, took account of nothing that could have weakened the obedience he owed to the Father, and the Virgin Mary obeyed in the most perfect fashion the conception of the eternal Word, making no judgment in that most mysterious of all events. So too did Abraham obey blindly in the sacrifice of Isaac.[60]

In addition, Nadal makes an argument from the "Principle and Foundation" of the *Spiritual Exercises*: in view of the fact that every creature exists to help man praise and reverence God, one ought to not choose one creature in preference to another except to the extent that one is moved by the will of God. It is through full abnegation and surrender of the intellect and the will that

---

own and dates from the period after the death of Ignatius, but that Nadal may very well have obtained some of the material from his conversations with the founder. See *Monumenta Historica Societatis Iesu: Epistolae et Monumenta P. Hieronymi Nadal*, vol. 5, *Comentarii de Instituto Societatis Jesu*, ed. Miguel Nicolau (Rome, 1962), 494–97. Similar ideas on obedience are expressed in Nadal's other works, notably, his 1554 talk in Spain. See Jerome Nadal, *Las pláticas del P. Jerónimo Nadal: La globalización ignaciana*, ed. and trans. Miguel Lop Sebastià, SJ (Bilbao: Mensajero, 2011), 90–94.

57. Martin O'Keefe, "Jerome Nadal, SJ, on the Virtue of Obedience," in *Spirit, Style, Story: Essays Honoring John W. Padberg, SJ*, ed. Thomas Lucas (Chicago: Loyola Press, 2002), 45–69, at 46.
58. O'Keefe, "Nadal," 47.
59. O'Keefe, "Nadal," 47.
60. O'Keefe, "Nadal," 56.

Jesuits arrive at this indifference to their own preferences.[61] This appeal to the *Spiritual Exercises* singles out Nadal among the Jesuit commentators under consideration, who appealed only to the founder's correspondence and the order's *Constitutions*. One might infer that Nadal wishes by means of this citation to give obedience an even deeper grounding in the order's spiritual tradition.

Nadal deals with the issue of commands that are impossible or sinful, saying that in such cases "obedience impels us to obey, taking no account of difficulty or impossibility."[62] If obedience is perfect, it overcomes in the power of Christ any natural impossibility or difficulty. If obedience is not perfect, but nevertheless true, it will lead the subject in simplicity of heart to tell the superior that it was impossible to do what was commanded. The subject will do so with shame, as if confessing a fault of his own. An obedient person never thinks that a superior would command what is impossible or sinful, and if he does think so, he will learn to regard this as a temptation that seeks to tear down the purity and simplicity of obedience.[63]

Nadal recommends as a remedy to this temptation that the subject not deliberate about the matter using his own private judgment, but rather accept the judgment of the superior. If the superior should be openly and clearly in the wrong, let the obedient person consider him so as a theoretical matter, and leave the determination to worthy professed fathers or his own confessor.[64] In other words, Nadal goes to extreme lengths to prevent the subject from exercising his own judgment. As he says, "only the will of the superior ought to be considered and nothing else; the intellect of the one who obeys ought to represent to his will only what the superior wills."[65] Nadal tells a subject who thinks he is being treated unjustly by a superior to "never take this in any other way but that he is doing this as your lack of merits warrants. And if he should do so even beyond what you in fact deserve, that truly would be for you a wonderful thing, for he, acting in the person of God himself, is testing you."[66]

In case any of the foregoing needed to be spelled out further, Nadal offers a list of forty-three canons on obedience. Here is a sample of them:

- One who examines the reasons why a superior issues a command is not an obedient person.
- One who entertains the idea of debating whether a superior has commanded properly is not an obedient person.

---

61. O'Keefe, "Nadal," 57.
62. O'Keefe, "Nadal," 48.
63. O'Keefe, "Nadal," 48.
64. O'Keefe, "Nadal," 48.
65. O'Keefe, "Nadal," 56–57.
66. O'Keefe, "Nadal," 58.

- One who obeys only the expressed will of the superior, and not the slightest sign of his will, is not an obedient person.
- One who obeys because of a given reason, and not solely because of the will of the superior in Christ, is not an obedient person.
- One who is not indifferent as to whatever the superior may command is not an obedient person.
- One who is not blind to all imperfections superiors may have or to whatever difficulties may stand in the way of obeying is not an obedient person.
- One who does not take in a good spirit what is commanded, and even examines it and weighs it, is not an obedient person.[67]

A telling feature of Nadal's treatise is how he deals with scholastic theologians and the expression of alternative viewpoints. He censures those who appeal to scholastic theologians: "for this is not to delineate one's obligations by the opinions of learned men, but rather to do by what one has convinced himself are the opinions of learned men."[68] He also classifies as not obedient anyone who himself thinks according to the word of the superior, but who says that it would not be impossible for some other opinion to be presented to him. "One who says that he is, indeed, obligated to obey according to the manner of the Society, but only in those matters that pertain to the rule and not to others, is not an obedient person. For he is obligated to obey in all things that are not sinful."[69] Although Nadal does not mention Aquinas's name here, the reference to the rule as a limiting condition strongly suggests him as the source.[70] Nadal was aware of the discrepancy between the scholastic doctors and the Society on this point, and wanted to establish the Jesuit view of the matter as not only one of a number of possible opinions, but as the only legitimate belief and practice for the order's members.

Nadal interprets Ignatius's teaching on obedience to give greater emphasis to the surrender of will and judgment, to the point that the limiting conditions almost disappear.[71] The possibility of error on the superior's part, and the possibility of a subject's identifying such an error, are nearly eclipsed, and Nadal, unlike Ignatius, makes no mention of representing. As in the case of the letter of 1553, no scholastic

---

67. O'Keefe, "Nadal," 50–55.
68. O'Keefe, "Nadal," 51–52.
69. O'Keefe, "Nadal," 53.
70. Another possible source is Bernard, whom Ignatius cites multiple times on the question of obedience.
71. A great expert on Nadal, who edited much of his corpus, does not identify these differences between him and Ignatius, saying only that the Mallorcan Jesuit explains obedience in more "scholastic" terms than the founder. Miguel Nicolau, *Jerónimo Nadal, S.I. (1507–1580): Sus obras y doctrinas espirituales* (Madrid: CSIC, 1949), 400–406.

authors are brought in for supporting evidence, but only Fathers like Leo, Cassian, and Bernard. One might also suggest that Nadal's opening argument—namely, that the religious vow of obedience is greatly different from any other kind—runs against a basic Thomistic principle: grace does not destroy nature but presupposes and perfects it. The Angelic Doctor treats obedience as a natural virtue elevated by charity, and, so to speak, nests the religious vow of obedience within it, whereas Nadal immediately moves to separate religious obedience from this context and seems to forestall appeals to its foundation in nature.

The teaching of Nadal is not to be taken lightly, in view of the enormous trust Ignatius placed in him as a transmitter of the Jesuit charism.[72] Observing the tension in Ignatius's own teaching between the absoluteness of obedience, on the one hand, and the limiting conditions and need for representation, on the other, O'Gorman has argued for viewing his thought in "dynamic" rather than "static" categories.[73] It is fair to say, however, that the most important early commentator and transmitter of the Jesuit way perceived the need to resolve the tension, and that he did so decisively in favor of the absoluteness of obedience.[74] This is not to say that Nadal wanted superiors to be oppressive; in his talks to Jesuit communities, he advises superiors to be practical and avoid imperiousness in their dealings with subjects.[75] Critics of the Jesuit notion of obedience can nevertheless be forgiven for seeing in Nadal's work a portrait of tyranny: the relentless attack on thoughts or expressions that deviate in any way from the superior's, the exalted comparisons of obedience to faith and original justice, the near disappearance of the limiting conditions found in Ignatius, and the rejection of appeal to the scholastic doctors.[76]

---

72. Aaron Pidel explains the majority opinion of scholars that Nadal was a privileged interpreter of Ignatius's spiritual vision. Dissenting views have focused on such matters as alleged departure from Ignatius concerning patterns of prayer or multiplying house rules, but not obedience. See Pidel, "Jerome Nadal's Apology for the Spiritual Exercises: A Study in Balanced Spirituality," *Studies in the Spirituality of Jesuits* 52, no. 1 (2020): 1–36, at 13–15.

73. O'Gorman, *Jesuit Obedience*, 28.

74. Personal reasons and experiences may have also played a factor in Nadal's views on obedience. In 1546, he had a confrontation with Ignatius over the character of a friend that may have led Nadal to more willingly submit his judgment to the superior. He also seems to have understood obedience in mystical terms, taking inspiration from Pseudo-Dionysius. See William Bangert and Thomas McCoog, *Jerome Nadal, SJ 1507–1580: Tracking the First Generation of Jesuits* (Chicago: Loyola University Press, 1992), 43–44, 257. Ignacio Ramos Riera suggests that obedience was particularly difficult for Nadal's strong personality: *Jerónimo Nadal (1507–1580) und der "verschriftlichte" Ignatius: Die Konstruktion einer individuellen und kollektiven Identität* (Boston: Brill, 2016), 262. Could these factors help explain his understanding of obedience in such absolute terms?

75. Ruiz Jurado, *Jerónimo Nadal*, 171.

76. It should be acknowledged that Nadal's thought defies easy integration. Mongini lays emphasis on other features that do not readily accord with his teaching on obedience, such as the

Robert Bellarmine

The long generalate of Claudio Acquaviva witnessed serious challenges to the Society's governance, as well as contests over the nature of its spirituality, coming especially from Spain and Italy. This is often referred to as the "*memorialistas* controversy," after the documents certain Jesuits composed to air their grievances. Both within and outside the order, objections were raised that the order's structure was excessively monarchical, whereas some Jesuits sought a spiritual reform in a more contemplative direction.[77] Ultimately, these challenges failed, and the order's response, in the view of some scholars, decisively shaped the order's definitive theological and disciplinary character.[78] According to Silvia Mostaccio, being a Jesuit in the time of Acquaviva entailed an act of collective obedience, the legitimacy of which lay in the exigencies of the missionary vocation and the realities of life as men religious. The "magic circle" of obedience was closed and reinforced in numerous texts published during these years.[79] Doris Moreno Martínez offers a fascinating study of the Society's treatment of real or imagined disobedience during these years. No less an authority than Pedro de Ribadeneyra authored a treatise on God's punishment of disobedient Jesuits *after* their departure from the order.[80]

While they lasted, however, these internal conflicts did produce literature on the issue of Jesuit obedience. Although numerous *memorialistas* omit any consideration of obedience among the things to be corrected in the Society,

---

allowance of liberty in non-essential theological matters (*en adiaphorois*) and his accommodation to non-Christians in administering the Spiritual Exercises. Guido Mongini, "Le teologie gesuitiche delle origini: Lo spiritualismo radicale come matrice commune del dissenso e della fedeltà all'ortodossia," in *Avventure dell'obbedienza nella Compagnia di Gesù: Teorie e prassi fra XVI e XIX secolo*, ed. Fernanda Alfieri and Claudio Ferlan (Bologna: Il Mulino, 2012), 19–47.

77. The features of the extreme monarchical character of the Society's organization have been discussed in many places. See, e.g., Harro Höpfl, "Ordered Passions: Commitment and Hierarchy in the Organizational Ideals of the Jesuit Founders," *Management Learning* 31, no. 3 (2000): 313–29. For the challenges from Spain and Italy, see Esther Jiménez Pablo, *La forja de una identidad: La Compañía de Jesús (1540–1640)* (Madrid: Editorial Polifemo, 2014).

78. Franco Motta, "Jesuit Theology, Politics, and Identity: The Generalate of Acquaviva and the Years of Formation," in *The Acquaviva Project: Claudio Acquaviva's Generalate (1581–1615) and the Emergence of Modern Catholicism*, ed. Pierre-Antoine Fabre and Flavio Rurale (Boston: Institute of Jesuit Sources, 2017), 353–74, at 358.

79. Silvia Mostaccio, "Debating Obedience in an Early Modern Context," in *The Acquaviva Project*, 59–80, at 75; Silvia Mostaccio, "Spiritual Exercises: Obedience, Conscience, Conquest," in *The Oxford Handbook of the Jesuits*, ed. Ines Županov (New York: Oxford University Press, 2019), 75–104, at 81–83.

80. Doris Moreno Martínez, "Obediencias negociadas y desobediencias silenciadas en la Compañía de Jesús en España, ss. XVI–XVII," *Hispania* 74, no. 248 (2014): 661–86. Acquaviva decided it would be imprudent to publish Ribadeneyra's work, but it circulated in manuscript.

others raised serious charges against it.[81] Francisco Abreo and Enrique Enríquez complained that disobedience to a superior's command was treated like heresy or a sin against the Holy Spirit and punished with reassignment to the Indies. Juan Ramírez, known for his itinerant preaching throughout Spain, took the unprecedented step in 1580 of denouncing the Society to the Spanish Inquisition, accusing the former of an erroneous understanding of Ignatius's letter on obedience. He claimed that if obedience to a superior went against the subject's understanding of the commandment of God, it could not prevail.[82]

In 1588, Diego de Santa Cruz, already seventy years old, wrote a *memorial* on obedience to the Holy Office in Rome.[83] Although appearing to defend in principle the order's "blind obedience," Santa Cruz was highly critical of the way it was commonly practiced, claiming that many in the Society were being seduced by the devil in understanding and exercising it. Not only did many superiors fall prey to vanity, but they also became guilty of "the heresy of the Pharisees" by saying it was licit to obey superiors against the law of God. Santa Cruz cited several sources, including Jesuit correspondence and a strange painting in the community at Caravaca, that demonstrated this false understanding of blind obedience.[84] His recommendation to the Holy Office was that certain propositions on obedience be anathematized, including "whoever says it is better to err through obedience than to be correct through one's own will," and "whoever says it is licit to break the divine law when superiors demand it." Santa Cruz also wanted the superior general to publicize this anathema with a letter

---

81. One catalogue of the Spanish *memoriales* of the 1580s, which include numerous complaints against the order's governance, does not mention Jesuit obedience as a malady in need of remedy. Jiménez Pablo, *La forja*, 178–81; Michela Catto, "The Jesuit Memoirists: How the Company of Jesus Contributed to Anti-Jesuitism," in *Los jesuitas: Religión, política y educación (siglos XVI–XVIII)*, ed. José Martínez Millán, Henar Pizarro Llorente, and Esther Jiménez Pablo (Madrid: Comillas, 2012), 927–41, at 939.

82. Doris Moreno, "La aportación española al debate sobre la obediencia ciega en la Compañía de Jesús durante el Papado de Sixto V (1585–1590)," *Investigaciones Históricas* 33 (2013): 63–88, at 74–75.

83. Santa Cruz had had a checkered career of nearly forty years in the order. A follower of Juan de Avila, Santa Cruz's activities in southern Spain elicited unwanted attention from both the Spanish Inquisition and Dominican critics of the Society. These and other disciplinary issues led Jesuit superiors to express doubts about his suitability for the solemn profession and eventually to restrict his movement. Doris Moreno Martínez, "Las *almas* de la Compañía de Jesús en el siglo XVI: ecos alumbrados," in *Jesuitas e Imperios de Ultramar: siglos XVI–XX*, ed. Alexandre Coello, Javier Burrieza and Doris Moreno (Madrid: Silex, 2012), 201–22.

84. Moreno, "La aportación española," 69–71. The painting in question depicted a religious about to kill his own son because his superior demanded it. The story was taken from a work of Cassian and obviously resonated with the biblical account of Abraham's sacrifice. The painting included the text of Mt 10:37: "He who loves father or mother more than me is not worthy of me; and he who loves son or daughter more than me is not worthy of me."

sent throughout the world, with the aid of the Spanish Inquisition. Santa Cruz explains such drastic recommendations and his appeal to the highest authorities in Rome and Madrid by the Society's repeated refusal to listen to his views. Not only had he been repeatedly criticized for talking about these matters, but his superiors had also prevented a number of his writings from being published. Francisco Borgia and Acquaviva had even ordered that they be collected so as to prevent their diffusion.[85]

What is surprising about these complaints against blind obedience is that even a cursory reading of Ignatius's letter of 1553 would provide ample defense against the claim that the will of superiors is to be obeyed even in sinful matters. Allowing for the other motives at work in the *memorialistas* controversy (the jockeying for supremacy between popes and kings, the desire of some Spaniards for greater independence, the *converso* question, and so forth) and the personal grievances of the authors, it seems that at least in some places, blind obedience was understood and enforced without regard for the limiting conditions Ignatius had identified, and dubious conclusions were being extrapolated from it.

Whereas the aforementioned instances of criticism were handled as administrative matters, the case of Julien Vincent elicited a reply from a major Jesuit theologian. In 1588, Vincent wrote the Holy Office with a formal censure of Ignatius's letter of 1553. This Vincent had had a checkered career in the Society. While imprisoned by the Inquisition in Rome, he wrote a letter explaining his actions to fellow Jesuits, saying that he had been in the order for thirteen years. At Bordeaux, he had clashed with numerous superiors over doctrinal issues, which resulted in his being sent on a solitary, penitential pilgrimage to Santiago de Compostela, dressed in sackcloth.[86] Despite his relative obscurity, Vincent's attack on the foremost monument of the founder's teaching on obedience was taken seriously: Acquaviva appealed to Robert Bellarmine to come to the Society's defense against Vincent, which he did with a *Tractatus de Obedientia, quae caeca nominatur*, and two additional works, which appeared in 1588 and 1589.[87]

The *Responsio* identifies ten articles in Vincent's letter, for which Bellarmine provides a point-by-point refutation. Examples of the criticisms are that Jesuit obedience allows for no limit to the scope of the superior's authority; it could

---

85. Moreno, "La aportación española," 72–73.
86. Mostaccio, *Early Modern Jesuits*, 89–90.
87. Robert Bellarmine, *Tractatus de Obedientia, quae caeca nominatur* (hereafter *Tractatus*), in *Auctarium Bellarminianum: Supplément aux Oeuvres du Cardinal Bellarmin* (Paris: Gabriel Beauchesne, 1913), 377–85; Bellarmine, *Responsio ad censuram P. Juliani Vincentii*, in *Auctarium Bellarminianum* (hereafter *Responsio*), 386–400; Bellarmine, *Brevis demonstratio quod ex constitutionibus et praxi Societatis non colligatur Praepositum Generalem errare non posse, contra calumnias Juliani Vincentii*, in *Auctarium Bellarminianum*, 400–403. The *Tractatus* was intended for Pope Sixtus V.

allow a superior to lead a subject into error and heresy; it presupposes that the superior cannot err, but this is only true of the Church; Jesuit obedience conflates the person of the superior with the superior as a vicar of Christ, and so forth.[88] At least some of the accusations pertained to live issues: the Spanish Jesuit Luis de Santander had been imprisoned by the Holy Office in 1588 for upholding the thesis that the superior general was infallible in matters of faith.[89] Vincent's accusations bear some similarity to the ones made by Hull and Lamont, although he does not seem to have made explicit contrast with the teaching of Thomas. As Mostaccio says, "It was exactly on the idea of the obedience of one's mind and intellect that Julien Vincent centered his censure of Ignatius's letter."[90]

Bellarmine does not mention Vincent in the *Tractatus*, but the *Responsio* does identify him by name and treats him rather contemptuously. Bellarmine is in high dudgeon over the fact that "a man I do not know (*hominem nescio quem*) would presume, without any support from Scripture or the Fathers, to attack the letter of a most eminent man and a religious order approved by the Holy See."[91] Bellarmine says that although his task is not to return a curse for a curse, but only refute arguments, he must nevertheless point out the fraudulence of Vincent's central claim: the 1553 letter to Portugal, which has been progressively corrupting the order, was not written by Ignatius, but by some other author.[92] Bellarmine follows with a thorough defense of the authenticity of the letter and its conformity to the order's teaching on obedience. The future cardinal underlines his low opinion of Vincent's character, as well as his own contrasting attitude toward authority, when he says that he wrote his works against Vincent to fulfill the demands of holy obedience, not because he judged the man worthy of a reply.[93]

Bellarmine's treatment of obedience has several main features. First, he leads with appeals to authority, offering proof-texts from Scripture, the Fathers, and the doctors, to show the pedigree of Ignatius's teaching. Second, Bellarmine wants to show that Ignatius's position, which he identifies with "blind obedience," is not merely a legitimate one particular to the Society of Jesus, but the common teaching of all religious orders as well as the foundation of ecclesiastical obedience. Third, his discussion of the limiting conditions highlights the issue of heresy, downplaying the idea that the Jesuit general or other superiors are infallible in matters of faith or otherwise incapable of error.

88. Bellarmine, *Responsio*, 387.
89. Moreno, "La aportación española," 76.
90. Mostaccio, *Early Modern Jesuits*, 98.
91. Bellarmine, *Responsio*, 400.
92. Bellarmine, *Responsio*, 386.
93. Bellarmine, *Responsio*, 400.

The *Tractatus* leads with a definition of blind obedience: "pure, perfect, and simple obedience without discussion of the reasons why something is commanded, but which is content only that it is commanded."[94] Most of the *Tractatus* is dedicated to sourcing blind obedience in positive theology. As Scripture shows, obedience given to men is really rendered to God. The Lord's words, "he who hears you, hears me" (Lk 10:16), along with Paul's exhortations in Ephesians 6 and Colossians 3, are Bellarmine's primary texts from the New Testament, and he brings in the examples of Abraham and Eve as well.[95] Next comes a catena of patristic authors who counsel blind obedience. Most of the citations are taken from texts on the monastic life, which serves Bellarmine's purpose of showing that Ignatius follows his predecessors; as the Jesuit doctor says, "there was never in the Church of God a profession of religious life that did not cultivate this obedience."[96] Basil's *Monastic Constitutions* provide numerous passages that enjoin obedience without asking the superior for reasons, comparing the monk to a tool in the hand of a craftsman. Bellarmine says that Ignatius drew on this passage when making his reference to a staff in the hand of an old man.[97] Jerome counsels the perfect monk in his letter to Rusticus to "fear the superior like a lord, love him like a parent, believe whatever he commands to be salutary, and do not judge the opinion of your elders."[98] Similar citations are taken from a host of other Fathers, including Augustine, Cassian, Benedict, Gregory the Great, and John Damascene.

Bellarmine selects several figures from the high medieval period to support his position, beginning with St. Francis of Assisi, who according to Bonaventure spoke of the truly obedient person as a dead body. Bellarmine says that this was Ignatius's source for this image of the obedient man in the sixth part of the *Constitutions*. The Jesuit theologian offers additional texts from the works of Bonaventure that explain the exercise of perfect obedience. Not content with Franciscans alone, Bellarmine also appeals to Dominican sources, beginning with Aquinas. In the *Tractatus* he cites *Summa Theologiae*, I-II, q. 13, a. 5, which says that the judgment of impossible tasks lies with the superior rather than the subject.[99] The *Responsio* adds more points from Thomas. Bellarmine uses the distinction between obedience that is sufficient for salvation and perfect obedience to argue that according to Thomas, it is not only licit, but pious and holy to vow absolute obedience in all things where sin is not manifest. In

---

94. Bellarmine, *Tractatus*, 377.
95. Bellarmine uses commentaries on these passages from Basil, Benedict, Bonaventure, and Vincent Ferrer to bolster his argument. *Tractatus*, 378–79.
96. Bellarmine, *Tractatus*, 379.
97. Bellarmine, *Tractatus*, 379.
98. Bellarmine, *Tractatus*, 380.
99. Bellarmine, *Tractatus*, 382.

Summa Theologiae, II-II, q. 88, Thomas teaches that the matter of the vow extends to every good act. Bellarmine reasons that if every good act falls under the vow, then much more so does every perfect act.[100] The Jesuit also cites a letter of Humbert of Romans, Minister General of the Dominicans during the thirteenth century, who counsels obedience in terms that correspond to Bellarmine's definition.

> So that your obedience may be acceptable to God, strive that it may be prompt without delay, devoted without disdain, voluntary without contradiction, simple without discussion, ordered without deviation, joyful without disorder, brisk without faintheartedness, universal without exception, persevering without ceasing.[101]

In the same vein, Humbert advises Dominicans to be like gold being shaped, or a flexible rod bent according to the craftsman's desire, a wheel moved by the wind, or a beast of burden, upon whose back anything is loaded.

Bellarmine is evidently eager to demonstrate that the Dominican order holds the same teaching as the Jesuit order. "St. Vincent, since he belonged to the order of St. Dominic, certainly did and taught what he had heard praised in that most glorious order according to what had been established by the holy Fathers Augustine and Dominic."[102] When defending the letter of 1553's assertion that superiors should be seen as vicars of Christ, Bellarmine says that "in this place Fr. Ignatius does not speak of religious of our order only, as the censor [Vincent] writes for the sake of inflaming envy, but of religious of all orders."[103] The reference to "inflaming envy" may well have the Dominicans in mind, since some of their members were among Society's severest critics.

This common teaching and practice, Bellarmine observes, faces the objection that perfect obedience, though suited to religious of ancient times, is no longer suited to the changed mores of the present. The Jesuit theologian replies that since perfect obedience has been maintained across the centuries by so many holy men, he sees no reason to change now. If so many other religious virtues, like asperity of life, poverty, silence, and dedication to prayer, are still praised as they were of old, so too should obedience, since it holds the first place in religious institutes, as Thomas says.[104] Here again Bellarmine presents the Society as upholding the tradition of the Church, rather than departing

---

100. Bellarmine, *Responsio*, 388. Thomas seems to have meant that only virtuous acts could be the matter of a vow, not that obedience required the fulfillment of every virtuous act.
101. Bellarmine, *Tractatus*, 383.
102. Bellarmine, *Tractatus*, 383.
103. Bellarmine, *Responsio*, 389.
104. Bellarmine, *Tractatus*, 385.

from or undermining it. As he says in the *Responsio*, "wherefore that novelty and den of many errors are not hiding in the letter of Fr. Ignatius, but in the open lie of the censor [Vincent]."[105]

Bellarmine argues not only that Scripture, the Fathers and doctors, and existing religious orders all uphold blind obedience, but also that this is the foundation of order in the Church.[106] Vincent's teaching not only opposes the common consensus of the Fathers, but also has the taste of "Lutheran leaven," because it tends toward the undermining of all ecclesiastical discipline. "What sort of face would the Church have, if all subjects were allowed to dispute the commands of bishops, abbots, or even temporal lords?"[107] Although the simple people do not vow obedience to their pastors and bishops, they are still bound to obey them blindly, because simple people are not able to determine the truth or falsehood of what they are taught. The liberty to believe whatever one wishes, as exists today among the Lutherans, is a far greater danger. In a religious order, where there are many learned men, the danger of obedience being used to lead people into heresy is far less.[108] Although this passage is consistent with Bellarmine's wider teaching on ecclesiastical polity, he does not develop the theme at any length, nor does he consider the role of obedience at the natural or civil level.

Bellarmine gives more attention to the limiting conditions of obedience than Nadal. The first of these conditions is that one does not owe obedience when something sinful is commanded.[109] Bellarmine is especially sensitive to the possibility that a superior could lead a subordinate into heresy, something that the other Jesuit commentators under consideration ignore. He parses the issue in the following way: obedience concerns human actions, not matters of faith, but it can apply when a superior commands conformity to theological opinion concerning matters not yet defined by the Church.[110] In other words, Bellarmine thinks that obedience primarily concerns practical commands rather than speculative propositions, but he does leave some space for the latter. Although Bellarmine admits that superiors can err, deceive, or be deceived, he is confident that any superior commanding heresy would not long be able to persist in so doing before being corrected by someone above him.[111] He also says that subordinates are allowed to represent to superiors, with due reverence

---

105. Bellarmine, *Responsio*, 389.
106. Moreno calls attention to Bellarmine's appeal to the role of the pope in Jesuit obedience as a "strong shield" and "unconquerable bulwark" in protecting its legitimacy. Moreno, "La aportación española," 81.
107. Bellarmine, *Responsio*, 391.
108. Bellarmine, *Tractatus*, 385.
109. Bellarmine, *Tractatus*, 384.
110. Bellarmine, *Responsio*, 388.
111. Bellarmine, *Tractatus*, 385.

and humility, and the disposition to conform his will and intellect, if something against the superior's command should occur to him.[112] Like Ignatius, he says that representing is compatible with blind obedience, without explaining how.

The Jesuit doctor provides personal testimony against the censures of Vincent when he says that in all his thirty years as a member of the Society, he has never witnessed the misdeeds that his letter of censure identifies, such as slow reception of papal instructions, or efforts to prevent Jesuits from going to the Inquisition. Bellarmine adds that if Vincent wishes to be taken seriously, he should identify particular misdeeds and their perpetrators, rather than indicting the whole order.[113]

Bellarmine's defense of Jesuit obedience differs from the approach of the other theologians. Aquinas grounds the vow of obedience in a natural virtue, whereas Nadal apparently separates it from nature. Bellarmine's tactic is grounding blind obedience in both the sources of theology and in ecclesiastical governance. His argument proceeds thus: the blind obedience of the Society is identical to the blind obedience of the whole tradition of religious life, and the blind obedience of religious life is, if not identical, then nearly, the same as the obedience that the simple faithful owe to their pastors and bishops.[114]

Francisco Suárez

The most thorough commentator under consideration on the question of Jesuit obedience is Francisco Suárez, who dedicates significant space to the topic in his massive *De religione*.[115] This work was begun at the behest of Acquaviva during the disturbances of the 1590s, but it was not completed until Suárez's death, and the final volumes were only published posthumously in 1625.[116] It was, in part, a response to external attacks on the Society, although obedience does not seem to have been at issue.[117] Like Bellarmine, Suárez

---

112. Bellarmine, *Tractatus*, 378.
113. Bellarmine, *Responsio*, 391.
114. Imbruglia notes the crucial place that obedience has in Bellarmine's vision of sanctity, particularly in the Society of Jesus. Girolamo Imbruglia, "La milizia come 'maniera di vivere' dei gesuiti: Missione, martirio, obbedienza," *Rivista di storia del cristianesimo* 15, no. 2 (2018): 271–84.
115. For an overview of Suárez's life in the Society, see Carlos Noreña, "Suárez and the Jesuits," *American Catholic Philosophical Quarterly* 65, no. 3 (1991): 267–86. For an explanation of what Suárez means by *religio*, see Aaron Pidel, "Francisco Suárez on Religion and Religious Pluralism," in *Francisco Suárez (1548–1617): Jesuits and the Complexities of Modernity*, ed. Robert Maryks and Juan Antonio Senent de Frutos (Boston: Brill, 2019), 128–53.
116. Paul Murphy, "'God's Porters:' The Jesuit Vocation according to Francisco Suárez," *Archivum Historicum Societatis Jesu* 70, no. 139 (2001): 3–28.
117. The Society, and even some of Suárez's own writings, were the target of blistering attacks by the Dominicans Alonso de Avendaño and García de Mondragón beginning in the late 1560s,

explicitly defends the teaching of Ignatius and provides grounding for it in the tradition of the Church, while also acknowledging certain limiting conditions. Also like Bellarmine, he tries to deal with objections to the teaching, although he is more perspicacious about the particular problem of the conformity of judgment. Suárez explicitly admits that blind obedience does not deprive the subject of all judgment, which is a crucial element of defending Jesuit teaching from the charges of its historical and contemporary critics.

The tenth book of *De religione* lays out Suárez's view of the vow of obedience in general, which he calls "the most excellent" (*praestantissimum*) of the three vows, because, "through obedience someone offers to the true God his soul, intellect, and will, and his whole self as a holocaust."[118] He cites *Summa Theologiae*, II–II, q. 186, a. 8, for this view, but he departs from Aquinas's actual words in two respects. First, Suárez calls obedience *praestantissimum* instead of *praecipuum*, and second, he explicitly includes the intellect along with the will among the things offered in holocaust to God. He proceeds to defend the legitimacy of simple religious vows against the objections of heretics. Appealing to Scripture and the Fathers, Suárez underlines the close connection between obeying Christ and obeying superiors.[119]

Suárez's general treatment also lays out limiting conditions, the first of which is *honestas*, by which he means that the act commanded has to be without sin.[120] Whatever is commanded must also be possible and not impede a greater good, as happens when a superior commands something contrary to the rule. Here Suárez cites two of Thomas's Quodlibetal questions (I, q. 8, a. 15 and I, q. 5, a. 10) in support of this stance.[121] When there is doubt about whether obedience binds in a particular case, the Jesuit says that it is better to obey.[122]

Suárez shifts from a general perspective on obedience to the special conditions of its exercise in the Society of Jesus in Tract Ten, Book Four of the *De religione*. He acknowledges that there is a discrepancy between the practice of

---

but they do not seem to have aimed at their rival's theory or practice of obedience. See Raoul de Scorraille, *François Suarez de la Compagnie de Jésus: D'après ses lettres, ses autres écrits inédits et un grand nombre de documents nouveaux*, vol. 1, *L'Etudiant-Le Maître* (Paris: P. Lethielleux, 1912), 264–77; Doris Moreno Martínez, "Crear opinión: El dominico Alonso de Avendaño y su predicación antijesuita (1567–1596)," in *Identidades y fronteras culturales en el mundo ibérico de la Edad Moderna*, ed. José Luis Betrán, Bernat Hernández, and Doris Moreno (Bellaterra: University of Barcelona, 2016), 399–413.

118. Francisco Suárez, *Opera Omnia*, ed. Charles Berton (Paris: Luis Vives, 1856), 15:863.
119. Suárez, *Opera Omnia*, 15:869.
120. Suárez, *Opera Omnia*, 15:865.
121. Suárez, *Opera Omnia* 15:876–77. Suárez seems to have erred in his citation. *Quodlibet* I, q. 8, a. 1 contains this explanation of the rule's limiting function, whereas *Quodlibet* I, q. 5 deals with contrition and does not have a tenth article.
122. Suárez, *Opera Omnia*, 15:878.

obedience among the Jesuits and in other orders, as the latter maintain a teaching of Thomas: the vow is limited by the rule that the religious professes. Suárez says that this limitation does not apply in the Society, because their obedience extends to "whatever particular acts of the religious" (*quoscumque actus particulares ipsius religiosi*), which is the widest possible scope. In consequence, the will of the superior, within the limits of *materia honesta*, becomes a living rule for the subject, taking the place of a written rule.[123]

Suárez attempts to mitigate the sweeping terms of this statement somewhat by appealing to the end for which the Society exists: in the words of the *Constitutions* (Part IX, Ch 3, paragraph 20), "the perfection and aid of its neighbors for the glory of God."[124] He raises this point against the objection that the ordinary exercise of Jesuit authority could impose even acts of heroic virtue on any of its members. Suárez says that everything that is necessary or conducive to the Society's end falls under the obligation of obedience, but not every possible act ordered toward perfection does so. He offers as examples the redemption of captives, or efforts on behalf of the external peace of a commonwealth, as actions that are good, but not per se ordered toward the spiritual good of one's neighbor. They would, therefore, not fall under obedience strictly speaking (*in rigore praecepti*).[125] This section helps clarify Suárez's statement that the superior's will is a living rule, because he says that it cannot go beyond the powers given to superiors in the *Constitutions*, which are in turn ordered toward the end for which the Society exists.[126] The practical force of this limiting condition is less significant than it may appear, however, for Suárez also says that any Jesuit can be obligated to go on missions to the Indies or other dangerous places, even if he has not professed the fourth vow, and that when such things are suggested rather than commanded, it is still better to comply.[127]

When Suárez treats Ignatius's three degrees of obedience, we find the most explicit acknowledgment among the authors under consideration of the inherent difficulties of the founder's teaching. Suárez is not long detained concerning the conformity of the will. He admits that Ignatius in his letter of 1553 exaggerates the necessity of this condition, but doing an action willingly is part of

---

123. Suárez, *Opera Omnia*, 16:762. I am grateful to Eric DeMeuse for the observation that the idea of the Christological unity of the Church, a prominent theme in Suárez's ecclesiology, influences his conception of the corporate unity and operation of the Society of Jesus.

124. Suárez, *Opera Omnia*, 16:763. Cf. Cons., §765.

125. Suárez, *Opera Omnia*, 16:764.

126. Suárez, *Opera Omnia*, 16:765.

127. Suárez, *Opera Omnia*, 16:766, 764. Murphy highlights the centrality of mission, especially preaching, in Suárez's understanding of the Society's particular charism. Murphy, "God's Porters," 13–17.

what makes that action moral and human—obeying without the conformity of will would be repugnant.[128]

By contrast, the vow of obedience *ex parte intellectus* is harder to explain. Suárez says that the Society expects two things here that seem contrary to each other. The first is that subjects in the Society are expected to see the superior not as man, but as God, and his commands as divine rather than human. The second is that obedience be blind.[129] Suárez raises the objection that these two conditions are contradictory because seeing the superior as God requires "great perceptiveness and reasoning" (*magna perspicacia et ratiocinatio*). How, therefore, can it at the same time be blind? Conformity of judgment also appears to be above the *ratio virtutis*, because perfect virtue does not require a false apprehension or judgment, but it is false to see the precept of man as that of God. If it is supposed that the superior can never deceive or wish to deceive, this is clearly a false supposition; if this is not supposed, then it is never possible to determine, according to examination of circumstances and persons, if a superior is in fact deceiving or attempting to deceive.[130] It is impossible to make a judgment without sufficient consideration, but Jesuit obedience seems to place the subject in the position of obeying a command from man that may be contrary to God.[131]

Before Suárez attempts reasoning through these difficulties, he presents, like Bellarmine, a catena of authorities in support of both propositions under consideration: of seeing the superior as God and blind obedience. Beginning with the words of Christ, *he who hears you, hears me*, Suárez proceeds to cite dozens of patristic sources, both eastern and western, as well as scholastic authors. Suárez includes all of Bellarmine's authors (except Vincent Ferrer) and adds several of his own, including John Chrysostom and his disciple Nilus, Lawrence Justinian, and Alonso Tostado (Abulensis). Suárez cites Tostado's commentary on Genesis 17, which says, "True obedience knows no delays, nor deliberates about acting when a command is given."[132] As for Dominicans, Suárez seizes upon Thomas's teaching in *Summa Theologiae*, I-II, q. 13, a. 5 that a subject does not judge whether something is impossible, but leaves that determination to the superior. Commenting on this point, he says,

> With these words he [Thomas] shows how the counsels of the saints are to be understood, when they say that one must obey even in impossible things. That is, where either the impossibility is not evident, or it is certainly evident, let a man begin and do what he can, until he can go no

---

128. Suárez, *Opera Omnia*, 16:769.
129. Suárez, *Opera Omnia*, 16:777.
130. Suárez, *Opera Omnia*, 16:777.
131. Suárez, *Opera Omnia*, 16:778.
132. Suárez, *Opera Omnia*, 16:782.

further, for in the meantime God opens a way for him to complete what seemed impossible at the beginning.[133]

Suárez also cites the aforementioned letter of Humbert of Romans in support of blind obedience without discussion.

Suárez's strategy here is the same as Bellarmine's: giving the teaching of Ignatius a solid foundation in Scripture and in the Fathers and doctors of the Church. He says explicitly that the Society's teaching on the perfection of obedience in the submission of the intellect "is not new, but most ancient, nor exceptional (*singularem*), but most widely shared (*communissimam*) and founded upon the highest authority." Obedience formally perfects the will; as Thomas says in q. 104, it is a moral virtue and a part of justice. In the same way that the will depends on the intellect in its actions, so the perfection of obedience depends on the perfection of the intellect.[134]

At this point, Suárez moves to resolve the objections raised at the outset. Seeing the superior as holding the place of God does not demand a false apprehension, but rather the elevation of the mind to considering the supreme reason and motivation for obeying, which is the divine will. The subject does not judge the superior to be God, but to represent God.[135] Nor is it necessary to judge the superior to be incapable of error or deception.[136] The correct understanding of blind obedience, according to Suárez, is not that the subject is deprived of all cognition and judgment, since he obeys as a man, not as a brute beast. The Fathers demand rather for perfect obedience "Lyncean eyes" for seeing God in the superior. Suárez cites several expressions that Ignatius uses in passages of the *Constitutions* to demonstrate that obedience is not blind *simpliciter*, but only under a certain aspect (*quadam ratione*). That is, blind obedience excludes merely human reasons for obeying the superior, such as his learning or prudence, or that he commands pleasant things, rather than looking to the will of God. This also means excluding "human reasoning" (*humanos discursus*) in examining why the superior commands one thing rather than another.[137]

"Human reasoning" is not coterminous with prudence, however, for Suárez seeks to defend the latter, distinguishing between the prudence of the flesh and spiritual, supernatural prudence. This means rejecting not all use of one's own will and liberty, but only insofar as it is vicious, as Thomas says in *Summa Theologiae*, II–II, q. 50, a. 2.[138] Suárez's citation might seem out of place, for this pas-

---

133. Suárez, *Opera Omnia*, 16:782.
134. Suárez, *Opera Omnia*, 16:782.
135. Suárez, *Opera Omnia*, 16:783.
136. Suárez, *Opera Omnia*, 16:783–84.
137. Suárez, *Opera Omnia*, 16:788.
138. Suárez, *Opera Omnia*, 16:789.

sage deals specifically with political rather than supernatural prudence and says nothing specifically about the vicious use of liberty. Yet, Thomas does say here that political subordinates are moved in such a way that their intellect and will must be engaged. Suárez seems to think that this stipulation applies analogously at the supernatural level, meaning that there is a kind of prudence legitimately exercised by subordinates within the context of Jesuit obedience. Although this approach seems to depart verbally from Ignatius's counsel to set aside one's own prudence in favor of the superior's, Suárez interprets the founder's teaching to exclude the sort of human prudence that looks only to natural motives and ends. One could argue in support of this idea that Ignatius's granting of wide discretionary powers, especially to Jesuits on foreign missions, presupposes the exercise of prudence.

Toward the end of this treatment on the conformity of judgment, Suárez attempts to ground blind obedience in the Society of Jesus in the exigencies of obedience at a natural level, saying that it is necessary to any kind of governance, whether political, economic, military, or any other. If the servant needed to understand and perceive reasons and causes that move his leader or lord to command, any governance at all would become difficult and morally impossible. A superior often commands according to higher and more universal reasons, which either the subject cannot understand or does not need to know.[139] It is curious, in view of his extensive contributions in the fields of law, authority, and political thought, that Suárez makes this point so tersely, almost as an afterthought.[140]

Suárez manifests a greater interest than the other Jesuit commentators in showing the conformity of Ignatius's teaching with Aquinas's. Not only does he cite him more frequently, but he also tries, if belatedly, to ground Jesuit obedience in nature. This Thomistic approach is conspicuously absent from the other Jesuit authors. That is not to say that Suárez's reading of Thomas is altogether convincing, but only that he is more sensitive to the need for continuity with the Angelic Doctor.

Conclusion

Although the foregoing is by no means a complete study of obedience in the writings of Ignatius, Aquinas, and the Jesuit commentators, it is now time to draw some tentative conclusions and make a partial reply to the charges of contemporary critics. The first point is that, from the beginning, the Society's

---

139. Suárez, *Opera Omnia*, 16:789.
140. As Doyle observes, Suárez's model society is a monarchy, in which lawmaking, judicial, interpretative, and enforcement powers all reside ultimately in the ruler. John P. Doyle, *Collected Studies on Francisco Suárez, SJ (1548–1617)*, ed. Victor Salas (Leuven: Leuven University Press, 2010), 373.

best minds have dealt with obedience in a variety of ways. A number of them ignored it altogether, including the supposedly central question of the conformity of will and judgment, neither opposing nor explicitly defending their founder's teaching. Even those who did defend Ignatius produced various interpretations of his writings.

There is no uniform position among the Jesuits about the relationship between the teaching of Aquinas and Ignatius on the subject of obedience. Whereas Ignatius neglected Thomas as a source, and Nadal implicitly rejected him, Bellarmine and Suárez sought to enlist him in support of Jesuit theory and practice. Their approach consists of highlighting those passages that best accord with their explanation, while ignoring or downplaying those that do not. Both Jesuits understand Thomas's distinction between obedience sufficient for salvation and perfect obedience in an expansive way: instead of interpreting it in terms of the limits this teaching places on obedience, they see it as an endorsement of conformity in all things where no sin is found. Aquinas's "perfect obedience" thus becomes the equivalent of Ignatius's "blind obedience," and Suárez takes Thomas's idea of the will's dependence on the intellect a step further by saying that the perfection of obedience depends on the perfection (that is, the conformity) of the intellect. Suárez, who is the most sensitive to the problems that conformity *ex parte intellectus* presents, makes the important concession that blind obedience does not deprive the subject of all vision and judgment.[141] These are the most promising avenues for reconciling the teachings of Thomas and Ignatius on this question.

At the same time, however, differences persist. Perhaps the most significant one is that for Thomas, the vow of obedience and its exercise has a clear foundation in nature, whereas for the Jesuits it does not. Ignatius mostly ignores the connection, Nadal denies it, and Bellarmine chooses to ground religious obedience in ecclesiastical obedience, that is, in another supernatural relationship. Only Suárez attempts to ground Jesuit obedience in nature, but this point is not central to his case. This distancing from nature may help explain both the Jesuit tendency toward a more absolute understanding of obedience and the Thomistic objection to it. Ignatius and his Jesuit commentators do not seem to recognize a kind of obedience that is merely sufficient for salvation, but instead make their understanding of perfection the standard of obedience as such.[142] Suárez is the only Jesuit author under consideration to explicitly identify a dis-

---

141. Although Suárez does not, curiously enough, appeal to the Ignatian theme of representing in his discussion of obedience, he does spell out what seems to be its underlying assumption: the subject must be allowed some judgment of his own.

142. Only Suárez is ambiguous on this point, as he recognizes that the practice of obedience in the Society differs from that of other orders.

crepancy between Aquinas and Ignatius, and his attempted solution is less than convincing. The idea that the "living rule" of the superior can substitute for the written rule of a religious order makes for, at best, verbal agreement with Thomas, since the rule's role as a stable limiting condition seems to be lost here. The emphasis on the conformity of will and judgment in Ignatius and all the Jesuit authors is simply absent from the works of the Angelic Doctor, and Thomists are well within their rights to underscore this point, even if the Society's Dominican critics of the sixteenth and seventeenth centuries did not do so.[143]

It would be premature, at this early stage of research, to offer a definitive reply to the criticisms of Jesuit obedience made by contemporary theologians. At the very least, they have identified important historical and theological matters at stake. I wish to suggest, however, that on this issue Ignatius and his commentators may differ from Thomas without thereby being in the wrong. Does "Jesuit obedience" have the resources to justify itself before the tradition and overcome its internal difficulties? Nadal's interpretation of Ignatius is not very promising in this regard, but there are other possibilities. Taken together, Bellarmine and Suárez may provide the necessary resources from within the order's own tradition of thought. Against the charge of novelty, they provide a pedigree for the teaching of Ignatius in Scripture, the Fathers, and the scholastic doctors; against the charge that Jesuit obedience leads into error or heresy, they explain that it primarily concerns human reasons and motivations rather than matters of faith or other speculative questions, while denying extreme claims of the indefectibility of superiors; against the charge of tyranny, they admit the right of representation, the reality of the subject's judgment, and the paradoxically greater perspicacity of the intellect that blind obedience entails. Such an interpretation of Ignatius would go a long way toward demonstrating that "blind obedience" forges not the shackles of tyranny, but rather the bonds of charity and apostolic service.

---

143. De Blignières says that the legitimate meaning of blind obedience is that a subordinate voluntarily executes a command for the sole formal reason that it is given by the superior, and not because the subject judges that what is commanded is prudent or expedient. In the author's words, the name "blind obedience" can be retained, but not the thing. "L'obéissance du jugement," 57, 65–67.

CHAPTER 10

"Therefore Israel First":
Francisco de Toledo, SJ's Thomistic Claims for *Converso* Christians[1]

Elisabeth Rain Kincaid

In Romans 11:1, the Apostle Paul asks, "Did God reject his people?" This question, in various guises, has reappeared again and again in Christian theology, often with answers leading to disastrous consequences for Jews and people of Jewish descent. Concerned by the horrors of the twentieth century, many contemporary theologians have engaged in a thoughtful analysis of these different answers and their repercussions. The theology of Thomas Aquinas has become an especially important *locus* of theological engagement on this question. Holly Taylor Coolman has mapped out an important division in the sources and conclusions in this scholarship.[2] On one hand, recent scholarship has highlighted—through a reclaiming of Aquinas's commentary on Romans—Aquinas's conviction that the Jews will eventually be saved in God's providential plan.[3] This positive claim, however, is often read as being in tension with Aquinas's condemnation of the practices of the ceremonial Jewish law contained in the *Summa*.[4]

---

1. For purposes of this paper, I will use the term "*conversos*" to refer to Spaniards of Jewish descent since this was the term generally in use in Ignatius and Toledo's time.

2. Holly Taylor Coolman, "Romans 9–11: Rereading Aquinas on the Jews" in *Reading Romans with St. Thomas Aquinas*, eds. Matthew Levering and Micahel Dauphinais (Washington, DC: The Catholic University of America Press, 2012), 103–5. For an argument regarding the possibility of Christian Jews continuing to fulfil Torah, see Matthew Levering, "Aquinas and Supersessionism One More Time: A Response to Matthew Tapie's *Aquinas on Israel and the Church*," *Pro Ecclesia* 25, no. 4 (2016): 401. See, e.g., Steven C. Boguslawski, *Thomas Aquinas on the Jews: Insights into His Commentary on Romans 9–11* (Mahwah, NJ: Paulist Press, 2008); Matthew Levering, *Christ's Fulfillment of Torah and Temple: Salvation according to Thomas Aquinas* (Notre Dame, IN: University of Notre Dame Press, 2002); Bruce D. Marshall, "Quasi in Figura: A Brief Reflection on Jewish Election, after Thomas Aquinas," *Nova et Vetera* 7, no. 2 (2009): 477–484.

3. Coolman herself attempts to mediate this tension by arguing that the positive claim of Jewish salvation in Aquinas's Romans commentary creates "an Israel-shaped gap" in his discussion of the promulgation of the Old Law to replace the new. Coolman, "Rereading Aquinas," 111.

4. Coolman, "Rereading Aquinas," 102–3. For more in-depth discussion of this point see Michael Wyschogrod, "A Jewish Reading of Thomas Aquinas on the Old Law," in *Understanding*

Along with the writings of St. Thomas, St. Ignatius of Loyola's engagement with Jews and Christians of Jewish descent has also occasioned significant contemporary theological study.[5] However, unlike the analysis of Aquinas's theological corpus, which has focused on tensions within a complex theological system, the Ignatian scholarship has focused on actions, including records of Ignatius's conversations regarding the value of Jewish lineage, his robust support of the incorporation of Jesuits of Jewish heritage into the Society, and his personal relationships with Christians of known Jewish lineage.

In this essay, I will argue that one of the early Jesuits, Francisco de Toledo, himself of *converso* descent, incorporated Ignatius's theological convictions regarding God's ongoing special relationship with the Jews and his defense of equal treatment of those of *converso* descent into a robust theological system, drawing creatively upon foundational insights of St. Thomas Aquinas. I will consider first the context for Toledo's work, including Ignatius's philo-semitism, Francisco de Toledo's Jewish heritage, his engagement with the issues of Jewishness within the Society, and his Thomistic formation as a member of the School of Salamanca. I will then consider the scriptural grounding of Toledo's understanding of Jewish election through analyzing his development of Thomistic thought in his commentary on the book of Romans. I will end with a reading of his commentary on the Summa and explore how he develops Thomas's arguments to challenge practices related to forced conversions of Jews and mistreatment of *conversos* in the Spain of *el siglo de oro*.

Conversos in the Society of Jesus and Spain

To begin, I will consider the formative influences upon Toledo's theological engagement with Judaism. First, I will consider in more depth the example set by St. Ignatius. Secondly, I will consider Toledo's own life and experience. Specifically, I will focus upon his training in Salamancan Thomism, his life within

---

the Scriptures, ed. Clemens Thoma and Michael Wyschogrod (Mahwah, NJ: Paulist Press, 1987); Jeremy Cohen, *Living Letters of the Law: Ideas of the Jew in Medieval Christianity* (Berkeley: University of California Press, 1999), 234–35; Matthew Tapie, *Aquinas on Israel and the Church: The Question of Supersessionism in the Theology of Thomas Aquinas* (Eugene, OR: Pickwick Publications, 2014), 23–24.

5. See, e.g., James W. Reites, SJ, "St. Ignatius of Loyola and the Jews," *Studies in the Spirituality of Jesuits* 13, no. 4 (1981): 1–48; Jose Gomez-Menor, "La Progenie Hebrea del Padre Pedro de Ribadeneira, SJ," *Sefarad* 36, no. 2 (1976): 308; and Eusebio Rey, SJ, "San Ignacio del Loyola y el problema de los 'cristianos nuevos,'" *Razón y Fe* 153 (1956): 178–204. The most recent and comprehensive scholarly output regarding Ignatius's interactions with Jews and Christians of Jewish heritage can be found in the work of Robert Maryks. See Robert Maryks, *The Jesuit Order as a Synagogue of Jews* (Leiden: Brill, 2009); Robert Maryks, "Ignatius of Loyola and the Converso Question," in *A Companion to Ignatius of Loyola* (Leiden: Brill, 2014), 88–89.

the Society of Jesus, and his own *converso* lineage to show how he develops Thomistic theology of Israel in a characteristically Ignatian direction. In Toledo's formation in the early Society of Jesus and in his own life experience, we see a unique convergence of the results of the early Jesuit promotion and support of Christians of Jewish heritage with the methodology of Salamancan Thomism.

As I mentioned above, demonstrations of St. Ignatius's engagement with Jews or Christians of Jewish descent, *conversos* or "New Christians" in the terminology of Spain, can be divided into two categories. First, there are records of Ignatius's numerous statements regarding the blessing of sharing a biological connection with both Jesus and Mary. Many of these instances were recorded in the first biography of Ignatius, written by an early member of the Society, Pedro Ribadeneyra, himself of secret *converso* descent.[6] The content seems to be consistent—an elevation of the continuing value and theological significance of Jewish lineage. A very representative example taken from a different source, Diego de Guzmán's letter to Claudio Aquaviva protesting the later discrimination against Jews in the Society provides this similar example, describing a conversation between Ignatius and a new Jewish Christian who had entered the society of catechumens established and funded by Ignatius in Rome.

> Chatting with him one day, [the new convert] told him: "I, my father Ignatius, would prefer, if God were served, not to be born of this lineage, for these people persecuted and crucified Jesus Christ our Lord." And our father answered him, "Do you want me to say what I feel about this? To tell you the truth, if our Lord would like me to choose this lineage to be born of, I would not choose other than yours. And the reason for this is that the Lord himself wanted to choose this lineage for him and to be son of Abraham and David and other patriarchs and kings; and of them was his most holy Mother, Virgin Mary, with her husband Saint Joseph, whom he used to call 'My Father.' And, the glorious Virgin, his mother...."[7]

Accounts of Ignatius's support of those of Jewish descent entering the Society and his inclusion of them within his personal circles constitute the second category.[8] This openness to those of Jewish descent, was, *de jure*, incorporated

---

6. Gomez-Menor, "La Progenie Hebrea," 308; See Maryks, "*Converso* Question," 42–45 for more on Ignatius's friendship and mentorship of Ribadeneira.

7. Maryks, "*Converso* Question," 46. For further excerpts of positive statements regarding Jews and *conversos* described by Ribadeneira, see Maryks, "*Converso* Question," 45. See Reites, "St. Ignatius of Loyola and the Jews," 12–13 for a discussion of Ignatius's provision for Jewish converts to Christianity in Rome.

8. Gomez-Menor, "La Progenie Hebrea," 307. See also Rey, "El problema de los 'cristianos nuevos,'" 173–204. For a thorough analysis of the *converso* connections in Ignatius's circle of friends and colleagues, see Maryks, *Jesuit Order as a Synagogue*, 50–71.

into the founding *Constitutions* of the Society.⁹ In addition, it was enacted *de facto* in Ignatius's robust support of those of Jewish descent entering the Society, even in the teeth of opposition from people with powerful influence in secular and ecclesiastical circles in Spain.¹⁰ This explicit openness to those of Jewish descent inspired many *conversos* to enter the early Society.¹¹ St. Ignatius doubled down on this support by robustly promoting many of these members to high offices within the Society and the Church at large. In fact, Robert Maryks has identified all four Jesuits (Polanco, Nadal, Madrid, and Laínez, the eventual second General) who exercised some governance over the Society after Ignatius's death until a congregation could be held to elect a new general as being of *converso* descent.¹² This openness and support of Jesuits of *converso* descent would continue through the administration of the third Superior General, St. Francisco de Borgia, the former Duke of Granja who was described as "a lover of Jews."¹³

Ignatius's staunch support of *conversos* entering the Society, and those of Jewish descent generally, was noted even in his own time because it ran contrary to much of the general sentiment in the Spain of *el siglo de oro*. In fact, this support was so distinctive that rumors began to circulate during Ignatius's life claiming that the only explanation for this care for *conversos* could be his own secret *converso* heritage. In contrast, the current scholarly consensus is that Ignatius's support was likely due both to his incarnational theology and the impact of friendship with *conversos* throughout his life.¹⁴ Ignatius's attitude was a noteworthy departure from the attitudes in his native Basque region, which had always been notorious in Spain for its focus on the prioritization of a purely "Christian" lineage.¹⁵ In addition, Ignatius's support of *conversos* stands in stark contrast to the dominant contemporary trends in Spain as a whole.¹⁶

---

9. For further discussion of St. Ignatius's decision to add this provision into the text of the 1556 *Constitutions*, see Maryks, "*Converso* Question," 100.

10. For discussion of Ignatius's conflict with the diocesan bishop with episcopal oversight over the college of Alcalá regarding Jesuit decisions to admit *conversos*, see Maryks, "*Converso* Question," 100.

11. Maryks, *Jesuit Order as a Synagogue*, 41–115.

12. Maryks, *Jesuit Order as a Synagogue*, 98.

13. Maryks, "Ignatius of Loyola and the *Converso* Question," 101.

14. For discussion of Ignatius's denial of this claim during his own life, see Reites, "St. Ignatius of Loyola and the Jews," 7. For contemporary scholarship on this question, see Markys, "*Converso* Question," 88–89.

15. Reites, "St. Ignatius of Loyola and the Jews," 7. For Polanco and Nadal's description of Ignatius's claims to blood purity and his Basque heritage, see Maryks, *Jesuit Order as a Synagogue*, 48–49.

16. For a discussion of the role in which anti-Judaism played as a common uniting factor contributing to the formation of a Visigothic cultural identity in the kingdom of Toledo from as early as the sixth century, see Wolfram Drews, *The Unknown Neighbour: The Jew in the Thought of Isidore of Seville* (Leiden: Brill, 2006): 294–303.

In his seminal work, *Neighboring Faiths*, David Nirenberg traces the shift in Spanish approaches to Jewish identity. Following the forced conversions of perhaps as many as 200,000 Jews in Spain (and most prominently in Toledo) at the end of the 14th century, Christian concerns about "secret Jews" were dramatically amplified.[17] Some of this was undoubtedly based on the fact that many of the victims of these forced conversions naturally returned to the practices and the faith of their fathers, that Jews and *conversos* still lived together, and that they remained bound to each other by family ties. In many cases, the continuing connections created the perception of a return to Jewish practices even among those who might have sincerely converted.[18] In addition, economic and political jealousy arose due to the fact that many converted Jews took advantage of the removal of the economic and political constraints which had bound Jews, thereby rising quickly both in economic success and political power, eventually coming to occupy many of the most important bureaucratic positions in the Spanish kingdom.[19] Throughout the 1400s, this suspicion led to a number of continuing purges and riots against *conversos*, and led the Inquisition to investigate alleged returns to the Jewish faith more zealously. Undoubtedly, the fear of *luteranismo* increased the skepticism and concern regarding possible heretical beliefs among *conversos*, as the Inquisition became ever more conflictual, mirroring the wider political and social conflict in early-modern Europe.[20]

Nirenberg also convincingly argues that after the 1492 expulsion of Jews, this cultural skepticism of those of Jewish heritage and resentment remained deeply embedded in Spanish culture. However, without the visual presence of the other of a different religion—the practicing Jew—it began to develop into strong racial rejection rather than religious discrimination. Thus, cultural suspicions expanded beyond first generation Jewish converts to also include suspicion of anybody of Jewish descent. This suspicion was characterized by attribution of negative characteristics to anybody who possessed Jewish blood—a taint of character which could not be erased even by baptism.[21] This conviction regarding a racial taint would, by the end of Toledo's life, permeate

---

17. David Nirenberg, *Neighboring Faiths: Christianity, Islam, and Judaism in the Middle Ages and Today* (Chicago: University of Chicago Press, 2014), 145, 155. See also Miriam Bodian, *Dying in the Law of Moses: Crypto-Jewish Martyrdom in the Iberian World* (Bloomington, IN: Indiana University Press, 2007), 12–13.

18. For an analysis of the relationships between *converso* Christians and Jews and the development of anti-Christian writing among Jews aimed toward *conversos* in response to the intensification of forced conversion across the fourteenth and fifteenth centuries, see Bodian, *Dying in the Law of Moses*, 9–10.

•19. See Jerome Friedman, "Jewish Conversion, the Spanish Pure Blood Laws, and Reformation, A Revisionist View of Racial and Religious Antisemitism," *The Sixteenth Century Journal* 18, no. 1 (Spring 1987): 8.

20. Bodian, *Dying in the Law of Moses*, 26–28.

the Society of Jesus in the *limpieza de sangre* controversies.²² In contrast, Ignatius's support of the *conversos* and rejection of this new racialization of anti-Semitism make the Society of Jesus in its early days a crucial and culturally distinct space for theological exploration of these questions.

Toledo's family and education prepared him to take full advantage of the opportunity for the type of theological reflection on Jews which was permitted in the early days of the Society of Jesus. Born in 1532 to a relatively impoverished family in the south of Spain, Francisco Toledo was sponsored by St. John of Avila to attend the university of Salamanca. While there, he studied under Domingo de Soto, one of the leaders of Thomistic revival at the School of Salamanca. Soto would later describe the young Toledo as a "prodigy," and Soto's Thomistic teaching would have a deep influence on Toledo's later teaching and scholarship.²³ In 1556, Toledo was ordained as a priest in Salamanca. Having encountered the Jesuit order in Salamanca, he entered it in 1558. Francisco de Borgia, familiar with Toledo due to his outstanding academic reputation, recommended him to the newly elected second general of the Jesuit order, Diego Laínez, who, soon after his novitiate, assigned him to teach at the newly formed Roman College.²⁴ At the appointment of Jerome Nadal, Toledo began teaching Aristotelian philosophy and then, from 1563 to 1569, was responsible for teaching moral and spiritual theology, where he innovated upon existing Roman College practices by continuing the tradition from the Universidad de Salamanca of lecturing on the *Summa*.²⁵ In this approach, he was revolutionary at the Roman College, and in fact stirred controversy by his departure from the formal mode of dictation and his use of the *Summa* as his textbook.²⁶ These lectures, which were preserved as student notes, and later published in 1869, constitute one of the first three, full commentaries by Jesuits written on the *Summa*.²⁷

This introduction of the methodology of the Salamancan school of Thomism, as well as the biblical humanist reforms of Cardinal Cisneros into the Jesuit educational system, would be the hallmarks of his teaching, which influenced subsequent generations of Jesuit pedagogy.²⁸ His career in Rome

21. Nirenberg, *Neighboring Faiths*, 158–85.
22. See Maryks, *Jesuit Order as a Synagogue*, 117–56 for a recounting of the political mechanism and cultural forces as well as their effect which led to the dramatic change in Jesuit policies toward Jews post Ignatius.
23. Luke Murray, *Jesuit Biblical Studies after Trent: Franciscus Toletus and Cornelius A. Lapide* (Göttingen: Vandenhoeck & Ruprecht, 2019), 59.
24. Murray, *Jesuit Biblical Studies after Trent*, 60.
25. Bernhard Knorn, SJ, "Theological Renewal after the Council of Trent? The Case of Jesuit Commentaries on the *Summa Theologiae*," *Theological Studies* 79, no. 1 (2018): 123.
26. Knorn, "Theological Renewal," 116.
27. Knorn, "Theological Renewal," 113.
28. Knorn, "Theological Renewal," 110–11.

was a series of continual elevations. In 1569, he left the Roman College to serve as preacher to the papal palace and, in 1570, he was appointed theologian to the Sacred Penitentiary.[29] In 1593, he was named the first Jesuit cardinal.[30] Along with his public offices, Toledo's biblical commentaries, most notably on John and Romans, gained praise and esteem.[31] In addition, he wrote a seminal work of early Jesuit casuistry, also developed out of his Roman College courses, *Summan Causam Conscientae*.[32] In this work, James Keenan has identified a "striking concern for the social conduct of Christians in the institutional world . . . [especially] sins arriving from behaviors within institutional structures."[33]

However, the end of his life was marked with turmoil within the Jesuit order and the Catholic Church. Toledo was a staunch theological defendant of the *converso* Archbishop of Toledo, Bartolomé Carranza de Miranda at his trial before the Inquisition for allegedly Judaizing.[34] The inquisitor sought to strike Toledo's testimony on the ground that his own *converso* family heritage made him suspect. According to the inquisitorial record, his paternal grandfather had been forced to do penance for "Judaizing" in Cordoba and his grandmother and great-grandparents had been burned at the stake.[35] Along with the rejection in the wider Church, Toledo also suffered a loss of influence in the Society under the anti-*converso* policies of the fourth and fifth Generals of the Society, Mercurian and Aquaviva, who, contrary to Ignatius's wishes and the practice of the Society, instituted the secular *limpieza de sangre* laws to forbid the entrance of most *conversos* into the society and to limit the influence of the *conversos* already part of the Society.[36] It is likely for this reason that Toledo, along with other Spanish Jesuits, was involved in an attempted coup to oust the first non-Spanish Superior General, Claudio Aquaviva.[37] The so-called memorialist controversy failed and Aquaviva continued in office and continued to enact a policy directly contrary to Ignatius, restricting the entry of Jesuits of Jewish heritage. At General Congregation 5, held in 1593 and convened at the urging of several prominent *converso* Jesuits, including Toledo, the pro-*converso* fac-

---

29. Murray, *Jesuit Biblical Studies after Trent*, 60.
30. Murray, *Jesuit Biblical Studies after Trent*, 60.
31. Murray, *Jesuit Biblical Studies after Trent*, 68–72.
32. For an in-depth discussion of Toledo's contribution to Jesuit casuistry, see James F. Keenan, SJ, "The Birth of Jesuit Casuistry," in *The Mercurian Project: Forming Jesuit Culture, 1573–1580* (Rome: IHSI, 2004), 461–82.
33. Keenan, "Birth of Jesuit Casuistry," 463.
34. Keenan, "Birth of Jesuit Casuistry," 465.
35. Maryks, *Jesuit Order as a Synagogue*, 104; quoting Ignacio Tellechea Idígoras from the document in the royal archives published as "Censura inédita del Padre Francisco de Toledo, SJ," *Revista Española de Teología* 29 (1969): 15–19.
36. Maryks, *Jesuit Order as a Synagogue*, 117–56.
37. Murray, *Jesuit Biblical Studies after Trent*, 61–62.

tion was defeated and an anti-*converso* policy was enacted barring entry into the Society for anybody of Jewish or Muslim heritage. With this official prohibition, Jesuits of Jewish heritage who had already taken final vows were marginalized, including Toledo throughout the rest of his life.

Commentary on Romans

In his commentary on Romans 9–11, Toledo presents a substantive, theological understanding of the place of the Jews in the *ordo salutis*. In this portion, I will argue that Toledo here expands upon Aquinas's commentary in Romans to address the two questions Coolman has identified: the place of Jews in God's plan of salvation and the status of the Old Law. In making this argument, I do not intend to make a full, descriptive statement regarding Aquinas's overall understanding of the relationship between Jews and the Church. Rather, I seek to highlight the unusual robustness of Toledo's theological argument in support of Jews by comparing selected passages in his commentary with the equivalent commentary from Aquinas. While Toledo follows the standard medieval interpretation of Paul that Jews in the eschaton will become Christians, he also focuses on the continued importance of Jewish identity—especially the continuance of Jewish identity for Christian converts. This argument stands in stark contrast to some of his contemporaries, such as those who argued that Jews after the apostolic age could not even become Christians. It significantly differs also from those, like Aquinas, who believed that Jews could convert, but that their Jewish identity was erased upon entering the Church.[38] In addition, while Toledo's strong arguments for the continuing importance of all types of law in God's plan of salvation are intended to challenge what he perceives as Lutheran anti-nomianism, they also entail an acceptance of some continuing validity of more than simply the moral aspects of the Old Law.

Toledo does not explicitly cite Aquinas's commentary on Romans in his own commentary, focusing instead on engaging with a small set of patristic commentators on Scripture (Ambrose, Jerome, Origen, and Chrysostom are especial favorites). However, he does cite the commentary on Romans in his *Enarratio*, making it clear that he was familiar with the work.[39] Luke Murray has also conclusively demonstrated that his theology of revelation itself is also based on Aquinas.[40] In addition, in many sections, his commentary follows the basic structure of much of Aquinas's commentary, even without directly citing Aquinas.

---

38. See Jeremy Cohen, "Supersessionism, the Epistle to the Romans, Thomas Aquinas, and the Jews of the Eschaton," *Journal of Ecumenical Studies* 52, no. 4 (Fall 2017): 529.

39. Francisco de Toledo, SJ, *In Summam Theologiae St. Thomae Aquinatis Enarratio* (Rome: Typis S. Congraegationis de Propoganda Fide, 1869–1870), 2:103.

40. Murray, *Jesuit Biblical Studies after Trent*, 85.

Toledo's emphasis on the continuing theological significance of Jewishness is apparent very early on in his commentary. He demonstrates this priority in his interpretation of the different meanings that St. Paul attaches to the use of "first" to describe the Jews in Romans 1 and 2. In Romans 1:16, St. Paul describes "the power of God for salvation to everyone who has Faith, to the Jew first and also to the Greek." According to Toledo, Aquinas interprets "first" to refer to the temporal order of salvation: the Jews are saved *first* "because the promises are made to them" and because Jesus was born of a Jew; the reward, however, remains the same, just as those arriving early or late to labor in the vineyard were paid the same in Matthew 20.[41] Toledo also affirms that part of Paul's meaning in saying "first" signifies the temporal order of salvation. In addition, he is clear that Paul is not exclusionary in his understanding of God's salvific plan. The offer first to the Jews does not exclude Gentiles—in the fullness of time—having equal access to salvation. Nor does the "first" nullify the significance of the rejection of the good news of the Gospel by the Jews, who persisted in believing that the Old Testament law was sufficient for salvation. However, Toledo's reading of "first" goes further than Aquinas's. Here, Toledo argues that the use of "first" assumes a continuing significance of Jewishness.[42] The status of the Jews, he argues, remains "preeminent" over the Gentiles, not that "the Jews are mixed with the people and stitched together with them in equal position."[43] This is because they are "God's chosen people" who received "the law, the prophets, promise, Christ according to the flesh, religion and worship to God . . . Paul magnifies all of this and, refusing to affirm equal condition for them, adds therefore Israel first."[44]

This continued preeminence does not mean that Israel does not need God's grace and mercy. The justice of God, forgiveness of sins, and reconciliation to God are all dependent upon faith that Christ is the Messiah who has come, as proclaimed in the good news of the Gospel. However, even this requirement does not change the fact that "Jewishness is necessary" in God's ongoing work of salvation, but rather implies that it will be changed to a "new state"—presumably a new form of Jewishness, not a rejection of Jewishness—by faith.[45] It is for this reason that Toledo departs from Thomas and Chrysostom (whom he cites as his theological opponents in this instance), who both read the verse, "The just shall live by faith," as a statement about the requirements of salvation

---

41. Thomas Aquinas, *Commentary on Romans*, trans. Fabian R. L'Archer, OP (Steubenville, OH: Emmaus Academic, 2020), §101.
42. Francisco de Toledo, *Commentarii et Annotationes in Epistolam B. Pauli Apostoli ad Romanos* (Rome: Sumptibus Paulini Arnolofini Lucensis, 1602), 45.
43. Toledo, *Commentarii*, 45.
44. Toledo, *Commentarii*, 45.
45. Toledo, *Commentarii*, 47.

in general. Toledo instead understands this statement to be directed at the Jews to remind them that true justice and relationship with God through Christ is required for redemption and life in God.[46]

Toledo goes on to consider a second instance where Paul uses the terminology to the Jews first and then to the Gentiles, namely, Romans 2:9. Here, Paul uses "first" to state that punishment is imposed first on the Jews. Both Chrysostom, whom Toledo again explicitly cites, and Aquinas argue that this use of "first" means that the punishment of the Jews will be more severe because they bear greater responsibility based on their greater knowledge of God's revelation—especially the Jews after Christ.[47] Toledo explicitly contradicts this reading based on the existence of faithful Jewish converts to Christianity. Specifically, there were faithful Jews both before and after the coming of Christ, who were among the elect and then received the Gospel. Surely Paul does not mean to include these in the statement that the punishment of these Jews will be worse than the Gentile. Rather, Toledo argues that this statement is simply a reference to the order of punishment allotted toward the unfaithful Jews before the proclamation of the Gospel—presumably the punishments to the unfaithful in the nation of Israel as recorded in the Old Testament.[48]

He takes the opposite approach in his reading of the following verse, Romans 2:10, where Paul states that "glory, honor and peace" will be returned "first to the Jew and then to the Gentile." Toledo here argues that Paul is discussing the rewards granted to the specific subsets of Jews and Gentiles living before the resurrection of Christ, those who followed the law of Moses and the natural law, respectively. He reads Paul as claiming that the good works of the Jews, which were guided by more strict precepts and clearer obligations, since they arose from divine, positive law received directly from God and included ceremonial and judicial as well as more precepts, were more meritorious before God than even the work of the righteous Gentiles who only obeyed the general moral precepts of the natural law. For this reason, the Jews would receive their reward first.[49] In contrast, Aquinas reads this statement more narrowly, in the same way as he reads first in Romans 1:16, that the offer of salvation through Christ came first to the Jews and then to the Gentiles.[50]

---

46. Toledo, *Commentarii*, 50–51.
47. Aquinas, *Commentary on Romans*, § 203.
48. Toledo, *Commentarii*, 111. For a stark contrast, see Simanca's claim that is impossible for *conversos* to ever truly accept Christ because they are "stained with the blood of their Jewish ancestors" who denied Christ. Simanca was the anti-*converso* bishop involved in the inquisitorial process against the *converso* Archbishop Bartolomé Carranza, whom Toledo defended. Maryks, *Jesuit Order as a Synagogue*, 33–34.
49. Toledo, *Commentarii*, 111.
50. Aquinas, *Commentary on Romans*, § 204.

Toledo continues his argument that God's special relationship with the Jews is ongoing throughout Romans. He explicitly begins his preview of Romans 9 by arguing that while it is true that Paul references the rejection of the Gospel by many Jews, the interpretation which has been handed down has always been that he continues to love them and does not want them subject to hate or harm.[51] In this way, he blocks any claims that the rejection of the Gospel by the Jews justifies persecution of them.[52] Following this contemporary reference in his introduction, his discussion of Romans 9:1–5 is almost an exact replication of Aquinas's discussion of why the Apostle Paul personally has such a passionate love for and commitment to the Jewish people. Both Aquinas and Toledo view this section of the chapter as building up to Paul's key theological point in Romans 9:6. What does Paul mean regarding the status of the Jews when he states that "the word of God does not fail?" Aquinas argues that Paul writes that "the word of God does not fail" because God has not given up on a relationship with Israel when Israel is understood spiritually, not as comprised of those physically descended from Jacob: "for all are not Israelites who are of Israel."[53] Rather, God's promise to Israel has not failed because Israel "refer[s] to the spiritual progeny chosen by God, which can include Jews and Gentiles."[54]

Toledo's emphasis is slightly, but significantly, different. In Romans 9:6, he argues that the word of God has not failed because God's plan for Israel has expanded. Rather than Israel simply referring to those descended from Israel according to the flesh, God has also brought Gentiles into Israel.[55] Toledo argues that Romans 9:8, where Paul says "it is not the children of the flesh who are the children of God," is not meant to exclude the possibility that sons of the flesh can also be sons of the promise. To argue that it means an exclusion of Christians of Jewish descent runs contrary to the historical fact that "there are indeed many Jews according to the flesh called to the faith."[56] Rather, Paul is emphasizing that the constitutive bond is (as it was throughout the Old Testament) God's promise to both Jews and Gentiles who are brought into his family.[57] In contrast, Aquinas does not explicitly mention Jews at all in his exegesis of this verse, but rather focuses on explaining the significance of the story of Ishmael and Isaac.[58]

Toledo again takes up this theme that faithful Jews constitute an important part of the Church in his exegesis of Romans 11. First, Toledo reads Paul's iden-

---

51. Toledo, *Commentarii*, 450.
52. Toledo, *Commentarii*, 450.
53. Aquinas, *Commentary on Romans*, § 750.
54. Aquinas, *Commentary on Romans*, §§ 748, 752.
55. Toledo, *Commentarii*, 466.
56. Toledo, *Commentarii*, 479.
57. Toledo, *Commentarii*, 479.
58. Aquinas, *Commentary on Romans*, § 753.

tification of his own Jewishness, especially his place among the tribe of Benjamin, which is the least of the tribes, as a sign that Paul envisions Jews continuing Jewish identity among Christians. If God had truly repudiated all his people, why would Paul say that he had called apostles and preachers out from among them, of whom Paul was one, even though of the least among the tribes?[59] Toledo goes on to analyze Paul's discussion of the seven thousand who have not bent the knee to Baal (1 Kings 19:18) as a further confirmation of God's promise that those of Jewish descent would continue to exist among Christians (Rom 11:4). The fact that there remain people of Jewish descent among the Christians is a sign of God's continuing faithfulness that he has not rejected all the people of Israel. Toledo reads Paul's reference to "until this present day" (Rom 11:5) to imply that those of Jewish descent will continue to be a part of the Church since God intends a continuing conversion of the Jews who were elect.[60] If seven thousand remained in the time of Elisha when grace was less, how many more will remain in the time of the Church by the election of God's grace?[61] In his discussion of this passage, Aquinas simply notes Paul's Jewishness and then reads "until this present day" as referencing Paul's context.[62]

In his reading of Romans 11:15, Toledo follows the standard eschatological reading that the consummation of the end of time will be marked by the conversion of the Jews and their being "reconciled to God and the church."[63] Like Thomas, he also argues that this theological conviction that God's story of creation both begins and ends with God's election of the Jews should provide a rebuke to any Gentile scorn of Jewish lineage.[64] Since the root of Israel on which God grafted his Church is holy, the branch proceeding out of this root by nature ("Jews according to the flesh") will be holy as well if they pursue faith; it "should not be excluded from salvation."[65] Rather than boasting or despising, the proper response of the Gentiles is to "build up those that you despised, to the salvation of those you neglect."[66] This care and concern applies both to the branches broken off—the Jews who reject Christ but may still be rejoined—as well as to the branches still integrated—those of Jewish descent united to the Church (Rom 11:15,17). The "bandage" and "the glue" by which the Gentile branches are united to the Church are far from firm, and rather than scorning Jewish descent, Gentiles should consider how much more easily they could be "per-

---

59. Toledo, *Commentarii*, 538.
60. Toledo, *Commentarii*, 542.
61. Toledo, *Commentarii*, 542.
62. Aquinas, *Commentary on Romans*, § 875
63. Toledo, *Commentarii*, 556.
64. Aquinas, *Commentary on Romans*, § 894.
65. Toledo, *Commentarii*, 558.
66. Toledo, *Commentarii*, 559.

mitted to fall away into unbelief" and replaced by the natural branches (Rom 11:21). [67] The Gentiles just as much as the Jews depend only upon God's mercy for their grafting to the roots, and thus all causes of pride are removed (Rom 11:22). In fact, even the failure of the Jews to believe is simply a gift to the Gentiles to allow more time for them to become part of the Church, a gift which should be received with humility, not scorn of those from whom they benefited.[68] In this section, Aquinas shares Toledo's emphasis on the importance of humility for the Gentiles, but mentions only the "natural branches" which have been broken off, not those which remain attached, who form such a significant part of Toledo's argument.[69] Toledo's emphasis here upon Paul's rebuke of Gentiles who scorn the Jewish branches can plausibly be read, therefore, as a rebuke of the attitude towards *conversos* in his own time.

Along with establishing God's continued care and selection of Jews and of Jewish converts to Christianity, Toledo at least obliquely explores the questions of what it means for Jewish-Christians to continue in their Jewish identity. In other words, what, if anything, is the continuing role of the practice of the ceremonial aspects of the law of Moses? Is this forbidden to Jews who accept Jesus Christ? Here, Toledo is more circumspect in his argument, but still clear. His claim is grounded on the analogy he sets up between divine and natural law in his discussion of Romans 2. Here, Toledo constructs the basic syllogism that Paul assumes that natural law is to the Gentiles as the divine positive law is to the Jews. The crucial point for my purposes here is not the discussion regarding grace and works, but rather the assumption throughout this passage, for Toledo, that the law of Moses (judicial, ceremonial, and moral) continues to be the Jewish equivalent of the natural law requirements for the Gentiles.[70] In Rom 3:31, Toledo also refuses to make the distinction that Aquinas does between the ceremonial and moral portions of the law.[71] Rather, he argues that Jews had to observe more laws, because they received the further revelation of the ceremonial and judicial laws, going beyond the moral laws which the Gentiles are bound to obey according to the law of reason engraved on the mind.[72] Thus, both Jews and Gentiles are guilty because they transgressed the laws which were revealed to each of them respectively. Justification is only possible through

---

67. Toledo, *Commentarii*, 561–62.
68. Toledo, *Commentarii*, 562–63.
69. Aquinas, *Commentary on Romans*, § 902.
70. In another interesting reference, which clearly ties to the Salamanca debates regarding the new world, Toledo also notes here that the Indians are also able, through grace, to carry out the natural law—a clear rejection of claims that non-Europeans should be accorded any type of lower moral status. *Commentarii*, 118.
71. See Aquinas, *Commentary on Romans*, § 321.
72. Toledo, *Commentarii*, 114.

God's gift of grace, since all have failed to be justified by the law. Ergo, salvation does not come through the law for anybody. But does this mean that the law should be disregarded or disobeyed by the Jews to whom it was divinely given?

Toledo addresses this question in his Annotation XIII to Chapter 2, where he moves beyond the text to consider the pressing theological issues of his own day. The presenting question is whether this reading of Paul justifies the claims of the Reformers that works do not justify man, only faith? No! This claim is, in fact, the exact opposite of what Paul is arguing here, he replies.[73] In this instance, he argues, we must remember that law means not only ceremonial and judicial precepts, but also moral law embodied by the Decalogue—which therefore encompasses the natural law binding Gentiles as well.[74] Of course, it is the justifying faith God plants within us which justifies, both for the Jew and the Gentile. It is this justifying faith which in fact makes it possible for us to do the works of the law. Although Toledo does not return to his early elaboration of the types of law included under Paul's general term of law, the logical conclusion is that the Jews are now fully empowered to obey the law given by God, not excused from it, in the same way that the Gentiles must still obey the natural law. Toledo elaborates on this point in his discussion of Romans 3:31. Here, he argues that for Jews and Gentiles Paul simply means that with the coming of Christ the law "of achievement" has been fulfilled. He does not, however, claim that the law has been destroyed by Christ—a position which would be very much at odds with his explicit argument against perceived Lutheran antinomianism earlier in Chapter 3.[75]

Toledo returns to this question in Romans 11, where in Annotation V he considers the argument, first made by Origen and followed by Chrysostom, that, "because the laws of the Jews erred, these laws are abolished by the Gospel."[76] Toledo again returns to his concerns about Lutheran antinomianism in Chapter 3. Claims such as these, he argues, exclude not only obedience to the Jewish law, but also the obedience to the natural law and, indeed, the significance of any work of merit or virtue carried out by man. His response is therefore to narrow the scope of this statement. The proper reading is that, of course, all works of the law are done in error if they are understood to justify in and of themselves. However, saying that works of laws do not justify does not mean that the disposition to the good is not required in the human for justification, such as "faith and penitence and love."[77] The error is assuming that a

---

73. Toledo, *Commentarii*, 118.
74. Toledo, *Commentarii*, 118.
75. Toledo, *Commentarii*, 198.
76. Toledo, *Commentarii*, 545.
77. Toledo, *Commentarii*, 546.

person achieves this disposition through his or her own actions; rather, these dispositions are only originally possible through Christ's virtues and God's will. Toledo then draws a comparison between the law and the work of Christ. In the way that God healed the people of Israel in the desert from the bites of the serpents through the vision of the serpent of bronze, the law serves as one of God's instruments of healing from sin—but the power is through God, not the serpent itself, which is merely God's instrument.

While Toledo never makes an explicit statement in these discussions that Christian Jews should continue in the practices of the Mosaic law, neither does he deny its continuing validity. However, Toledo's continual insistence on the syllogism that the natural law, which does remain valid, is to the Gentiles as the law of Moses is to the Jews, as well as his emphasis on the Jewish practices of the earlier apostles, does at the very least open lines for further theological arguments justifying the practices of Jewish ceremonial law by Jewish converts to Christianity.

Conversion of Jews in Toledo's *Enarratio*

Toledo's commentary on Romans provides a tacit development of Aquinas in line with Ignatius. I will now consider another project in which this synthesis is much more explicit: Toledo's *Enarratio* on the *Summa*, the transcription of his lectures on the *Summa* at the Roman College.[78] As I noted above, Toledo's lectures were a departure from the traditional Roman style in being less formal and scripted. This more conversational approach is the rationale for the title of his eventually published lectures: *Enarratio*, or "narration," rather than simply a commentary.[79] While his style was his own, his methodological approach follows the example of his mentors at the University of Salamanca, Francisco de Vitoria and Soto. In these discussions, Toledo uses the structure and basic ideas of the Summa as a launching pad both to convey timeless theological truths as explicated by St. Thomas and to engage with the pressing moral and theological questions of the day.[80] Throughout the work, he rarely disagrees directly with Thomas's conclusions, although he does not hesitate at times to disagree with

---

78. These lectures from 1569 were collected and almost all published (except for the *Prima Secundae*) in 1869. Knorn, "Theological Renewal," 117.

79. Knorn, "Theological Renewal," 117.

80. Knorn identifies this constructive retrieval of St. Thomas as a key distinguishing factor of post-Tridentine commentaries on the *Summa* in "Theological Renewal," 110, 126. For a discussion of the development of commentary on the *Summa* as a genre to address contemporary issues among Dominicans in the School of Salamanca and Jesuits, see Annabel Brett, "Later Scholastic Philosophy of Law," in *A Treatise of Legal Philosophy and General Jurisprudence*, vol. 6, *A History of the Philosophy of Law from the Ancient Greeks to the Scholastics*, eds. Fred D. Miller Jr. and Carrie-Ann Biondi (New York: Springer, 2015), 337–38.

Cajetan, the most important Thomistic commentator of the time.[81] Rather, he spends much of his time supplementing and defending Thomas's claims. He clearly seeks to expand his reader's engagement with the work by raising new *dubia* which need to be addressed in light of contemporary circumstances.[82] In addition, drawing upon his training and research as a biblical scholar engaged in the humanist recovery of Scripture of his day (and his facility in Greek and at least some Hebrew), Toledo integrated extensive scriptural commentary into his "narration" of the *Summa*. Throughout these passages, the same concern with social structures which Keenan identified in his casuistical writings appears of great significance as well.[83]

Toledo uses as the launching point of his argument for the humane treatment of the Jews St. Thomas's discussion of the infused virtue of faith. He considers this question most explicitly in his analysis of ST II-II, q. 10, a. 8, on whether forced conversion of unbelievers can ever be licit. Following the standard development of the tradition, Toledo identifies two different lines of argument for the basic question of whether forced conversions of infidels are theologically permitted and fall within the Church's spiritual authority to condone. The minority view, of whom the most standard representatives are Duns Scotus and Gabriel Biel, do in fact hold that the Church has the authority to compel infidels into the faith through baptism for their own ultimate benefit and the salvation of their soul.[84] The majority view, with which he identifies Aquinas, Bonaventure, and the modern theologians Soto and Cajetan as the prominent proponents, rejects these claims and instead states that it is neither "licit" nor even "possible" to compel infidels to the acceptance of the faith.[85] Toledo, not surprisingly, claims that Aquinas's statement in the corpus of the question is the most theologically correct: "Among unbelievers there are some who have never received the faith, such as the heathens and the Jews: and these are by no means to be compelled to the faith, in order that they may believe, because to believe depends on the will."[86]

Toledo then follows this clarification on the meaning of conversion by considering the *dubia* which he thinks are most likely to conflict with Aquinas's

---

81. Knorn, "Theological Renewal," 117.
82. Knorn, "Theological Renewal," 117.
83. Keenan, "Birth of Jesuit Casuistry," 463.
84. Francisco de Toledo, SJ, *In Summam Theologiae St. Thomae Aquinatis Enarratio* (Rome: Typis S. Congraegationis de Propoganda Fide, 1869–1870), 2:105.
85. Toledo, *Enarratio*, 2:105.
86. ST II-II, q. 10, a. 8. See Francisco de Vitoria, "On the American Indians," in *Political Writings*, ed. Anthony Pagden and Jeremy Lawrence, Cambridge Texts in the History of Political Thought (Cambridge: Cambridge University Press, 1991), 272 for a similar account claiming the majority of theologians reject forced conversions of the Jews.

rejection of the forced conversions of infidels. Rather than following Toledo's exact order in these questions, I will consider first his general and more universal arguments and then his arguments which specifically address the issues of forced conversion in Spain.

Toledo carefully exegetes each of the Gospel texts which have been read at various points to explicitly support coercion of non-believers into the faith, such as Matthew 10 (shake the dust from your feet), Luke 9 (Samaritan does not receive Jesus), Mark 16 (whoever does not believe will be condemned). In each of these, he notes that Jesus does not give any authority to impose temporal penalties on unbelievers, but rather focuses on the power of persuasive preaching of the Gospel.[87] In contrast, in 1 Corinthians 5 we see Paul rejecting this temporal authority, asking rhetorically, "What is to me to judge those who are outside?"[88] Thus, there is no grounding in the teaching of the Gospel to support a forced conversion. Instead, Toledo presents 2 Timothy 4 as the example of the only type of accepted coercion to be used on non-believers: "effective preaching and persuasion."[89]

Toledo then considers the teaching of the Church, both through official doctrine and the teaching of the saints. He cites a wide range of Church teaching, including teachings by Pope Leo the Great, Pope Innocent III, Pope Clement VI, all of which deny the validity of forced conversions.[90] In the Canon *Qui sincera* (*Decretum* D.45.3), Pope Gregory I writes that the proper way of evangelism consists of "blandishment not ... roughness."[91] He also consults important Catholic sources especially close to home for Spaniards, specifically the Fourth Counsel of Toledo and the writings of St. Isidore, both of which denied the licit forced conversions of the Jews.[92] In addition, he pinpoints specific teaching by St. Augustine and St. Ambrose that reject the claims that the Church has authority to compel infidels and a reliance upon the intrinsically compelling nature of the Gospel for a true conversion.[93]

However, despite the weight of the tradition on his side, Toledo knows that he must differentiate his claims from Augustine's reading of several key scriptural texts in the Donatist controversy. These passages include the example in Luke 14 of the king sending out wedding invitations with orders to "compel them to come in," and in Acts 9, where Paul's description of how the fear of

---

87. Toledo, *Enarratio*, 2:105.
88. Toledo, *Enarratio*, 2:105.
89. Toledo, *Enarratio*, 2:107.
90. Toledo, *Enarratio*, 2:106. See Drews, *Unknown Neighbour*, 233–34 for a comparison of the firmness of Gregory's rejection with the more hesitant condemnation by Isidore.
91. Toledo, *Enarratio*, 2:106.
92. Toledo, *Enarratio*, 2:106.
93. Toledo, *Enarratio*, 2:106.

God compels him to a confession of faith becomes, by analogy, a justification for compelling conversions. Toledo distinguishes both claims from his own argument on the grounds that Augustine only uses them to make an analogous point about heretics—never about Jews or other infidels.[94]

The combination of Church teaching and Scripture demonstrates "that the church has the right to show and preach the good news, but also not to force them, because they are not its subjects."[95] Under this understanding, the words of the preacher should not exercise the will to power but lift up the doctrine of humility. This type of evangelical preaching should be the opposite of coercion, modeled instead on Christ, the head of the Church, who "was peaceful, never forcing, never punishing" vis-à-vis his earthly hearers during his time on earth.[96] Thus, rather than relying on temporal authority to force conversions, Christians should remember that they are always sent out as "sheep among wolves," given power to "cure the sick, heal the lepers, raise the dead, cast out demons," but never to compel.[97] The power of the Gospel is not the power of this world and, in the early Church, we never see them confused. Coercion involves a sacrifice of the Church's own self-identity in that it places the Church under a law of hate and substitutes force of arms and oppression in place of its duty "to converse in fraternal love."[98]

In these arguments, Toledo has simply distilled and clarified the majority view as articulated in Scripture and Tradition. Building upon these arguments, he innovates in two different ways—both intended to explicate the Thomistic tradition in the controversies of his own day.

First Innovation: Defining Coerced Conversion

For his first innovation, he explores in more depth what precisely constitutes a coerced conversion. The obvious meaning of coercion indicates direct force: to "drag those unwilling and resisting" to baptism.[99] Most theologians, he argues, have been most concerned with defining the proper and improper use of direct force.[100] However, Toledo identifies the day's more pressing question as to whether indirect coercion—in which the person is not physically forced but chooses baptism due to the infliction of any type of pain or fear—is also illicit.

---

94. Toledo, *Enarratio*, 2:105, 107. For an overview of Toledo's radically different approach to the coercion of heretics see Kevin Flannery's entry in this volume.
 95. Toledo, *Enarratio*, 2:108.
 96. Toledo, *Enarratio*, 2:107.
 97. Toledo, *Enarratio*, 2:106.
 98. Toledo, *Enarratio*, 2:107.
 99. Toledo, *Enarratio*, 2:105.
 100. Toledo, *Enarratio*, 2:105.

Theologians traditionally rejected direct, forced conversions because they resulted in a destruction of the freedom of the will and substituted human action for divine action. Toledo explains that faith is, by definition, a supernatural virtue necessary for salvation, acquired not according to human reason or our own strength, but only with the supernatural help of God, who "opens the hearts of the infidels and illuminates minds."[101] In this description, Toledo assumes Aquinas's two-part structure of faith: faith is the assent of the intellect "insofar as the will moves it to assent."[102] The object of the will in faith is "to believe in God."[103] However, any form of external oppression is insufficient to "change the desire of the will."[104] Coercion simply replaces the actions of reason and will. It overpowers the reason and instead imposes some "belief or desire to believe which is not according to the truth but rather stems only from fear."[105] Thus, a forced convert might make what is apparently an external profession of faith, but the object would not be belief in God, but rather the necessities of survival. Even setting aside the scriptural limits on the Church's power described above, it is obvious that it is impossible for the Church through external coercion to command changes to internal acts of will and reason, which are necessary for true baptismal vows.[106] Rather, God alone can bestow the "supernatural participation of divine goodness" that is necessary for salvation beyond natural reason. To this end, "the best weapon in the conversion of infidels is not violence but rather prayer, asking God to give the gift he already desired to give."[107]

In arguing against indirect coercion, Toledo claims that fear should be understood as having the same impact on the will as direct force—a statement which has implicit unstated echoes of both Thomas Aquinas and St. Ignatius. In his earlier discussion of the relationship between fear and faith, Aquinas distinguishes between servile fear, fear of divine punishment, and filial fear, which is dread of separation from God.[108] Ignatius repeats this distinction in §370 of the *Spiritual Exercises*, where he provides a more positive reading than Aquinas on the role of servile fear, which he describes as "pious and very holy."[109] The fear that God causes, either servile or filial, "is able to soften the heart and the will to

---

101. Toledo, *Enarratio*, 2:106.
102. ST II-II, q. 2, a. 2.
103. ST II-II, q. 2, a. 2.
104. Toledo, *Enarratio*, 2:106.
105. Toledo, *Enarratio*, 2:106.
106. Toledo, *Enarratio*, 2:107.
107. Toledo, *Enarratio*, 2:107.
108. ST II-II, q. 7, a. 1.
109. Ignatius of Loyola, *The Spiritual Exercises of St. Ignatius*, trans. Louis J. Puhl, SJ, 1951. Reprint, (Chicago, IL: Loyola University Press, 1961), 161.

conversion."[110] However, this is only something God can do, since he is able to "command interior acts, which the church is not able to command."[111] The fear inflicted by God results in "the desire of God," thus creating a "perfect will" in the person and leading to "perfect works." This type of fear Aquinas describes as the effect of faith.[112] Both Ignatius and Thomas also identify a third category of fear: "worldly fear." For St. Ignatius, worldly fear is described in §9 as fear of disgrace in the world's eyes which may interfere with moving forward in spiritual progress in the exercises.[113] Aquinas identifies worldly fear as fear which "turns men away from God and which God's enemies sometimes inflict."[114]

Toledo, however, elaborates on what is presumably natural fear, which, according to Aquinas, is a pre-moral shrinking from objects that are contrary to nature.[115] It is only this fear, he believes, which the Church or secular government may instill by the persecution of the infidels to force into relationship with God. On the other hand, all that humanly induced fear can create is a desire to avoid the penalty. The external works which stem from this fear, even seeking baptism, contradicts the person's internal desires. The reason is plain— coercion does not serve to protect infidels from future sin but actually places them in a new state of mortal sin, by forcing them to commit sacrilege by accepting the baptism and sacraments in which they do not believe.[116] Therefore, the works which stem out of this fear are not oriented to God or relationship with God, but rather can result in a sacrilege, not a sacrament.[117] This understanding of the evils of coercion override the argument that forced conversion is a gift to those who are forced, because they are spared the sins of idolatry which otherwise they would commit, made by the adherents of the minority opinion, such as Duns Scotus.[118]

This question of "indirect" conversion is in fact much more important for the "present controversies."[119] This is because indirect coercion to conversion had become the main mode of conversion imposed upon Jews in Spain at this time. In seeing this question as an occasion for discussion of this type of issue, Toledo is following in the footsteps of his Dominican Thomistic predecessors

---

110. Toledo, *Enarratio*, 2:107 (ad 2).
111. Toledo, *Enarratio*, 2:107 (ad. 2).
112. ST II-II, q. 7, ad 1.
113. Ignatius, *SpEx*, 4.
114. ST II-II, q. 19, a. 2, ad 4. For a more in-depth analysis of the difference between Toledo and Aquinas on the will, see Kevin Flannery's essay included in this volume.
115. ST II-II, q. 41, a. 2.
116. Toledo, *Enarratio*, 2:106.
117. Toledo, *Enarratio*, 2:107.
118. Toledo, *Enarratio*, 2:105.
119. Toledo, *Enarratio*, 2:105.

from the school of Salamanca, Vitoria and Soto. For both Vitoria and Soto, commentary on the question of coercion to faith had direct implications for the Spanish persecution and forced conversions in the New World.[120] In the same way that Vitoria and Soto challenge Spanish action in the new world using this passage, Toledo presents subtle and engaged understanding of the effects of forced conversion on the Jewish people, especially related to new Christians in the Spain of his own day.

Toledo sets this direct versus indirect coercion question into context by comparing the potentially coercive actions of two Spanish kings: one remote and one recent. This consideration of princes and rulers, the enforcers of secular jurisdiction, also raises the question as to whether they have the authority as "custodians and executors" to compel infidels to accept the faith in accordance with divine law?[121] This specific argument had become a standard *topos* in the Salamanca school related especially to the questions as to whether forced conversions were permitted in the Americas.[122]

In answering this question, Toledo considers two specific instances in Spanish history. The first is described in Gratian's canon de Iudaies (*Decretum* D.45.5), which considers the actions of the Visigoth King Sisebut who compelled the Jews to assent to baptism in the sixth century.[123] As Wolfram Drews has plausibly argued, this forced conversion represented a key moment in defining the boundaries of the Visigoth political kingdom—a delineation of outsiders and insiders, in which Jews in a sense stood in for all "outsiders."[124] In referring back to this moment, Toledo is therefore gesturing back to a key archetypal moment in Spanish Old Christian identity. While he is careful not to completely demolish Sisebut by claiming that his actions may have come out of good intentions, he nevertheless maintains that they were reasons of zeal, which do not spring from reason or knowledge. They were harmful to those coerced because they had been required to follow Christianity unsuitably and they run explicitly against Scripture and Church teaching.[125] This both provides a classic example of direct coercion and demonstrates that the Church does not consider kings to have the divine authority to impart the gift of faith, which is only given by God.

---

120. See Vitoria, "On the American Indians," passim; Domingo de Soto, "De Dominio," in *Relecciones y opusculos*, vol. 1, ed. and trans. Jaime Brufau Prats (Salamanca: Editorial Sebastian, 1995), 99–192.

121. Toledo, *Enarratio*, 2:105.

122. Vitoria, "On the American Indians," 271–72. See also Soto, "De Dominio," 126–27: "God gives us freely grace and glory . . . humans do not have ownership."

123. Toledo, *Enarratio*, 2:104–5.

124. Drews, *Unknown Neighbour*, 296–300.

125. Toledo, *Enarratio*, 2:108.

Toledo then considers a second more contemporary Spanish king's actions against the Jews: the 1492 expulsion of Jews and Muslims from the kingdom of Spain by Ferdinand, *El Rey Católico*,[126] according to which only those who had accepted baptism were permitted to remain.[127] Toledo hedges on this question in a way which is more disturbing to modern rulers. But even while making the politically savvy move of not condemning the great ruler of contemporary Spanish history, Toledo makes some important delineations to prove his underlying point. Ferdinand's decree was licit because the intention was not to force conversions at all. Rather, it was to exile bad citizens who were corrupting the citizenry. If Ferdinand had intended to indirectly coerce conversion by his decree, then his actions would have been unacceptable. Thus, Toledo nods to the standard narrative while also carefully delineating the types of actions which are in fact acceptable theologically.

Second Innovation: Rejecting Consequentialism

For his second innovation, Toledo states the corollary argument that the true gift of forced conversion is to the children of the *conversos* because the children are, presumably, true Christians after only a few generations.[128] This was, of course, Toledo's own experience. By setting this up as an objection, Toledo not only gestures to the living memory of the justifications of forced conversions in Spain but also, implicitly, raises the question as to whether the children of the forced converts are necessarily placed under the Church's jurisdiction—an important point for the Spanish inquisition's investigation into claims of Judaizing in *converso* families. As discussed above, this goes against the understanding of how faith transforms the will. In addition, it fails in several ways in its goals. First, it reduces all the evangelical power of the Gospel, which Toledo finds a grave concern, making the faith "odious" and actually "hiding the gate of infidel salvation."[129] Secondly, rather than rescuing infidels from sins, it forces even more occasion for sins, such as blasphemy, upon the infidels, as they seek to avoid death.[130] Toledo thus rejects the consequentialist argument

---

126. It is intriguing that Toledo does not mention Ferdinand's co-ruler, Isabel, as potentially culpable. The fact that he is not willing to consider Isabel's transgression is probably due to the extreme respect in which she was held in Spain even for years after her death. See Liss, Peggy. "Isabel of Castile (1451–1504), Her Self-Representation and Its Context," in *Queenship and Political Power in Medieval and Early Modern Spain*, ed. Theresa Earenfight (New York: Routledge, 2005), 120–44, at 121–22.
127. Toledo, *Enarratio*, 2:108.
128. Toledo, *Enarratio*, 2:105.
129. Toledo, *Enarratio*, 2:108.
130. Toledo, *Enarratio*, 2:108.

that gaining the children for the Church after several generations justifies the original violation of the will.

How far does indirect coercion go? What constitutes coercive proselytizing? Like Soto and Vitoria, Toledo does argue that the Church has opposed tyrants who refuse to let the Gospel be taught in their lands.[131] However, this requirement of the freedom to proclaim the Gospel does not carry the corollary assumption that the Church has any type of jurisdictional powers over nonbelievers, including even forcing them to listen to sermons and the proclamation of the Gospel—a policy toward Spanish Jews common for centuries.[132] This too would constitute illicit coercion. In addition, the proof to which Toledo points is Soto's exegesis of Matthew 10, "whoever does not receive you or listen to your sermons, leave them," as well as Pope Gregory's statement that the Jews (specifically) should be given the opportunity to hear the Gospel, but only "benignly and without oppression."[133] The Church may preach in Jewish temples and synagogues—Toledo extends the freedom of preaching to an extent uncomfortable to most modern readers here—under this divinely granted jurisdiction, but cannot force anybody using those synagogues to remain or even listen.[134]

Having established these fundamental principles, Toledo then turns to consider the engagement in daily life with infidels. Contrary to the prevalent trend in Spain and in Italy, Toledo argues for a minimalist understanding of these limitations. Rejecting the claims of a Jewish taint, and going even further than Ignatius in arguing for openness to a pluralist society, Toledo adopts and expands upon Thomas's statement that: "these are not to be forbidden to communicate with unbelievers who have not received the faith, such as pagans or Jews, especially if there be some urgent necessity for so doing."[135] The only reason he argues that a Christian should consider not communicating with unbelievers is out of a fear of possible subversion or conversion arising in the communication.[136] He seems to consider this a remote or exceptional possibil-

---

131. Vitoria, "On the American Indians," 284. Vitoria also makes a similar argument that the Church does not have the authority to grant civil rulers these powers (260).

132. Vitoria, "On the American Indians," 271–72.

133. Toledo, *Enarratio*, 2:107.

134. Here, in some ways, he goes farther than Vitoria, who argues that the barbarians are required to listen to the faith. However, Vitoria also claims that the obligation is moral, since listening to the Gospel is required to avoid falling into pains of mortal sin. He does not seem to imply that the existence of this moral obligation means that the civil or ecclesiastical officers have authority to enforce it (Vitoria, "On the American Indians," 270–71). One can sense the much more immediate context of concern for Toledo, who knew of situations in which Jews were locked inside synagogues and forced to listen to preaching.

135. ST II-II, q. 10, a. 9.

136. For the opposite extreme of rhetoric, contrast St. Vincent Ferrer in 1412: "And above all there should be no communication with them in the home, for Christian and infidel should

ity, not something which Christians should approach with normal concern. Secondly, as is always indicated by natural and divine law, communication should be limited out of the desire to avoid scandal to neighbors. Aquinas raises the same concern about the danger of scandal. However, Aquinas's solution is to urge the enactment of laws which prohibit the "simple" from engaging with the Jews at all in order to protect them. Toledo takes a much more moderate stance. He simply claims that there is *no law*—presumably natural or divine—prohibiting communication or transaction, assuming scandal can be avoided.[137] In making this claim, Toledo goes beyond Ignatius, who supported the bill *Cum Nimis Absurdum* promulgated in 1555 by Pope Paul IV, which severely limited Jewish and Christian engagement in daily life. Thus, Toledo's conclusion has the effect of bringing Jews back into medieval society, rather than exiling them.

Conclusion

In conclusion, Toledo's theology as expressed in the Commentary on Romans and his *Enarratio* provides a robust schema for Christian engagement with Jews on multiple levels which challenged the dominant view of his day. First, God's continuing faithfulness and commitment to the Jews as his chosen people neither disappears nor is diminished by the incorporation of Gentiles. This special election of the Jews continues even when they are a part of the Church—the place of the *converso*. As children of the flesh and the promise, they are not scorned or tainted or replaced, but rather their presence is essential to the Church's identity as the new Israel. The continuance of their Jewish identity may in fact include or even necessitate a continued adherence to the law of Moses, understood as having reached its fulfilment, not its destruction, in Christ.

In addition, the role of the Church is not to interfere or act as God in trying to force faith upon Jews through forced coercion—whether direct or indirect. Rather, the Church is also called to express faith in God's faithfulness and power by preaching persuasively rather than forcing belief. The presence of those of other faiths in a community—whether Jews or pagans—is not a hindrance to the Gospel or even, when approached according to the virtue of prudence, a danger to the Christian faithful. Thus, Christian protection of Jews, whether within or outside of the Church, becomes a testimony to God's faithfulness to the Church and Israel: a conclusion in line with the spirit of both St. Thomas and St. Ignatius.

---

not dwell together in the same house, for it is an evil which is contagious, that is, luxury, for many are thought to be the children of Jews, and are really Christian, and vice versa. And therefore just as Jews and Muslims are different from Christians in law, they should be different from them in habitation." Cited in Nirenberg, *Neighboring Faiths*, 148.

137. Reites, "St. Ignatius of Loyola and the Jews," 13–15.

CHAPTER 11

Francisco de Toledo on Thomas Aquinas and the Possibility of Coerced Faith

Kevin Flannery, SJ

In the *Constitutions of the Society of Jesus*, under the heading, "Regarding the books to be lectured upon," St. Ignatius affirms that, "In theology, to be read are the Old and New Testament and the scholastic teaching of St. Thomas."[1] The purpose of the present essay is to say something about the way in which this rule, as it pertains to Thomas Aquinas, was received by Francisco de Toledo (1532–1596), one of the earliest professors of philosophy and theology at the Roman College, later to become the Pontifical Gregorian University. De Toledo has not attracted a great deal of scholarly attention in recent years, although that may be changing somewhat because of a current controversy.[2] His surviving works—which appeared under his Latinized name, Franciscus Toletus—are many, including as they do commentaries on Aristotle, on Thomas Aquinas's *Summa Theologiae*, and on Holy Scripture. The intention of the present essay is not, however, to treat de Toledo's scholarly works in general—nor even to treat his use of Thomas in general; it is rather to consider what he has to say in his massive *Enarratio* on Thomas's *Summa* about the question whether faith can be coerced.[3] This will provide us with at least some information regarding the use of Thomas Aquinas in the nascent Society of Jesus.

---

1. Societas Iesu, *Constitutiones Societatis Iesu et normae complementarae* (Rome: Curia Praepositi Generalis Societatis Iesu, 1995), 171 (§ 464).
2. The controversy, into which we cannot enter here, concerns the relationship between the teaching of the Second Vatican Council's document *Dignitatis humanae* and the Church's tradition regarding religious liberty. See Thomas Pink, "The Right to Religious Liberty and the Coercion of Belief: A Note on Dignitatis Humanae," in *Reason, Morality, and Law: The Philosophy of John Finnis*, eds John Keown and Robert P. George (Oxford: Oxford University Press, 2013), 427–42; and John Finnis, "John Finnis on Thomas Pink," in *Reason, Morality, and Law: The Philosophy of John Finnis*, ed. John Keown and Robert P. George (Oxford: Oxford University Press, 2013), 566–77.
3. Franciscus Toletus, *In Summam Theologiae S. Thomae Aquinatis Enarratio*, ed. Iosephus Paria (Rome/Turin/Paris: S. Congregatio de Propaganda Fide/Marietti/Victorium Palmé, 1869–70). In what follows, in referring to this work I shall speak simply of the *Enarratio*, followed by the volume number, followed by the page number(s) and, where appropriate, the column (a or b).

In the first section of the following, the basic details of de Toledo's life, especially as a Jesuit, are presented, including a controversy in which he was involved regarding God's predestination of some souls for glory, others for reprobation. As is argued later in the essay (in particular but not solely in the seventh section), this controversy is relevant to the issue of coercion, since a proper understanding of God's predestination must recognize the part that man's free will plays in any act of faith. In the second section, two ecclesial positions that (as explained in the fifth section) figure into remarks that de Toledo makes regarding coercion and faith are discussed. The first position was maintained by the Fourth Council of Toledo and has to do with the coercion of Jews. The other was maintained by the Council of Trent and has to do with ideas originating in remarks by Erasmus of Rotterdam regarding individuals baptized as infants who, having reached adolescence, choose not to continue as Catholics. In the third section, Thomas Aquinas's early ideas regarding religious liberty are expounded; in section four are expounded his later ideas (in the *Summa Theologiae*) on the same topic. In the fifth section, de Toledo's commentary on these later ideas by Thomas regarding religious liberty is considered. In sections six and seven, illustrated respectively are Thomas's ideas on predestination and then de Toledo's own position regarding the same, which he presents as an alternative to Thomas's. The final section is a conclusion in which are summarized the ways in which de Toledo's agreements and disagreements with Thomas regarding coercion and predestination relate to Church teaching, especially as put forward by the Council of Trent, regarding coercion.

Francisco de Toledo

Francisco de Toledo was born in Córdoba in 1532, the son of Christians of Jewish extraction.[4] He received his master of arts degree at the University of Zaragoza, which was at the time a center for Aristotelian studies. Between the years 1554 and 1558, he studied at Salamanca under the Dominican Domingo de Soto, who described his student as "prodigious." Already during those years, he was teaching philosophy; there is, however, disagreement among scholars regarding just when he began teaching. Thomas Campbell states that "he occupied a chair of philosophy when he was fifteen," which seems unlikely, and Campbell cites no evidence.[5] Hugo von Hurter speaks of his beginning as a

---

4. J. P. Donnelly, "Toledo, Francisco de," in *Diccionario Histórico de la Compañía de Jesús, Biográfico-Temático*, ed. Charles E. O'Neill and Joaquín M. Domínguez (Rome/Madrid: IHSI/Universidad Pontificia Comillas, 2001), 3807–8.

5. Thomas J. Campbell, *Jesuits, 1534–1921: A History of the Society of Jesus* (New York: Encyclopedia Press, 1921), 113. As indicated by an anonymous referee, "most historians now use Campbell as an instance of pious historiography."

professor in 1555, that is to say, at twenty-three years of age.[6] In 1556, the year St. Ignatius died, de Toledo was ordained and in 1558 he entered the Society of Jesus. The very next year he was summoned to become a professor at the Roman College.

Although he was praised for the clarity and energy of his lectures at the Roman College, de Toledo's tenure there was not entirely happy. In 1562, one of his colleagues there, Juan de Mariana, expressed dislike "for the method he adopted in his lectures."[7] It is likely that this complaint had to do with a certain eclecticism in de Toledo's thought.[8] Rather boldly for one only four years in the Society, de Toledo immediately brought the matter raised by de Mariana before the General of the Society, Diego Laínez, who at the time was participating in the third and final period (1562–1563) of the Council of Trent.

The dispute with the volatile de Mariana was eventually resolved, but it was soon succeeded by a theologically more charged dispute that involved other professors at the Roman College and concluded with a recantation imposed upon de Toledo by another General of the Society of Jesus, St. Francis Borgia.[9] Regarding God's predestination of some souls for glory, others for reprobation, de Toledo taught in his lectures on the *Summa Theologiae* the following:

> Foreseen good acts are the proximate reason for predestination; the primary reason, however, is the unique will of God. This conclusion goes contrary to St. Thomas, Scotus, and many others; but, with the help of God, we will demonstrate it sufficiently. . . .
>
> Now, if you ask regarding the proximate reason, why he elects this one and not that, I answer: in this one he foresees good acts, in that bad. And if you ask further, why because of [*propter*] good acts he elects and

---

6. Hugo von Hurter, ed., *Nomenclator literarius theologiae Catholicae theologos exhibens aetate, natione, disciplinis distinctos* (Innsbruck: Libraria Academica Wagneriana, 1903–1913), col. 248. Anna Tropia (together with others) speaks of a course in 1557–1558; see Anna Tropia, "Francisco de Toledo: Setting a Standard for Jesuit Philosophy," in *Jesuit Philosophy on the Eve of Modernity*, ed. Cristiano Casalini (Leiden: Brill, 2019), 251n3.

7. Feliciano Cereceda, "En el cuarto centenario del nascimento del P. Francisco Toledo," *Estudios eclesiásticos: Revista de investigación e información teológica y canónica* 13 (1934): 94.

8. Although in his writings he sides with Thomas more often than not, when he does not agree, he often frames the disagreement as disagreement rather with Cajetan. Anna Tropia gives an example of this: "Toledo only recognizes that the thesis of the direct intellection of the singulars goes against Thomas Cajetan (1469–1534), with whom he does not associate Aquinas. Although the indirect intellection of the singulars is a Thomistic doctrine, with a history and controversies internal to the Dominican order, the point here is that Toledo does not openly contradict Aquinas. Like most of his peers, he prefers to refute Cajetan instead." Tropia, "Setting a Standard," 259. As we shall see, however, de Toledo does occasionally explicitly reject what Thomas says.

9. See Cereceda, "En el cuarto centenario," 96–103 and Tropia, "Setting a Standard," 262–65. Borgia was General of the Society from 1565–1572.

because of [*propter*] evil acts reprobates, I answer: because he has so willed and established; he has acted, therefore, as one who is just. And if you ask further, why has he so willed, I answer finally: because it so pleased him.[10]

As we shall see, this thesis regarding predestination—the central issue in the *De auxiliis* controversy—is, especially for de Toledo, intimately tied up with the issue of coerced faith.

De Toledo continued to teach at the Roman College until 1569. In that year Pius V named him theologian of the Sacred Penitentiary and ordinary preacher to the pope and to the college of cardinals. Pius V also arranged for him to live in the papal palace, thereby establishing a certain distance between de Toledo and the Society of Jesus. Under popes Gregory XIII, Sixtus V, and Clement VIII, he exercised great influence not only as a theologian but also as a diplomat. In 1593, three years before his death, he was named a cardinal-priest, the first Jesuit so to be named; he was assigned to the church Santa Maria in Traspontina. According to Carlo Giacon, SJ, toward the end of his life, de Toledo wanted to renounce the title of cardinal and so return to living as a Jesuit but the pope at the time, Clement VIII, would not have that.[11]

The Fourth Council of Toledo and the Council of Trent on Coercion and Faith

Before entering into the details of de Toledo's, and Thomas's, ideas concerning coercion as it relates to faith, it is important, of course, to understand the historico-theological context within which he developed those ideas. Especially significant in this regard are the seventh century (633) Fourth Council of Toledo and the sixteenth century (1545–1563) Council of Trent— the former, because a provincial council, being less authoritative than the latter.

There is no doubt that in Visigothic Spain, whose capital was Toledo, baptism was forced upon certain Jews well into the seventh century.[12] At the

---

10. *Enarratio* 1.287b–88°: "Praedestinationis ratio proxima sunt praevisa opera bona; ratio tamen prima sola Dei voluntas. Haec conclusio est contra S.Thomam, Scotum, et alios multos; sed adiutorio Dei sufficienter probabimus eam. . . . Modo si rationem petas proximam: quare hunc elegit, non illum? dico, quia in illo opera bona, in hoc mala praevidit. At si rursus: quare propter bona opera eligit, propter mala reprobat? dico, quia sic voluit et statuit: tanquam ergo iustus facit. Rursus: quare ipse hoc ita voluit? dicam ultimo, quia sic placitum est illi." On de Toledo's use of the term "reason" (*ratio*) instead of "cause," see note 58 below.

11. Carlo Giacon, *Seconda Scolastica*, vol. 2, *Precedenze teoretiche ai problemi giuridici* (Milan: Fratelli Bocca, 1946), 32.

12. Marcia Colish, however, in a recent book argues that the prevalence of coerced baptism of Jews ought not to be exaggerated. "So, while we can indeed document an increasingly harsh series of enactments against Jews, including their forced baptism, they look to be the campaign

Fourth Council of Toledo, it was decreed, regarding Jews, that "henceforth, force is to be inflicted upon no one in order that he might believe," although the Council also went on to say that, "On the other hand, those who in the past were coerced to accept Christianity [*ad Christianitatem coacti sunt*], . . . it is fitting also that they be coerced to hold the faith they were coerced by force or necessity to accept." The Council also acknowledged that in the past coerced baptisms had been imposed by "the most religious prince Sisebut," the Visigoth king deposed in 621.[13] It would be a mistake, however, to assume that the Fourth Council of Toledo was wholly on Sisebut's side. It was presided over by the renowned scholar Isidore of Seville (d. 636). Some years before the council, Isidore said of Sisebut, whom he does describe as *christianissimus*, that, "at the beginning of his reign, in moving Jews to the Christian faith, he had certainly zeal, but it was not in accordance with knowledge, for by force he compelled those whom it is fitting to challenge by the reason of faith."[14]

The pertinent edict from the Council of Trent is canon 14, passed in 1547 at the Council's seventh session. It has to do with remarks found in Erasmus of Rotterdam's prologue to his own *Paraphrase of the Gospel of Matthew*, first published in 1522. That prologue ("To the pious reader"), which Erasmus says he wrote because his printer complained that otherwise he would have to leave

---

promises of a series of short-lived and unstable kings, ignored by them in practice and frequently overturned by their successors." Marcia L. Colish, *Faith, Force and Fiction in Medieval Baptismal Debates* (Washington, DC: The Catholic University of America Press, 2014), 242.

13. The decree can be found in Gratian, *Decretum Magistri Gratiani*, vol. 1 of *Corpus Iuris Canonici*, ed. Aemilius Ludovicus Richter and Aemilius Friedberg (Leipzig: B. Tauchnitz, 1879), cols. 161–62, where it is referred to as canon 56. It can also be found at J. D. Mansi, P. Labbeus, and G. Cossartius, eds., *Sacrorum conciliorum nova et amplissima collectio*, vol. 10 (Florence: A. Zatta, 1764), col. 633, where it is identified as chapter 57. The entire decree reads as follows: "De Iudeis autem praecepit sancta synodus, nemini deinceps ad credendum vim inferre. Cui enim vult Deus miseretur, et quem vult indurat. Non enim tales inviti salvandi sunt, sed volentes ut integra sit forma iustitiae. Sicut enim homo propria arbitrii voluntate serpenti oboediens periit, sic vocante se gratia Dei propriae mentis conversione homo quisque credendo salvatur. Ergo non vi sed libera arbitrii facultate ut convertantur suadendi sunt non potius impellendi. Qui autem iam pridem ad Christianitatem coacti sunt, sicut factum est temporibus religiosissimi principis Sisebuti quia iam constat eos sacramentis divinis adsociatos, et baptismi gratiam suscepisse, et chrismate unctos esse, et corporis domini et sanguinis extitisse participes, oportet ut fidem etiam quam vi vel necessitate susceperunt tenere cogantur, ne nomen Domini blasphemetur, et fides quam susceperunt, vilis ac contemptibilis habeatur."

14. Isidore of Seville (Isidorus Hispalensis), *Historia de regibus Gothorum, Vandalorum et Sueborum*, in PL 83, ed. J.-P. Migne (Paris, 1850), col. 1073, § 60: ". . . qui initio regni Judaeos ad fidem Christianam permovens, aemulationem quidem habuit, sed non secundum scientiam; potestate enim compulit quos provocare fidei ratione oportuit." See also Colish, *Faith, Force and Fiction*, 243. In his *Enarratio*, de Toledo appears to agree with Isidore, for he uses very similar language: "Quod si laudatur Sisibutus dum dicitur religiosissimus, id est non ratione facti, sed ratione zeli, qui ex bona intentione processit, sed non secundum scientiam." *Enarratio* 2.108.

some pages blank in the book being prepared, is basically an exhortation to all Christians, whatever their level of education, to study Holy Scripture with graced enthusiasm and affection. He imagines a community of such committed Christians, suggesting that within it, once youths, baptized as babies, reach adolescence, they "would be asked whether they confirm what their sponsors promised [*polliciti sunt*] on their behalf at baptism."[15] If they should confirm these promises, a sort of ceremony would take place: a "profession" of the original baptismal promises, analogous to the commemorative professions by monks of their original of vows. If, however, a youth should not be willing to confirm what their sponsors have promised,

> every effort must be made lest anyone slide back from his early faith [*a prima fide*]. If this cannot be prevented, perhaps it will be expedient that such a person not be compelled, but left to his own inclination until he returns to his senses. Nor in the meantime ought he to be subject to any other punishment, except that he be prevented from receiving the eucharist and the other sacraments. For the rest, he should be excluded neither from ceremonies nor from assemblies.[16]

A few years later (1526), in responding to attacks by Paris theologian Noël Beda, Erasmus, having first reiterated the above (including the reference to faith), explains that his reason for proposing such an approach was "that we might have [in the Church] those who are purely and truly Christians rather than coerced persons and hypocrites." They should live as do the Jews, he argues, "who are not prevented from attending Christian assemblies but are punished for hurling blasphemies at the name of Christ."[17] "If," he says, "it is feared that the life [of such a one] shall grow more criminal, in this case the profane laws will prevail: if he should steal, murder, provoke tumult, or speak blasphemy against Christ."[18]

---

15. Desiderius Erasmus, *Opera Omnia*, vol. 7 (Leiden: P. Vander, 1703–1706), **3v: "... interrogentur ratum ne habeant, quod susceptores illorum nomine polliciti sunt in baptismo." The translation is taken from Desiderius Erasmus, *Paraphrase on Matthew*, CWE 35, ed. and trans. Dean Simpson (Toronto: University of Toronto Press, 2008), 20.

16. Erasmus, *Opera Omnia*, vol. 7, **3v: "Sed omnia tentanda sunt, ne quis resiliat a prima fide. Quod si non potest obtineri, fortassis expediet illum non cogi, sed suo relinqui animo, donec resipiscat: nec ad aliam interim vocari pænam, nisi ut ab Eucharistia sumenda reliquisque sacramentis arceatur. Ceterum nec a sacris, nec a concionibus excludatur."

17. Erasmus, *Opera Omnia*, vol. 9, 459E: "Quod si qui resilirent, sic finerentur inter nos vivere, quemadmodum vivunt Judai, qui non arcentur ab Ecclesiasticis concionibus: puniuntur tamen blasphemiam jaculantes in nomen Christi. Hæc eo tendunt ut habeamus pure vereque Chriftianos, potius quam coactos & hypocritas." See also 561A–563B.

18. Erasmus, *Opera Omnia*, vol. 9, 563A: "Quod si metuitur vita sceleratior, hic valebunt profanæ leges, si furetur, si occidat, si moveat tumultum, si blasphemiam dicat in Christum."

Canon 14 of the seventh session of the Council of Trent does not mention Erasmus by name, although the connection with his 1522 prologue is apparent. The canon reads:

> If any one says (a) that those who have been thus baptized as children, are, when they have grown up, to be asked whether they wish to ratify what their sponsors promised [*polliciti sunt*] in their names when they were baptized; and (b) that, in case they answer that they choose not to, they are to be left to their own decision and are meanwhile not to be coerced by any other penalty to a Christian life save that they be impeded from reception of the Eucharist and of the other sacraments, until they return to their senses: let him be anathema.[19]

The crucial question—as we shall see, also for Francisco de Toledo—was (and is) whether with this canon the Council of Trent recognized such a right to coerce belief or faith. Important for answering this question was the influence had by Jerome Seripando, General of the Augustinian order, who was directly involved in the wording of canon 14. In an intervention made at the Council, Seripando puts forward an argument very similar to Erasmus's defense of his own position: that it does not help the Church to have within it "coerced persons and hypocrites."[20] One notes that in the canon's final form, all reference to faith has been removed. What was left was the Council's rejection of the thesis that coercion might never be used even to ensure that *any* of the original baptismal promises be fulfilled—that is to say, even a promise mentioned in the baptismal rite but obligatory for all, irrespective of the faith. If one does not recognize that the condemnation of canon 14 includes also these latter types of promises, it must be read as countering *simply* opposition to coercion regarding the faith—or, conversely, as defending such coercion.

What were these promises? The Council of Trent eventually settled upon thirteen errors regarding baptism to be condemned. That in which Erasmus and the baptismal promises are mentioned became #11. Error #13 also had to do with promises (called there *vota*); it was formulated as follows: "The *votum* of baptism has no condition other than faith, and it abolishes all other *vota*."[21]

---

19. Heinrich Denzinger, ed., *Enchiridion Symbolorum Definitionum et Declarationum de Rebus Fidei et Morum* (Freiburg im Breisgau: Herder, 2009), § 1627: "Si quis dixerit huiusmodi parvulos baptizatos cum adoleverint interrogandos esse an ratum habere velint quod patrini eorum nomine dum baptizarentur polliciti sunt et, ubi se nolle responderint, suo esse arbitrio relinquendos nec alia interim poena ad christianam vitam cogendos nisi ut ab Eucharistiae aliorumque sacramentorum perceptione arceantur donec resipiscant: anathema sit."

20. See *Concilium Tridentinum: Diariorum, actorum, epistularum, tractatuum nova collectio* (Freiburg im Breisgau: Herder, 1901–2001), 5:965, lines 10–16. See also 12:756, lines 42–47.

21. *Concilium Tridentinum*, 5:838: "Votum baptismi non habere conditionem nisi fidei, et alia omnia vota evacuare."

Considering these errors in order, in a tract that was part of the Council's proceedings, immediately after a brief mention of the Erasmian error (#11), Seripando says things that enable us to understand what these promises [*vota*] were understood to be.

Seripando considers separately the two parts of error #13.[22] The first part, which says that baptism involves no condition other than faith, he counters with what is said during the baptismal rite: "If you wish to enter into life, observe the mandates."[23] It is apparent that "the mandates" are conditions distinct from the condition of faith (and that, like the condition of faith, they are involved in baptism). Regarding the second part of error #13, that is, the idea that the *votum* of baptism abolishes all other *vota*, Seripando cites Augustine who, in commenting on Psalm 75:12, identifies many *vota*, some of which are obligatory for all. Among these latter, Seripando mentions "living properly according to the common mode, not to steal, etc."[24] It is apparent, therefore, that "the mandates" agreed to in—as conditions of—baptism are in fact *vota* and that they include promises to abide by moral precepts obligatory for all. Understanding also the condemnation of the Erasmian error in

---

22. *Concilium Tridentinum* 12:757: "Tertium decimum articulum sic intelligo quoad primam partem; votum baptismi non habere condtitionem nisi fidei, ut baptizatus scilicet ad aliud non teneatur pro consequenda salute nisi ad fidem. Quod damnatum est per illud, quod in baptismo proponitur, 'Si vis ad vitam ingredi, serva mandata.' Quoad partem alteram: votum baptismi omnia alta vota evacuare, destruitur et damnatur Augustini auctoritate in Ps. 75, ubi ponit vota communia omnibus christianis, credendi scilicet in Deum, sperandi ab eo vitam aeternam, bene vivendi secundum communem modum, furtum non facere etc."

23. See the baptismal rite issued by authority of the Council of Trent: *Rituale Romanum, Editio Princeps (1614)*, ed. Manlio Sodi and Juan Javier Flores Arcas, *Monumenta Liturgica Concilii Tridentini*, vol. 5 (Vatican City: Libreria Editrice Vaticana, 1614), 13, 23. In the rite, the presiding priest first asks of the one to be baptized or his sponsors: "What do you ask of the Church of God?" The answer: "Faith." He asks what faith offers; the answer is: "Eternal life." And then he says: "If, therefore, you wish to enter into life, observe the mandates." In comparison with the rite for infants (p. 13), the rite for adults (p. 23) distinguishes more explicitly the *vota* connected strictly with the faith from those obligatory for all (which are nonetheless also connected with the faith affirmed in baptism). In the rite for adults the *vota* connected strictly with the faith are listed second and introduced by the words: "On the other hand, faith is . . ." ["*Fides autem est . . .*"]: "Si vis habere vitam aeternam, serva mandata. Diliges Dominum Deum tuum ex toto corde tuo, & ex tota anima tua, & ex tota mente tua, & proximum tuum sicut teipsum. In his duobus mandatis tota lex pendat, & Prophetae. Fides autem est, ut unum Deum in Trinitate, & Trinitatem in unitate venereris, neque confundendo personas, neque substantiam separando. Alia est enim persona Patris, alia Filii, alia Spiritus Sancti; sed horum trium, una est substantia, & non nisi una Divinitas."

24. See above, note 21. Augustine's list of *vota* obligatory for all includes the following: "Credere in Illum, sperare ab Illo vitam aeternam, bene vivere secundum communem modum. Est enim quidam modus communis omnibus. Furtum non facere, non castimoniali praecipitur, et nuptae non praecipitur: adulterium non facere, omnibus praecipitur." Augustine, *Enarrationes in Psalmos*, in *Sancti Aurelii Augustini Hipponensis Opera Omnia*, PL 36–37 (Paris: Migne, J.-P., 1845), 36:967.

accordance with these terms, the promises made by a young adult's sponsors (godparents) and which remain obligatory even if he turns away from the faith, include promises not strictly bound up with the faith.

Thomas Aquinas's Early Remarks on Religious Liberty

Early on in his career, Thomas Aquinas addressed the issue of what today we would call "religious freedom." He does so in his commentary on Peter Lombard's *Sentences* in an article entitled "Whether heretics are to be tolerated" [*Utrum haeretici sint sustinendi*].[25] He does so more extensively in an article in the *Summa Theologiae* (and which we will consider in the next section of the present essay).

While reading Thomas's various comments in this regard, it is important to bear in mind that he lived in a society very different from our own: in a society, that is, that was largely Christian and in which the relationship between the Church and the civil authorities was much closer than in our present, more pluralistic society. Some of the standard penalties of which he expresses approval—imprisonment or even death for heretics, for instance—would be unacceptable in our society. That said, however, it is important to bear in mind that Thomas is always in search of the concepts and distinctions that will make possible the construction of a just system of laws—and so a just society— independently of the particular, concrete means that a particular society might choose to adopt. As we shall see, Thomas makes a distinction between coercion with respect to faith itself and coercion for the purpose of protecting the vulnerable who might be corrupted regarding the faith. Regarding the latter, we can in our application of his thought substitute less drastic means, such as laws (with penalties) regarding the rights of parents in the education of their children. The important things are the concepts and the distinctions.

When in the pertinent article in the commentary on the *Sentences* he considers the question whether heretics are to be tolerated, Thomas cites a principle put forward by Augustine which is the foundation of his own thought in these regards. That is to say, in the fifth objection, we read: "As Augustine says, no one believes unwillingly." (The objection continues: "But heretics err in faith; therefore, they are not to be coerced.")[26] In setting out this principle,

---

25. He does this in book four, distinction 13, question 2, article 3, of the *Sentences* commentary [*Scriptum super libros Sententiarum Magistri Petri Lombardi Episcopi Parisiensis*, ed. Pierre Mandonnet & Maria Fabianus Moos (Paris: Lethielleux, 1929-47)], which I abbreviate as *Sent.* 4.13.2.3.

26. *Sent.*, 4.13.2.3, obj. 5: "Nullus credit non volens, ut dicit Augustinus. Sed haeretici in fide errant. Ergo non sunt cogendi." The quotation comes from Augustine's commentary on the Gospel of St. John; the passage actually reads as follows: "Intrare quisquam ecclesiam potest

Augustine is commenting upon John 6:44: "No one can come to me unless the Father who sent me draws him." As we shall see, it is not insignificant that, immediately after quoting this biblical verse and before saying that "it is not possible to believe unless doing so willingly," Augustine raises the very question that de Toledo raises regarding justification and predestination: "Whom he [the Father] draws and whom He does not draw, and why he draws that one and does not draw that one, do not wish to judge if you do not wish to err."[27] Notwithstanding Augustine's hesitation in these regards, it is apparent that the question of predestination and the involvement of free will—"*why* he draws that one and does *not* draw that one"—is related to the question of coercion with respect to the faith.

In the corpus of *Sent.* 4.13.2.3, Thomas does not address the issue of justification and predestination but addresses rather the specific question he has posed: whether heretics might be tolerated rather than coerced. His basic argument is that coercion can be used but primarily in order to prevent harm to the uneducated (the *simplices*), who are easily corrupted. In this case the Church might use either imprisonment or expulsion; if the heretics are not corrupting others, they might still be sequestered. Given, however, a "secular judgment," they might also be killed and despoiled of their property, even if they are not corrupting others, for they blaspheme God and maintain a "false faith," and so there is even more reason to punish them than to punish those who are guilty of "criminal harm to the sovereign or than those who produce false coinage."[28]

In line with what was said just above, what interests us here is not the particular means of coercion deemed acceptable but rather the fact that Thomas implicitly opposes the idea of the Church's or the state's coercing with respect to faith itself, although he will allow coercion of those who stray from the faith,

---

nolens, accedere ad altare potest nolens, accipere Sacramentum potest nolens: credere non potest nisi volens." Augustine, *In Iohannis Evangelium Tractatus*, ed. Radbodus Willems, CCSL 36 (Turnhout: Brepols, 1954), tract 26, 260, lines 12–14.

27. Augustine, *In Iohannis Evangelium Tractatus*, tract 26, 260, lines 7–8: "Quem trahat et quem non trahat, quare illum trahat et illum non trahat, noli velle iudicare, si non vis errare." For de Toledo's similar query ("quare hunc elegit, non illum"), see above, note 10.

28. Thomas Aquinas, *Scriptum super Libros Sententiarum*, 4.13.2.3c: ". . . Ecclesia eos a consortio fidelium excludit, et praecipue illos qui alios corrumpunt. Et simplices, qui de facili corrumpi possunt, ab eis sunt segregati non solum mente, sed etiam corporaliter; unde per Ecclesiam incarcerantur et expelluntur. Si autem alios non corrumperent, possent etiam celari. Sed illi qui sunt firmi in fide, possunt cum eis corpore conversari, ut eos convertant; non tamen in divinis, quia excommunicati sunt. Sed judicio saeculari possunt licite occidi et a bonis suis spoliari, etsi alios non corrumpant; quia sunt blasphemi in Deum, cum fidem falsam observant. Unde magis possunt puniri juste isti quam illi qui sunt rei criminis laesae majestatis et illi qui falsam monetam cudunt."

especially when the innocent (or uneducated) might otherwise be corrupted. It is also worth noting that Thomas puts professing a "false faith" within the same general category as criminal harm to the sovereign and the production of false coinage [*falsam monetam*], both crimes that harm the state.

What is implicit in the corpus of *Sent.* 4.13.2.3, becomes more apparent in Thomas's response to the fifth objection (the objection arguing that, according to Augustine, "no one believes unwillingly" and so heretics ought not to be coerced). He writes: "the Church does not pursue them so that through force they might be brought to believe, but lest they corrupt others and lest such a sin remain unpunished."[29]

Thomas Aquinas's Later Remarks on Religious Liberty

We turn now to Thomas's ST II-II, q. 10, a. 8 and (in the subsequent section) to de Toledo's commentary upon it. In this article Thomas says things not dissimilar to what he says in *Sent.* 4.13.2.3. The question posed (to translate literally) is "whether infidels are to be compelled toward the faith" [*Utrum infideles compellendi sint ad fidem*].[30] In the corpus of the article he draws a distinction between two types of "infidel": those who have never accepted the faith, such as Gentiles and Jews, and those who "at one time did accept the faith and profess it" but no longer do so, such as heretics and apostates. Regarding the first type, he says that they are "by no means to be compelled toward the faith so that they might believe, for to believe is of the will" [*nullo modo sunt ad fidem compellendi ut ipsi credant, quia credere voluntatis est*]—although they might be compelled *from* the faithful [*compellendi a fidelibus,*] in order that they might not impede the faith by means of "blasphemies, persuasions, or even open persecutions." He mentions in this regard that Christians frequently wage war against such infidels to prevent them from impeding the faith.

Thomas's remarks (in the article's corpus) regarding the second type of infidel are much more succinct: they are "to be compelled even bodily in order that they might fulfill what they have promised and to hold what at one time they accepted" [*Et tales sunt etiam corporaliter compellendi ut impleant quod promiserunt et teneant quod semel susceperunt*]. One notices here Thomas's

---

29. Thomas Aquinas, *Sent.*, 4.13.2.3 ad 5: "Ad quintum dicendum quod Ecclesia non persequitur eos ut per violentiam inducantur ad credendum, sed ne alios corrumpant, et ne tantum peccatum inultum remaneat."
30. In what follows, I translate the phrase *ad fidem* in this way as "toward the faith." Thomas accepts various sorts of coercion connected with the faith, and many of these—such as coercion for the promotion or protection of faith—might be called coercion of faith without being coercion precisely *to believe*. What he rejects is the idea that someone can be coerced *toward* the faith, for it is the will that takes one toward the faith.

speaking—not unlike the Council of Trent in canon 14 of its seventh session—of *promises*, and one wonders accordingly whether this passage might not have influenced that canon's wording. In any case, since in the earlier section of the corpus he has stated that "to believe is of the will" and that this is the reason why infidels such as Gentiles and Jews ought not to be compelled toward the faith, we must understand compulsion of heretics and apostates "to hold to [*teneant*] what at one time they accepted"—and so to fulfill what they have promised—as stopping short of compulsion toward the faith. As we shall see, in ST II-II, q. 10, a. 8, ad 3 he makes another distinction—or, perhaps better, the same distinction expressed differently—saying that "to accept the faith is of the will but to hold to [*tenere*] the faith once accepted is of necessity."

Among the responses to the objections in ST II-II, q. 10, a. 8, the ones most relevant to present concerns are, indeed, the first and the third. In the first, quoted is a remark by John Chrysostom regarding the parable of the weeds among the wheat (Mt 13:24–30) in which the master tells the servants not to pull up the weeds lest they pull up the wheat along with them. Chrysostom understands this as implying that heretics ought not to be killed since in doing so "it is necessary that many of the saints be subverted" [*necesse est multos sanctorum simul subverti*]. In his response, Thomas points out, first of all, that Chrysostom does not rule out *any* coercion of heretics (such as the threat of excommunication) but only killing them. He then notes that even Augustine retracted his earlier position that any coercion should be by means of words and disputation, arguing later in life (in his letter 93) that "fear of the laws has been so profitable that many say, 'Thanks be to the Lord who has broken our chains.'"[31] Neither Augustine nor Thomas here says that the threat of execution—and so execution itself—might be used against heretics, although the implication is that it could be. Still, nothing in this response contradicts the principle put forward in the corpus that, because "to believe is of the will," coercion *toward* the faith—as distinct from erecting disincentives to measures hostile to the faith—is not acceptable.

The third response also involves Augustine and even more directly his principle that "it is not possible to believe unless one does so willingly," to which Thomas makes reference in the corresponding objection. The objection argues that this principle entails that infidels (and, in particular, heretics) "are not to be compelled toward the faith" [*infideles non sint ad fidem cogendi*]. Thomas's response is very nuanced. He begins by saying that, "Just as to vow is of the will but to render in return [*reddere*] is of necessity, so also to accept the faith is of the will but to hold to [*tenere*] the faith once accepted is of necessity; and so

---

31. Augustine, *Sancti Aurelii Augustini Hipponiensis episcopi: Epistulae: Pars II, Ep. XXXI–CXXIII*, CSEL 34.2, *Epistulae II*, ed. Alois Goldbacher (Prague: Tempsky, 1898), 462–63.

heretics are to be compelled in order that they might hold to the faith [*ut fidem teneant*]."³² And then he quotes one of Augustine's letters: "How is it that those ones typically cry out, 'To believe or not to believe is free; upon whom did Christ use force'? They ought to recall that, in the case of Paul, Christ first coerced and afterwards taught."³³ In the case of Paul, the coercion comes first and then the faith. If (as we must) we are to understand this response as consistent with what Thomas says in the corpus of the article (and, in fact, in *Sent.* 4.13.2.3), Augustine must be understood, at least according to Thomas's interpretation, as saying that the act of faith—the act of going toward faith [*ad fidem*]—is to be separated from any coercion in whatever way linked with it. In the case of heretics, as distinct from the case of Paul, the coercion "in order that they might hold to [*tenere*] the faith" is subsequent (at least logically) to their initial holding of the faith. Nonetheless, as with Paul, it is quite different from coercion toward the faith. To use the language employed in the corpus of ST II-II, q. 10, a. 8, it has to do with fulfilling what was earlier promised—or, as he says here in ST II-II, q. 10, a. 8, ad 3, with rendering in return [*reddere*] what was initially proffered. For a society to institute incentives and disincentives aimed at not obstructing the performance of genuine acts of faith is not to exercise coercion toward the faith.

Francisco de Toledo on Thomas Aquinas's Remarks on Religious Liberty

What then does de Toledo make of all this? We have come across no reference by him to *Sent.* 4.13.2.3; but, given the length of his remarks on ST II-II, q. 10, a. 8 in the *Enarratio*, he is clearly very interested in the issue itself.³⁴ Not unlike the corpus in ST II-II, q. 10, a. 8, de Toledo's remarks on the article

---

32. ST II-II, q. 10, a. 8, ad 3: "Ad tertium dicendum quod, sicut vovere est voluntatis, reddere autem est ecessitates, ita accipere fidem est voluntatis, sed tenere iam acceptam est necessitatis; et ideo haeretici sunt compellendi ut fidem teneant." At *Sent.* 4.38.1.3.1, s.c. 2, Thomas remarks, "Praeterea, Augustinus dicit, quod vovere est voluntatis, sed reddere necessitatis." The Parma edition of the *Sentences* commentary gives as the reference Augustine's letter 43.

33. The passage in Augustine actually reads as follows: "Ubi est quod isti clamare consueverunt: 'Liberum est credere, vel non credere? Cui vim Christus intulit? Quem coegit?' Ecce habent Paulum apostolum; agnoscant in eo prius cogentem Christum, et postea docentem, prius ferientem et postea consolantem." Augustine, *Sancti Aurelii Augustini Hipponiensis episcopi: Epistulae: Pars IV, Ep. CLXXXV–CCLXX*, CSEL 57, ed. Alois Goldbacher (Prague: Tempsky, 1911), 21. Goldbacher mentions a variant: instead of *consolantem*, *consulentem*. The variant makes more sense: Augustine would be employing the proportion *"cogentem:docentem::ferientem: consulentem."*

34. ST II-II, q. 10 contains twelve articles. Seven of these de Toledo does not comment upon; two others (articles 1 and 9) he discusses very briefly. To article 8 he devotes considerably more space than to either of the remaining two articles (4 and 10).

are divided into two sections—*Enarratio* 2.104a–108a and 2.108a–111b—each introduced by a question. The first question asks whether infidels who have never professed the faith "can and ought to be coerced toward the acceptance of the faith." De Toledo thinks not. None of the positions that he sets out in this first section is wholly incompatible with what Thomas says in ST II-II, q. 10, a. 8, although de Toledo does assert that "the *Church* has the right of punishing and castigating even by death" those who impede the preaching of the Gospel (*Enarratio* 2.105b).[35] At least in *Sent.* 4.13.2.3, as we have seen, Thomas appears to locate such authority in the state.

De Toledo does in this first section introduce concepts that do not enter into ST II-II, q. 10, a. 8 at all: God's grace and our free will, concepts central to the *De auxiliis* controversy. De Toledo makes reference to *De Iudeis*, that is to say, to the decree from the Fourth Council of Toledo which we have already seen, and remarks that "force is to be inflicted upon no one in order that he might believe, for God has mercy upon whom he wills and he hardens [the heart] of whom he wills."[36] He also quotes the passage from the Gospel of John that (as we have seen) Augustine quotes when dealing with predestination—"No one can come to me unless the Father who sent me draws him"—and goes on immediately to speak of God's opening minds and hearts (*Enarratio* 2.106b).[37] So, it is apparent that, in de Toledo's mind, religious freedom (discussed in ST II-II, q. 10, a. 8) and predestination are closely linked. And a bit later in this first section he also says that, "Since, therefore, faith is supernatural, it is to be sought not by force from men but by prayer from God, as he wishes to give it" (*Enarratio* 2.107a).

The initial question of the second section is whether heretics "are to be coerced by suffering the penalty of death, toward accepting the faith" [*sint cogendi sub poena mortis ad fidem suscipiendam*] that they accepted in the past (*Enarratio* 2.108a). De Toledo maintains that pertinacious heretics ought to suffer the ultimate punishment and that to maintain otherwise is heretical (*Enarratio* 2.108b). He mentions in a positive manner Augustine's letter 93, mentioned also by Thomas in ST II-II, q. 10, a. 8, in which Augustine recants his earlier position that coercion should be limited to verbal disputation (*Enarratio* 2.109a). Also, one of the objections (the third) to de Toledo's own position regarding coercion "toward accepting the faith" by means of the death penalty invokes Christ's remark to the Twelve, "Do you also wish to go away?"

---

35. Emphasis added.
36. *Enarratio* 2.106a: "Nemini ad credendum vis inferatur: cui enim vult Deus miseretur et quem vult indurat." The decree of the Fourth Council of Toledo (see above, note 13) begins with the words, "De Iudeis autem praecepit sancta synodus, nemini deinceps ad credendum vim inferre. Cui enim vult Deus miseretur, et quem vult indurat."
37. The passage from John is 6:44, although our text gives the reference as "Ioann. 17."

(Jn 6:67). "Therefore, the Church too, imitating Christ, ought to allow heretics to go away" (*Enarratio* 2.108b). De Toledo's response is that Christ, for various reasons, including the fact that those others had "not yet professed the faith," allowed them to go away. "But the Church, which has accepted from Christ justice and power, quite properly uses severity against evil ones" (*Enarratio* 2.110b). As we shall see, this thesis is connected with de Toledo's understanding of the way in which God's grace operates on us, *through* the Church.

But the most important remark in this second section has to do with Erasmus. It is contained in what de Toledo numbers as his "fifth conclusion" and is worth quoting in its entirety:

Fifth conclusion:

Young persons baptized before the use of reason, when they have arrived at the use of reason, are by all means to be coerced to maintain the faith, even suffering the ultimate punishment. This conclusion is against Erasmus, who in a certain preface to a version of the New Testament says that it is more advisable that these young persons, supposing that they arrive at the use of reason, be questioned about the faith—and that, if they do not wish to continue [*perseverare*], they be left to their liberty: they would only be deprived of sharing in the sacraments.

But this teaching is heresy and [this fifth] conclusion is Catholic. In the first place, this heresy is regarded as condemned in canon 14 of the seventh session of the Council of Trent. And moreover, because according to divine right it is possible for baptism to be conferred upon children, for this reason they can be bound by God himself even before the use of reason, for God can demand from a human being whatever he pleases. Regarding this, however, we have said more in the material regarding baptism.[38]

There are a number of things in this fifth conclusion worth noting. First of all, although, as we have seen, the anathema, which is canon 14 of the seventh session of the Council of Trent, does not mention faith but rather, quite generally, promises—which would include promises made by a child's sponsors to live a life

---

38. *Enarratio* 2.110a: "Quinta conclusio. Parvuli ante usum rationis baptizati, quum ad rationis usum pervenerint, sunt cogendi prorsus servare fidem, etiam sub ultimo supplicio. Ista est contra Erasmum, qui in quadam praefatione versionis novi testamenti dicit esse consultius, si isti parvuli ad usum rationis pervenientes interrogarentur de fide: et si nollent perseverare, in sua relinquerentur libertate; solum communione sacramentorum privarentur. Sed haec doctrina est haeresis, et conclusio est catholica. Habetur in primis haec haeresis damnata in Conc. Trid. sess. 7 can. 14. Et praeterea quia sicut iure divino potest conferri baptismus parvulis, sic ab ipso Deo potuerunt obligari, etiam ante usum rationis; potest enim Deus ab homine exigere, quidquid ipsi fuerit beneplacitum. De hoc tamen plura diximus in materia de baptismo."

consistent with those Christian values that are also values for all humans (respect for justice, etc.)—the implication of de Toledo's remarks is that the canon allows for coercion toward the faith, for he cites it as support for his conclusion that youth, once they have arrived at the use of reason, "are by all means to be coerced to maintain the faith." Secondly, the theological basis for this conclusion has to do with predestination and the issues inherent in the *De auxiliis* controversy: whether or in what sense what God requires of a man depends wholly upon God. De Toledo adds immediately that he discusses this matter later in the *Enarratio*: that is to say, in the section of the *Enarratio* we shall examine shortly.

In the very last paragraph of his commentary on ST II-II, q. 10, a. 8, de Toledo summarizes that article's response to its third objection, i.e., the place where Thomas, following Augustine, draws the distinction between vowing and rendering in return, the one being voluntary, the other of necessity. The objection, as abbreviated by de Toledo, reads: "Infidels are not to be coerced since faith is to be voluntary; therefore, neither are heretics" (*Enarratio* 2.108b). De Toledo says in response:

> The arguments are dissimilar, for infidels have not promised faith. For this reason they are not to be coerced. But heretics have promised. Granted, therefore, that per se they are not bound *toward* the faith since it is voluntary; nonetheless, by reason of the bond they can be coerced. For to vow is voluntary; to fulfill what has been promised is a matter of justice—and there can be coercion toward the corresponding fulfillment.[39]

Noticeable here is the idea that any promising (such as that mentioned in canon 14) has to do explicitly with faith. Moreover, the subsequent coercion towards fulfillment is toward fulfillment of what was initially voluntarily promised: faith. This leaves little room for saying that the Council of Trent condemns the thesis that coercion can never be imposed, not even coercion not intrinsically of the faith. What de Toledo says here is not very different from what Thomas says in ST II-II, q. 10, a. 8, ad 3—"and so heretics are to be compelled in order that they might hold to the faith"—at least verbally. That phrase, however, "in order that they might hold to the faith" [*ut fidem teneant*], when not interpreted in the way that de Toledo interprets it, can be understood as referring to disincentives aimed at keeping open the possibility of faith in others (the *simplices*) and of actions issuing from genuine faith.

---

39. *Enarratio* 2.111b: "Ad 6um dico, non esse similem rationem. Infideles enim non promiserunt fidem; ob id non sunt cogendi: at haeretici promiserunt. Licet ergo ad fidem per se non obligentur, quia voluntaria est; tamen ratione obligationis cogi possunt: vovere enim *voluntarium est; tamen implere quod promissum est, iustitiae est*, et ad impletionem talem potest esse coactio." Italics added to translation.

When de Toledo says at the end of the fifth conclusion (*Enarratio* 2.110a) that, regarding the meaning of canon 14 in Trent's seventh session, "we have said more in the material regarding baptism," he is referring to remarks he makes upon ST III, q. 68, a. 9, the article in which Thomas asks, "Whether children [*pueri*] are to be baptized." Thomas's answer to this question is, of course, that they should be. De Toledo agrees with Thomas and draws from that position three conclusions: (1) that baptism benefits infants [*infantes*] (*Enarratio* 4.81a), (2) that baptized infants are to be counted among the faithful (*Enarratio* 4.81b–82a), and (3) that "baptized children [*parvuli*], when they arrive at the use of reason, are not to be left to their own choice so that they might recede from the faith, if they wish."[40] In support of this third conclusion he remarks:

> This [conclusion] is against Erasmus, who, in his prologue upon Matthew, says that they ought to be left to their own choice so that they might elect to remain in the faith accepted. The Anabaptists have also taught this.
> But this position is the heresy damned during the Council of Trent, session seven, canon 14, where that is expressly rejected. And before the Council's determination the rite of the universal Church and plain reason ought to have been sufficient in opposition to Erasmus. For, since Christ the Lord had deigned to give them faith—and grace and the supernatural gifts—without their consent, it was most fitting that they should be bound, even from that moment, to observe the law in which they had been sanctified.[41]

We see here once again that, according to de Toledo, canon 14 has only to do with faith, whether at or well after baptism. He does not mention Trent's specification that persons, once they arrive at the use of reason, are to respect the *promises* made in their name by their sponsors. Once capable of using of reason, they would continue to be bound by the very "law in which they had been sanctified." With respect to faith, including acts of faith or acts inspired by faith, there is no difference whatsoever between the state of things at baptism and the

---

40. De Toledo describes conclusions one and two as "Catholic"; the contrary of the third he describes as heretical.

41. "Ista est contra Erasmum in prologo super Matthaeum, qui dicit illos debere suo arbitrio relinqui, ut eligant permanere in fide suscepta. Hoc etiam docuerunt Anabaptistae. Sed ista sententia est haeresis damnata in Concilio Tridentino sess. VII can. 14 ubi expresse id reprobatur. Et ante Concilii determinationem sufficere debuissent Erasmo ritus universalis Ecclesiae in contrarium, et ratio aperta. Nam quum Christus Dominus dignatus fuerit ipsis sine suo consensu dare fidem, et gratiam, et dona supernaturalia; decentissimum fuit, ut obligarentur etiam ex tunc servare legem, in qua sanctificati fuerunt."

state of things once the person has arrived at the use of reason. Finally, the legitimacy, once they have been baptized, of coercing persons with respect to the faith depends upon the fact that "Christ the Lord had deigned to give them faith."

Thomas Aquinas on Predestination

That brings us back finally to God's predestination of some to glory, others to reprobation. Although, as we have seen, in his comments upon ST II-II, q. 10, a. 8 and ST III, q. 68, a. 9 de Toledo's interpretation does not always correspond to what Thomas says in those articles, he presents his interpretation as Thomas's position. That is not the case with what he says about Thomas's ST I, q. 23, a. 5, the article on the question, "Whether pre-knowledge of merits is the cause of predestination." De Toledo acknowledges quite openly that his position that "foreseen good acts are the proximate reason for predestination; the primary reason, however, is the unique will of God" is "contrary to St. Thomas, Scotus, and many others . . ."[42] As mentioned above, these "others" included at least some of his colleagues at the Roman College.

What then does Thomas say about the question? Early on in the corpus of ST I, q. 23, a. 5, he refers back to what he says in ST I, q. 19, a. 5, which is essential for understanding his position. In that earlier article Thomas asks whether, when we speak about God's will, we can introduce talk of a cause. The reason this is an issue is that, very often when we speak about a cause and an effect, we presuppose a certain separation—often a temporal separation—between the two. God, however, is absolutely simple and also above time, and so anything we say about his will must be understood as not implying his moving from one state to another.

A philosopher, for instance, grasps the meaning of a pair of premises, and that leads him to draw the appropriate conclusion. A similar thing happens in the practical sphere: a person might, with one act of the will, will a particular end and with another "that which is for the end" (which phrase would include the means).[43] But even with human beings this separation is sometimes only what we might call a "formal" separation. In understanding the premises, a

---

42. *Enarratio* 1.287b: "Secunda conclusio. Praedestinationis ratio proxima sunt praevisa opera bona; ratio tamen prima sola Dei voluntas. Haec conclusio est contra S. Thomam, Scotum, et alios multos; sed adiutorio Dei sufficienter probabimus eam." At *Enarratio* 1.289a he identifies one of these others: William Durandus.

43. Thomas's Latin is "ea quae sunt ad finem." This phrase is often translated "means," but, especially in this context, it is important to recognize the more general signification: "that which is for the end" (or, more literally, "things that are for the end"). On this issue, see David Wiggins, "Deliberation and practical reason," *Proceedings of the Aristotelian Society (1975–1976)* 76 (1976): 30–36.

person already sees the conclusion; a person wills an end but, in that very act, he wills that which is for the end. In this latter case it is better not to speak of the person's act of willing the end as the cause of his act of willing that which is for the end since there is only one act and (as Thomas notes) nothing can be a cause of itself. Still, however, he says, "it will be right to say that he wills to order that which is for the end toward the end."[44]

In the case of God, we must be especially careful not to introduce cause/effect separation. Even when a person wills the end and that which is for the end in the one act, his understanding of the end and his understanding of that which is for the end are distinct. Moreover, such thinking presumes a situation—the spatial, temporal universe—in which one is without certain things and must move (in some sense or another) in order to reach those things. But God's thoughts are not distinct from one another as are human thoughts, one consequence of which is that he does not operate with syllogisms, speculative or practical—not even those involving propositions (premises and conclusions) that are not really distinct one from the other. And he does not move with the hope—or even the expectation—of bringing something about in the future: he is present, so to speak, at both ends of the event. And so, says Thomas,

> to will an end is not for [God] a cause of willing that which is for the end; still, however, he wills that which is for the end *to be ordered toward* the end. He, therefore, wills this to *be* because of [*propter*] that, but not because of [*propter*] this does he will that.[45]

In ST I, q. 23, a. 5, Thomas expresses the latter point somewhat differently. He says, that is, that "a *cause* of the divine will is not to be assigned with respect to the act of *willing*; but it is possible for a *reason* to be assigned with respect to the things willed, in as much, that is, as God wills something to *be* because of [*propter*] another."[46] In other words, in speaking about such matters, it would be illegitimate to speak of something causing God to will something, although we can look to the realm of effects, i.e., to the effects of predestination, and,

---

44. ST I, q. 19, a. 5: "Et tamen erit verum dicere quod velit ordinare ea quae sunt ad finem, in finem."

45. ST I, q. 19, a. 5, c. Here is the larger passage: "Unde, sicut in Deo intelligere causam non est causa intelligendi effectus, sed ipse intelligit effectus in causa; ita velle finem non est ei causa volendi ea quae sunt ad finem, sed tamen vult ea quae sunt ad finem, ordinari in finem. Vult ergo hoc esse propter hoc, sed non propter hoc vult hoc."

46. ST I, q. 23, a. 5, c: "Dictum est autem supra quod non est assignare causam divinae voluntatis ex parte actus volendi; sed potest assignari ratio ex parte volitorum, inquantum scilicet Deus vult esse aliquid propter aliud." The emphasis is (obviously) not in Thomas's text but is added in the hope that it makes the train of Thomas's very abstract reasoning more apparent.

bearing in mind His particular characteristics, give an account of God's influence: how he wants things to be. This amounts to a denial that the foreknowledge of merits causes God to effect predestination—a position, he says, that no one of sound mind could hold—but it amounts also to an acknowledgement that there is another issue to address: "whether, with respect to the *effect*, predestination has some cause." He immediately adds: "And this is to inquire whether God would preordain himself to give the *effect* of predestination to someone because of certain merits."[47] He turns his attention, therefore, away from the cause of predestination (God) to the universe in which predestination has its effect.

Thomas identifies three ways of answering the question "whether, with respect to the effect, predestination has some cause"—with none of which he agrees. The first, which can be traced back to Plato but appears also in Origen, says that the effect of someone's predestination depends on merits in a previous life. That this position is not Christian is obvious. The second, which Thomas attributes to the Pelagians, places the pre-existent causal merits not in a previous life but in the subject's present (and only) life: it sees the initial factor (the word Thomas uses is *initium*) in becoming blessed as coming from the individual, although its consummation comes from God. Thomas's answer focuses in upon the idea that an individual, in preparing himself for beatitude, might give himself this *initium*. He quotes St. Paul's 2 Corinthians 3:5: "We are not able to think anything by ourselves as if from ourselves." Since, in any such preparation, the *initium* must be thought and since, according to Paul, thoughts cannot ultimately originate within the individual, it cannot be true that the *initium* (the initial thought) is within us.[48]

The third way of answering the question "whether, on the part of the effect, predestination has some cause," Thomas attributes to no one in particular. It is in fact a way of dealing with the previous argument, by simply acknowledging that the *initium* of predestination is *God*'s thought: "God gives grace to someone and preordains himself to give it to him *because* he has foreknown that the

---

47. ST I, q. 23, a. 5, c: "Sed hoc sub quaestione vertitur, utrum ex parte effectus, praedestinatio habeat aliquam causam. Et hoc est quaerere, utrum Deus praeordinaverit se daturum effectum praedestinationis alicui, propter merita aliqua."

48. ST I, q. 23, a. 5, c: "Posuerunt enim Pelagiani quod initium benefaciendi sit ex nobis, consummatio autem a Deo. Et sic, ex hoc contingit quod alicui datur praedestinationis effectus, et non alteri, quia unus initium dedit se praeparando, et non alius. Sed contra hoc est quod dicit apostolus, 2 Cor 3.5, quod non sumus sufficientes cogitare aliquid a nobis, quasi ex nobis. Nullum autem anterius principium inveniri potest quam cogitatio. Unde non potest dici quod aliquod in nobis initium existat, quod sit ratio effectus praedestinationis." Thomas might here have quoted Aristotle's *Eudemian Ethics* 7.14.1248a15–27. See in this regard Kevin L. Flannery, *Acts Amid Precepts: The Aristotelian Logical Structure of Thomas Aquinas's Moral Theory* (Washington, DC: The Catholic University of America Press, 2001), 136–37.

person will use the grace well."⁴⁹ Thomas goes on to compare such a scenario to a king who "might give to some soldier a horse, which he knows will be well used by him." Those who hold this position, he says, "appear to distinguish between that [effect] which is from grace and that which is from free will—as if it could not be one and the same thing from both."⁵⁰ But, since God is not bound by our temporal and physical limitations, there is nothing preventing God from arranging that a single effect issue from the two causes: grace and free will.

Thomas points out that this is true not just with respect to predestination but universally: God is just as much present in secondary causes as in primary. He refers back to what he has said in ST I, q. 22, a. 3: "In his intellect he [God] has the reason [*rationem*] of everything, even the most minor things, and to whatever causes he sets up as governing certain effects, He gives the power of producing those effects."⁵¹ He contrasts this approach with that which he attributes to Plato and the Platonists, who posit a high god in charge of things universal, secondary gods who move the heavenly bodies, and the lesser spirits [*daemonibus*] who influence human affairs. The high god of these thinkers, he would no doubt say, is like the king who gives his soldier a horse because he knows he will use it well.⁵²

De Toledo on Predestination

It has already been mentioned that de Toledo states explicitly that he does not agree with St. Thomas regarding predestination and that he maintains rather that "the proximate reason of predestination are foreseen good acts; the primary reason, however, is the unique will of God."⁵³ This is the "second conclusion" of his commentary on ST I, q. 23, a. 5. In this, the final section of the present essay,

---

49. ST I, q. 23, a. 5, c: "Deus dat gratiam alicui, et praeordinavit se ei daturum, quia praescivit eum bene usurum gratia."

50. ST I, q. 23, a. 5, c: ". . . sicut si rex det alicui militi equum, quem scit eo bene usurum. Sed isti videntur distinxisse inter id quod est ex gratia, et id quod est ex libero arbitrio, quasi non possit esse idem ex utroque."

51. ST I, q. 22, a. 3, c: "Quia in suo intellectu habet rationem omnium, etiam minimorum, et quascumque causas aliquibus effectibus praefecit, dedit eis virtutem ad illos effectus producendos."

52. See also SCG 3.70.8. (For this reference I am grateful to John Finnis.) In ST I, q. 23, a. 5, Thomas goes on to point out that an effect of predestination can be considered under two distinct titles: either "in particular" or "in common." Under the first title, nothing prevents an effect of predestination from being also a cause. Under the second title, in which we consider not particular causal chains or situations but the whole predestined universe, we must ultimately acknowledge a cause external to it all, the whole predestined universe itself being this first mover's effect.

53. *Enarratio* 1.287b. See above, note 41.

it will be referred to as the "proximate-primary thesis." The dual task of this final section is to set out de Toledo's reasons for maintaining the proximate-primary thesis rather than Thomas's position and to explain how that thesis bears upon the issue of predestination and (in the end) coercion toward faith.

As mentioned, toward the beginning of the corpus in ST I, q. 23, a. 5, Thomas cites his own ST I, q. 19, a. 5, the primary conclusion of which is that God "wills this to *be* because of [*propter*] that, but not because of [*propter*] this does he will that."[54] In his commentary on ST I, q. 19, a. 5, de Toledo faithfully reports that "God wills one thing to *be* because of [*propter*] another, i.e., the means because of [*propter*] the end, but he does not will one thing because of [*propter*] another." De Toledo understands, however, the import of this principle not to be, as in Thomas, that God is not bound by the logical structure that governs causality in the physical-temporal universe, but to be simply that God's will rules, for de Toledo adds immediately (as part of the same sentence) "thus, of his willing, there is no cause other than his will."[55]

When we turn to de Toledo's commentary upon ST I, q. 23, a. 5, we find that he does not mention ST I, q. 19, a. 5 and that he ignores the details of Thomas's argument—which is an application of what is said in ST I, q. 19, a. 5c—against the third way of answering the question "whether, with respect to the effect, predestination has some cause." De Toledo also ignores Thomas's likening the third way's thesis, that "God gives grace to someone and preordains Himself to give it to him because he has foreknown that the person will use the grace well," to a king's giving a soldier a horse, knowing that he will use it well. In other words, he fails to recognize Thomas's key idea that God does not have to initiate movements that go out from himself in order to bring about what he wants them to achieve: he is already there at the conclusion of the enterprise. Thomas's realization that predestination is at most *analogous* to the king-soldier-horse story allows him to show that we need not distinguish two effects: one from grace and the other from the person's free will.[56]

In his analysis of ST I, q. 23, a. 5, de Toledo chooses rather to emphasize God's power—a power which, as we have seen, he holds that God passes on to the Church.[57] Here is what he offers as an explanation of his proximate-primary thesis:[58]

---

54. See above, note 43.

55. *Enarratio* 1.256a: "Deus vult unum esse propter aliud, scilicet media propter finem; sed non vult unum propter aliud: unde volitionis eius non est alia causa a voluntate."

56. See above, note 49.

57. See *Enarratio* 1.105 and 2.110b, both discussed above in the fifth section ("Francisco de Toledo on Thomas Aquinas's remarks on religious liberty").

58. Having stated the proximate-primary thesis, de Toledo first explains it ("*Explicatur primo*") (*Enarratio* 1.287a); this explanation is then followed by a series of nine proofs, finishing at *Enarratio* 1.291b.

According to our way of understanding, even so it is necessary to consider what happens in God. *First*, with his own intellect he sees that all men are capable of beatitude, simultaneously seeing the means and aids by which, if they should wish, they might possess glory and such beatitude. *Secondly*, he has willed that those men *do*—and he in turn to bestow sufficient means of achieving beatitude if they should choose and execute—that which is within him. *Thirdly*, he has willed to give glory to those who perform that which is within him and who make use of the bestowed means; those, however, who do not but rather misuse those means, he has willed to reject. *Fourthly*, he has known, in his foreknowledge, who *these* are and who *those*, and, at that moment [*tunc*], by virtue of his immutable will, he has chosen certain individuals because of [*ex*] foreseen acts which, by his grace, are good, and he has reprobated others because of [*ex*] foreseen iniquities.

Now, if you ask regarding the proximate reason, why he elects this one and not that, I answer: in this one he foresees good acts, in that bad. And if you ask further, why because of [*propter*] good acts he elects and because of [*propter*] evil acts reprobates, I answer: because he has so willed and established; he has acted, therefore, as one who is just. And if you ask further, why has he so willed, I answer finally: because it so pleased him. Behold the supreme reason, the divine free will; behold the proximate reason, foreseen good or evil acts.

Moreover notice that I say "reason" and not "cause," for a cause is not properly said to be in God but rather a reason, in accordance with what we have said.[59] Foreknowledge is the reason for his volition, and one thing is the reason of another. Our merits do not oblige God with respect to predestination but rather the fact that he so wills. For this reason many ancient teachers have denied that there is a cause of predestination but have said that there is some reason. Say, therefore, that he reproves because of [*propter*] evil acts and that he predestines because of [*propter*] foreseen good acts.[60]

---

59. As we have seen, Thomas makes a distinction between cause and reason in ST I, q. 23, a. 5 (see above, note 45). Despite what he says here in the *Enarratio*, de Toledo goes on to speak occasionally of God as cause. See, for instance, *Enarratio* 1.291b: "Unde sequitur, quod Deus sit causa praecipua boni operis per gratiam suam."

60. *Enarratio* 1.287b–288a: "Secundum nostrum intelligendi modum ita oportet considerare in Deo. *Prius* intellectu suo vidit omnes homines capaces beatitudinis, simul videns media et auxilia, quibus, si ipsi vellent, consequi possent gloriam et beatitudinem talem. *Secundo* voluit homines ipsos facere (et rursus dare media sufficientia consequendi beatitudinem, si ipsi velint et adhibeant) quod in se est. *Tertio* voluit his, qui, quod in se est, faciunt, et datis mediis utuntur, dare gloriam; hos vero, qui non, sed eis abutuntur, reiicere. *Quarto* cognovit in sua praescientia, qui hi, qui illi essent; et tunc voluntate sua immutabili elegit quosdam ex praevisis bonis operibus cum gratia sua, reprobavit alios ex praevisis iniquitatibus."

One notices in this explanation of his own position that de Toledo does not avoid saying what Thomas says we ought not to say, that is, that God does something "because of [*propter*]" something else; in fact, de Toledo says twice that God reproves or predestines "because of [*propter*]" foreseen good or evil acts. One cannot really say that de Toledo contradicts Thomas, for he understands all of this as occurring "in God," and God, also according to de Toledo, is absolutely simple (without articulated thoughts).[61] What this does, however, is to put all the action of predestination in the mind of God, even "the foreseen good acts" which (as he says in the proximate-primary thesis) are "the proximate reason of predestination." This is to eliminate Thomas's understanding of how God is present in that which occurs in the physical-temporal universe. Thomas says, God "wills this to *be* because of [*propter*] that, but not because of [*propter*] this does he will that."[62] It also, therefore, eliminates Thomas's explanation of how the effect of both grace and free will can be "one and the same thing from both."[63]

Finally, it so emphasizes "the unique will of God" as the primary and supreme reason of predestination that the proximate reason—"foreseen good acts," the products of human free will—pales into insignificance. Since, then, as we have seen a number of times, de Toledo understands God as expressing his supreme authority—and will—in the Church,[64] it is not at all surprising that de Toledo is open to the idea that the Church (or those she sanctions) might coerce toward the faith.

"Modo si rationem petas proximam: quare hunc elegit, non illum? dico, quia in illo opera bona, in hoc mala praevidit. At si rursus: quare propter bona opera eligit, propter mala reprobat? dico, quia sic voluit et statuit: tanquam ergo iustus facit. Rursus: quare ipse hoc ita voluit? dicam ultimo, quia sic placitum est illi. Vide supremam rationem divinam voluntatem liberam; vide proximam opera bona vel mala praevisa.

"Attende rursus, quod dico rationem, non causam; quia causa non dicitur proprie in Deo, sed ratio, secundum quod dicimus: praescientia est ratio volitionis, et unum est ratio alterius. Nec merita nostra obligant Deum ad praedestinandum, sed quia ipse sic vult. Ob hoc multi antiqui Doctores negaverunt causam praedestinationis, sed dixerunt esse rationem aliquam. Dic ergo, quod reprobat propter mala opera, praedestinat propter bona praevisa." (I have altered the punctuation of the sentence beginning "*Secundo*.")

61. See *Enarratio* 1.85–89.
62. See above, note 44.
63. See above, note 49.
64. As noted above, at *Enarratio* 2.105b, de Toledo asserts that "the *Church* has the right of punishing and castigating even by death" those who impede the preaching of the Gospel. Also, at *Enarratio* 2.110b, he says that "the Church, which has accepted from Christ justice and power, quite properly uses severity against evil ones."

Conclusion

To conclude then and to summarize, it is apparent that Francisco de Toledo is considerably more open to the use of coercion with respect to faith than is Thomas Aquinas. His understanding of canon 14 of the Council of Trent's seventh session fails to recognize that it condemns those who would oppose coercion even, for instance, of efforts to promote justice. This failure to recognize the distinction between coercion regarding faith itself and coercion to promote the justice which even non-Christians are obliged to respect entails an understanding of Trent's canon as countering *simply* opposition to coercion regarding the faith—or, conversely, as defending such coercion. By taking this line, de Toledo allows greater limitation of religious liberty than would Thomas Aquinas, according to remarks that the latter makes in his commentary on Peter Lombard's *Sentences* and in the *Summa Theologiae*.

One sees this greater tolerance for limitations on religious liberty in de Toledo's interpretation of ST II-II, q. 10, a. 8, although it becomes even more apparent in his remarks regarding God's predestination of some to glory, others to reprobation. Unlike his treatment of Thomas's remarks on religious liberty in the *Summa*, de Toledo's treatment of predestination is explicitly divergent from Thomas's. Thomas puts forward a metaphysically subtle analysis of the relationship between God's predestination that avoids any downplaying of the role of free will in man's act of faith; de Toledo's approach so emphasizes God's power that free will fades into theoretical insignificance. And, since he also sees God as bestowing that same power upon the Church, which can then delegate it to secular authorities, the result is even more manifestly a theory that would permit coercion with respect to the faith.

Works Cited

Primary Sources

Albertus Magnus. *Alberti Magni Opera omnia*. Edited by Auguste Borgnet and Êmile Borgnet. 38 vols. Paris: Vivès, 1890–1899.

Ambrose of Milan. *Theological and Dogmatic Works*. Translated by Roy J. Deferrari. Fathers of the Church, vol. 44. Washington, DC: The Catholic University of America Press, 1963.

Aquaviva, Claudio. "The Official Directory of 1599." In *On Giving the Spiritual Exercises: The Early Jesuit Manuscript Directories and the Official Directory of 1599*. Edited and translated by Martin E. Palmer. St. Louis, MO: Institute of Jesuit Sources, 1996.

Aquinas, Thomas. *Commentary on Aristotle's Nicomachean Ethics*. Translated by C. I. Litzinger. 1964. Reprint, Notre Dame, IN: Dumb Ox Books, 1993.

———. *Commentary on Aristotle's Politics*. Translated by Richard J. Regan. Indianapolis, IN: Hackett, 2007.

———. *Commentary on Romans*. Translated by Fabian R. L'Archer. Steubenville, OH: Emmaus Academic, 2020.

———. *Commentary on the Sentences Book IV, 1–13*. Translated by Beth Mortensen. Green Bay, WI: Aquinas Institute, Inc., 2017.

———. *De Regno*. Translated by Gerard B. Phelan. Toronto: Pontifical Institute of Medieval Studies, 1949.

———. *De Veritate*. Text available at https://www.corpusthomisticum.org/iopera.html.

———. *Devotissima Expositio super Salutatione Angelica. Opuscula Theologica*. Vol. 2. Rome: Marietti, 1954.

———. *Devoutly I Adore Thee*. Translated and edited by Robert Anderson and Johann Moser. Manchester, NH: Sophia Institute Press, 1933.

———. *Expositio in Evangelium Joannis*. Text available at https://www.corpusthomisticum.org/iopera.html.

———. *Expositio Libri Posteriorum Analyticorum*. Text available at https://www.corpusthomisticum.org/iopera.html.

———. *Opera Omnia*. Vol. 11, *Tertia Pars a quaestione LX ad quaestionem XC, cum commentariis Thomae de Vio Caietani*. Rome: Ex Typographia Polyglotta, 1906.

———. *Opera Omnia*. Vol. 14, *In psalmos Davidis expositio*. Typis Petri Fiaccadori: Parmae, 1863.

———. *Opera Omnia*. Vol. 27, *Opuscula varia*. Paris: Vives, 1875.

———. *Scriptum super Libros Sententiarum Magistri Petri Lombardi Episcopi Parisiensis*. Edited by Pierre Mandonnet and Maria Fabianus Moos. Paris: Lethielleux, 1929–1947.

———. *Sententia libri de Anima*. Text available at https://www.corpus thomisticum.org/iopera.html.

———. *Somme théologique*. Translated by Jean-Pierre Torrell. Paris: Éditions du Cerf, 1985.

———. *Summa Theologiae*. 61 vols. Edited by Blackfriars. New York: McGraw-Hill, 1963–1980.

———. *Summa contra Gentiles Book Four: Salvation*. Translated by Charles J. O'Neil. Notre Dame, IN: University of Notre Dame Press, 1975.

———. *Super Epistolas S. Pauli Lectura*. Book 1, *Super Primam Epistolam ad Corinthios Lectura*. Edited by R. Cai. 8th ed. Taurini-Romae: Marietti, 1953.

———. *Super Iob*. Text available at https://www.corpusthomisticum.org/iopera.html.

———. *Thomas Aquinas's Quodlibetal Questions*. Translated by Turner Nevitt and Brian Davies. Oxford: Oxford University Press, 2020.

Augustine of Hippo. *Epistulae I–LV*. Edited by K. D. Daur. CCSL 31. Turnhout: Brepols, 2004.

———. *Sancti Aurelii Augustini Hipponiensis episcopi: Epistulae: Pars II, Ep. XXXI–CXXIII*. Edited by Alois Goldbacher. CSEL 34.2. Vienna: Tempsky, 1898.

———. *Sancti Aurelii Augustini Hipponiensis episcopi: Epistulae: Pars IV, Ep. CLXXXV–CCLXX*. Edited by Alois Goldbacher. CSEL 57. Vienna: Tempsky, 1911.

———. *In Iohannis Evangelium Tractatus*. Edited by Radbodus Willems. CCSL 36. Turnhout: Brepols, 1954.

———. *Sancti Aurelii Augustini Opera Omnia, Tomus quartus, Pars prior; pars altera*. Edited by the Congregation of Saint Maur. PL 36–37. Paris: J. P. Migne, 1865.

———. *Letters 1–99*. Translated by Roland Teske. Edited by Boniface Ramsey. Works of Saint Augustine II, vol. 1. Hyde Park, NY: New City Press, 2001.

Bellarmine, Robert. *Tractatus de Obedientia, quae caeca nominatur*. In *Auctarium Bellarminianum: Supplément aux Oeuvres du Cardinal Bellarmin*. Paris: Gabriel Beauchesne, 1913.

Bernard of Clairvaux. *Sermons on the Blessed Virgin Mary*. Chulmleigh, UK: Augustine, 1984.

Bobadilla, Nicholas Alphonsus. *Bobadillae monumenta: Nicolai Alphonsi de Bobadilla, sacerdotis e Societate Jesu, gesta et scripta ex autographis aut archetypis potissimum deprompta*. MHSI 46. Madrid: Typis Gabrielis Lopez del Horno, 1913.

Bonaventure. *Commentary on the Sentences: Sacraments*. Works of Bonaventure, vol. 17. Translated by J. A. Wayne Hellman, Timothy R. LeCroy, and Luke Davis Townsend. St. Bonaventure, NY: Franciscan Institute Publications, 2016.

———. *The Mirror of the Blessed Virgin Mary and the Psalter of Our Lady*. Translated by Sr. Mary Emmanuel. St. Louis, MO: Herder, 1932.

———. *Opera Omnia*. Vols. 4–8. Quaracchi: Collegii S. Bonaventurae, 1891–1898.

———. *Works of St. Bonaventure*. Vol. 5. Translated by Dominic Monti. St. Bonaventure, NY: The Franciscan Institute, 1994.

Cano, Melchor. *De Locis Theologicis*. Salamanca: Mathius Gastius, 1563.

Cicero. *Tusculan Disputations*. Loeb Classical Library 141. Edited and translated by J. E. King. Cambridge, MA: Harvard University Press, 1945.

Concilium Tridentinum: Diariorum, actorum, epistularum, tractatuum nova collectio. Freiburg im Breisgau: Herder, 1901–2001.

Constitutiones Societatis Iesu et normae complementariae. Rome: Curia Praepositi Generalis Societatis Iesu, 1995. English translation: *The Constitutions of the Society of Jesus and Their Complementary Norms: A Complete English Translation of the Official Latin Texts*. Translated by George Ganss, SJ. St. Louis, MO: The Institute of Jesuit sources, 1996.

Descartes, René. *The Passions of the Soul*. Translated by S. H. Voss. Indianapolis: Hackett, 1989.

Epistolae mixtae ex variis Europae locis ab anno 1537 ad 1556 scriptae. 5 vols. MHSI 12, 14, 17, 18, 20. Madrid: Aügustinus Avrial, 1898–1901.

Erasmus, Desiderius. *Desiderii Erasmi Roterodami Opera Omnia*. Edited by Jean LeClerc. 10 vols. Leiden: Peter van der Aa, 1703–1706.

———. *Moriae Encomium*. In *Opera Omnia Desiderii Erasmi Roterodami*. Ordo IV, t. 3. Edited by Clarence H. Miller. Amsterdam: North-Holland, 1979. English translation in CWE 27, *Literary and Educational Writings 5*. Edited by A. H. T. Levi. Toronto: University of Toronto Press, 1988.

———. *Paraphrase on Matthew*. Edited and translated by Dean Simpson. CWE 45. Toronto: University of Toronto Press, 2008.

———. Preface to Hilary of Poitiers. In *The Correspondence of Erasmus: Letters 1252–1355*. Translated by John C. Olin and James F. Brady, Jr. CWE 9, 246–274. Toronto: University of Toronto Press, 1989.

Gratian. *Decretum Magistri Gratiani*. Vol. 1 of *Corpus Iuris Canonici*, edited by Aemilius Ludovicus Richter and Aemilius Friedberg. Leipzig: B. Tauchnitz, 1879. 2nd ed., 1922.

Gregory of Valencia. *Commentariorum Theologicorum Tomi Quatuor*. Vol. 1. Ingolstadt, 1603.

Ignatius of Loyola. *Ignatius of Loyola: Letters and Instructions*. Edited by John W. Padberg, SJ, and John L. McCarthy, SJ. Translated by Martin E. Palmer, SJ. St. Louis, MO: Institute of Jesuit Sources, 2006.

———. *Ignatius of Loyola: Spiritual Exercises and Selected Works*. Classics of Western Spirituality. Edited by George E. Ganss, SJ. New York: Paulist Press, 1991.

———. *Letters and Instructions of St. Ignatius of Loyola*. Vol. 1, *1524–1547*. Edited by A. Goodier. Translated by D. F. O'Leary. 1914. Reprint, New York: Cosimo, 2007.

———. *Monumenta Ignatiana ex autographis vel ex antiquioribus exemplis. Series Prima: Sancti Ignatii Epistolae et Instructiones. Tomus primus: 1524–1548*. MHSI 22. Madrid: Typis Gabrielis Lopez del Horno, 1903.

———. *Monumenta Ignatiana: Exercitia Spiritualia Sancti Ignatii de Loyola et eorum directoria*. MHSI 57. Madrid: Typis Successorum Rivadeneyrae, 1919.

———. *Monumenta Ignatiana, series secunda: Exercitia spiritualia S. Ignatii et eorum Directoria*. Nova editio. Tomus I, *Exercitia Spiritualia*. Edited by Josephus Calveras and Candidus de Dalmases. MHSI 100. Rome: IHSI, 1969.

———. *Monumenta Ignatiana, series tertia: Sancti Ignatii de Loyola Constitutiones Societatis Jesu*. Vol. 1, *Monumenta Constitutionum Praevia*. MHSI 63. Rome, IHSI, 1934.

———. *Obras Completas*. 2nd ed. Edited by Ignacio Iparraguirre and Candido de Dalmases. Madrid: Biblioteca de Autores Cristianos, 1963.

———. *The Spiritual Exercises of Saint Ignatius: A Translation and Commentary by George E. Ganss*. Translated and edited by George E. Ganss, SJ. St. Louis, MO: The Institute of Jesuit Sources, 1992.

———. *The Spiritual Exercises of Saint Ignatius of Loyola. Translated from the Spanish with a Commentary and a Translation of the* Directorium in Exercitia. Translated by William F. Longridge. London: Robert Scott, 1919.

———. *The Spiritual Exercises of St. Ignatius: Based on Studies in the Language of the Autograph*. Translated by Louis J. Puhl, SJ. 1951. Reprint, Chicago: Loyola University Press, 1961.

———. *Ignatius Writes to His Brethren: Fifty Selected Letters and Instructions of St. Ignatius of Loyola*. With commentary by Joseph N. Tylenda, SJ. St. Louis, MO: Institute of Jesuit Sources, 2006.

———. *Letters of St. Ignatius of Loyola.* Translated by William J. Young. Chicago: Loyola University Press, 1959.

———. *Personal Writings: Reminiscences, Spiritual Diary, Select Letters including the Text of the Spiritual Exercises.* Translated by Joseph A Munitiz, SJ, and Philip Endean, SJ London: Penguin, 2004.

Ludolph of Saxony. *Vita Jesu Christi.* Edited by A.-C. Bolard, L.-M. Rigollot, and J. Carnadet. Paris/Rome: Palmé, 1865.

Madridii, R. P. Christophori. *De Frequenti Usu Sanctissimi Eucharistiae Sacramenti Libellus.* Cologne: Apud Balthasarum Clypeum, 1604.

Mair, John. *In secundum sententiarum.* Paris: Badius, 1528.

More, Thomas. *The Complete Works of St. Thomas More,* vol. 15. Edited and translated by Daniel Kinney. New Haven, CT: Yale University Press, 1986.

Nadal, Jerome. *Commentarii de Instituto Societatis Iesu.* Edited by Michael Nicolau. MHSI 90. Rome: MHSI, 1962.

———. *Epistolae P. Hieronymi Nadal Societatis Jesu ab anno 1546 ad 1577.* 5 vols. Madrid, 1898–1905.

———. *Evangelicae historiae imagines ex ordine euangeliorum, quae toto anno in missae sacrificio recitantur, in ordinem temporis vitae Christi digestae.* Edited by IHSI. Sassari, Italy: Casa editrice Scriptorium, 2002.

———. *Orationis Observationes.* Edited by Miguel Nicolau. MHSI 90A. Rome: IHSI, 1964.

———. *Las pláticas del P. Jerónimo Nadal: La globalización ignaciana.* Edited and translated by Miguel Lop Sebastià, SJ. Bilbao, Spain: Mensajero, 2011.

———. *Scholia in Constitutiones S.I.* Edited by Manuel Ruiz Jurado. Granada: Facultad de Teologia, 1976.

Peter Lombard. *Sententiae in IV libris distinctae.* 3rd rev. ed. Edited by Ignatius C. Brady. 2 vols. Grottaferrata: Collegii S. Bonaventurae ad Claras Aquas, 1971–1981.

———. *The Sentences. Book 4: On the Doctrine of Signs.* Translated by Giulio Silano. Mediaeval Sources in Translation, vol. 48. Toronto: Pontifical Institute of Mediaeval Studies, 2010.

Polanco, Juan Alfonso de. *Vita Ignatii Loiolae et rerum Societatis Jesu historia, auctore Joanne Alphonso de Polanco, ejusdem societatis sacerdote.* 6 vols. MHSI 1, 3, 5, 7, 9, 11. Madrid: Typographorum societas, 1894–1898.

Pseudo-Dionysius. *Corpus Dionysiacum.* Vol. 2, *De coelesti hierarchia. De ecclesiastica hierarchia. De mystica theologia. Epistulae.* Edited by Günter Heil and Adolf Martin Ritter. Patristische Texte und Studien 36. Berlin: De Gruyter, 1991.

———. *Pseudo-Dionysius: The Complete Works*. Translated by Colm Lubheid. Classics of Western Spirituality. New York: Paulist, 1987.

Ribadeneyra, Pedro de. *Monumenta Ignatiana. Series quarta. Scripta de S. Ignatio. Fontes narrativi de Sancto Ignatio de Loyola et de Societatis Iesu initiis*. Vol. 4, *Vita Ignatii Loyolae*. MHSI 93. Edited by Candidus de Dalmases. Rome: MHSI, 1965.

Salmerón, Alfonso. *Commentarii in Evangelicam Historiam et in Acta Apostolorum*. Madrid, 1598; Cologne: Antonius Hierat and Johannes Gynmnicus, 1612–1614.

Soto, Domingo de. "De Dominio." In *Relecciones y opusculos*. Edited and translated by Jaime Brufau Prats, 99–192. Salamanca: Editorial Sebastian, 1995.

Suárez, Francisco. *Opera Omnia*. Edited by Charles Berton. Paris: Luis Vives, 1856.

Tanner, Norman P., SJ, ed. *Decrees of the Ecumenical Councils*. 2 vols. Washington, DC: Georgetown University Press, 1990.

Toledo, Francisco de. *Commentarii et Annotationes in Epistolam B. Pauli Apostoli Ad Romanos*. Rome: Sumptibus Paulini Arnolofini Lucensis, 1602.

———. *In Summam Theologiae St. Thomae Aquinatis Enarratio*, vol. 2. Rome: Typis S. Congraegationis de Propoganda Fide, 1869–1870.

Vázquez, Gabriel. *Commentariorum ac disputationionum in Summam S. Thomae tomus primus*. Alcalá, 1598.

Vitoria, Francisco de. "On the American Indians." In *Political Writings*. Edited by Anthony Pagden and Jeremy Lawrence, 231–84. Cambridge: Cambridge University Press, 1991.

Wesley, Charles. *Hymns for Those That Seek, and Those That Have Redemption in the Blood of Jesus Christ*. London: Strahan, 1747.

Xavier, Francis. *Monumenta Xaveriana, ex autographis vel ex antiquioribus exemplis collecta*. 2 vols. Madrid, Typis Augustini Avrial, 1899–1900.

———. *Francis Xavier: His Life, His Times*. 2 vols. Translated by Joseph Costelloe. Rome: Jesuit Historical Institute, 1973.

Secondary Sources

Alburquerque, Antonio. *Diego Lainez, SJ: First Biographer of Saint Ignatius of Loyola*. Translated by John Montag. St. Louis, MO: Institute of Jesuit Sources, 2010.

Aldama, Antonio M. de. *The Constitutions of the Society of Jesus: Jesuit Religious Life*. Translated by Ignacio Echániz, SJ. St. Louis, MO: Institute of Jesuit Sources, 1995.

———. *The Constitutions of the Society of Jesus: Missioning*. Translated by Ignacio Echániz, SJ. St. Louis, MO: Institute of Jesuit Sources, 1996.

Alonso-Schökel, Luis. *The Inspired Word: Scripture in the Light of Language and Literature*. New York: Herder and Herder, 1965.

Andrés, Melquiades. "*Alumbrados*, Erasmians, 'Lutherans', and Mystics: The Risks of a More 'Intimate' Spirituality." In *The Spanish Inquisition and the Inquisitorial Mind*, edited by Ángel Alcalá. Translated by Esther da Costa-Frankel, 457–94. Highland Lakes, NJ: Atlantic Research and Publications, 1987.

Astell, Ann W. *Eating Beauty: The Eucharist and the Spiritual Arts in the Middle Ages*. Ithaca, NY: Cornell University Press, 2006.

Augé, Robert. *Connaître Dieu par expérience: la connaissance expérimentale de Dieu selon saint Thomas d'Aquin, coll. Sed Contra*. Paris: Artège-Lethielleux, 2016.

Aumann, Jordan. *Spiritual Theology*. Huntington, IN: Our Sunday Visitor Press, 1980.

Balthasar, Hans Urs von. *The Glory of the Lord: A Theological Aesthetics*. Vol. 1, *Seeing the Form*. San Francisco: Ignatius Press, 1983.

———. *The Glory of the Lord: A Theological Aesthetics*. Vol. 5, *The Realm of Metaphysics in the Modern Age*. Translated by Oliver Davies, et al. Edited by Brian McNeil, C.R.V., and John Riches. San Francisco: Ignatius Press, 1991.

Bangert, William V. *Claude Jay and Alfonso Salmerón: Two Early Jesuits*. Chicago: Loyola University Press, 1985.

Bangert, William V. and Thomas M. McCoog. *Jerome Nadal, SJ 1507–1580: Tracking the First Generation of Jesuits*. Chicago: Loyola University Press, 1992.

Barclay, John M. G. *Paul and the Gift*. Grand Rapids, MI: Eerdmans, 2015.

Barron, Robert. Introduction to *Ignatian Collection* by Ignatius of Loyola, Gerard Manley Hopkins, and St. Francis Xavier. Edited by Holly Ordway and Daniel Seseske. Translated by Louis J. Puhl, SJ. Park Ridge, IL: Word on Fire, 2020.

———. *Thomas Aquinas, Spiritual Master*. New York: Crossroad, 1996.

Bartók, Tibor. *Un interprète et une interprétation: Le Père Louis Lallemant et sa Doctrine spirituelle au carrefour de l'histoire, de l'analyse institutionnelle et de la pensée d'auteurs jésuites antérieurs et contemporains*. Rome: Gregorian & Biblical Press, 2016.

Bataillon, Marcel. "D'Érasme a la Compagnie de Jésus." *Archives de sociologie des religions* 24 (1967): 57–81.

Bauerschmidt, Frederick Christian. "Imagination and Theology in Thomas Aquinas." *Louvain Studies* 34 (2009–2010): 169–84.

Bedouelle, Guy. "Attacks on the Biblical Humanism of Jacques Lefèvre d'Étaples." In *Biblical Humanism and Scholasticism in the Age of Erasmus*, edited by Erika Rummel, translated by Anna Machado-Matheson, 117–41. Leiden: Brill, 2008.

Beguiriztáin, Justo. *The Eucharistic Apostolate of St. Ignatius Loyola.* Translated by John H. Collins. Cambridge, MA: B. Herder, 1955.

———. *Ignacio de Loyola: apóstol de la comunión frecuente.* Barcelona: E. Subirana, 1909.

Black, Christopher F. *Italian Confraternities in the Sixteenth Century.* Cambridge: Cambridge University Press, 2003 (hardback ed., 1989).

Blankenhorn, Bernhard-Thomas. "The Good as Self-Diffusive in Thomas Aquinas." *Angelicum* 79 (2002): 800–837.

———. *The Mystery of Union with God: Dionysian Mysticism in Albert the Great and Thomas Aquinas.* Thomistic Ressourcement 4. Washington DC: The Catholic University of America Press, 2015.

Blignières, Louis-Marie de. "L'obéissance du jugement." *Sedes Sapientiae* 126 (2013): 43–69.

Boeft, Jan de. "Erasmus and the Church Fathers." In *The Reception of The Church Fathers in the West: From the Carolingians to the Maurists*, edited by Irena Backus, 537–72. Leiden: Brill 1997.

Boguslawski, Steven C. *Thomas Aquinas on the Jews: Insights into His Commentary on Romans, 9–11.* Mahwah, NJ: Paulist Press, 2008.

Bohineust, Hughes. *Obéissance du Christ, obéissance du chrétien: Christologie et morale chez saint Thomas d'Aquin.* Paris: Éditions Parole et Silence, 2017.

Boland, Vivian. "*Non Solum Discens Sed et Patiens Divina*: The Wanderings of an Aristotelian Fragment." In *Roma, magistra mundi: Itineraria culturae medievalis: Mélanges offerts au Père L.E. Boyle à l'occasion de son 75e anniversaire*, edited by Jaqueline Hamesse, 55–69. Turnhout: Brepols, 1998.

Bonacci, Louis, *The Marian Presence in the Life and Works of Saint Ignatius Loyola: From Private Revelation to Spiritual Exercises—The Cloth of Loyola's Allegiance.* PhD diss., International Marian Research Institute at the University of Dayton, 2002.

Bonino, Serge-Thomas. "Rôle de l'image dans la connaissance prophétique d'après Saint Thomas d'Aquin." *Revue Thomiste* 89, no. 4 (1989): 533–68.

Boulay, C. E. du. *Historia Universitatis Parisiensis.* 6 vols. Paris, Typographum Reginae ordinarium & Bibliopolam juratum Universitatis Parisiensis, 1665–1673.

Brann, Eva. *Feeling Our Feelings: What Philosophers Think and People Know.* Philadelphia: Paul Dry Books, 2008.

Bremond, Henri. *Histoire littéraire du sentiment religieux en France depuis la fin des guerres de religion jusqu'à nos jours jours.* Vol. 3, *La conquête mystique: L'école française*; vol. 5, *L'école du Père Lallemant et la tradition mystique dans la Compagnie de Jésus.* Paris: Bloud et Gay, 1920.

Brett, Annabel. "Later Scholastic Philosophy of Law." In *A Treatise of Legal Philosophy and General Jurisprudence*. Vol. 6, *A History of the Philosophy of Law from the Ancient Greeks to the Scholastics*, edited by Fred D. Miller Jr. and Carrie-Ann Biondi, 337–38. New York: Springer, 2015.

Brown, Benjamin. "The Integration of Law and Virtue: Obedience in Aquinas's Moral Theology." *Irish Theological Quarterly* 67 (2002): 333–51.

Buser, Thomas. "Jerome Nadal and Early Jesuit Art in Rome." *The Art Bulletin* 58, no. 3 (1976): 424–33.

Butler, Richard. *Religious Vocation: An Unnecessary Mystery*. 1961. Reorint, Rockford, IL: TAN, 2005.

Caldera, Rafael-Thomas. *Le Jugement par Inclination chez Saint Thomas D'Aquin*. Paris: Vrin, 1980.

Calveras, J. *San Ignacio en Montserrat y Manresa, a través de los procesos de canonización*. Barcelona: Editorial Libreria religiosa, 1956.

Câmara, Luís Gonçalves da. *Remembering Iñigo: Glimpses of the Life of Saint Ignatius Loyola*. Translated by Alexander Eaglestone and Joseph A. Munitiz. St. Louis, MO: Gracewing, 2004.

Campbell, Thomas J. *Jesuits, 1534–1921: A History of the Society of Jesus*. New York: Encyclopedia Press, 1921.

Cañellas, Juan Nadal. *Jerónimo Nadal: Vida e influjo*. Bilbao, Spain: Mensajero, 2007.

Carruthers, Mary. *The Book of Memory: A Study of Memory in Medieval Culture*. 2nd ed. Cambridge: Cambridge University Press, 2002.

———. *The Craft of Thought: Meditation, Rhetoric, and the Making of Images, 400–1200*. Cambridge: Cambridge University Press, 1998.

Castro Valdés, José García de. "Companionship in the Spirit. A History of the Spirituality of the Society of Jesus." *Estudios Eclesiásticos* 91, no. 356 (2016): 87–141.

Cates, Diana Fritz. *Aquinas on the Emotions: A Religious-Ethical Inquiry*. Washington, DC: Georgetown University Press, 2009.

Catto, Michela. *La Compagnia divisa: Il dissenso nell'ordine gesuitico tra '500 e '600*. Brescia, Italy: Editrice Morcelliana, 2009.

———. "The Jesuit Memoirists: How the Company of Jesus Contributed to Anti-Jesuitism." In *Los jesuitas: Religión, política y educación (siglos XVI–XVIII)*, edited by José Martínez Millán, Henar Pizarro Llorente, and Esther Jiménez Pablo, 927–41. Madrid: Comillas, 2012.

Cereceda, Feliciano. "En el cuarto centenario del nascimento del P. Francisco Toledo." *Estudios eclesiásticos: Revista de investigación e información teológica y canónica* 13 (1934): 90–110.

Cessario, Romanus. "Molina and Aquinas." In *A Companion to Luis de Molina*, edited by Matthias Kaufmann and Alexander Aichele, 291–323. Leiden: Brill, 2014.

———. "Sacrifice, Social and Sacramental: The Witness of Louis Billot, SJ." *Nova et Vetera* 14 (2016): 127–49.

Cessario, Romanus and Cajetan Cuddy. *Thomas and the Thomists: The Achievement of Thomas Aquinas and His Interpreters*. Minneapolis, MN: Fortress Press, 2017.

Chadwick, Owen. *From Bossuet to Newman*. 2nd ed. Cambridge: Cambridge University Press, 1987.

Chantraine, Pierre. *Dictionnaire étymologique de la langue grecque*. Paris: Klincksieck, 1968–1980.

Chenu, M-D. *La Théologie comme Science au XIIIe Siècle*. 3rd ed. Paris: Vrin, 1957.

Chesterton, G. K. *St. Thomas Aquinas*. Mineola, NY: Dover Publications, 2009.

Clarke, W. Norris. *The One and the Many: A Contemporary Thomistic Metaphysics*. Notre Dame, IN: University of Notre Dame Press, 2001.

Cline, Erin M. *A World on Fire: Sharing the Ignatian Spiritual Exercises with Other Religions*. Washington, DC: The Catholic University of America Press, 2018.

Cohen, Jeremy. *Living Letters of the Law: Ideas of the Jew in Medieval Christianity*. Berkeley: University of California Press, 1999.

———. "Supersessionism, the Epistle to the Romans, Thomas Aquinas, and the Jews of the Eschaton." *Journal of Ecumenical Studies* 52, no. 4 (Fall 2017): 527–53.

Cole, Basil. "Consecrated Obedience and Spirituality." *Angelicum* 73 (1996): 569–87.

Colish, Marcia L. *Faith, Force and Fiction in Medieval Baptismal Debates*. Washington, DC: The Catholic University of America Press, 2014.

———. *Peter Lombard*. 2 vols. Brill Studies in Intellectual History 41. Leiden: Brill, 1994.

Colunga, Emilio. "Intelectualistas y místicos en la Teología española del siglo XVI." *Ciencia Tomista* 9 (1914): 209–21.

———. "Intelectualistas y místicos en la Teología española del siglo XVI." *Ciencia Tomista* 10 (1915): 377–94.

Combes, André. "Le P. John F. Dedek et la connaissance quasi-experimentale des Personnes divines selon Saint Thomas d'Aquin." *Divinitas* 7, no. 1 (1963): 3–83.

Conedera, Sam Zeno. "Forgotten Saint: The Life and Writings of Alfonso Salmerón, SJ." *Studies in the Spirituality of Jesuits* 52, no. 4 (2020): 1–34.

Congar, Yves. "Aspects ecclésiologiques de la querelle entre mendiants et séculiers dans la seconde moitié du XIIIe siècle et le début du XIVe." *Archives d'histoire doctrinale et littéraire du Moyen Age* 28 (1961): 35–151.

———. *L'Église de saint Augustin à l'époque moderne*. Histoire du Dogma, vol. 3, part 3. Paris: Éditions du Cerf, 1970.

———. *Tradition and the Traditions: An Historical and Theological Essay*. 2 vols. Translated by Michael Naseby and Thomas Rainborough. London: Burns and Oates, 1966.

Coolman, Holly Taylor. "Romans 9–11: Rereading Aquinas on the Jews." In *Reading Romans with St. Thomas Aquinas*, edited by Matthew Levering, 103–5. Washington, DC: The Catholic University of America Press, 2012.

Cooper, Adam G. "Hierarchy, Humility, and Holiness: The Meaning of Ecclesial Ranks according to Dionysius the Areopagite." *Nova et Vetera* 11, vol. 3 (2013): 649–61.

Copleston, Frederick. *Aquinas*. London: Penguin Books, 1955.

Cordonier, Valérie. *Aristoteles Latinus, Ethica Eudemica (fragmentum); Liber de bona fortuna, Translatio Moerbekana, Recensio Vulgata, textus praevius praeparatus a Valérie Cordonier*. Series "Aristoteles Latinus Database." Release 3 (ALD-3), 2016.

Coroleu, Alejando. "Anti-Erasmianism in Spain." In *Biblical Humanism and Scholasticism and Scholasticism in the Age of Erasmus*, edited by Erika Rummel, translated by Anna Machado-Matheson, 73–92. Leiden: Brill, 2008.

Courtine, Jean-François. *Suarez et le système de la métaphysique*. Paris: PUF Epiméthée, 1990.

Cros, L. Joseph-Marie. "Saint Ignace de Loyola et la Communion Quotidienne." *Études* 115 (April, May, June, 1908): 752–65.

Daley, Brian. *Mary on the Eve of the Council*. Notre Dame University Press, 2017.

Decloux, Simon. "Our Lady in Ignatian Spirituality: Mary in the Spiritual Diary of St. Ignatius." *Centrum Ignatianum Spiritualitatis* 19 (1988): 1–144.

Dedek, John F. *Experimental Knowledge of the Indwelling Trinity: An Historical Study of the Doctrine of St. Thomas*. Mundelein, IL: Saint Mary of the Lake Seminary, 1958.

———. "*Quasi Experimentalis Cognitio*: A Historical Approach to the Meaning of St. Thomas." *Theological Studies* 22 (Sept. 1961): 357–90.

Dekoninck, Ralph. "Jesuit Emblematics Between Theory and Practice." *Jesuit Historiography Online*. Brill, 2017. https://referenceworks.brillonline.com/entries/jesuit-historiography-online/jesuit-emblematics-between-theory-and-practice-COM_192540.

Denzinger, Henrich, Peter Hünermann, and Helmut Hoping, eds. *Enchiridion Symbolorum Definitionum et Declarationum de Rebus Fidei et Morum*. Freiburg im Breisgau: Herder, 2009.

Dhôtel, Jean-Claude. Introduction to *Récit écrit par le Père Louis Gonçalves aussitôt qu'il l'eut recueilli de la bouche même du Père Ignace*, by Ignace de Loyola, 9–41. Paris: Desclée de Brouwer-Bellarmin, 1988.

Donnelly, John Patrick. "Religious Orders for Men." In *The Cambridge History of Christianity*. Vol. 6, *Reform and Expansion 1500–1660*, edited by R. Po-Chia Hsia, 162–79. Cambridge: Cambridge University Press, 2007.

———. "Toledo, Francisco de." In *Diccionario Histórico de la Companía de Jesús, Biográfico-Temático*, edited by Charles E. O'Neill and Joaquín M. Domínguez, 3807–8. Rome: Institutum Historicum, S.I., 2001.

Dougherty, Joseph. *From Altar-Throne to Table: The Campaign for Frequent Holy Communion in the Catholic Church*. ATLA Monograph Series 50. Lanham, MD: Scarecrow Press, 2010.

Doyle, John P. *Collected Studies on Francisco Suárez, SJ (1548–1617)*. Edited by Victor Salas. Leuven: Leuven University Press, 2010.

Drews, Wolfram. *The Unknown Neighbour: The Jew in the Thought of Isidore of Seville*. Leiden: Brill, 2006.

Dublanchy, E. "Communion Fréquente." In *Dictionnaire de Théologie Catholique*. Vol. 3, *Clarke–Czepanski*. Paris, 1908.

Dulles, Avery. *The Assurance of Things Hoped For: A Theology of Christian Faith*. Oxford: Oxford University Press, 1994.

———. "Saint Ignatius and the Jesuit Theological Tradition." *Studies in the Spirituality of Jesuits* 14, no. 2 (March 1982): 1–21.

———. "The Theology of Worship: Saint Thomas." In *Rediscovering Aquinas and the Sacraments: Studies in Sacramental Theology*, edited by Matthew Levering and Michael Dauphinais, 1–13. Chicago: Hillenbrand Books, 2009.

Egan, Harvey D. *The Spiritual Exercises and the Ignatian Mystical Horizon*. St. Louis, MO: Institute of Jesuit Studies, 1976.

———. *Ignatius Loyola The Mystic*. Wilmington, DE: Michael Glazier, 1987.

Endean, Philip. "Our Lady and the Graces of the Fourth Week." *The Way Supplement* 99 (2000): 44–60.

———. "Who Do You Say Ignatius Is? Jesuit Fundamentalism and Beyond." *Studies in the Spirituality of Jesuits* 19, no. 5 (November 1987): 1–53.

English, John. *Spiritual Freedom: From an Experience of the Ignatian Exercises to the Art of Spiritual Guidance*. 2nd ed. Chicago: Loyola University Press, 1995.

Emery, John. "Aquinas's Christology of Communication." In *Thomas Aquinas and the Crisis of Christology*, edited by Michael A. Dauphinais, Andrew Hofer, OP, and Roger W. Nutt, 171–94. Ave Maria, FL: Sapientia Press, 2021.

Erb, Heather McAdam. "'*Pati Divina*': Mystical Union in Aquinas." In *Faith, Scholarship, and Culture in the 21st Century*, edited by Alice Ramos and Marie George, 73–96. Washington, DC: The Catholic University of America Press, 2002.

Fabre, Pierre-Antoine. Introduction to "Journal des motions intérieures." In *Écrits*, by Ignace de Loyola, edited by Maurice Giuliani, 313–18. Paris: Desclée de Brouwer-Bellarmin, 1991.

———. "L'obéissance comme 'représentation' dans la Compagnie de Jésus." In *Negociar la obediencia: autoridad y consentimiento en el mundo ibérico en la Edad Moderna*, edited by Jean-Paul Zúñiga, 189–95. Granada: Comares, 2013.

———. *The Spiritual Writings of Pierre Favre: The Memoriale and Selected Letters and Instructions*. Translated by Edmond C. Murphy and Martin E. Palmer. St. Louis, MO: Institute of Jesuit Sources, 1996.

Fanfani, Ludovicus I. *De Confraternitaibus Aliisque Associationibus Ordini Fr. Praedicatorum Propriis. In Appendice de Confraternite SS. Sacramentum*. Rome: Apud Domum Generalitiam, 1934.

Farge, James K. *Biographical Register of Paris Doctors of Theology 1500–1536*. Toronto: PIMS, 1980.

———. "Noël Beda and the Defense of the Tradition." In *Biblical Humanism and Scholasticism in the Age of Erasmus*, edited by Erika Rummel, 143–64. Leiden: Brill, 2008.

———. *Orthodoxy and Reform in Early Reformation France: The Faculty of Theology of Paris (1500–1543)*. Studies in Medieval and Reformation Thought 32. Leiden: Brill, 1985.

———. "The University of Paris in the Time of Ignatius of Loyola." In *Ignacio de Loyola y Su Tiempo*, edited by Juan Plazaola, 221–43. Congreso Internacional de Historia, 9–13 Setiembre 1991. Bilbao, Spain: Mensajero, 1992.

———, ed. *Registre des Procès-Verbaux de la Faculté de Théologie de l'Université de Paris de janvier 1524 à novembre 1533*. Paris: Aux Amateurs de Livres, 1990.

Farkasfalvy, Denis. *The Marian Mystery: The Outline of a Mariology*. New York: St. Pauls, 2014.

Feingold, Lawrence. *The Eucharist: Mystery of Presence, Sacrifice, and Communion*. Steubenville, OH: Emmaus Academic, 2018.

Feldhay, Rivka. *From Knowledge and Faith to Science and Religion: The Jesuit Way to Modernity (2003–2005); Galileo and the Church: Political Inquisition or Critical Dialogue?* Cambridge: Cambridge University Press, 2008.

───. "The Use and Abuse of Mathematical Entities: Galileo and the Jesuits Revisited." In *A Companion to Galileo*, edited by P. Machamer, 80–146. Cambridge University Press, 1998.

───. "On Wonderful Machines: The Transmission of Mechanical Knowledge by Jesuits." *Science and Education* 15 (2006): 151–72.

Ferlita, Ernest C. "The Road to Bethlehem—Is It Level or Winding? The Use of the Imagination in the *Spiritual Exercises*." *Studies in the Spirituality of Jesuits* 29, no. 5 (1997): 1–23.

Fernández, Luis. "Íñigo de Loyola y Los Alumbrados." *Hispania Sacra* 35 (1983): 585–680.

Ferreyrolles, Gérard. *Les reines du monde: L'imagination et la coutume chez Pascal*. Paris: Honoré Champion, 1995.

Finnis, John. "John Finnis on Thomas Pink." In *Reason, Morality, and Law: The Philosophy of John Finnis*, edited by John Keown and Robert P. George, 574. Oxford: Oxford University Press, 2013.

Flannery, Kevin L. *Acts Amid Precepts: The Aristotelian Logical Structure of Thomas Aquinas's Moral Theory*. Washington, DC: The Catholic University of America Press, 2001.

Friedman, Jerome. "Jewish Conversion, the Spanish Pure Blood Laws, and Reformation." *The Sixteenth Century Journal* 18, no. 1 (Spring 1987): 3–30.

Frost, Robert. "Mending Wall" (1914). In *North of Boston*. Boston MA: Henry Holt & Co., 1917.

Füessli, Peter. *Peter Füesslis Jerusalemfahrt 1523 und Brief über den Fall von Rohodos 1522*. Zurich: Schulthess, 1981.

Gaetano, Matthew T. "The Catholic Reception of Aquinas in the *De auxiliis* Controversy." In *The Oxford Handbook of the Reception of Aquinas*, edited by Matthew Levering and Marcus Plested, 255–79. Oxford: Oxford University Press, 2021.

Gallagher, Michael Paul. *Clashing Symbols: An Introduction to Faith and Culture*. London: Darton, Longman and Todd, 1997.

Gallagher, Timothy M. *The Discernment of Spirits: An Ignatian Guide for Everyday Living*. New York: Crossroad, 2005.

───. *Overcoming Spiritual Discouragement: The Spiritual Teachings of Venerable Bruno Lanteri*. Manchester, NH: Sophia Institute Press, 2019.

García Villoslada, Ricardo. *La universidad de Paris durante los estudios de Victoria, OP (1507–1522)*. Rome: Gregorian University Press, 1938.

Garrigou-Lagrange, Réginald. *Christian Perfection and Contemplation according to St. Thomas Aquinas and St. John of the Cross*. Translated by Sr. Timothea Doyle. St. Louis, MO: Herder Books, 1937.

———. *De Christo Salvatore*. Torino-Roma: Marietti, 1946.

———. *De gratia: commentarius in Summam theologicam S. Thomae Iae Iiae q. 109–114*. Torino-Roma: Marietti, 1946.

———. *The Mother of the Savior*. Translated by B. Kelly. St. Louis, MO: Herder Books, 1948.

Giacon, Carlo. *Seconda Scolastica*. Vol. 2, *Precedenze teoretiche ai problemi giuridici*. Milan: Fratelli Bocca, 1946.

Gilmore, Myron P. "Valla, Érasme et Bédier a propos du Nouveau Testament." In *L'Humanisme Français au début de la Renaisaance*, edited by André Stegmann, 175–84. Paris: Vrin, 1973.

Giuliani, Maurice. "Le mystère de Notre Dame dans les Exercices." *Christus* 1 (July 1, 1954): 32–49.

Gomez-Menor, Jose. "La Progenie Hebrea del Padre Pedro de Ribadeneira, SJ." *Sefarad* 36, no. 2 (1976): 307–32.

Gondreau, Paul. "The Passions and the Moral Life: Appreciating the Originality of Aquinas." *The Thomist* 71, no. 3 (2007): 419–50.

———. *The Passions of Christ's Soul in the Theology of St. Thomas Aquinas*. Münster: Aschendorff Werlag Gmbh & Co., 2002. Reprint, Providence, RI: Cluny Media LLC, 2018.

Gratian. *Decretum Magistri Gratiani*. Vol. 1 of *Corpus Iuris Canonici*. Edited by Aemilius Ludovicus Richter and Aemilius Friedberg. Leipzig: B. Tauchnitz, 1879.

Graver, Margaret. *Stoicism and Emotions*. Chicago: University of Chicago Press, 2007.

Gregory, Brad. *The Unintended Reformation: How a Religious Revolution Secularized Society*. Cambridge, MA: Belknap Press, 2012.

Grendler, Paul F. *The Jesuits and Italian Universities*. Washington, DC: The Catholic University of America Press, 2017.

Guibert, Joseph de. *The Jesuits: Their Spiritual Doctrine and Practice*. Translated by William J. Young. Chicago: Institute of Jesuit Sources and Loyola Press, 1964.

Guillausseau, Axelle. "Les récits des miracles d'Ignace de Loyola. Un exemple du renouvellement des pratiques hagiographiques à la fin du XVIe siècle et au début du XVIIe siècle." *Mélanges de la Casa de Velázquez* 36, no. 2 (2006): 233–54.

Guiellet, Jacques, Gustave Bardy, Francois Vandenbroucke, eds. *Discernment of Spirits*. Collegeville, MN: The Liturgical Press, 1970.

Guy, Jean-Claude. "L'apparition à Notre Dame." *Christus* 95 (1977): 356–62.

Hall, Pamela M. "Towards a Narrative Understanding of Thomistic Natural Law." *Medieval Philosophy and Theology* 2 (1992): 53–73.

Hamel, J. Thomas. "Our Lady's Presence in the Spiritual Exercises." *Review for Religious* 63, no. 2 (2004): 182–91.

Hankey, Wayne. "Dionysian Hierarchy in Thomas Aquinas: Tradition and Transformation." In *Denys l'Aréopagite et sa postérité en Orient et en Occident*, edited by Y. de Andia, 405–38. Paris: Études Augustiniennes, 1996.

Hardon, John A. *All My Liberty: Theology of the Spiritual Exercises*. Bardstown, KY: Eternal Life, 1998.

———. "Historical Antecedents of St. Pius X's Decree on Frequent Communion." *Theological Studies* 16, no. 4 (1955): 493–522.

Heiding, Fredrik. "Our Lady, Lead us to Christ! Early Jesuit Devotion to Mary." *The Way* 50, no. 2 (April 2011): 25–35.

Heydt, Margo and Sarah Melcher. "Mary, the Hidden Catalyst: Reflections from an Ignatian Pilgrimage to Spain and Rome." In *Jesuit and Feminist Education: Intersections in Teaching and Learning from the Twenty-first Century*, edited by Joceyln Boryczka and Elizabeth Petrino, 37–55. New York: Fordham University Press, 2012.

Hofer, Andrew. "Dionysian Elements in the Christology of Thomas Aquinas: A Case of the Authority and Ambiguity of Pseudo-Dionysius." *The Thomist* 72, no. 3 (2008): 409–42.

———. "St. Thomas Aquinas on St. Benedict." *American Benedictine Review* 71 (2020): 410–34.

Homza, Lu Ann. "Hero or Heretic? Spanish Humanism and the Valladolid Assembly of 1527." *Renaissance Quarterly* 50 (1997): 78–118.

———, trans. *Spanish Inquisition, 1478–1614: An Anthology of Sources*. Indianapolis: Hackett, 2006.

Höpfl, Harro. "Ordered Passions: Commitment and Hierarchy in the Organizational Ideals of the Jesuit Founders." *Management Learning* 31, no. 3 (2000): 313–29.

Horst, Ulrich. *Bischöfe und Ordensleute: cura principalis animarum und via perfectionis in der Ekklesiologie des hl. Thomas von Aquin*. Berlin: Akademie Verlag, 1999.

———. *The Dominicans and the Pope: Papal Teaching Authority in the Medieval and Early Modern Thomist Tradition*. Translated by James D. Mixson. Notre Dame, IN: University of Notre Dame Press, 2006.

Huizinga, Johann. *Autumntide of the Middle Ages: A Study of Forms of Life and Thought of the Fourteenth and Fifteenth Centuries in France and the Low Countries*. Leiden: Leiden University Press, 2020.

Hull, Geoffrey. *The Banished Heart: Origins of Heteropraxis in the Catholic Church*. New York: T&T Clark, 2010.

Humphries, Thomas. "'These Words are Spirit and Life': Thomas's Use of Augustine in *Summa Theologiae*, III, 73–83." *Recherches de Théologie et Philosophie médiévales* 78, no. 1 (2011): 59–96.

Hurter, Hugo von, ed. *Nomenclator literarius theologiae Catholicae theologos exhibens aetate, natione, disciplinis distinctos*. Oeniponte Innsbruck: Libraria Academica Wagneriana, 1903–1913.

Idígoras, Ignacio Tellechea. "Censura inédita del Padre Francisco de Toledo, SJ" *Revista Española de Teología* 29 (1969): 15–19.

———, ed. *Bartolomé de Carranza: Documentos históricos*. Madrid: Real Academia de la Historia, 1981.

Iparraguirre, Ignacio. *Historia de la Práctica de los Ejercicios de San Ignacio de Loyola en Vida de su Autor (1522–1556)*, vol. 1. Roma: IHSI, 1946.

Ivens, Michael. *Understanding the Spiritual Exercises: Text and Commentary, A Handbook for Retreat Directors*. Trowbridge, England: Cromwell Press, 1998.

Izbicki, Thomas M. *The Eucharist in Medieval Canon Law*. New York: Cambridge University Press, 2015.

Jensen, Steven J. *The Human Person: A Beginner's Thomistic Psychology*. Washington, DC: The Catholic University of America Press, 2018.

Jiménez Pablo, Esther. *La forja de una identidad: La Compañía de Jesús (1540–1640)*. Madrid: Editorial Polifemo, 2014.

———. "El P. Alfonso Salmerón y el gobierno de los colegios de Nápoles." *Magallánica* 2, no. 4 (2016): 57–79.

Jurado, SJ, Manuel Ruiz. *Jerónimo Nadal: El teólogo de la gracia de la vocación*. Madrid: Biblioteca de Autores Cristianos, 2011.

Kahn, Nicholas. *Aquinas on Emotion's Participation in Reason*. Washington, DC: The Catholic University of America Press, 2019.

Kavanaugh, Aidan. *On Liturgical Theology: The Hale Memorial Lectures of Seabury-Western Theological Seminary 1981*. Collegeville, MN: Liturgical Press, 1984.

Kearney, Richard. *Poetics of Imagining: Modern to Post-Modern*. New York: Fordham University Press, 1998.

———. *The Wake of the Imagination: Toward a Post-Modern Culture*. London: Routledge 1988.

Keenan, James F. "The Birth of Jesuit Casuistry." In *The Mercurian Project: Forming Jesuit Culture, 1573–1580*, edited by Thomas M. McCoog, SJ, 461–82. Rome: IHSI, 2004.

Knight, David. "Joy and Judgment in Religious Obedience." *Studies in the Spirituality of Jesuits* 6 (1974): 131–67.

Knorn, Bernhard. "Theological Renewal after the Council of Trent? The Case of Jesuit Commentaries on the *Summa Theologiae*." *Theologial Studies* 79 (2018): 107–22.

Knuuttila, Simo. *Emotions in Ancient and Medieval Philosophy*. Oxford UK: Clarendon Press, 2004.

Kolvenbach, Peter-Hans. *Road from La Storta: Peter-Hans Kolvenbach, SJ, on Ignatian Spirituality*. St. Louis, MO: The Institute of Jesuit Sources, 2000.

Koning, Robin. "Revisiting the Marian Dimension of Ignatian Spirituality." In *Mariology at the Beginning of the Third Millennium*, edited by Kevin Wagner, et al, 140–62. Eugene, OR: Wipf and Stock, 2017.

König-Nordhoff, Ursula. *Ignatius von Loyola. Studien zur Entwicklung einer neuen Heiligen-Ikonographie im Rahmen einer Kanonisationskampagne um 1600*. Berlin: Gebr. Mann Verlag, 1982.

Korosac, B. *Mariologia sancti Alberti Magni eiusque coaequalium*. Rome: Acad. Mariana, 1954.

Kramp, Igna. "Der Jesuit Alfonso Salmerón (1515–1585) als humanistischer Theologe." *Theologie und Philosophie* 90 (2015): 504–27.

Kristeller, Paul Oskar. *Renaissance Thought: The Classic, Scholastic, and Humanist Strains*. New York: Harper and Row, 1961.

———. *Medieval Aspects of Renaissance Learning*. Rev. ed. Edited and translated by Edward P. Mahoney. New York: Columbia University Press, 1992.

Labourdette, Michel-Marie. "La vertu d'obeissance selon S. Thomas." *Revue thomiste* 57 (1957): 626–56.

Lafontaine, René. *L'originalité des Exercices d'Ignace de Loyola*. Namur-Paris: Éditions jésuites, 2016.

Lamont, John. "Tyranny and Sexual Abuse in the Catholic Church: A Jesuit Tragedy." *Rorate Caeli*. October 27, 2018. https://rorate-caeli.blogspot.com/2018/10/tyranny-and-sexual-abuse-in-catholic.html.

Lane, Dermot A. "Imagination and Theology: The *Status Quaestionis*." *Louvain Studies* 34 (2009–2010): 119–45.

Laplace, Jean. *An Experience of Life in the Spirit: Ten Days in the Tradition of the Spiritual Exercises*. Chicago: Veritas Publications, 1977.

Latourelle, René. "Teologia fondamentale." In *Dizionario di teologia fondamentale*, edited by René Latourelle and Rino Fisichella, 1248–58. Assisi: Citadella editrice, 1990.

Laurentin, René. *A Short Treatise on the Virgin Mary*. Washington, DC: Ami Press, 1991.

Lazar, Lance Gabriel. *Working in the Vineyard of the Lord: Jesuit Confraternities in Early Modern Italy*. Toronto: University of Toronto Press, 2005.

Lécrivain, Phillipe. *Paris in the Time of Ignatius of Loyola (1528–1535)*. Translated by Ralph C. Renner. St. Louis, MO: Institute of Jesuit Sources, 2011.

———. "La 'Somme théologique' de Thomas d'Aquin aux XVIe-XVIIIe siècles." *Recherches de Science Religieuse* 91, no. 3 (2003): 397–427.

Lepers, Étienne. "Rendre visible ce qui est invisible. La comparaison dans les deux premiers Exercices." *Christus* 133 (1987): 100–110.

Levering, Matthew. "Aquinas and Supersessionism One More Time: A Response to Matthew Tapie's *Aquinas on Israel and the Church*." *Pro Ecclesia* 25, no. 4 (2016): 395–412.

———. *Christ's Fulfillment of Torah and Temple: Salvation according to Thomas Aquinas*. Notre Dame, IN: University of Notre Dame Press, 2002.

Levering, Matthew and Marcus Plested, ed. *The Oxford Handbook of the Reception of Aquinas.* Oxford: Oxford University Press, 2021.

Lewis, C. S. *The Discarded Image: An Introduction to Medieval and Renaissance Literature*. Cambridge: Cambridge University Press, 1964.

Lewis, Mark and Jennifer Selwyn. "Jesuit Activity in Southern Italy during the Generalate of Everard Mercurian." In *The Mercurian Project: Forming Jesuit Culture, 1573–1580*, edited by Thomas M. McCoog, SJ, 532–57. St. Louis, MO: Institute of Jesuit Sources, 2004.

Liss, Peggy. "Isabel of Castile (1451–1504), Her Self-Representation and Its Context." In *Queenship and Political Power in Medieval and Early Modern Spain*, edited by Theresa Earenfight, 120–44. New York: Routledge, 2005.

Lisska, Anthony J. *Aquinas's Theory of Perception: An Analytic Reconstruction*. Oxford: Oxford University Press, 2016.

Lombardo, Nicholas. *The Logic of Desire: Aquinas on Emotion*. Washington, DC: Catholic University Press, 2011.

Lubac, Henri de. *Paradoxes of Faith*. San Francisco: Ignatius Press, 1987.

Lucas, Thomas. "Virtual Vessels, Mystical Signs. Contemplating Mary's Images in the Jesuit Tradition." *Studies in the Spirituality of Jesuits* 35, no. 5 (2003): 1–46.

Luscombe, David E. "Thomas Aquinas and Conceptions of Hierarchy in the Thirteenth Century." In *Thomas Aquin: Werk und Wirkung im Licht neuerer Forschung*, edited by Albert Zimmermann and Clemens Kopp, 261–77. Berlin: Walter de Gruyter, 1988.

Lynch, Reginald M. "The Reception of the *Summa Theologiae* on the Question of Eucharistic Sacrifice in the Early Modern Period." Ph.D. diss., University of Notre Dame, 2020. https://doi.org/10.7274/qb98mc9146k.

Lynch, William F. *Images of Hope: Imagination as Healer of the Hopeless*. Notre Dame, IN: University of Notre Dame Press, 1965.

Maas, A. "Did the Blessed Virgin Help St. Ignatius in the Composition of the *Spiritual Exercises*?" *Woodstock Letters* 24 (February 1895): 52–70.

Macy, Gary. *The Theologies of the Eucharist in the Early Scholastic Period: A Study of the Salvific Function of the Sacrament according to the Theologians c. 1080–c. 1220*. Oxford: Clarendon Press, 1984.

Madrigal Terrazas, Santiago. *Estudios de eclesiología ignaciana*. Madrid: Universidad de Comillas and Desclée de Brouwer, 2002.

Marcel, Gabriel. *Creative Fidelity*. New York: Fordham University Press, 2002.

Margoin, Jean-Claude. "Essai de Mise au Point sur l'Érasmisme dans le sillage d'Alcalá et la Lumière de Quelques Travaux Récents." In *Ignacio de Loyola y su Tiempo*, edited by Juan Plazaola, 245–70. Congreso Internacional de Historia, 9–13 Setiembre 1991. Bilbao, Spain: Mensajero, 1992.

Marien, Francis J. "Our Lady and the Exercises." *Woodstock Letters* 82 (1953): 224–37.

Maritain, Jacques. *The Degrees of Knowledge*. London: Centenary Press, 1937.

Márquez, Antonio. *Los alumbrados: Orígenes y filosofía (1525–1529)*. Madrid: Taurus, 1980.

Marshall, Bruce D. "Quasi in Figura: A Brief Reflection on Jewish Election, after Thomas Aquinas." *Nova et Vetera* 7, no. 2 (2009): 477–84.

Marthaler, Bernhard L., ed. *The New Catholic Encyclopedia*. New York: McGraw-Hill, 1967.

Martin, Ralph. *The Fulfillment of All Desire: A Guidebook for the Journey to God based on the Wisdom of the Saints*. Steubenville, OH: Emmaus Road, 2006.

Martínez, Doris Moreno. "Crear opinión: El dominico Alonso de Avendaño y su predicación antijesuita (1567–1596)." In *Identidades y fronteras culturales en el mundo ibérico de la Edad Moderna*, edited by José Luis Betrán, Bernat Hernández, and Doris Moreno, 399–413. Bellaterra, Spain: University of Barcelona, 2016.

———. "Las *almas* de la Compañía de Jesús en el siglo XVI: ecos alumbrados." In *Jesuitas e Imperios de Ultramar: siglos XVI–XX*, edited by Alexandre Coello, Javier Burrieza, and Doris Moreno, 201–22. Madrid: Silex, 2012.

———. "Obediencias negociadas y desobediencias silenciadas en la Compañía de Jesús en España, ss. XVI–XVII." *Hispania* 74, no. 248 (2014): 661–86.

Martini, Angelo. "Gli studi teologici di Giovanni de Polanco alle origine della legislazione scolastica della Compagnia di Gesù." *Archivum Historicum Societatis Iesu* 21, no. 42 (1952): 225–81.

Marty, François. *Sentir et goûter, les sens dans les « Exercices spirituels » de saint Ignace*. Cogitatio fidei series. Paris: Cerf, 2005.

Maryks, Robert. *A Companion to Ignatius of Loyola*. Leiden: Brill, 2014.

———. *The Jesuit Order as a Synagogue of Jews*. Leiden: Brill, 2009.

Mateo, Rogelio García. "El pensiamento aristotélico en los *Ejercicios Esprituales* y el influjo de éstos en Descartes." *Gregorianum* 98, no. 4 (2017): 763–83.

McAleer, G. J. "The Politics of the Flesh: Rahner and Aquinas on *Concupiscentia*." *Modern Theology* 15, no. 3 (July 1999): 355–65.

McCabe, Herbert. *On Aquinas*. Edited by Brian Davies. London-New York: Burns & Oates-Continuum, 2008.

McCool, Gerald A. *The Neo-Thomists*. Milwaukee, WI: Marquette University Press, 1994.

McGinn, Bernard. *Mysticism in the Golden Age of Spain (1500–1650)*. New York: Crossroad, 2017.

McLeod, Frederick G. "The Use of the Imagination in the Ignatian Exercises." In *Images and the Imagination in the Ignatian Exercises*, 33–92. Rome: Centrum Ignatianum Spiritualitatis, 1987.

Meissner, W. W. *Ignatius of Loyola: The Psychology of a Saint*. New Haven, CT: Yale University Press, 1992.

———. *To the Greater Glory: A Psychological Study of Ignatian Spirituality*. Marquette Studies in Theology. Milwaukee, WI: Marquette University Press, 1999.

Meyer, Michael. *Philosophy and the Passions: Toward a History of Human Nature*. Translated by Robert F. Barsky. University Park, PA: Pennsylvania State University Press, 2000.

Miner, Robert. "Thomas Aquinas and Hans Urs Von Balthasar: A Dialogue on Love and Charity." *New Blackfriars* 95, no. 1059 (2014): 504–24.

———. *Thomas Aquinas on the Passions*. New York: Cambridge University Press, 2009.

Minnich, Nelson. "Alberto Pio's Defense of Scholastic Theology." In *Biblical Humanism and Scholasticism*, edited by Erika Rummel, translated by Anna Machado-Matheson, 277–95. Leiden: Brill, 2008.

Mongini, Guido. "Le teologie gesuitiche delle origini: Lo spiritualismo radicale come matrice commune del dissenso e della fedeltà all'ortodossia." In *Avventure dell'obbedienza nella Compagnia di Gesù: Teorie e prassi fra XVI e XIX secolo*, edited by Fernanda Alfieri and Claudio Ferlan, 19–47. Bologna: Il Mulino, 2012.

Mostaccio, Silvia. "Debating Obedience in an Early Modern Context." In *The Acquaviva Project: Claudio Acquaviva's Generalate (1581–1615) and the Emergence of Modern Catholicism*, edited by Pierre-Antoine Fabre and Flavio Rurale, 59–80. Boston: Institute of Jesuit Sources, 2017.

———. *Early Modern Jesuits between Obedience and Conscience During the Generalate of Claudio Acquaviva (1581–1615)*. Burlington, VT: Ashgate, 2014.

———. "Spiritual Exercises: Obedience, Conscience, Conquest." In *The Oxford Handbook of the Jesuits*, edited by Ines Županov, 75–104. New York: Oxford University Press, 2019.

Motta, Francis. "Jesuit Theology, Politics, and Identity: The Generalate of Acquaviva and the Years of Formation." In *The Acquaviva Project: Claudio Acquaviva's Generalate (1581–1615) and the Emergence of Modern Catholicism*, edited by Pierre-Antoine Fabre and Flavio Rurale, 353–74. Boston: Institute of Jesuit Sources, 2017.

Munitiz, Joseph A. *Inigo: Discernment Log-Book*. London: Inigo Enterprises, 1987.

Murphy, Paul. "'God's Porters:' The Jesuit Vocation according to Francisco Suárez." *Archivum Historicum Societatis Jesu* 70, no. 139 (2001): 3–28.

Murray, Luke. *Jesuit Biblical Studies after Trent: Franciscus Toletus and Cornelius A. Lapide*. Göttingen: Vandenhoeck & Ruprecht, 2019.

Nardoni, Enrique. "The Concept of Charism in Paul." *The Catholic Biblical Quarterly* 55, no. 1 (1993): 68–80.

Nauert, Charles G. "Humanism as Method: Roots of Conflict with the Scholastics." *The Sixteenth Century Journal* 29 (1998): 427–38.

Newman, John Henry. *Discussions and Arguments on Various Subjects*. London: Longmans, Green, and Co., 1907.

———. *An Essay in Aid of a Grammar of Assent*. London: Longmans, Green, and Co., 1903.

———. *Fifteen Sermons Preached before the University of Oxford*. London: Longmans, Green, and Co., 1909.

Nicolau, Miguel. *Jerónimo Nadal, S.I. (1507–1580): Sus obras y doctrinas espirituales*. Madrid: CSIC, 1949.

Nirenberg, David. *Neighboring Faiths: Christianity, Islam, and Judaism in the Middle Ages and Today*. Chicago: University of Chicago Press, 2014.

Nisi, Ludovico. *Fuori dell'anima: Ignazio di Loyola e l'immaginazione*. Milan: Mimesis, 2020.

Noreña, Carlos. "Suárez and the Jesuits." *American Catholic Philosophical Quarterly* 65, no. 3 (1991): 267–86.

O'Connor, Edward, ed. *The Dogma of the Immaculate Conception*. Notre Dame, IN: University of Notre Dame Press, 1958. Reprint, 2017.

———. "The Fundamental Principle of Mariology in Scholastic Theology." *Marian Studies Journal* 10, no. 1 (1959): 60–103.

O'Gorman, Thomas. *Jesuit Obedience from Life to Law: The Development of the Ignatian Idea of Obedience in the Jesuit Constitutions, 1539–1556*. Manila: Ateneo University, 1971.

O'Keefe, Martin. "Jerome Nadal, SJ, on the Virtue of Obedience." In *Spirit, Style, Story: Essays Honoring John W. Padberg, SJ*, edited by Thomas Lucas, 45–69. Chicago: Loyola Press, 2002.

Olin, John C. *Six Essays on Erasmus*. New York: Fordham University Press, 1979.

Olphe-Galliard, Michel. "La letter de Saint Ignace de Loyola sur la vertu d'obéissance." *Revue d'Ascétique et de Mystique* 30 (1954): 7–28.

O'Malley, John W. *The First Jesuits*. Cambridge, MA: Harvard University Press, 1993.

———. *Praise and Blame in Renaissance Rome: Rhetoric, Doctrine, and Reform in the Sacred Orators of the Papal Court, c. 1450–1521*. Durham, NC: Duke University Press, 1979.

———. "Renaissance Humanism and the Religious Culture of the First Jesuits." *Heythrop Journal* 31 (1990): 471–87.

———. "Some Distinctive Characteristics of Jesuit Spirituality in the Sixteenth Century." In *Saints or Devils Incarnate? Studies in Jesuit History*. Jesuit Studies: Modernity through the Prism of Jesuit History 1. Leiden: Brill, 2013; originally published in *Jesuit Spirituality: A Now and Future Resource*, ed. John W. O'Malley, SJ, John W. Padberg, SJ, and Vincent T. O'Keefe, SJ, 1–20. Chicago, IL: Loyola Press, 1990.

———. "Some Renaissance Panegyrics of Aquinas." *Renaissance Quarterly* 27, no. 2 (1974): 174–92.

———. *Trent: What Happened at the Council*. Cambridge, MA: Harvard University Press, 2013.

O'Malley, John W. and Timothy W. O'Brien. "The Twentieth-Century Construction of Ignatian Spirituality: A Sketch." *Studies in the Spirituality of Jesuits* 52, no. 3 (2020): 1–40.

Ong, Walter. "A.M.D.G.: Dedication or Directive?" *Review for Religious* (September 1952). Reprint, *Review for Religious* 50, no. 1 (January–February 1991): 35–42.

O'Reilly, Terence. "Erasmus, Ignatius Loyola, and Orthodoxy." *The Journal of Theological Studies* 39 (1979): 115–27.

———. "Melchor Cano and the Spirituality of St. Ignatius Loyola: The *Censura y parecer contra el Instituto de los Padres Jesuitas*." *Journal of Jesuit Studies* 4 (2017): 365–94.

———. "The Spiritual Exercises and Illuminism in Spain: Dominican Critics of the Early Society of Jesus." In *Ite Inflammate Omnia: Selected Historical Papers from Conferences Held at Loyola and Rome in 2006*, edited by Thomas McCoog, SJ, 199–228. Rome: IHSI, 2006.

Osborne, Thomas. *Human Action in Thomas Aquinas, John Duns Scotus, and William of Ockham*. Washington, DC: The Catholic University of America Press, 2014.

Pabel, Hilmar M. "Praise and Blame: Peter Canisius's Ambivalent Assessment of Erasmus." In *The Reception of Erasmus in the Early Modern Period*, edited by Karl A. E. Enenkel, 129–59. Leiden: Brill, 2013.

Pasnau, Robert. *Thomas Aquinas on Human Nature: A Philosophical Study of Summa Theologiae 1a 75–89*. Cambridge: Cambridge University Press, 2002.

Pastore, Stephanie. "Jesuits, *Conversos*, and *Alumbrados* in the Iberian World." In *The Oxford Handbook of the Jesuits*, edited by Ines G. Županov, 269–92. Oxford University Press, 2019.

Patfoort, Albert. "Cognitio ista est quasi experimentalis (I Sent, d. 14, q. 2, a. 2, ad 3 m)." *Angelicum* 63 (1986): 3–13.

———. "Missions divines et expérience des personnes divines selon S. Thomas." *Angelicum* 63 (1986): 545–59.

Petri, Thomas. *Aquinas and the Theology of the Body: The Thomistic Foundations of John Paul II's Anthropology*. Washington, DC: The Catholic University of America Press, 2016.

Pidel, Aaron. "Francisco Suárez on Religion and Religious Pluralism." In *Francisco Suárez (1548–1617): Jesuits and the Complexities of Modernity*, edited Robert Maryks and Juan Antonio Senent de Frutos, 128–53. Boston: Brill, 2019.

———. "Jerome Nadal's Apology for the Spiritual Exercises: A Study in Balanced Spirituality." *Studies in the Spirituality of Jesuits* 52, no. 1 (2020): 1–36.

Pieper, Josef. *The Four Cardinal Virtues: Prudence, Justice, Fortitude, Temperance*. Notre Dame, IN: University of Notre Dame Press, 1966.

Pink, Thomas. "The Right to Religious Liberty and the Coercion of Belief: A Note on Dignitatis Humanae." In *Reason, Morality, and Law: The Philosophy of John Finnis*, edited by John Keown and Robert P. George, 428. Oxford: Oxford University Press, 2013.

Pope Francis. "'Avere coraggio e audacia profetica': Dialogo di papa Francesco con I gesuiti riuniti nella 36ª Congregazione Generale." *La Civiltà Cattolica* 3995 (2016): 421.

Prodi, Paolo. *Il paradigma tridentino: un'epoca della storia della Chiesa.* Brescia, Italy: Morcelliana, 2010.

Rahner, Hugo. *Ignatius the Theologian.* London: Geoffrey Chapman, 1968.

———. *The Vision of St. Ignatius in the Chapel of La Storta.* 2nd ed. Rome: Centrum Ignatianum, 1979.

Rahner, Karl. "Eine ignatianische Grundhaltung: Marginialen über den Gehorsam." *Stimmen der Zeit* 158 (1955–56): 253–67.

Ramos Riera, Ignacio. *Jerónimo Nadal (1507–1580) unter der "verschriftliche" Ignatius: Die Konstruktion einer individuellen und kollektiven Identität.* Boston: Brill, 2016.

Ratzinger, Joseph. "Der Einfluss des Bettelordenstreites auf die Entwicklung der Lehre vom päpstlichen Universalprimat, unter besonderer Berücksichtigung des heiligen Bonaventura." In *Theologie in Geschichte und Gegenwart: Michael Schmaus zum sechzigsten Geburtstag,* edited by J. Auer and H. Volk, 697–724. München: K. Zink, 1957.

Reinhardt, Nicole. "Hernando de Mendoça (1562–1617), General Acquaviva, and the Controversy over Confession, Counsel, and Obedience." *Journal of Jesuit Studies* 4 (2017): 209–29.

Reiser, Willaim. "The *Spiritual Exercises* in a Religiously Pluralistic World." *Spiritus* 10 (Fall 2010): 135–57.

Reites, James W. "St. Ignatius of Loyola and the Jews." *Studies in the Spirituality of Jesuits* 13, no. 4 (1981): 1–48

Renaudet, A. *Études Érasmiennes (1521–1529).* Paris: Droz, 1939.

Rey, Eusebio. "San Ignacio del Loyola y el problema de los 'cristianos nuevos.'" *Razón y Fe* 153 (1956): 178–204.

Rocques, René. "Denys l'Aréopagite." In *Dictionnaire de spiritualité,* vol. 3, 244–86. Paris: Beauchesne, 1957.

Rodrigues, Simão. *A Brief and Exact Account: The Recollections of Simão on the Origin and Progress of the Society of Jesus.* St. Louis, MO: The Institute of Jesuit Sources, 2004.

Rodriguez-Grahit, I. "Ignace de Loyola et le Collège Montaigu: L'Influence de Standonk sur Ignace." *Bibliothèque d'Humanisme et Renaissance* 20 (1958): 388–401.

Roldán-Figueroa, Rady. *The Ascetic Spirituality of Juan de Ávila (1499–1569).* Studies in the History of Christian Traditions. Leiden: Brill, 2010.

Roschini, G. *La mariolgia di San Tommaso.* Rome: Belardetti, 1950.

Rose, Steward. *Ignatius and the Early Jesuits.* 2nd ed. London: Longmans-Green, 1871.

Rowland, Tracey. *Catholic Theology*. London: Bloomsbury T&T Clark, 2017.

Rummel, Erika. *Erasmus and His Catholic Critics*. 2 vols. Nieuwkoop, Netherlands: De Graaf Publishers, 1989.

———. *The Humanist-Scholastic Debate in the Renaissance and Reformation*. Cambridge, MA: Harvard University Press, 1995.

Ryan, Tom. "Aquinas' Integrated View of Emotions, Morality and the Person." *Pacifica* 14 (February 2001): 55–70.

Sartre, Jean-Paul. *L'imagination*. Paris: Félix Alcan, 1936.

———. *L'imaginaire: Psychologie phénoménologique de l'imagination*. Paris: Gallimard, 1940.

Schnoor, Antje. "Transformational Ethics: The Concept of Obedience in Post-Conciliar Jesuit Thinking." *Religions* 10, no. 5 (2019): 1–16.

Schurhammer, George. *Francis Xavier: His Life, His Times*. Vol. 1, *Europe (1506–1541)*. Translated by M. Joseph Costelloe. Rome: Jesuit Historical Institute, 1973.

Scorraille, Raoul de. *François Suarez de la Compagnie de Jésus: D'après ses lettres, ses autres écrits inédits et un grand nombre de documents nouveaux*. Vol. 1, *L'Etudiant-Le Maître*. Paris: P. Lethielleux, 1912.

Seasoltz, R. Kevin, ed. *The New Liturgy: A Documentation, 1903–1965*. New York: Herder and Herder, 1966.

Segarra Pijuan, Joan. *Manresa and Saint Ignatius of Loyola*. Translated by Patricia Mathews. Manresa, Spain: Ajunament de Manresa, 1992. Original Catalon edition in 1990, Spanish in 1991.

Shore, Paul. "The *Vita Christi* of Ludolph of Saxony and Its Influence on the *Spiritual Exercises* of Ignatius of Loyola." *Studies in the Spirituality of Jesuits* 30, no. 1 (1998): 1–32.

Sieben, Hermann Josef. "Option für den Papst: Die Jesuiten auf dem Konzil von Trient, Dritte Sitzungsperiode 1562/1563." In *Ignatianisch: Eigenart und Methode der Gesellschaft Jesu*, edited by Michael Sievernich and Günter Switek, 235–53. Freiburg: Herder, 1990.

Sodi, Manlio and Juan Javier Flores Arcas, eds. *Rituale Romanum, Editio princeps (1614)*. Monumenta Liturgica Concilii Tridentini 5. Vatican City: Libreria Editrice Vaticana, 1614.

Sokolon, Marlene K. *Political Emotions: Aristotle and the Symphony of Reason and Emotion*. Dekalb, IL: Northern Illinois University Press, 2006.

Sommervogel, Carlos. *Bibliothéque de la Compagnie de Jésus*. Nouv ed. Bruxelles/Paris: Shepens/Picard, 1898.

Spadaro, Antonio. "Intervista a Papa Francesco." *La Civiltà Cattolica* 3918 (2013): 476.

Stadler, Joseph Nicholas. *Frequent Holy Communion: A Historical Synopsis and a Commentary*. The Catholic University of America Canon Law Series 263. Washington, DC: The Catholic University of America Press, 1947.

Staudt, Jared. "Religion as a Virtue: Thomas Aquinas on Worship through Justice, Law, and Charity." Ph.D. diss., Ave Maria University, 2008.

Steeves, Nicolas. *Grâce à l'imagination. Intégrer l'imagination en théologie fondamentale*. Paris: Éditions du Cerf, 2019.

———. "L'immaginazione è preghiera?" *Ignaziana* 21 (2016): 61–68.

Taft, Robert F. *Beyond East and West: Problems in Liturgical Understanding*. 2nd rev. and enlarged ed. Rome: Pontifical Oriental Institute, 1997.

Tandonnet, Roger. "L'obeissance religieuse, obeisance parfait." *Christus* 7 (1955): 332–49.

Tapie, Matthew. *Aquinas on Israel and the Church: The Question of Supersessionism in the Theology of Thomas Aquinas*. Eugene, OR: Pickwick Publications, 2014.

Toner, Jules. *A Commentary on St. Ignatius' Rules for Discernment of Spirits*. St. Louis, MO: Institute of Jesuit Sources, 1982.

Torrell, Jean-Pierre. *Christ and the Spirituality in St. Thomas Aquinas*. Thomistic Ressourcement. Washington, DC: The Catholic University of America Press, 2011.

———. "La pratique pastorale d'un théologien du XIII siècle: Thomas d'Aquin prédicateur." *Revue thomiste* 82, no. 2 (1982): 213–45.

———. *Saint Thomas Aquinas*. Vol. 2, *Spiritual Master*. Translated by Robert Royal. Washington, DC: The Catholic University of America Press, 2003.

Tropia, Anna. "Francisco de Toledo: Setting a Standard for Jesuit Philosophy." In *Jesuit Philosophy on the Eve of Modernity*, edited by Cristiano Casalini, 251–69. Leiden: Brill, 2019.

Vicaire, Humbert. *L'imitation des Apôtres*. Paris: Éditions du Cerf, 1963.

Visser, Arnould. "Erasmus, the Church Fathers and the Ideological Implications of Philology." *Erasmus of Roterdam Society Yearbook* 31 (2011): 7–31.

Vogel, C. J. de. "Erasmus and His Attitude Towards Church Dogma." In *Scrinium Erasmianum*. 2 vols. Edited by J. Coppens. Leiden: Brill, 1969.

Wawrykow, Joseph. "The Greek Fathers in the Eucharistic Theology of Thomas Aquinas." In *Thomas Aquinas and the Greek Fathers*, edited by Michael Dauphinais, Andrew Hofer, OP, and Roger Nutt, 274–302. Ave Maria, FL: Sapientia Press, 2019.

White, Kevin. "The Passions of the Soul (IaIIae, qq. 22–48)." In *The Ethics of Aquinas*, edited by Stephen J. Pope, 103–15. Washington, DC: Georgetown University Press, 2002.

Wiggins, David. "Deliberation and Practical Reason." *Proceedings of the Aristotelian Society (1975–1976)* 76 (1976): 30–36.

Wright, A. D. "The Jesuits and the Older Religious Orders in Spain." In *The Mercurian Project: Forming Jesuit Culture, 1573–1580*, edited by Thomas McCoog, SJ, 913–44. St. Louis, MO: Institute of Jesuit Sources, 2004.

Wyschogrod, Michael. "A Jewish Reading of Thomas Aquinas on the Old Law." In *Understanding the Scriptures*, edited by Clemens Thoma and Michael Wyschogrod, 125–38. Mahwah, NJ: Paulist Press, 1987.

Author and Editor Biographies

Justin M. Anderson is professor and chair of moral theology at Immaculate Conception Seminary School of Theology at Seton Hall University.

Sam Zeno Conedera, SJ, is assistant professor of history at Saint Louis University.

Kevin Flannery, SJ, is ordinary professor at the Pontifical Gregorian University, Rome.

Andrew Hofer, OP, is ordinary professor of patristics and ancient languages at the Dominican House of Studies, Washington, DC.

Margaret I. Hughes is tutor at the New England campus of Thomas Aquinas College.

Elisabeth Rain Kincaid is the Legendre-Soulé Chair of Business Ethics at Loyola University New Orleans.

Joseph W. Koterski, SJ, was associate professor of philosophy at Fordham University.

Matthew Levering is the James N. Jr. and Mary D. Perry Chair of Theology at the University of St. Mary of the Lake, Mundelein, IL.

Theresa Marie Chau Nguyen, OP, is assistant professor of theology at the University of St. Thomas, Houston.

Thomas M. Osborne is professor and chair of philosophy at the University of St. Thomas, Houston.

Aaron Pidel, SJ, is *docente incaricato associato* at the Pontifical Gregorian University, Rome.

Nicolas Steeves, SJ, is extraordinary professor at the Pontifical Gregorian University, Rome.

Index

A Life of the Blessed Virgin, 180
abandonment, 32–33, 217
Abreo, Francisco, 232
affection(s), xii, 1, 55, 70–72, 91, 96, 158, 164, 193, 276
affectivity, xvi, 64, 94–95, 97, 129, 130
Albert the Great, 17, 24, 181, 187
Alcalá, xi, xiii, 15, 35–36, 42n50, 127, 154, 250n10
Alexander of Hales, 17, 24
alms, 81
alumbradismo, 31–32, 35, 37n32, 38, 40–42
alumbrado(s), 31–37, 39, 40–42, 106n7, 178n57, 225
Ambrose, St., 8, 140, 147–49, 153n77, 160, 255, 263
Anabaptists, 287
Anacletus, Pope, 141, 150
analogia entis, x, xi
anathema, 232, 277, 285
Andrés, Melquiades, 33, 37n33
angelology, 198, 210–12
angels, 41, 59, 62, 71, 73, 78, 86, 114, 119, 126, 131, 164, 181, 184, 190, 193, 199, 200–206, 209–13, 216
Anima Christi, 177
Animation, 187, 190
Annunciation, 169, 171, 175–76, 192
Anselm of Canterbury, St., 24, 187n85
appetite(s), 49, 61–63, 65–66, 69, 73–74, 76, 80, 94–96, 101
Aquaviva, Claudio (Acquaviva, Claudio), 225n48, 226, 231, 233, 238, 249, 253
Aquinas, Thomas (works of): *Compendium theologiae*, 182–83, 187, 189; *Contra impugnantes*, 205–06; *De Veritate*, 109n15, 115–19n78, 162n120; *Devotissima Expositio Salutationis Angelicae*, 182–84, 189–90; *In psalmos Davidis expositio*, 29n2, 45–46, 53, 57n109; *Quodlibet*, 189, 223, 239; *Scriptum super Sententiarum*, 44n58, 48, 52n91, 106n6, 111n28, 136, 142, 144–45, 148–49, 189, 193, 200n18–202n25, 222, 279–81n29; *Summa contra gentiles*, 56, 109n15, 182, 204–5n36; 291n52; Summa theologiae, xi, xiii-xiv, 4–5, 21, 42, 53, 55, 80, 106n6, 111, 115, 122, 131, 136, 139, 148–51, 155n88, 164–66, 182–84, 187, 189, 201–3, 208–9, 222–23, 235–36, 239, 241–42, 247–48, 252, 261–62, 271–74, 279, 283n32, 295; *Super de Trinitate*, 118n71, 120n82; *Super epistolam ad Romanos*, 115n54, 247–48, 254–59, 261; *Super evangelium Ioannis*, 42n49, 45n61, 182–83; *Super Iob*, 45–46n67; *Super primam Epistolam ad Corinthios*, xviin22, 147n54
Aristotle, 4, 50, 56, 80, 93, 95–96, 102, 109, 113, 117, 120, 123, 129–30n132, 156n87, 185, 200, 204, 271, 290n48
Ascension, 72
Assumption, 172
attachment(s), 71, 80–86, 88, 90–91, 169, 192–93
Augé, Robert, 56
Augustine of Hippo, St., xii, 1, 8, 16–17, 48n73, 123n100, 125, 140–46, 148–50, 153n77, 159–60, 235–36, 263–64, 278–84, 286
Austin, Nicholas, ix
Avicenna, 110–11
Azpeitia, 152, 158, 160
Bañez, Domingo, x, 225
Bangert, William, 17
baptism, 149, 175, 251, 262, 264, 266–68, 274–78, 285, 287
baptismal rite, 277–78
Barclay, John, xiii
Barron, Robert, xiv
Basil, St., 8, 235
Basilica of St. Mary Major, 173, 176
battle at Pamplona, 126, 169
Bauerschmidt, Frederick, 120–21, 134
beatific vision, xvi, 74–75, 116
beatitude, xii, 73, 131, 214n73, 290, 293
beatos, 33–34
Bechs, Gràcia, 154
Beda, Noel (Noël), 5n15–6n18, 9n30–11, 13n44, 15, 276,
Beguiriztáin, Justo, 138, 159
Bellarmine, Robert, St., 218, 231, 233–39, 241–42, 244–45
Benedict, St., 12, 162n120, 235
Benoist, Jean, 13n43, 155

327

328 | INDEX

Bernard of Clairvaux, St., 180, 184, 187, 219, 229n70, 230
Betz, John, x
Biblical philology, 6, 10, 13, 26
Biel, Gabriel, 262
Billot, Louis, x
Black Madonna, 171
Black, Christopher, 156–57
Blankenhorn, Bernhard, 45n59, 48n74, 49, 51–52, 55, 146n51
Blindness, 192, 220, 227
Bobadilla, Nicholas, 12–13, 15, 137n8, 218n3
Bonaventure, St., xiii, 1, 17, 31n6, 54–55, 136, 138, 142–46, 149, 150–51, 156n90, 165, 180, 187, 213n73, 235, 262
Bonino, Serge-Thomas, ix, 115–19
Borgia, Francis, St. (Francis Borja, Borgia, Francisco, Francisco de Borgia), 129n130, 179, 233, 250, 252, 273
Brethren of the Common Life, 5, 10
Brown, Benjamin, 222
Cabrera, Antoni Joan, 154
Cajetan (Thomas de Vio Cajetan, Cardinal), x, 5, 23, 153n77, 156n91, 164n125, 208, 262, 273n8
Campbell, Thomas, 272
Canisius, Peter, 23n75, 224
Cano, Melchor, 24–25, 27, 31, 32n9, 35–43, 153n75, 225
Caravaca, 232
Cardoner, 34, 128, 171
Carmelites, 180
Carranza, Bartolomé, 37n33, 39, 41–42, 152, 153n75, 153n76, 253, 256n48
Carruthers, Mary, 112n33, 122, 134
Cassian, 219–20, 230, 232n84, 235
Catherine of Siena, St., 156n91, 204
causality, xi, 203, 211, 292
celestial hierarchy, 198–99, 202, 205, 209–10
Cessario, Romanus, x, 153n76
Chadwick, Owen, ix
charity, xiv, 42, 44–45, 49–52, 54, 88, 131, 140, 146, 159, 162, 219, 222, 230, 245
Christocentrism, 182
Christology, xiv, 122n96, 146n51, 182, 194
Chrysostom, John, 8, 176, 241, 254–56, 260, 282
Church of Sancta Maria della Strada, 173
Church of the Gesù (Gesù), 157, 168, 173
Church militant, 66n28, 123n100, 202, 204–5

Cicero, 18–19, 25, 27
Circumspection, 100
Cisneros, Cardinal, 252
Cistercian(s), 134n155, 180, 206
Clarke, Norris, xi, 146n51
Clement VI, Pope, 263
Clement VIII, Pope, 274
Cline, Erin, xiv
coercion, 95, 263–67, 269–70, 272, 274, 277, 279–84, 286, 292, 295
cogitative power, 111
Coimbra, 220
Colish, Marcia, 141, 274n12
College of Gandia, 219
College of Montaigu, 5, 10, 12, 15
College of Sainte-Barbe, 12, 15
Colunga, Emilio, 38–39
Combes, André, 46
Confession (sacrament of confession), 91, 136–37, 144, 150, 152, 157, 159n105, 162–63, 171, 206n41, 225n48
confessor(s), 32, 34, 36, 42, 125, 171, 225n48, 228
Confraternity of the Holy Spirit, 157
Confraternity of the Most Blessed Sacrament (Minerva confraternity), 156–57, 166
Congar, Yves-Marie, 197
Conscience, 87, 126, 160–61
consecration, 185–86
consequentialism (consequentialist argument), 80, 268
consolation, 33, 41–42, 54n98, 56, 87–89, 91, 127, 169, 173, 207, 209–12
contemplation, 3–4, 30, 40, 48, 50–53, 56, 68, 73–74, 81, 124, 132, 174–75, 179, 184, 192, 195, 207, 210, 219
contemplative life, 45
convent(s), 12, 13n43, 39, 137, 154n84
conversion(s), ix, xi, 81, 126, 153, 167, 169–70, 248, 251, 258, 261–69
converso(s), vi, xvi, 233, 247–54, 256n48, 259, 268, 270
Coolman, Holly Taylor, 247, 254
Copleston, Fredrick, xi, 61n7
Corbin, Michel, xiv
Córdoba, 253
Cornibus, Master de, 12–13, 123n99
Costurier, Pierre, 10
Council of Basel-Ferrara-Florence, 190

Council of Trent, 16, 136, 138, 162–64, 191, 214n75, 272–75, 277, 278n23, 282, 285–87, 295
counsel(s), 12, 40–42, 66, 89, 97–98, 100–101, 144, 147, 149, 162–63, 165, 220, 223, 235–36, 241, 243
Crockaert, Pieter, 208
Cros, L. Joseph-Marie, 138
d'Étaples, Jacques Lefèvre, 6–7, 10, 15, 26
da Câmara, Luis Gonçalves, 125, 130
Damascene, John, St., 17, 24, 93n11, 235
de Alcaraz, Pedro Ruiz, 32n8, 34
De Auxiliis controversy, ix, xiii, xiv, 21, 274, 284, 286
de Bedoya, Gaspar, 34
de Blignières, Louis-Marie, 217–18n3, 245n143
de Carranza, Bartolomé, 37n33, 39, 41–42, 152–53n75, 253, 256n48
de Castillo, Juan, 36
de Châtillon, Romée, 37
de Figueroa, Juan Rodríguez, 35
de Finance, Joseph, xi
de Guibert, Joseph, 124n104, 168
de Guzman, Diego, 249
de la Cruz, Isabel, 32n8, 34
de la Cruz, Juan, 152
de la Fuente, Alonso, 225
de Lubac, Henri, x, xi, 109, 110n14
de Lugo, Francisco, ix
de Madrid, Christopher, 138, 144, 152, 250
de Mariana, Juan, 273
de Miona, Manuel, 36
de Miranda, Bartolomé Carranza, 253
de Molina, Luis, 21, 155n87
de Orellan, Juan, 225
de Pedroche, Tomas, 31, 38–42, 54n98, 225
de Peña, Juan, 12, 37n33
de Polanco, Juan Alfonso, 3–4, 23, 31n6, 33n16, 250
de Ribadeneira, Pedro, 5–6, 129n130, 249n6
de Salazar, Hernando Chirino, 191
de Santa Cruz, Diego, 232–33
de Santander, Luis, 234
de Soto, Domingo (Dominic), 3–4, 23, 27, 252, 261–62, 267, 269, 272
de Toledo, Francisco (Francisco Toledo; Toletus, Franciscus), xvi, 20–21, 24, 27, 224, 247–70, 271–75, 277, 280–81, 283–88, 291–95
de Torres, Miguel, 36–37n32

de Valdés, Juan, 36
de Valtanás, Domingo, 153
de Vitoria, Francisco, x, 25, 261, 267, 269
Decree on Frequent and Daily Reception of Holy Communion, 137
Dedek, John F., 46
Della Mirandola, Giovanni Pico, 7
demons, 44n58, 119, 131, 181, 212, 264
Descartes, 101
Desert Fathers, 221
desire(s), 30, 63, 67, 70–72, 75, 77, 79, 82, 87–88, 91–92, 94–97, 102, 130, 136, 145, 148–49, 158, 166, 170, 173, 193, 233, 236, 265–66, 270
desolation, 41, 87–89, 100, 171
devil, 41–42n48, 67, 127, 129, 162, 172n23, 232
devotio moderna, 5, 134n155
devotion, 9, 14–15, 45, 59–60, 64–65, 75, 136, 143–45, 149–50, 157, 159–60, 166, 173, 178–81, 184, 186, 189, 195, 198, 206, 213n72, 217, 219
Diatessaron, 175
Dionysius the Areopagite, xii, 43, 48, 52, 55, 57n108, 67, 116, 151n68, 198–206, 208, 210–12, 216, 230n74
discernment, v, xvi, 30, 32, 35, 41–42, 79–82, 85, 88–89, 91–93, 97–98, 100, 103, 127, 129–30, 139, 165, 198, 201, 203, 210–12
discretio spirituum, 97–98
Divine Essence, 50, 69
docilitas, 100
Dominican(s), ix–xi, xiii, 4–5, 12–13, 23–25, 27, 31–32n12, 35–40, 42–43, 51, 56, 105, 107n7, 122, 125, 129, 138, 152–58, 165–66, 169, 171–72, 180, 190–91, 197, 205, 208, 214, 225, 232n83, 235–36, 238n117, 241, 245, 261n80, 267, 272, 273n8,
Donatist controversy, 263
Donnelly, John Patrick, xiii
Drews, Wolfram, 263n90, 267
dubia, 262
Dublanchy, Edmond, 135–36
Dulles, Avery Cardinal, xv, 167, 194n112–95
Duns Scotus, John, xiii, 13, 123–24, 187, 190, 192n105, 262, 266, 273, 288
Easter duty, 140
ecclesiastical hierarchy, 198–99, 202, 204–6, 212–13
Eck, Johannes, 23
ecstasis, xiv

Edict of 1525, 31–32n8, 34, 42
Eikasia, 109–10
Emery, Gilles, ix
emotion(s), 64, 79–80, 82, 87, 90–97, 101–2, 129–30, 134
Enríquez, Enrique, 232
Ephrem the Syrian, 176
Erasmian(s), 32–33, 278
Erasmus, Desiderius, viii, xvi, 5–12, 15, 18–19, 22–23, 25–27, 33n14, 272, 275–77, 285, 287
Eucharist (Blessed Sacrament), xii, 128, 135–37n8, 139–42, 144–49, 151, 153n77, 155n88–58, 161, 163–64, 166, 276–77
Eucharistic devotion, 143, 150
Evangelicae Historiae Imagines, 124
evangelical counsels, 40
Every, Louis, 190
evil spirit, 87–89, 131, 211–212n70
Faber, Peter St., 12, 157, 179
Fabian, Pope, 141, 150
Fabre, Pierre-Antoine, 130–31, 221n21
Farge, James, 6, 208
fear, 31n7, 63–64, 66, 85, 94, 145–47n54, 149–50, 208, 235, 251, 263–66, 269, 282
feeling(s) (see also: Ignatius, Rules for Thinking, Judging, and Feeling with the Church), 1, 41, 55, 64–65, 72, 75, 79–80, 82, 87–88, 90–97, 129, 133, 207–8, 214n73, 215
Fernández, Luis, 32–33
Ferrer, Vincent, 235n95, 241, 269n136
Ferreyrolles, Gérard, 110, 122
Fourth Council of Toledo (Fourth Counsel of Toledo), 263, 272, 274–75, 284
Fourth Lateran Council (Lateran IV), 139, 142, 150
Francis I, King of France, 7, 9, 11
Francis of Assisi, St., 126, 156n90, 235
Franciscan(s), xiii, xvi, 12–13, 31, 54–55, 123n99, 134, 180, 190–91, 194, 235
free will, xii, 21, 62, 67, 225, 272, 280, 284, 291–95
freedom, x, xiii, 34, 37n33, 76, 80–83, 86, 90, 94–95, 133–34, 182, 189, 219, 224, 265, 269, 279, 284
Gaetano, Matthew, xiii
Gallagher, Timothy, 88
Ganss, George E., xii, xiii, 155, 168
Garrigou-Lagrange, Reginald, 45n59, 105–106, 189n92

Gennadius of Marseilles, 141, 144–45n47, 159–60
Gerson, Jean, 32n13, 137, 139, 166
Gesù Church, 157, 168, 173
Giacon, Carlo, 274
good spirit, 59, 87–89, 229
grace(s), x–xv, 4, 21, 29, 41–42, 44, 47–48, 51–52, 54, 56, 59, 65, 68, 71–72, 77, 81–82, 85, 87, 90, 100n32, 106, 116, 119, 129, 131–32, 150n65, 153n77, 155n88, 159n105, 161, 169n11–71n23, 173, 176–78, 180–88, 191–93, 199, 203, 205–206, 210, 213n73, 216, 225, 230, 255, 258–60, 267n122, 284–85, 287, 290–94; gratuitous grace, 98; prevenient grace, 190; theology of grace, 105
Gratian, 141, 267, 275n13,
Gregory of Valencia, xv, 20–21, 26–27
Gregory XIII, Pope, 274
Grendler, Paul, 15
Gui, Bernard, 121
habit(s), 4, 67, 76, 81, 83–84, 91, 96n21, 99, 209
habitus, 101
happiness, 60–70, 74–75, 78
Hardon, John, 137n4–38
Henry of Navarre, 24
heresy (heresies), 9, 12–13, 18–19, 21, 27, 31, 37–38, 128n127, 153n76–54, 178n58, 202, 232, 234, 237, 245, 285, 287
heretic(s), 10, 18–19, 24, 33n16, 37n33, 239, 264, 279–86
Hernández, Francisca, 36
Heydt, Margo, 168
hierarchical Church, v, xvi, 33, 66n28, 197–98
Hierotheos, 43, 48
Hilary of Poitiers, 10, 19, 22
Holy Land, 35, 127
Holy Trinity, 128
hope, xv, 63, 70, 88, 94, 99, 131, 150, 171n21, 289
Hospital of Santa Lucía, 171
Hull, Geoffrey, 217–18n3, 234
Humanism, xv, 5–7, 15, 18, 26
humanist(s), xv, 1, 2, 5–7, 9–10, 13–17, 19, 25–27, 252, 262
Humbert of Romans, 236, 242
humility, 87, 90, 121, 146n50, 149, 238, 259, 264
Hütter, Reinhard, ix
hylomorphism, 93

Iberian Peninsula, 31, 39
iconoclasm, 132
iconolatry, 132
Ignatius of Loyola (works of): *Constitutions of the Society of Jesus (Constitutions)*, 2, 12–15, 27, 61n8, 89, 123, 129, 147n53, 155, 166, 173–74, 209, 214–15, 218–21, 226, 228, 235, 240, 242, 250, 271; Contemplation to Attain the Love of God ("Contemplation for Attaining Love"; "Contemplation to Attain Divine Love"), 30, 68, 81, 207; First Principle and Foundation, 67, 70–71, 81–82, 84–86, 88–90; "Letter on Obedience", 212–13, 232; *Autobiography*, 34, 64, 67, 116, 123, 125–30, 153–54, 169–70, 206–209; Call of the King, 90; Instruction for the Sojourn at Trent, 162; Meditation on the Two Standards, 90; Meditations on Sin, 133; Rules for the Discernment of Spirits, 79–80, 82, 88–89, 201–210; "Rules for Thinking with the Church" ("Rules for Thinking, Judging, and Feeling with the Church"), 1, 27, 33, 136–137n8, 142, 152, 155n88, 198; *Spiritual Diary (Diary)*, 59, 64–65, 89n7, 116, 123, 130–31, 173, 177–78, 185, 210; *Spiritual Exercises*, xiv–xvi, 12–13, 15, 29–31, 35–42, 54–56, 59, 65, 67–68, 70–72, 76–77, 79–82, 85–90, 116, 122n96–25, 129, 131–34, 136n3, 154, 162, 167, 174–77, 179, 185, 192–94, 197–98, 207–8, 210, 215, 225, 227–28, 231n76, 265–66; Three Classes of Men, 90; Three Degrees of Humility, 90
illumination(s), 34, 40, 116–17, 178, 199–200, 206, 209n57, 216
illuminative way, 81
image of God, 60–61, 68–69, 77–78
Imitation of Christ, xii, 14, 137, 139, 166
Immaculate Conception, ix, 186–88, 190–92n105
"immaculist thesis", 190
Imprudence, 99, 218n3
Incarnation, xii, 82, 88, 151, 175–76, 184, 186, 192–94
indifferent (indifference), 32n12, 40–41, 82–84, 220, 225, 228–29
indulgences, 156–58
infidel(s), 262–69, 281–82, 284, 286
initium, 290

Innocent III, Pope, 140, 150, 206, 263
instinctus, 50, 56
intellect, 33, 46–47, 50, 52, 55, 60–61, 65, 69, 72–75, 77, 111, 113–14, 116–19, 126, 129, 192, 201, 211, 226–28, 234, 238–39, 242–45, 265, 291, 293
intellectual nature, 61n7, 68, 216
intelligentia, 100
Isaac of Stella, St., 180
Isidore, St., 263, 275
Ivens, Michael, 30, 55
Jacopo of Varagine (James of Voragine), 153, 169
Jansen, Cornelius, 165
Jansenism, 165
Januarius, 141–43
Jerome, St., 1, 8, 123n100, 235, 254
Jews, 17, 202, 247–52, 254–64, 266–70, 272, 274–76, 281–82
John of Avila, St., 252
John of St. Thomas, x, 110n21
Julius III, Pope, 37
justice, 45, 102, 182, 186, 188, 192–94, 203n30, 218n3, 222, 227, 230, 242, 255–56, 285–86, 294n64–95
justification, 164, 259–60, 280
Justin Martyr, St., 16
Justinian, Lawrence, 241
Kavanaugh, Aidan, 52
Kearney, Richard, 108
Keenan, James, 253, 262
Kenny, Anthony, 112
King Ferdinand, 268
King Sisebut, 275, 267
Kleutgen, Josef, xi
Kolvenbach, Peter Hans, 174
Koning, Robin, 177–178n57, 193
Kretzmann, Norman, 114, 146n51
Kristeller, Paul Oskar, 7
La Storta, 172, 174, 209
Lafontaine, René, 122n96, 133
Laínez, Diego (Lainez), xiii, 15, 36n32, 214n75, 221n26, 225, 250, 252, 273,
Lamont, John, 217–18n3, 234
Laurent, Thomas, 154–55
law: ecclesial law, 33; Jewish law, 247, 260; Mosaic law, 261; natural law, 92, 201, 256, 259–61
Leo the Great, Pope, 230, 262
lex divinitatis, 200–201, 206–8, 213, 215–16

Liberatore, Matteo, xi
liturgical rituals, 33
Lombard, Peter, xiii, 17, 22, 24, 26, 119n78, 136, 140–42, 145, 147–48, 155, 187, 208, 279, 295
Lombardo, Nicholas, 64
Lonergan, Bernard, x, xiii, 114, 124
Ludolph of Saxony (Ludoph), xiii, 14, 31n6, 153, 169, 176
Luther, Martin, 9, 16, 24, 208
Lutheranism, 31n7, 40
Lutherans, 10, 33, 237
"maculist thesis", 191
Madrid, 233, 250
magisterium, 136
Maior, John, 10
Manresa, xi, 34, 127, 137, 153, 154, 170–72, 174, 207–9n57
Marcel, Gabriel, 121
Maréchal, Joseph, 124
Mariology, 167, 179, 180n64–81, 191, 194–95
Marty, François, 54n100, 124
Maryks, Robert, 250
Mass, x, 9, 59, 65, 130, 137, 145, 153n77–54, 162–64, 171–73, 176, 185–86, 297, 207, 209
Master de Cornibus, 12–13, 123n99
Maternity, 183–84
McCabe, Herbert, 120
mediadores, 209–210, 216
Mediatrix, 182–83
Meissner, W.W., 30n5, 169, 172
Melanchthon, Philip, 24
Melcher, Sara, 168
"*memorialistas* (memorialist) controversy", 231, 233, 253
memory (memories) (*memoria*), 68, 99, 111–13, 118, 122, 126, 134, 191, 268
mental prayer, 33, 40, 81, 105
Mercurian, Everard, 226, 253
mercy, 87, 143, 145, 180, 183, 255, 259, 284
merit(s), xii, 70, 94, 183, 202, 228, 260, 288, 290, 293
"middle knowledge", xiii
Minnich, Nelson, 6
monastery (monasteries), 52, 137, 186
Mongeau, Gilles, ix
Montserrat, 137, 153, 170–71, 174
moral science, 4
moral theory, 85, 93, 95

More, Thomas St., 8
Moreno Martínez, Doris, 231
Moses, 55, 256, 259, 261, 270
Mostaccio, Silvia, 231, 234
Mother of God, xvi, 179, 190–91, 193
Munitiz, Joseph A. 130
Murray, Luke, 254
mysticism, xi, 32n6, 43, 54, 106n7
mystic(s), xii, 33, 39, 106, 169, 198
Nadal, Jerome (Jérôme, Jerónimo), 3–4, 13–15, 38n36, 61n8, 124, 167, 179, 218, 226–30, 237–38, 244–45, 250, 252
natural law theory, 92
Navarrete, 170
Newman, John Henry, ix, 107, 128n127
Nirenberg, David, 251
Norman Conquest, 186
Nuñes, Juan, 152
O'Gorman, Thomas, 221, 230
O'Malley, John W., xi–xii, 2–4, 30, 33n16, 37, 61n8, 137, 139, 153, 155–57, 163
O'Reilly, Terence, 36n32, 39, 41–42
Ockham, William of, xiii, 110n21, 124
Oñate, 170
Origen, 254, 260, 290
original justice, 182, 186, 188, 192–94, 227, 230
Our Lady of Aránzazu, 170, 174
Our Lady of the Way, 172–73, 179
Our Lady of Villadordis, 171
Palace of Mendoza, 32
Paris, xi–xiii, 1–2, 5–7, 9–10, 12–15, 18, 24, 26, 35–37, 56, 123, 127, 129, 154–55, 172, 185, 208, 214, 276
Parisian Gallicanism, 209
Pascual, Mateo, 36
Pasnau, Robert, 111–15, 117
Pastore, Stefanie, 35–36n31, 42
Patfoort, Albert, 46
patiens divina, 48, 56–57n108
Paul III, Pope, 156–57, 162, 173
Paul IV, Pope, 37, 270
Pedroche, Thomas (Tomas), 31, 38–42, 54n98, 225
Pelagians, 290
penance(s), 38, 126, 139, 171, 221, 225, 253
phantasia, 109–13, 131
phantasms, 111–19, 126, 133, 201, 212
Philip of Macedon, 18
Philip the Chancellor, 14

Pieper, Josef, 99
Piety, 154, 156n90–57, 162, 165, 169, 179–80, 187, 190
pilgrim(s), 65, 67, 69, 73, 127, 168–69, 171n23, 174–75, 179
pilgrimage(s), xvi, 8, 35, 60, 67–68, 75, 137, 164, 168, 171–72, 233
Pius X, Pope, 136, 138, 152, 159, 165
Plato, 95n17, 101–102, 109, 155n87, 290–91
Platonic position, 101
Platonism, 95, 97
Platonists, 200n17, 291
Pontifical Gregorian University, 106n6, 271
Portugal, 213n71, 217–18, 221, 234
Possevino, Antonio, 224
potency, 94
poverty, 19, 40, 65, 82, 84, 89–90, 130–31, 161, 172, 210, 236
poverty of spirit, 84
Premonstratensian Canons, 180
predestination, xiii, 225, 272–74, 280, 284, 286, 288–95
Protestantism (Protestant Controversy), 21, 23, 181
providentia, 100
"proximate-primary thesis", 292, 294
prudence (*prudentia*), v, xvi, 4, 79–80, 84, 92, 97–101, 103, 220, 242–43, 270
Przywara, Erich, x
Pullen, Robert, 142
punishment, 76, 231, 256, 265, 276, 284–85
purgative way, 81
quietism, 32
Rahner, Hugo, 122n96, 123n99, 167, 194n112, 209n58
Rahner, Karl, 124, 218n3
Ramírez, Juan, 232
rational appetite, 62, 69, 76, 94
rational creature(s), xii, 48, 187
rational powers, 69
rational soul, 94, 187, 190
rationes divinas, 50
Redemption, xii, 184, 187–90, 192, 194, 207, 240, 256
Reformation (Protestant Reformation), 8, 9, 26, 106n7
Regimini militantis ecclesiae, 158
Reginald of Piperno, 183
Rejadell, Teresa (Theresia), 66, 139, 152, 158n100–60, 166

religious liberty, 271n2–72, 279, 281, 283, 295
ressourcement, 136, 155n88
resurrected body, 74
Resurrection, xii, 45n61, 72, 82, 86, 94, 175–76, 256
retreat (retreatant), 30, 65, 68, 70, 77, 80–82, 85–92, 100, 175–78, 192–93, 207, 210
Ribadeneyra, Pedro, 231n80, 249
Ricœur, Paul, 108
Rocques, René, 199
Roldán-Figueroa, Rady, 138n11, 152, 163
Roman College, 252–53, 261, 271, 273–74, 288
"Roman School", ix–x
Rome, ix, 21, 27, 36, 132n144, 153n76, 155n88–57, 159, 168, 172–74, 176, 208–9, 232–33, 249, 252
rosary, 173, 179–80
Rotsaert, Mark, 133
Rousselot, Pierre, xi, 124
Ruben, Peter Paul, 59
sacra doctrina, 56, 120–21
Sacra Tridentina Synodus, 136, 163, 165
sacrament(s), 33, 39, 84, 128, 136, 138n11–39, 141–42, 145–49, 152, 154, 156–58, 160, 163–64, 166, 198, 201, 225, 266, 276–77, 285
Sacred Penitentiary, 253, 274
Sacrilege, 151, 266
Salamanca, xi, xiii, 35, 37n33, 43, 154, 248, 252, 259n70, 261, 267, 272
Salmerón, Alfonso, xv, 2–3, 15–21, 23–27, 36n32, 225–26
salvation, xiv, 1, 16, 20, 32n8, 83, 125, 141–42n31, 175, 185, 190, 194–95, 199, 202, 223, 235, 244, 247n3, 254–56, 258, 260, 262, 265, 268
San Esteban, 35–36
Sanctification, 182, 187–89, 192–93
Santa Maria sopra Minerva, 156n91, 166
Santiago de Compostela, 233
scholasticism, xi, 2, 5–7, 9, 11, 13–15, 24, 26, 55, 105n1, 164, 198, 216
school of Saint Jacques, 154
Scotism, 7
Scotus, John Duns, xiii, 13, 110n21, 123–24, 187, 190, 192n105, 262, 266, 273, 288
scruples, 81, 126, 154
Second Vatican Council, 137, 152, 165, 166, 168, 178, 218n3, 271n2
self-determination, 95
self-knowledge, 85

self-offering, 222
Seripando, Jerome, 277–78
Serry, Jacques-Hyacinthe, xiii
sickbed, 67, 126
silence, 102, 133, 236
Silíceo, Juan Martínez, 37–38
sin(s), 32n8, 41, 53, 65–66, 68, 71–72, 75, 80–81, 86–88, 91, 112, 115, 126, 131–32, 137n8, 139–41, 147n54, 149, 151, 159, 161–62, 182, 187–90, 192n105, 194, 220, 232, 235, 239, 244, 253, 255, 261, 266, 268, 281; mortal sin(s), 86, 88, 141, 151, 161, 266, 269n134; Original Sin, 187–92; venial sin(s), 36, 112n36, 145, 147, 190
situation ethics, 80
Sixtus IV, Pope, 191
Sixtus V, Pope, 233n87, 274
spiritual director(s) (director), 29–30, 77, 81, 92–93, 100, 133, 171
Socrates, 101–102
solertia, 100
Sordi, Serafino, xi
Sorrow, xvi, 60, 63, 65, 71–72, 74–75, 78, 88, 94, 178
Soter, Pope, 150
Soto, Domingo (Soto, Domingo de–Soto, Dominic), 3, 4, 23, 27, 252, 261–62, 267, 269, 272
Spanish Inquisition, 31–32n8, 34–36, 153, 232–33, 238, 251, 253
spiritual direction, 80, 92, 97, 100
spiritual warfare, 126–27
St. Denis of Montmartre, 192
Stella, Tommaso, 156–58, 166
Stoicism (Stoic position), 80, 83, 95, 97, 101
Suárez, Francisco, ix-x, 21, 110n21, 124, 181n69, 191, 218, 238–45
suffering(s), 48n74–50, 52, 72, 82, 118, 172, 284–85
Taparelli, Luigi, xi
Tatian, 175
tears, 54, 59, 60, 64–65, 71–75, 78, 87, 106n7, 130, 141
The Imitation of Christ, xii, 14, 139, 166
theology: dialectical theology, 17; Eucharistic theology, xvi; fundamental theology, 108, 115; imaginative theology, 120; monastic theology, 52; moral theology, ix, 92; mystical theology, 3–4, 43; patristic theology, 22; positive theology, 1, 8, 10–11, 13, 155, 235; speculative theology, 3; scholastic theology, xv, 1–27, 105, 142n31, 155n88
Thomas de Vio (Cajetan), x, 5, 23, 153n77, 156n91, 164n125, 208, 262, 273n8
Toletus, Francisco (Toletus, Franciscus), 20–21, 24, 27, 271
Torrell, Jean-Pierre, ix, xiv, 44, 46n65–47, 49, 52, 117, 122n96
Tostado, Alonso, 241
transmutation, 62, 74
triumphant Church, 204–5
unitive way, 81–82
universal jurisdiction, 206, 213–14
universal vicar, 213, 215–16
University of Alcalá, xi, xiii, 15, 35–36, 42n50, 127, 154, 250n10
University of Ávila, 138
University of Padua, 5
University of Valencia, xi
University of Zaragoza, 272
utilitarian casuistry, 92
Valencia, Gregory of, xv, 20–27, 224
Valladolid, 11n41–12, 36
van Dorp, Maarten, 7
Vázquez, Gabriel, xv, 2–3, 20–21, 24–27, 224
Vincent, Julien, 233–38
virginity, 186
virtue(s), ix, xii, xvi, 20, 36n27, 40–42, 44, 49–52, 54, 66, 84, 91–92, 95–97, 99–102, 131, 140, 146, 149, 151, 169, 181n71, 184, 218, 222–23n37, 226–27, 230, 236, 238, 240–42, 260–62, 265, 270, 293
virtue: acquired virtue, 50; natural virtue, 222, 230, 238; supernatural virtue(s), 92, 265; theological virtue(s), 20, 42, 44, 49, 51, 131, 222
Vitoria, Francisco, x, 25, 261, 267, 269
von Balthasar, Hans Urs, xi, 105n2, 124, 134
von Hurter, Hugo, 273
vow(s), 33, 172–73, 198–99, 212, 214–16, 218, 221–23, 227, 230, 235–41, 244, 254, 265, 276, 282, 286
wayfarer, 67, 70, 73, 202
Wernher the Swiss, 180
White, Thomas Joseph, ix
Wilkins, Jeremy, x
wisdom, 39–40, 42, 44–45, 48n73–52, 54–56, 99, 129, 181n71, 212, 218n3–19
Xavier, Francis St., 12–13, 15